D1203867

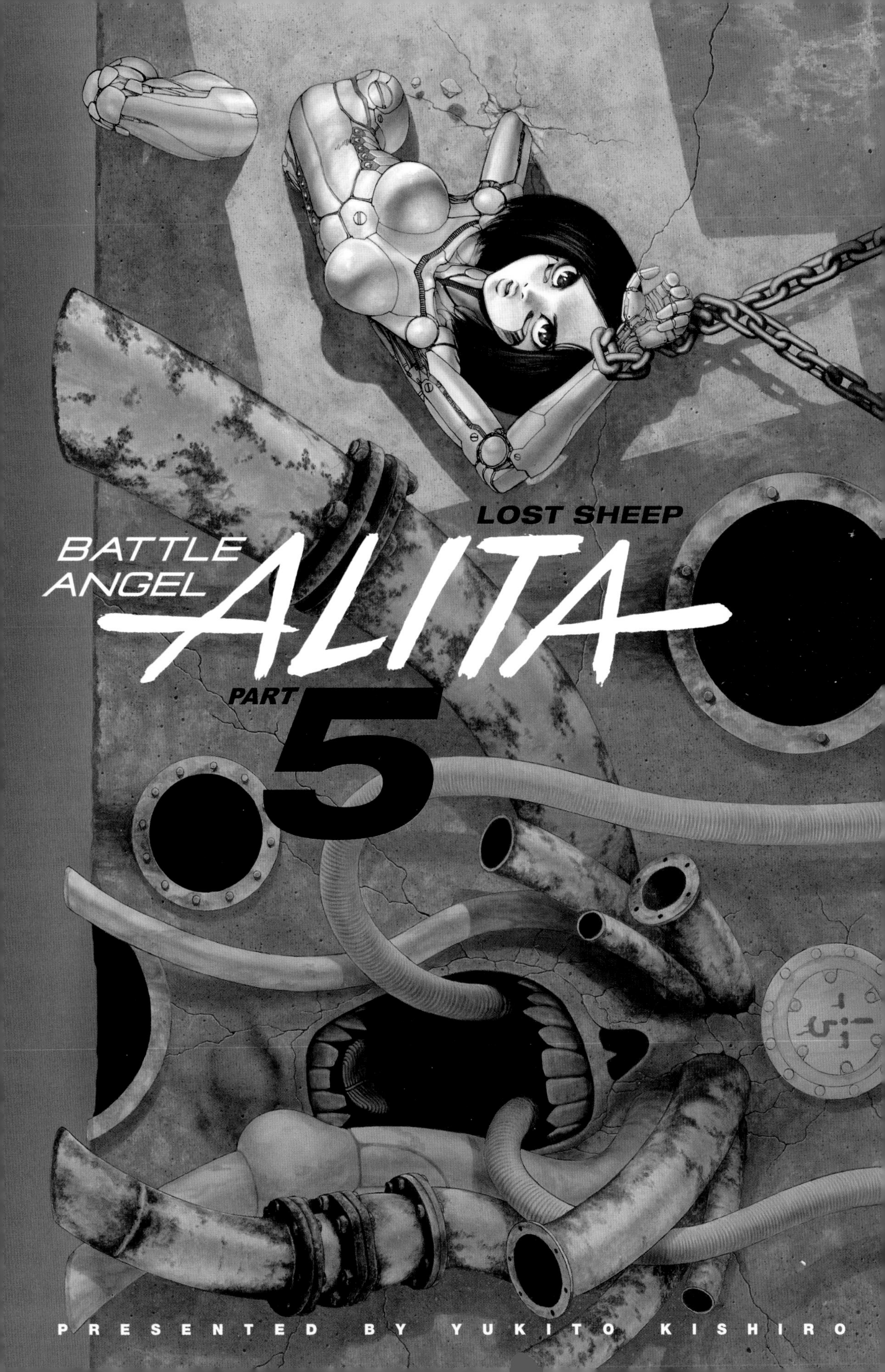
LOST SHEEP
BATTLE ANGEL
ALITA
PART 5
PRESENTED BY YUKITO KISHIRO

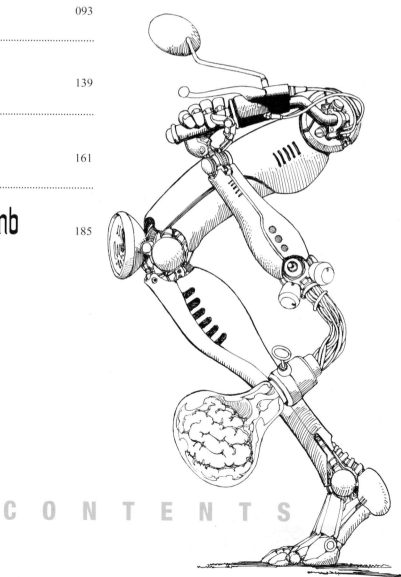

CONTENTS

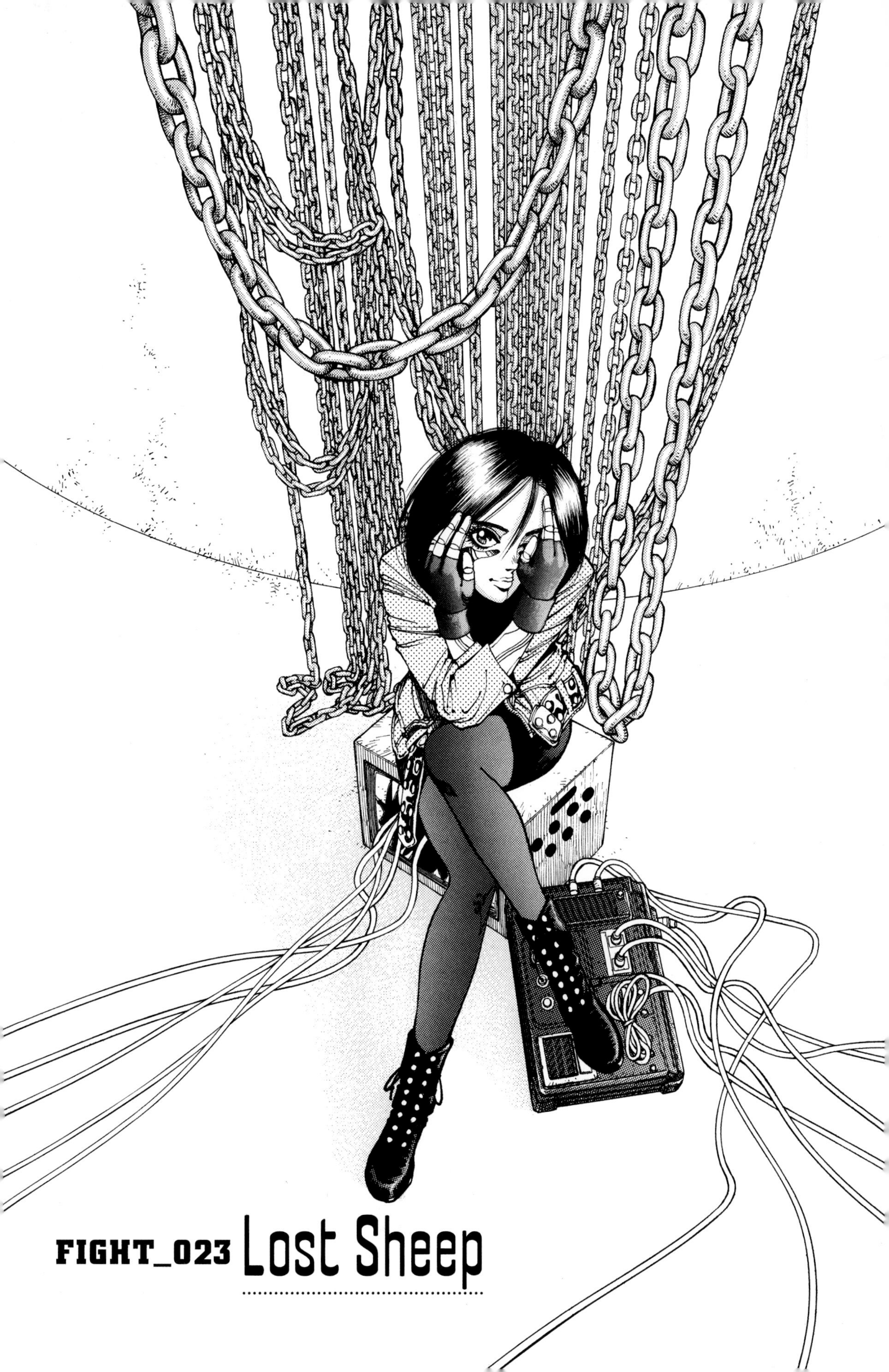

FIGHT_023 Lost Sheep

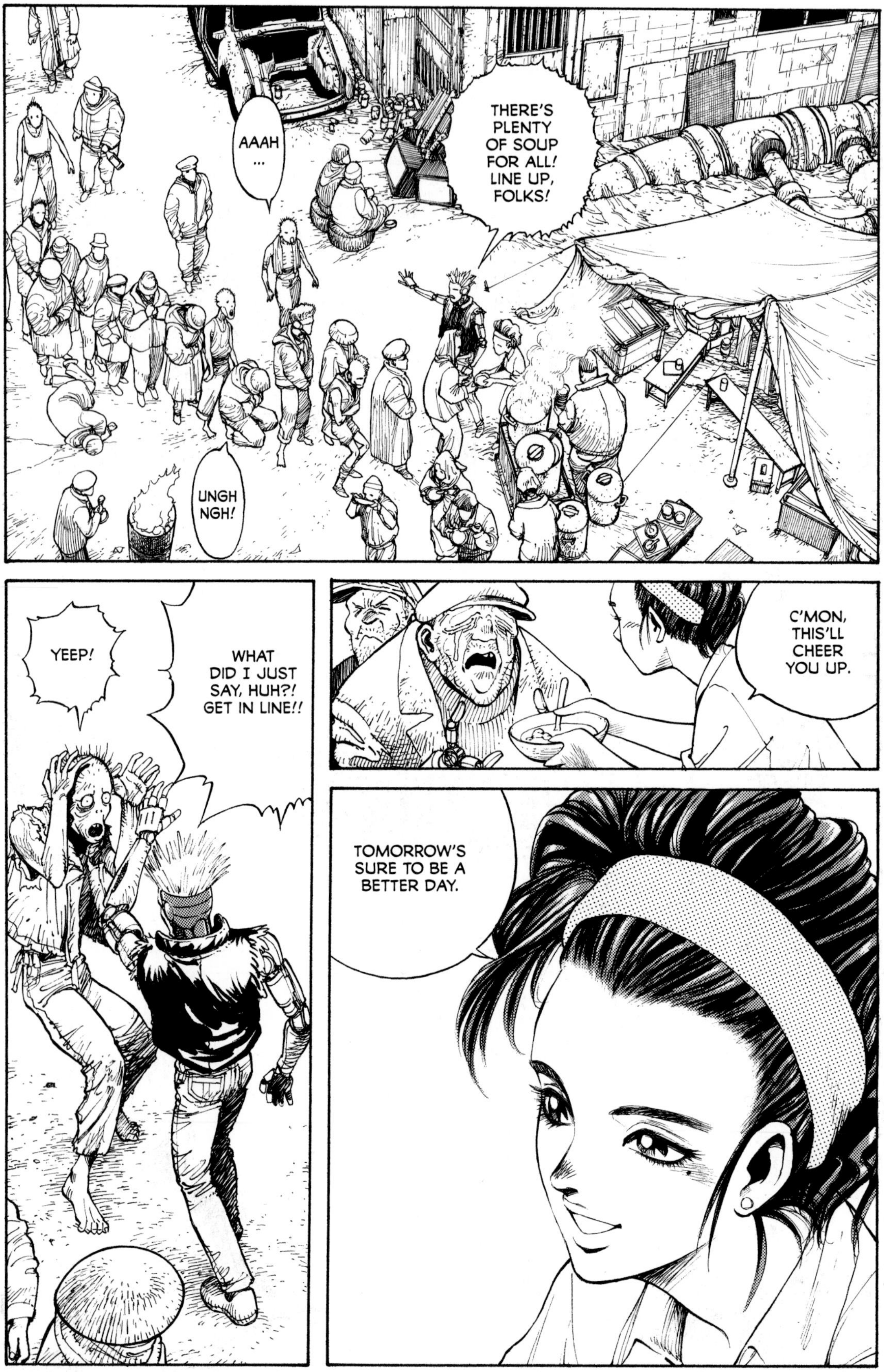
THERE'S PLENTY OF SOUP FOR ALL! LINE UP, FOLKS!
AAAH ...
UNGH NGH!
C'MON, THIS'LL CHEER YOU UP.
TOMORROW'S SURE TO BE A BETTER DAY.
WHAT DID I JUST SAY, HUH?! GET IN LINE!!
YEEP!

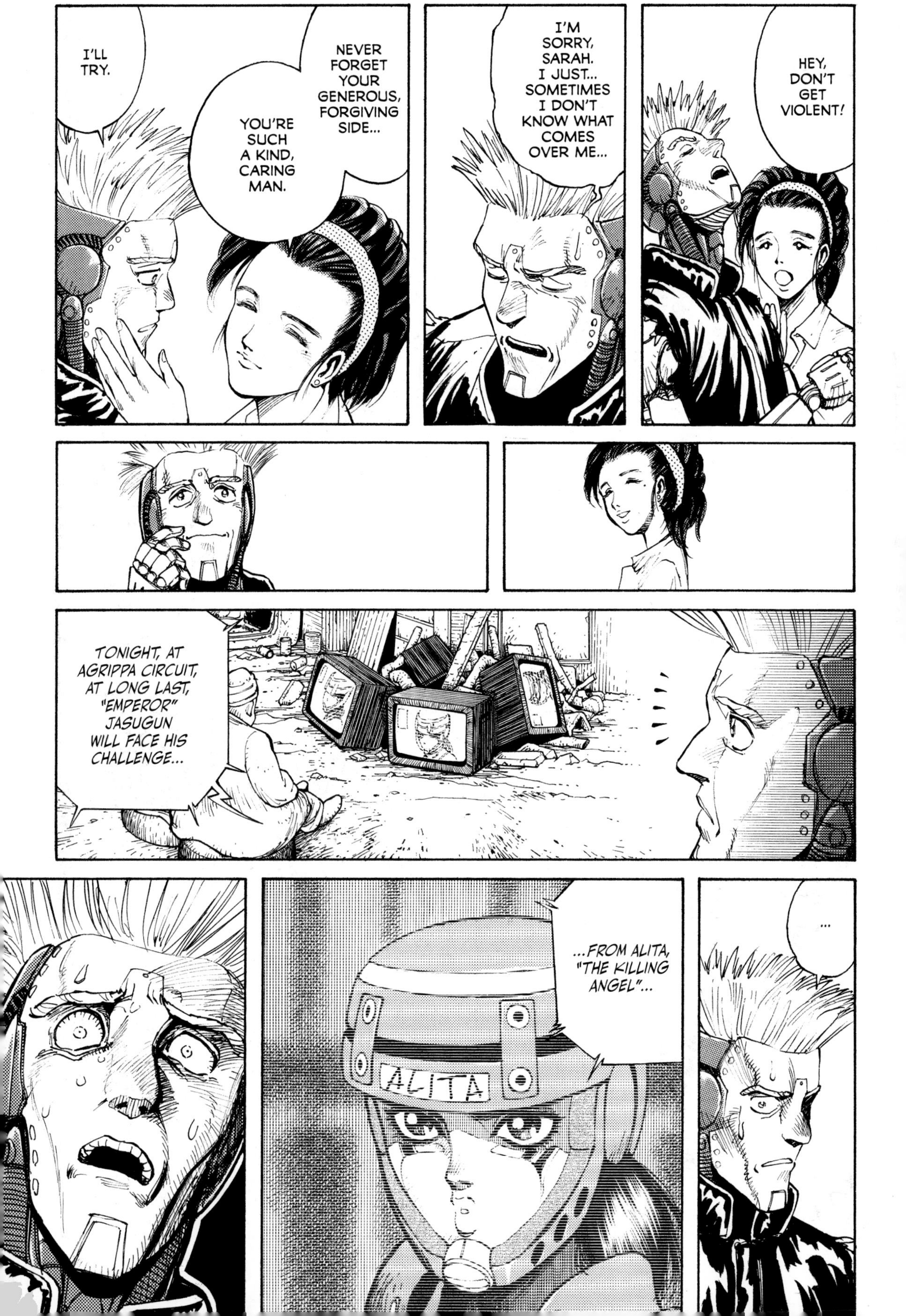
HEY, DON'T GET VIOLENT!
I'M SORRY, SARAH. I JUST... SOMETIMES I DON'T KNOW WHAT COMES OVER ME...
NEVER FORGET YOUR GENEROUS, FORGIVING SIDE...
YOU'RE SUCH A KIND, CARING MAN.
I'LL TRY.
TONIGHT, AT AGRIPPA CIRCUIT, AT LONG LAST, "EMPEROR" JASUGUN WILL FACE HIS CHALLENGE...
...
...FROM ALITA, "THE KILLING ANGEL"...
ALITA

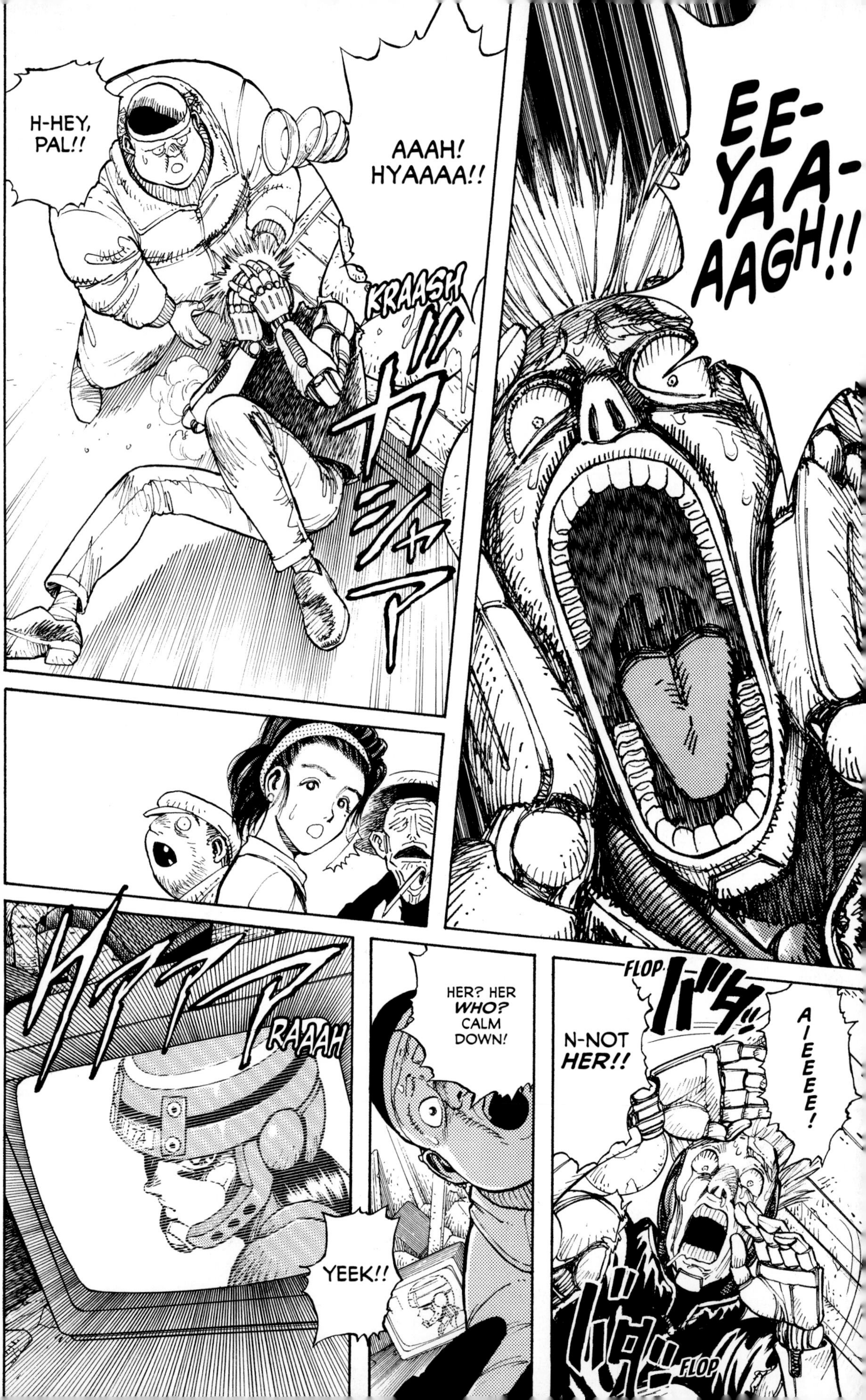
EE-YAA-AAGH!!
AAAH! HYAAAA!!
H-HEY, PAL!!
KRAASH
AIEEEEE!
FLOP
N-NOT HER!!
FLOP
HER? HER WHO? CALM DOWN!
YEEK!!
RAAAH

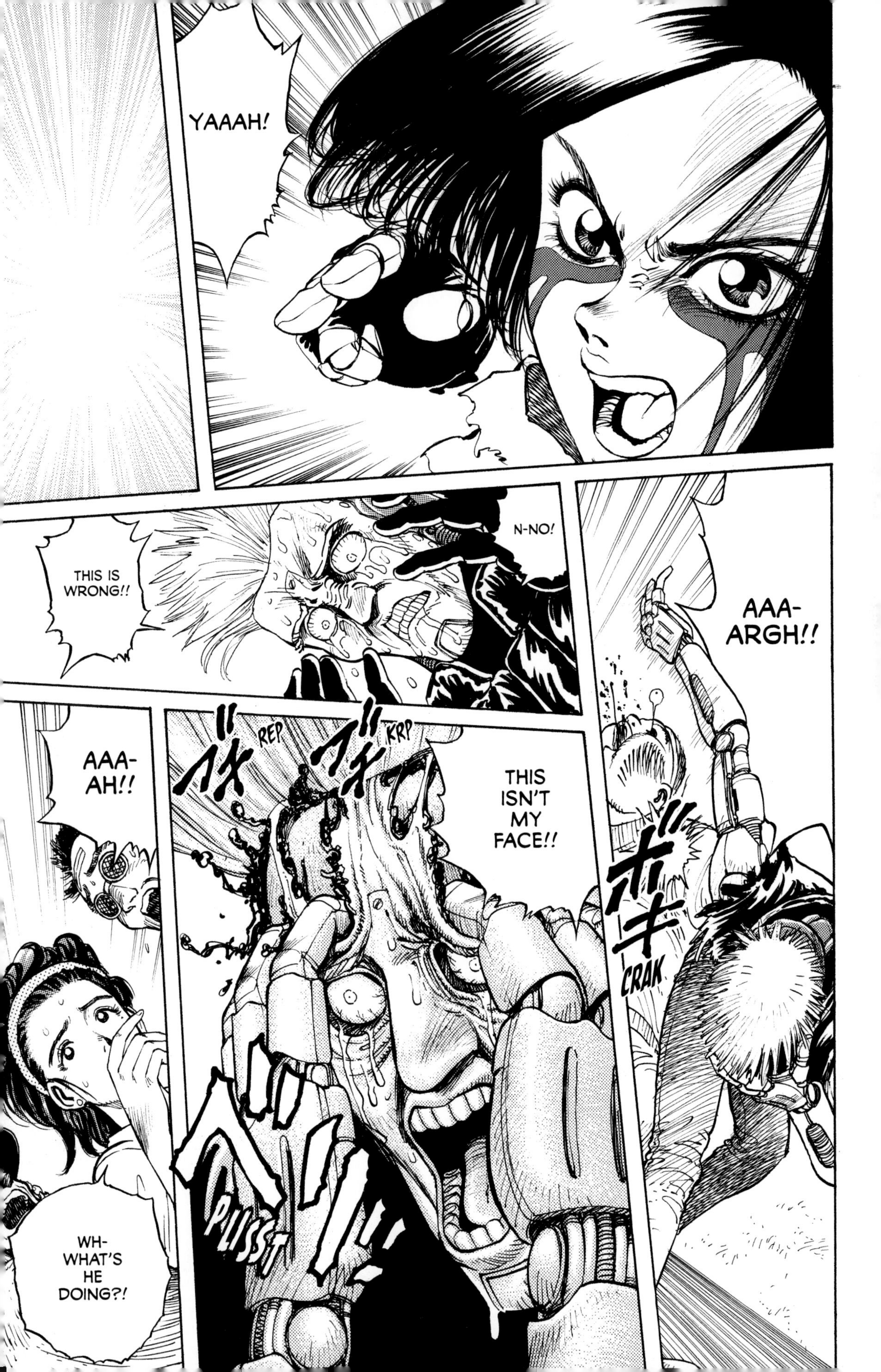
YAAAH!
AAA-ARGH!!
CRAK
N-NO!
THIS IS WRONG!!
REP
KRP
THIS ISN'T MY FACE!!
PLISST
AAA-AH!!
WH-WHAT'S HE DOING?!

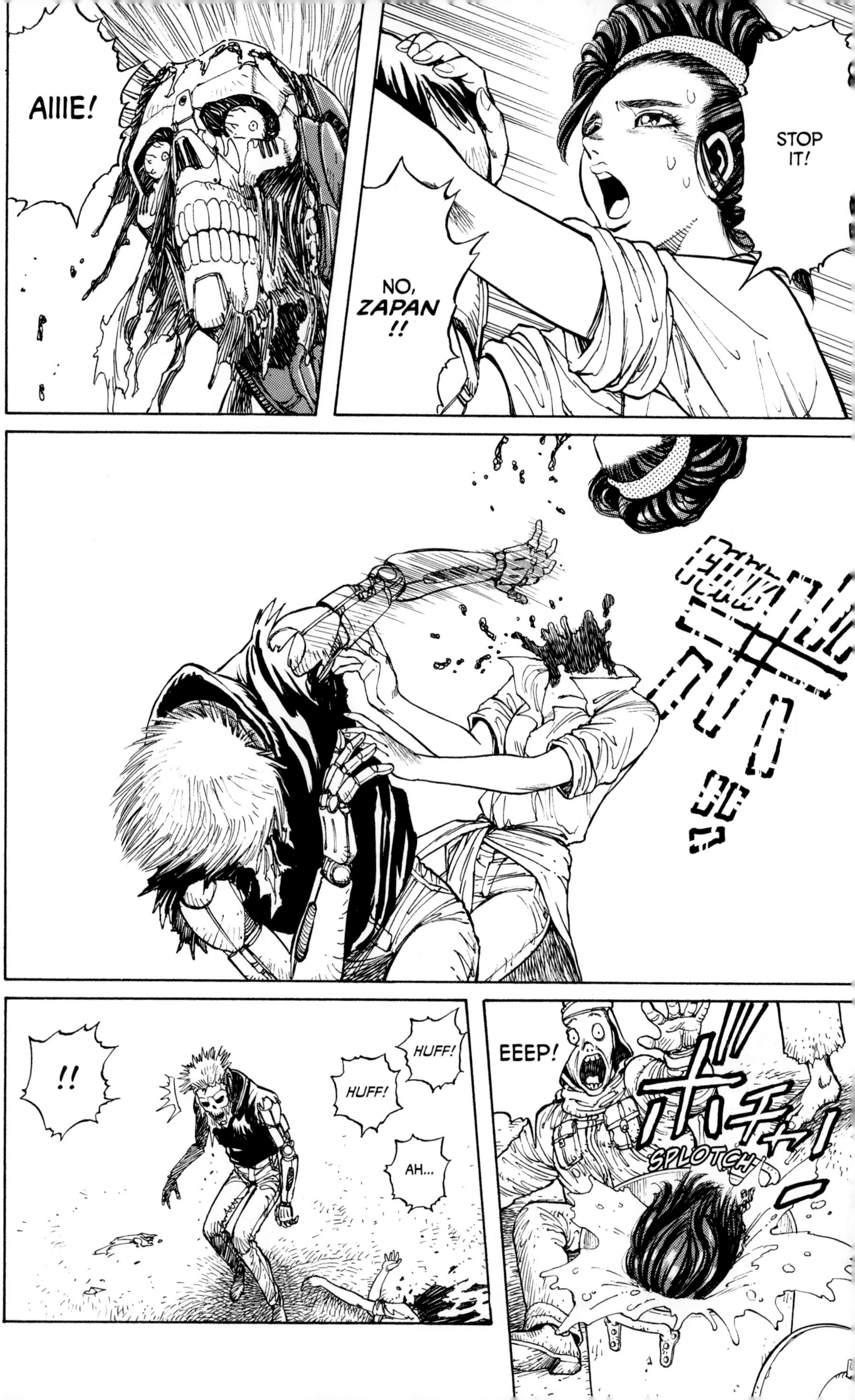
STOP IT!
NO, ZAPAN!!
AIIIE!
EEEP!
SPLOTCH
HUFF!
HUFF!
AH...
!!

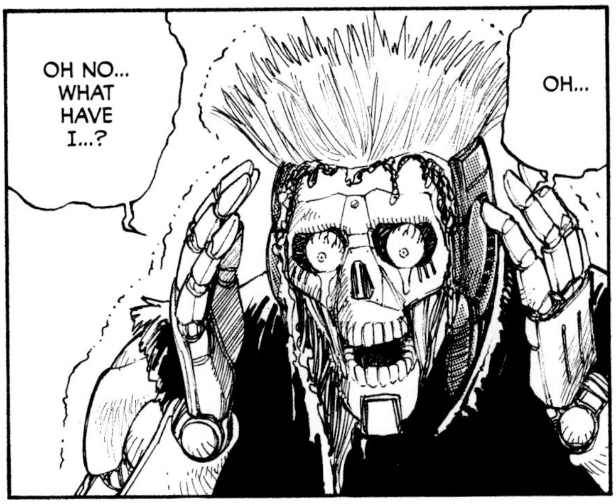
OH...
OH NO... WHAT HAVE I...?

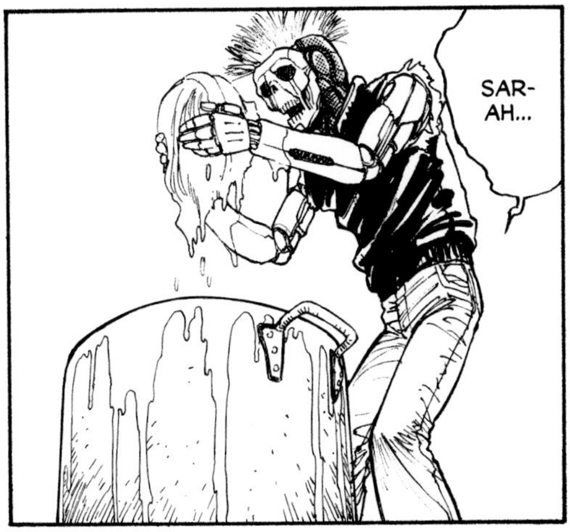
SAR-AH...

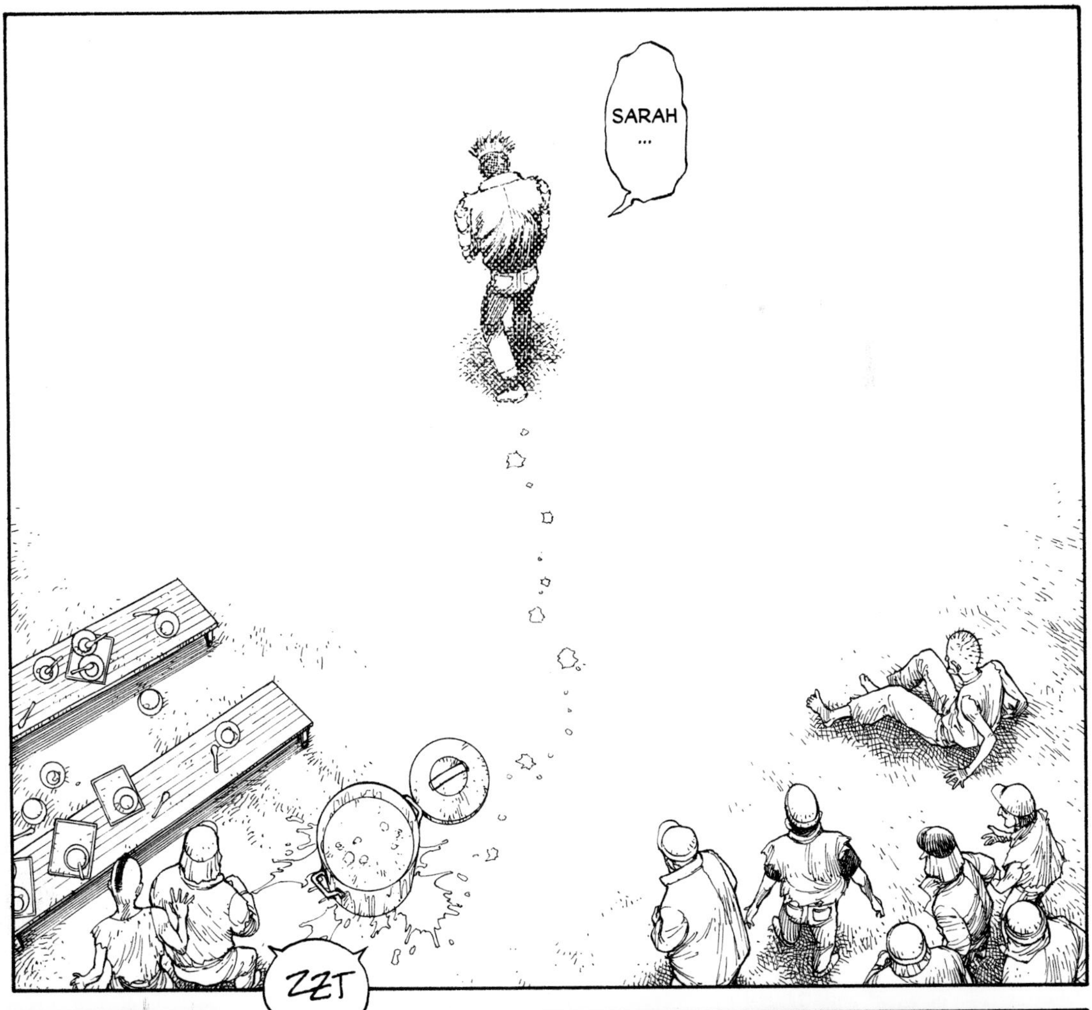
SARAH ...

ZAPAN

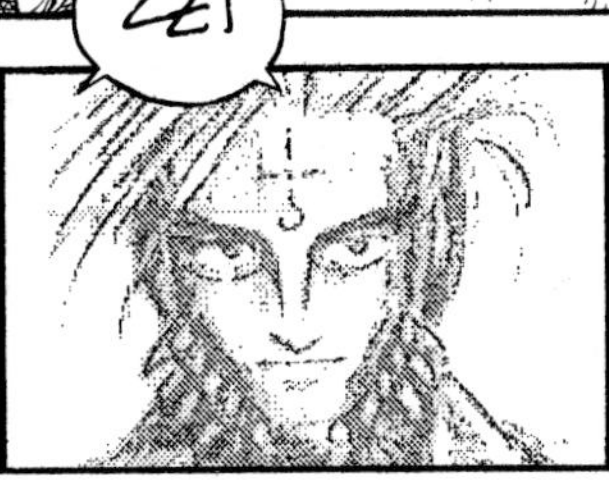
ZZT

Former Hunter-Warrior:
Wanted for murder
50,000 chip bounty
Note: Injured face

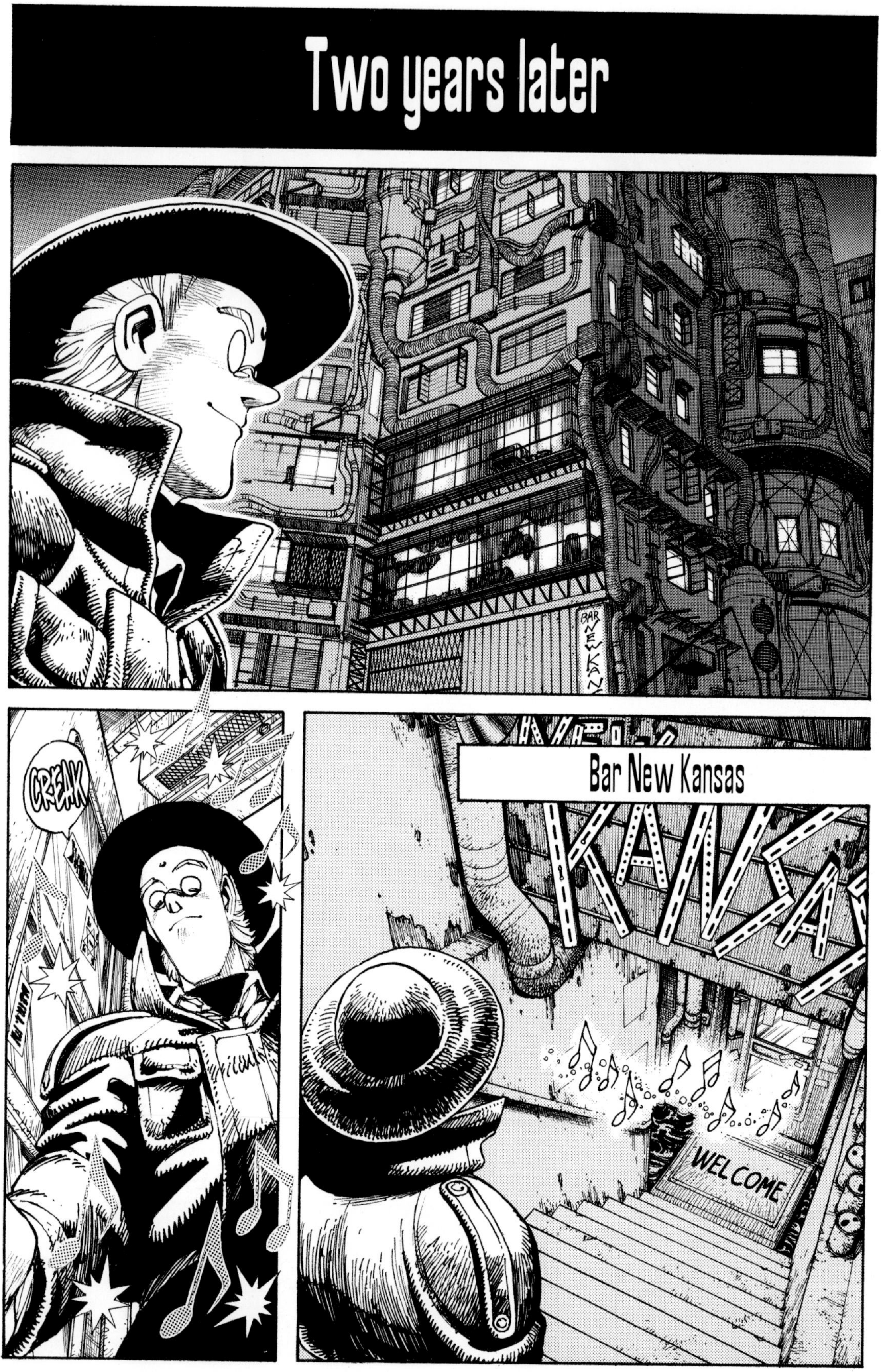
Two years later
Bar New Kansas
WELCOME
CREAK

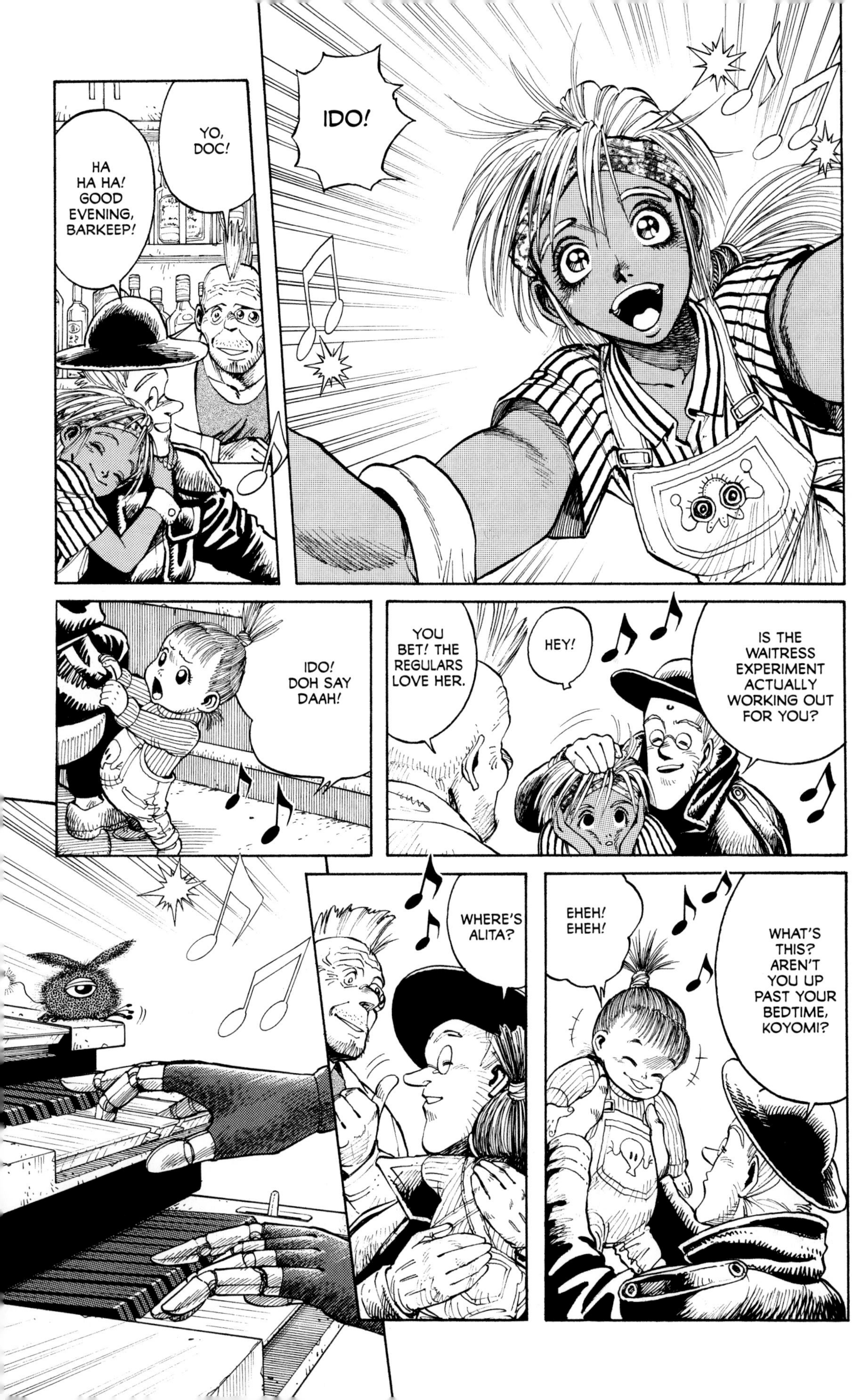
IDO!
YO, DOC!
HA HA HA! GOOD EVENING, BARKEEP!
IS THE WAITRESS EXPERIMENT ACTUALLY WORKING OUT FOR YOU?
HEY!
YOU BET! THE REGULARS LOVE HER.
IDO! DOH SAY DAAH!
WHAT'S THIS? AREN'T YOU UP PAST YOUR BEDTIME, KOYOMI?
EHEH! EHEH!
WHERE'S ALITA?

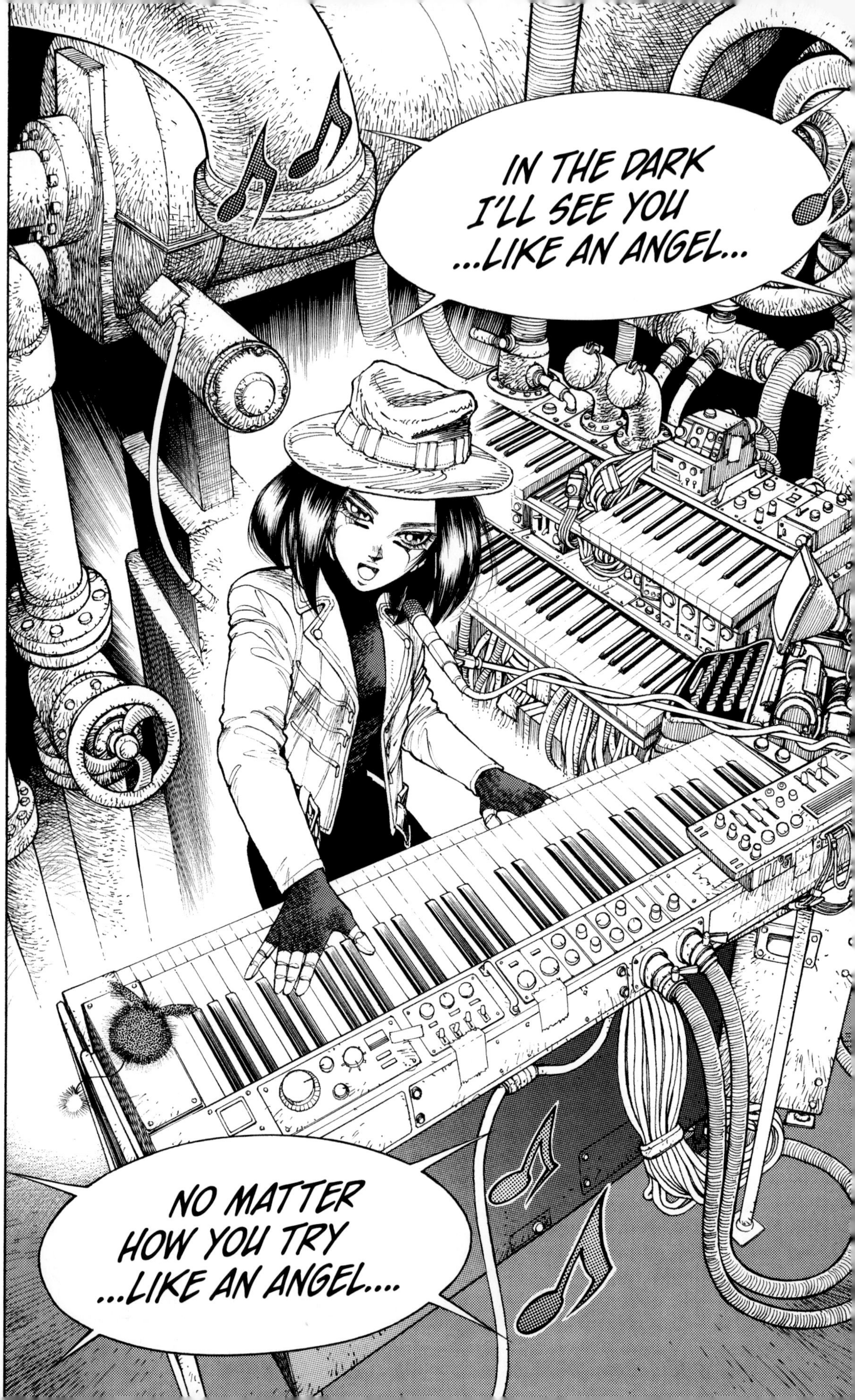
IN THE DARK I'LL SEE YOU ...LIKE AN ANGEL...
NO MATTER HOW YOU TRY ...LIKE AN ANGEL....

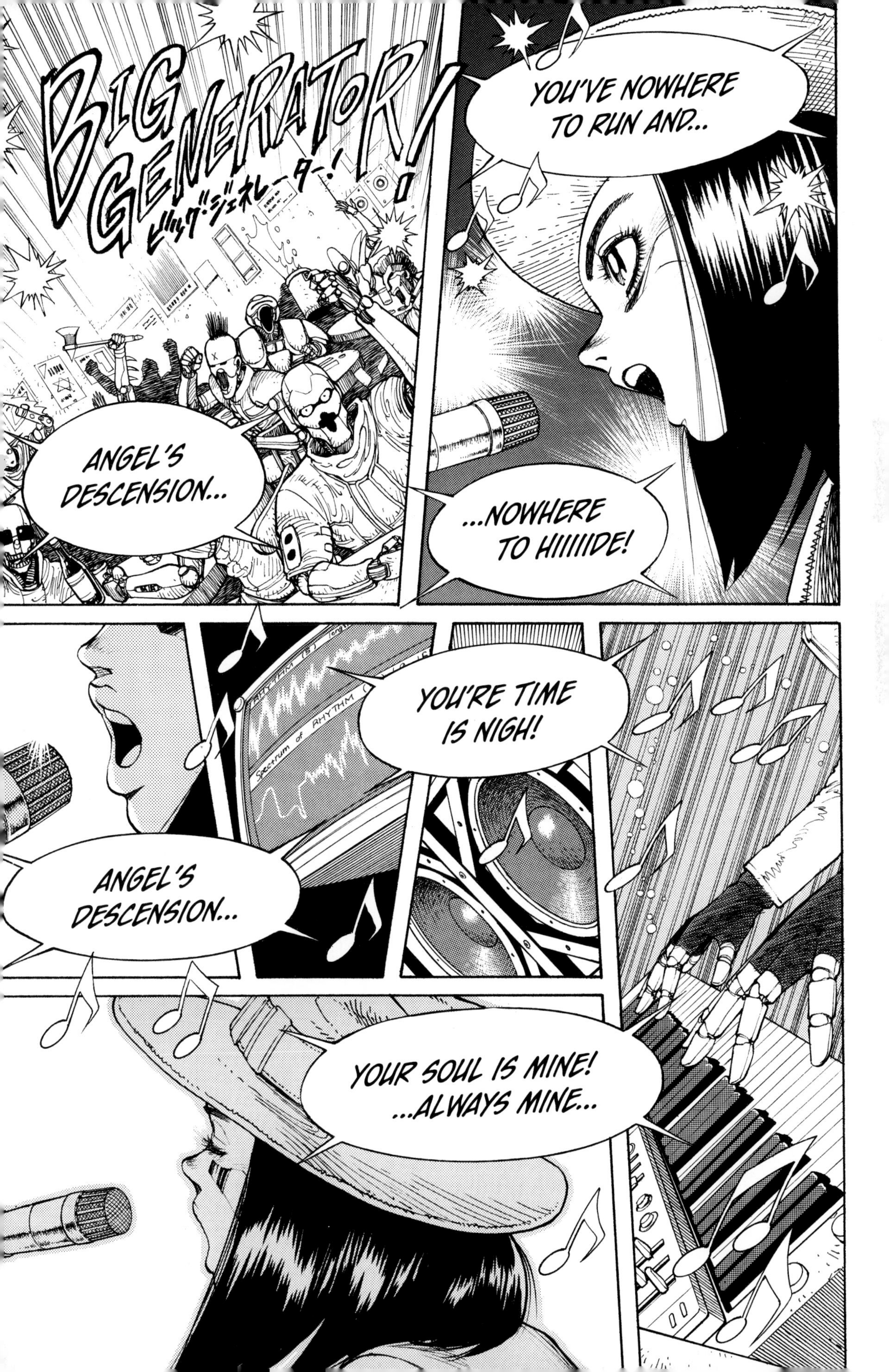
YOU'VE NOWHERE TO RUN AND...
...NOWHERE TO HIIIIIDE!
BIG GENERATOR!
ビッグ・ジェネレーター！
ANGEL'S DESCENSION...
Spectrum of RHYTHM
YOU'RE TIME IS NIGH!
ANGEL'S DESCENSION...
YOUR SOUL IS MINE! ...ALWAYS MINE...

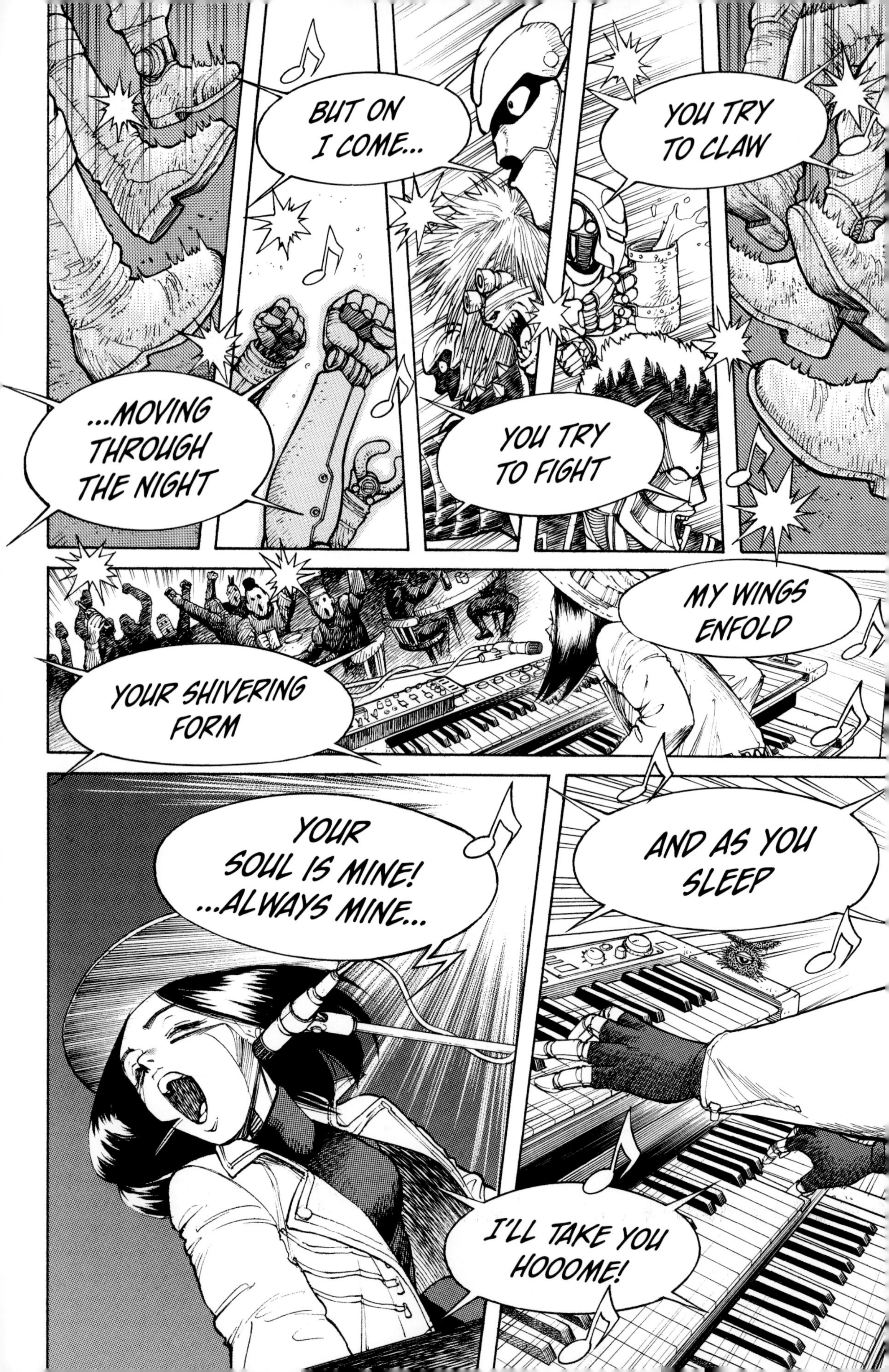
YOU TRY TO CLAW
BUT ON I COME...
YOU TRY TO FIGHT
...MOVING THROUGH THE NIGHT
MY WINGS ENFOLD
YOUR SHIVERING FORM
AND AS YOU SLEEP
YOUR SOUL IS MINE! ...ALWAYS MINE...
I'LL TAKE YOU HOOOME!

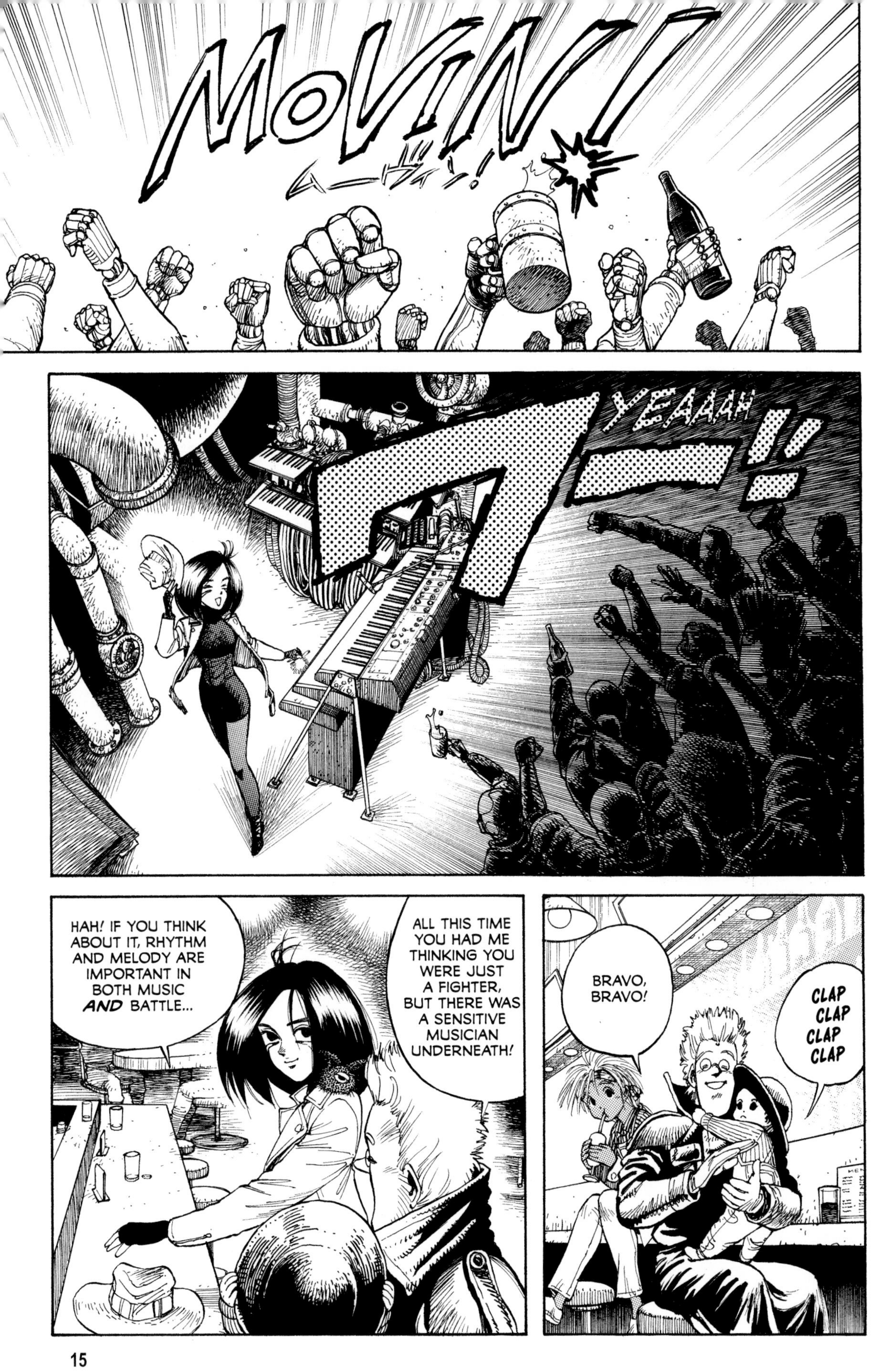
MoVIN'!
ムーヴィン!
YEAAAH
!!
BRAVO, BRAVO!
CLAP CLAP CLAP CLAP
ALL THIS TIME YOU HAD ME THINKING YOU WERE JUST A FIGHTER, BUT THERE WAS A SENSITIVE MUSICIAN UNDERNEATH!
HAH! IF YOU THINK ABOUT IT, RHYTHM AND MELODY ARE IMPORTANT IN BOTH MUSIC ***AND*** BATTLE...

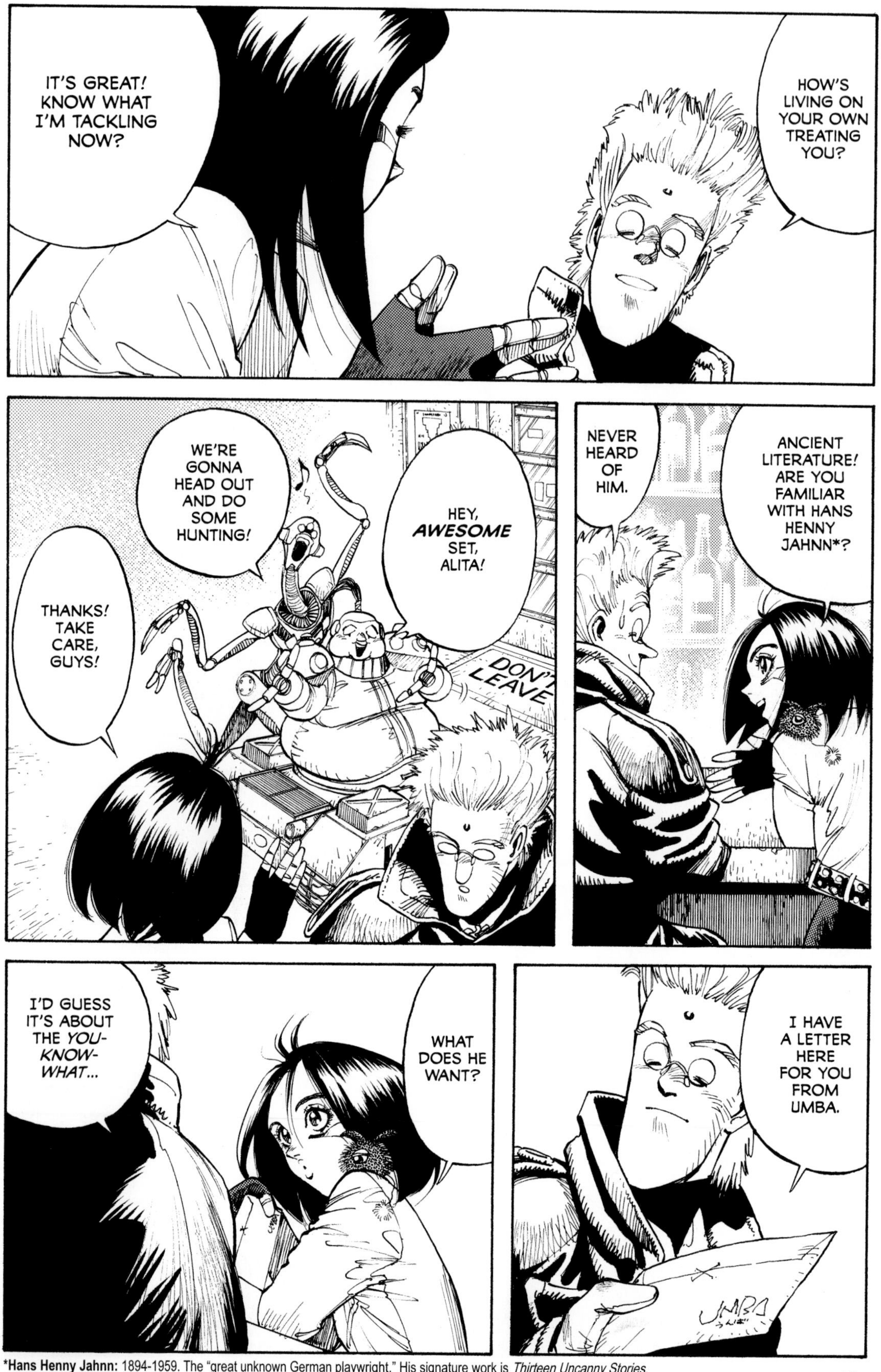
HOW'S LIVING ON YOUR OWN TREATING YOU?
IT'S GREAT! KNOW WHAT I'M TACKLING NOW?
ANCIENT LITERATURE! ARE YOU FAMILIAR WITH HANS HENNY JAHNN*?
NEVER HEARD OF HIM.
HEY, AWESOME SET, ALITA!
WE'RE GONNA HEAD OUT AND DO SOME HUNTING!
DON'T LEAVE
THANKS! TAKE CARE, GUYS!
I HAVE A LETTER HERE FOR YOU FROM UMBA.
UMBA
WHAT DOES HE WANT?
I'D GUESS IT'S ABOUT THE YOU-KNOW-WHAT...

***Hans Henny Jahnn:** 1894-1959. The "great unknown German playwright." His signature work is *Thirteen Uncanny Stories*.

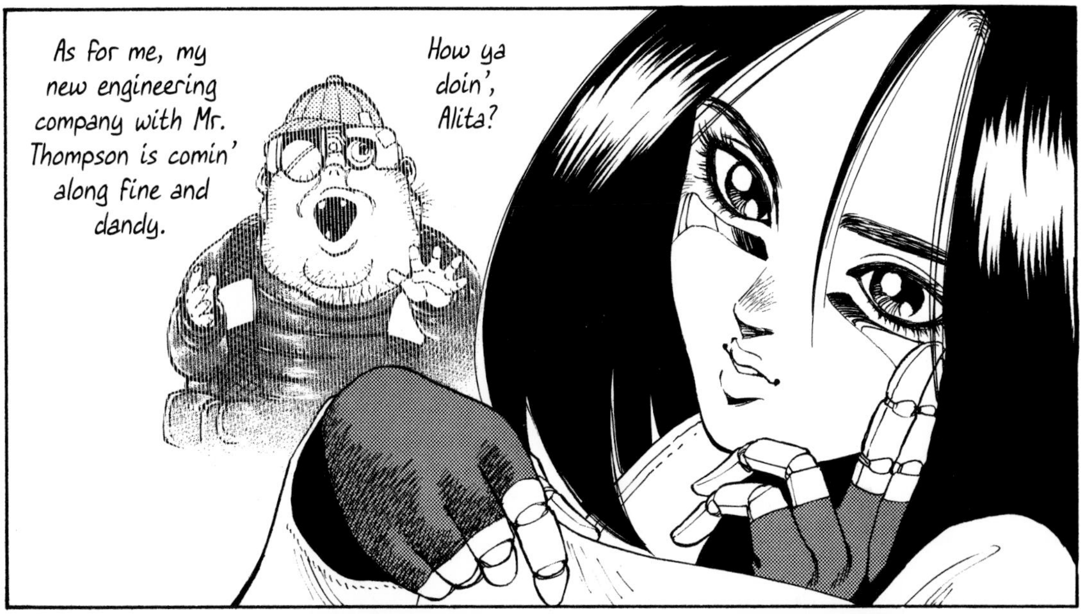
How ya doin', Alita?
As for me, my new engineering company with Mr. Thompson is comin' along fine and dandy.

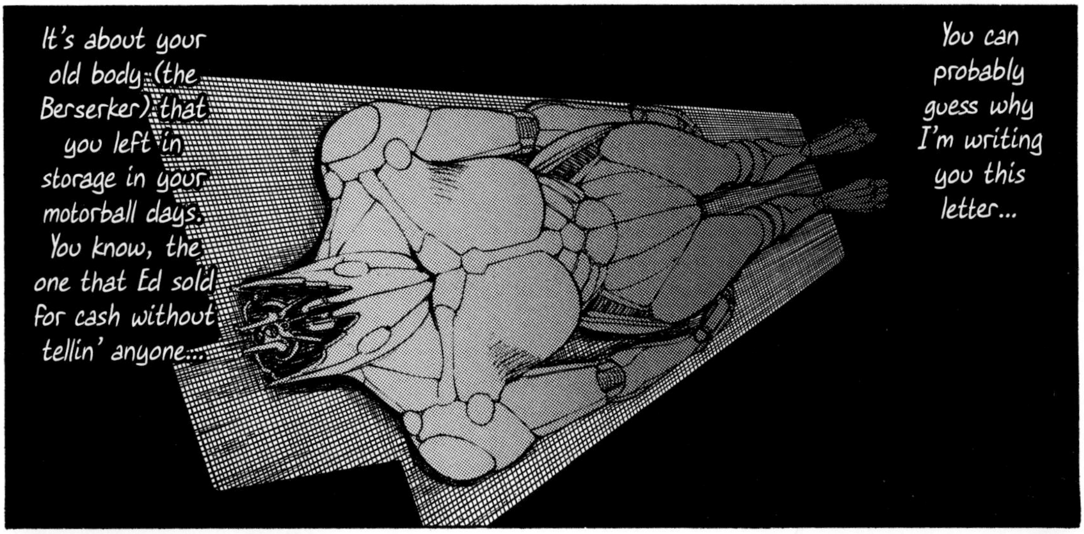
You can probably guess why I'm writing you this letter...
It's about your old body (the Berserker) that you left in storage in your motorball days. You know, the one that Ed sold for cash without tellin' anyone...

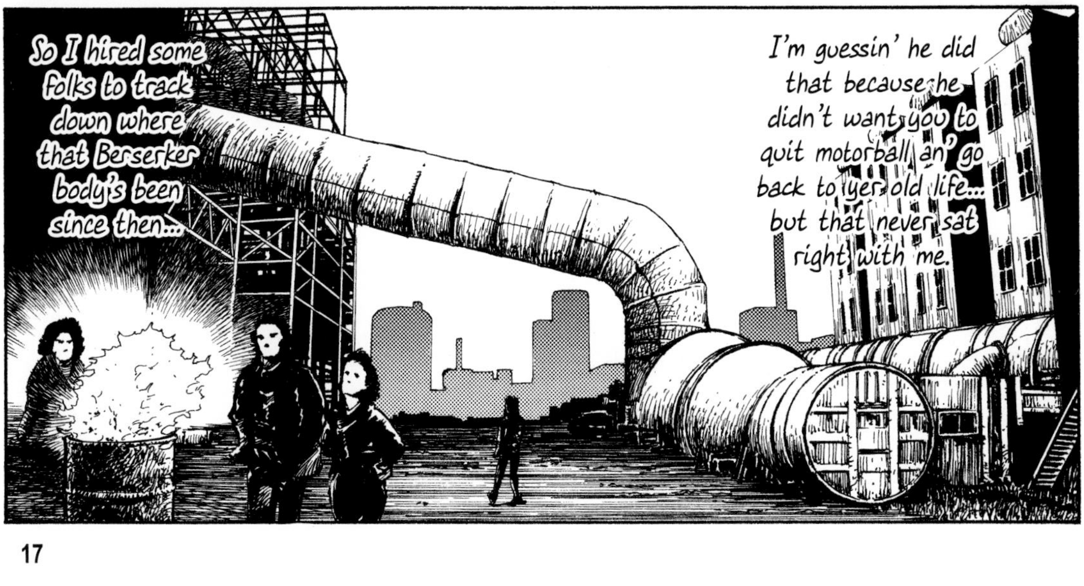
I'm guessin' he did that because he didn't want you to quit motorball an' go back to yer old life... but that never sat right with me.
So I hired some folks to track down where that Berserker body's been since then...

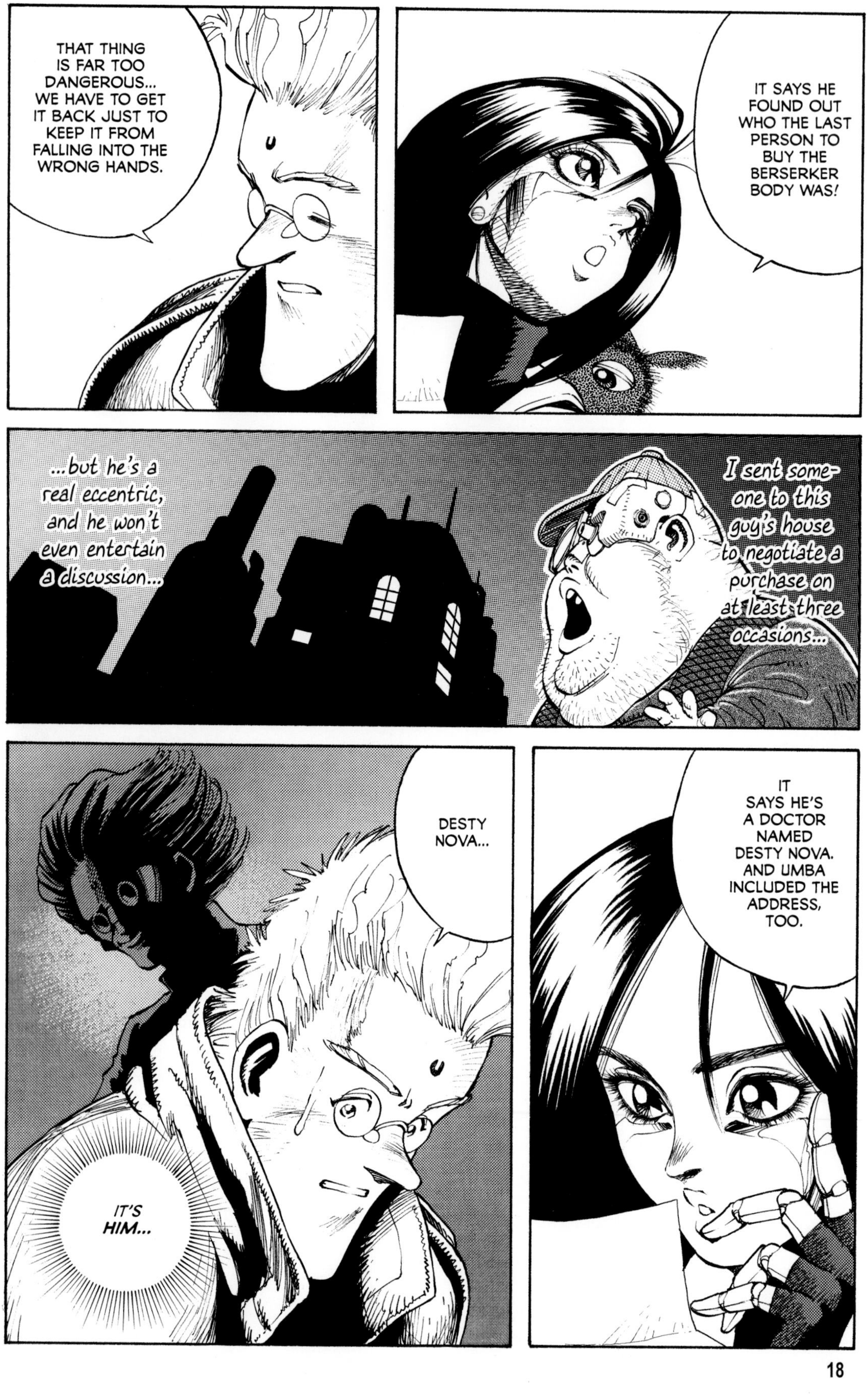
IT SAYS HE FOUND OUT WHO THE LAST PERSON TO BUY THE BERSERKER BODY WAS!
THAT THING IS FAR TOO DANGEROUS... WE HAVE TO GET IT BACK JUST TO KEEP IT FROM FALLING INTO THE WRONG HANDS.
I sent someone to this guy's house to negotiate a purchase on at least three occasions...
...but he's a real eccentric, and he won't even entertain a discussion...
IT SAYS HE'S A DOCTOR NAMED DESTY NOVA. AND UMBA INCLUDED THE ADDRESS, TOO.
DESTY NOVA...
IT'S HIM...

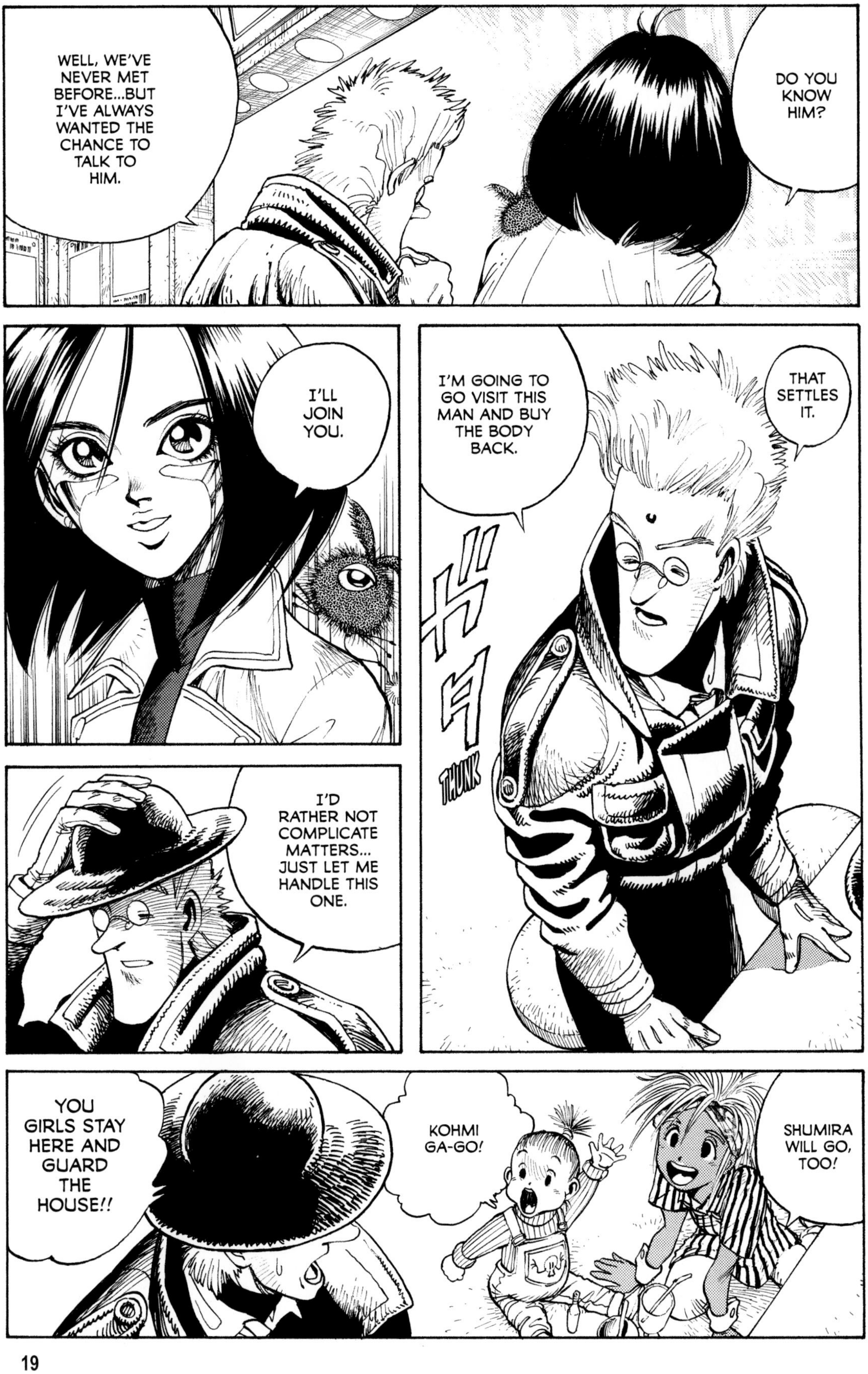
DO YOU KNOW HIM?
WELL, WE'VE NEVER MET BEFORE...BUT I'VE ALWAYS WANTED THE CHANCE TO TALK TO HIM.
THAT SETTLES IT.
I'M GOING TO GO VISIT THIS MAN AND BUY THE BODY BACK.
THUNK
I'LL JOIN YOU.
I'D RATHER NOT COMPLICATE MATTERS... JUST LET ME HANDLE THIS ONE.
SHUMIRA WILL GO, TOO!
KOHMI GA-GO!
YOU GIRLS STAY HERE AND GUARD THE HOUSE!!

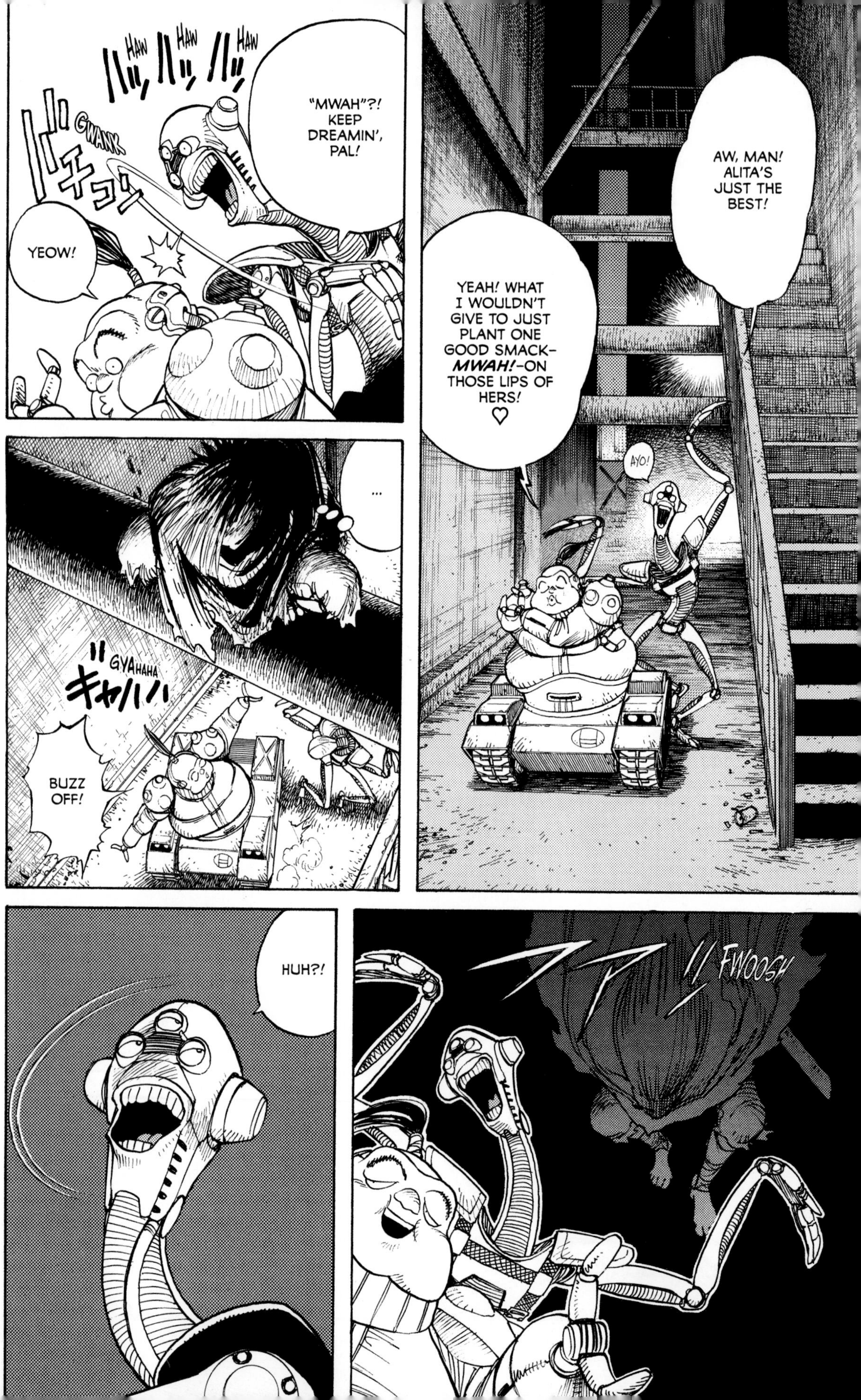
AW, MAN! ALITA'S JUST THE BEST!
YEAH! WHAT I WOULDN'T GIVE TO JUST PLANT ONE GOOD SMACK—*MWAH!*—ON THOSE LIPS OF HERS! ♡
AYO!
HAW HAW HAW
"MWAH"?! KEEP DREAMIN', PAL!
GWANK
YEOW!
...
GYAHAHA
BUZZ OFF!
FWOOSH
HUH?!

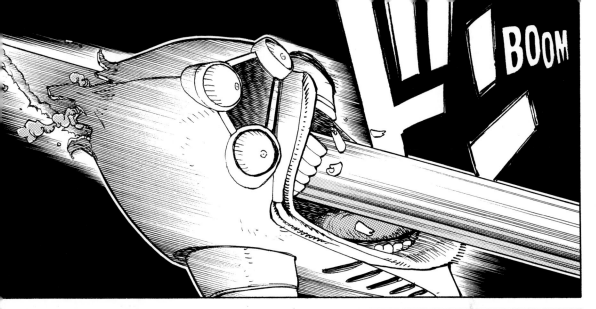

BOOM

AAAH...!

THWAM

FWOP

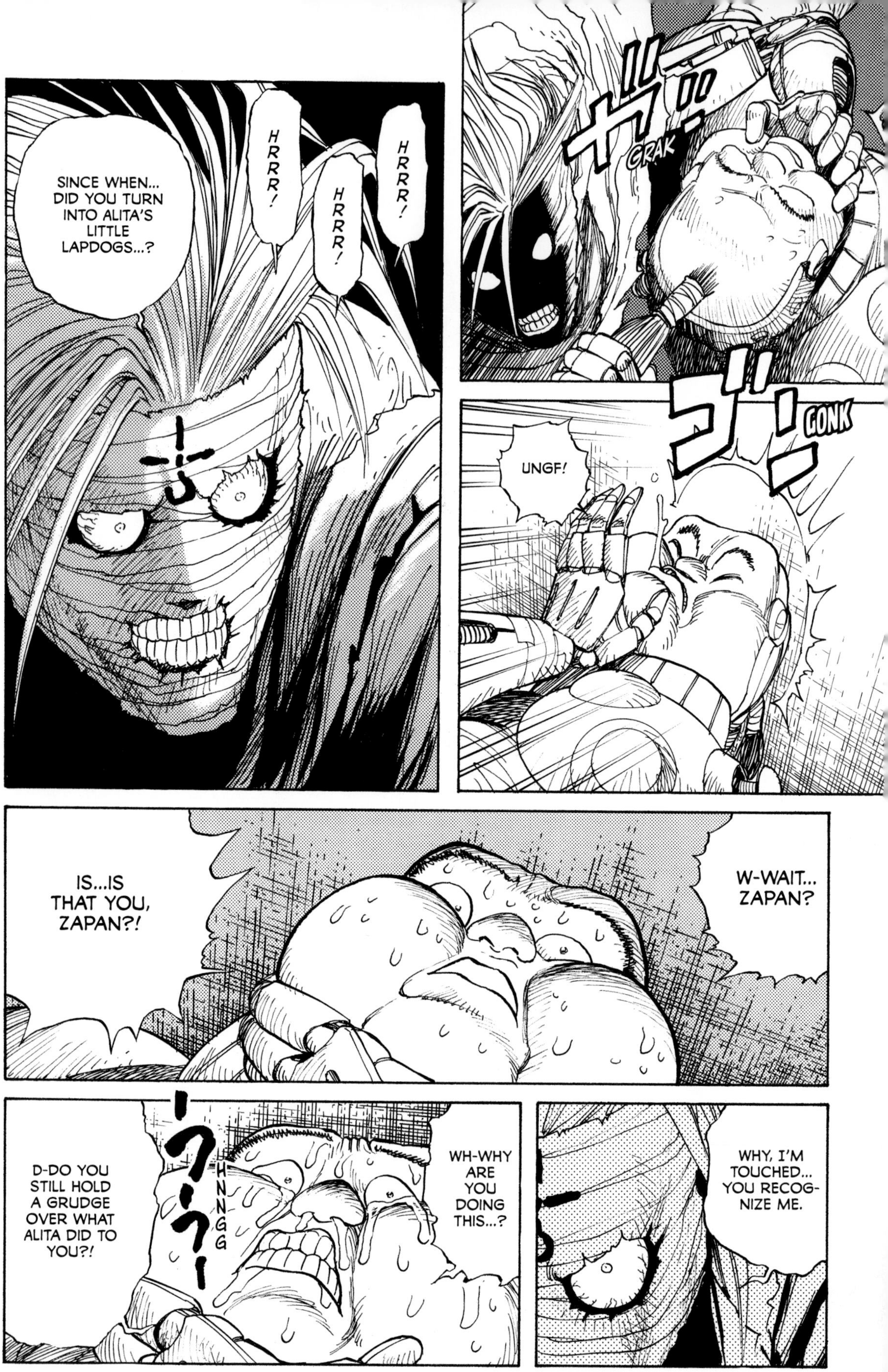
GRAK
GONK
UNGF!
HRRR!
HRRR!
HRRR!
SINCE WHEN... DID YOU TURN INTO ALITA'S LITTLE LAPDOGS...?
W-WAIT... ZAPAN?
IS...IS THAT YOU, ZAPAN?!
WHY, I'M TOUCHED... YOU RECOGNIZE ME.
WH-WHY ARE YOU DOING THIS...?
HNNGG
D-DO YOU STILL HOLD A GRUDGE OVER WHAT ALITA DID TO YOU?!

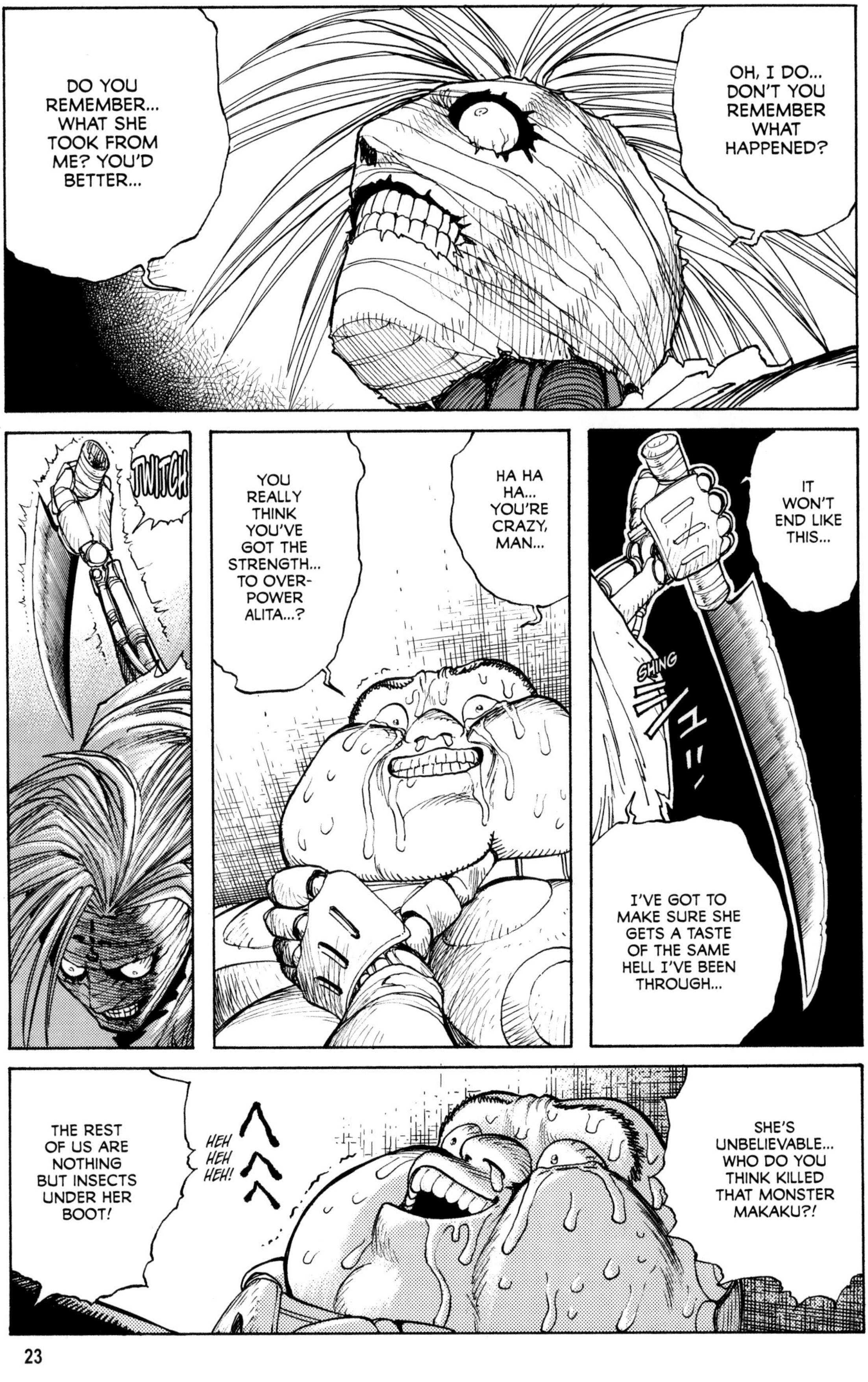
OH, I DO... DON'T YOU REMEMBER WHAT HAPPENED?
DO YOU REMEMBER... WHAT SHE TOOK FROM ME? YOU'D BETTER...
IT WON'T END LIKE THIS...
SHING
I'VE GOT TO MAKE SURE SHE GETS A TASTE OF THE SAME HELL I'VE BEEN THROUGH...
HA HA HA... YOU'RE CRAZY, MAN...
YOU REALLY THINK YOU'VE GOT THE STRENGTH... TO OVER-POWER ALITA...?
TWITCH
SHE'S UNBELIEVABLE... WHO DO YOU THINK KILLED THAT MONSTER MAKAKU?!
HEH HEH HEH!
THE REST OF US ARE NOTHING BUT INSECTS UNDER HER BOOT!

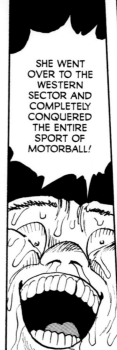

RRRGH...!
BRRR
SHE WENT OVER TO THE WESTERN SECTOR AND COMPLETELY CONQUERED THE ENTIRE SPORT OF MOTORBALL!
AAAAH!
RATTLE
RATTLE
SHE'S A DEMON! A *DEVIL!!*
THAT'S RIGHT! AND SHE'S FAR MORE POWERFUL THAN A MISERABLE CAST-OFF LIKE YOU!
NOW'S MY CHANCE!
CHKING
DIE, YOU PSYCHO!

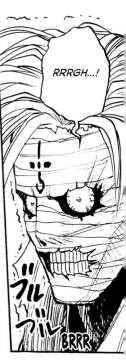

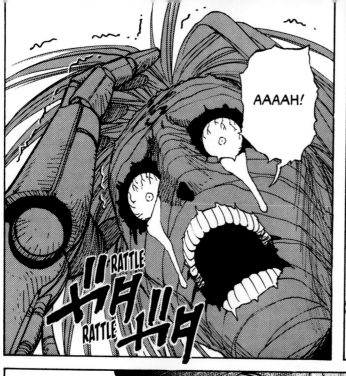

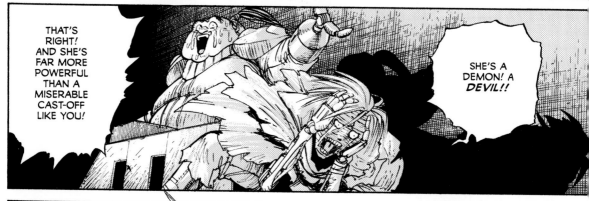

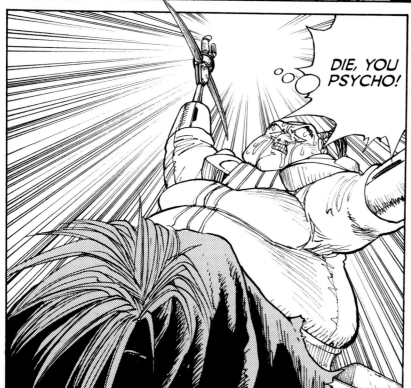

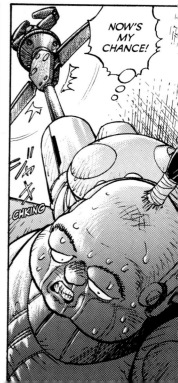

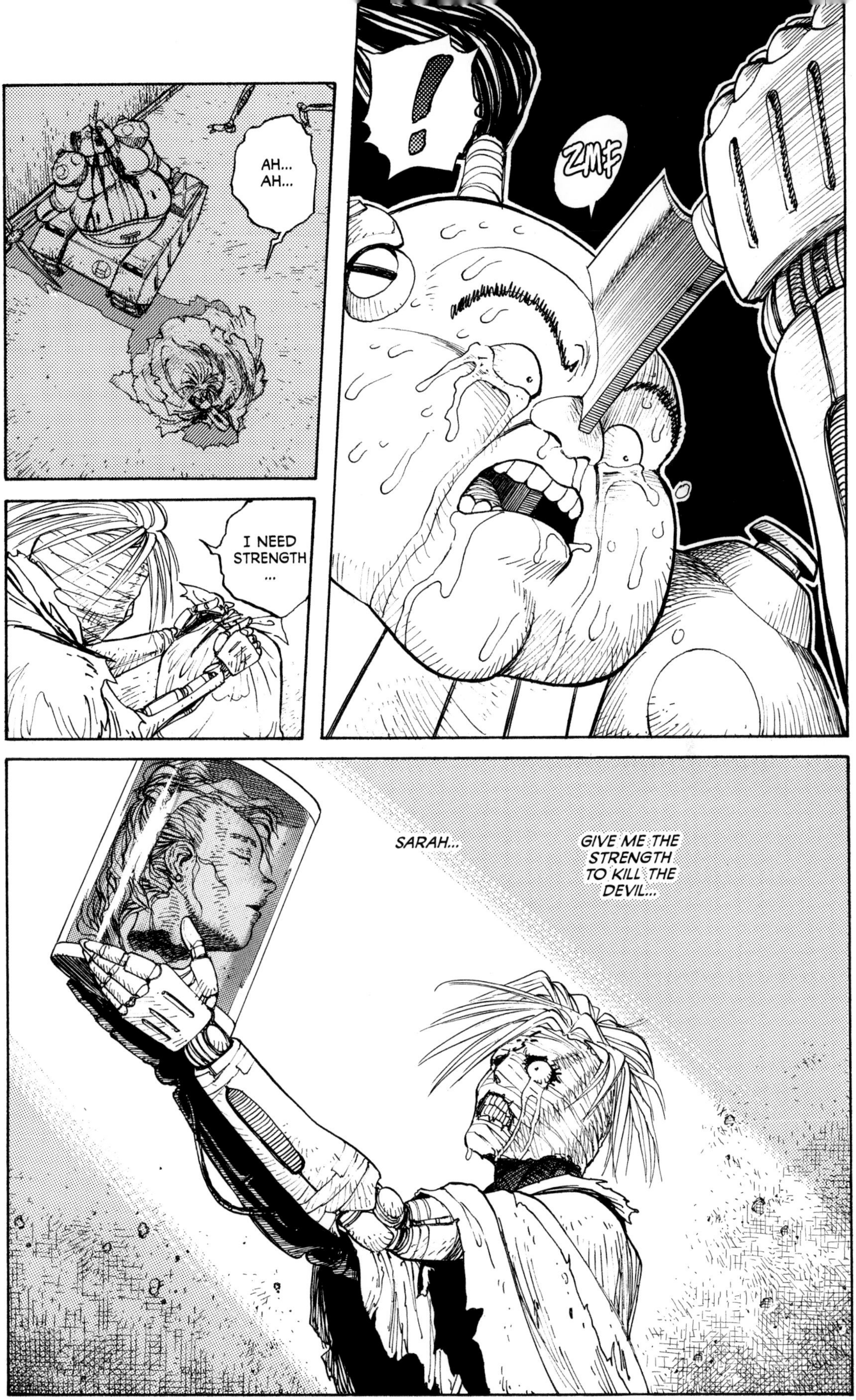
!
ZMF
AH... AH...
I NEED STRENGTH ...
GIVE ME THE STRENGTH TO KILL THE DEVIL...
SARAH...

FIGHT_024 Dog Master

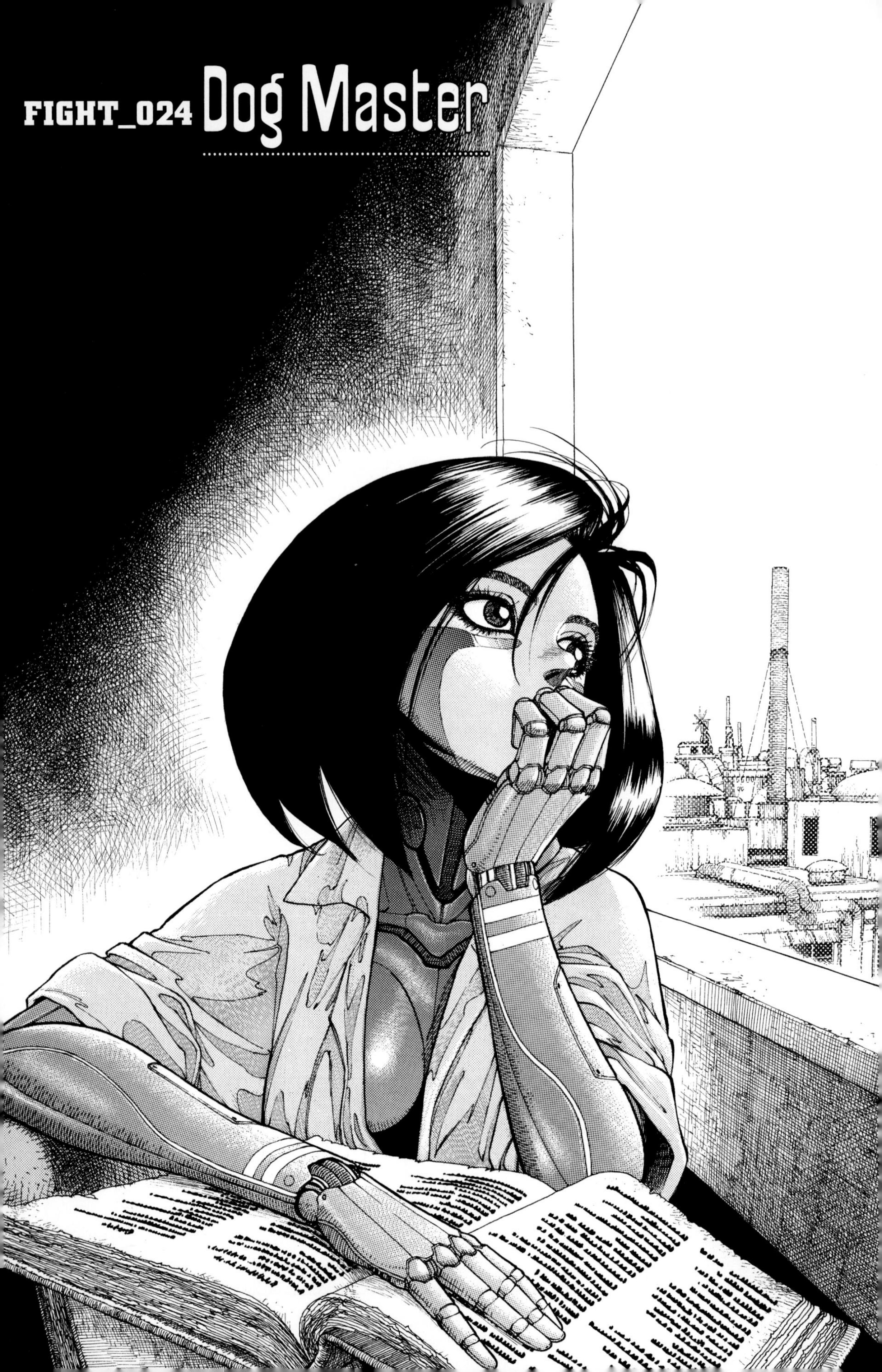

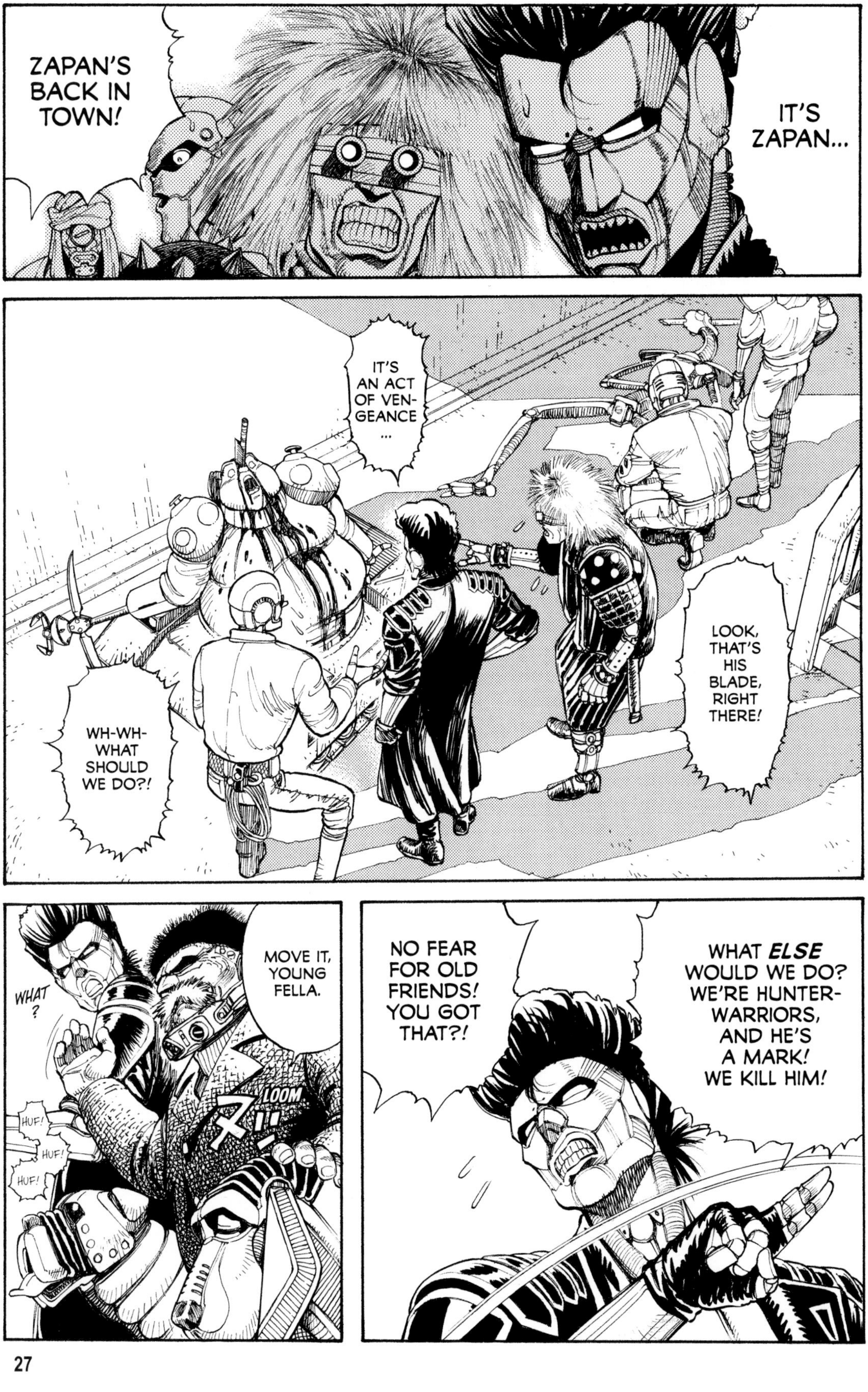
IT'S ZAPAN...
ZAPAN'S BACK IN TOWN!
IT'S AN ACT OF VENGEANCE ...
LOOK, THAT'S HIS BLADE, RIGHT THERE!
WH-WH-WHAT SHOULD WE DO?!
WHAT *ELSE* WOULD WE DO? WE'RE HUNTER-WARRIORS, AND HE'S A MARK! WE KILL HIM!
NO FEAR FOR OLD FRIENDS! YOU GOT THAT?!
MOVE IT, YOUNG FELLA.
WHAT ?
LOOM
HUF!
HUF!
HUF!

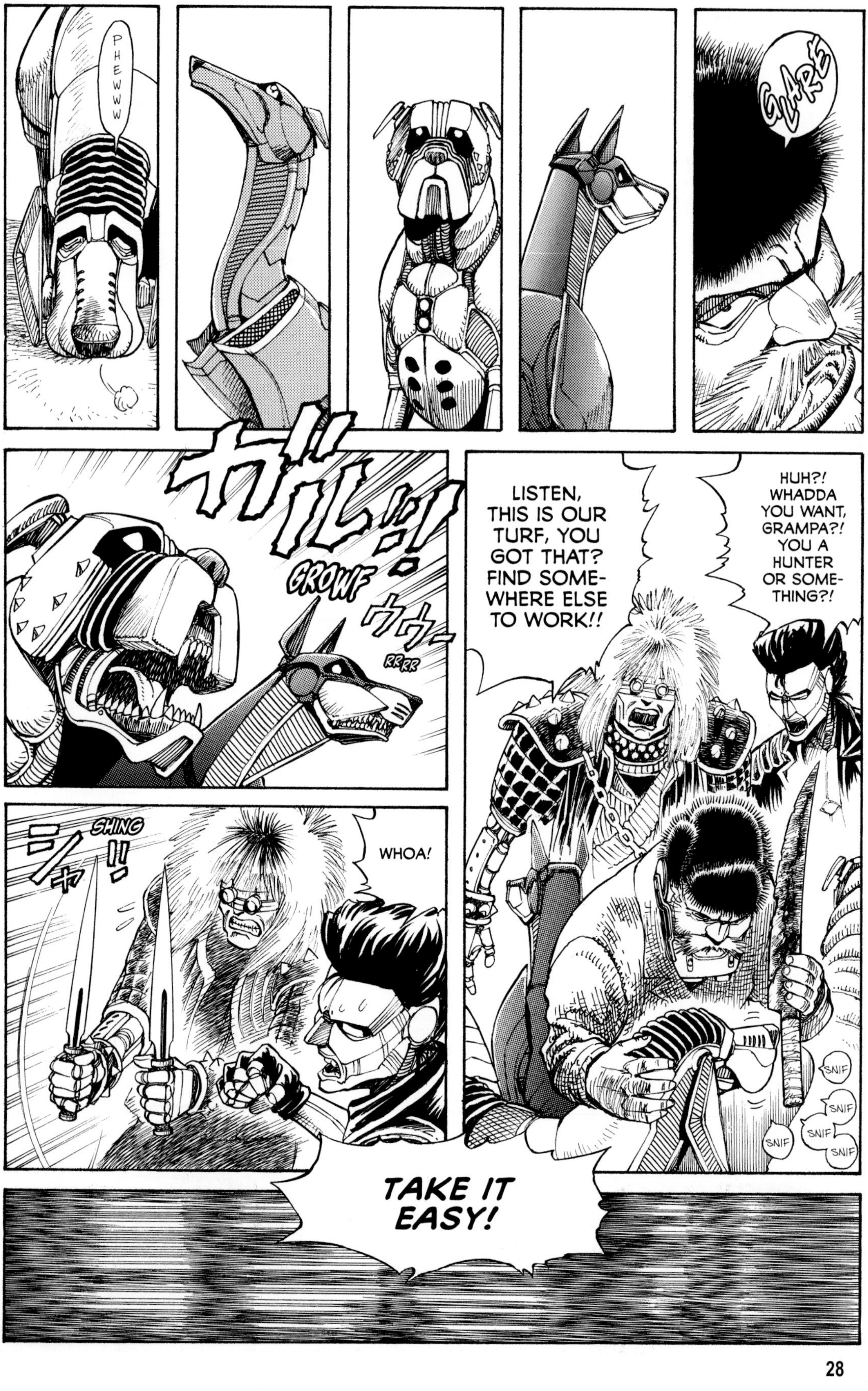
GLARE
PHEWWW
HUH?! WHADDA YOU WANT, GRAMPA?! YOU A HUNTER OR SOME-THING?!
LISTEN, THIS IS OUR TURF, YOU GOT THAT? FIND SOME-WHERE ELSE TO WORK!!
SNIF
SNIF
SNIF
SNIF
SNIF
ガルッ!!
GROWF
ウウー
RRRR
SHING
シャ!!
WHOA!
TAKE IT EASY!

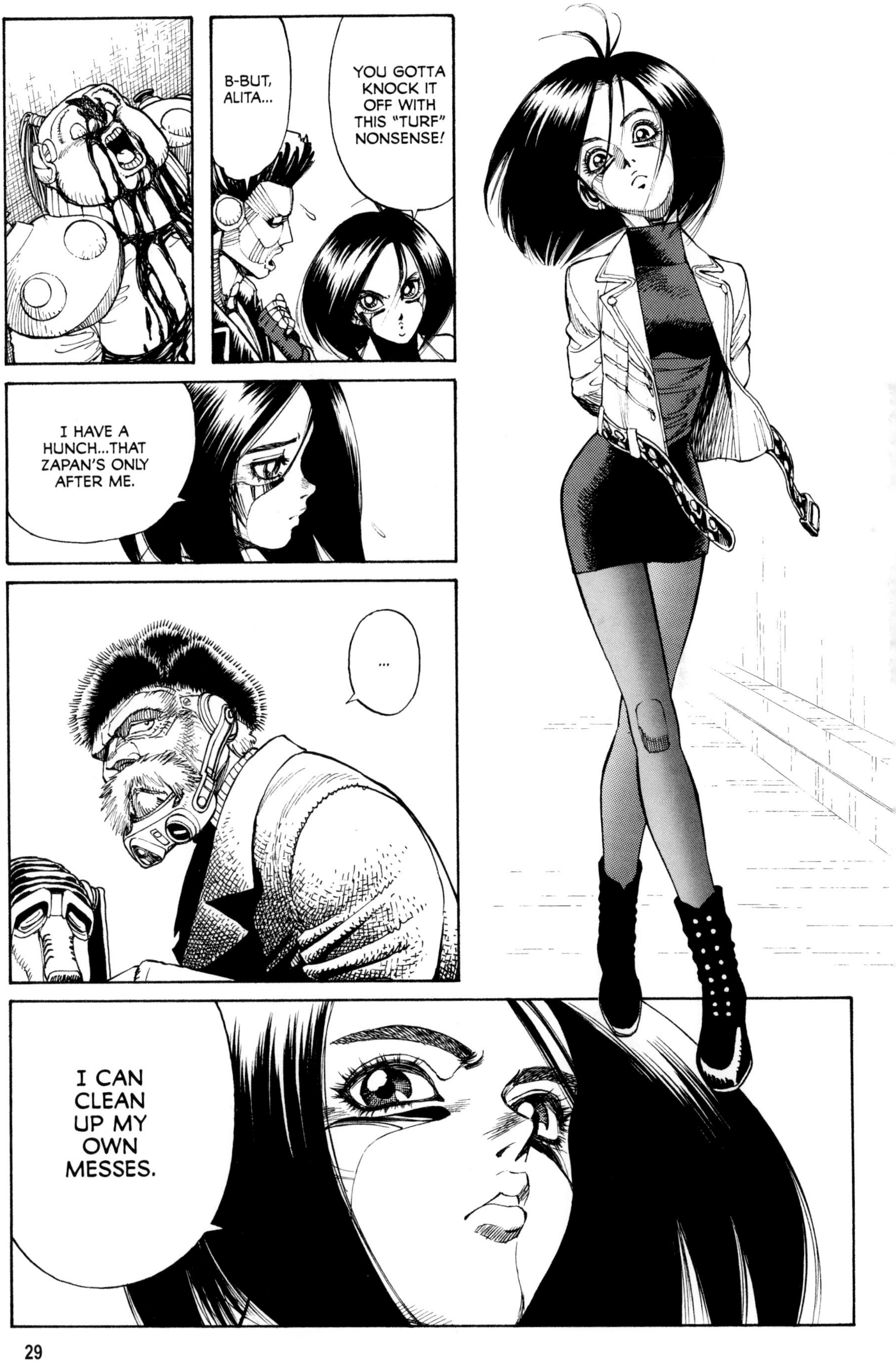
YOU GOTTA KNOCK IT OFF WITH THIS "TURF" NONSENSE!
B-BUT, ALITA...
I HAVE A HUNCH...THAT ZAPAN'S ONLY AFTER ME.
...
I CAN CLEAN UP MY OWN MESSES.

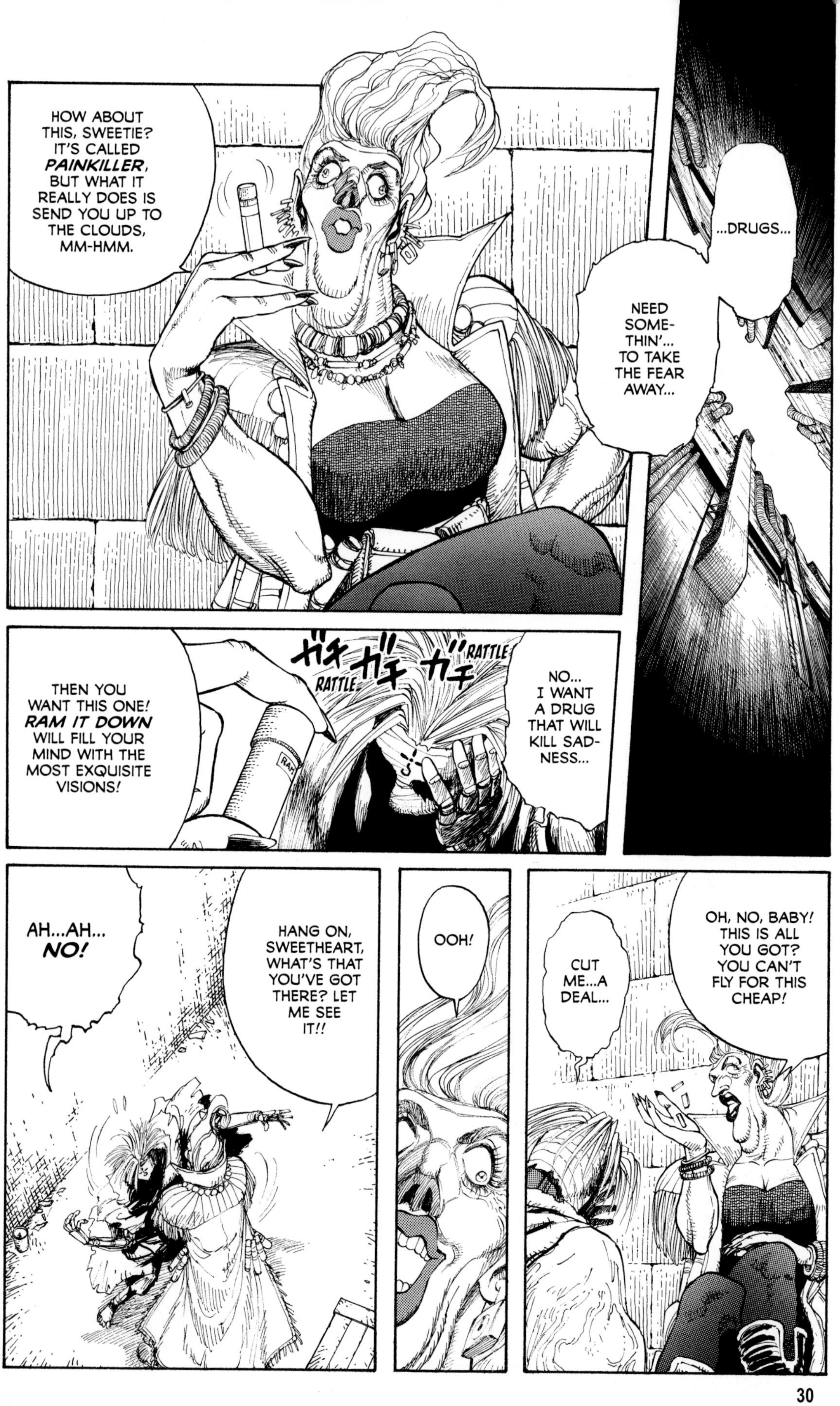
...DRUGS...
NEED SOME-THIN'... TO TAKE THE FEAR AWAY...
HOW ABOUT THIS, SWEETIE? IT'S CALLED ***PAINKILLER***, BUT WHAT IT REALLY DOES IS SEND YOU UP TO THE CLOUDS, MM-HMM.
NO... I WANT A DRUG THAT WILL KILL SAD-NESS...
ガチ RATTLE
ガチ
ガチ RATTLE
THEN YOU WANT THIS ONE! ***RAM IT DOWN*** WILL FILL YOUR MIND WITH THE MOST EXQUISITE VISIONS!
OH, NO, BABY! THIS IS ALL YOU GOT? YOU CAN'T FLY FOR THIS CHEAP!
CUT ME...A DEAL...
OOH!
HANG ON, SWEETHEART, WHAT'S THAT YOU'VE GOT THERE? LET ME SEE IT!!
AH...AH... ***NO!***

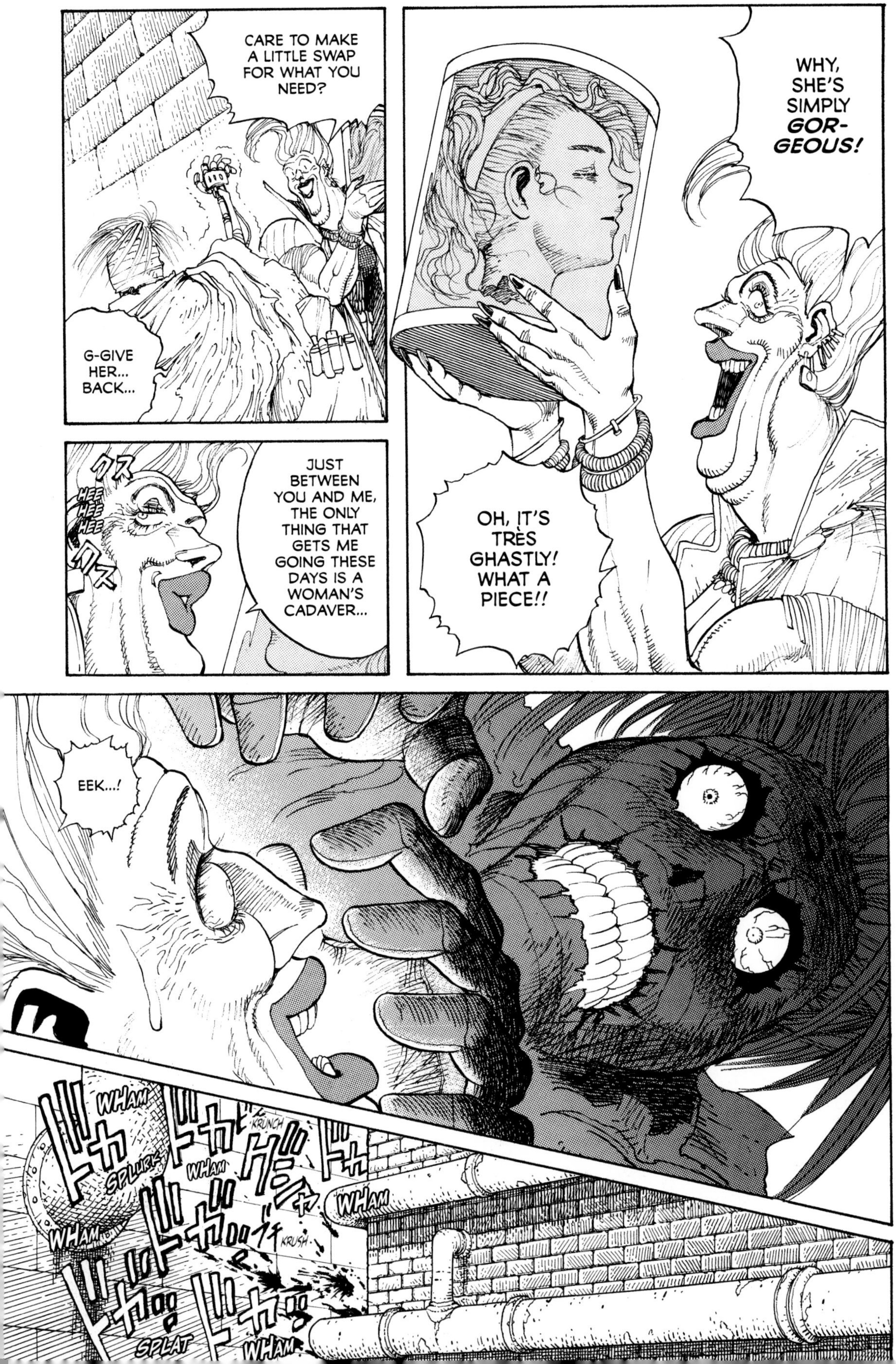
WHY, SHE'S SIMPLY ***GOR-GEOUS!***
OH, IT'S TRÈS GHASTLY! WHAT A PIECE!!
CARE TO MAKE A LITTLE SWAP FOR WHAT YOU NEED?
G-GIVE HER... BACK...
JUST BETWEEN YOU AND ME, THE ONLY THING THAT GETS ME GOING THESE DAYS IS A WOMAN'S CADAVER...
クス
HEE HEE HEE
クス
EEK...!
WHAM
KRUNCH
WHAM
SPLURK
WHAM
WHAM
KRUSH
SPLAT
WHAM

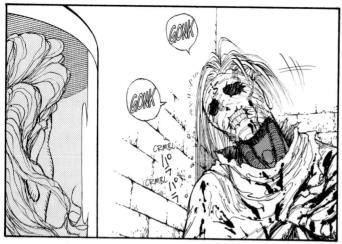

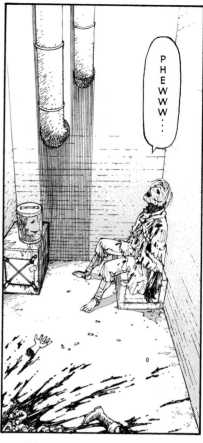

PHEWWW...
GONK
GONK
CRMBL
CRMBL
I DESERVE TO DIE LIKE THIS, SARAH...
I'M JUST YOUR GARDEN-VARIETY LOSER...
CLIK
AND YET...FOR SOME REASON...
...YOU TRIED TO HELP ME... TO SAVE ME...
WHY DID YOU HAVE TO DO THAT?!
"YOU THINK...
...THE SAME WAY MY FATHER DOES..."

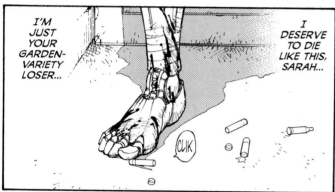

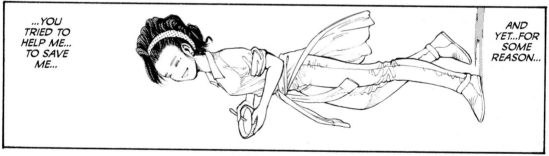

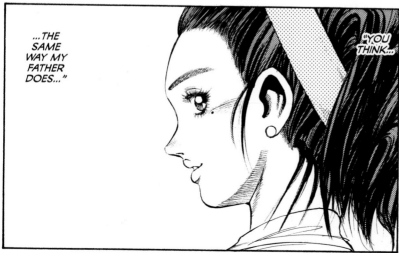

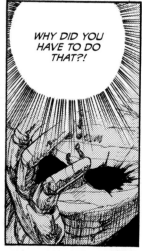

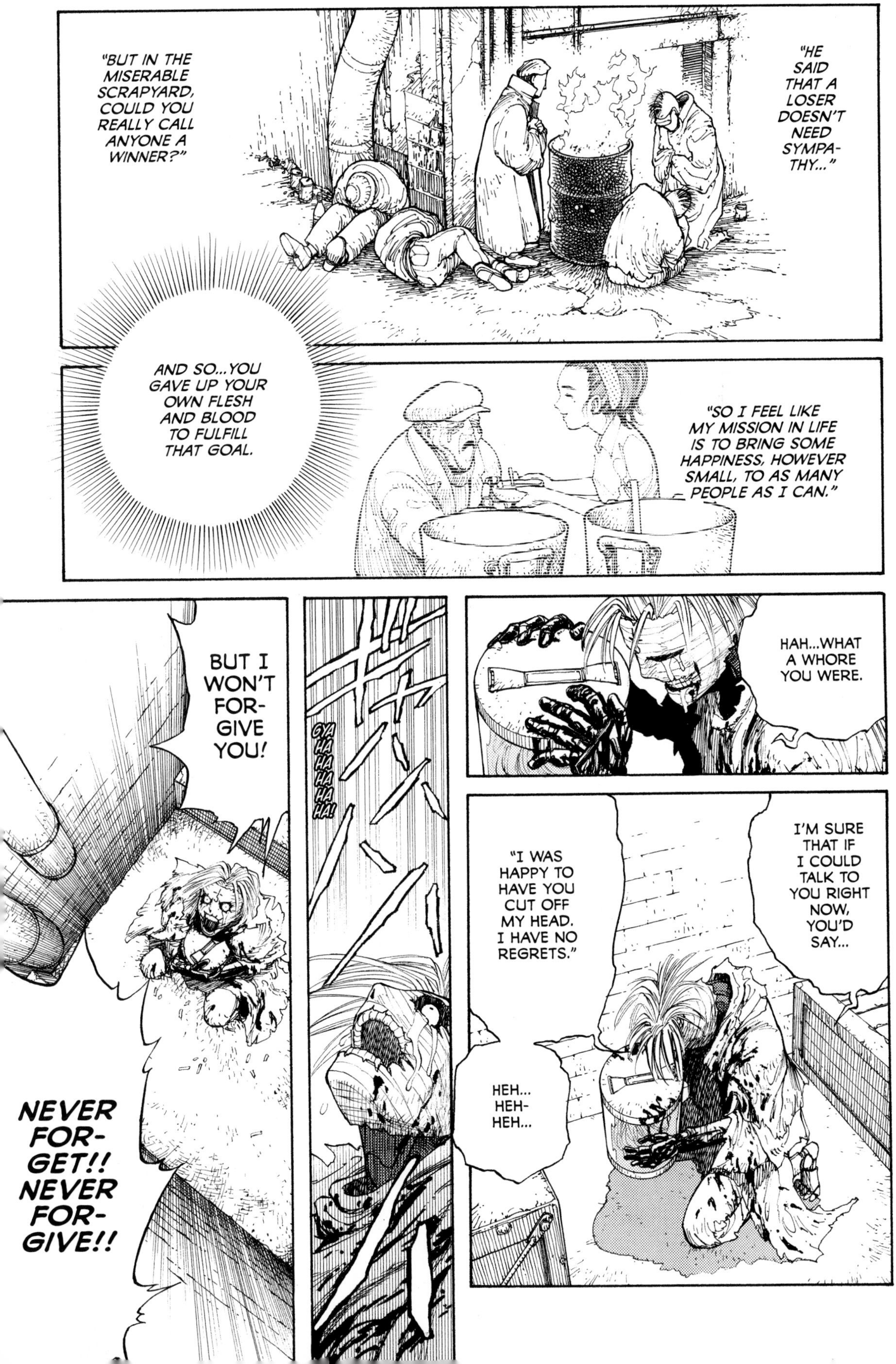
"HE SAID THAT A LOSER DOESN'T NEED SYMPATHY..."
"BUT IN THE MISERABLE SCRAPYARD, COULD YOU REALLY CALL ANYONE A WINNER?"
"SO I FEEL LIKE MY MISSION IN LIFE IS TO BRING SOME HAPPINESS, HOWEVER SMALL, TO AS MANY PEOPLE AS I CAN."
AND SO...YOU GAVE UP YOUR OWN FLESH AND BLOOD TO FULFILL THAT GOAL.
HAH...WHAT A WHORE YOU WERE.
I'M SURE THAT IF I COULD TALK TO YOU RIGHT NOW, YOU'D SAY...
"I WAS HAPPY TO HAVE YOU CUT OFF MY HEAD. I HAVE NO REGRETS."
HEH... HEH-HEH...
GYAHAHAHAHAHA!
BUT I WON'T FORGIVE YOU!
NEVER FORGET!! NEVER FORGIVE!!

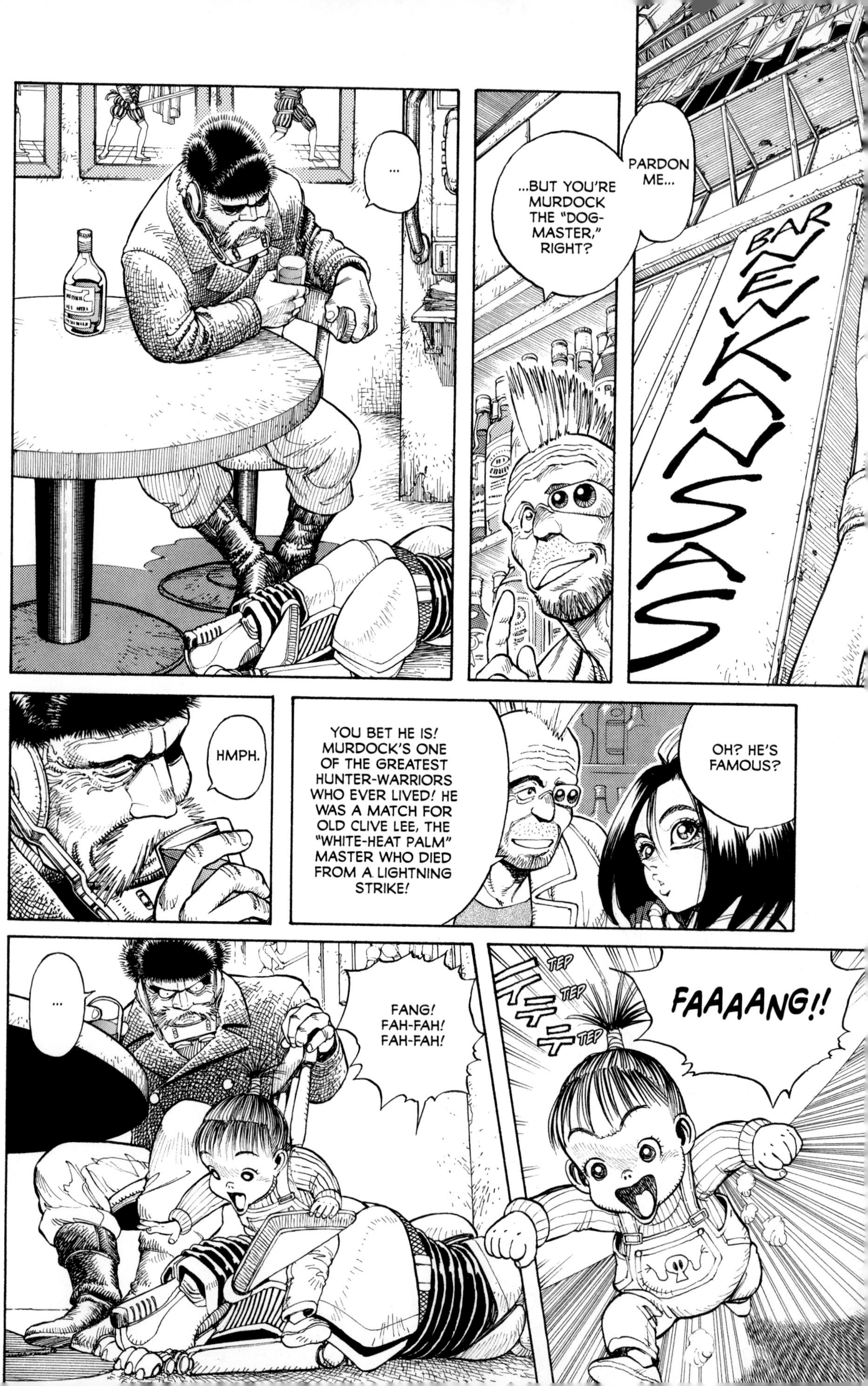
BAR NEW KANSAS
PARDON ME...
...BUT YOU'RE MURDOCK THE "DOG-MASTER," RIGHT?
...
OH? HE'S FAMOUS?
YOU BET HE IS! MURDOCK'S ONE OF THE GREATEST HUNTER-WARRIORS WHO EVER LIVED! HE WAS A MATCH FOR OLD CLIVE LEE, THE "WHITE-HEAT PALM" MASTER WHO DIED FROM A LIGHTNING STRIKE!
HMPH.
TEP TEP TEP
FAAAANG!!
FANG! FAH-FAH! FAH-FAH!
...

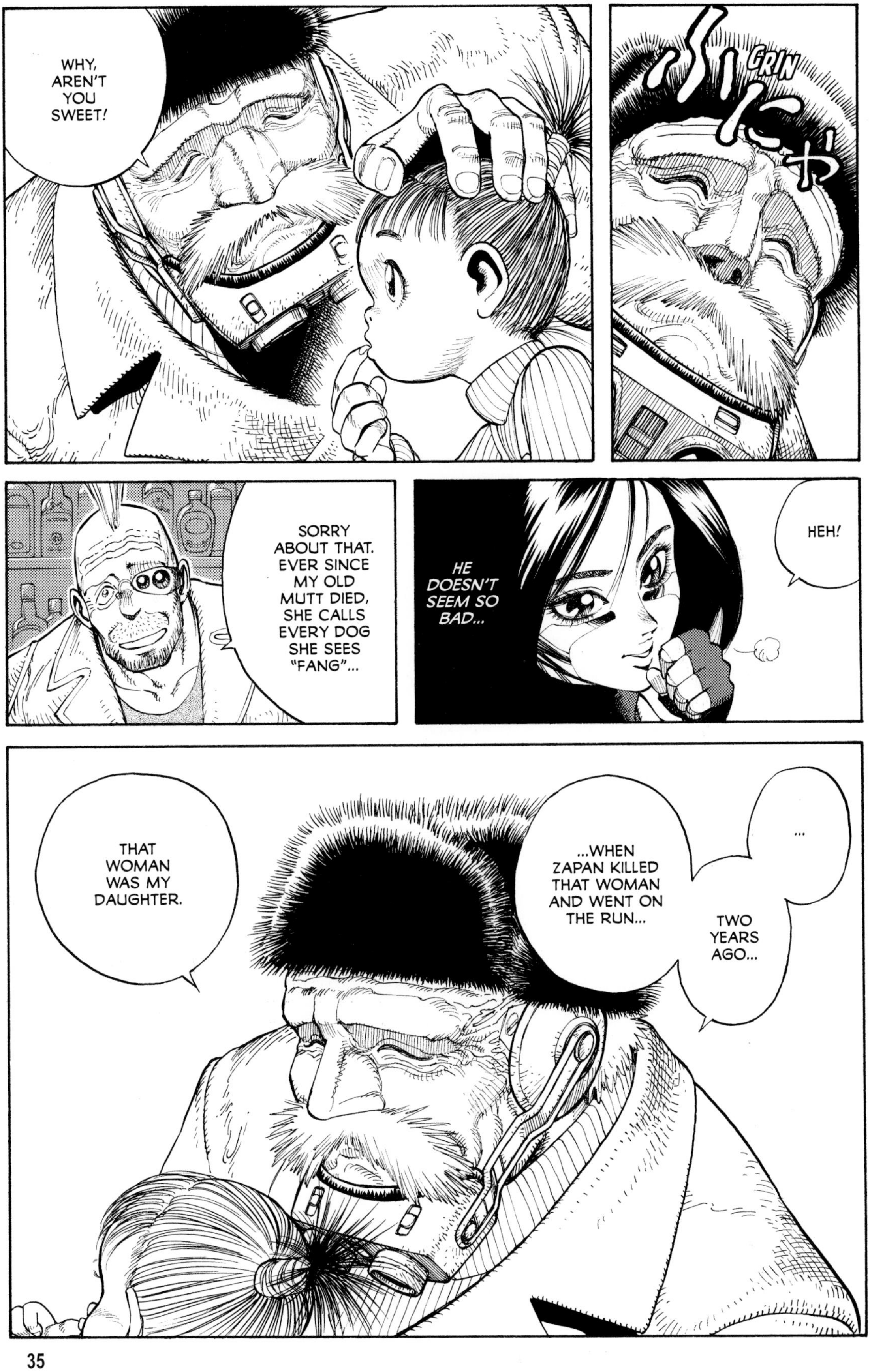
GRIN
WHY, AREN'T YOU SWEET!
HEH!
HE DOESN'T SEEM SO BAD...
SORRY ABOUT THAT. EVER SINCE MY OLD MUTT DIED, SHE CALLS EVERY DOG SHE SEES "FANG"...
...
TWO YEARS AGO...
...WHEN ZAPAN KILLED THAT WOMAN AND WENT ON THE RUN...
THAT WOMAN WAS MY DAUGHTER.

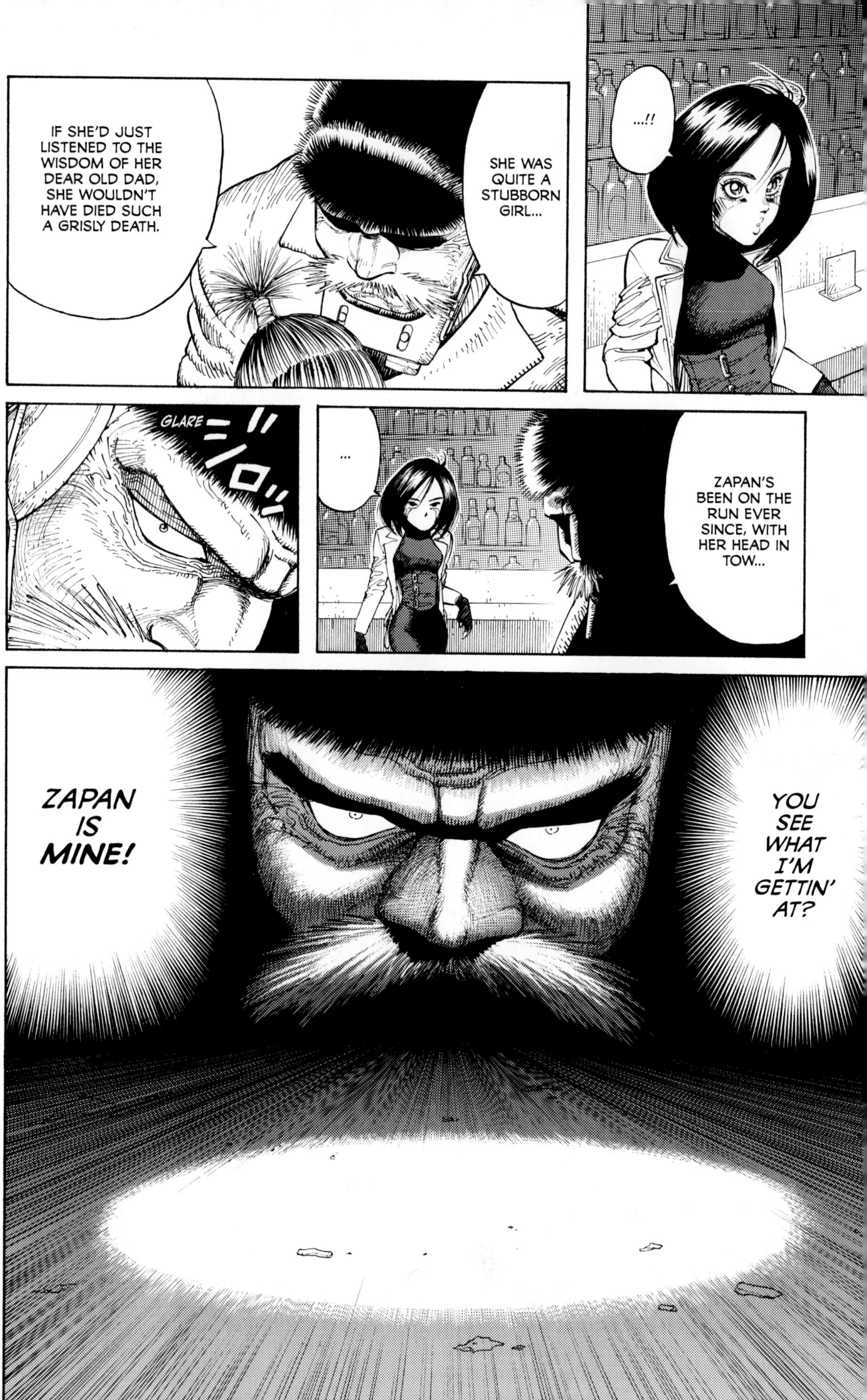
...!!
SHE WAS QUITE A STUBBORN GIRL...
IF SHE'D JUST LISTENED TO THE WISDOM OF HER DEAR OLD DAD, SHE WOULDN'T HAVE DIED SUCH A GRISLY DEATH.
ZAPAN'S BEEN ON THE RUN EVER SINCE, WITH HER HEAD IN TOW...
...
GLARE
YOU SEE WHAT I'M GETTIN' AT?
ZAPAN IS MINE!

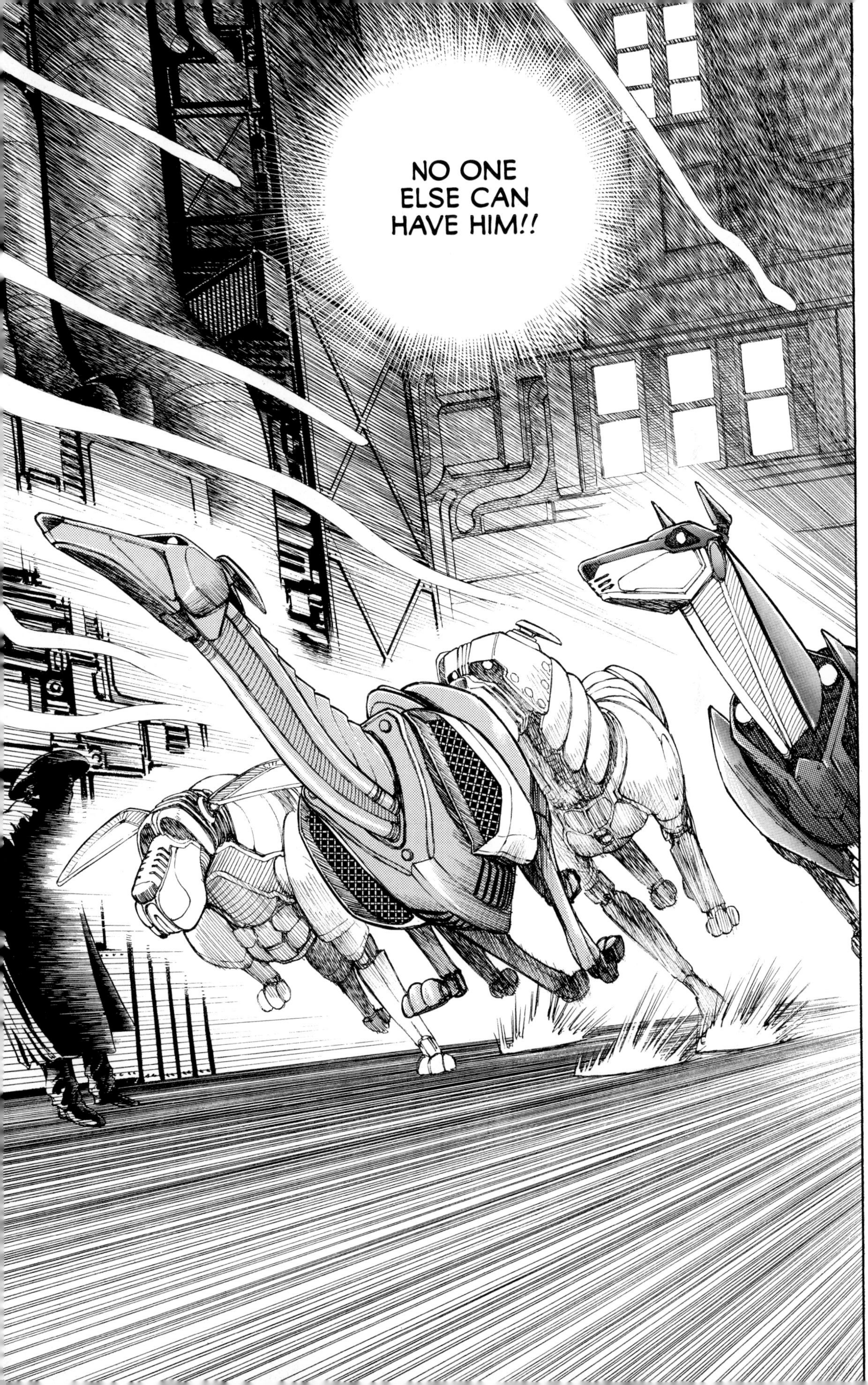
NO ONE
ELSE CAN
HAVE HIM!!

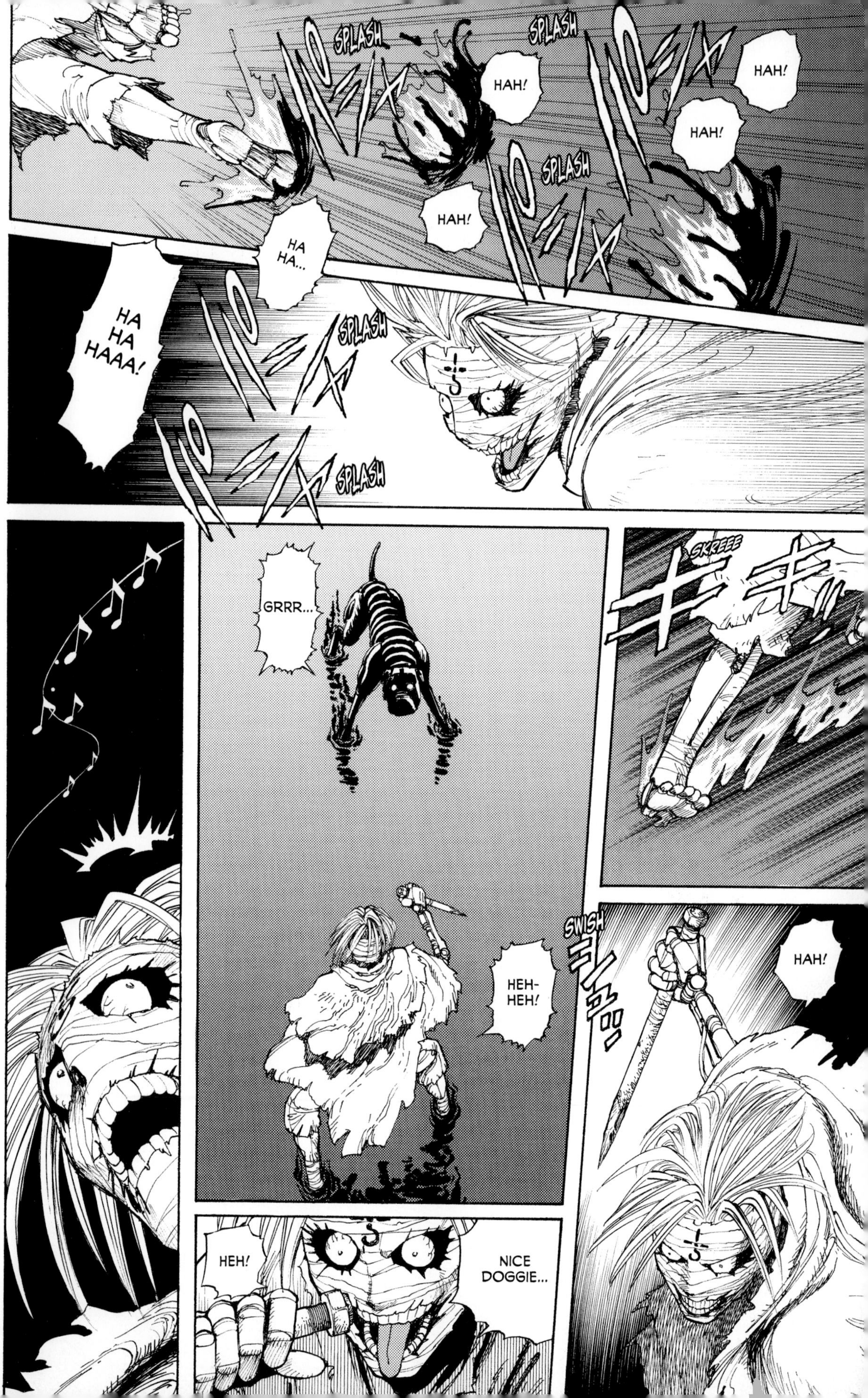
HAH!
HAH!
SPLASH
HAH!
SPLASH
SPLASH
HAH!
HA HA...
SPLASH
SPLASH
HA HA HAAA!
SKREEE
HAH!
SWISH
GRRR...
HEH-HEH!
NICE DOGGIE...
HEH!

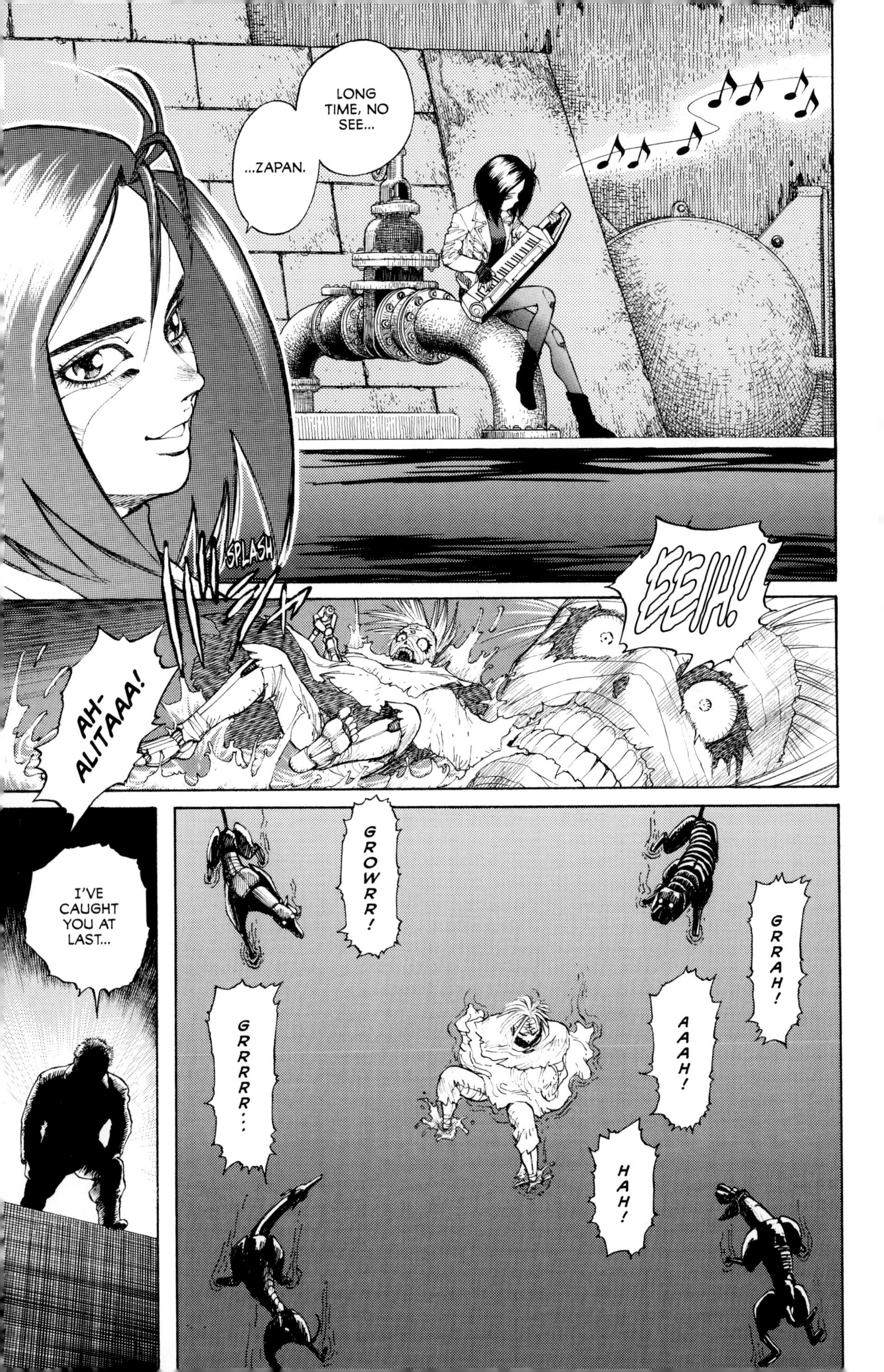
LONG TIME, NO SEE...
...ZAPAN.
SPLASH
EEH!
AH-ALITAAA!
GRRAH!
GROWRR!
AAAH!
HAH!
GRRRRR...
I'VE CAUGHT YOU AT LAST...

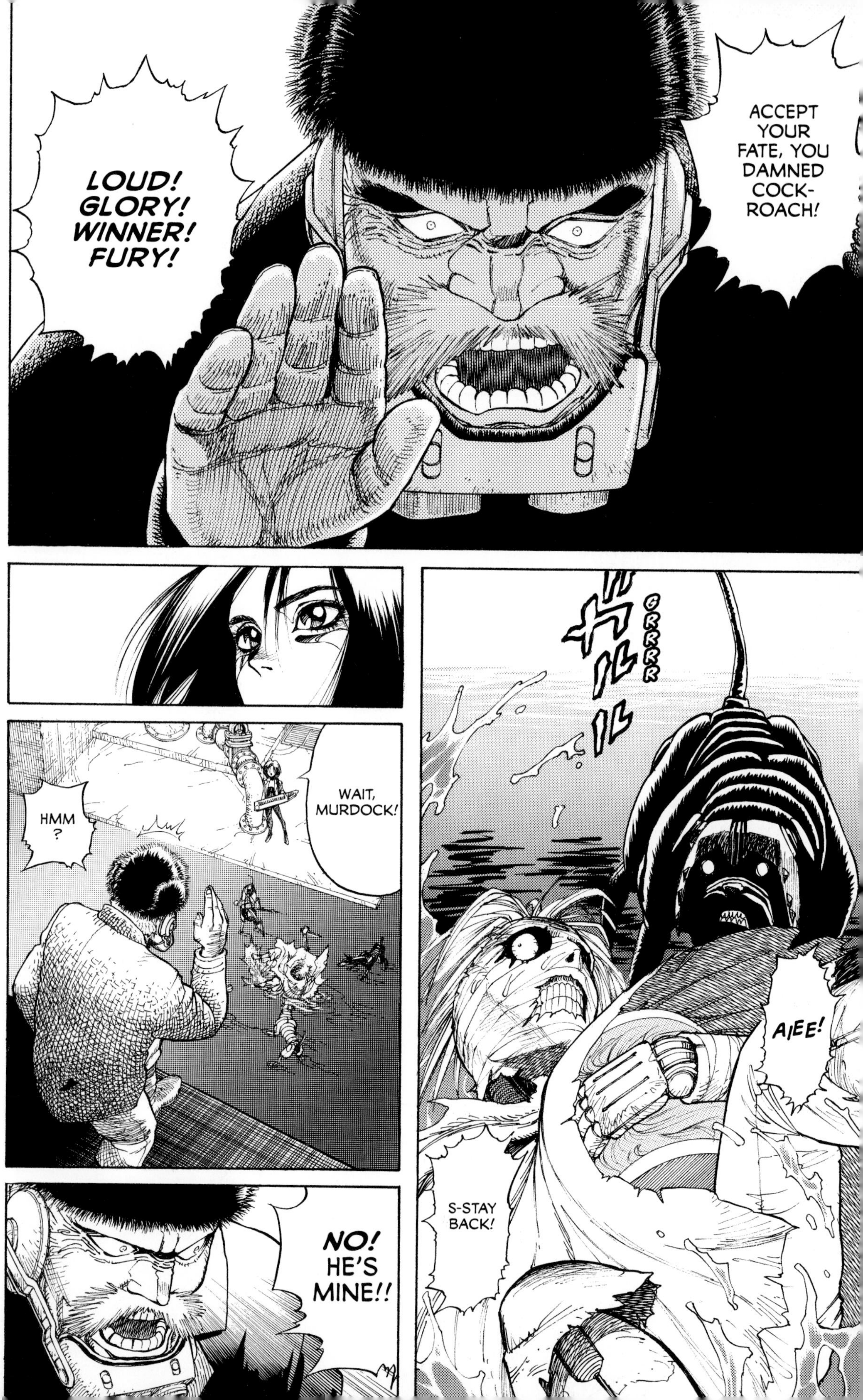
ACCEPT YOUR FATE, YOU DAMNED COCK-ROACH!
LOUD! GLORY! WINNER! FURY!
GRRRR
AIEE!
S-STAY BACK!
WAIT, MURDOCK!
HMM?
NO! HE'S MINE!!

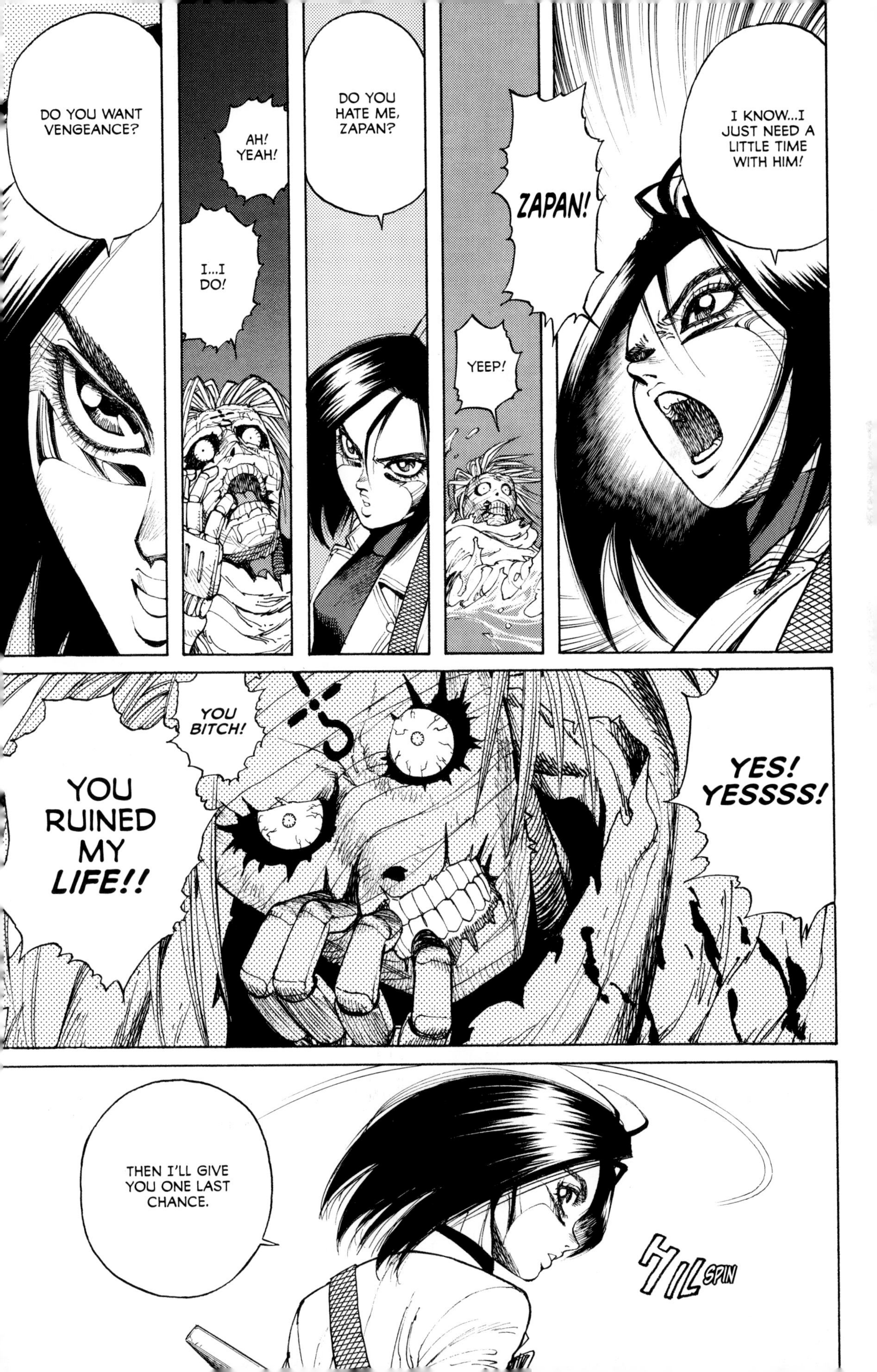
I KNOW...I JUST NEED A LITTLE TIME WITH HIM!
ZAPAN!
YEEP!
DO YOU HATE ME, ZAPAN?
AH! YEAH!
I...I DO!
DO YOU WANT VENGEANCE?
YES! YESSSS!
YOU BITCH!
YOU RUINED MY LIFE!!
THEN I'LL GIVE YOU ONE LAST CHANCE.
SPIN

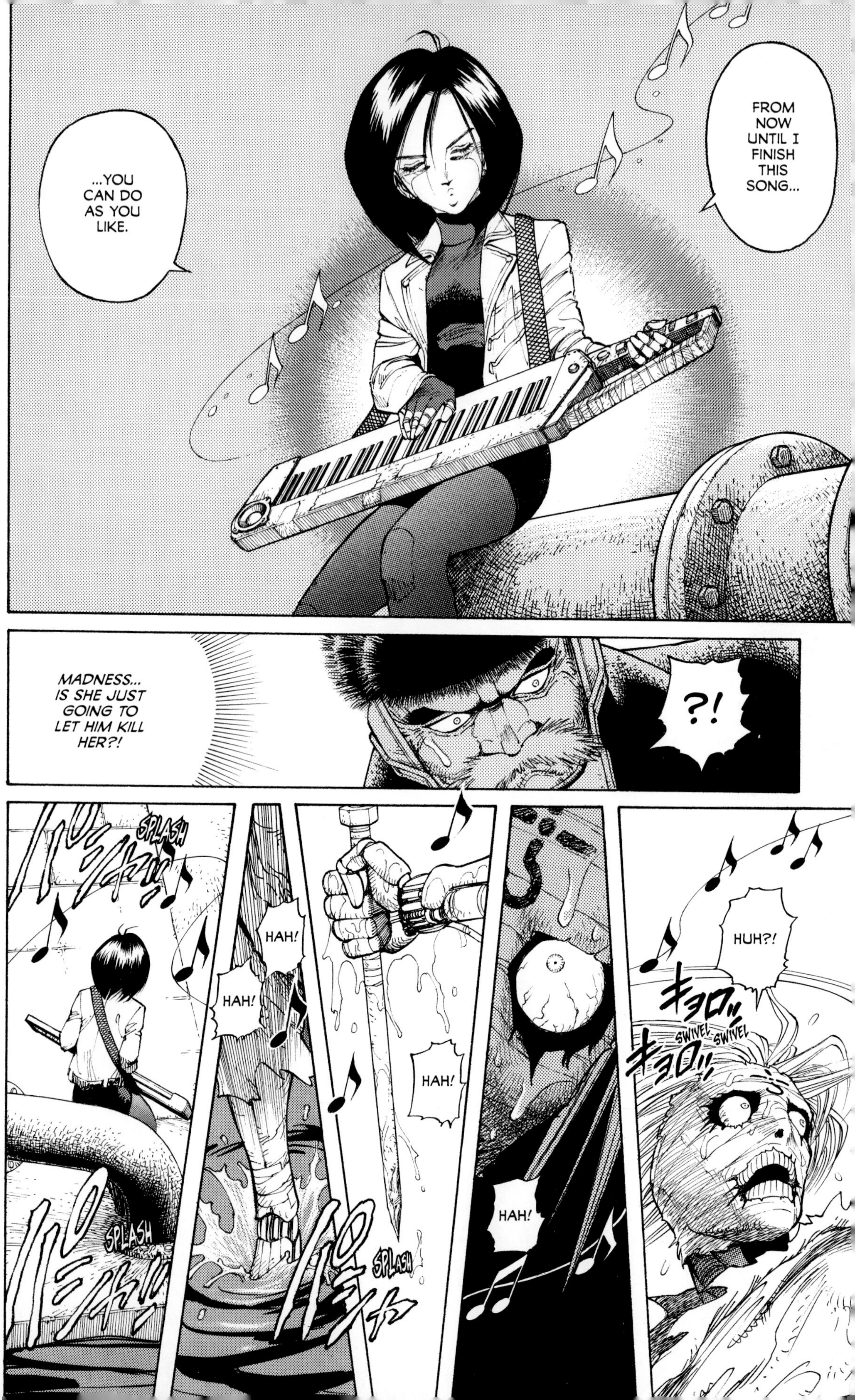
FROM NOW UNTIL I FINISH THIS SONG...
...YOU CAN DO AS YOU LIKE.
?!
MADNESS... IS SHE JUST GOING TO LET HIM KILL HER?!
HUH?!
キョロッ SWIVEL
キョロッ SWIVEL
HAH!
HAH!
HAH!
HAH!
SPLASH
SPLASH
SPLASH

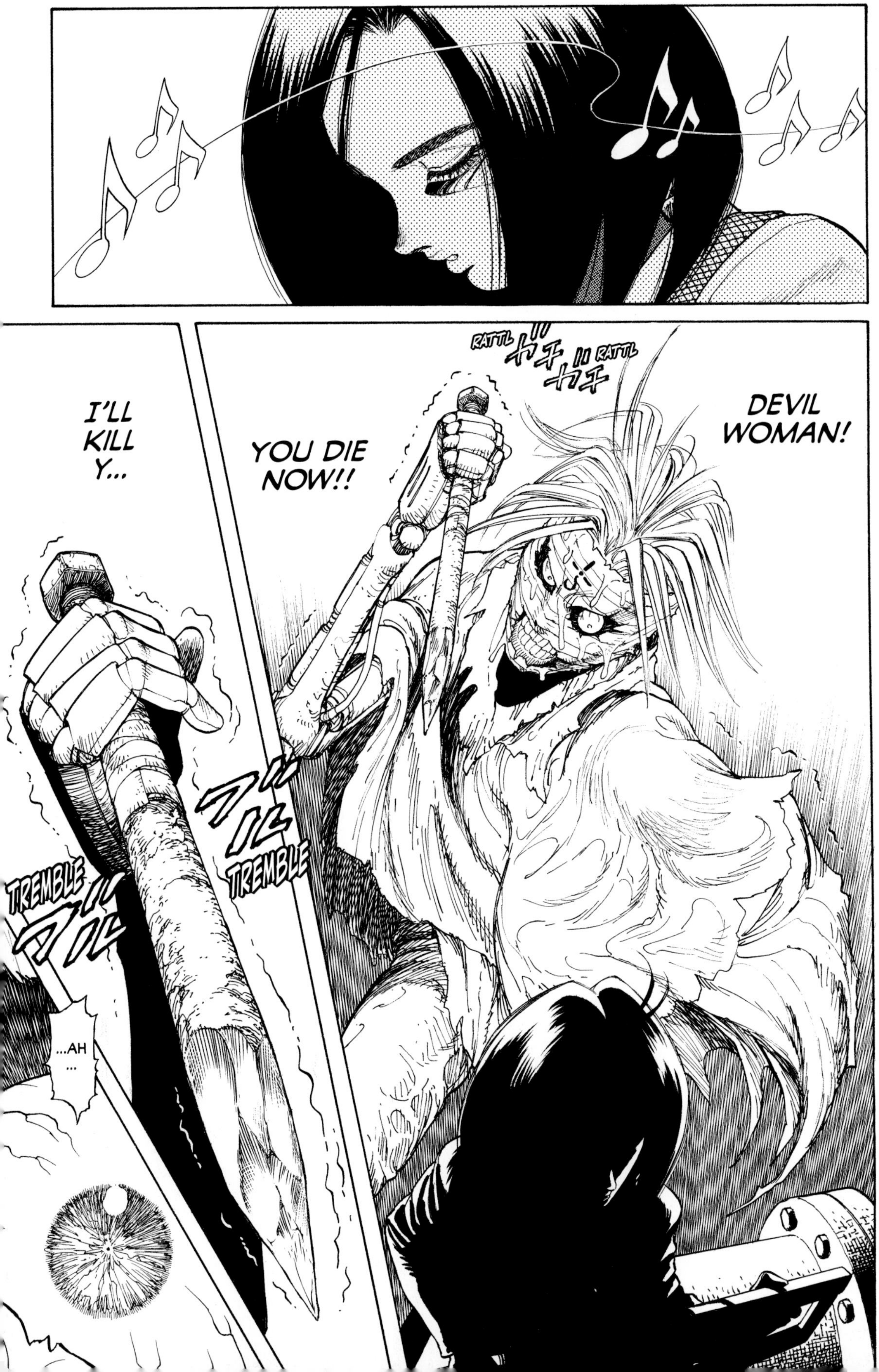
RATTL
RATTL
DEVIL WOMAN!
YOU DIE NOW!!
TREMBLE
I'LL KILL Y...
TREMBLE
...AH ...

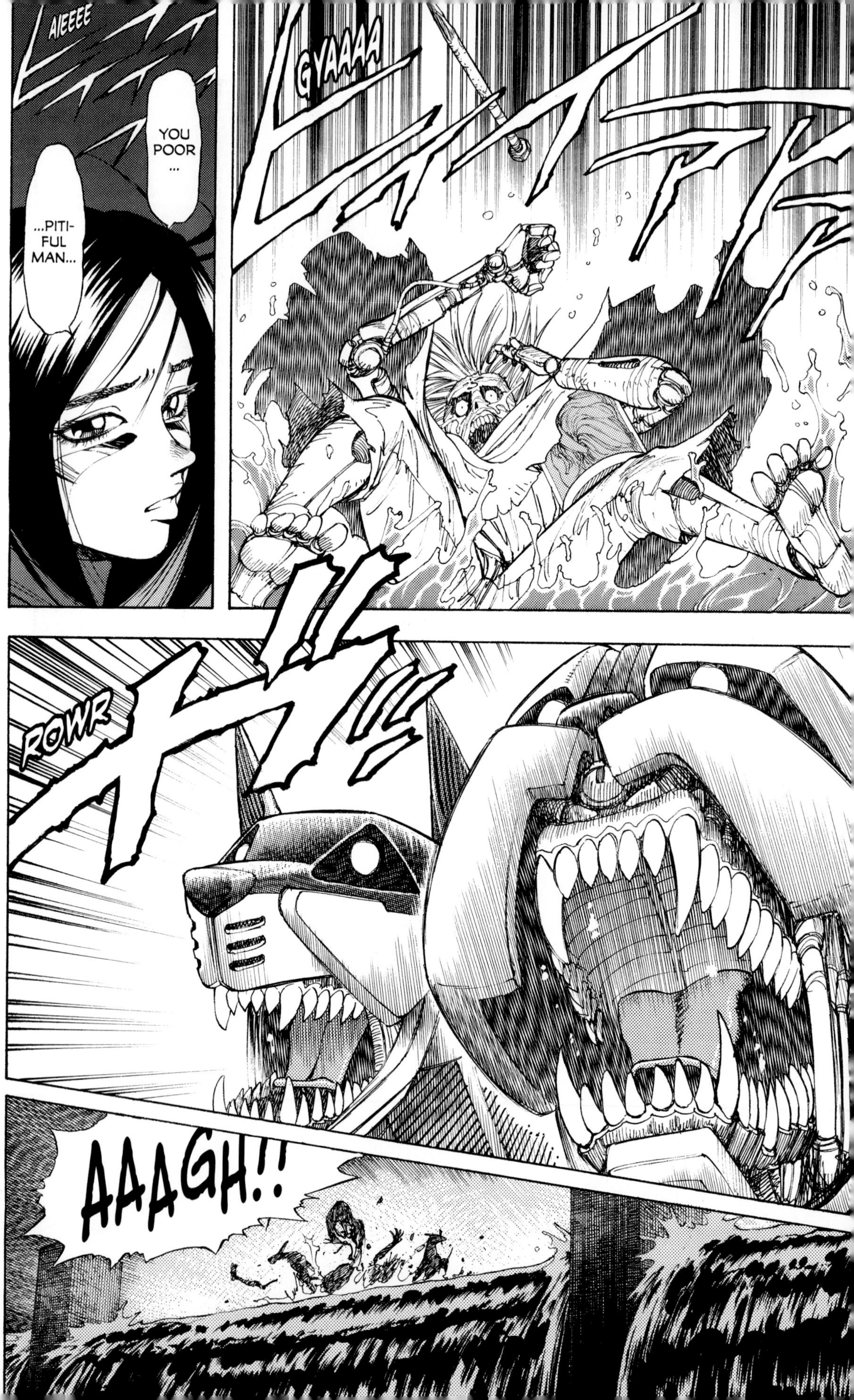
GYAAAA
AIEEEE
YOU POOR ...
...PITI-FUL MAN...
ROWR
AAAGH!!

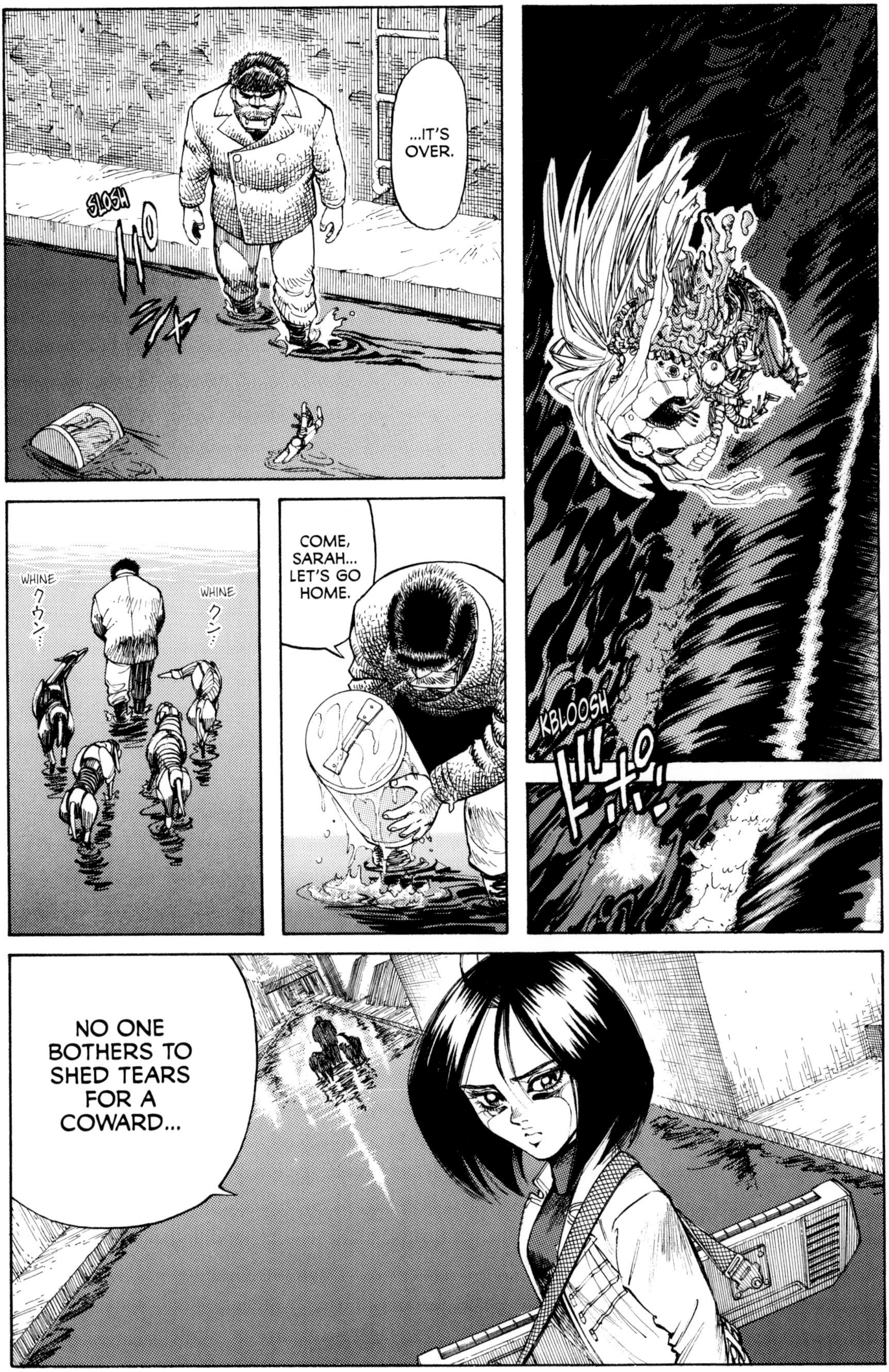
KBLOOSH
ドポッ
SLOSH
...IT'S OVER.
COME, SARAH... LET'S GO HOME.
WHINE
クン…
WHINE
クゥン…
NO ONE BOTHERS TO SHED TEARS FOR A COWARD...

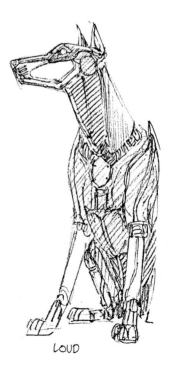

LOUD

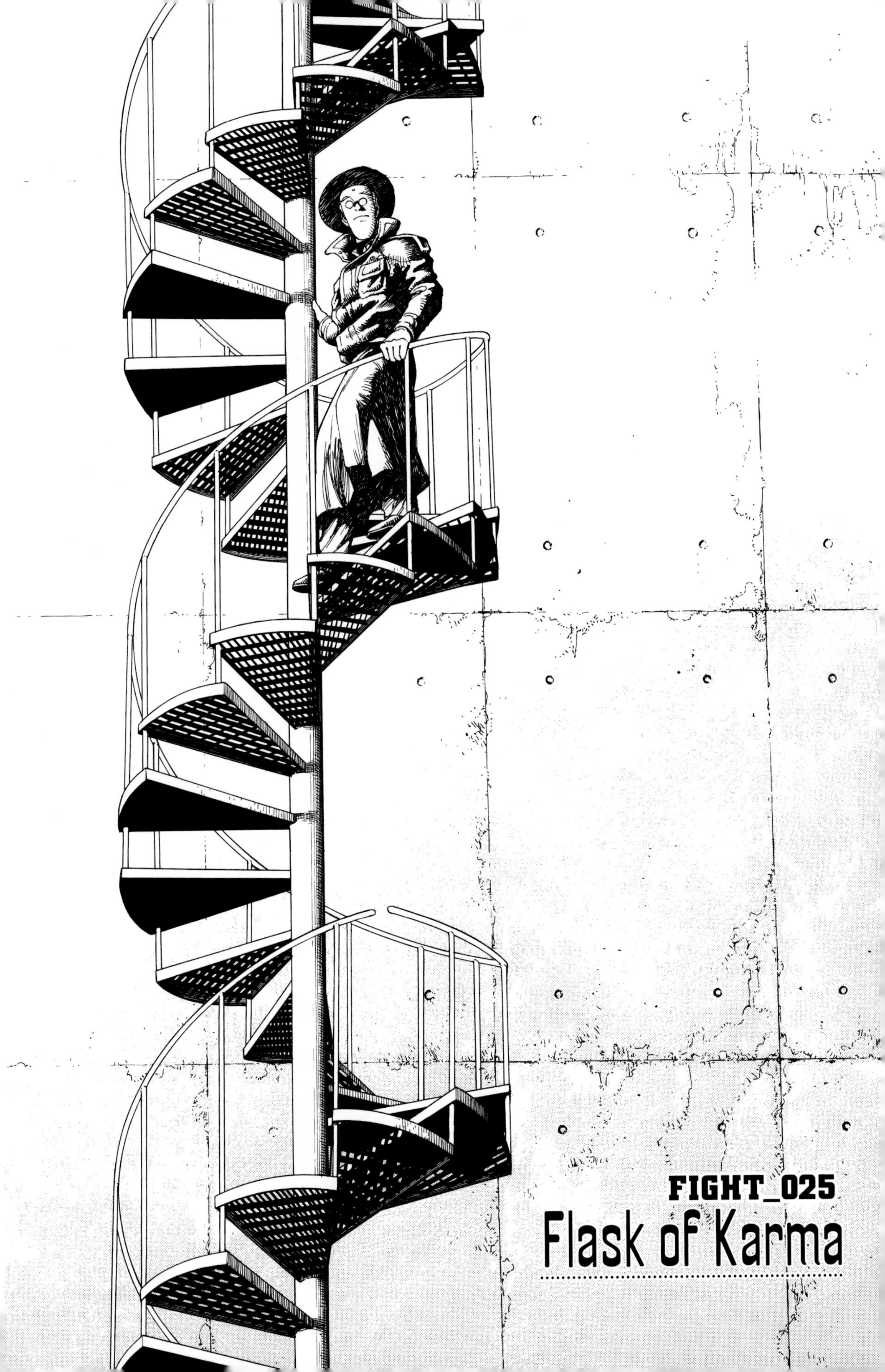
FIGHT_025
Flask of Karma

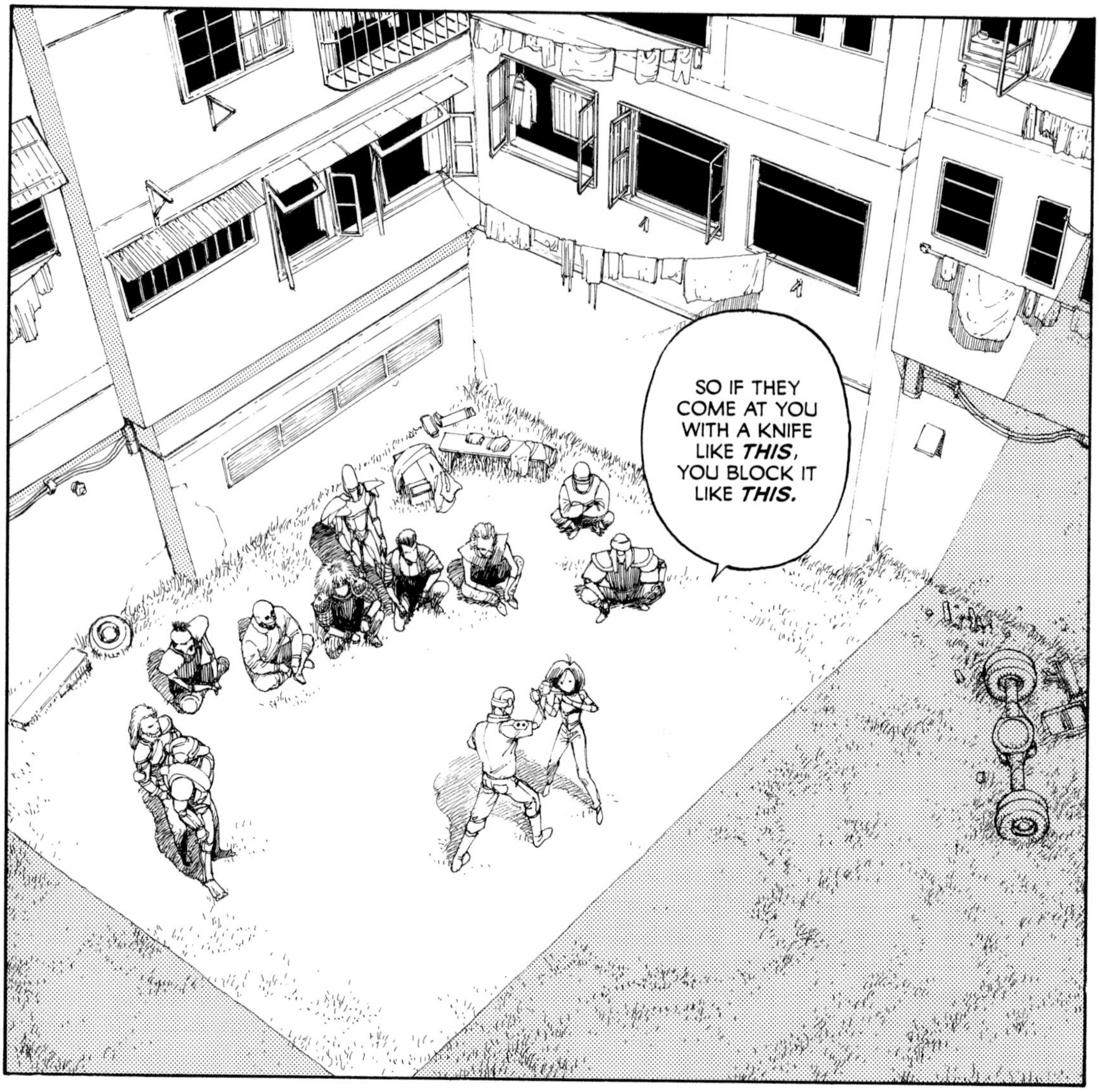
SO IF THEY COME AT YOU WITH A KNIFE LIKE ***THIS***, YOU BLOCK IT LIKE ***THIS.***

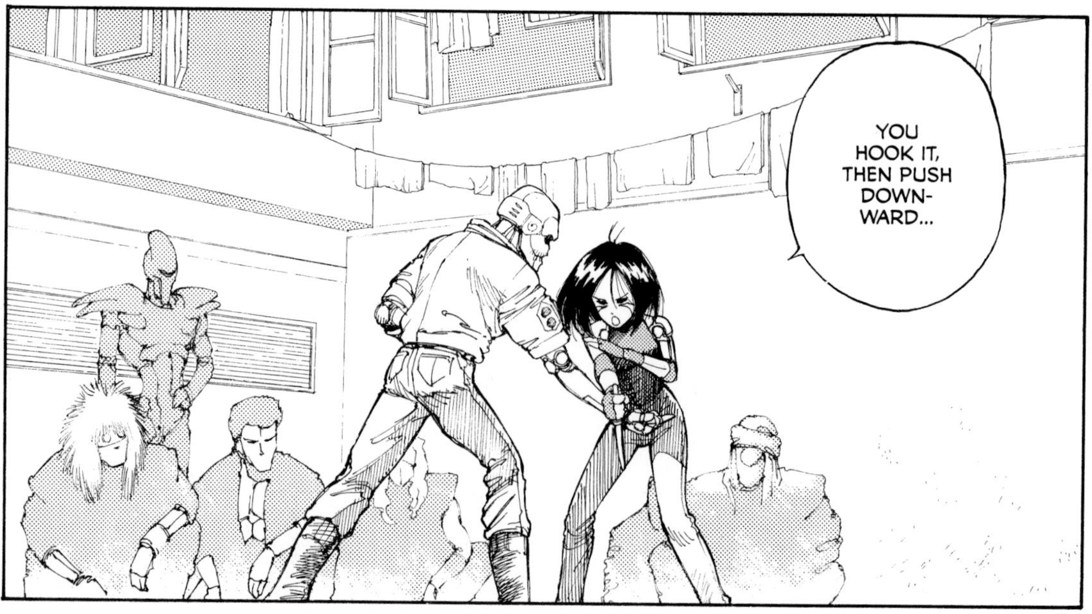
YOU HOOK IT, THEN PUSH DOWN-WARD...

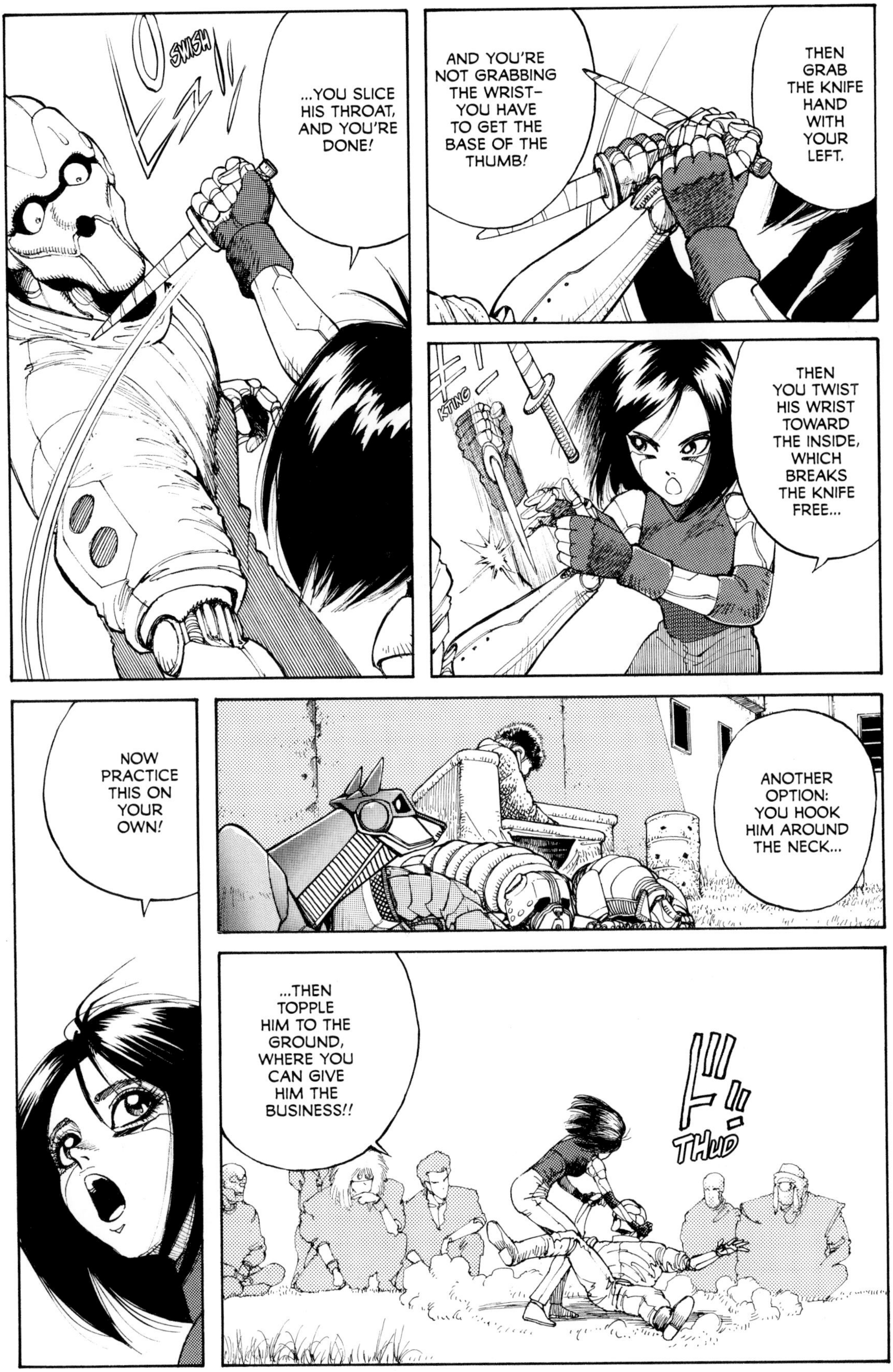

THEN GRAB THE KNIFE HAND WITH YOUR LEFT.
AND YOU'RE NOT GRABBING THE WRIST– YOU HAVE TO GET THE BASE OF THE THUMB!
KTING
THEN YOU TWIST HIS WRIST TOWARD THE INSIDE, WHICH BREAKS THE KNIFE FREE...
SWISH
...YOU SLICE HIS THROAT, AND YOU'RE DONE!
ANOTHER OPTION: YOU HOOK HIM AROUND THE NECK...
...THEN TOPPLE HIM TO THE GROUND, WHERE YOU CAN GIVE HIM THE BUSINESS!!
THUD
NOW PRACTICE THIS ON YOUR OWN!

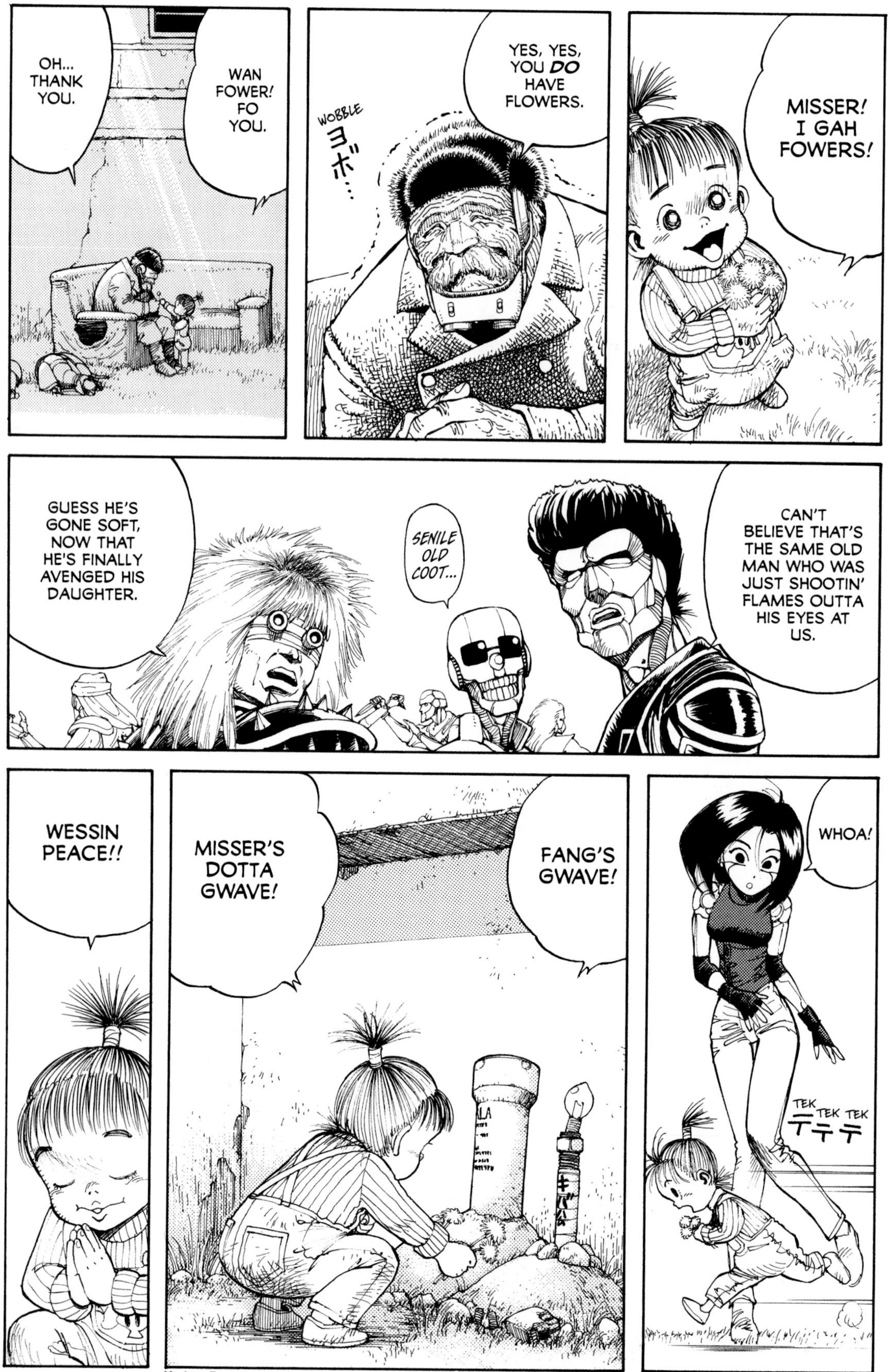
MISSER! I GAH FOWERS!
YES, YES, YOU *DO* HAVE FLOWERS.
WOBBLE ヨボ…
WAN FOWER! FO YOU.
OH... THANK YOU.
CAN'T BELIEVE THAT'S THE SAME OLD MAN WHO WAS JUST SHOOTIN' FLAMES OUTTA HIS EYES AT US.
SENILE OLD COOT...
GUESS HE'S GONE SOFT, NOW THAT HE'S FINALLY AVENGED HIS DAUGHTER.
WHOA!
TEK TEK TEK テテテ
FANG'S GWAVE!
MISSER'S DOTTA GWAVE!
WESSIN PEACE!!
Marker: Fang

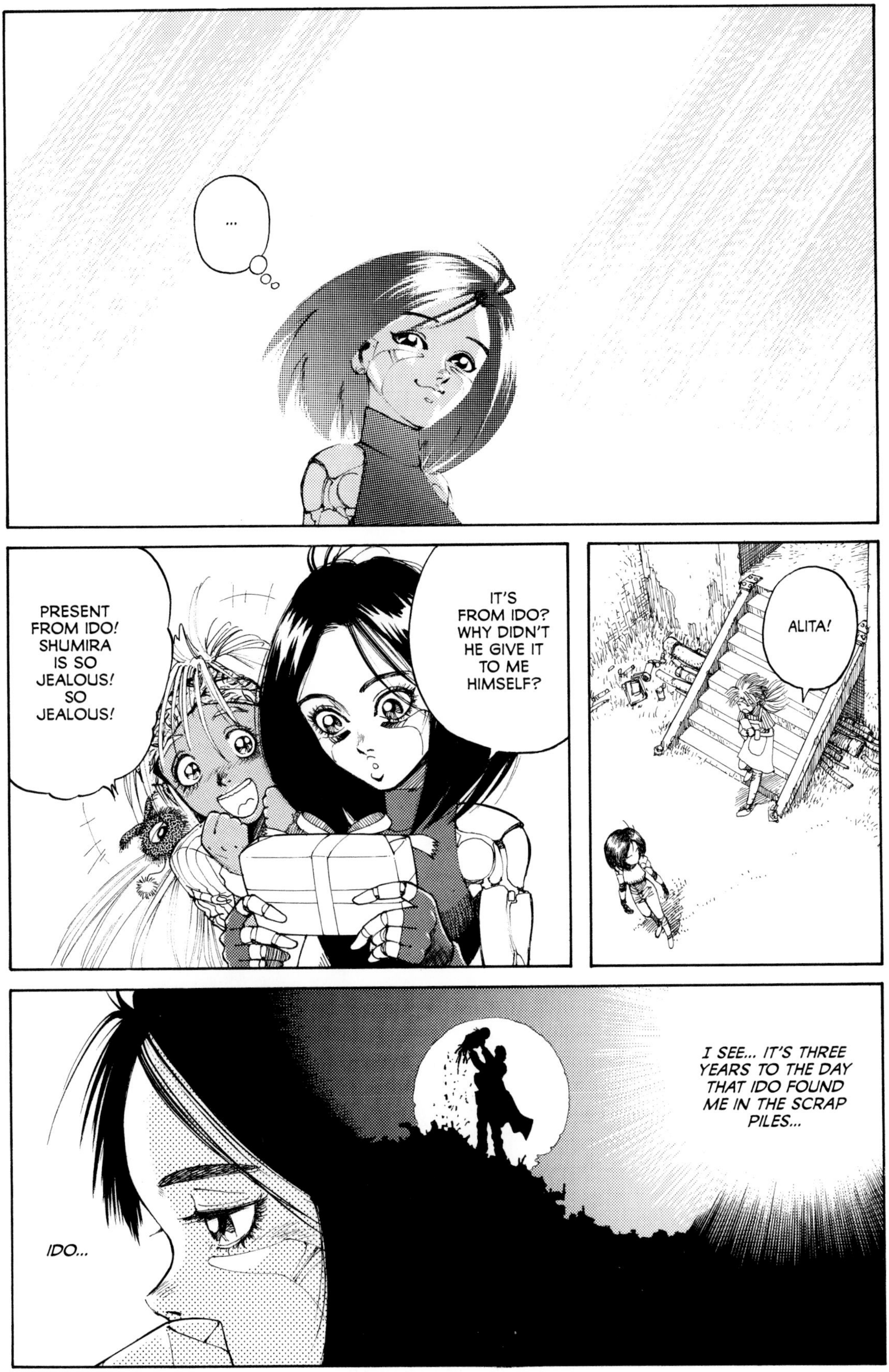
...
ALITA!
IT'S FROM IDO? WHY DIDN'T HE GIVE IT TO ME HIMSELF?
PRESENT FROM IDO! SHUMIRA IS SO JEALOUS! SO JEALOUS!
I SEE... IT'S THREE YEARS TO THE DAY THAT IDO FOUND ME IN THE SCRAP PILES...
IDO...

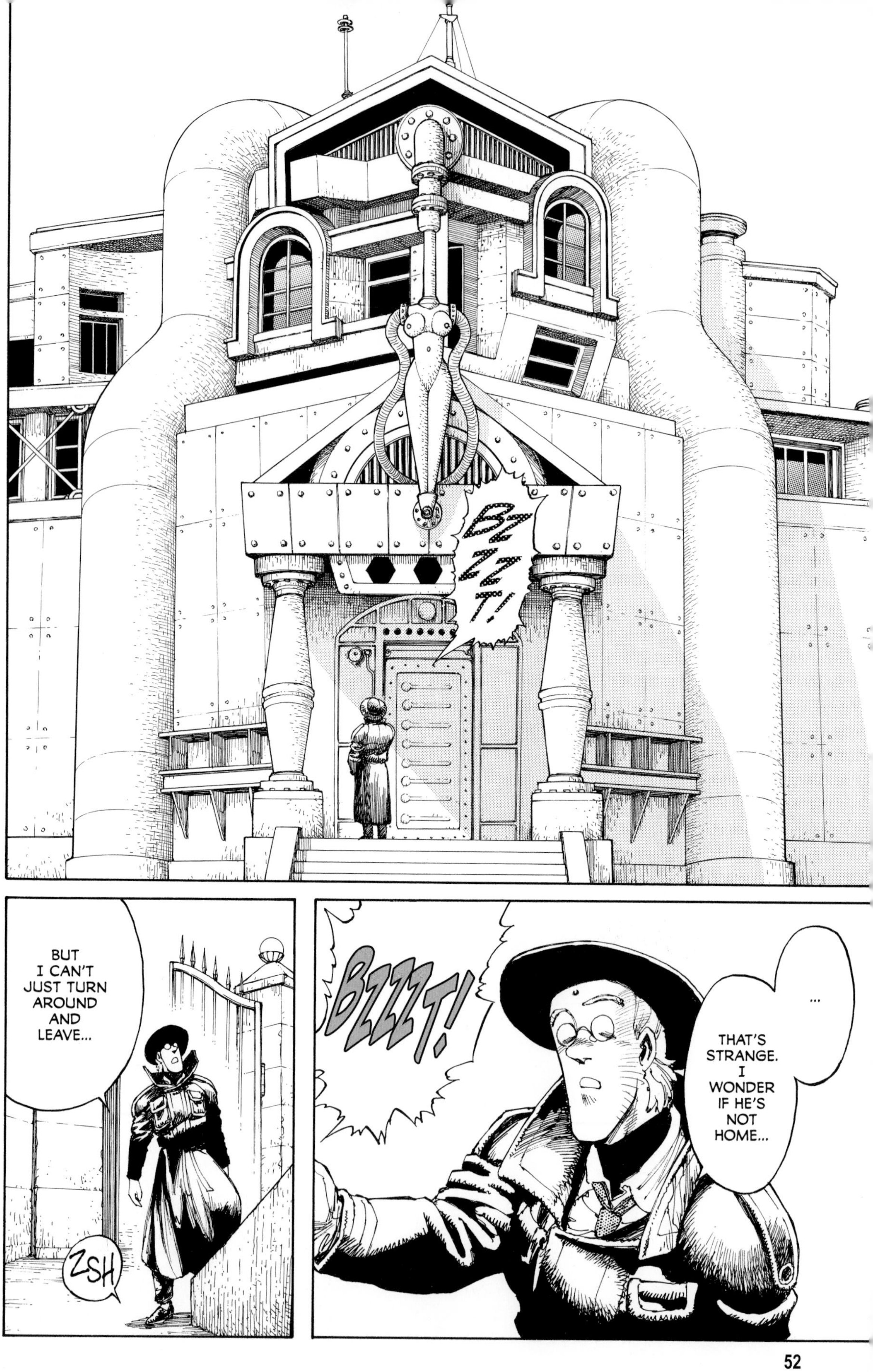
BZZZZT!!
BZZZT!
...
THAT'S STRANGE. I WONDER IF HE'S NOT HOME...
BUT I CAN'T JUST TURN AROUND AND LEAVE...
ZSH

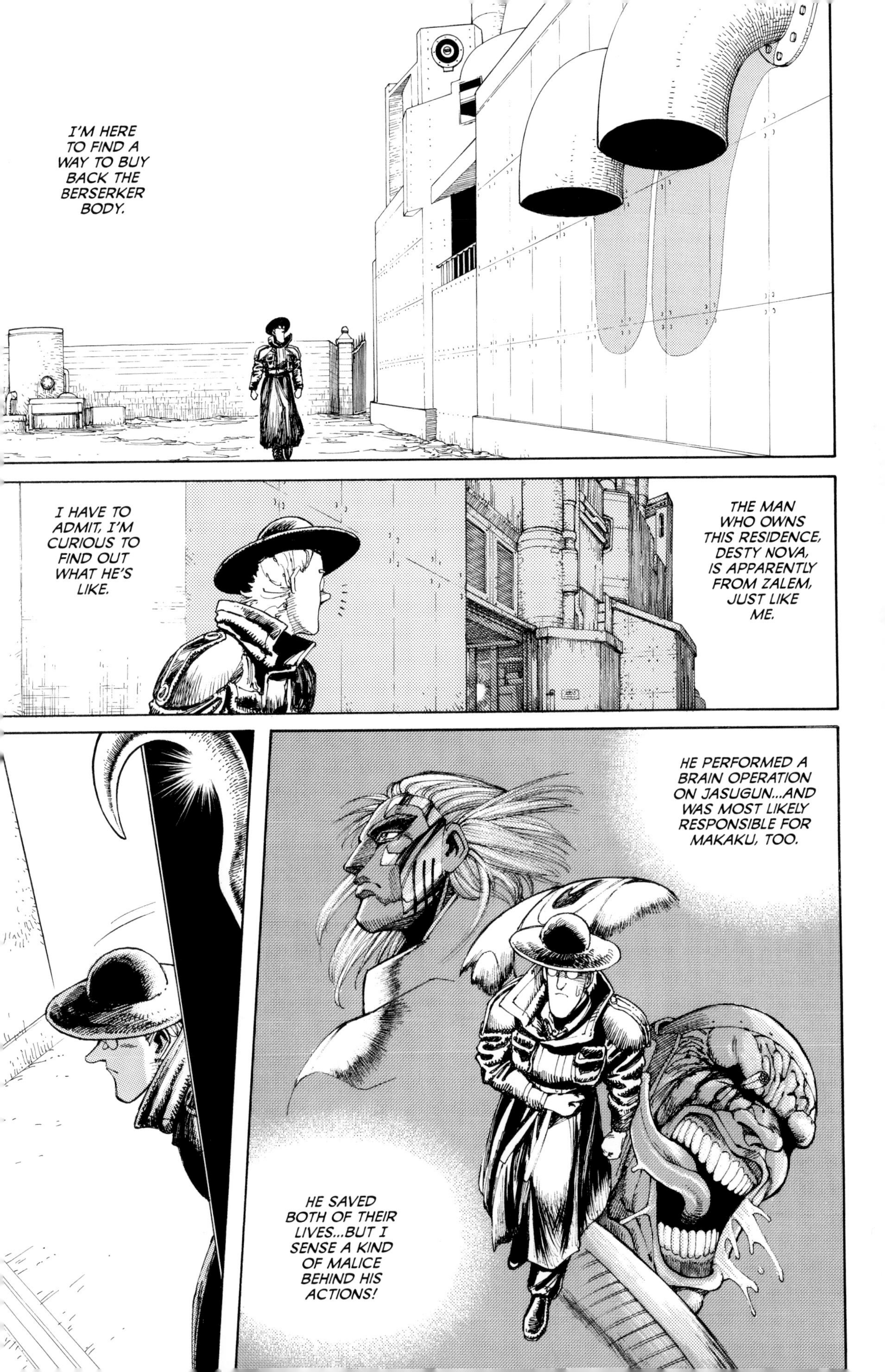
I'M HERE TO FIND A WAY TO BUY BACK THE BERSERKER BODY.
THE MAN WHO OWNS THIS RESIDENCE, DESTY NOVA, IS APPARENTLY FROM ZALEM, JUST LIKE ME.
I HAVE TO ADMIT, I'M CURIOUS TO FIND OUT WHAT HE'S LIKE.
HE PERFORMED A BRAIN OPERATION ON JASUGUN...AND WAS MOST LIKELY RESPONSIBLE FOR MAKAKU, TOO.
HE SAVED BOTH OF THEIR LIVES...BUT I SENSE A KIND OF MALICE BEHIND HIS ACTIONS!

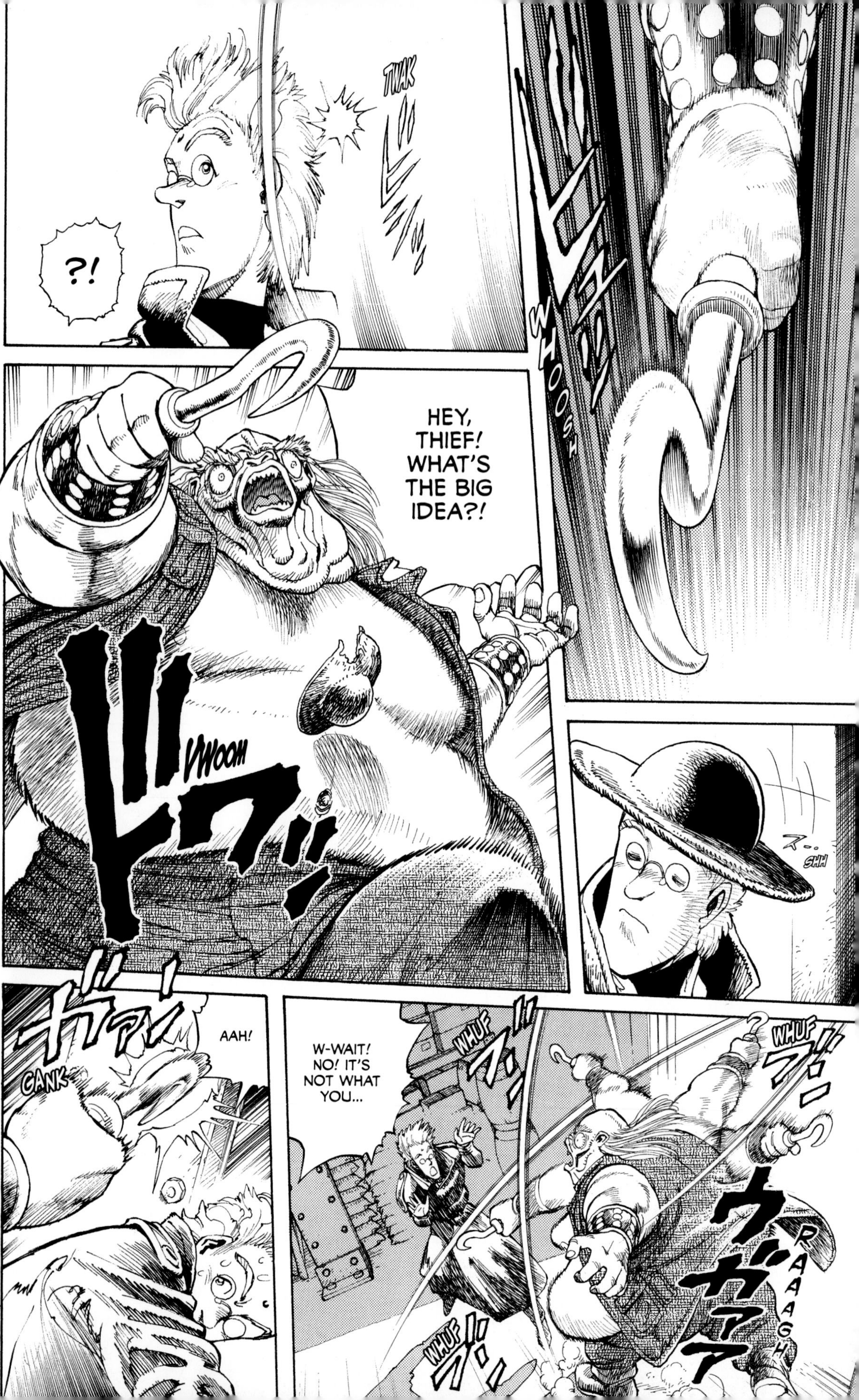

WHOOSH
TWAK
?!
HEY, THIEF! WHAT'S THE BIG IDEA?!
VWOOM
SHH
WHUF
W-WAIT! NO! IT'S NOT WHAT YOU...
WHUF
RAAAGH
WHUF
CANK
AAH!

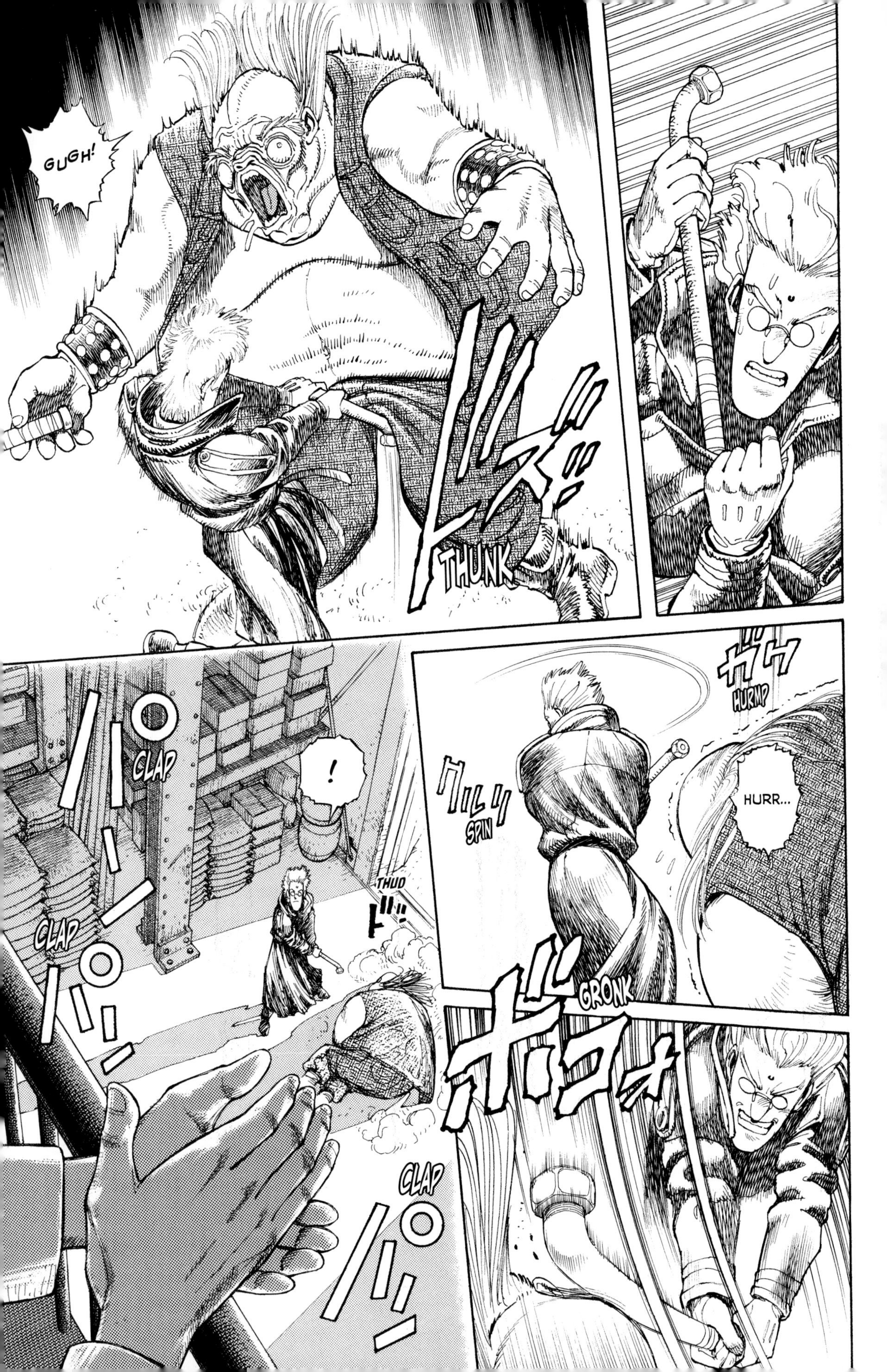
GUGH!
THUNK
HURMP
HURR...
SPIN
GRONK
CLAP
!
THUD
CLAP
CLAP

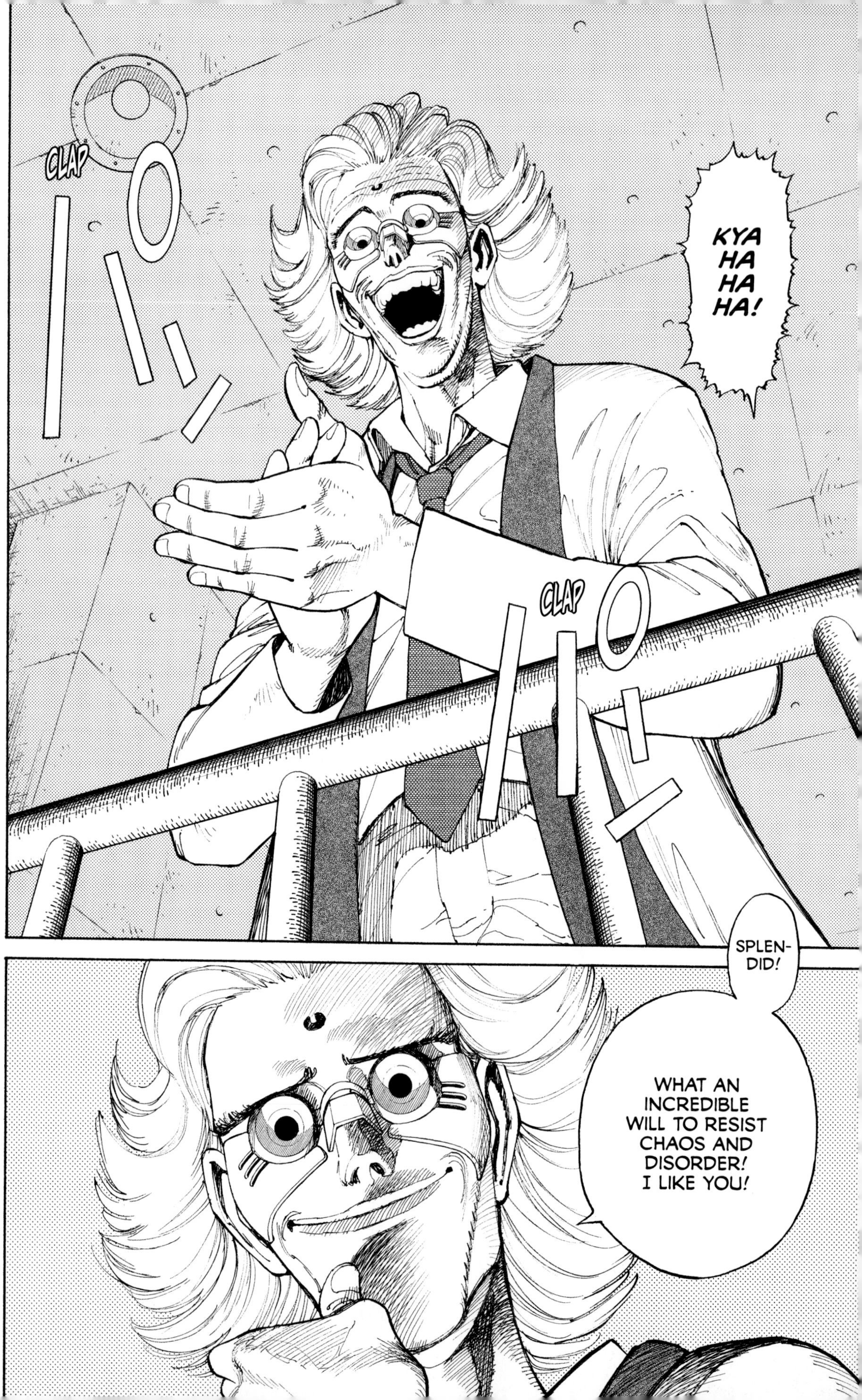
KYA HA HA HA!
CLAP
CLAP
SPLEN-DID!
WHAT AN INCREDIBLE WILL TO RESIST CHAOS AND DISORDER! I LIKE YOU!

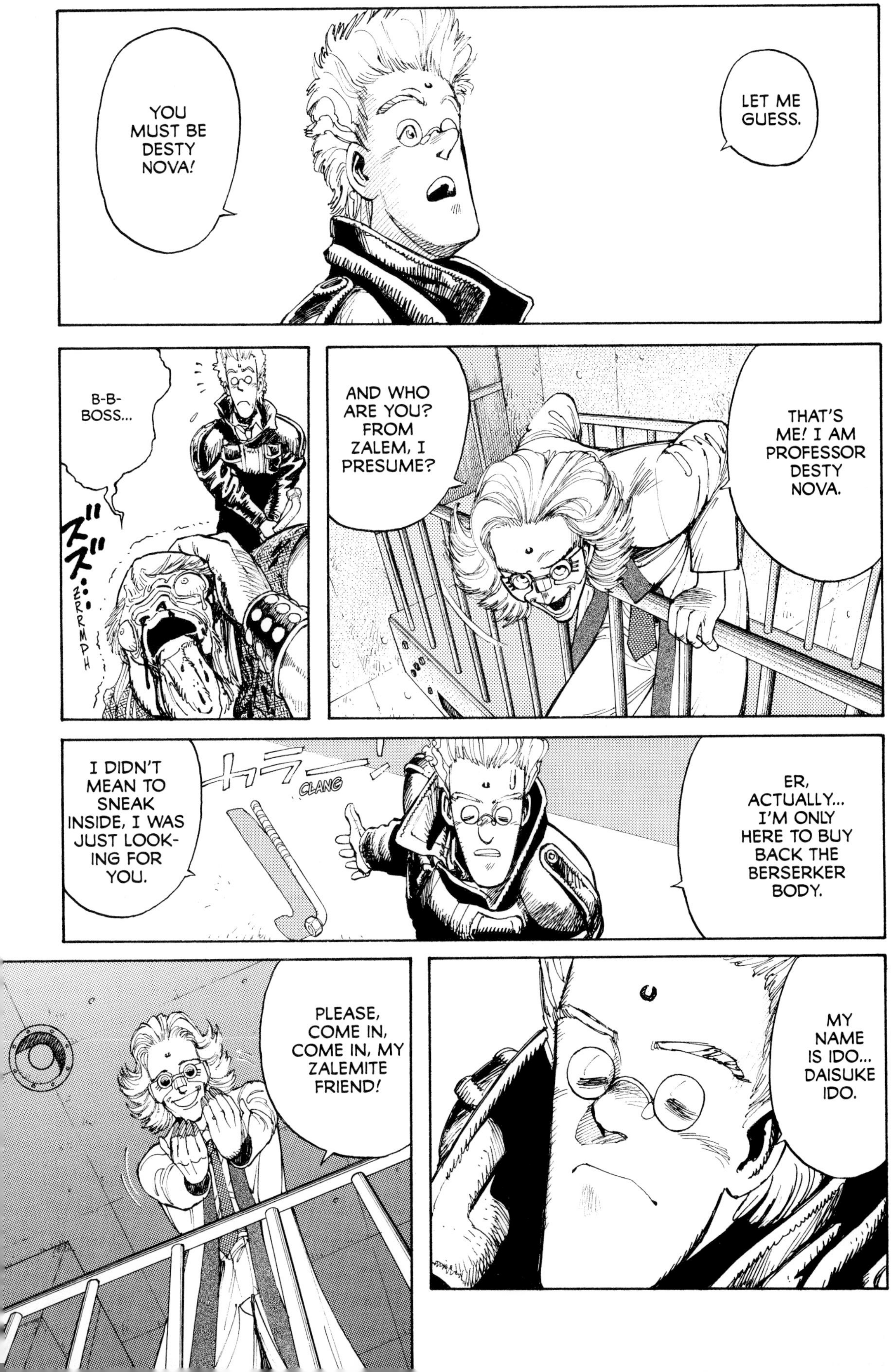
LET ME GUESS.
YOU MUST BE DESTY NOVA!
THAT'S ME! I AM PROFESSOR DESTY NOVA.
AND WHO ARE YOU? FROM ZALEM, I PRESUME?
B-B-BOSS...
ERRRMPH
ER, ACTUALLY... I'M ONLY HERE TO BUY BACK THE BERSERKER BODY.
CLANG
I DIDN'T MEAN TO SNEAK INSIDE, I WAS JUST LOOKING FOR YOU.
MY NAME IS IDO... DAISUKE IDO.
PLEASE, COME IN, COME IN, MY ZALEMITE FRIEND!

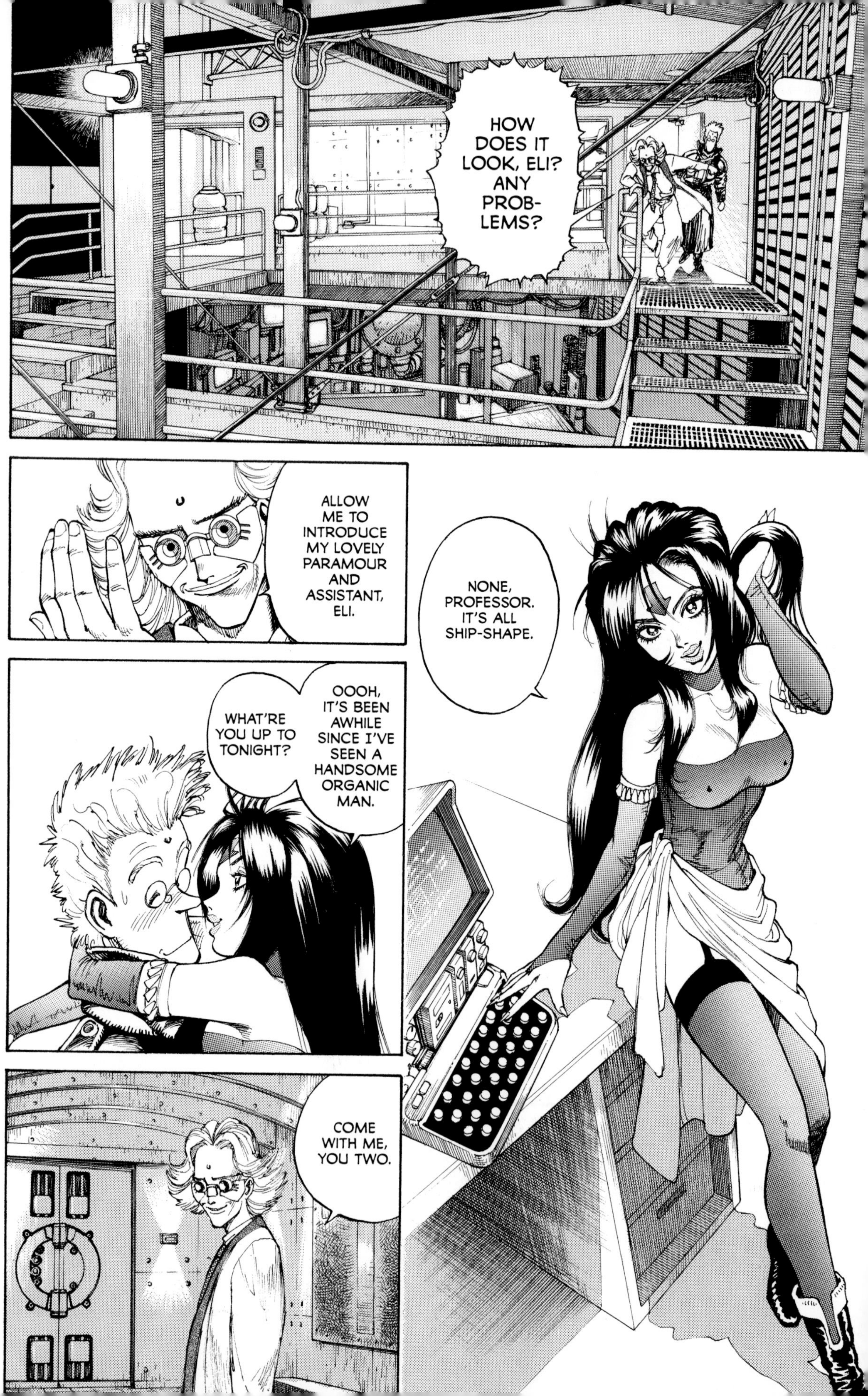
HOW DOES IT LOOK, ELI? ANY PROB-LEMS?
NONE, PROFESSOR. IT'S ALL SHIP-SHAPE.
ALLOW ME TO INTRODUCE MY LOVELY PARAMOUR AND ASSISTANT, ELI.
OOOH, IT'S BEEN AWHILE SINCE I'VE SEEN A HANDSOME ORGANIC MAN.
WHAT'RE YOU UP TO TONIGHT?
COME WITH ME, YOU TWO.

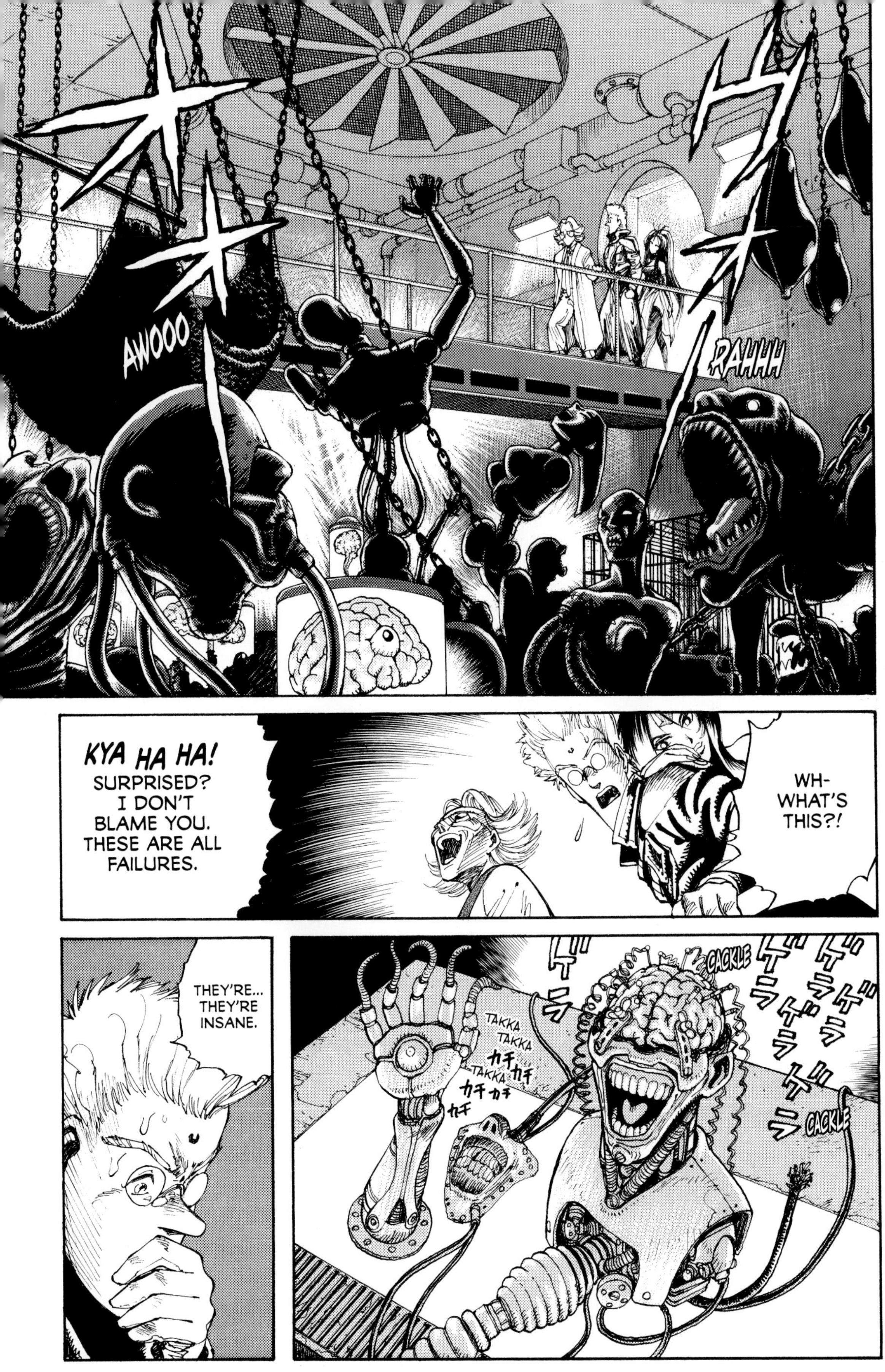
RAHHH
AWOOO
WH- WHAT'S THIS?!
KYA HA HA! SURPRISED? I DON'T BLAME YOU. THESE ARE ALL FAILURES.
CACKLE
ゲラゲラゲラゲラ
TAKKA TAKKA
カチカチ
TAKKA
カチカチ
カチ
CACKLE
THEY'RE... THEY'RE INSANE.

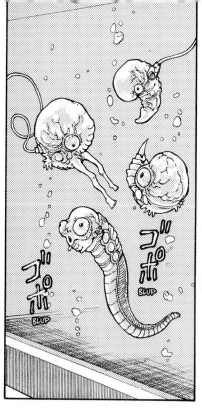

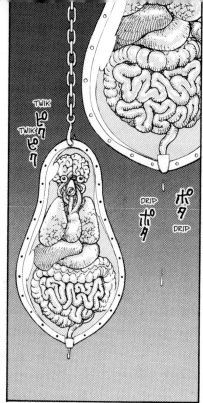

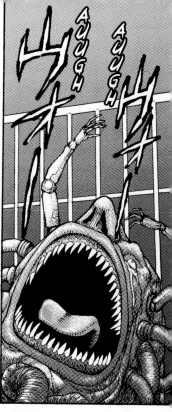

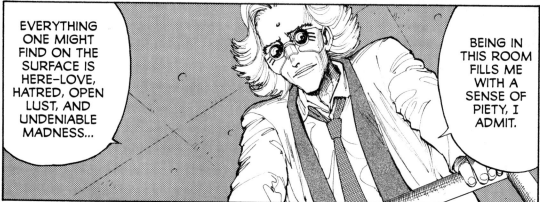

AUGH
AUGH
TWIK
TWIK
ピク
ピク
DRIP
DRIP
ポタ
ポタ
BLUP
BLUP
ゴポ
ゴポ
BEING IN THIS ROOM FILLS ME WITH A SENSE OF PIETY, I ADMIT.
EVERYTHING ONE MIGHT FIND ON THE SURFACE IS HERE–LOVE, HATRED, OPEN LUST, AND UNDENIABLE MADNESS...
WH-WHAT IS THE TRUE PURPOSE OF YOUR RESEARCH, PROFESSOR NOVA?!

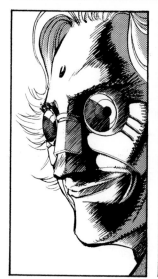

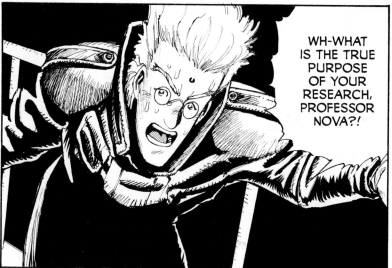

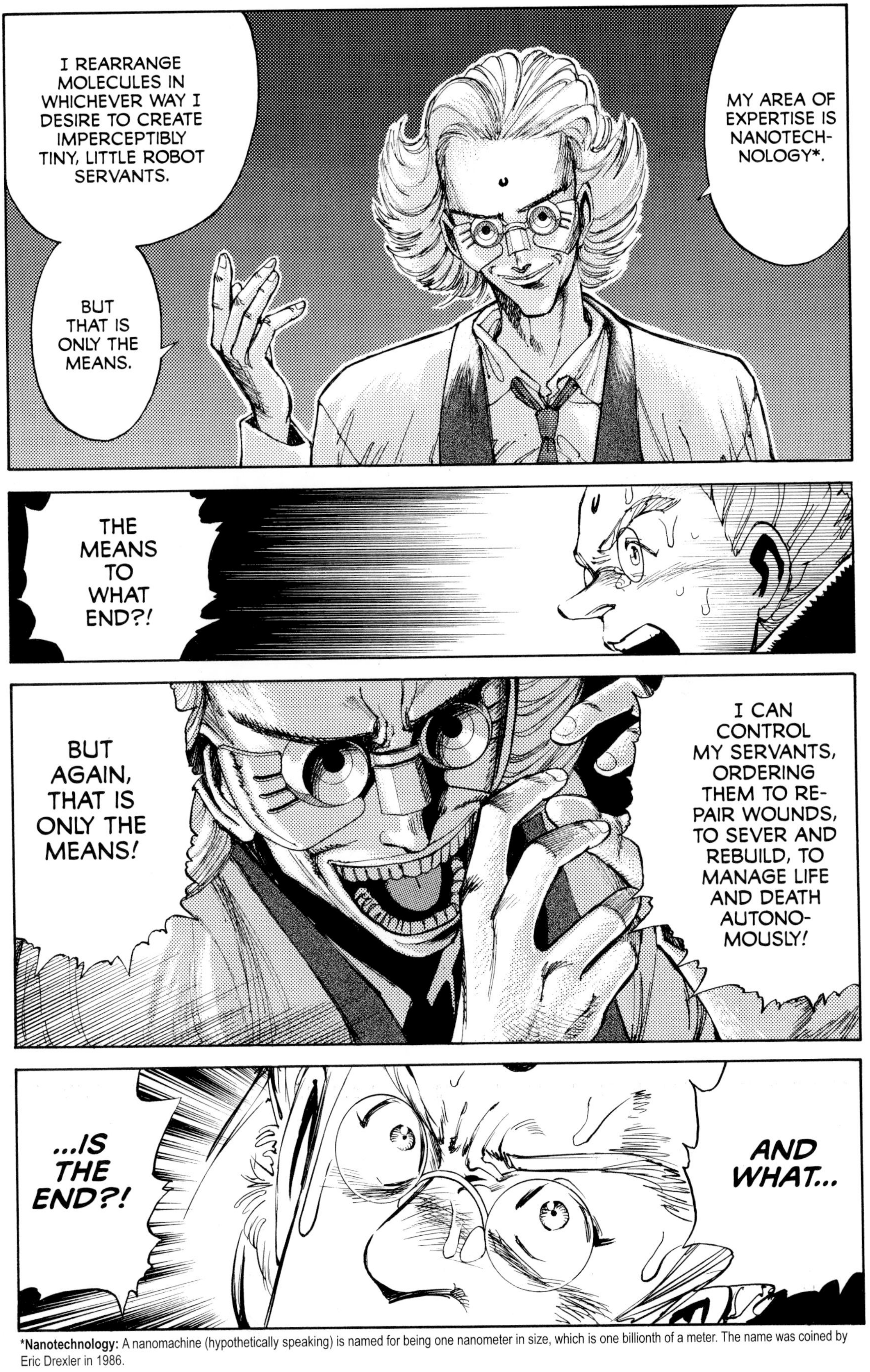
MY AREA OF EXPERTISE IS NANOTECH-NOLOGY*.
I REARRANGE MOLECULES IN WHICHEVER WAY I DESIRE TO CREATE IMPERCEPTIBLY TINY, LITTLE ROBOT SERVANTS.
BUT THAT IS ONLY THE MEANS.
THE MEANS TO WHAT END?!
I CAN CONTROL MY SERVANTS, ORDERING THEM TO RE-PAIR WOUNDS, TO SEVER AND REBUILD, TO MANAGE LIFE AND DEATH AUTONO-MOUSLY!
BUT AGAIN, THAT IS ONLY THE MEANS!
AND WHAT...
...IS THE END?!

***Nanotechnology:** A nanomachine (hypothetically speaking) is named for being one nanometer in size, which is one billionth of a meter. The name was coined by Eric Drexler in 1986.

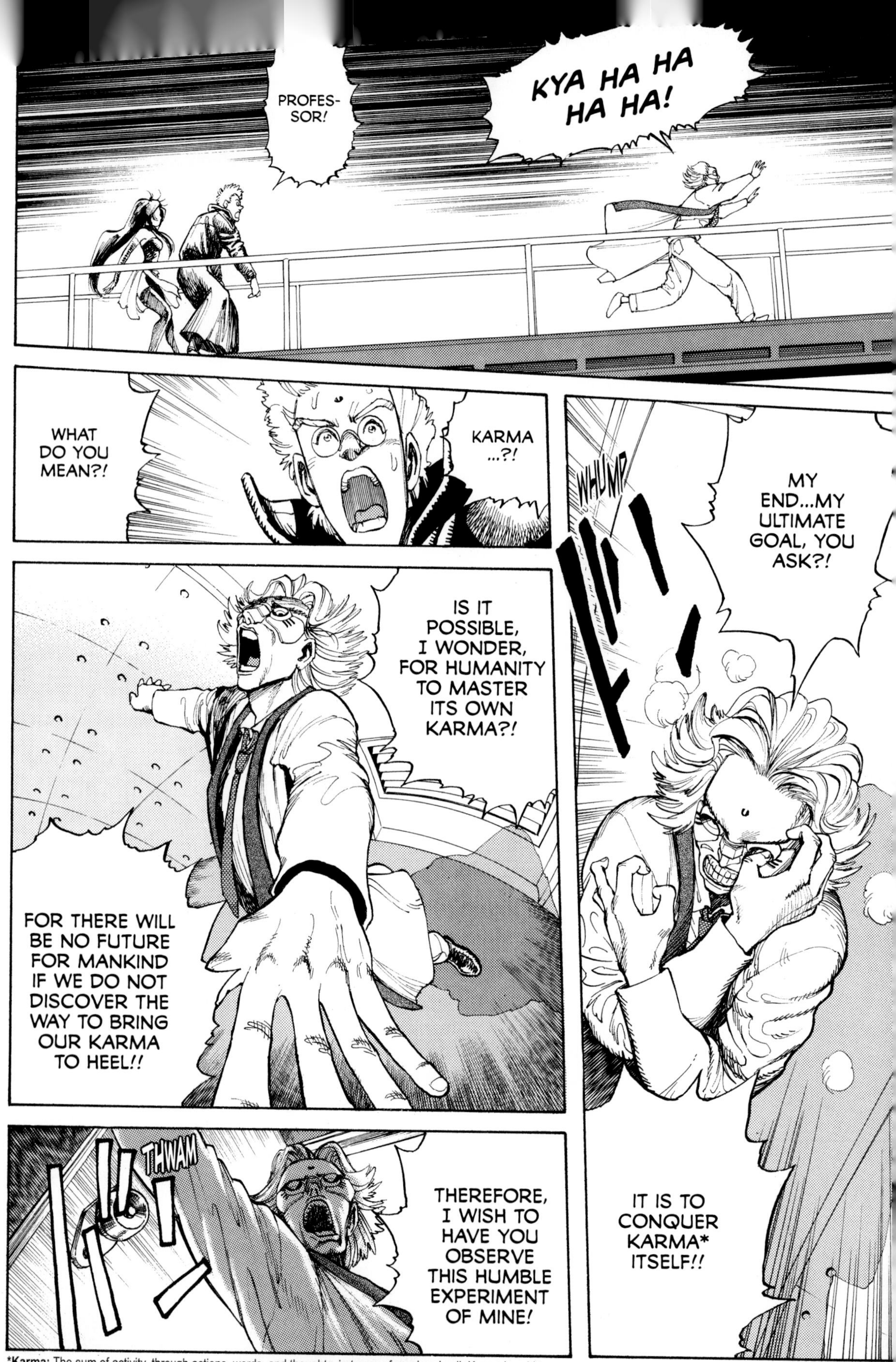
KYA HA HA HA HA!
PROFES-SOR!
MY END...MY ULTIMATE GOAL, YOU ASK?!
WHUMP
IT IS TO CONQUER KARMA* ITSELF!!
KARMA ...?!
WHAT DO YOU MEAN?!
IS IT POSSIBLE, I WONDER, FOR HUMANITY TO MASTER ITS OWN KARMA?!
FOR THERE WILL BE NO FUTURE FOR MANKIND IF WE DO NOT DISCOVER THE WAY TO BRING OUR KARMA TO HEEL!!
THWAM
THEREFORE, I WISH TO HAVE YOU OBSERVE THIS HUMBLE EXPERIMENT OF MINE!

***Karma:** The sum of activity, through actions, words, and thoughts, in terms of good and evil. Karma is said to influence the outcome of the events of one's life. The term is from Sanskrit, and means "action" or "deed."

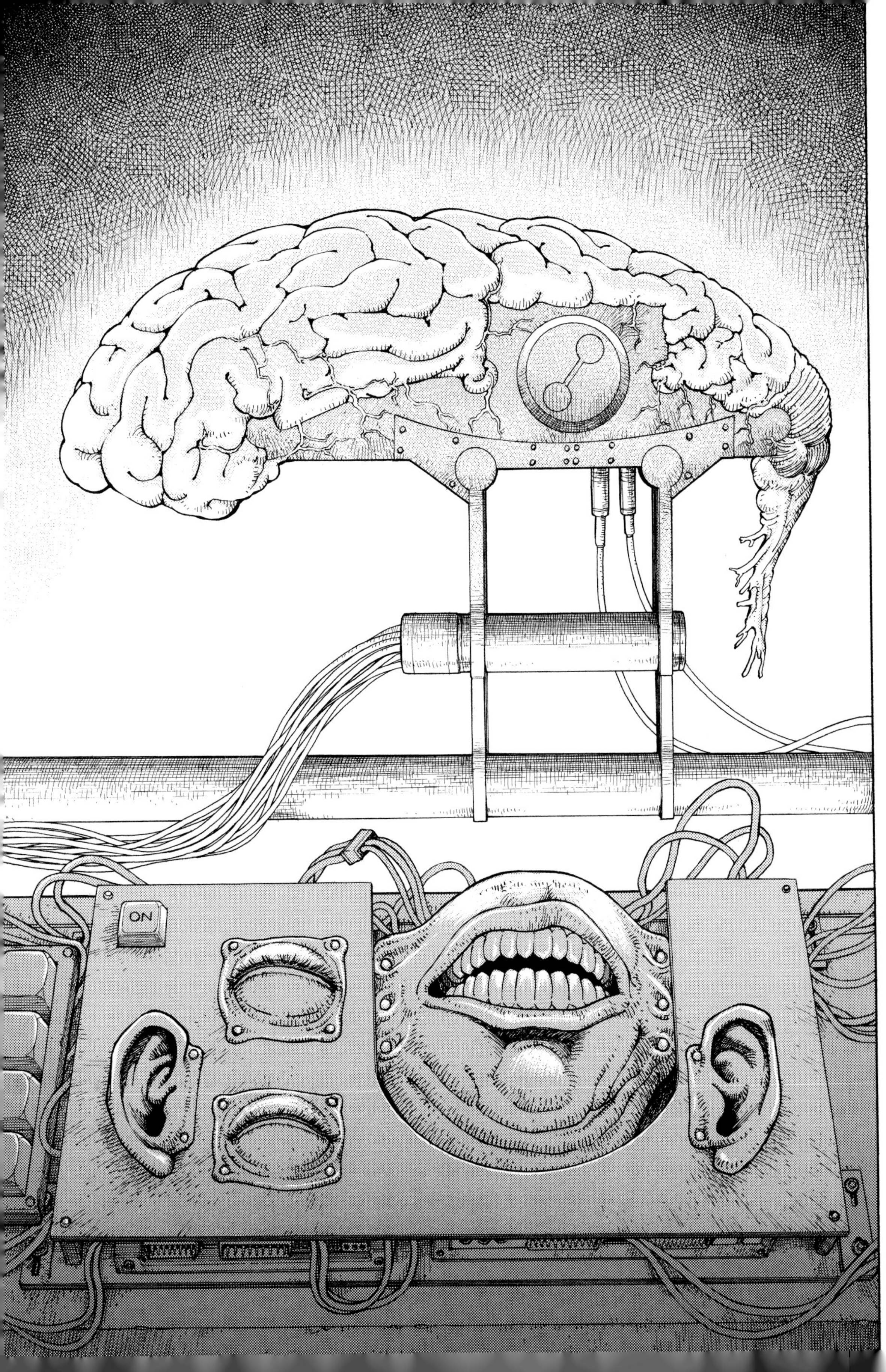
ON

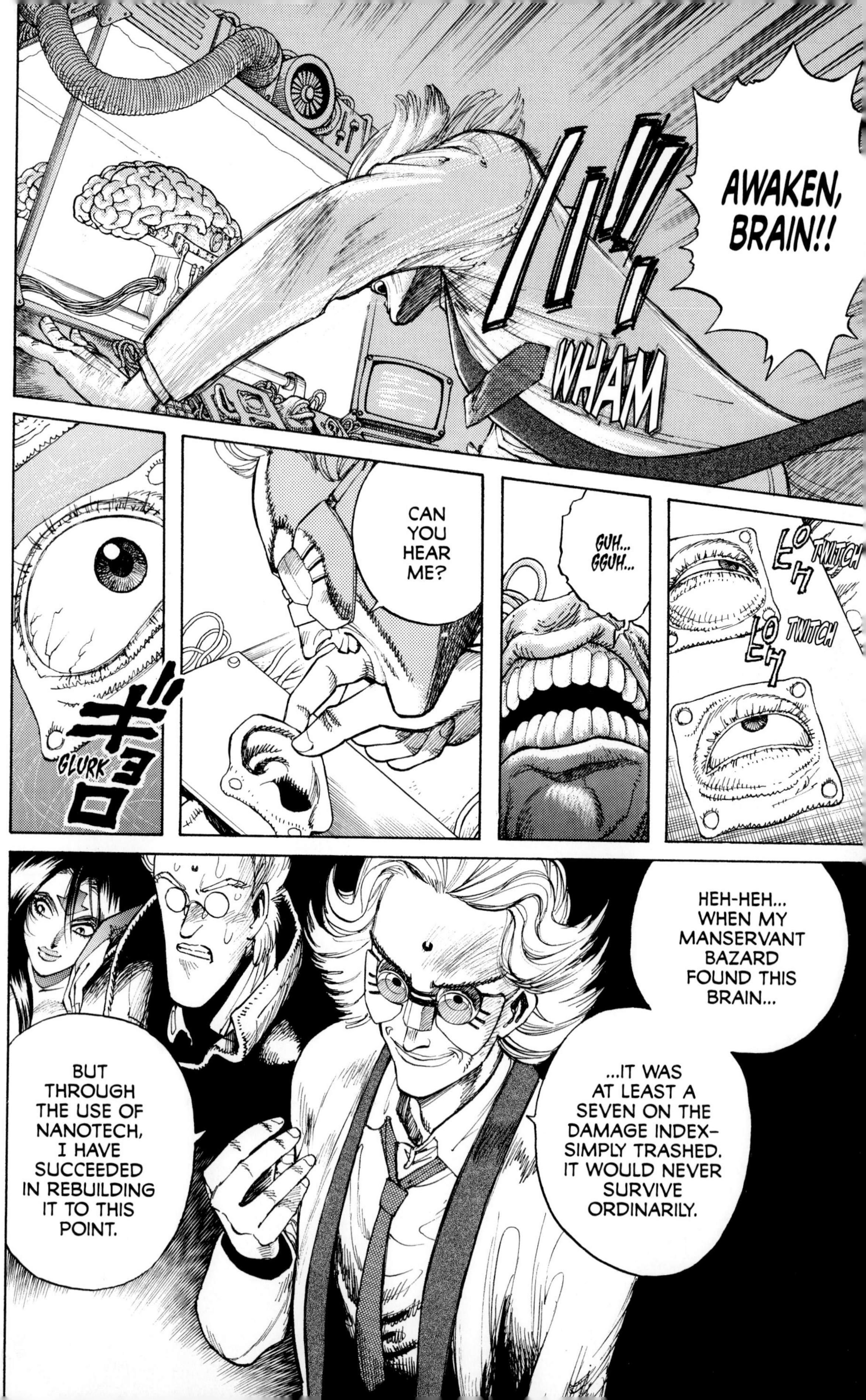
AWAKEN, BRAIN!!
WHAM
TWITCH
TWITCH
GUH... GGUH...
CAN YOU HEAR ME?
ギョロ
GLURK
HEH-HEH... WHEN MY MANSERVANT BAZARD FOUND THIS BRAIN...
...IT WAS AT LEAST A SEVEN ON THE DAMAGE INDEX–SIMPLY TRASHED. IT WOULD NEVER SURVIVE ORDINARILY.
BUT THROUGH THE USE OF NANOTECH, I HAVE SUCCEEDED IN REBUILDING IT TO THIS POINT.

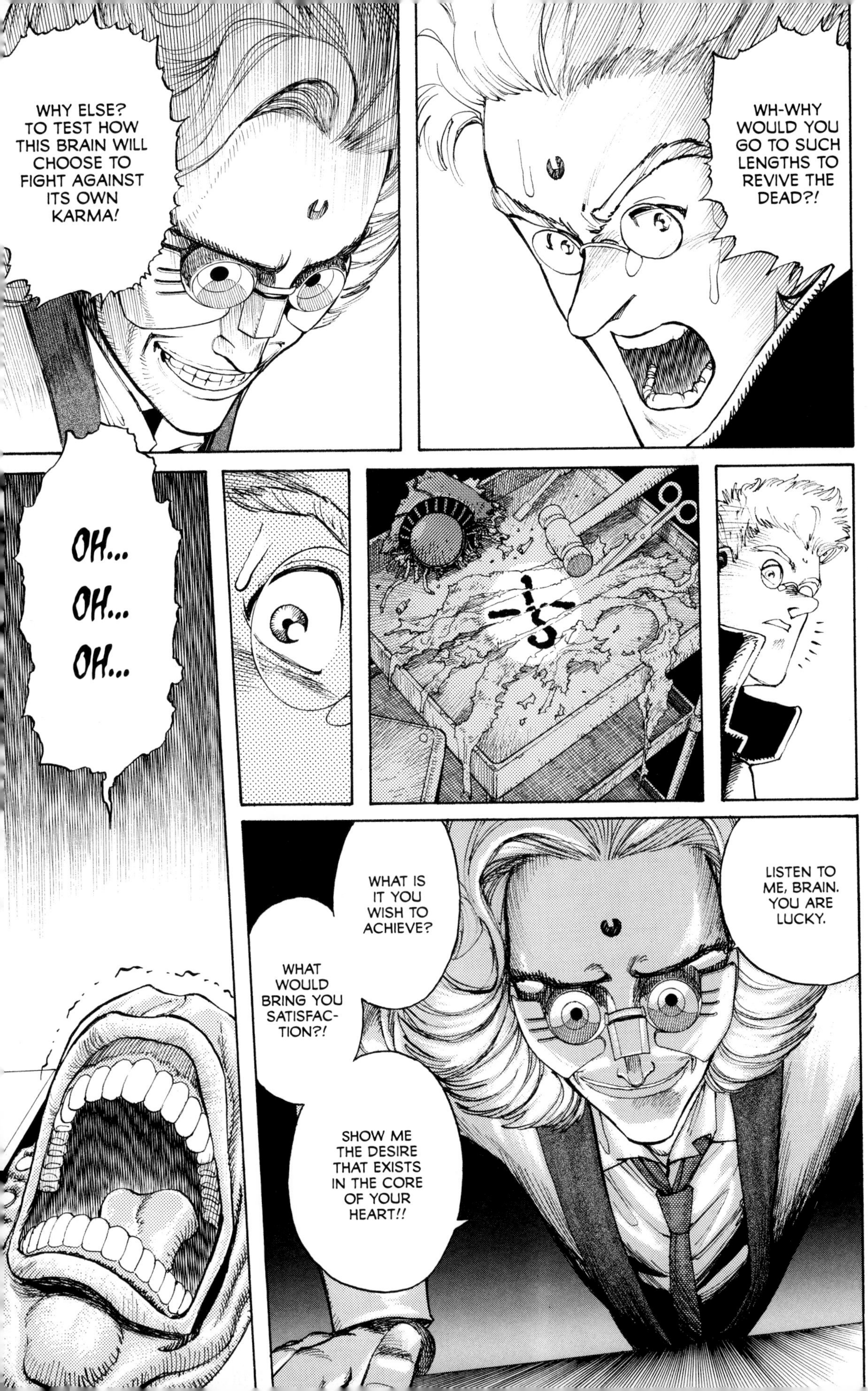
WH-WHY WOULD YOU GO TO SUCH LENGTHS TO REVIVE THE DEAD?!
WHY ELSE? TO TEST HOW THIS BRAIN WILL CHOOSE TO FIGHT AGAINST ITS OWN KARMA!
LISTEN TO ME, BRAIN. YOU ARE LUCKY.
WHAT IS IT YOU WISH TO ACHIEVE?
WHAT WOULD BRING YOU SATISFAC-TION?!
SHOW ME THE DESIRE THAT EXISTS IN THE CORE OF YOUR HEART!!
OH... OH... OH...

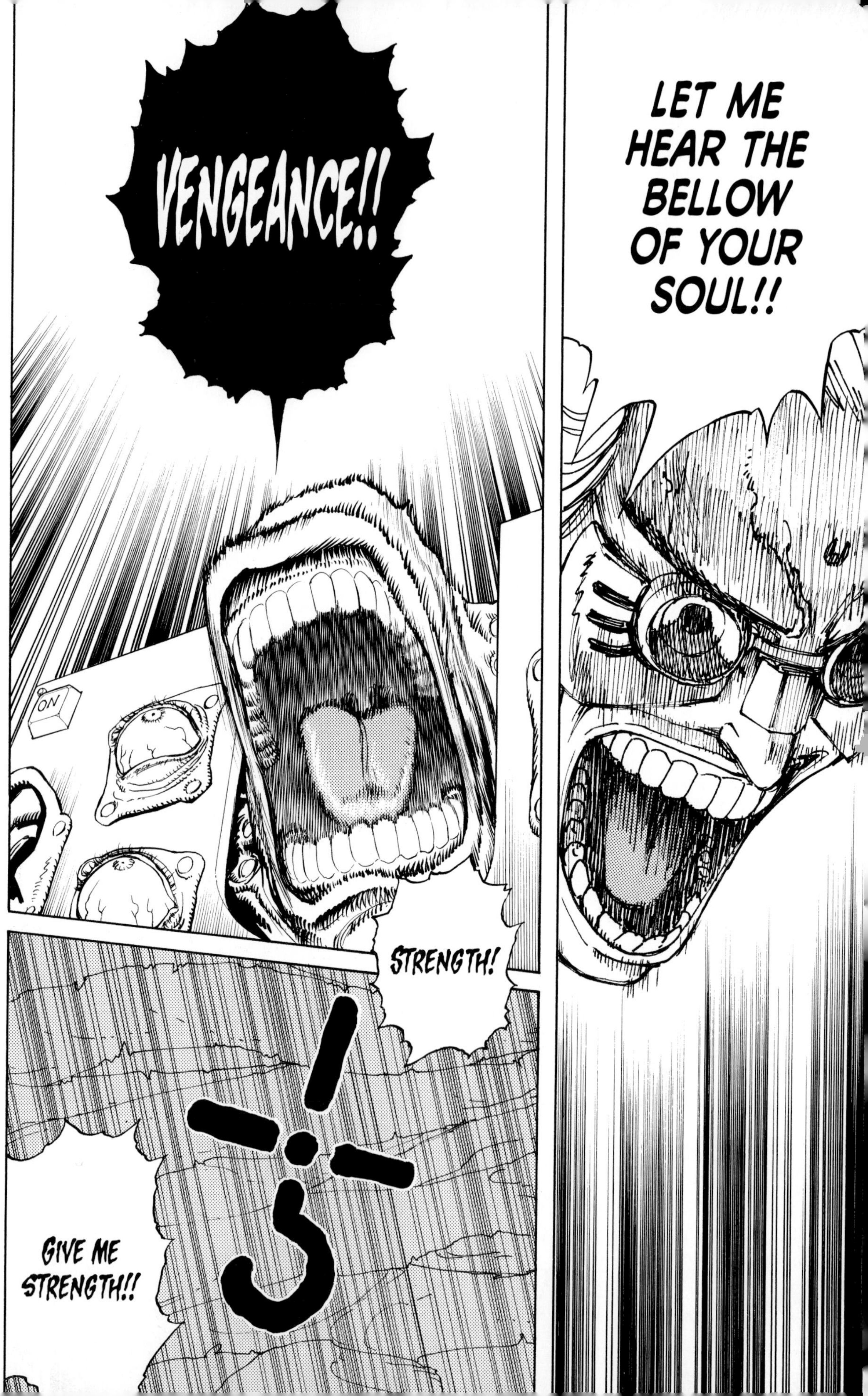
LET ME HEAR THE BELLOW OF YOUR SOUL!!
VENGEANCE!!
STRENGTH!
GIVE ME STRENGTH!!

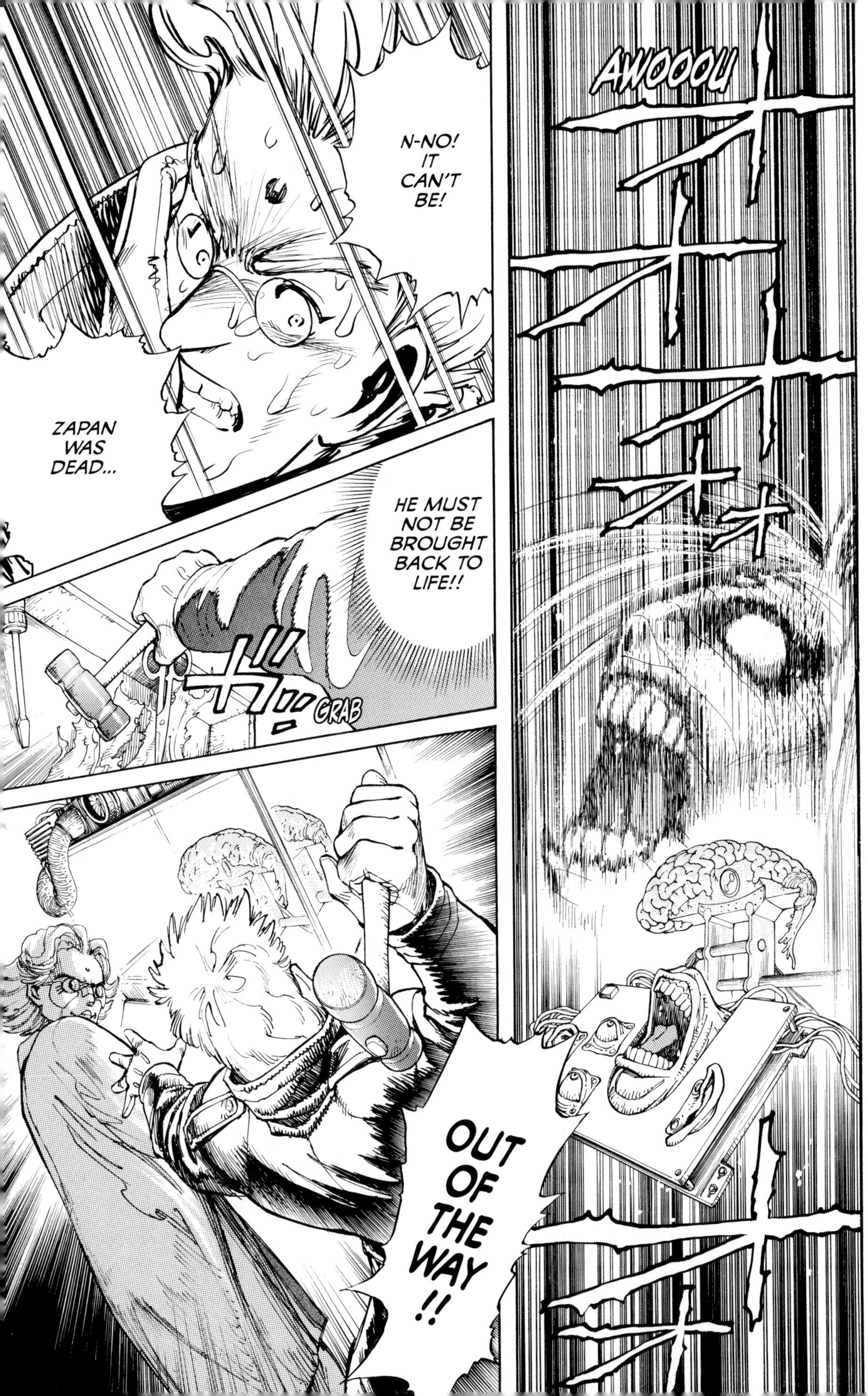
AWOOOU
N-NO! IT CAN'T BE!
ZAPAN WAS DEAD...
HE MUST NOT BE BROUGHT BACK TO LIFE!!
GRAB
OUT OF THE WAY!!

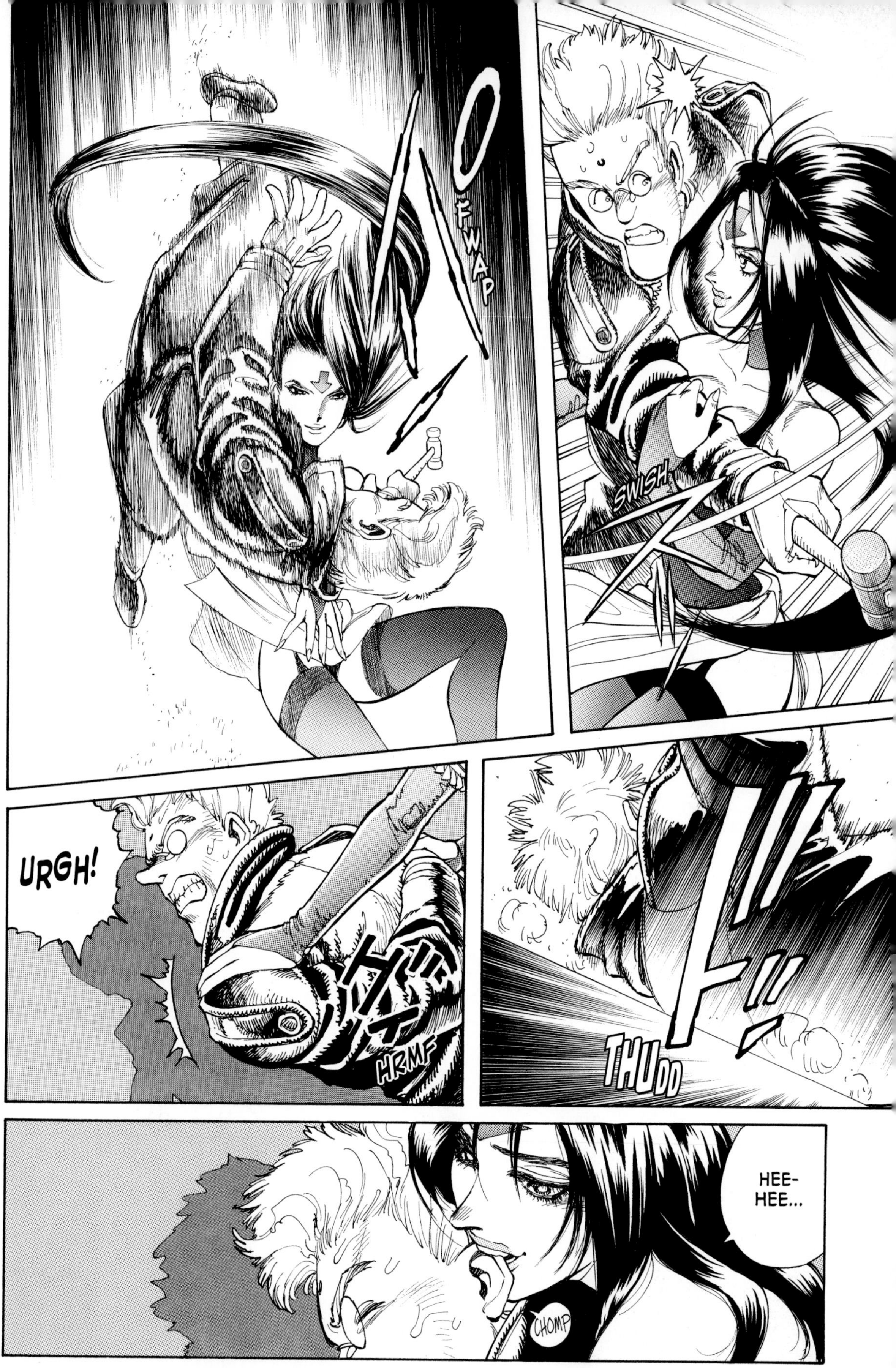
SWISH
FWAP
THUDD
URGH!
HRMF
HEE-HEE...
CHOMP

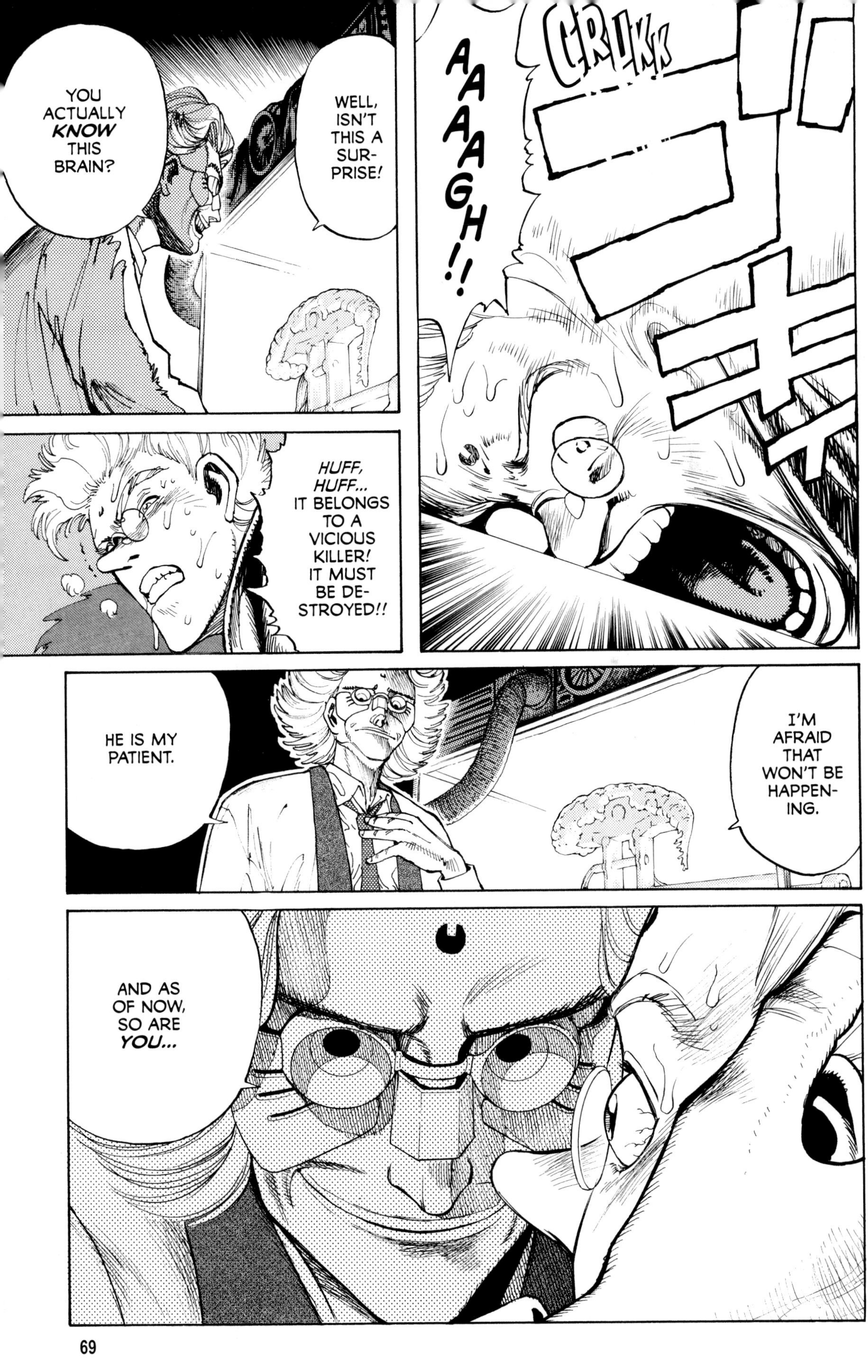
ゴキ
CRUKK
AAAAAGH!!
WELL, ISN'T THIS A SUR-PRISE!
YOU ACTUALLY *KNOW* THIS BRAIN?
HUFF, HUFF... IT BELONGS TO A VICIOUS KILLER! IT MUST BE DE-STROYED!!
I'M AFRAID THAT WON'T BE HAPPEN-ING.
HE IS MY PATIENT.
AND AS OF NOW, SO ARE *YOU...*

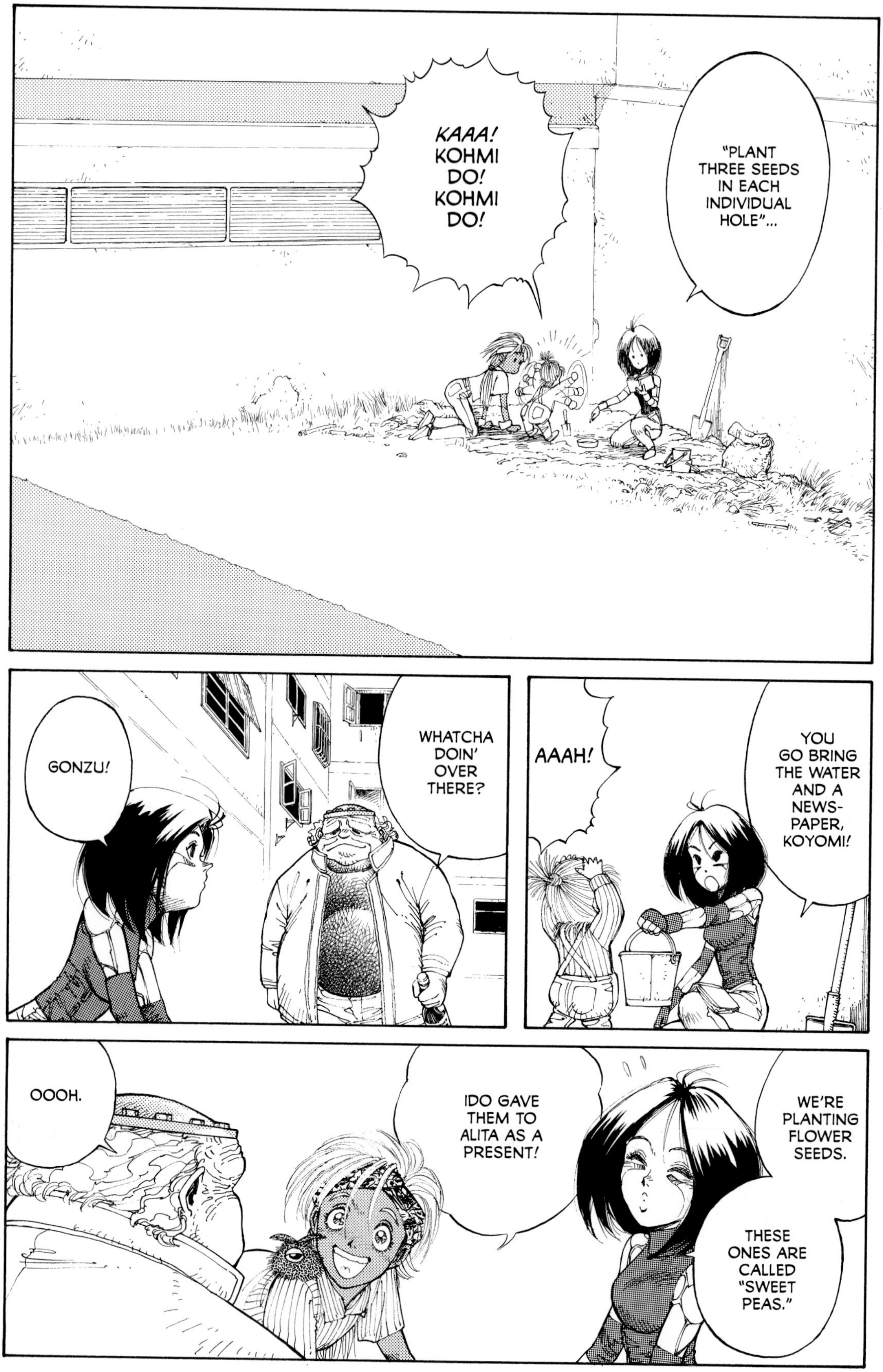
"PLANT THREE SEEDS IN EACH INDIVIDUAL HOLE"...
KAAA! KOHMI DO! KOHMI DO!
YOU GO BRING THE WATER AND A NEWS-PAPER, KOYOMI!
AAAH!
WHATCHA DOIN' OVER THERE?
GONZU!
WE'RE PLANTING FLOWER SEEDS.
THESE ONES ARE CALLED "SWEET PEAS."
IDO GAVE THEM TO ALITA AS A PRESENT!
OOOH.

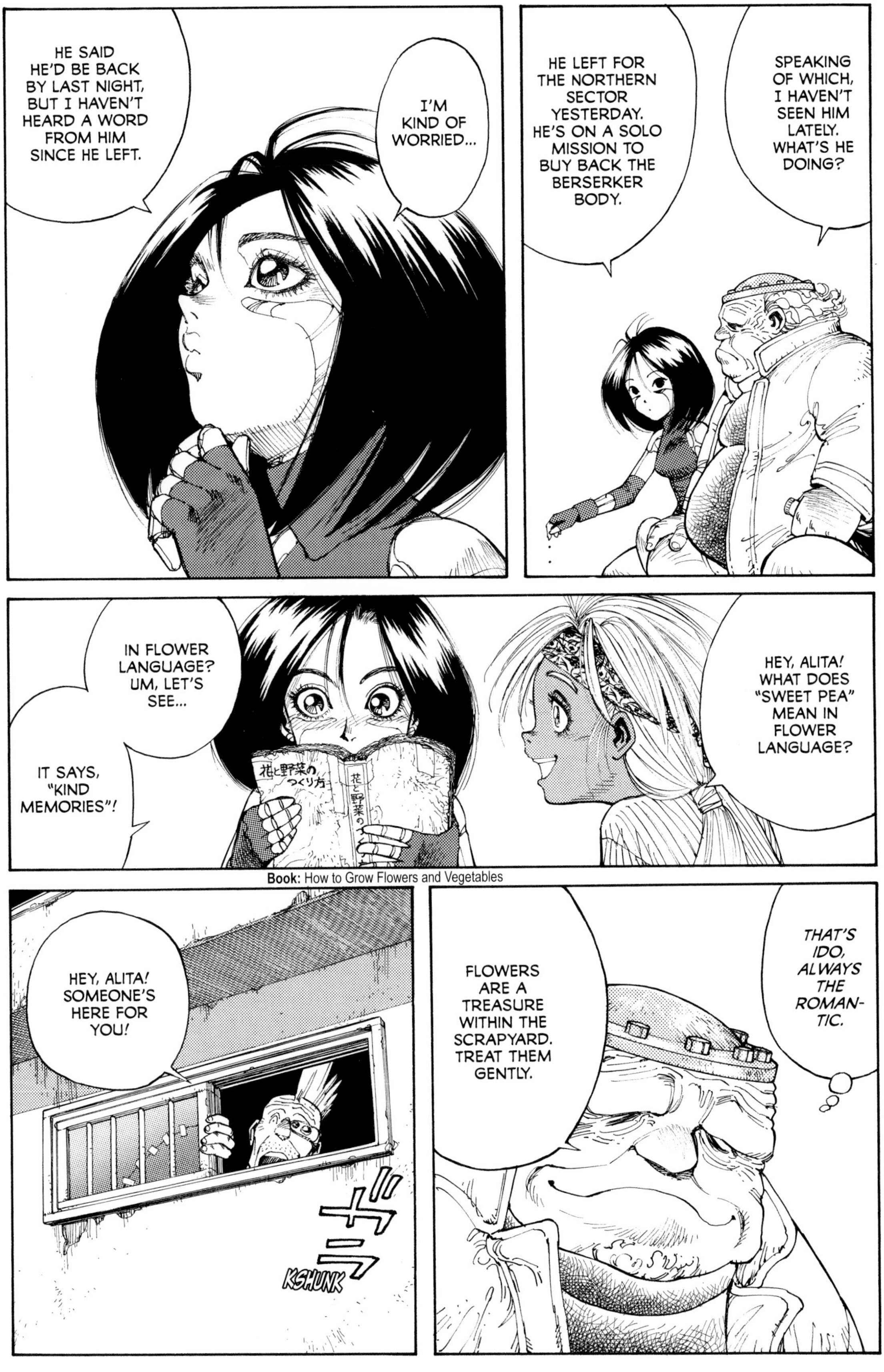
SPEAKING OF WHICH, I HAVEN'T SEEN HIM LATELY. WHAT'S HE DOING?
HE LEFT FOR THE NORTHERN SECTOR YESTERDAY. HE'S ON A SOLO MISSION TO BUY BACK THE BERSERKER BODY.
I'M KIND OF WORRIED...
HE SAID HE'D BE BACK BY LAST NIGHT, BUT I HAVEN'T HEARD A WORD FROM HIM SINCE HE LEFT.
HEY, ALITA! WHAT DOES "SWEET PEA" MEAN IN FLOWER LANGUAGE?
IN FLOWER LANGUAGE? UM, LET'S SEE...
花と野菜のつくり方
IT SAYS, "KIND MEMORIES"!
Book: How to Grow Flowers and Vegetables
THAT'S IDO, ALWAYS THE ROMANTIC.
FLOWERS ARE A TREASURE WITHIN THE SCRAPYARD. TREAT THEM GENTLY.
HEY, ALITA! SOMEONE'S HERE FOR YOU!
ガラ
KSHUNK

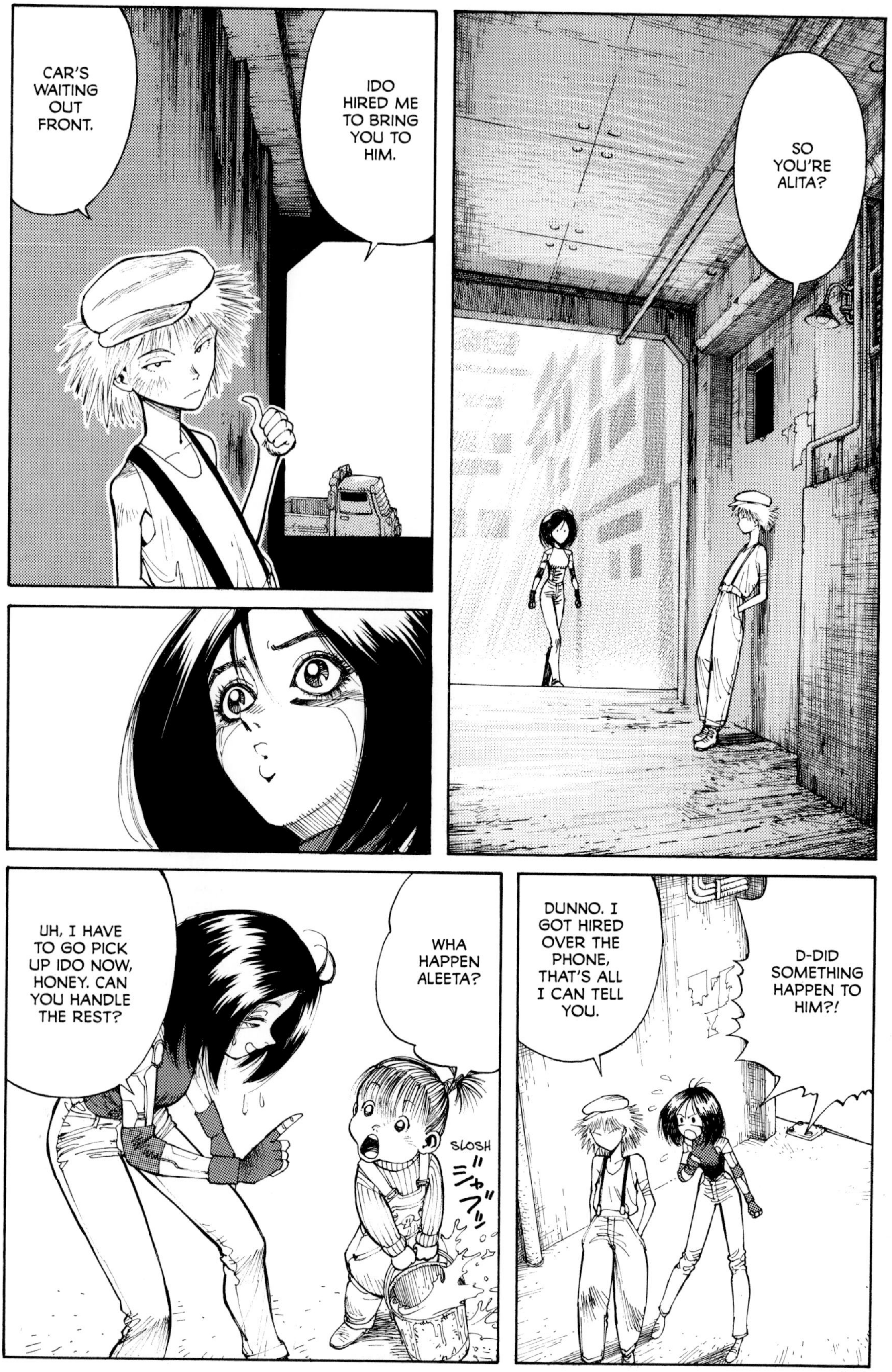
SO YOU'RE ALITA?
IDO HIRED ME TO BRING YOU TO HIM.
CAR'S WAITING OUT FRONT.
D-DID SOMETHING HAPPEN TO HIM?!
DUNNO. I GOT HIRED OVER THE PHONE, THAT'S ALL I CAN TELL YOU.
WHA HAPPEN ALEETA?
SLOSH
ジャブッ
UH, I HAVE TO GO PICK UP IDO NOW, HONEY. CAN YOU HANDLE THE REST?

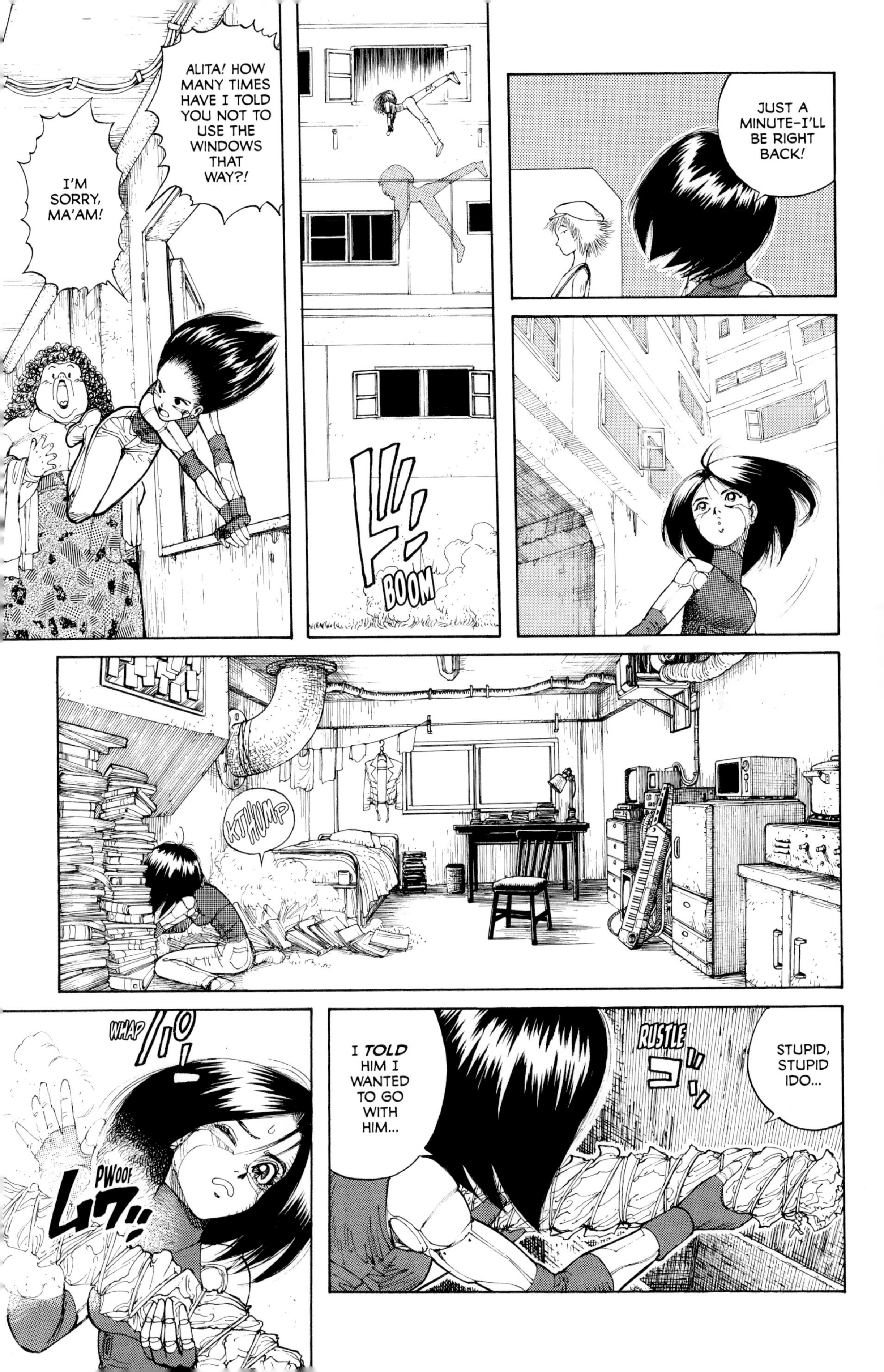
JUST A MINUTE—I'LL BE RIGHT BACK!
BOOM
ALITA! HOW MANY TIMES HAVE I TOLD YOU NOT TO USE THE WINDOWS THAT WAY?!
I'M SORRY, MA'AM!
KTHUMP
STUPID, STUPID IDO...
RUSTLE
I *TOLD* HIM I WANTED TO GO WITH HIM...
WHAP
PWOOF

DON'T WORRY, I'M COMING TO SAVE YOU...

LET'S GO!

SORRY!

ALITA!

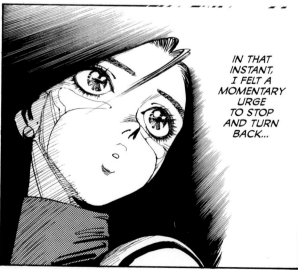

IN THAT INSTANT, I FELT A MOMENTARY URGE TO STOP AND TURN BACK...

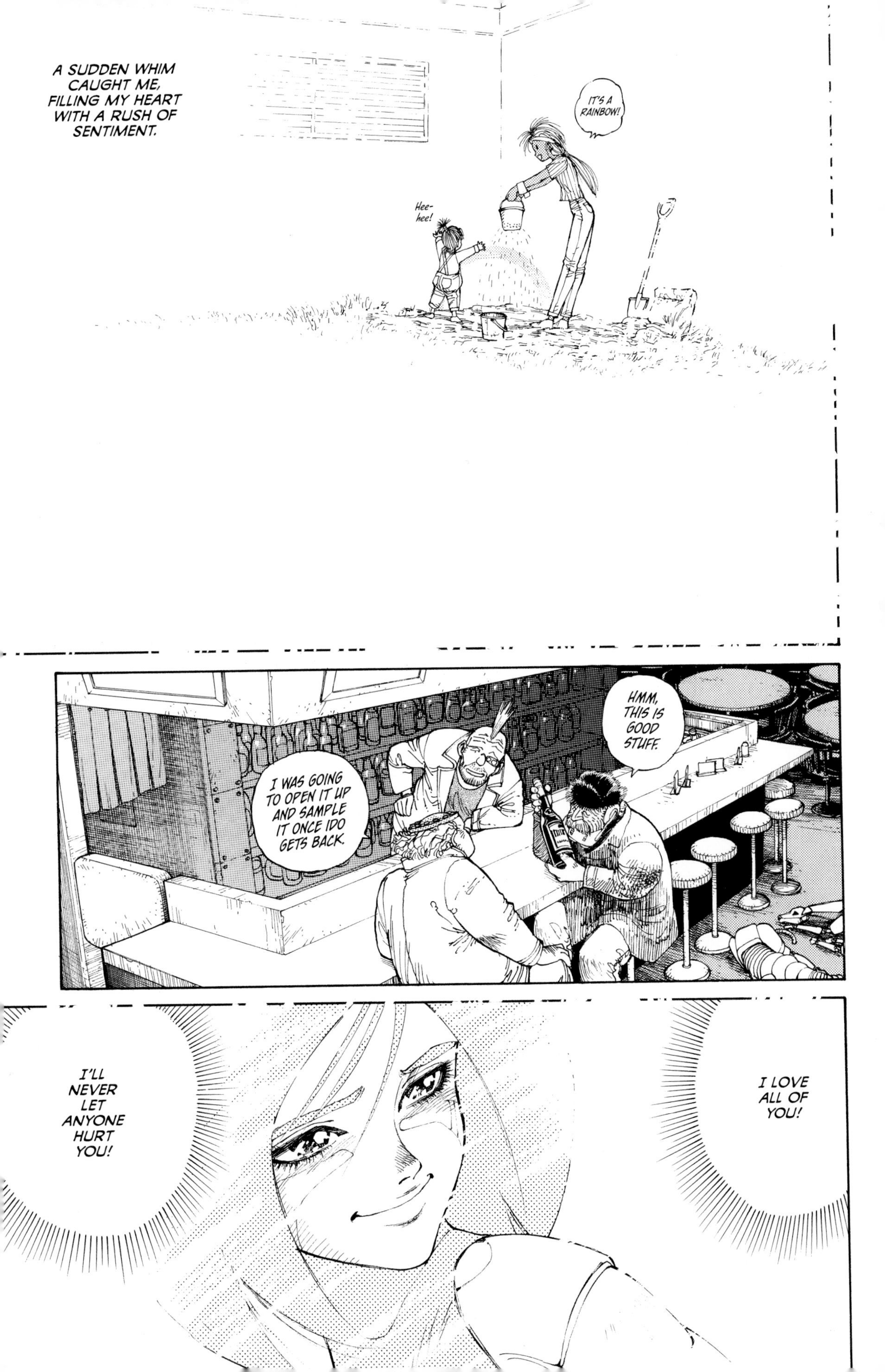
IT'S A RAINBOW!
Hee-hee!
A SUDDEN WHIM CAUGHT ME, FILLING MY HEART WITH A RUSH OF SENTIMENT.
HMM, THIS IS GOOD STUFF.
I WAS GOING TO OPEN IT UP AND SAMPLE IT ONCE IDO GETS BACK.
I LOVE ALL OF YOU!
I'LL NEVER LET ANYONE HURT YOU!

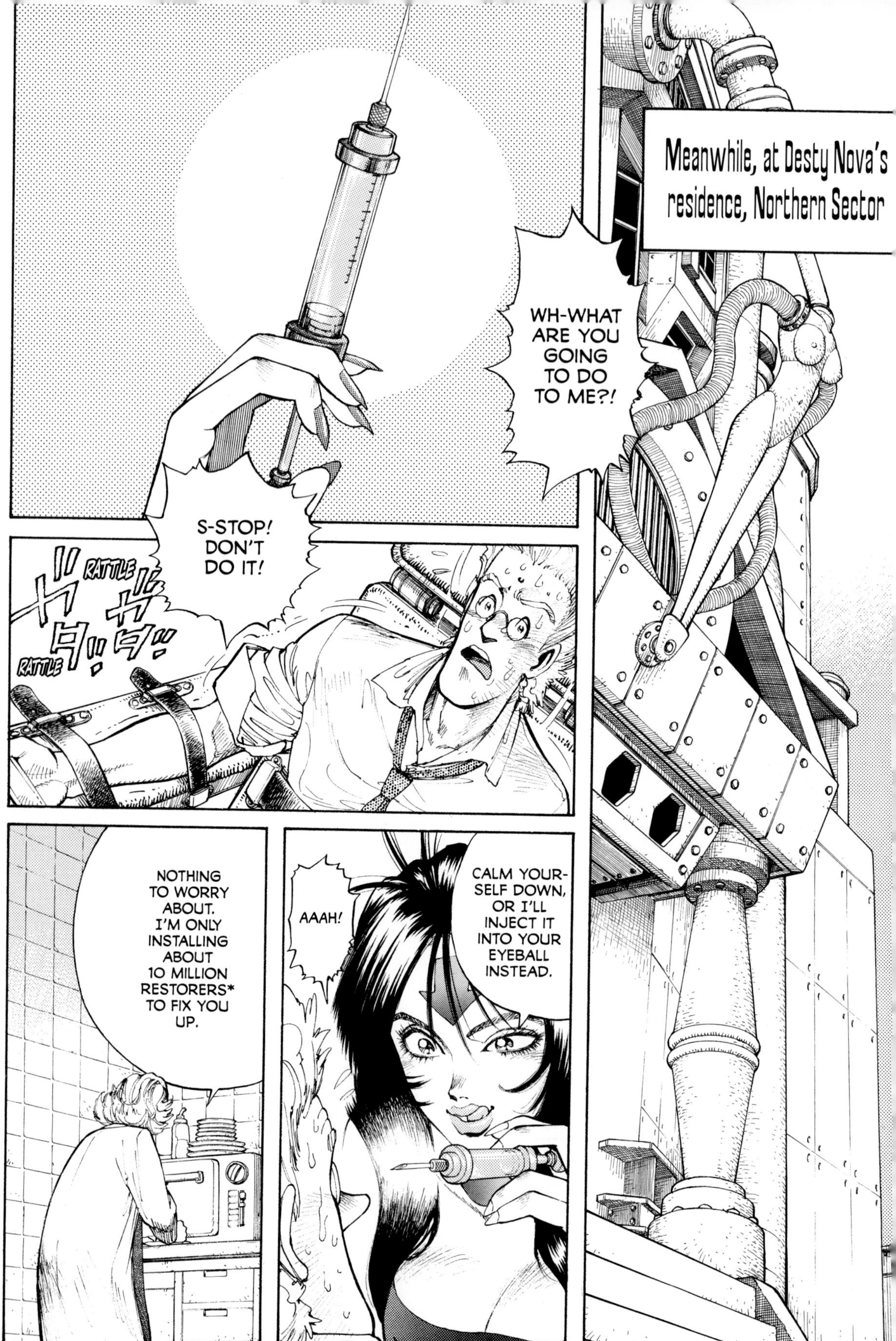
Meanwhile, at Desty Nova's residence, Northern Sector
WH-WHAT ARE YOU GOING TO DO TO ME?!
S-STOP! DON'T DO IT!
RATTLE
RATTLE
CALM YOURSELF DOWN, OR I'LL INJECT IT INTO YOUR EYEBALL INSTEAD.
AAAH!
NOTHING TO WORRY ABOUT. I'M ONLY INSTALLING ABOUT 10 MILLION RESTORERS* TO FIX YOU UP.

***Restorer:** A type of nanomachine that performs bodily repair on the cellular level. People with these nanobots in their body will have dramatically faster self-healing capabilities.

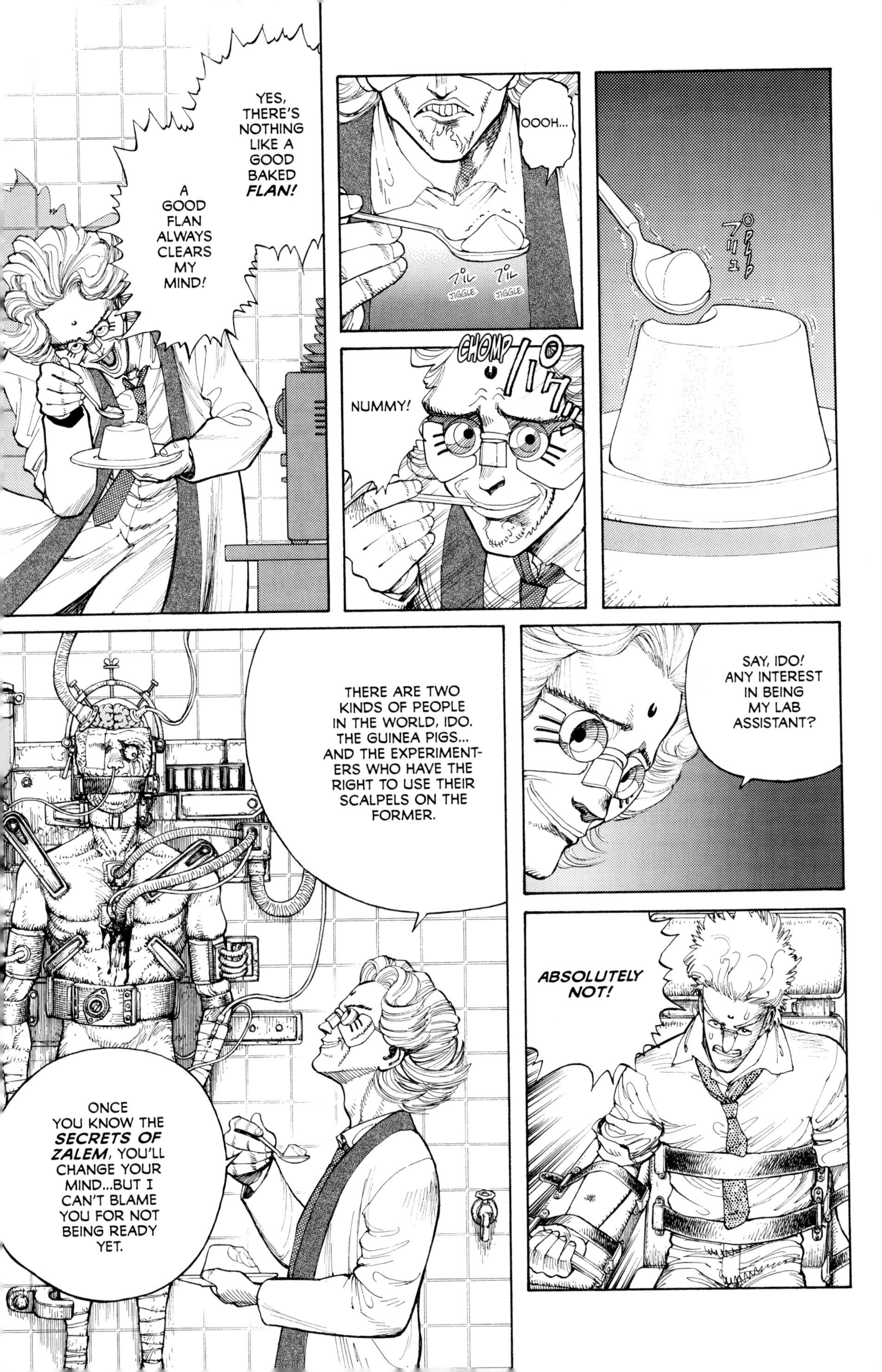
OOOH...
プル JIGGLE
プル JIGGLE
CHOMP
NUMMY!
YES, THERE'S NOTHING LIKE A GOOD BAKED *FLAN!*
A GOOD FLAN ALWAYS CLEARS MY MIND!
SAY, IDO! ANY INTEREST IN BEING MY LAB ASSISTANT?
ABSOLUTELY NOT!
THERE ARE TWO KINDS OF PEOPLE IN THE WORLD, IDO. THE GUINEA PIGS... AND THE EXPERIMENTERS WHO HAVE THE RIGHT TO USE THEIR SCALPELS ON THE FORMER.
ONCE YOU KNOW THE *SECRETS OF ZALEM*, YOU'LL CHANGE YOUR MIND...BUT I CAN'T BLAME YOU FOR NOT BEING READY YET.

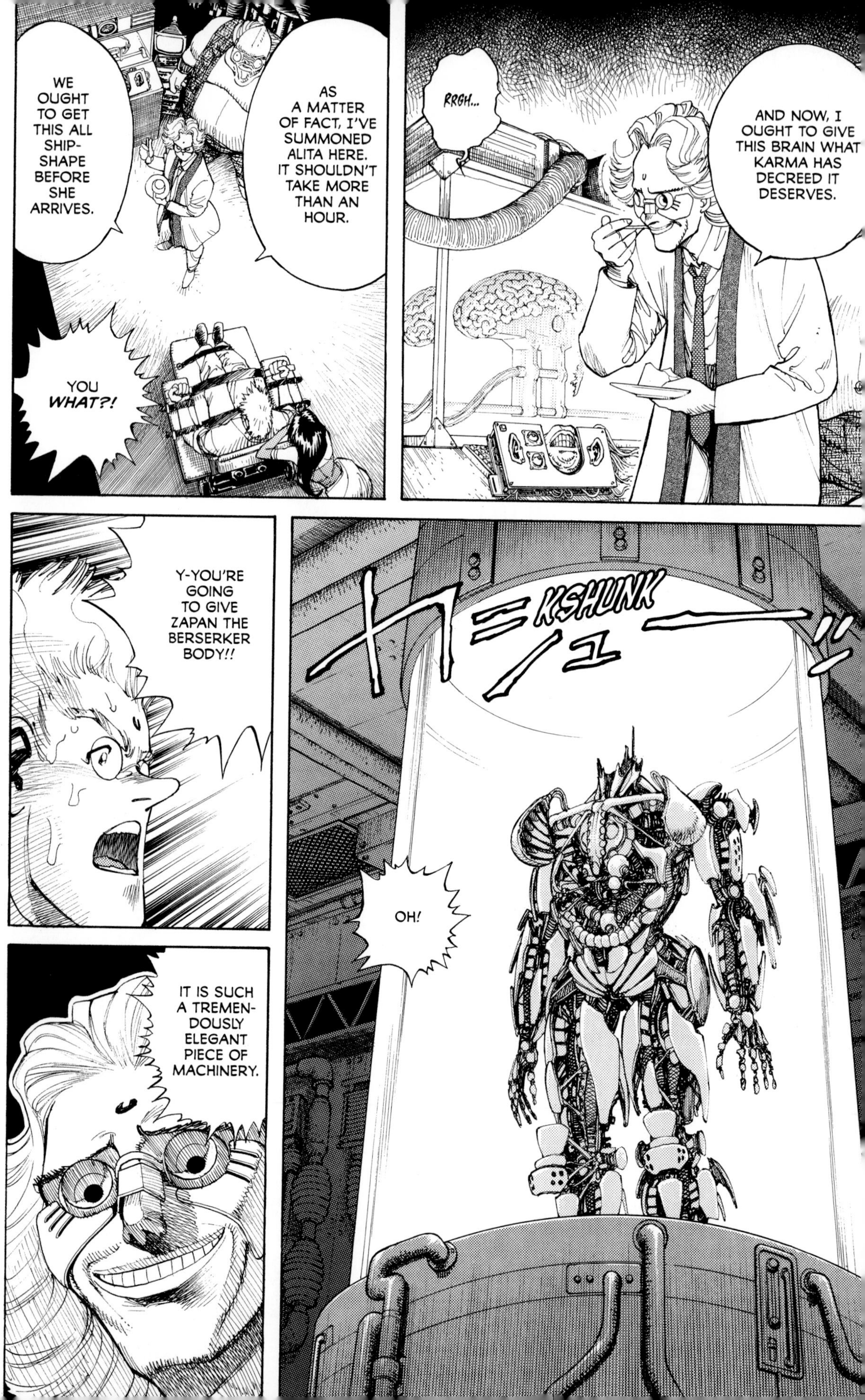
RRGH...
AND NOW, I OUGHT TO GIVE THIS BRAIN WHAT KARMA HAS DECREED IT DESERVES.
AS A MATTER OF FACT, I'VE SUMMONED ALITA HERE. IT SHOULDN'T TAKE MORE THAN AN HOUR.
WE OUGHT TO GET THIS ALL SHIP-SHAPE BEFORE SHE ARRIVES.
YOU *WHAT?!*
KSHUNK
OH!
Y-YOU'RE GOING TO GIVE ZAPAN THE BERSERKER BODY!!
IT IS SUCH A TREMEN-DOUSLY ELEGANT PIECE OF MACHINERY.

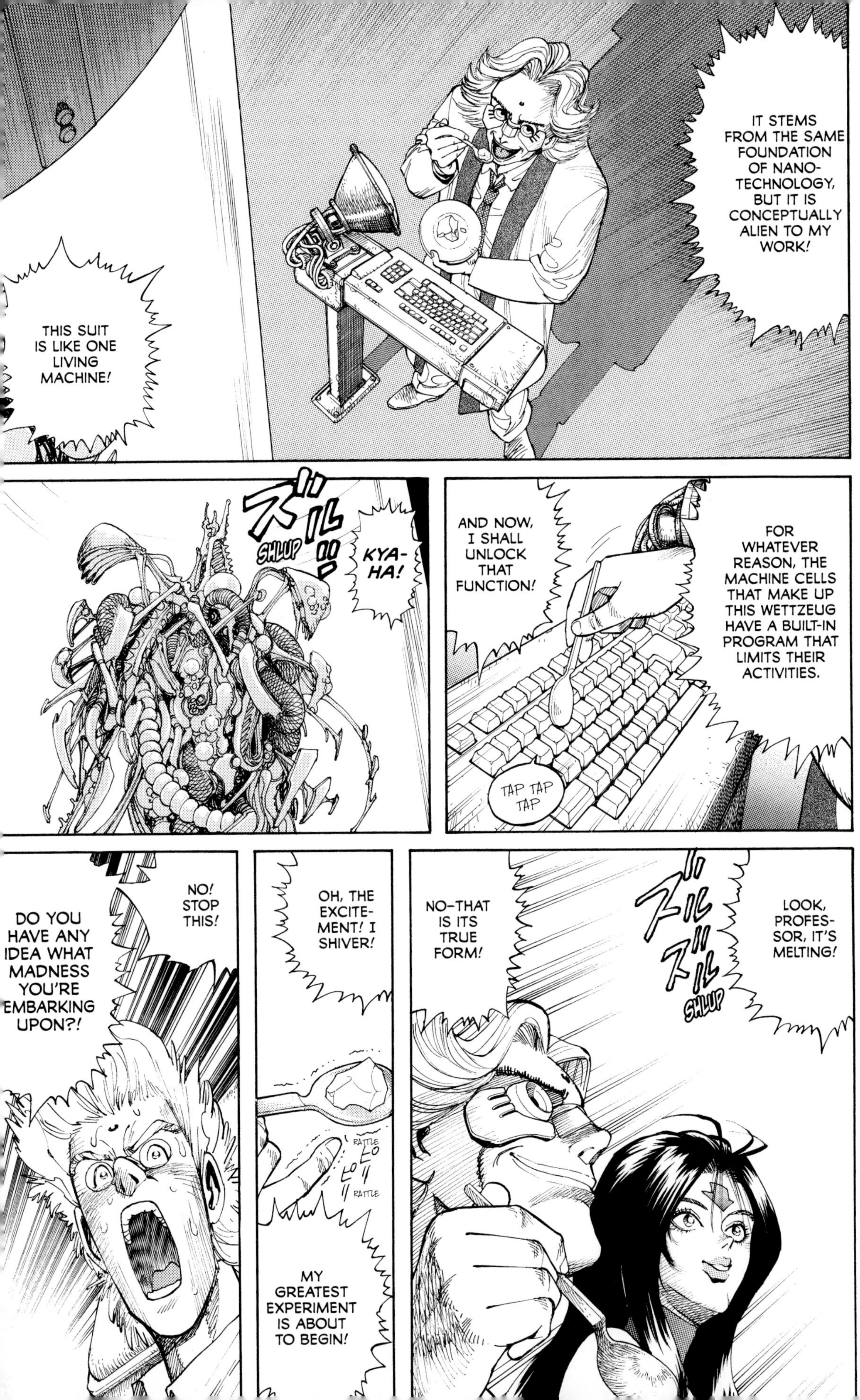
IT STEMS FROM THE SAME FOUNDATION OF NANO-TECHNOLOGY, BUT IT IS CONCEPTUALLY ALIEN TO MY WORK!
THIS SUIT IS LIKE ONE LIVING MACHINE!
FOR WHATEVER REASON, THE MACHINE CELLS THAT MAKE UP THIS WETTZEUG HAVE A BUILT-IN PROGRAM THAT LIMITS THEIR ACTIVITIES.
AND NOW, I SHALL UNLOCK THAT FUNCTION!
TAP TAP TAP
SHLUP
KYA-HA!
SHLUP
LOOK, PROFESSOR, IT'S MELTING!
NO—THAT IS ITS TRUE FORM!
OH, THE EXCITEMENT! I SHIVER!
RATTLE
RATTLE
MY GREATEST EXPERIMENT IS ABOUT TO BEGIN!
NO! STOP THIS!
DO YOU HAVE ANY IDEA WHAT MADNESS YOU'RE EMBARKING UPON?!

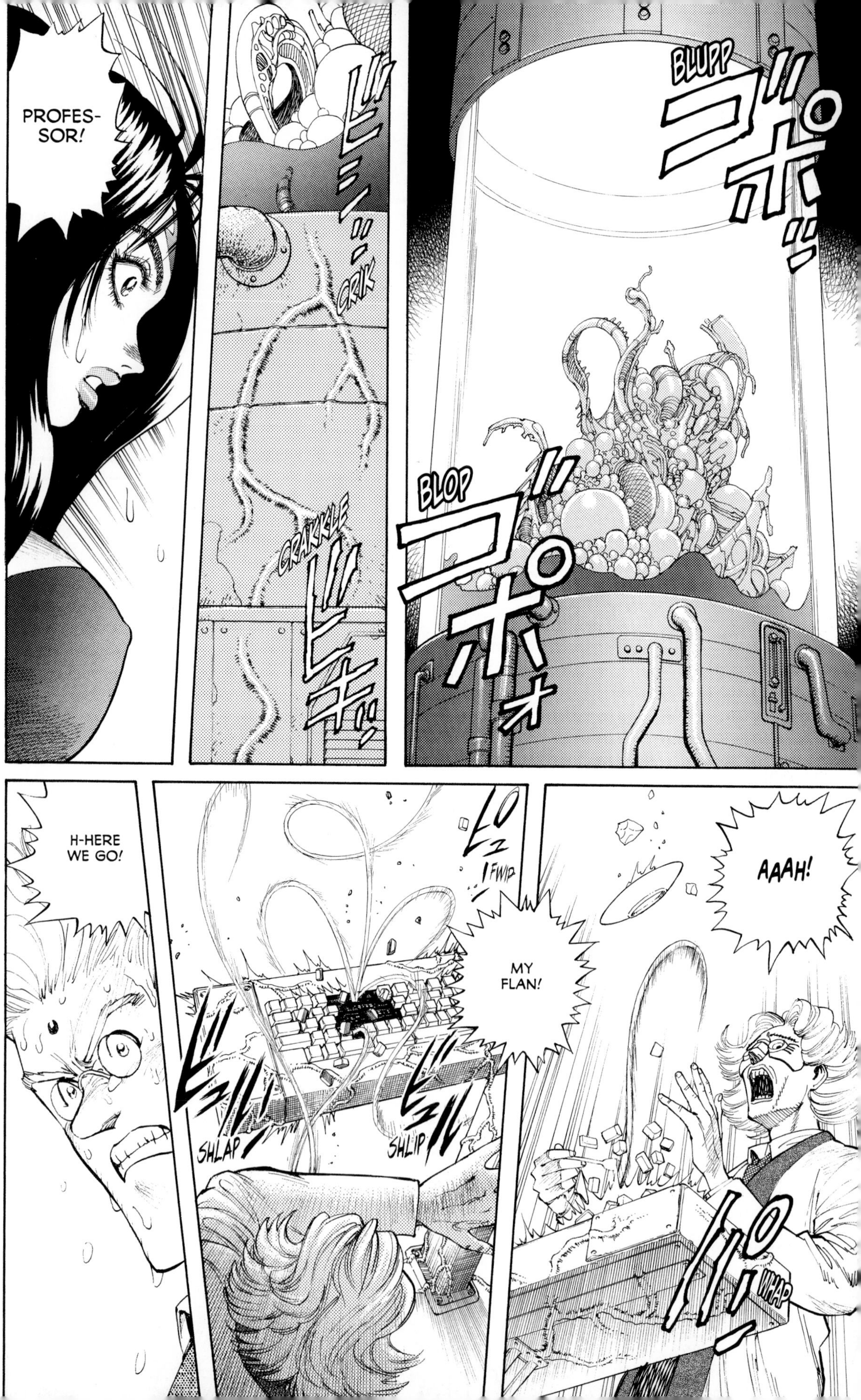

BLUPP
BLOP
CRIK
CRAKKLE
PROFES-
SOR!
AAAH!
MY
FLAN!
WHAP
FWIP
SHLIP
SHLAP
H-HERE
WE GO!

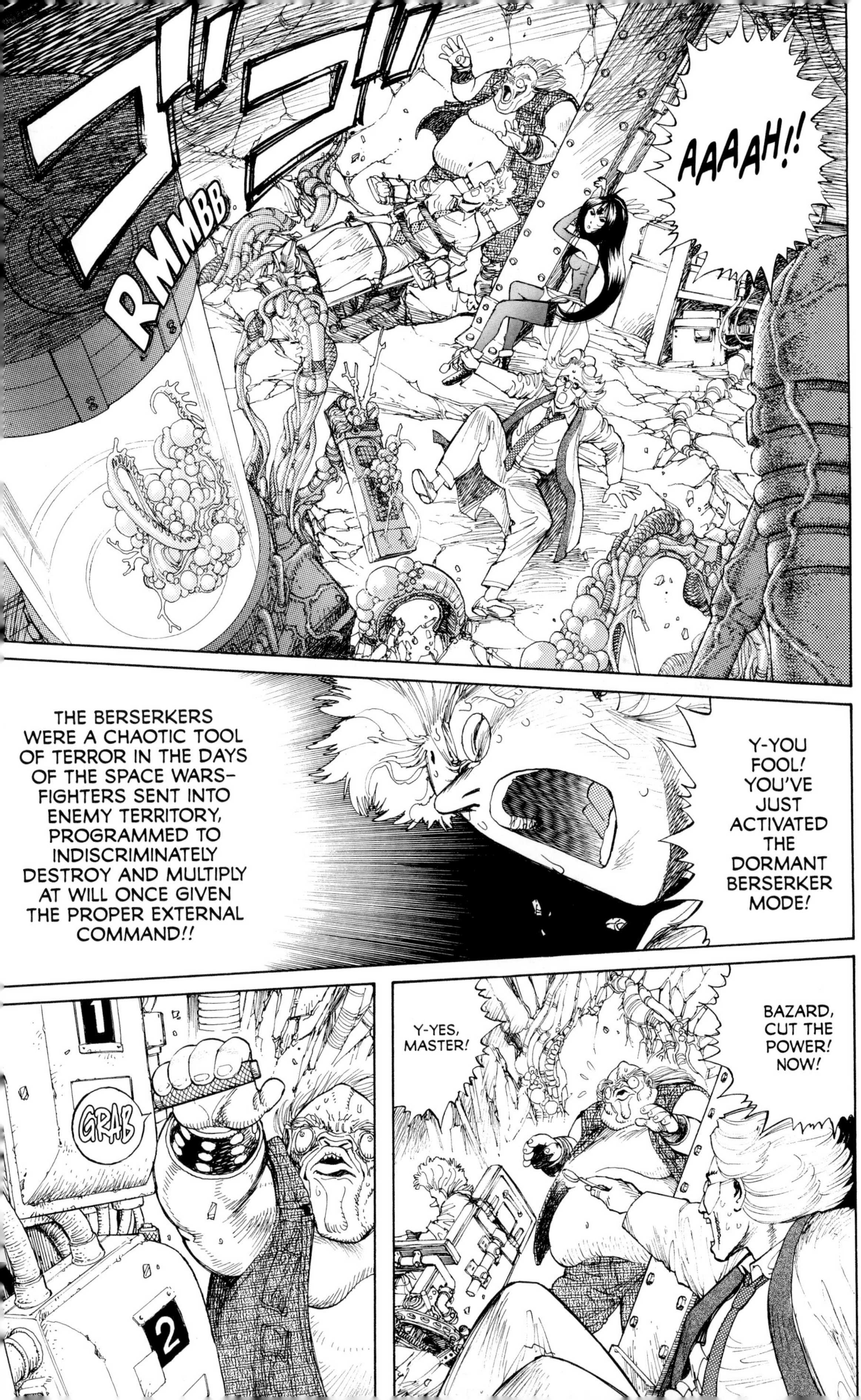
AAAAH!!
RMMBB
Y-YOU FOOL! YOU'VE JUST ACTIVATED THE DORMANT BERSERKER MODE!
THE BERSERKERS WERE A CHAOTIC TOOL OF TERROR IN THE DAYS OF THE SPACE WARS–FIGHTERS SENT INTO ENEMY TERRITORY, PROGRAMMED TO INDISCRIMINATELY DESTROY AND MULTIPLY AT WILL ONCE GIVEN THE PROPER EXTERNAL COMMAND!!
BAZARD, CUT THE POWER! NOW!
Y-YES, MASTER!
GRAB
1
2

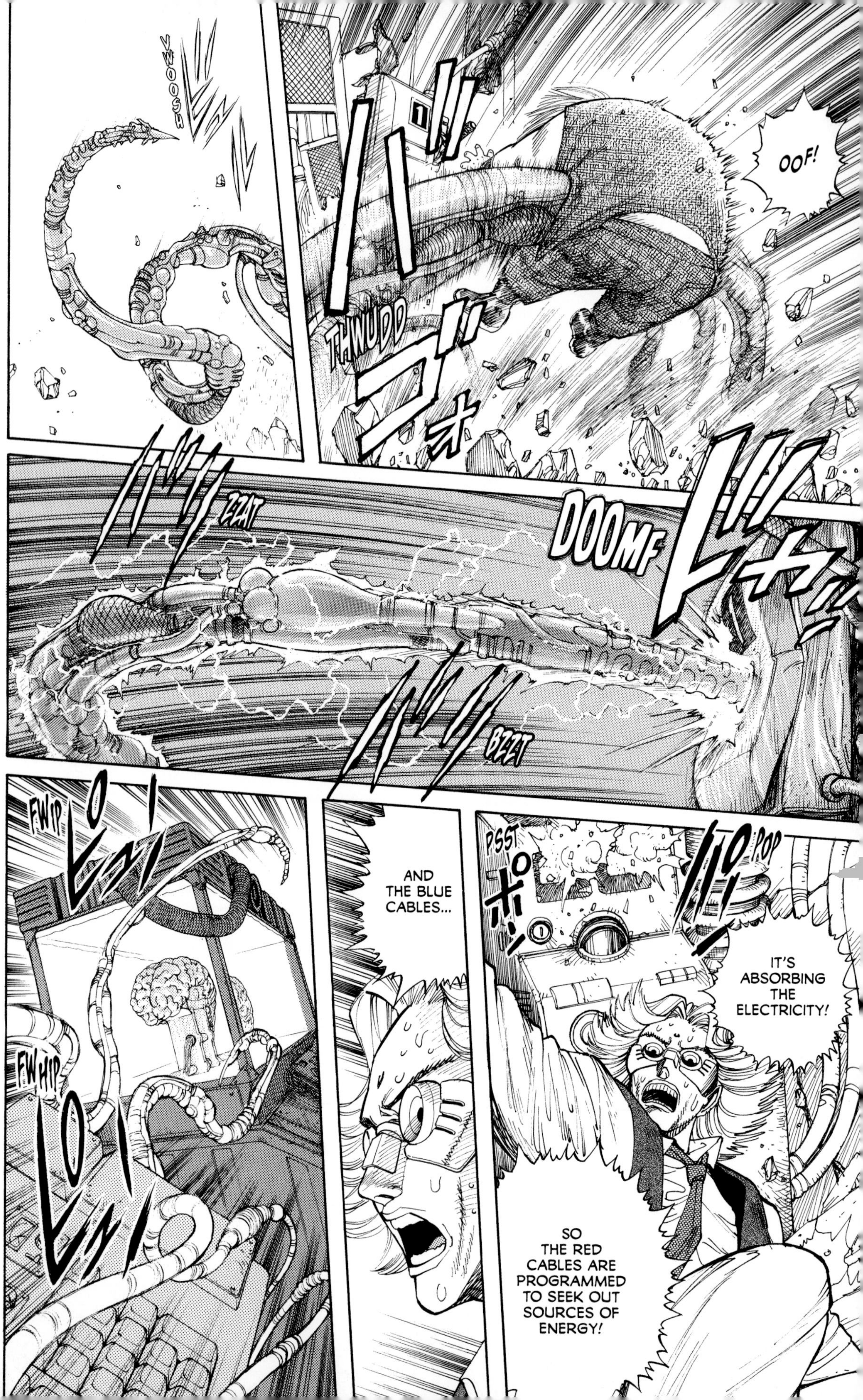
OOF!
THWUDD
VWOOSH
DOOMF
ZZAT
BZZT
POP
PSST
IT'S ABSORBING THE ELECTRICITY!
SO THE RED CABLES ARE PROGRAMMED TO SEEK OUT SOURCES OF ENERGY!
AND THE BLUE CABLES...
FWIP
FWHIP

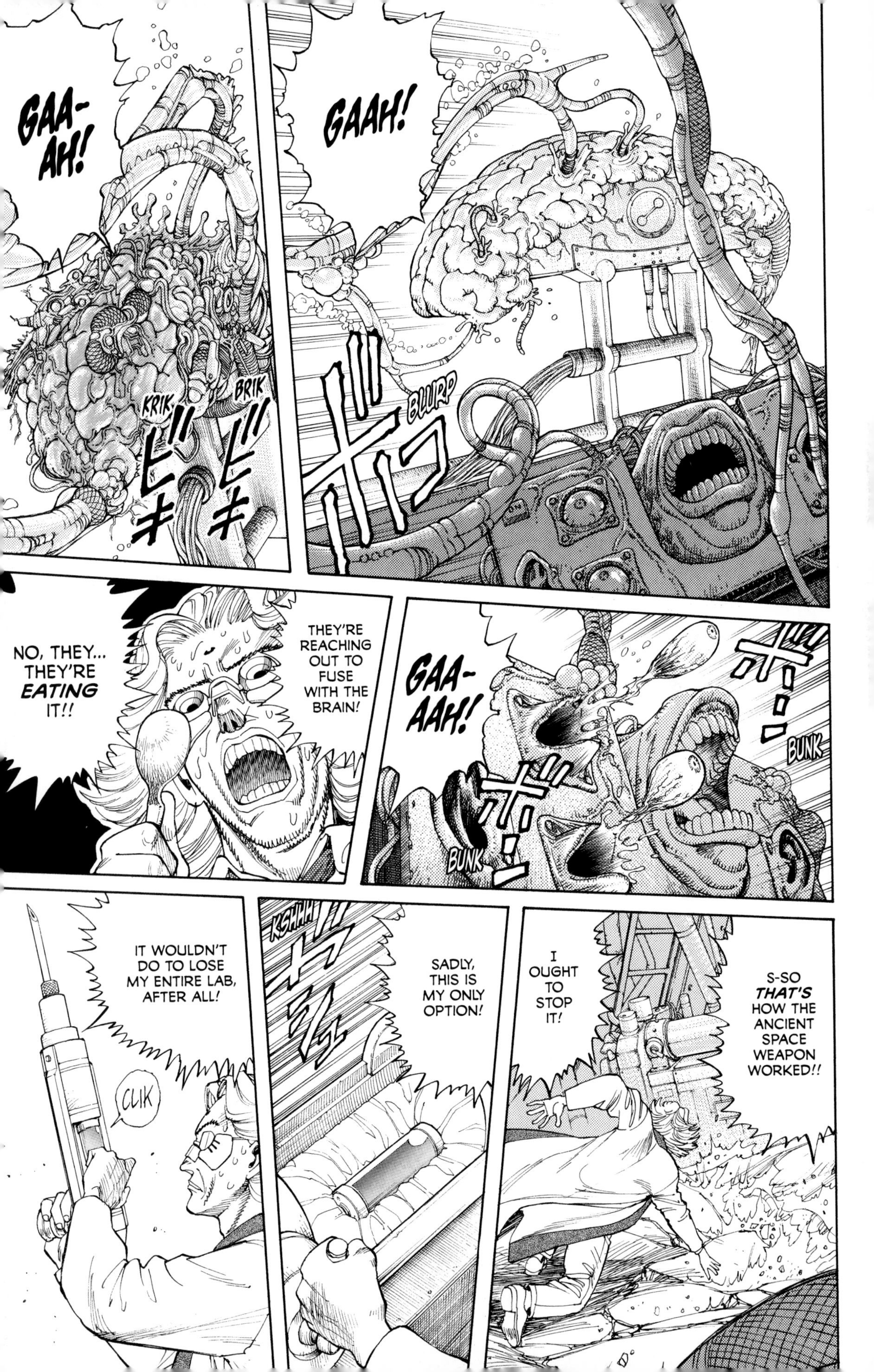
GAAH!
BLURP
GAA-AH!
KRIK
BRIK
GAA-AAH!
BUNK
BUNK
THEY'RE REACHING OUT TO FUSE WITH THE BRAIN!
NO, THEY... THEY'RE *EATING* IT!!
S-SO *THAT'S* HOW THE ANCIENT SPACE WEAPON WORKED!!
I OUGHT TO STOP IT!
KSHHH
SADLY, THIS IS MY ONLY OPTION!
IT WOULDN'T DO TO LOSE MY ENTIRE LAB, AFTER ALL!
CLIK

BOOOM

KRAK

CRAK

LOOK OUT, PROFESSOR!

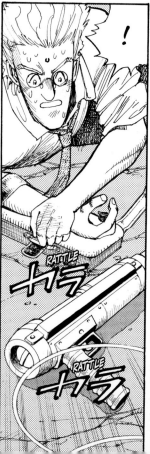

!

RATTLE

RATTLE

KBOOM

RGH!

AIEEE!

KSHUNK

CLANK

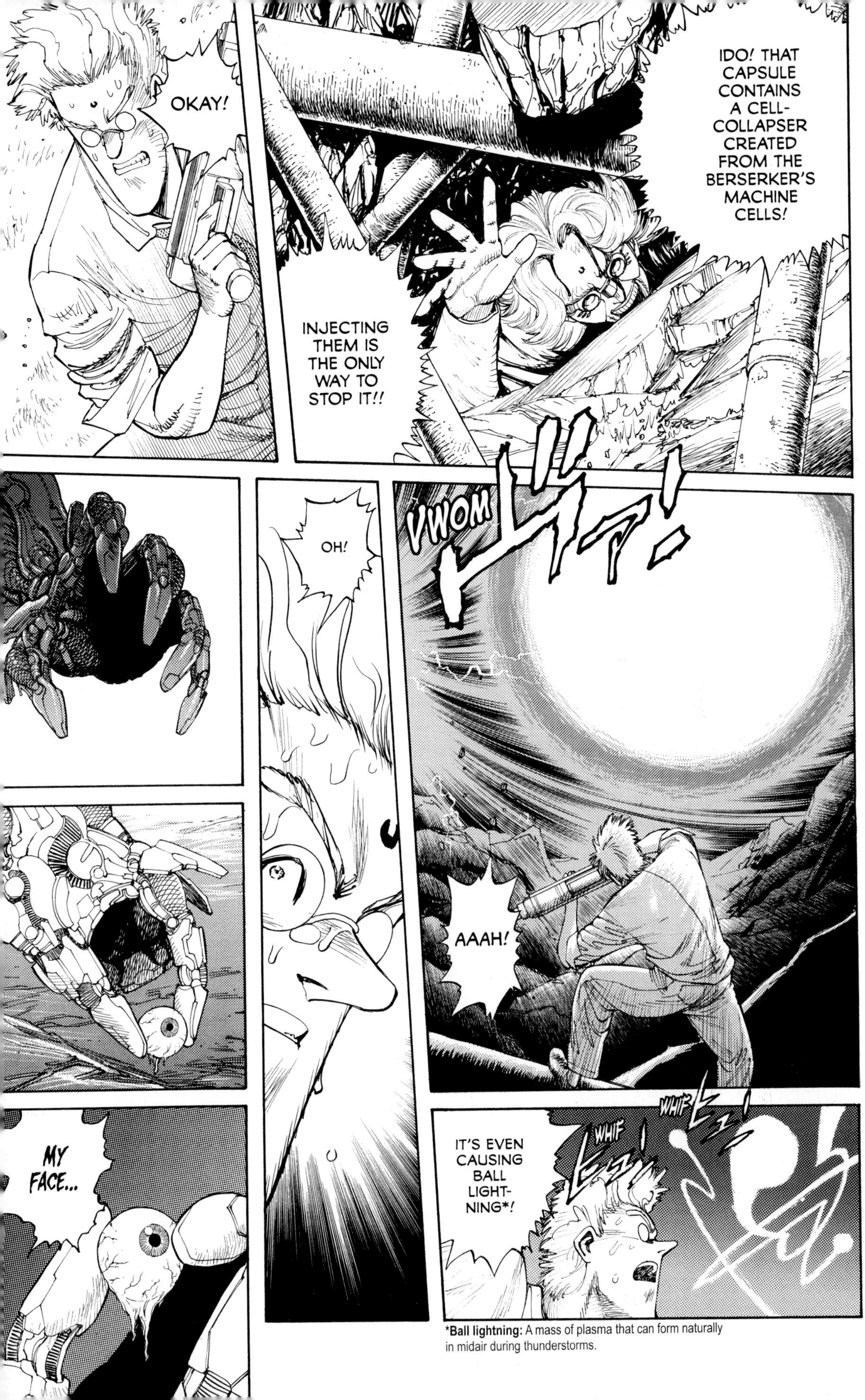
IDO! THAT CAPSULE CONTAINS A CELL-COLLAPSER CREATED FROM THE BERSERKER'S MACHINE CELLS!
INJECTING THEM IS THE ONLY WAY TO STOP IT!!
OKAY!
VWOM
AAAH!
IT'S EVEN CAUSING BALL LIGHT-NING*!
WHIF
WHIF
OH!
MY FACE...

***Ball lightning:** A mass of plasma that can form naturally in midair during thunderstorms.

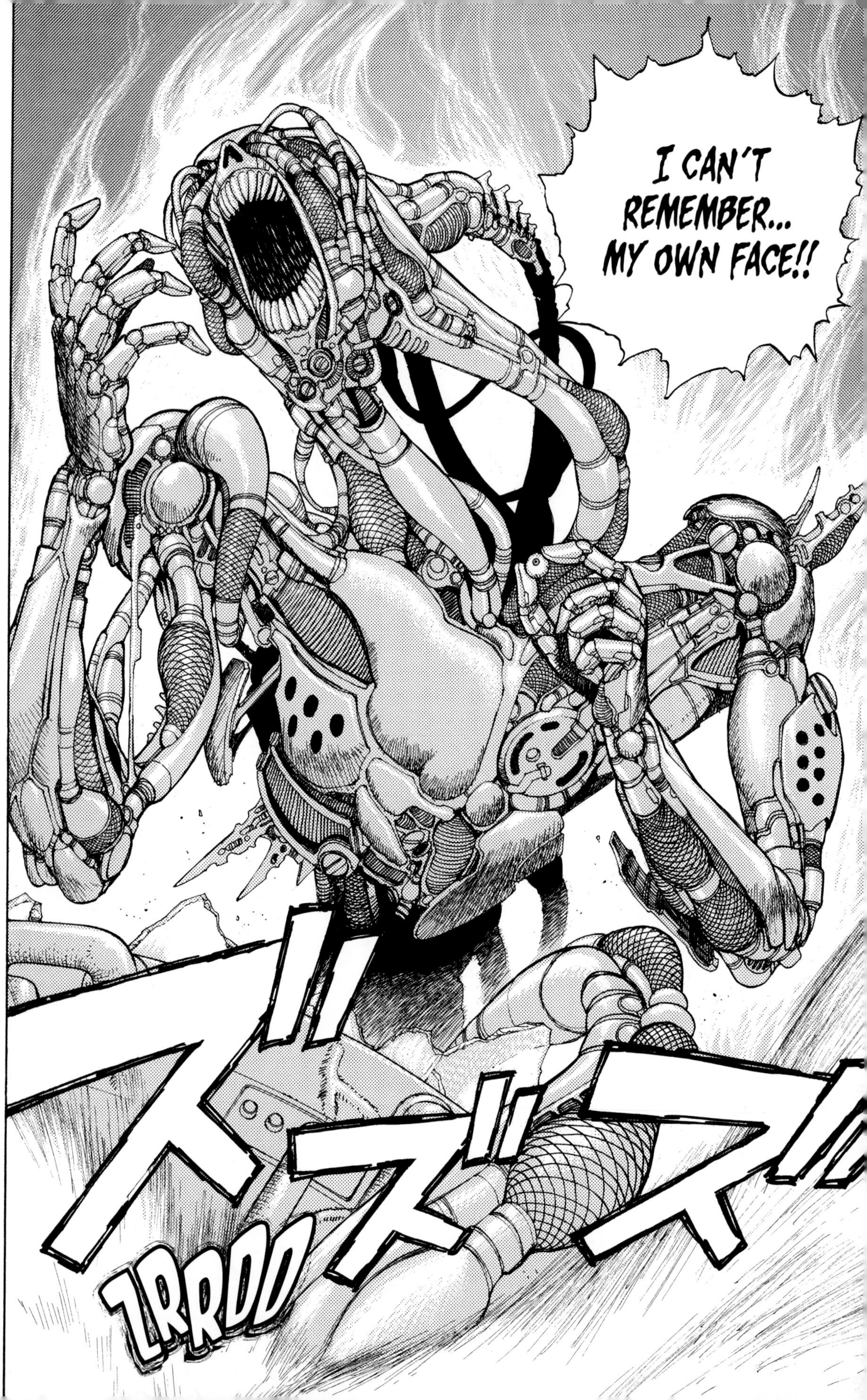
I CAN'T REMEMBER... MY OWN FACE!!
ズズズ
ZRRDD

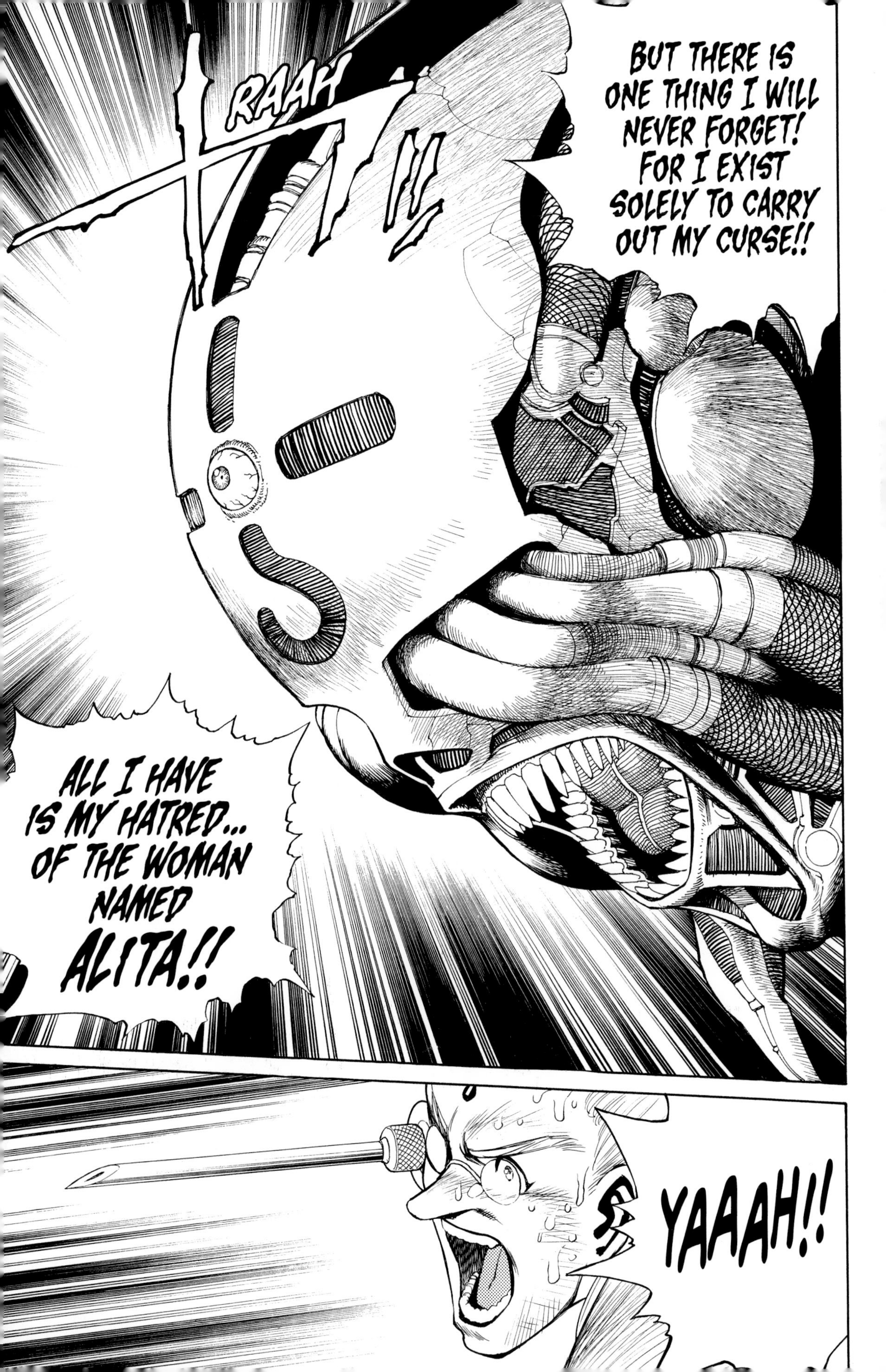
BUT THERE IS ONE THING I WILL NEVER FORGET! FOR I EXIST SOLELY TO CARRY OUT MY CURSE!!
RAAH
ALL I HAVE IS MY HATRED... OF THE WOMAN NAMED ALITA!!
YAAAH!!

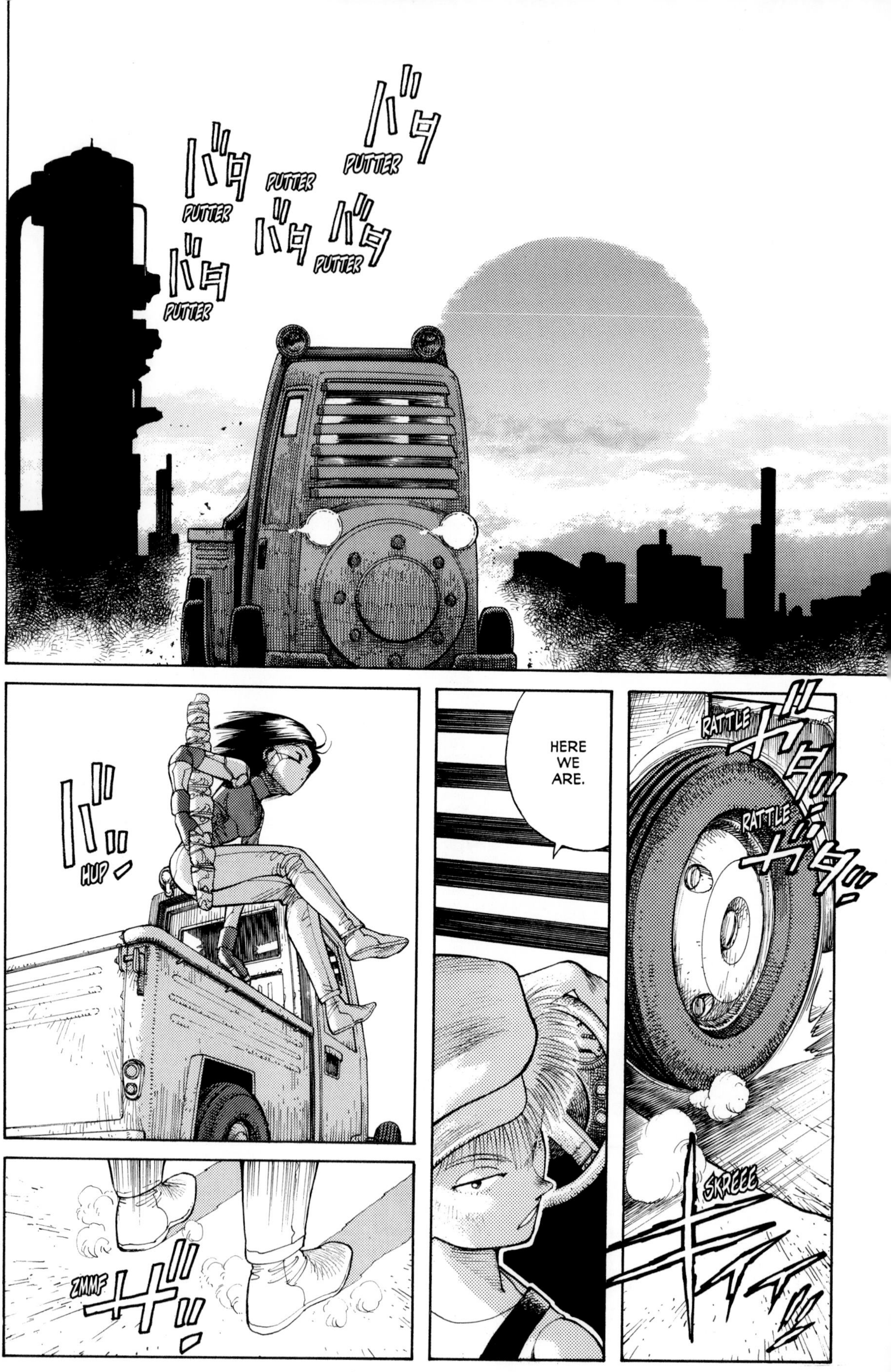
PUTTER
PUTTER
PUTTER
PUTTER
PUTTER
PUTTER
RATTLE
RATTLE
SKREEE
HERE WE ARE.
HUP
ZMMF

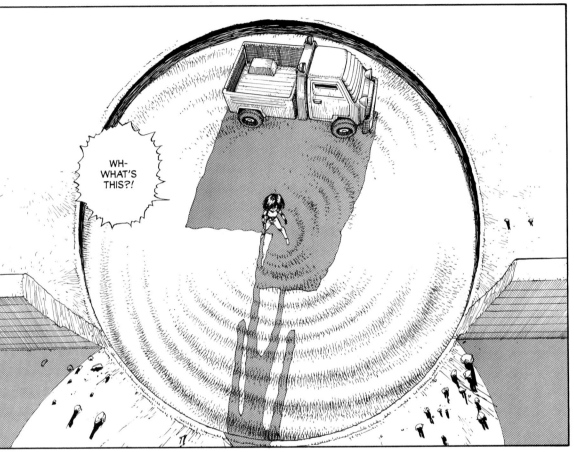

WH-
WHAT'S
THIS?!

IT'S BEEN
MELTED
AWAY INTO
GLASS...

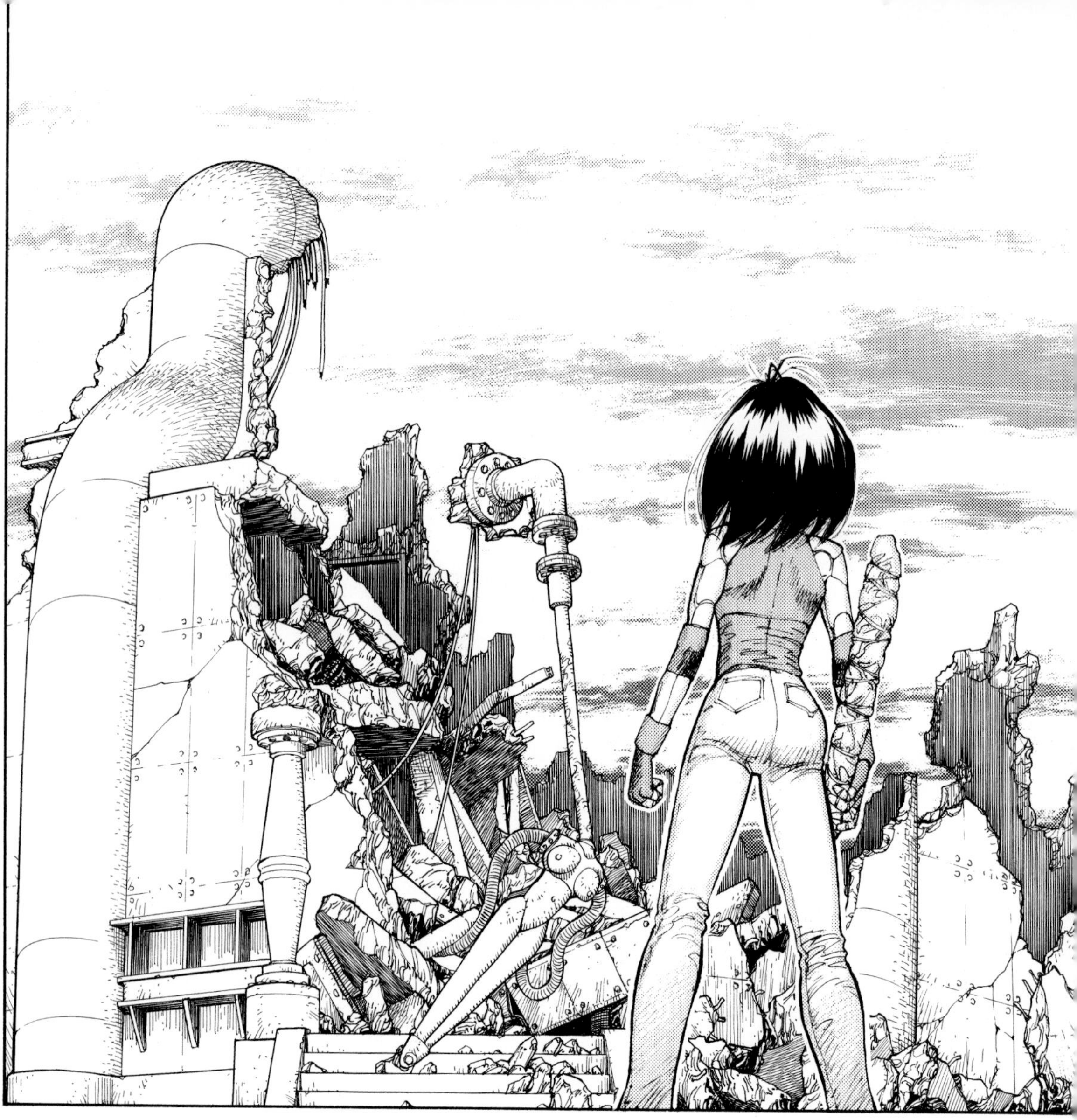

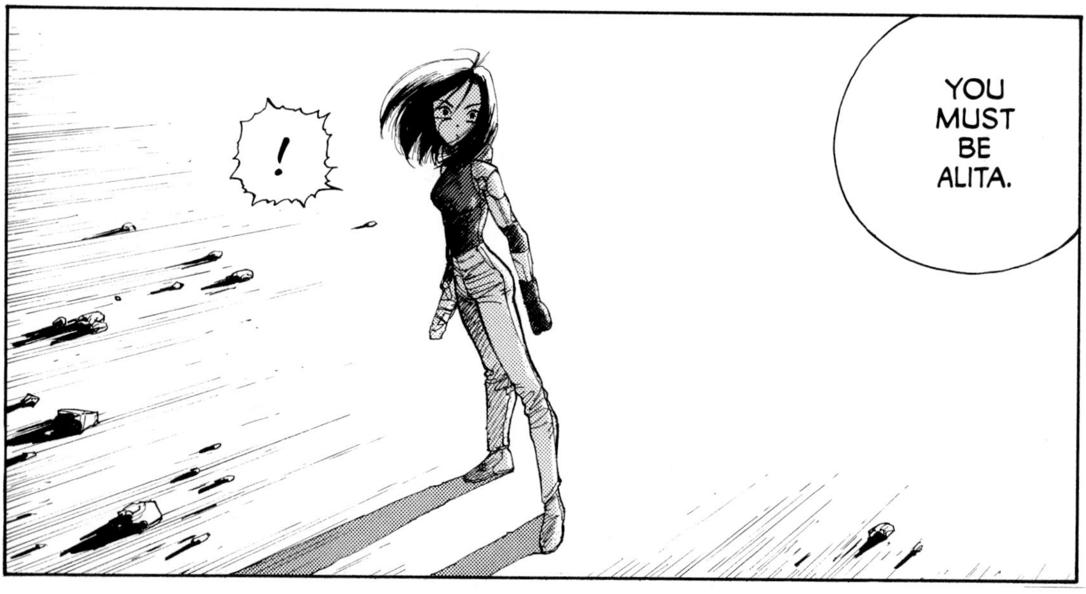
YOU MUST BE ALITA.
!

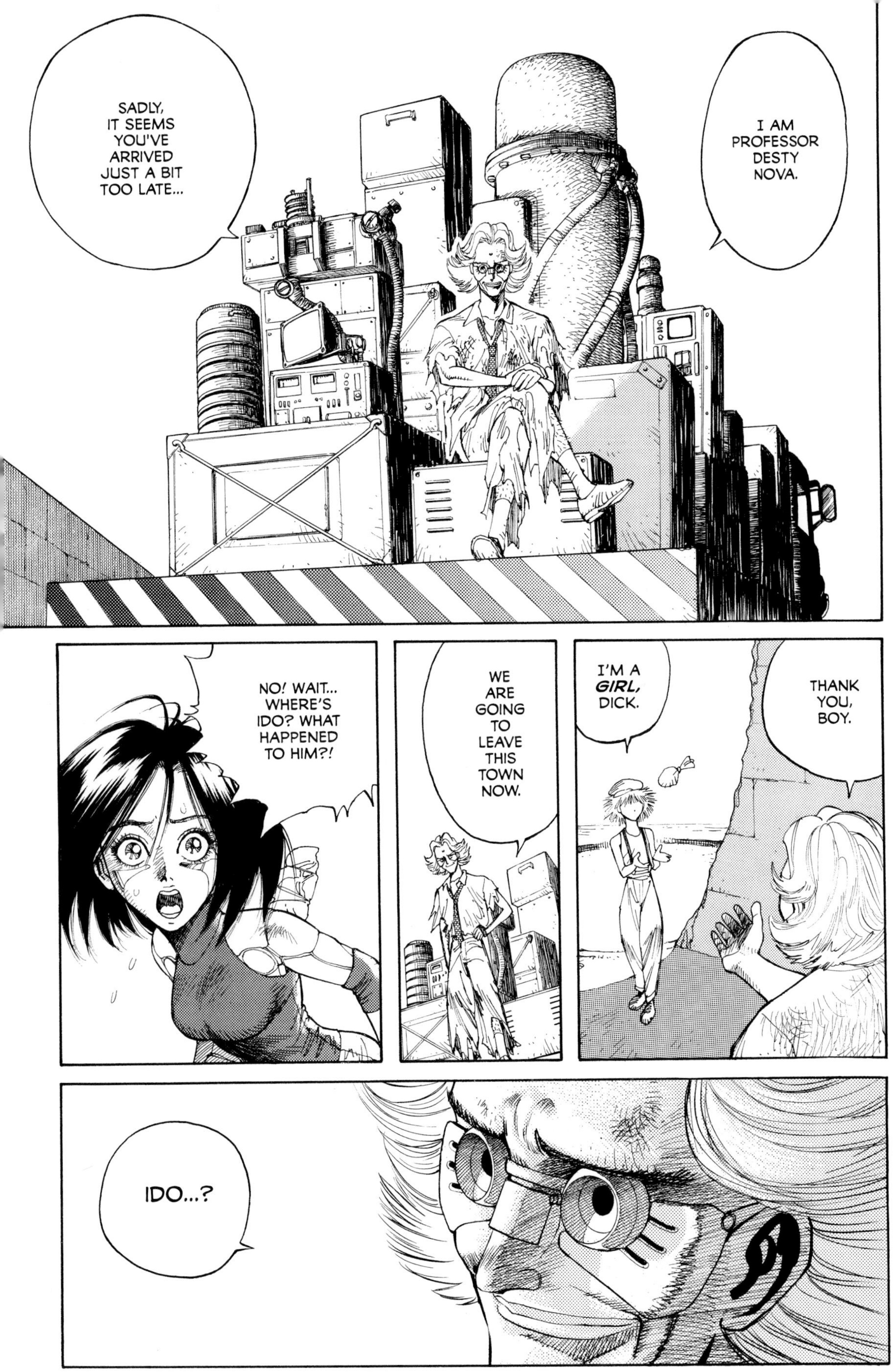
I AM PROFESSOR DESTY NOVA.
SADLY, IT SEEMS YOU'VE ARRIVED JUST A BIT TOO LATE...
THANK YOU, BOY.
I'M A *GIRL,* DICK.
WE ARE GOING TO LEAVE THIS TOWN NOW.
NO! WAIT... WHERE'S IDO? WHAT HAPPENED TO HIM?!
IDO...?

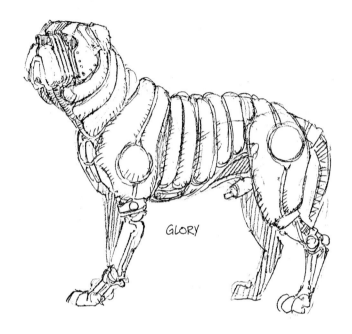

GLORY

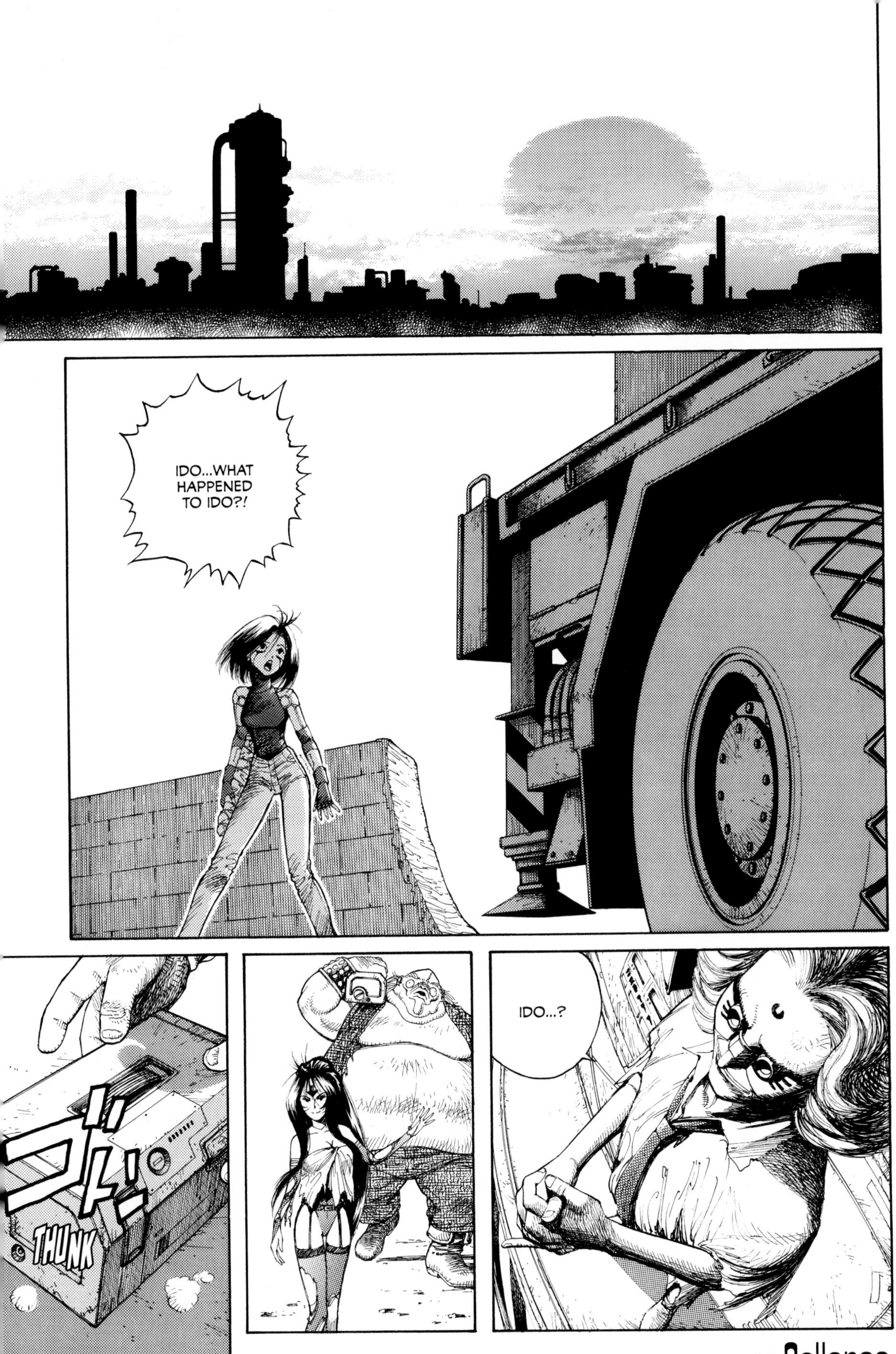
IDO...WHAT HAPPENED TO IDO?!
IDO...?
THUNK

FIGHT_026 Collapse

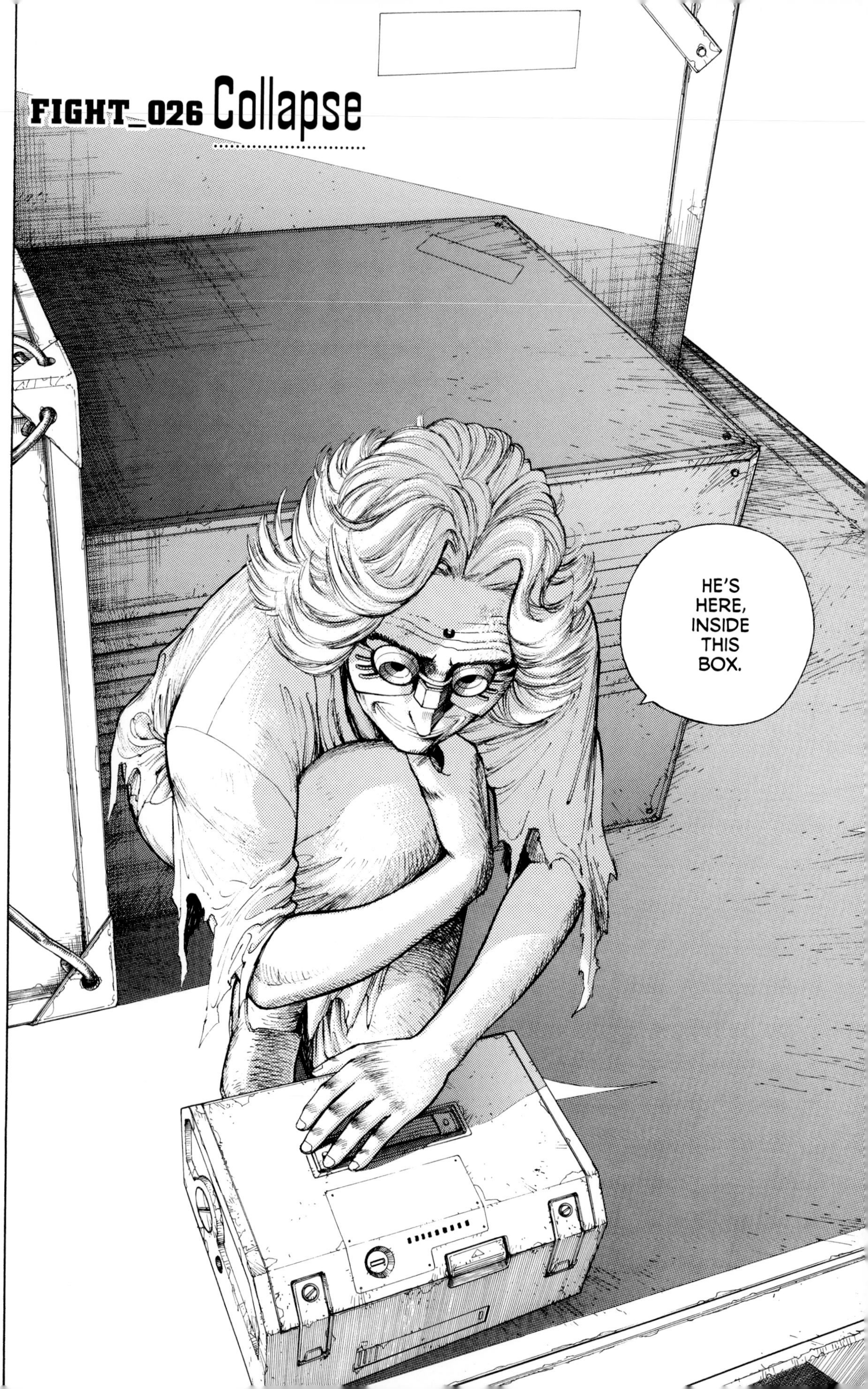
FIGHT_026 Collapse
HE'S HERE, INSIDE THIS BOX.

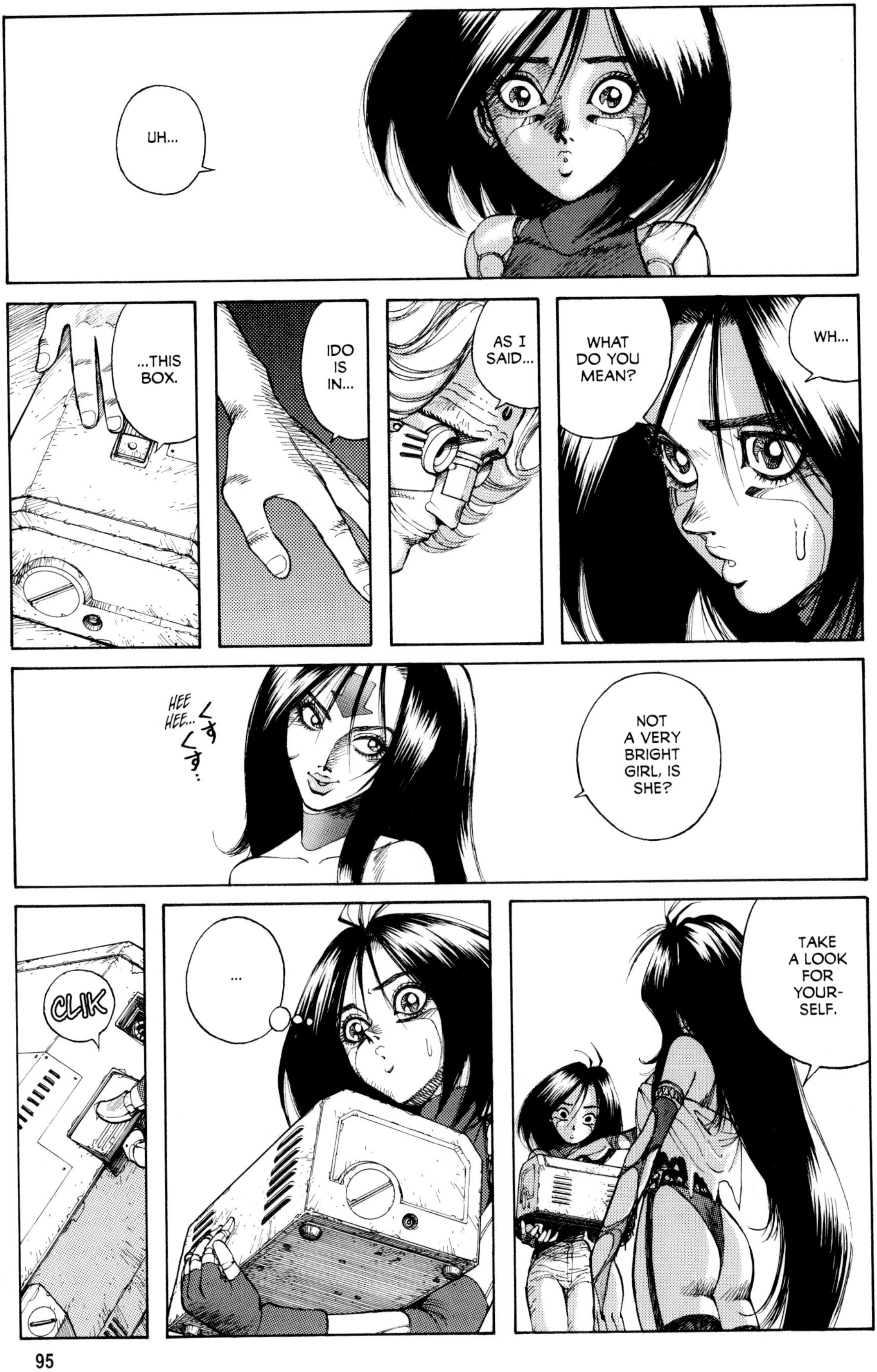

UH...
WH...
WHAT DO YOU MEAN?
AS I SAID...
IDO IS IN...
...THIS BOX.
NOT A VERY BRIGHT GIRL, IS SHE?
HEE HEE... くすくす...
TAKE A LOOK FOR YOUR-SELF.
...
CLIK

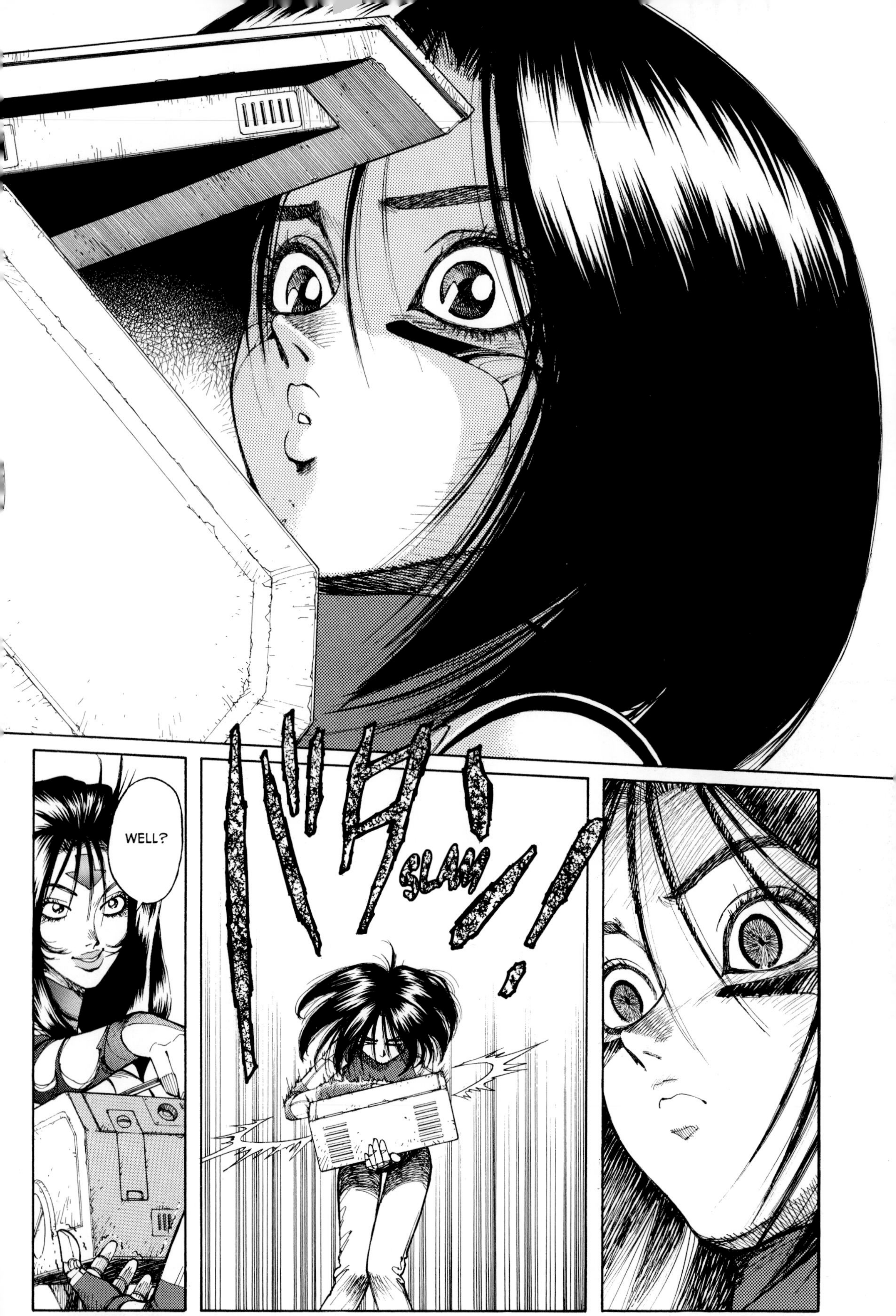
SLAM
WELL?

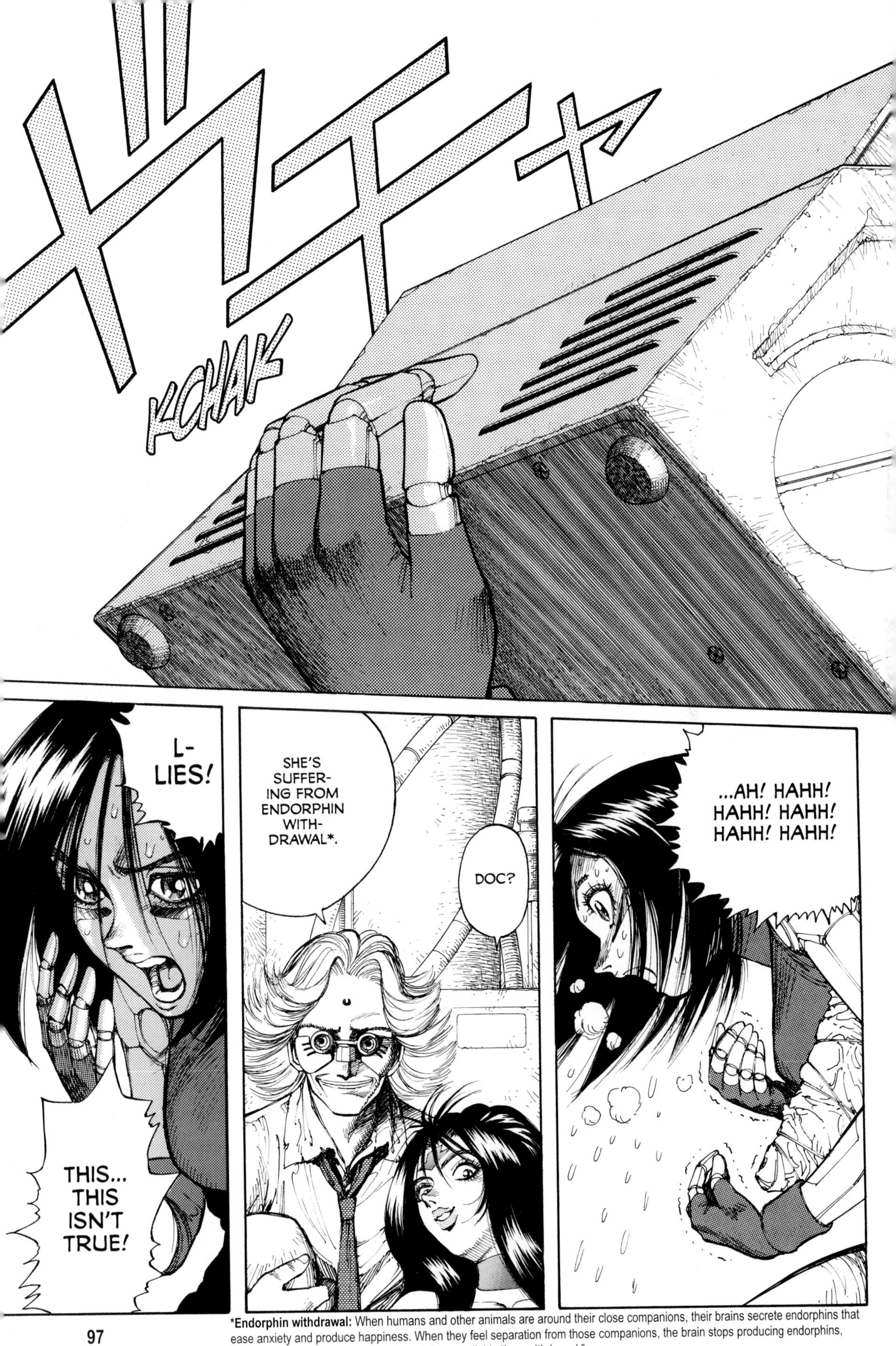
KCHAK
...AH! HAHH! HAHH! HAHH! HAHH! HAHH!
DOC?
SHE'S SUFFERING FROM ENDORPHIN WITHDRAWAL*.
L-LIES!
THIS... THIS ISN'T TRUE!

***Endorphin withdrawal:** When humans and other animals are around their close companions, their brains secrete endorphins that ease anxiety and produce happiness. When they feel separation from those companions, the brain stops producing endorphins, leading to a kind of chemical withdrawal. Some call this "love withdrawal."

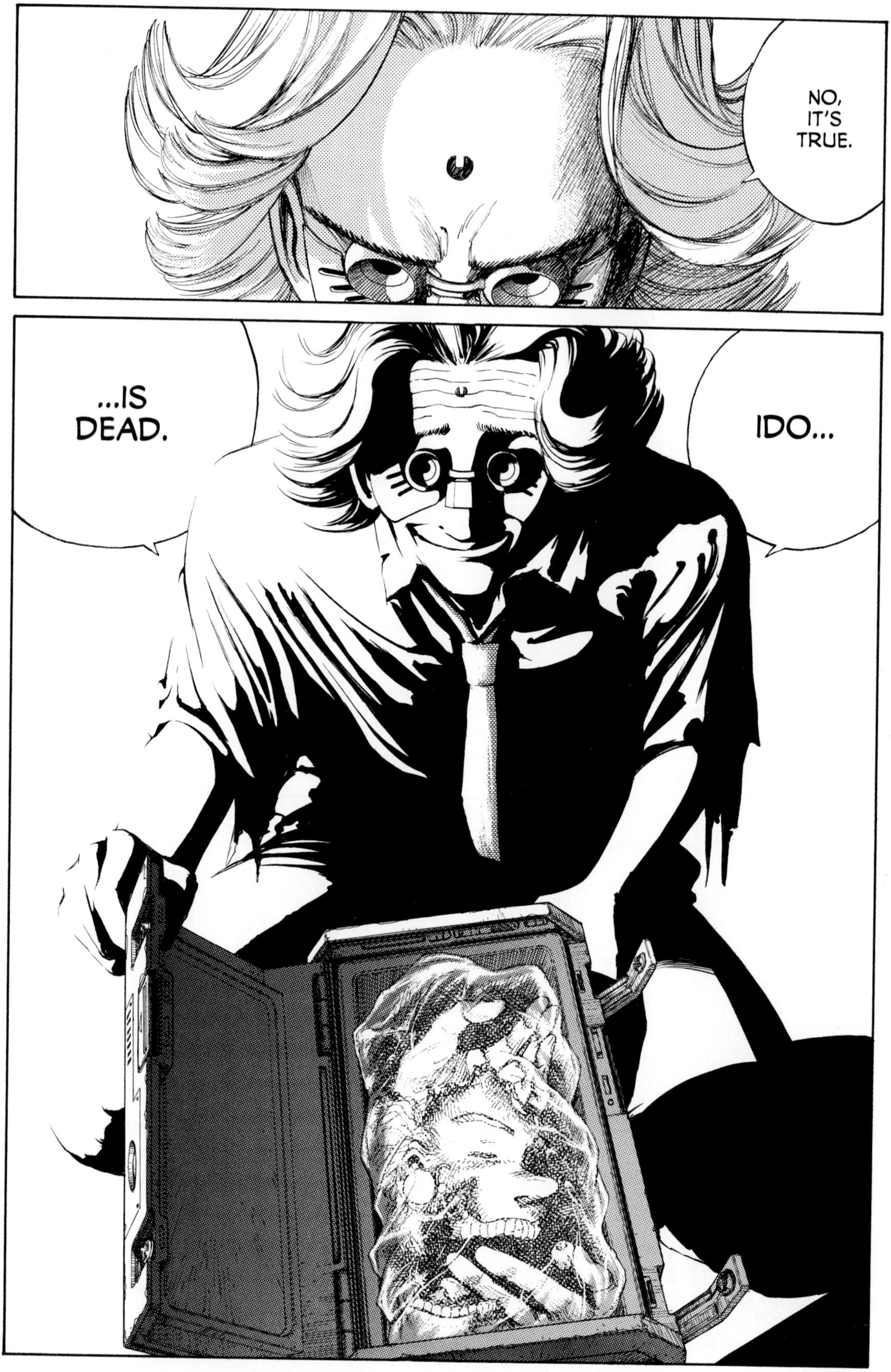
NO, IT'S TRUE.
IDO...
...IS DEAD.

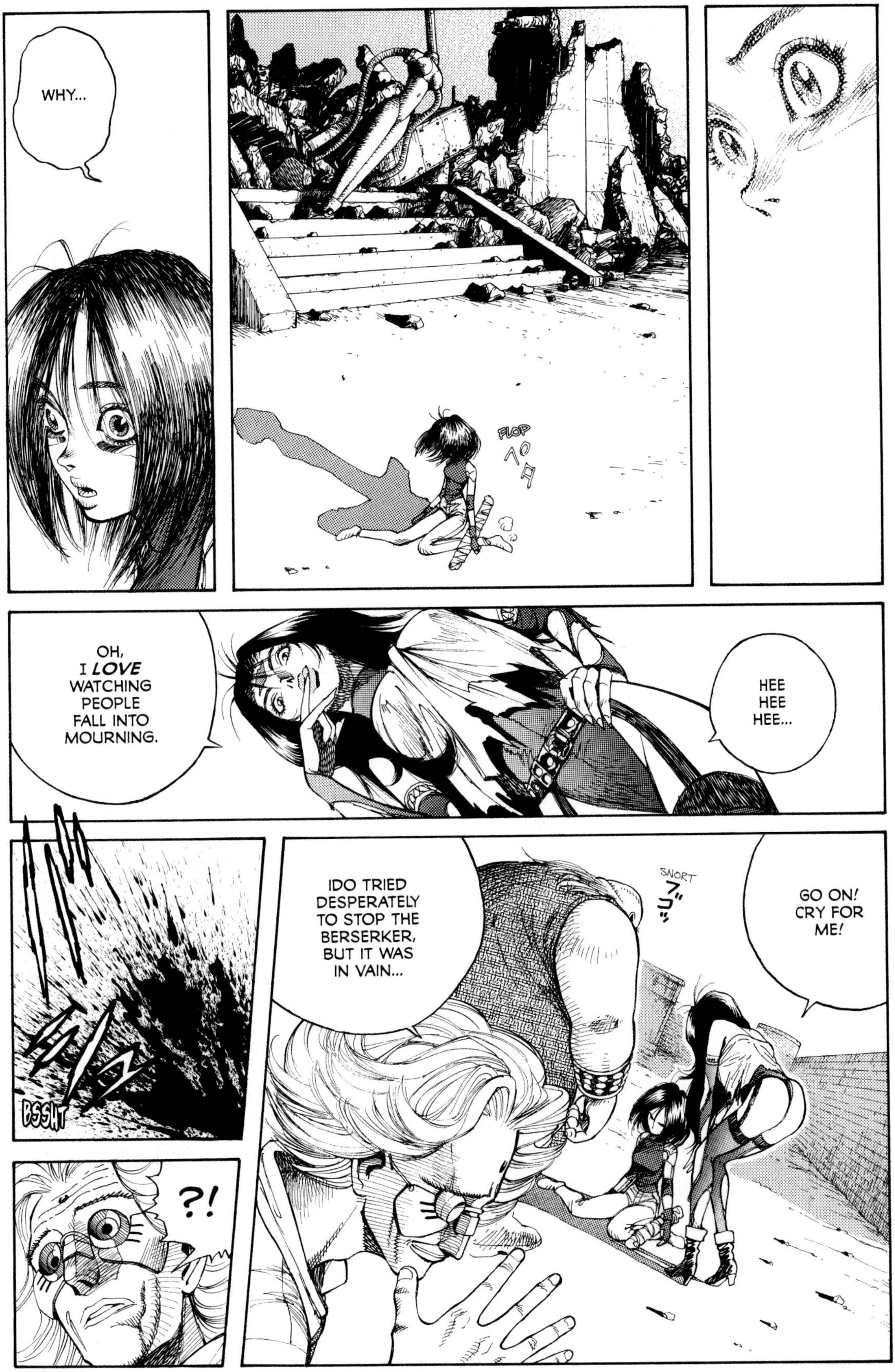
FLOP
WHY...
HEE HEE HEE...
OH, I *LOVE* WATCHING PEOPLE FALL INTO MOURNING.
GO ON! CRY FOR ME!
SNORT
IDO TRIED DESPERATELY TO STOP THE BERSERKER, BUT IT WAS IN VAIN...
BSSHT
?!

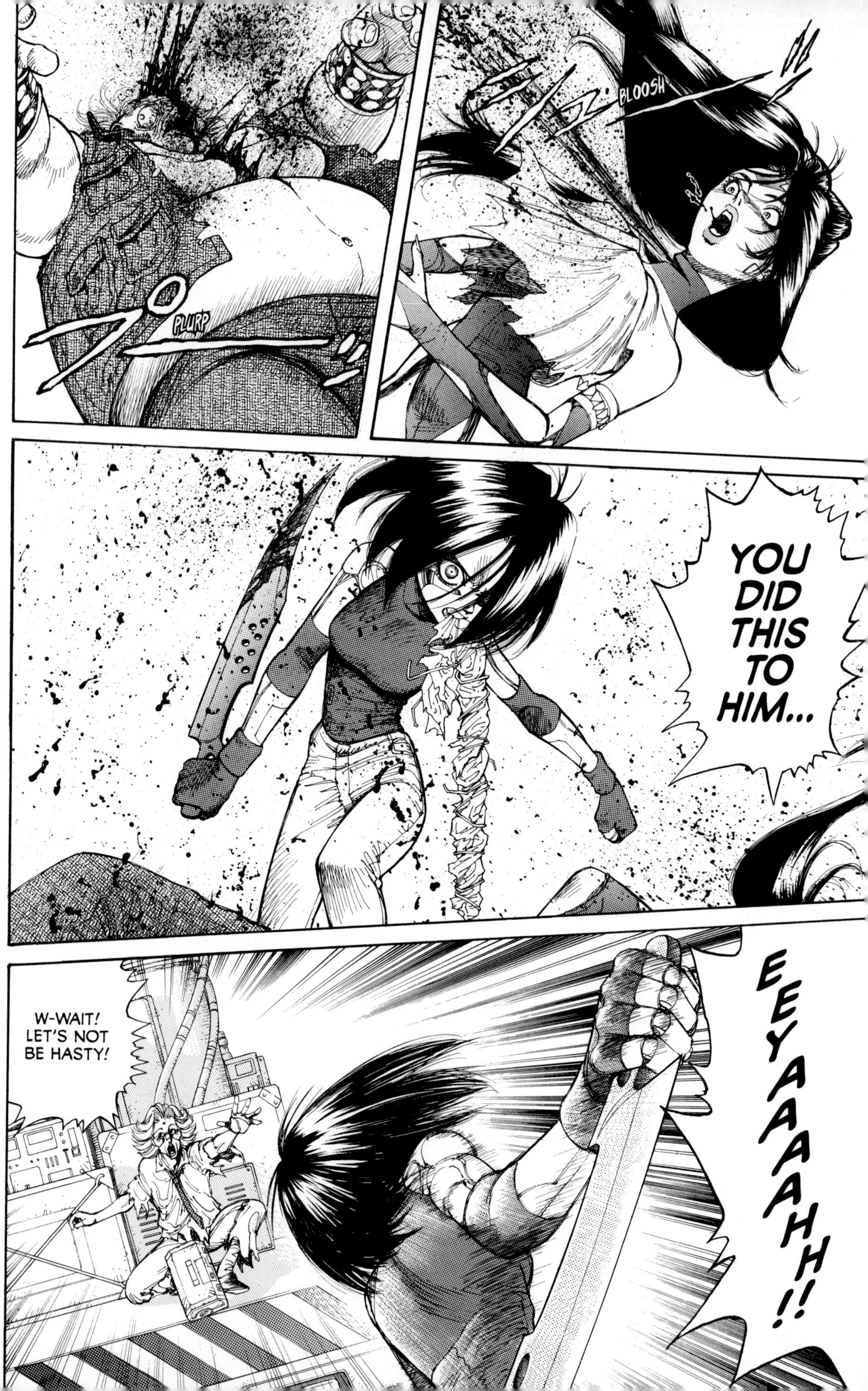
BLOOSH
PLURP
YOU DID THIS TO HIM...
EEYAAAAHH!!
W-WAIT! LET'S NOT BE HASTY!

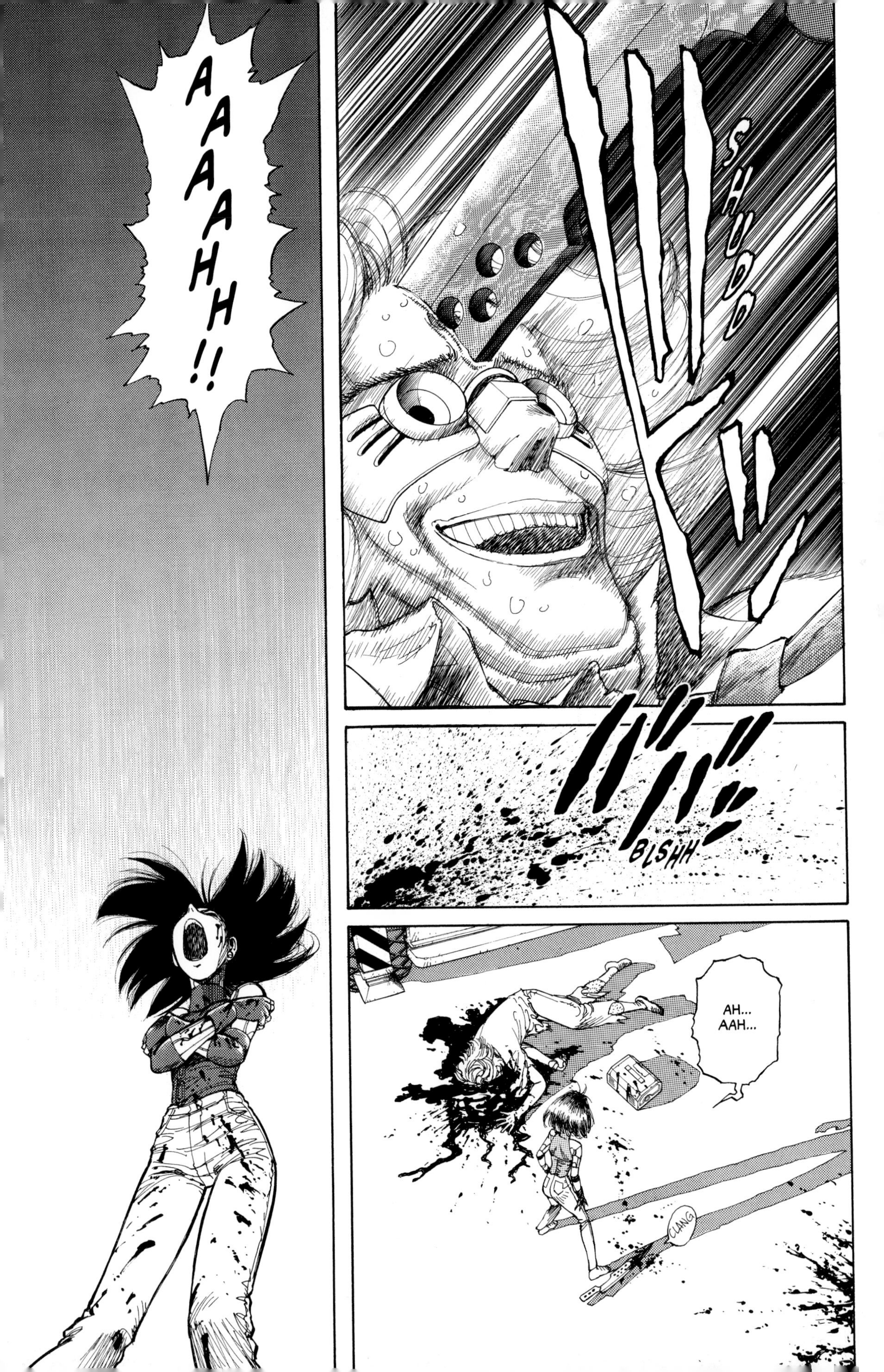
SHUDD
BLSHH
AH... AAH...
CLANG
AAAAAHH!!

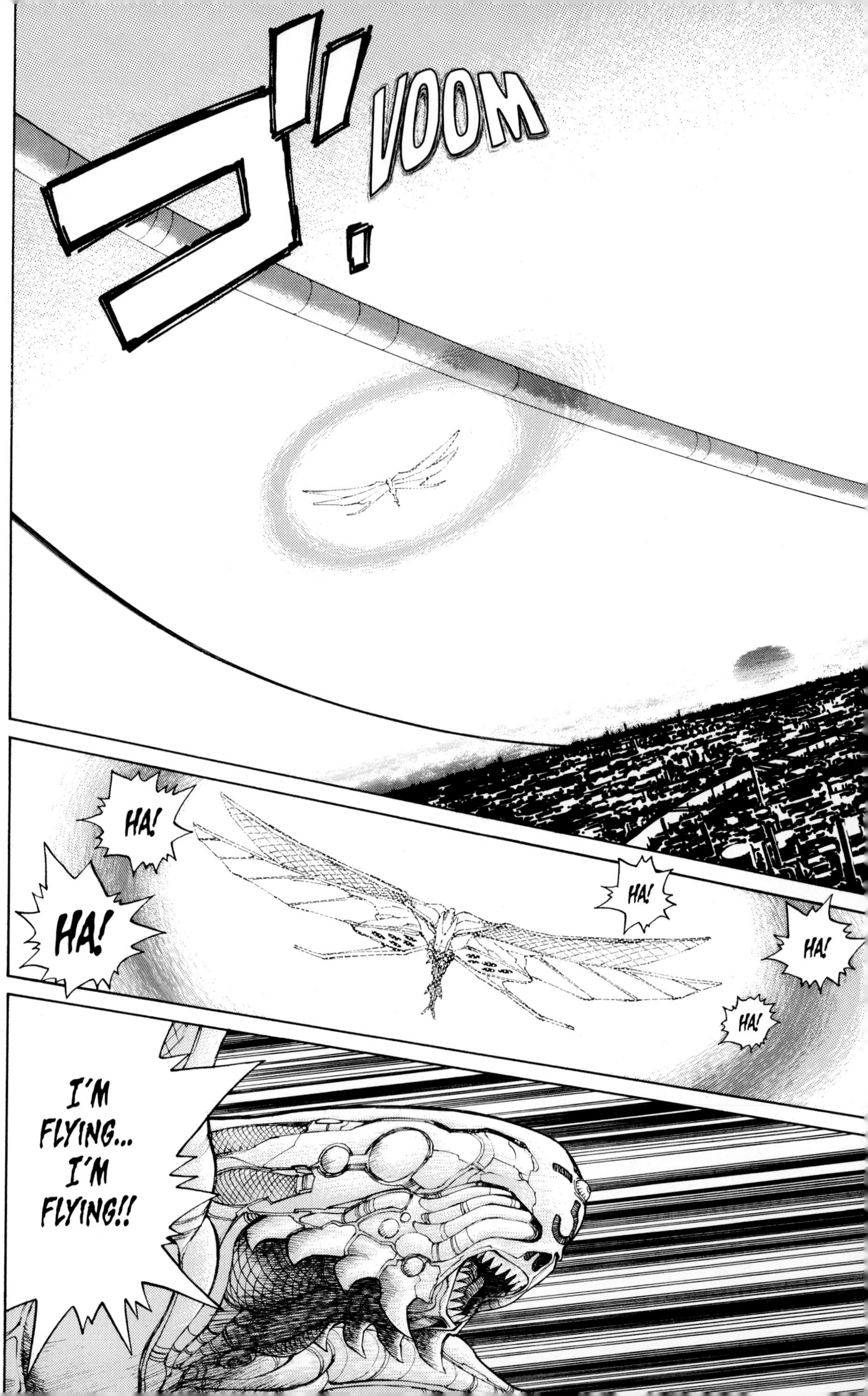
VOOM
HA!
HA!
HA!
HA!
HA!
I'M FLYING... I'M FLYING!!

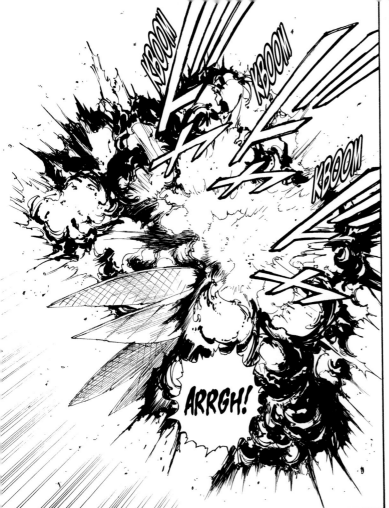

WHA-?!
HYUMM
KBOOM
KBOOM
KBOOM
ARRGH!
FACTORY 99
CLASS-A VIOLATION UNIDENTIFIED FLYING OBJECT* ELIMINATED!!
ELIMINATION CONFIRMED! BZZT!
FACTORY LAW
FACTORY LAW
FACTORY LAW
CTORY
CTORY
CTORY

***Class-A violation UFO:** All flying objects within Zalem airspace are shot down by the Netmen for Class-A crimes. This is why there are no birds in the Scrapyard.

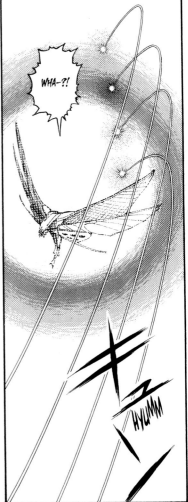

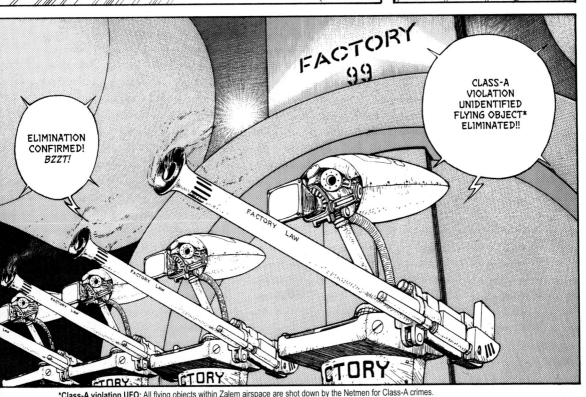

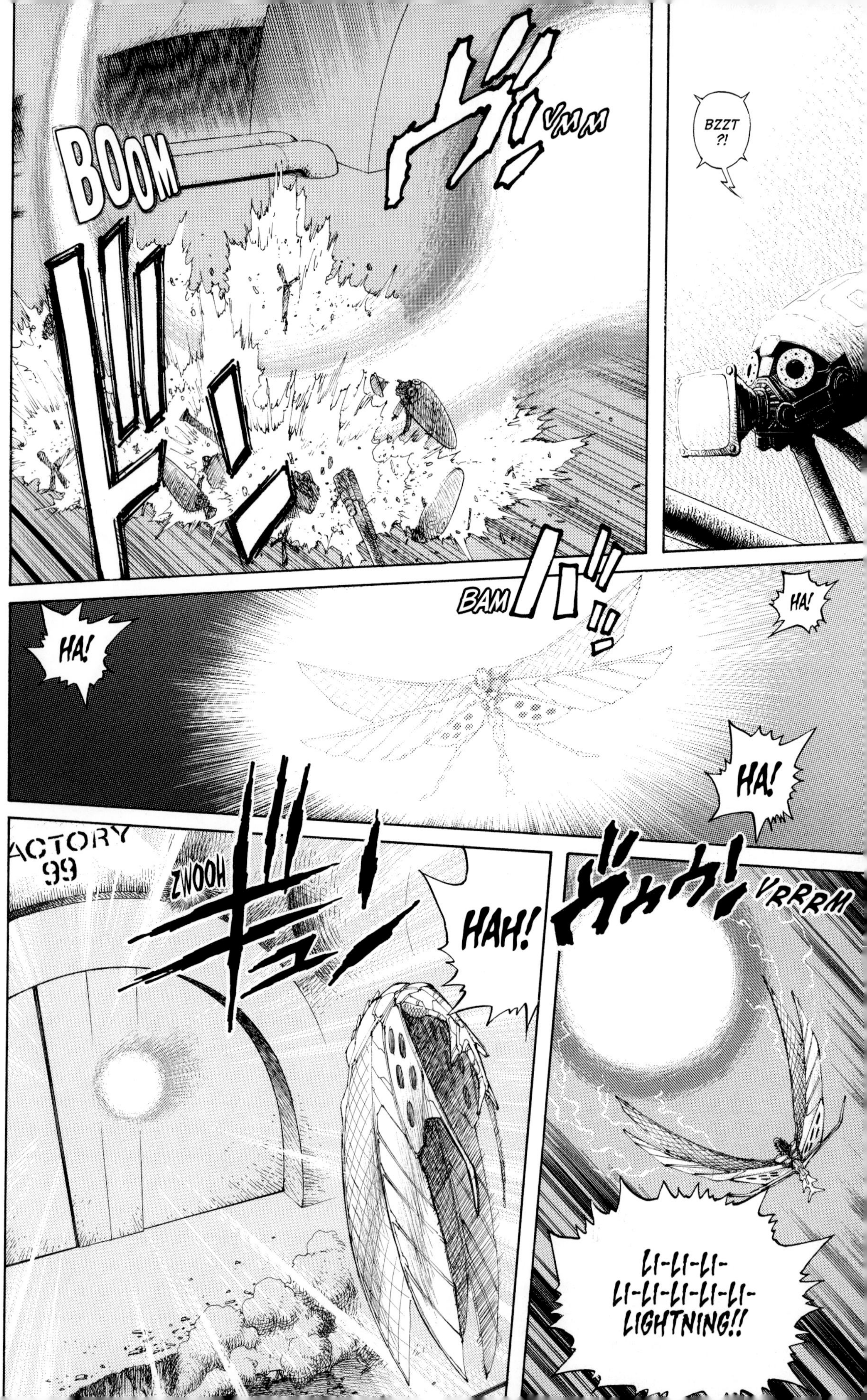
BZZT ?!
VMM
BOOM
HA!
BAM
HA!
HA!
VRRRM
LI-LI-LI-
LI-LI-LI-LI-LI-
LIGHTNING!!
HAH!
ZWOOH
ACTORY
99

VOOM

KABOOM

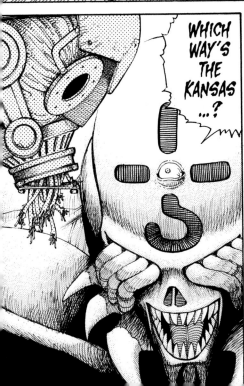
WHICH WAY'S THE KANSAS...?

BZZT.

FWOOO

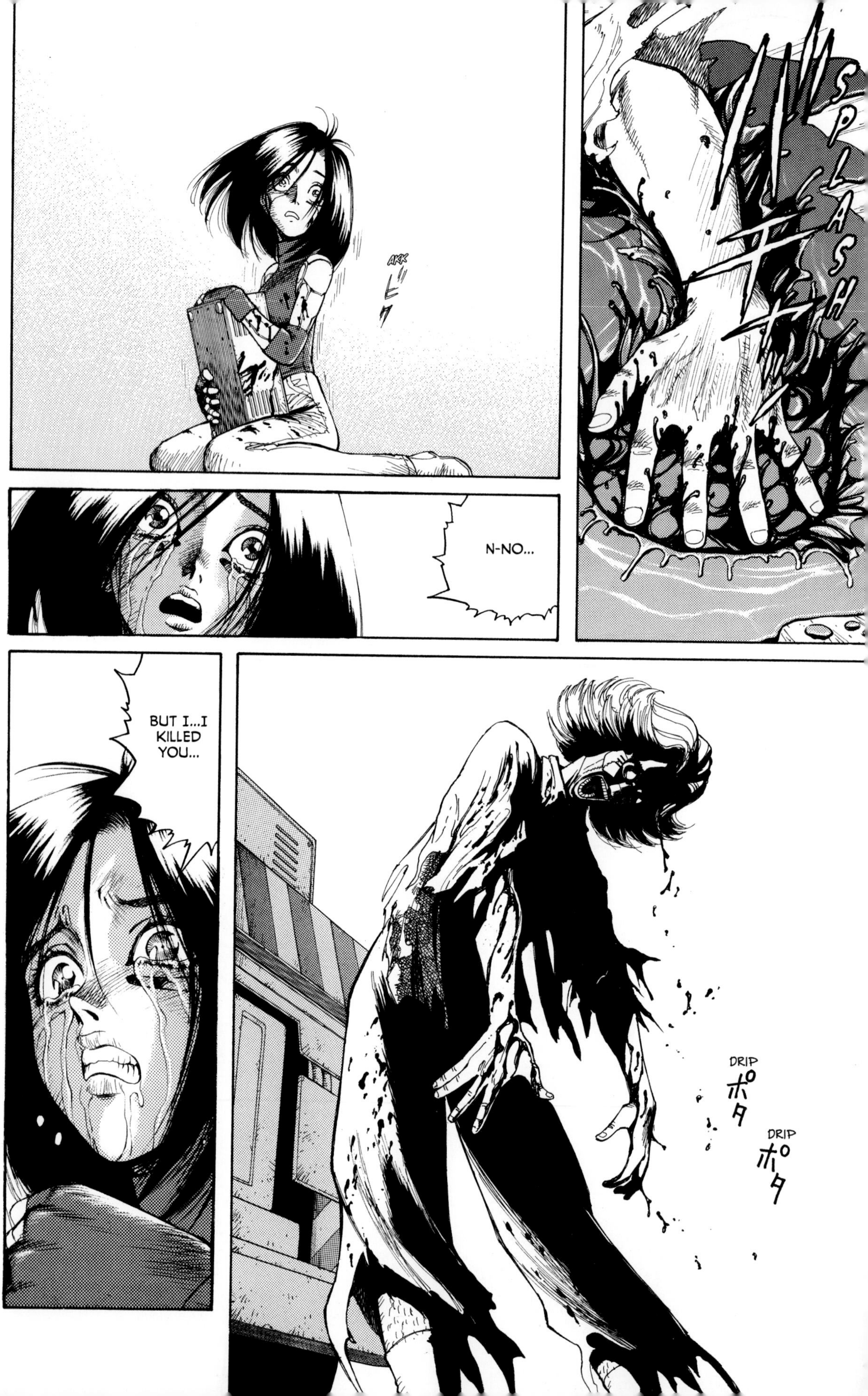
SPLASH
AKK
N-NO...
DRIP
ポタ
DRIP
ポタ
BUT I...I KILLED YOU...

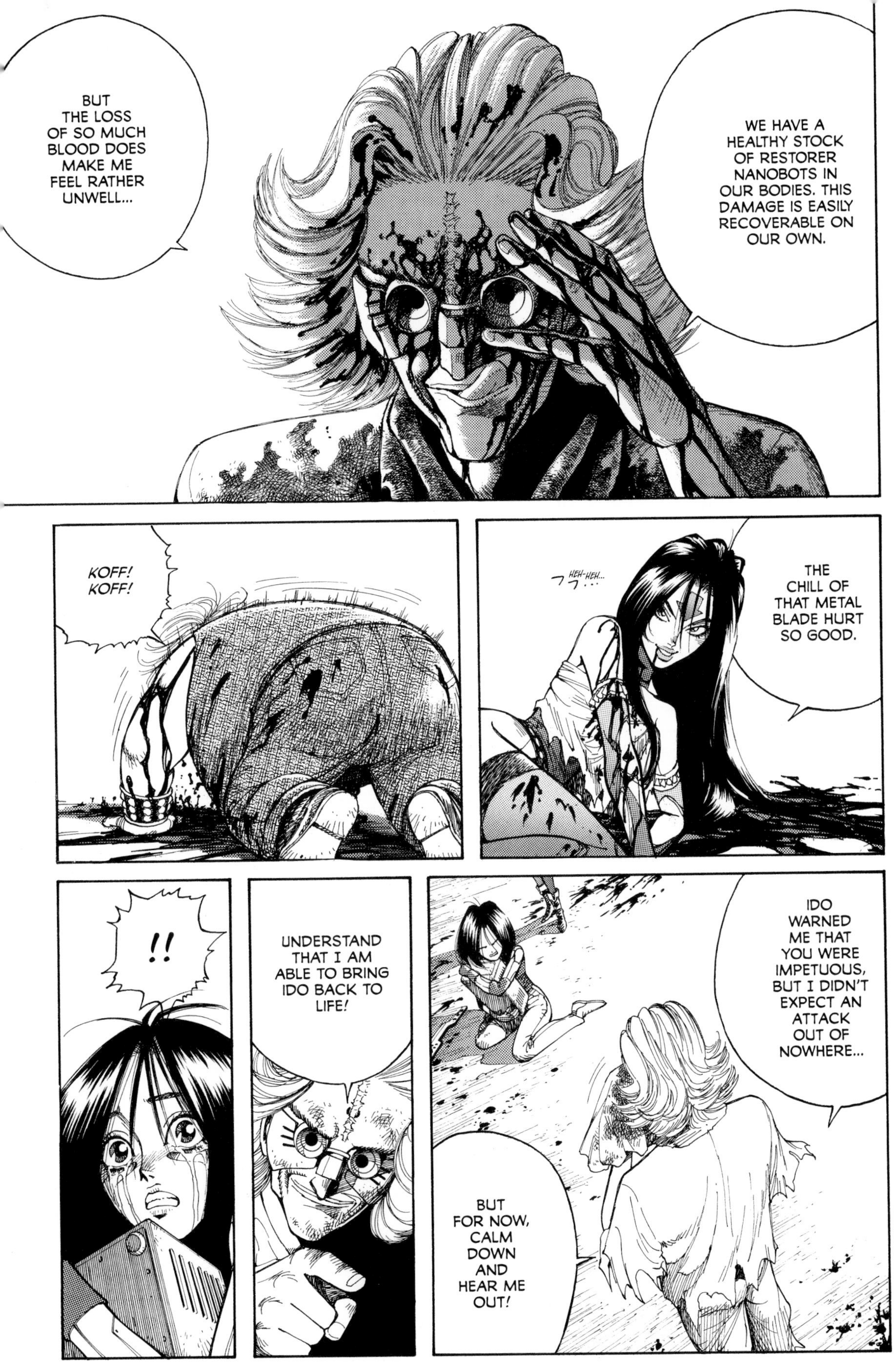

WE HAVE A HEALTHY STOCK OF RESTORER NANOBOTS IN OUR BODIES. THIS DAMAGE IS EASILY RECOVERABLE ON OUR OWN.
BUT THE LOSS OF SO MUCH BLOOD DOES MAKE ME FEEL RATHER UNWELL...
THE CHILL OF THAT METAL BLADE HURT SO GOOD.
HEH-HEH...
KOFF! KOFF!
IDO WARNED ME THAT YOU WERE IMPETUOUS, BUT I DIDN'T EXPECT AN ATTACK OUT OF NOWHERE...
BUT FOR NOW, CALM DOWN AND HEAR ME OUT!
UNDERSTAND THAT I AM ABLE TO BRING IDO BACK TO LIFE!
!!

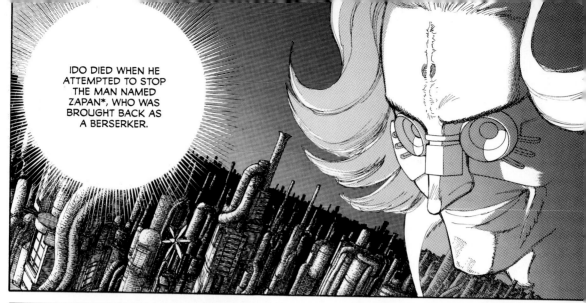

IDO DIED WHEN HE ATTEMPTED TO STOP THE MAN NAMED ZAPAN*, WHO WAS BROUGHT BACK AS A BERSERKER.

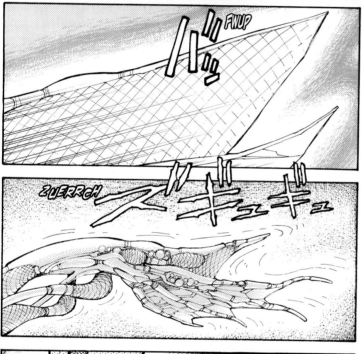

FWUP

ZUERRCH

AAAAH!

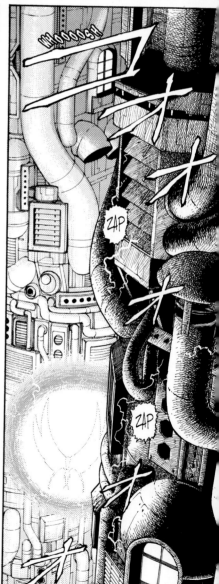

Nooooosh!

ZAP

ZAP

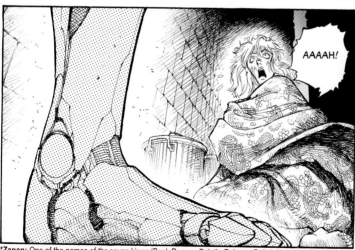

*Zapan: One of the names of the seven kings (Bael, Pursan, Beleth, Paimon, Belial, Asmoday, Zapan) who rule the four directions of Hell, according to the demonologist Johann Weyer (1516-1588).

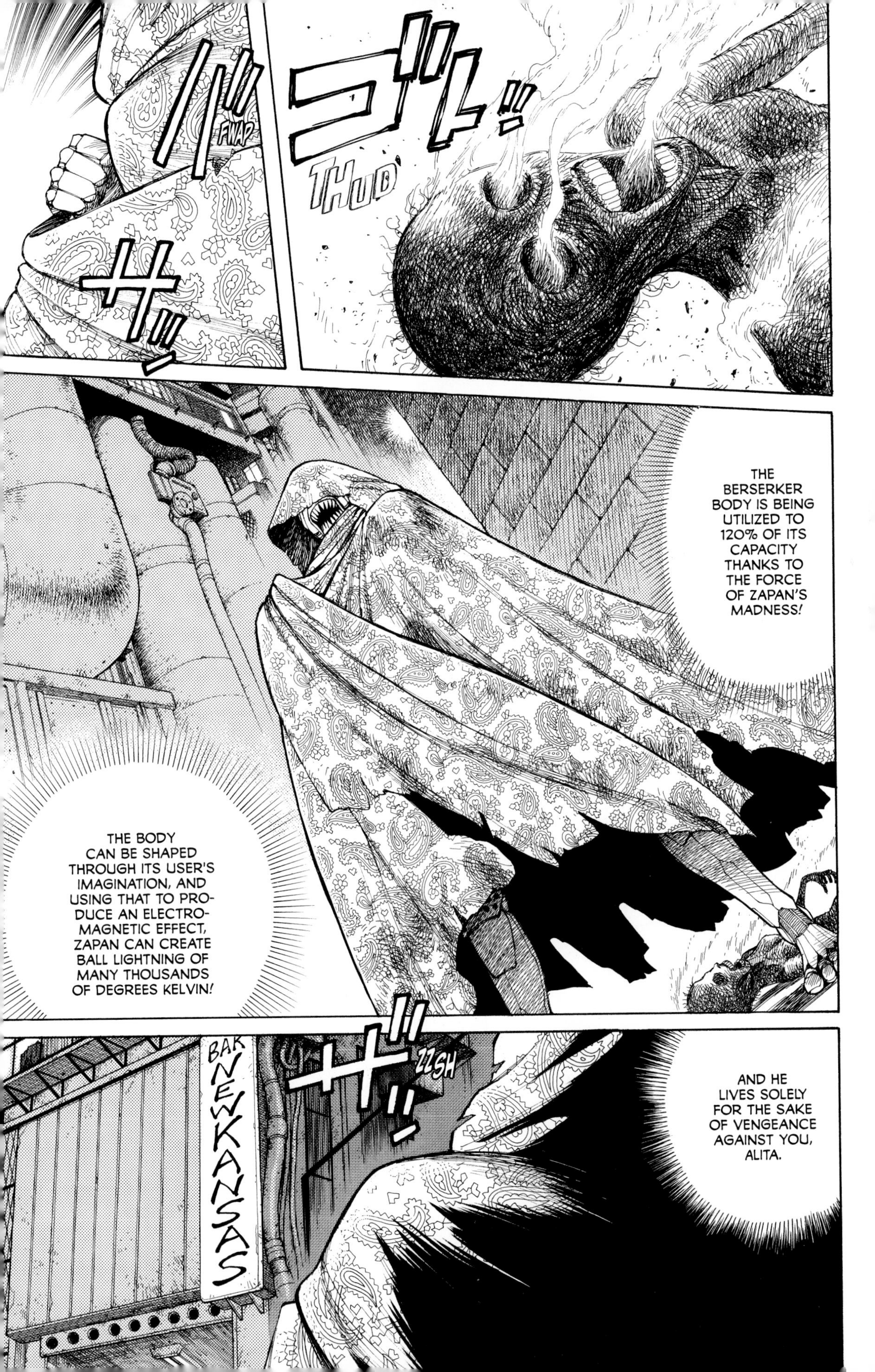
THUD
FWAP
THE BERSERKER BODY IS BEING UTILIZED TO 120% OF ITS CAPACITY THANKS TO THE FORCE OF ZAPAN'S MADNESS!
THE BODY CAN BE SHAPED THROUGH ITS USER'S IMAGINATION, AND USING THAT TO PRODUCE AN ELECTROMAGNETIC EFFECT, ZAPAN CAN CREATE BALL LIGHTNING OF MANY THOUSANDS OF DEGREES KELVIN!
AND HE LIVES SOLELY FOR THE SAKE OF VENGEANCE AGAINST YOU, ALITA.
ZZSH
BAK
NEWKANSAS

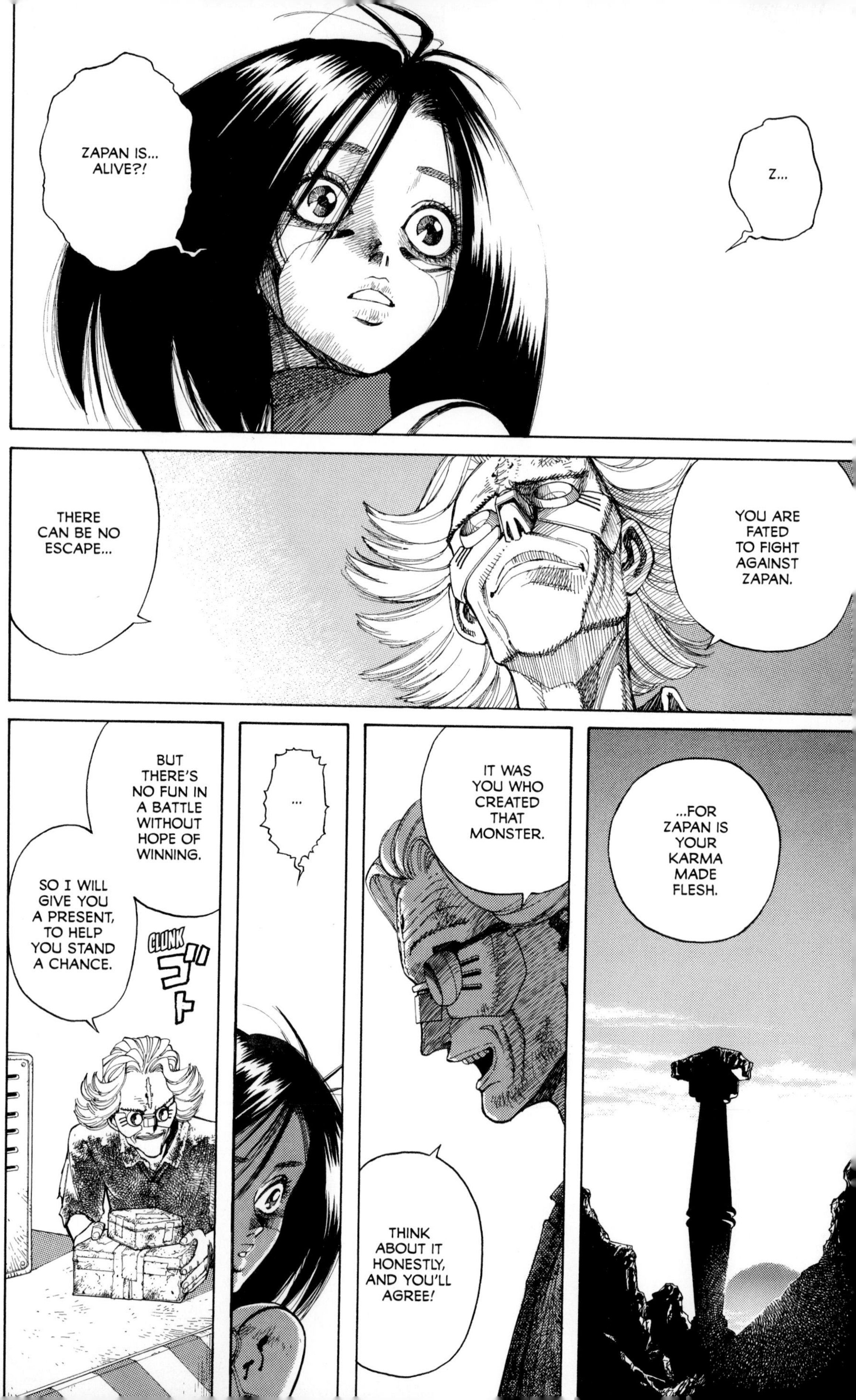
Z...
ZAPAN IS... ALIVE?!
YOU ARE FATED TO FIGHT AGAINST ZAPAN.
THERE CAN BE NO ESCAPE...
...FOR ZAPAN IS YOUR KARMA MADE FLESH.
IT WAS YOU WHO CREATED THAT MONSTER.
THINK ABOUT IT HONESTLY, AND YOU'LL AGREE!
...
BUT THERE'S NO FUN IN A BATTLE WITHOUT HOPE OF WINNING.
SO I WILL GIVE YOU A PRESENT, TO HELP YOU STAND A CHANCE.
CLUNK

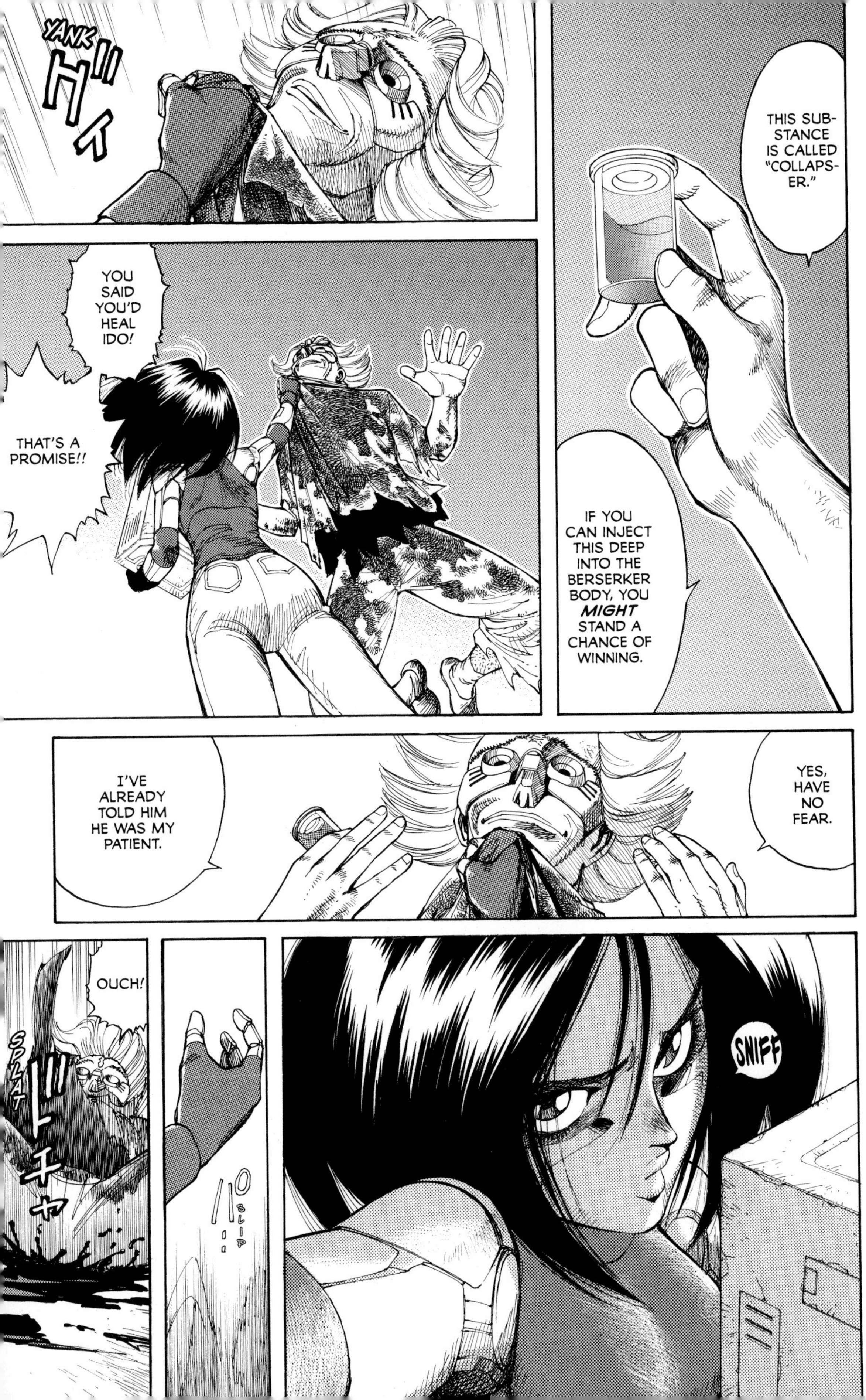
THIS SUBSTANCE IS CALLED "COLLAPSER."
IF YOU CAN INJECT THIS DEEP INTO THE BERSERKER BODY, YOU ***MIGHT*** STAND A CHANCE OF WINNING.
YANK
YOU SAID YOU'D HEAL IDO!
THAT'S A PROMISE!!
YES, HAVE NO FEAR.
I'VE ALREADY TOLD HIM HE WAS MY PATIENT.
SNIFF
SLIP
OUCH!
SPLAT

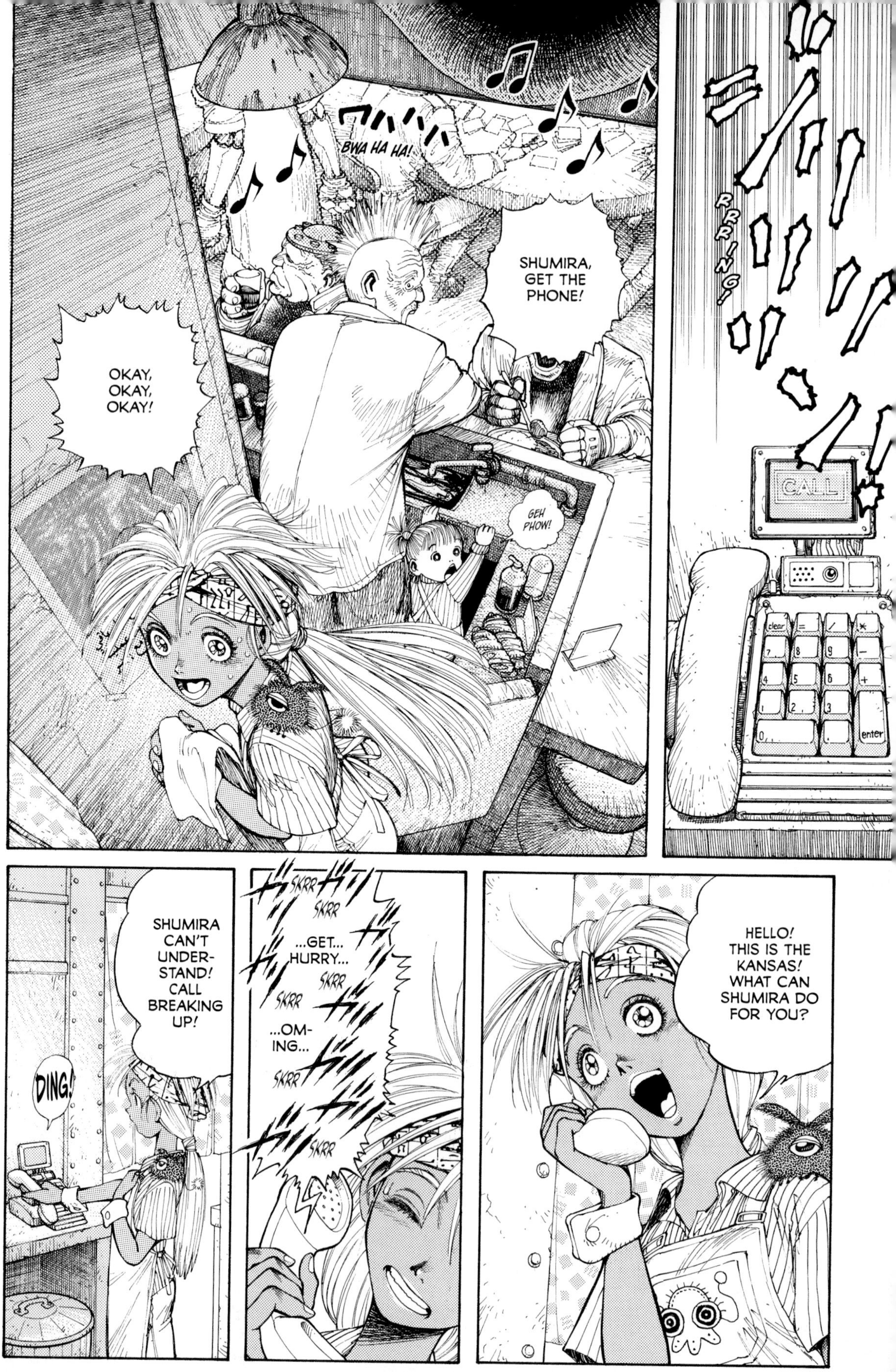
RRRING!
CALL
BWA HA HA!
SHUMIRA, GET THE PHONE!
OKAY, OKAY, OKAY!
GEH PHOW!
HELLO! THIS IS THE KANSAS! WHAT CAN SHUMIRA DO FOR YOU?
SKRR
SKRR
...GET... HURRY...
SKRR
SKRR
...OM- ING...
SKRR
SKRR
SHUMIRA CAN'T UNDER- STAND! CALL BREAKING UP!
DING!

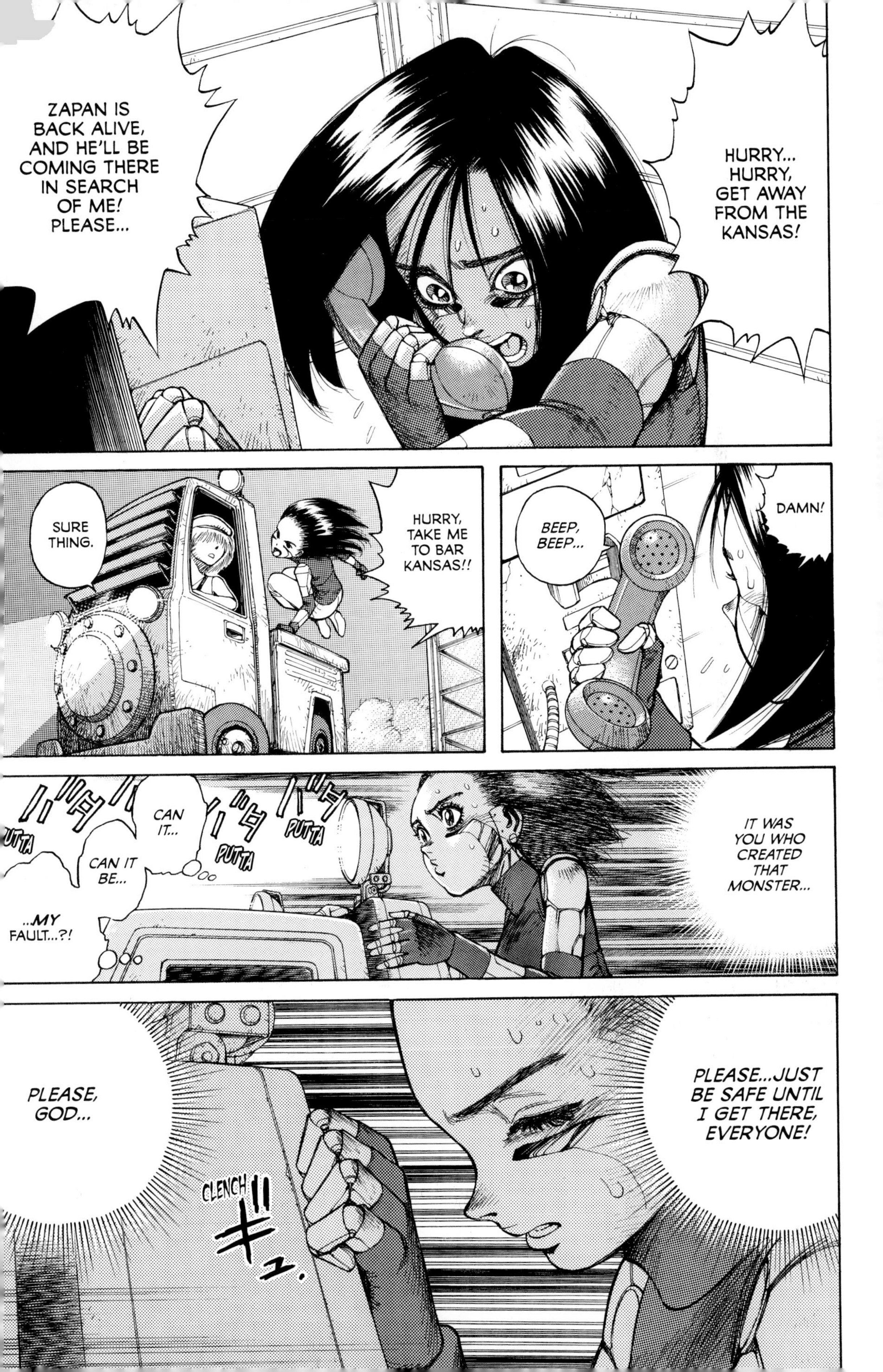

HURRY... HURRY, GET AWAY FROM THE KANSAS!
ZAPAN IS BACK ALIVE, AND HE'LL BE COMING THERE IN SEARCH OF ME! PLEASE...
DAMN!
BEEP, BEEP...
HURRY, TAKE ME TO BAR KANSAS!!
SURE THING.
IT WAS YOU WHO CREATED THAT MONSTER...
PUTTA
CAN IT...
PUTTA
CAN IT BE...
...MY FAULT...?!
PLEASE...JUST BE SAFE UNTIL I GET THERE, EVERYONE!
CLENCH
PLEASE, GOD...

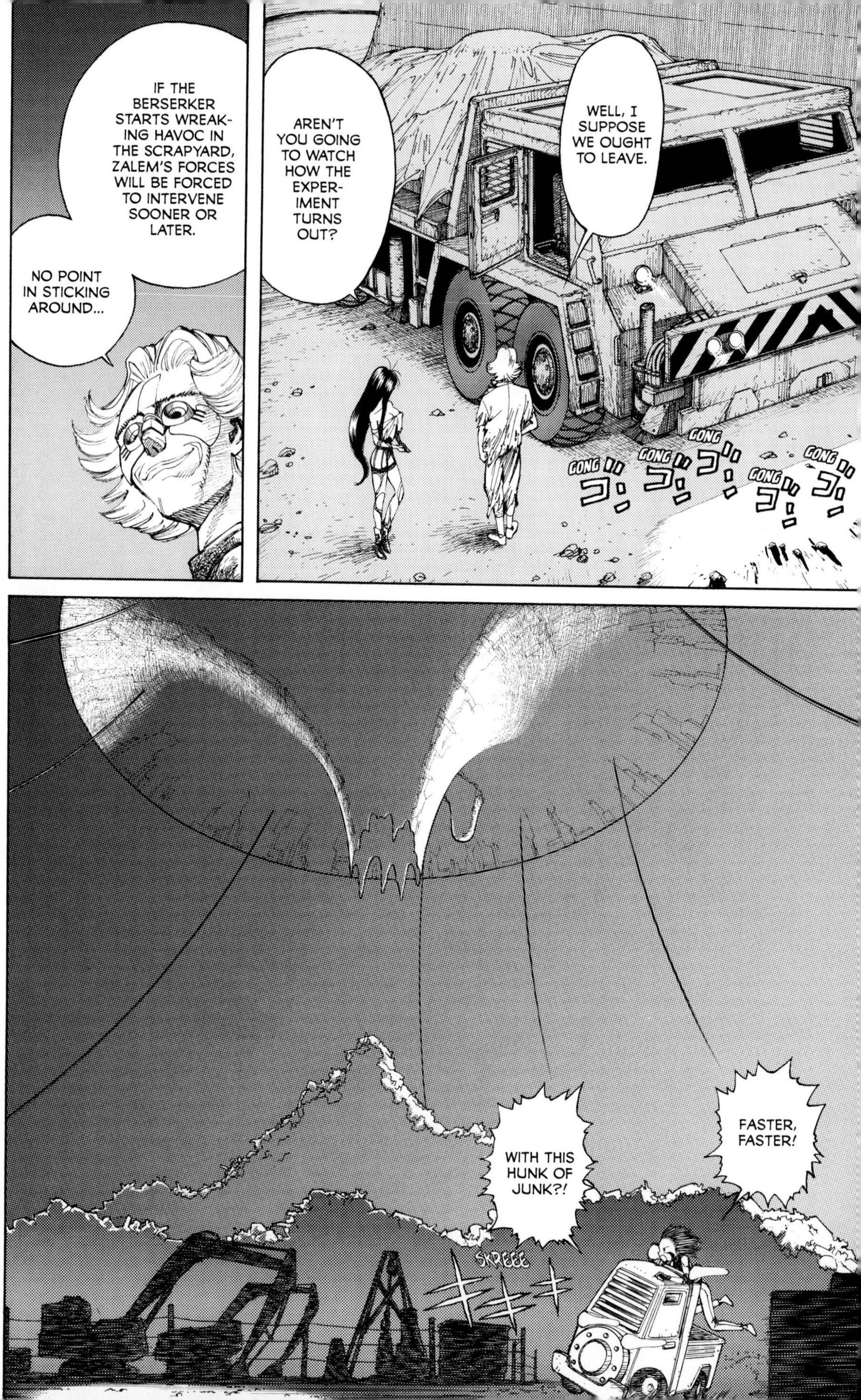
WELL, I SUPPOSE WE OUGHT TO LEAVE.
AREN'T YOU GOING TO WATCH HOW THE EXPERIMENT TURNS OUT?
GONG GONG GONG GONG GONG
IF THE BERSERKER STARTS WREAKING HAVOC IN THE SCRAPYARD, ZALEM'S FORCES WILL BE FORCED TO INTERVENE SOONER OR LATER.
NO POINT IN STICKING AROUND...
FASTER, FASTER!
WITH THIS HUNK OF JUNK?!
SKREEE

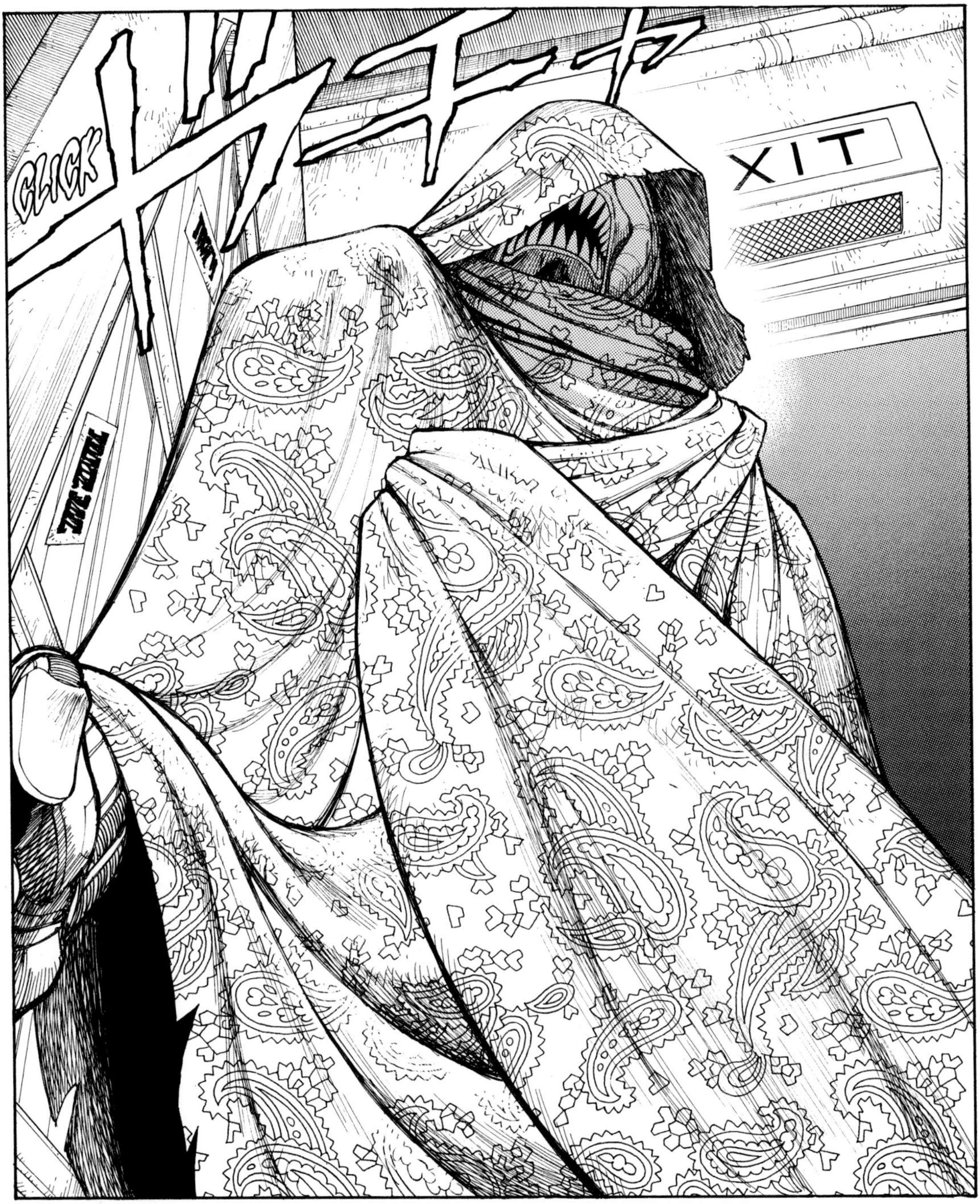
CLICK
XIT
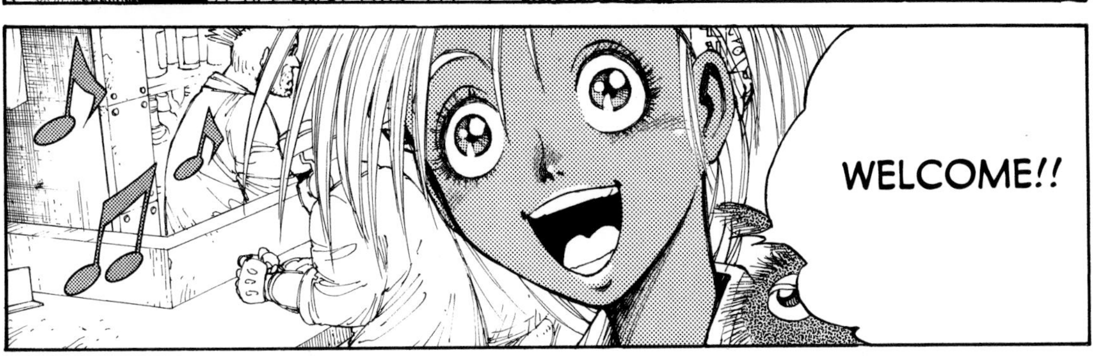
WELCOME!!

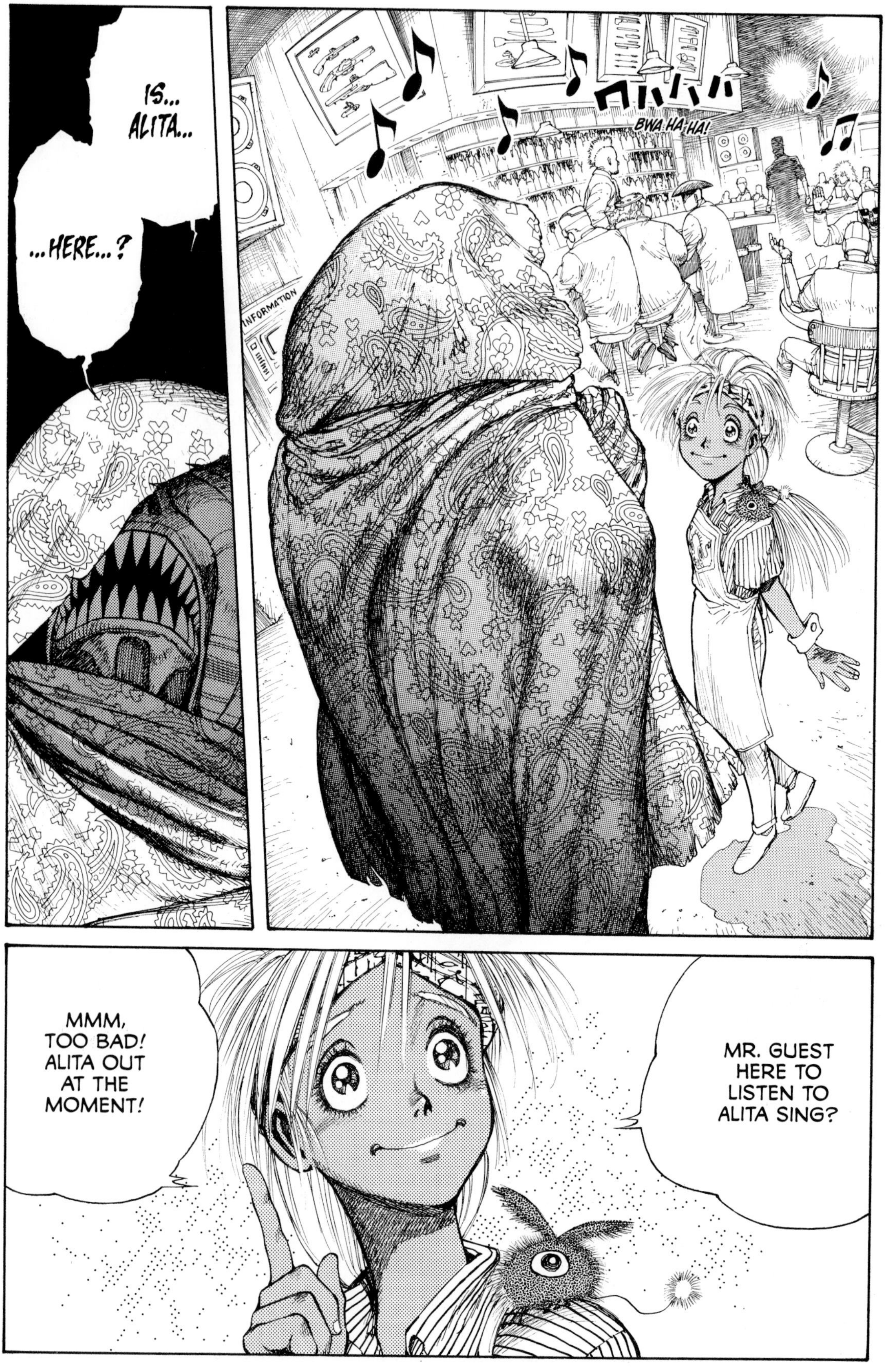
BWA HA HA!
IS... ALITA...
...HERE...?
MR. GUEST HERE TO LISTEN TO ALITA SING?
MMM, TOO BAD! ALITA OUT AT THE MOMENT!

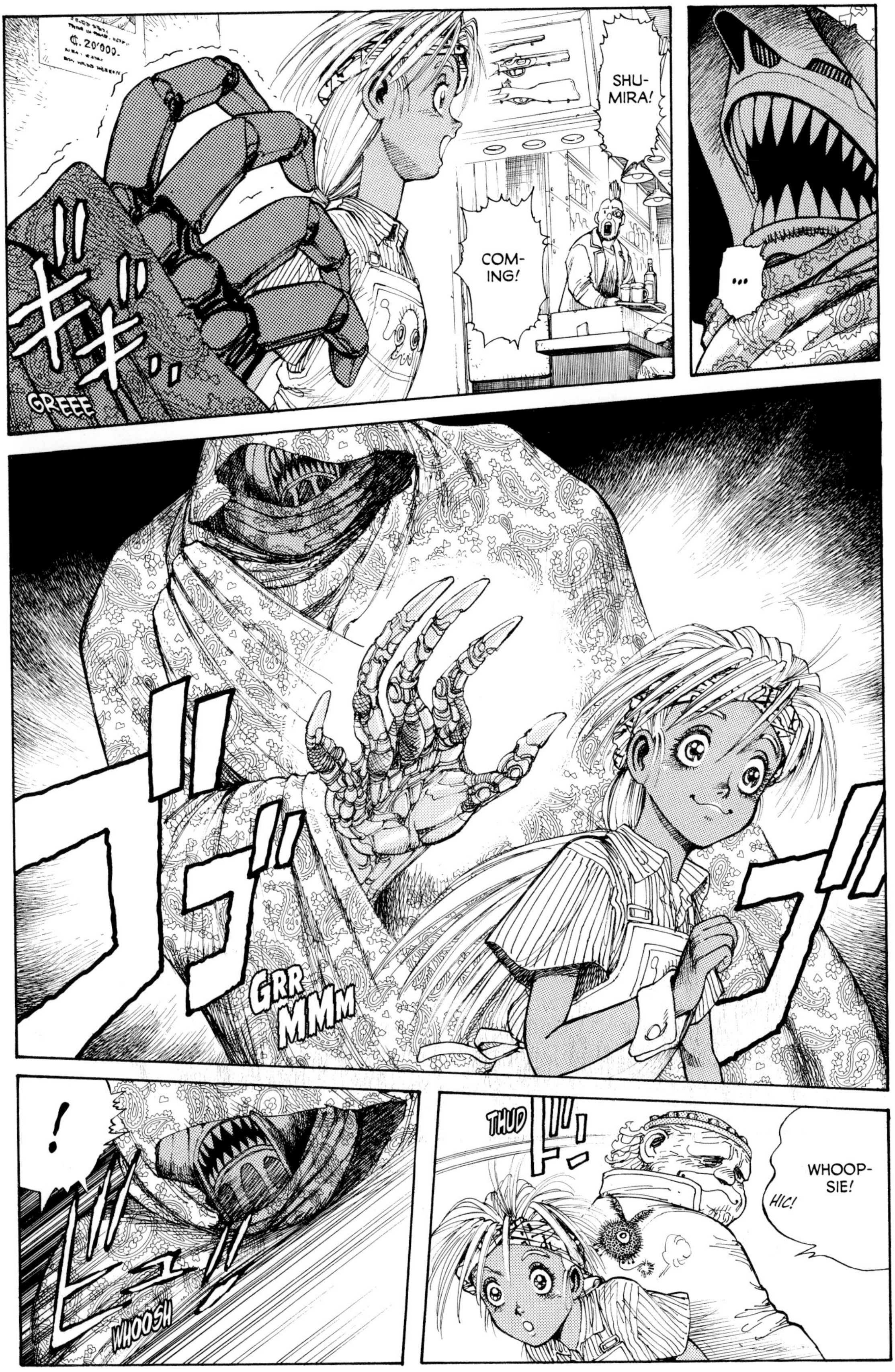
...
SHU-MIRA!
COMING!
GREEE
GRR MMM
WHOOP-SIE!
HIC!
THUD
!
WHOOSH

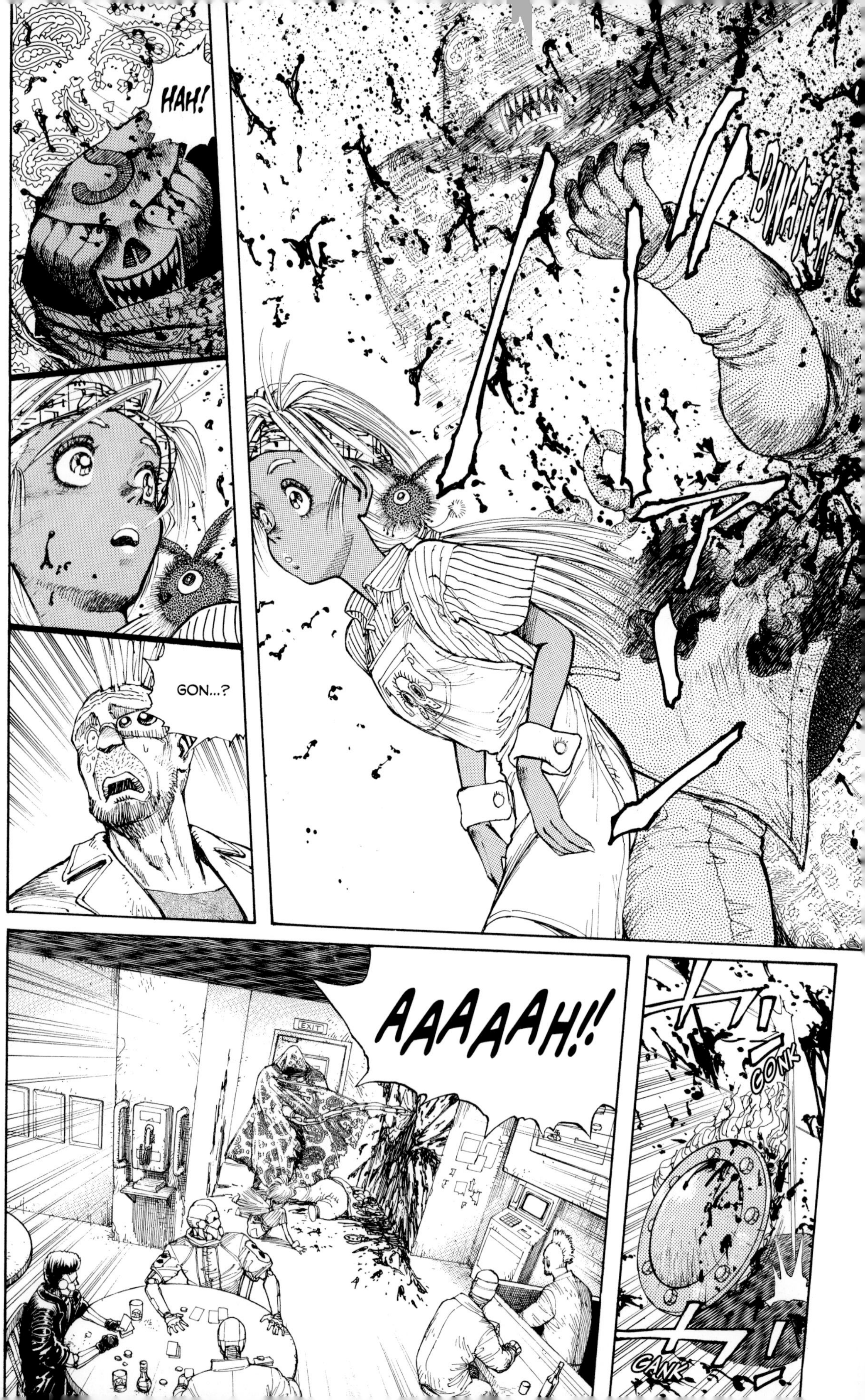
BWATCH
HAH!
GON...?
CONK
CANK
AAAAAH!!

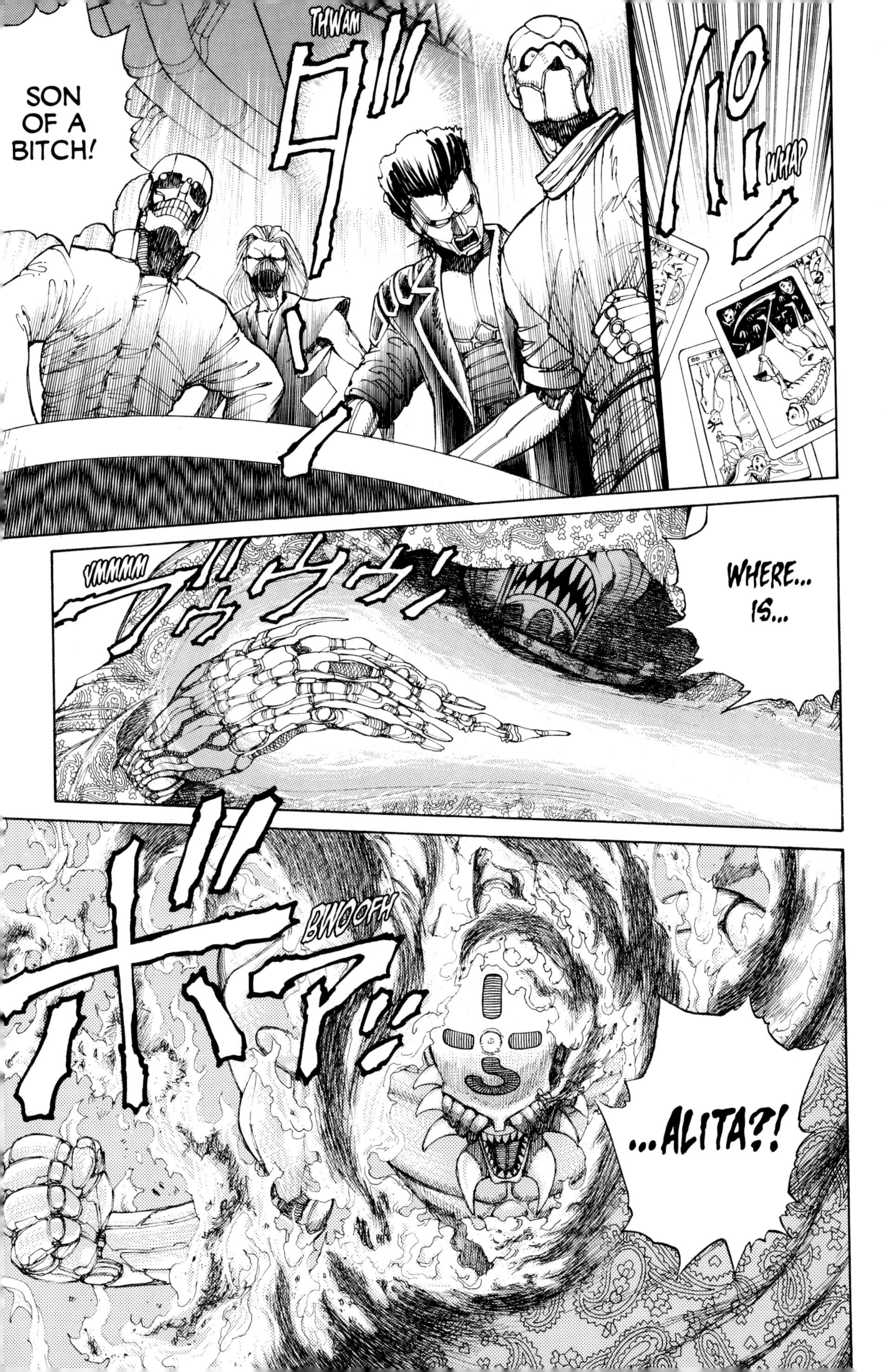
WHAP
THWAM
SON OF A BITCH!
WHERE... IS...
VMMMM
BWOOFH
...ALITA?!

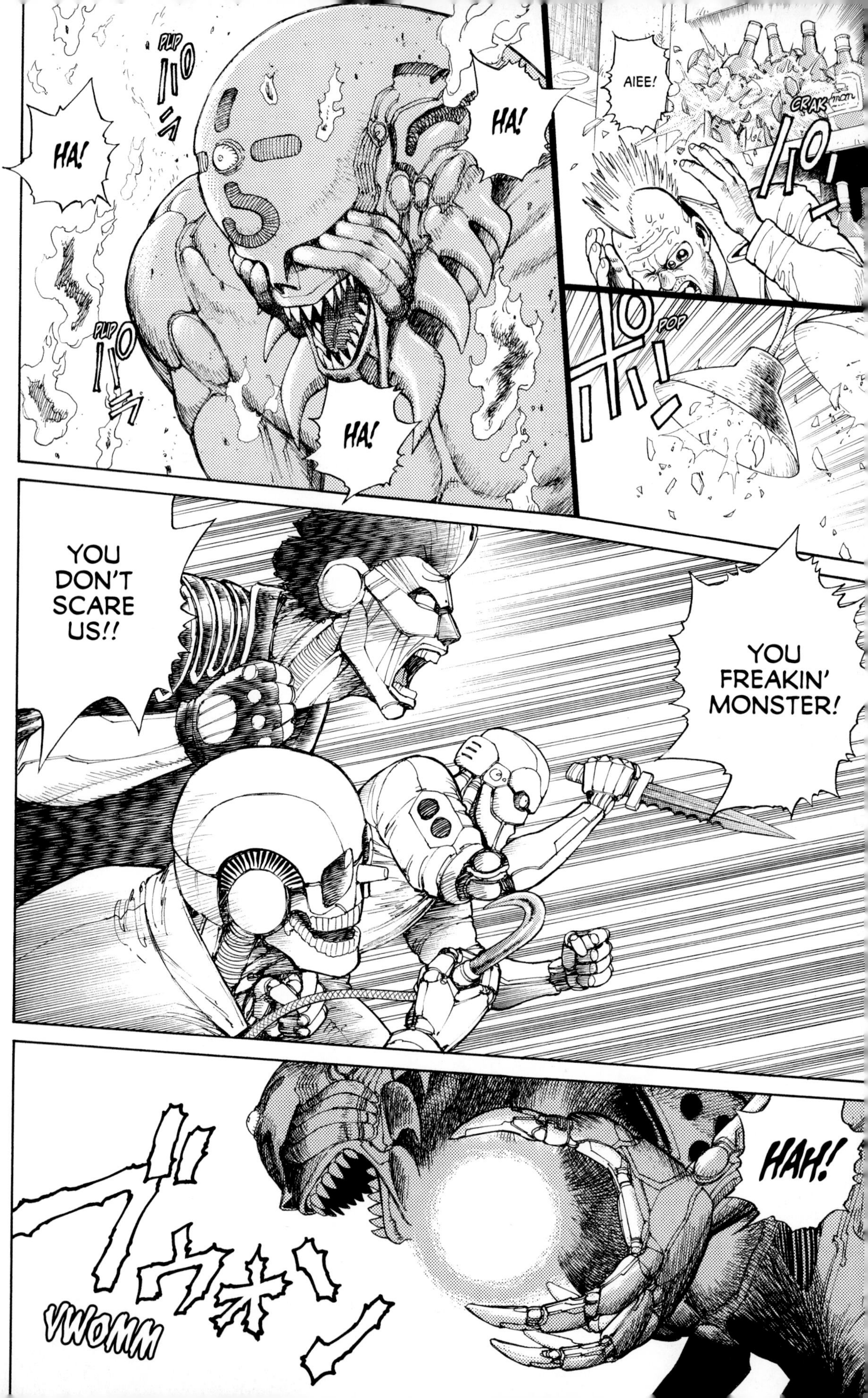
AIEE!
CRAK
POP
HA!
PLIP
HA!
PLIP
HA!
YOU FREAKIN' MONSTER!
YOU DON'T SCARE US!!
HAH!
VWOMM

BOOOM

BZT

BZT

BAR NEWKANS

CLUNK

KRSSH

TNK....

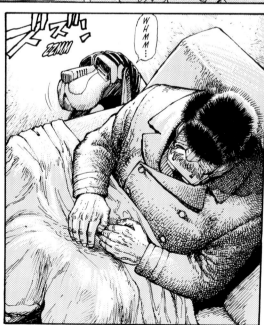

ZZMM

WHMM....

AA-AH!

BAM

EE-EI!

BAM

BAM

BLAM

BAR NEW

121

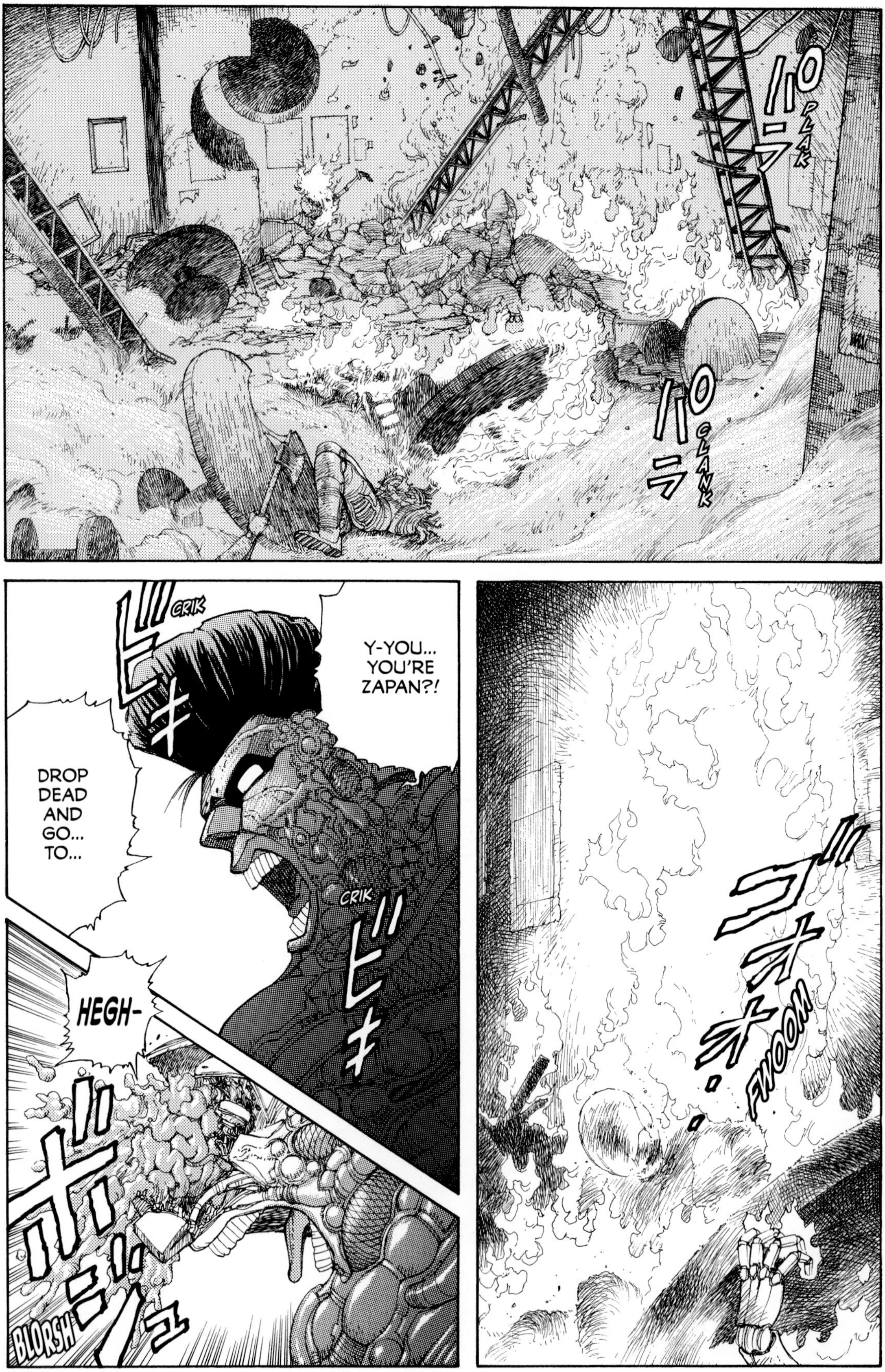
PLAK
CLANK
FWOOM
Y-YOU... YOU'RE ZAPAN?!
CRIK
DROP DEAD AND GO... TO...
CRIK
HEGH-
BLORSH

RATTLE RATTLE

HEEP!

HEEP!

AH... AAAH!

SPLAT

...IS ALITAAAA?

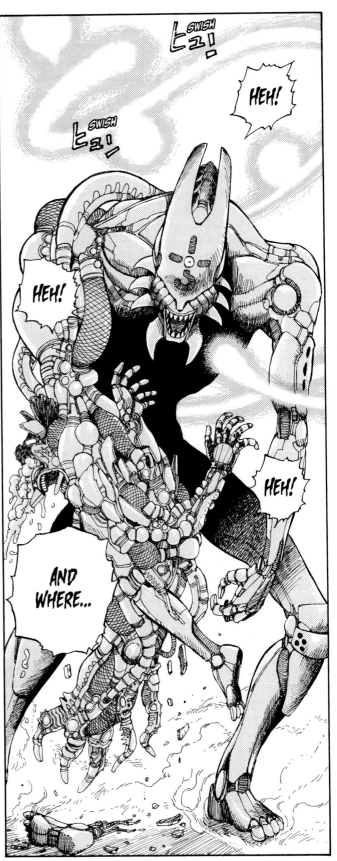

SWISH

SWISH

HEH!

HEH!

HEH!

AND WHERE...

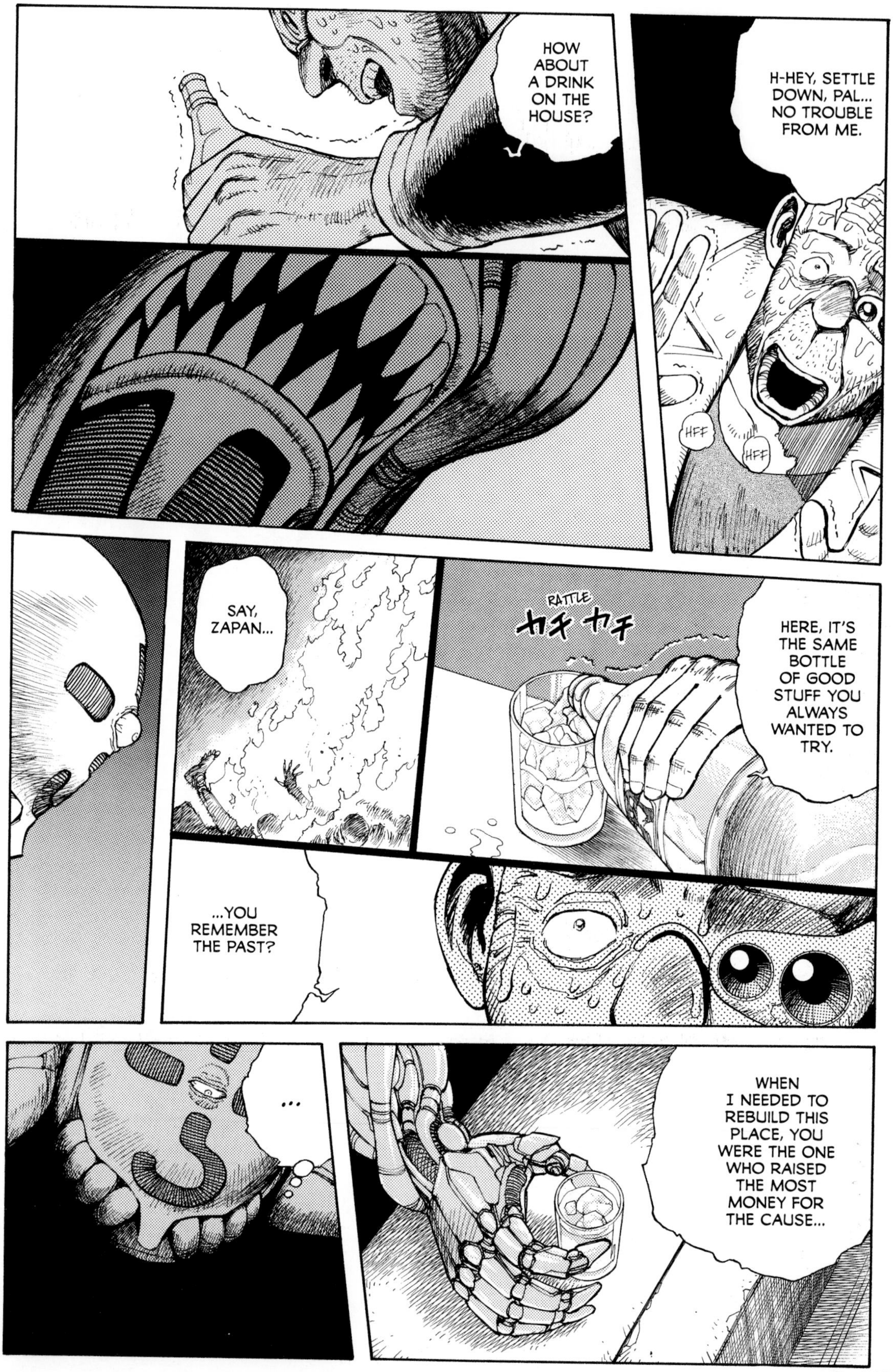
H-HEY, SETTLE DOWN, PAL... NO TROUBLE FROM ME.
HFF
HFF
HOW ABOUT A DRINK ON THE HOUSE?
RATTLE
カチ カチ
HERE, IT'S THE SAME BOTTLE OF GOOD STUFF YOU ALWAYS WANTED TO TRY.
SAY, ZAPAN...
...YOU REMEMBER THE PAST?
WHEN I NEEDED TO REBUILD THIS PLACE, YOU WERE THE ONE WHO RAISED THE MOST MONEY FOR THE CAUSE...
...

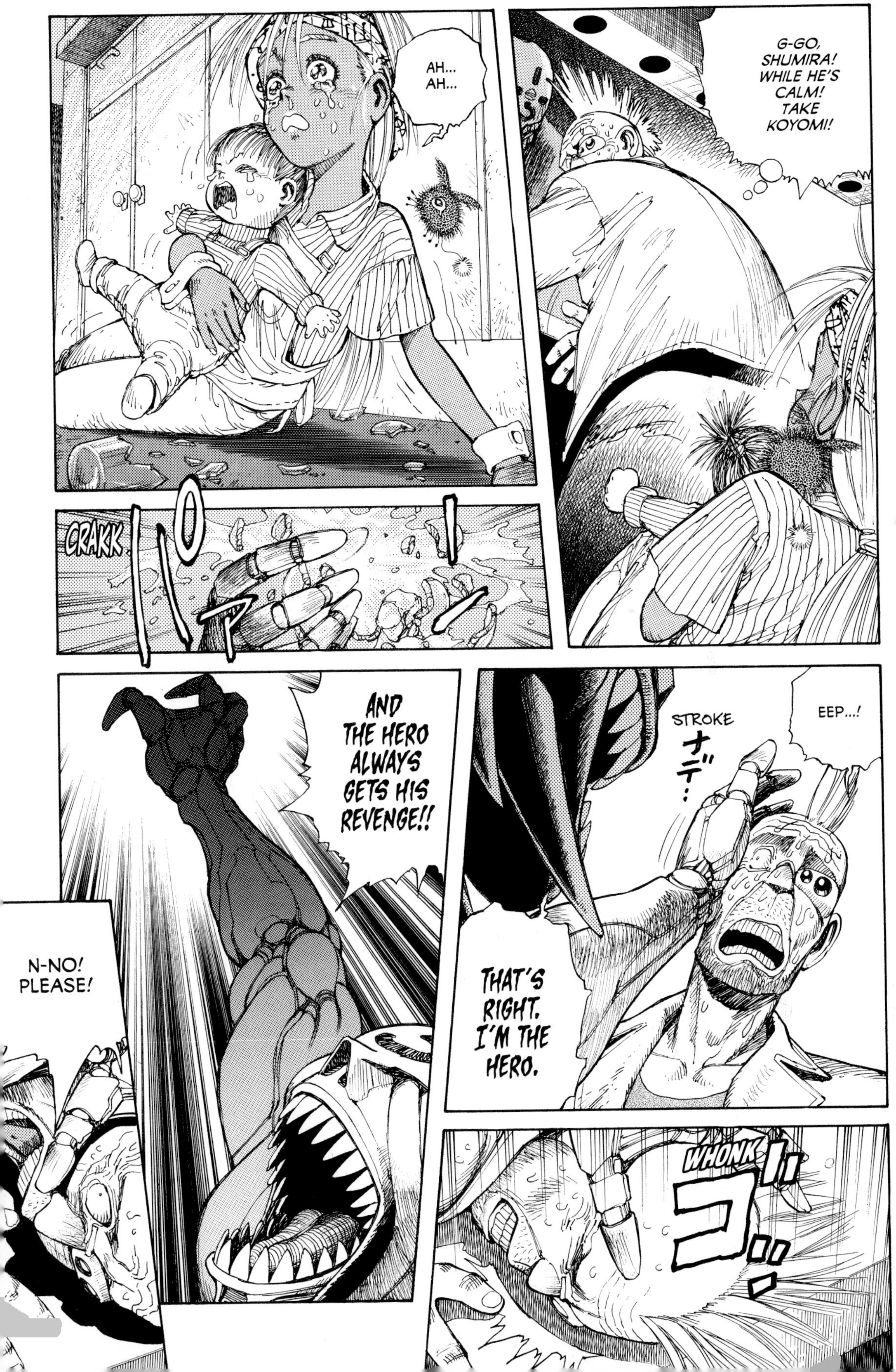
G-GO, SHUMIRA! WHILE HE'S CALM! TAKE KOYOMI!
AH... AH...
CRAKK
EEP...!
STROKE
THAT'S RIGHT. I'M THE HERO.
AND THE HERO ALWAYS GETS HIS REVENGE!!
N-NO! PLEASE!
WHONK!!

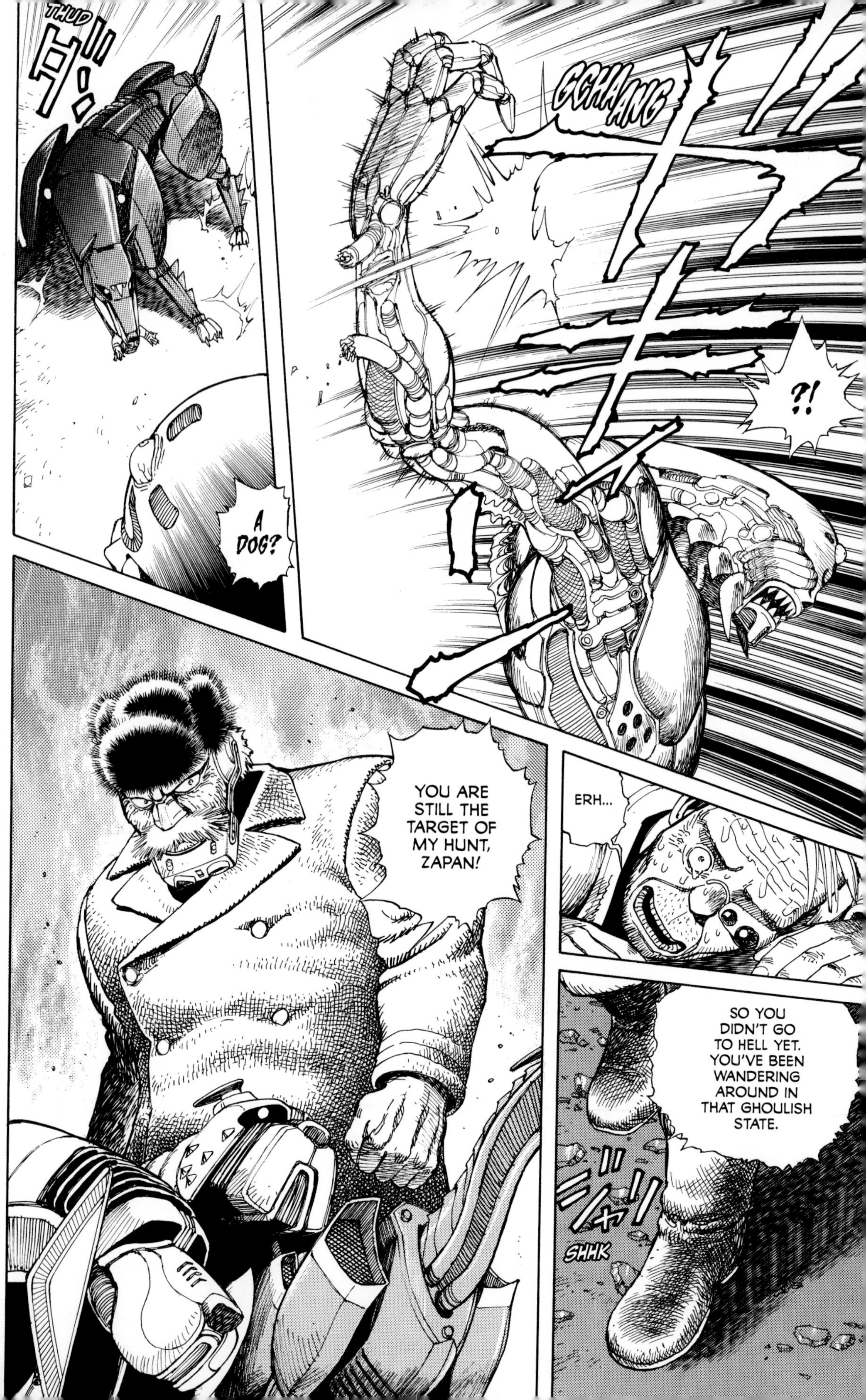
GCHANG
?!
THUD
A DOG?
ERH...
SO YOU DIDN'T GO TO HELL YET. YOU'VE BEEN WANDERING AROUND IN THAT GHOULISH STATE.
SHHK
YOU ARE STILL THE TARGET OF MY HUNT, ZAPAN!

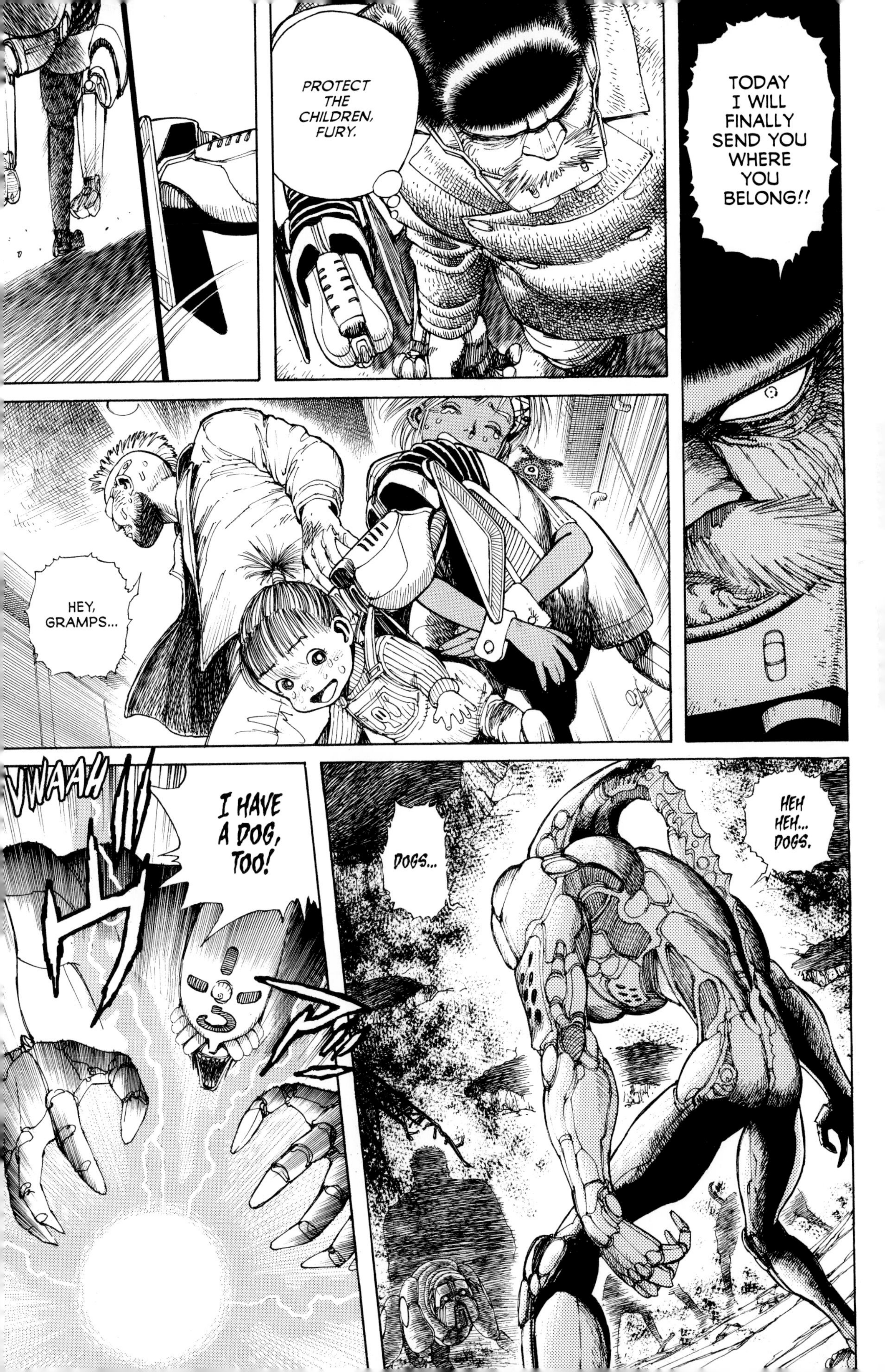
TODAY I WILL FINALLY SEND YOU WHERE YOU BELONG!!
PROTECT THE CHILDREN, FURY.
HEY, GRAMPS...
HEH HEH... DOGS.
DOGS...
I HAVE A DOG, TOO!
VWAAH

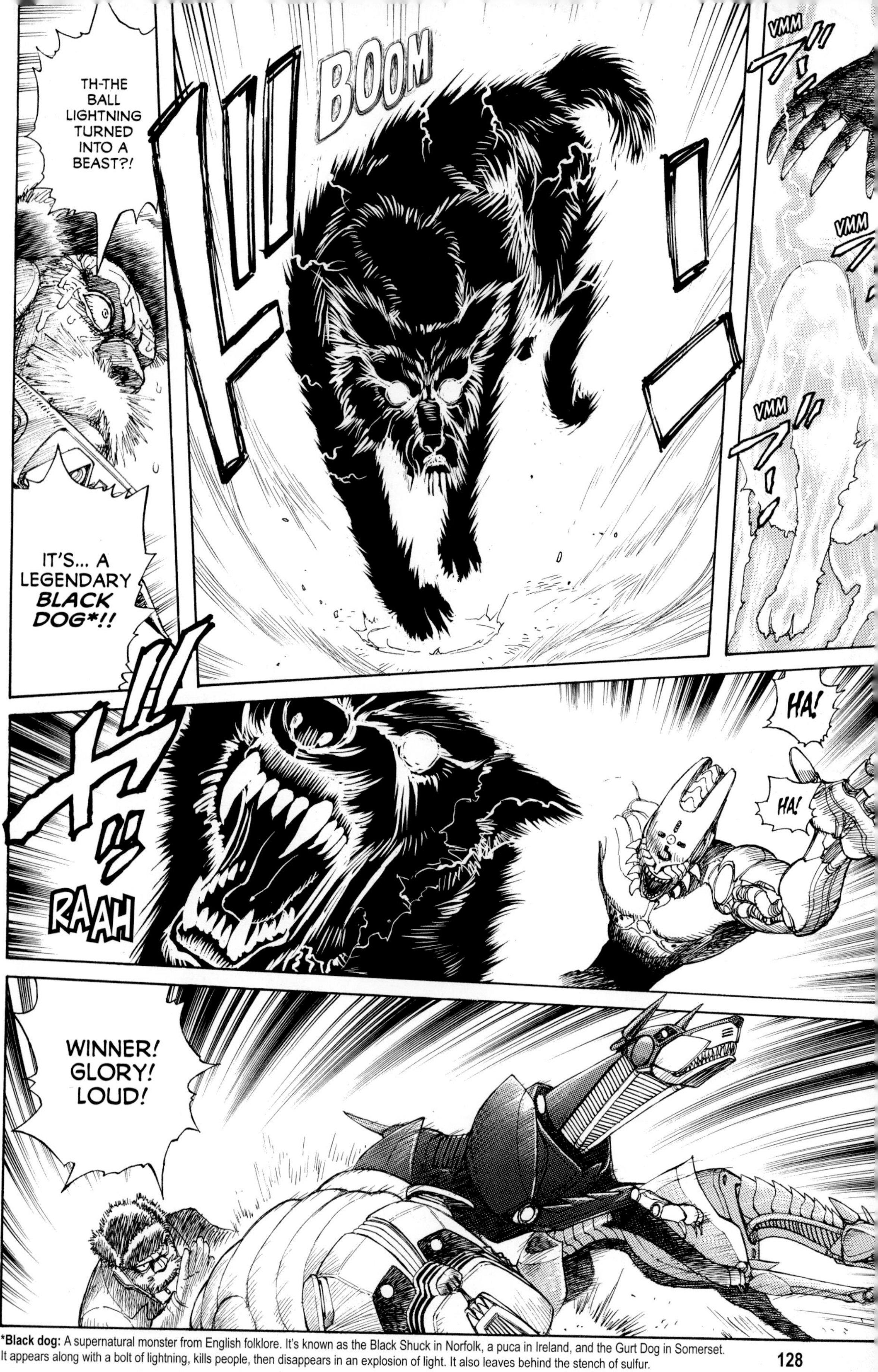
VMM
VMM
VMM
BOOM
TH-THE BALL LIGHTNING TURNED INTO A BEAST?!
IT'S... A LEGENDARY *BLACK DOG*!!*
HA!
HA!
RAAH
WINNER! GLORY! LOUD!

***Black dog:** A supernatural monster from English folklore. It's known as the Black Shuck in Norfolk, a puca in Ireland, and the Gurt Dog in Somerset. It appears along with a bolt of lightning, kills people, then disappears in an explosion of light. It also leaves behind the stench of sulfur.

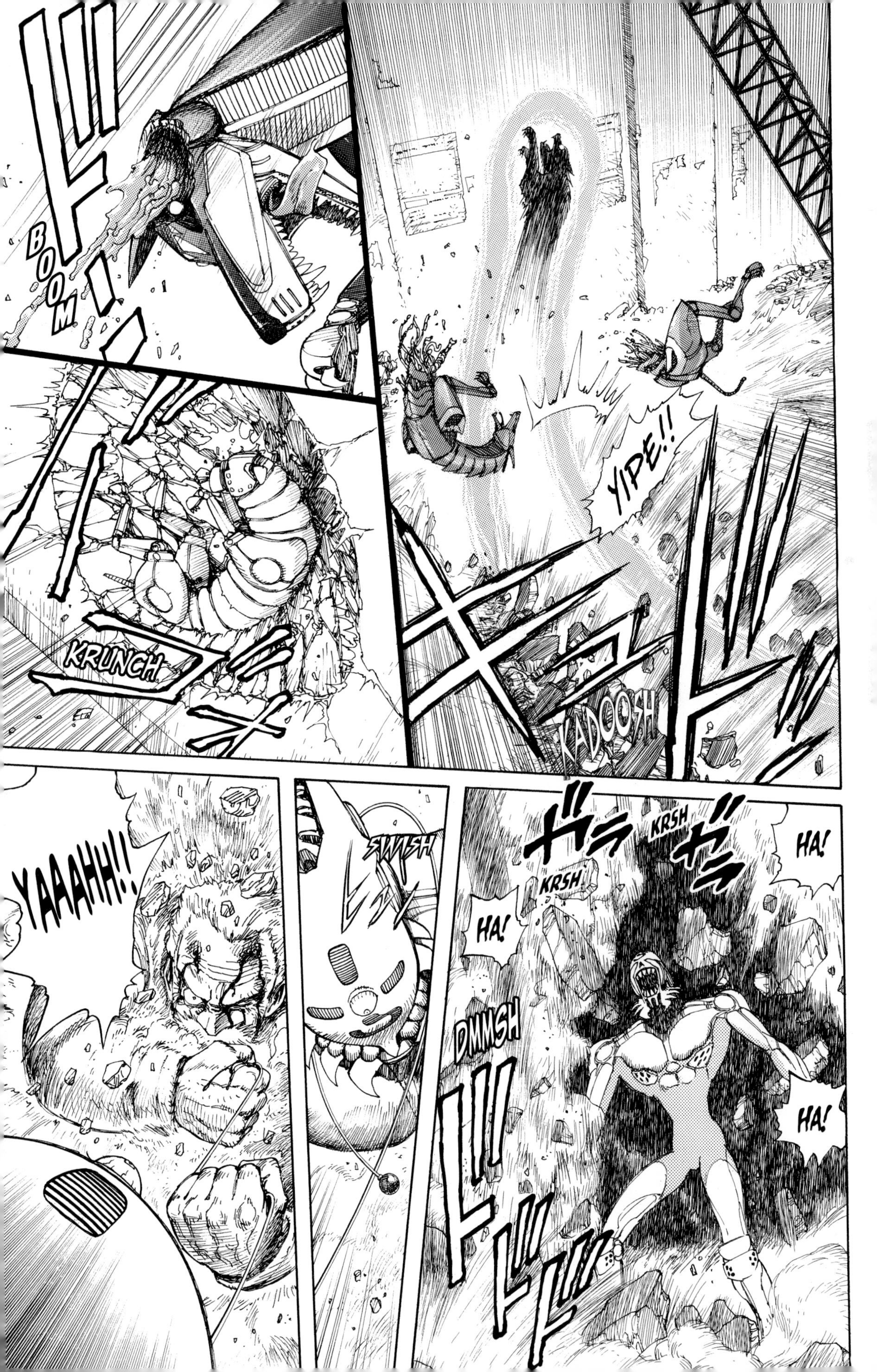
YIPE!!
KADOOSH
BOOM
KRUNCH
HA!
KRSH
KRSH
HA!
DMMSH
HA!
SWISH
YAAAHH!!

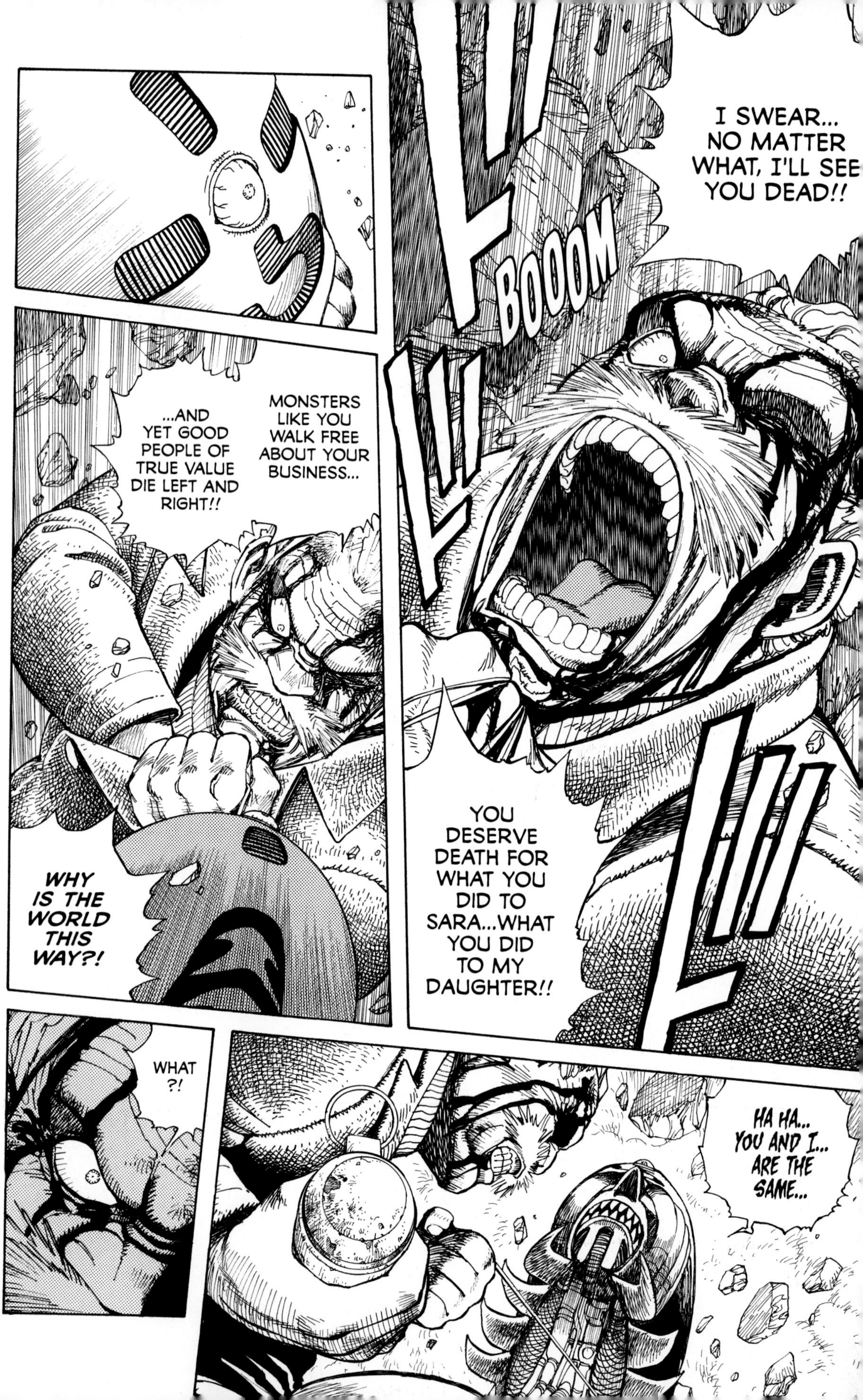
I SWEAR... NO MATTER WHAT, I'LL SEE YOU DEAD!!
BOOOM
YOU DESERVE DEATH FOR WHAT YOU DID TO SARA...WHAT YOU DID TO MY DAUGHTER!!
MONSTERS LIKE YOU WALK FREE ABOUT YOUR BUSINESS...
...AND YET GOOD PEOPLE OF TRUE VALUE DIE LEFT AND RIGHT!!
WHY IS THE WORLD THIS WAY?!
HA HA... YOU AND I... ARE THE SAME...
WHAT ?!

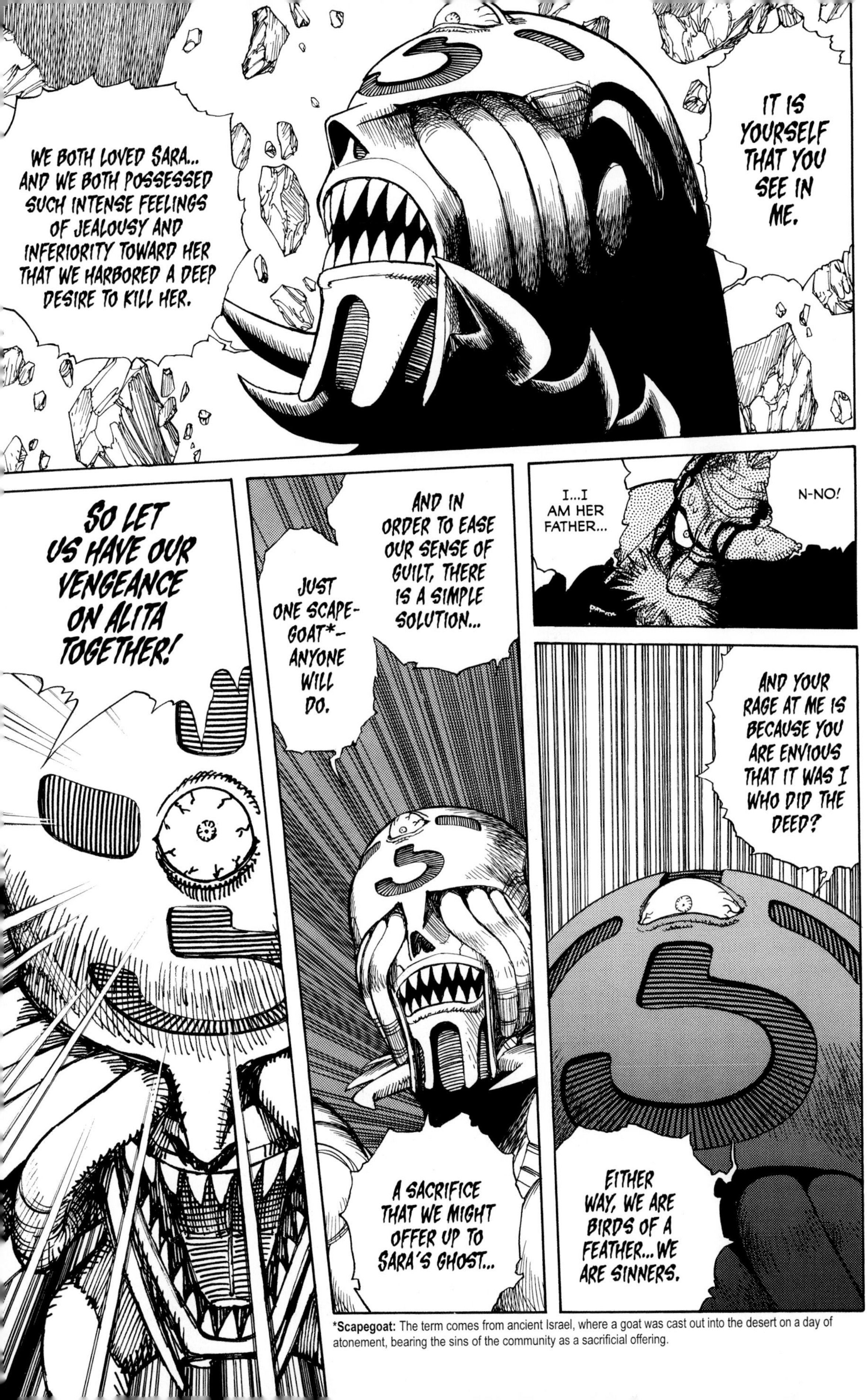
IT IS YOURSELF THAT YOU SEE IN ME.
WE BOTH LOVED SARA... AND WE BOTH POSSESSED SUCH INTENSE FEELINGS OF JEALOUSY AND INFERIORITY TOWARD HER THAT WE HARBORED A DEEP DESIRE TO KILL HER.
N-NO!
I...I AM HER FATHER...
AND YOUR RAGE AT ME IS BECAUSE YOU ARE ENVIOUS THAT IT WAS I WHO DID THE DEED?
EITHER WAY, WE ARE BIRDS OF A FEATHER...WE ARE SINNERS.
AND IN ORDER TO EASE OUR SENSE OF GUILT, THERE IS A SIMPLE SOLUTION...
JUST ONE SCAPE-GOAT*–ANYONE WILL DO.
A SACRIFICE THAT WE MIGHT OFFER UP TO SARA'S GHOST...
SO LET US HAVE OUR VENGEANCE ON ALITA TOGETHER!

***Scapegoat:** The term comes from ancient Israel, where a goat was cast out into the desert on a day of atonement, bearing the sins of the community as a sacrificial offering.

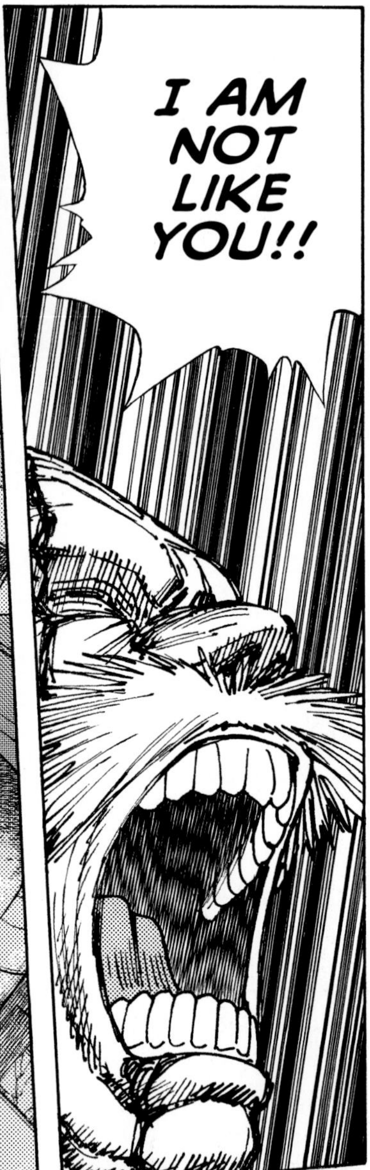
I AM NOT LIKE YOU!!
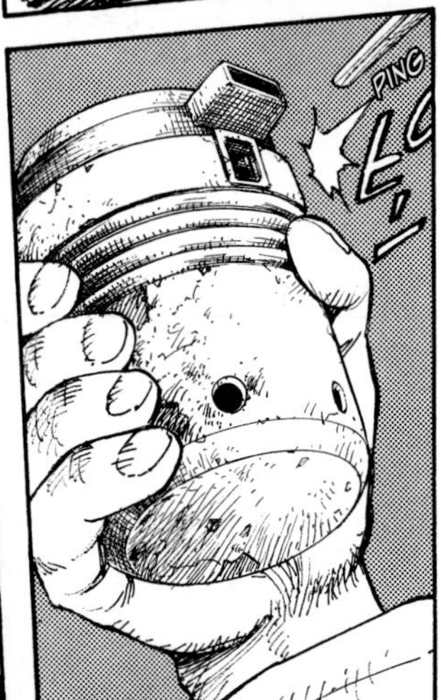
PING
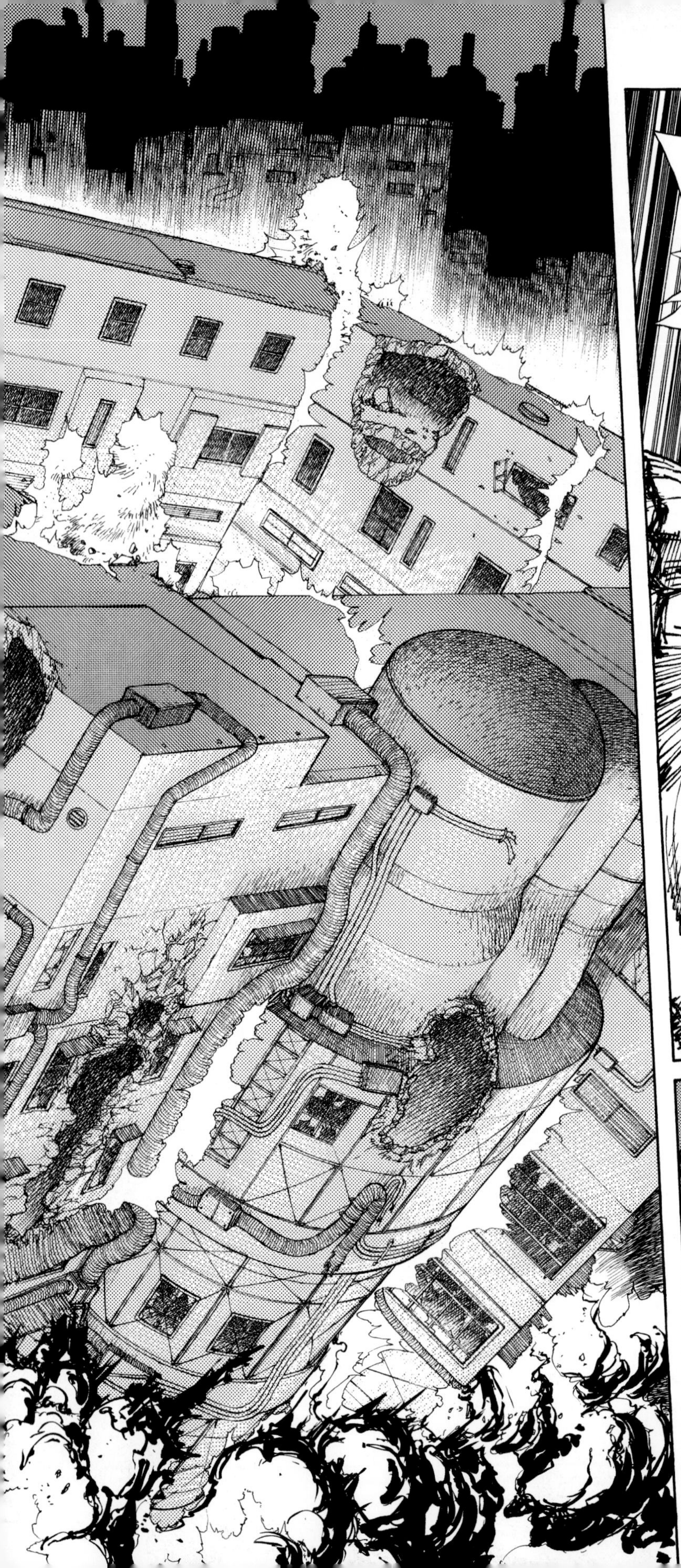

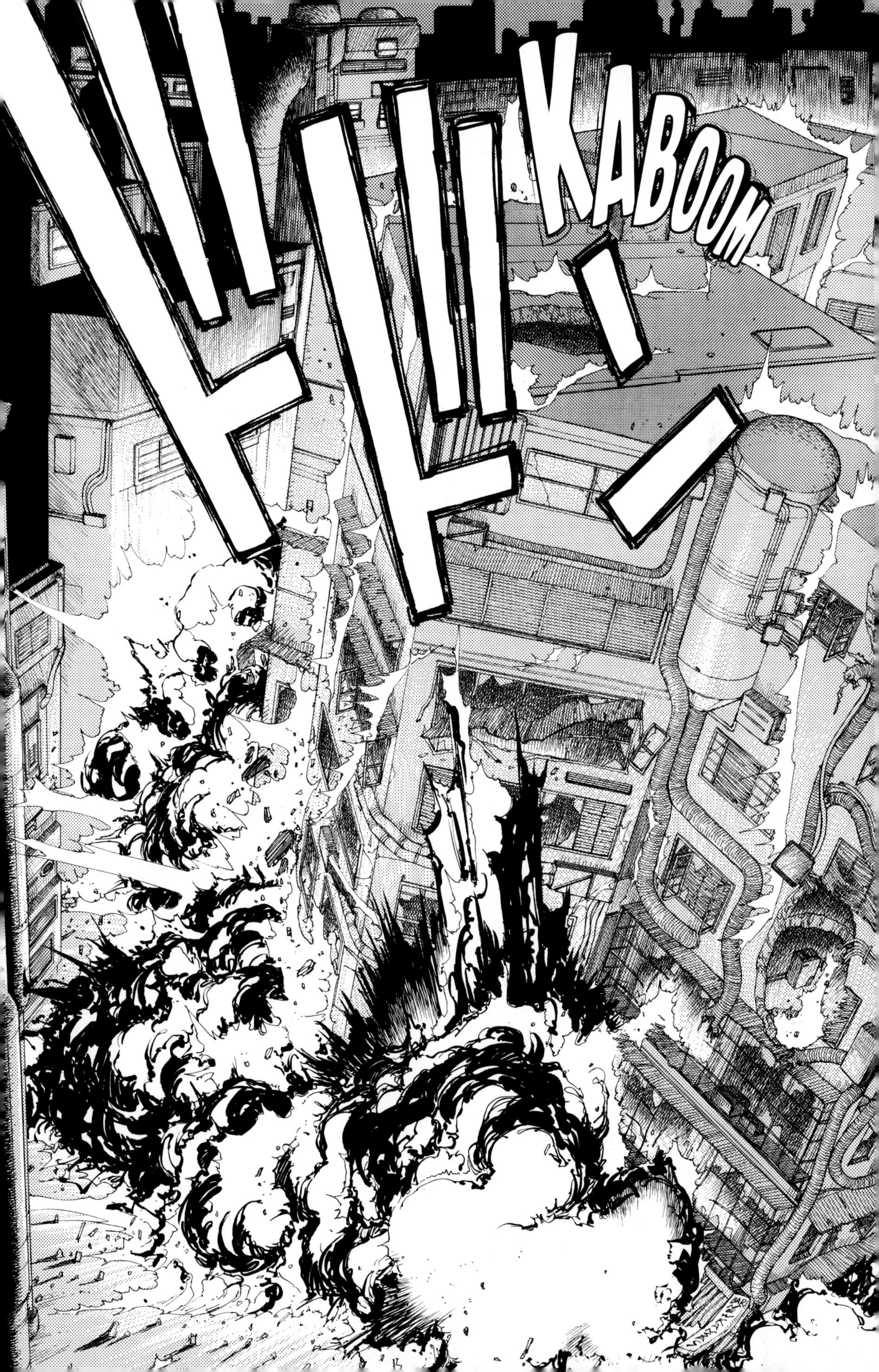
KABOOM

Marker: Fang

Sign: Don't step on the flowers!

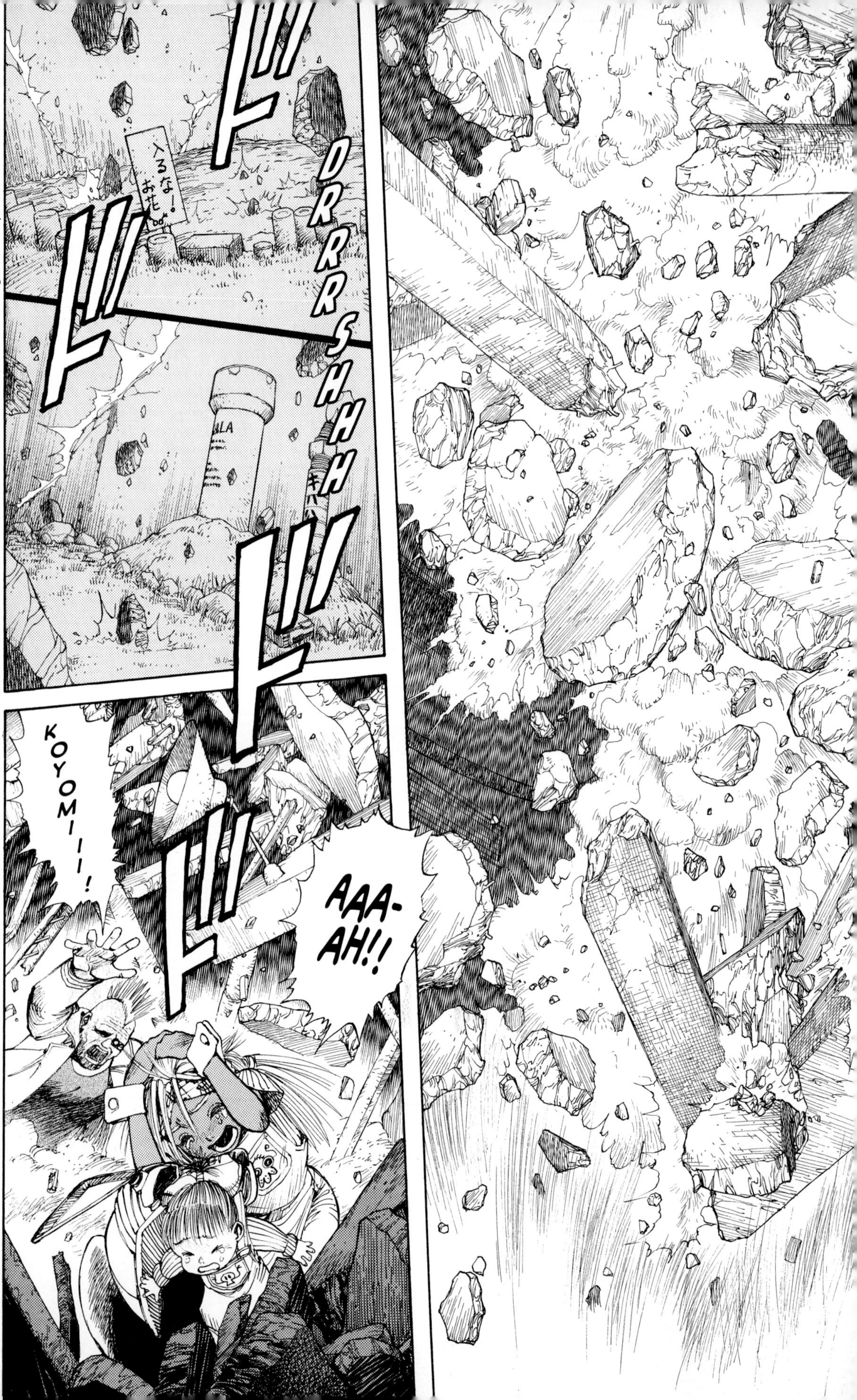
ド
DRRRSHHHH
入るな！
お花
ド
ド
KOYOMI!!!
ド
AAA-AH!!

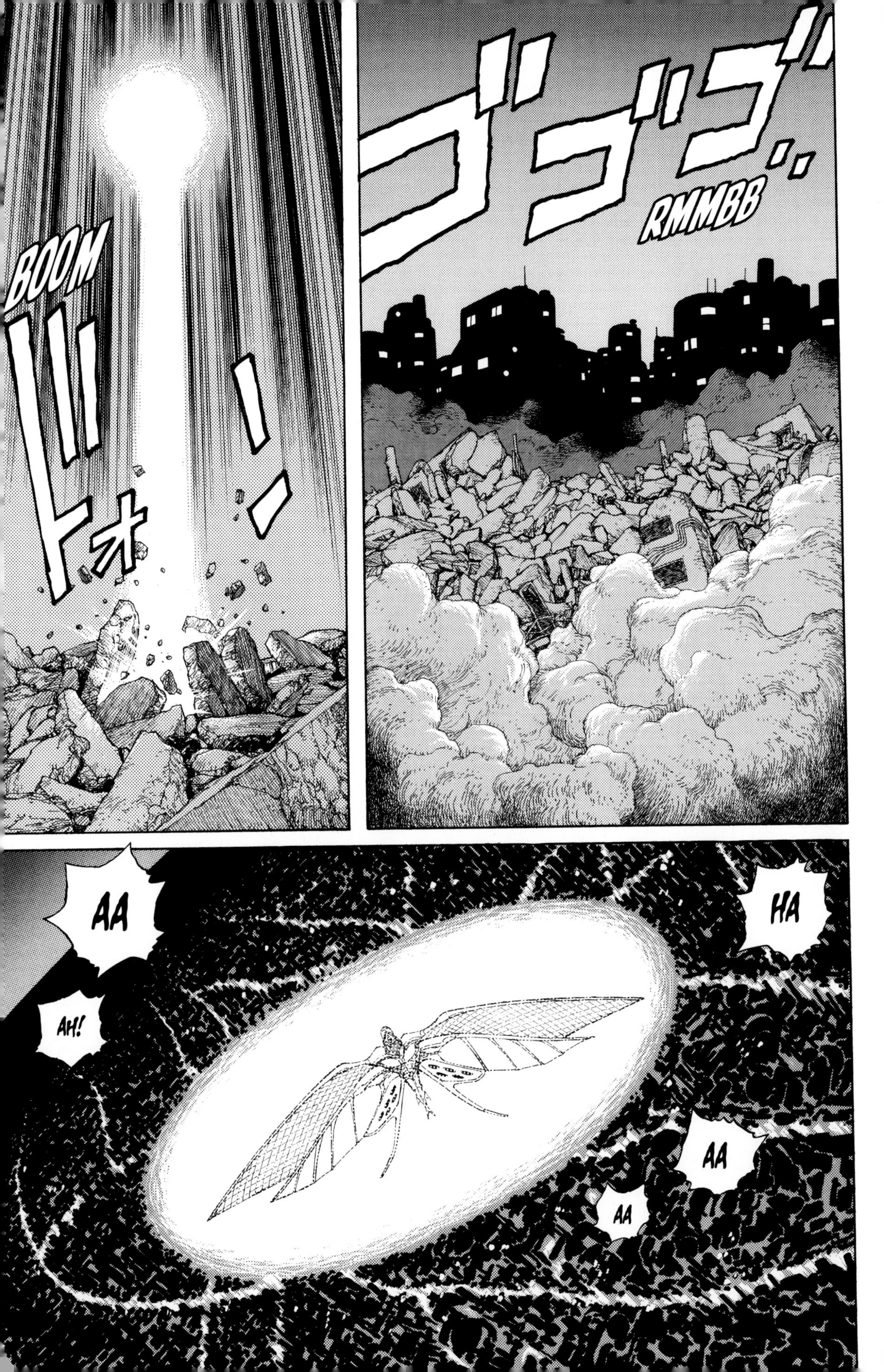
ゴゴゴ
RMMBB
BOOM
ドォーン
HA
AA
AA
AA
AH!

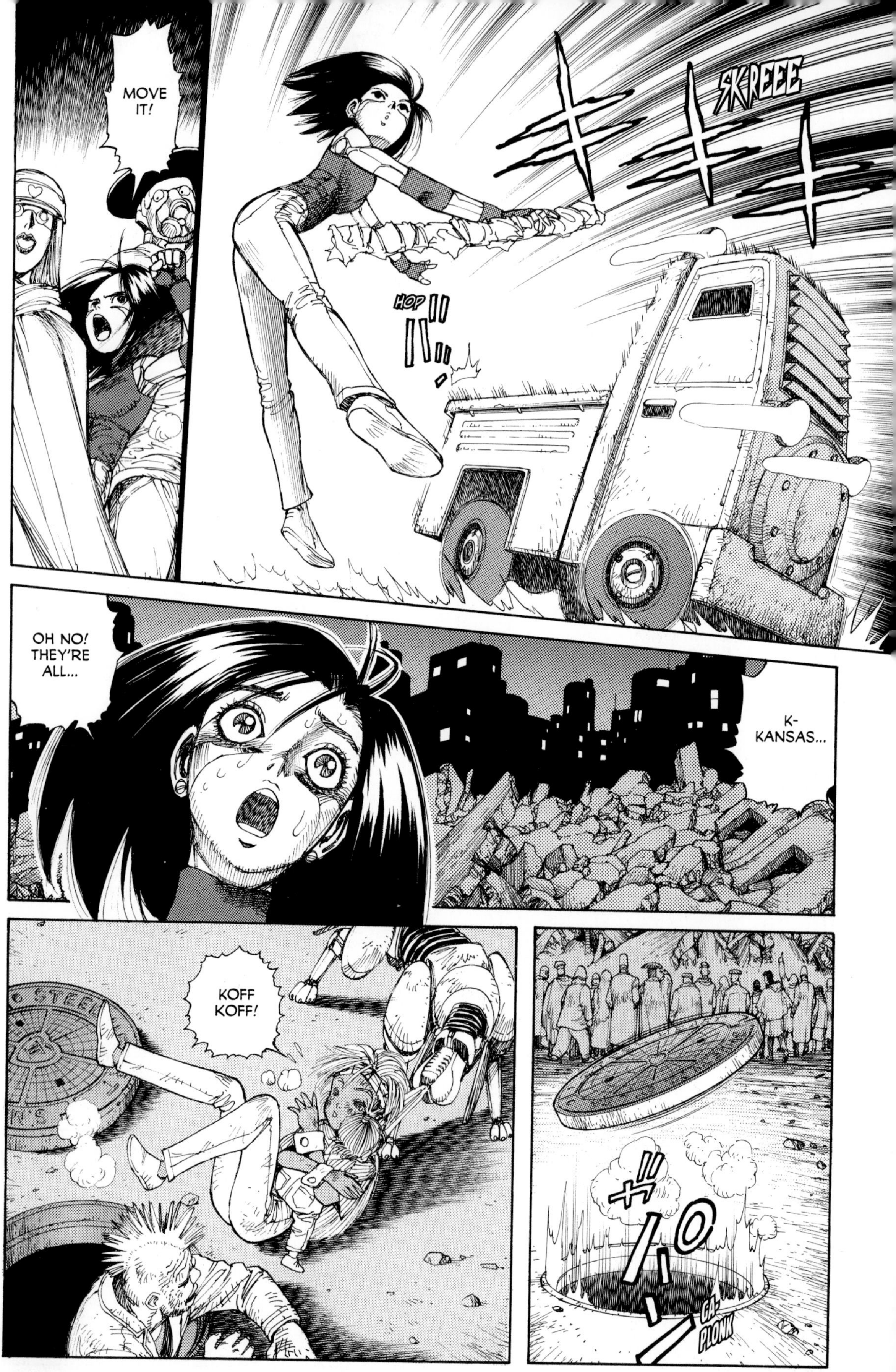
SK-REEE
HOP
MOVE IT!
OH NO! THEY'RE ALL...
K-KANSAS...
GA-PLONK
KOFF KOFF!

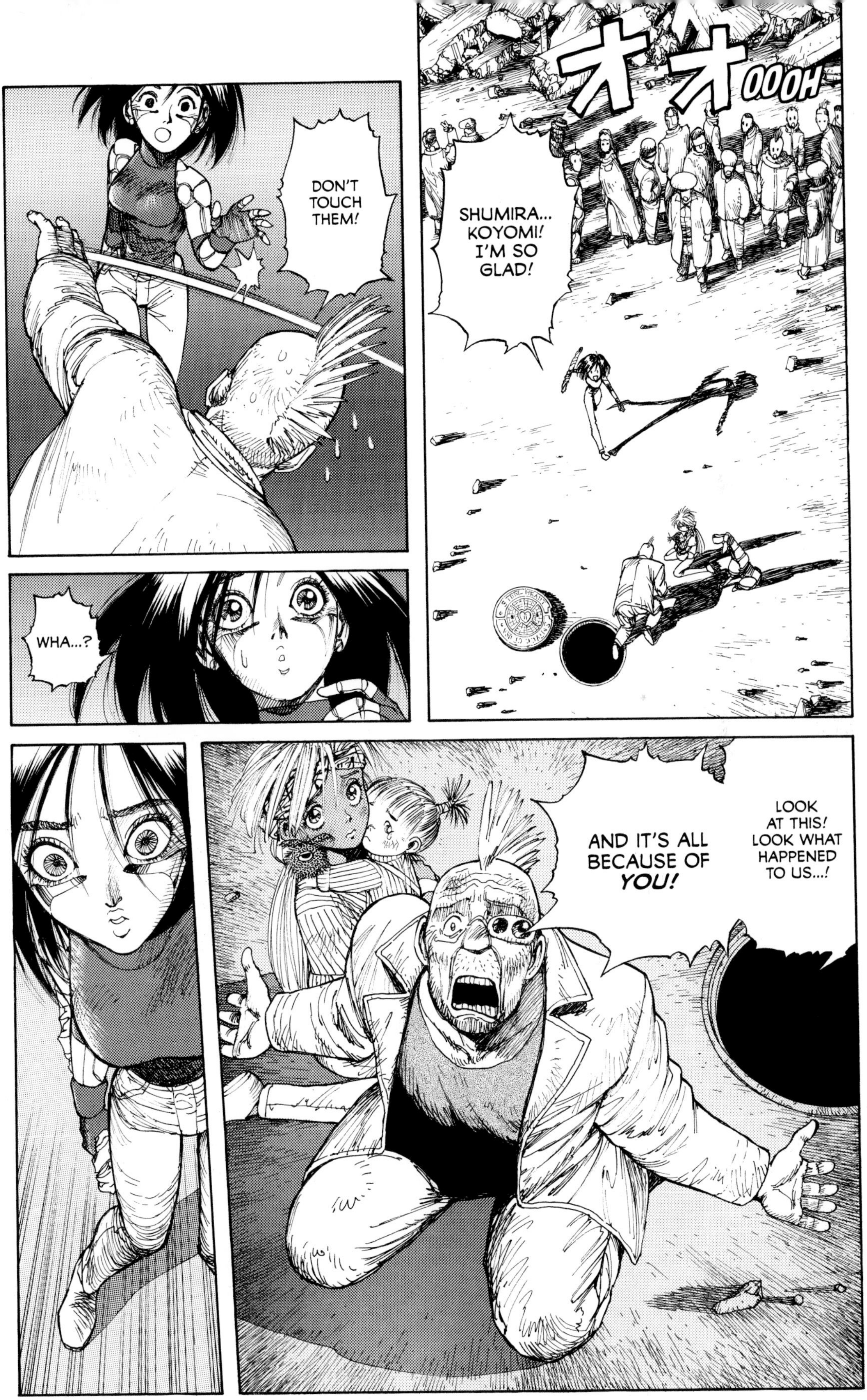
オオ OOOH
SHUMIRA... KOYOMI! I'M SO GLAD!
DON'T TOUCH THEM!
WHA...?
LOOK AT THIS! LOOK WHAT HAPPENED TO US...!
AND IT'S ALL BECAUSE OF *YOU!*

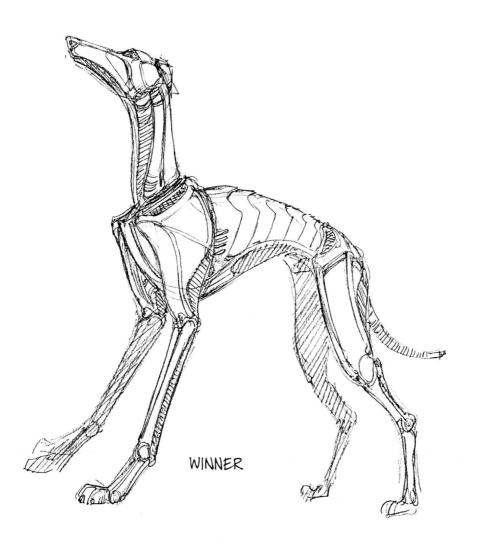

WINNER

FIGHT_027 Scapegoat

Sign: Daisuke Ido Repairs • Cyborgs, Androids, Robots; Repairs, Tuning & Maintenance for all models!

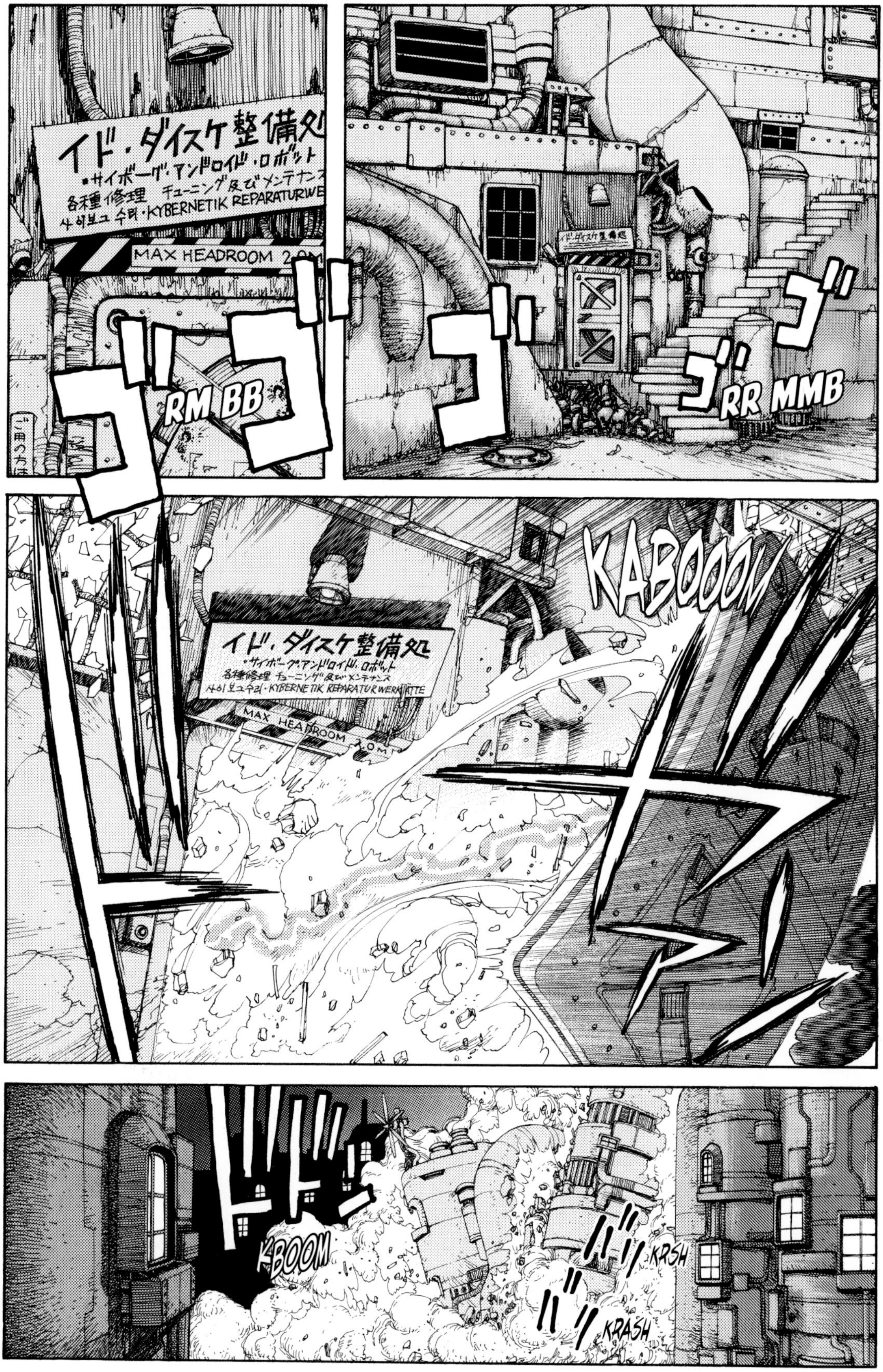
ゴゴ
RR MMB
イド・ダイスケ整備処
ゴゴ
ゴゴ
RM BB
イド・ダイスケ整備処
•サイボーグ・アンドロイド・ロボット
各種修理 チューニング及びメンテナンス
사이보그 수리・KYBERNETIK REPARATURWE
MAX HEADROOM 2.0M
KABOOOM
ドガ
イド・ダイスケ整備処
•サイボーグ・アンドロイド・ロボット
各種修理 チューニング及びメンテナンス
사이보그 수리・KYBERNETIK REPARATURWERKSTATTE
MAX HEADROOM 2.0M
ドドドド
KBOOM
バババ
KRSH
KRASH

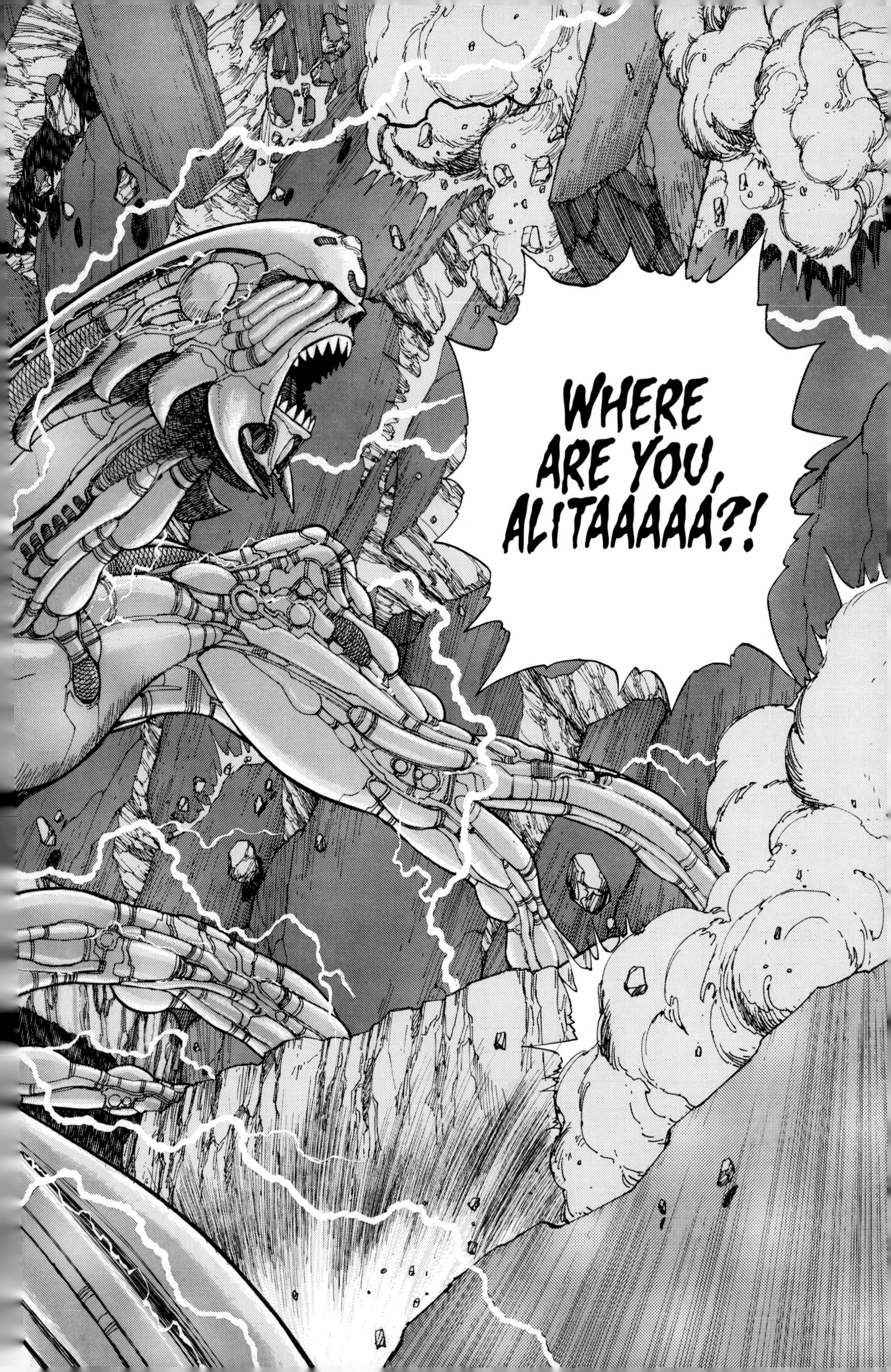
WHERE ARE YOU, ALITAAAAA?!

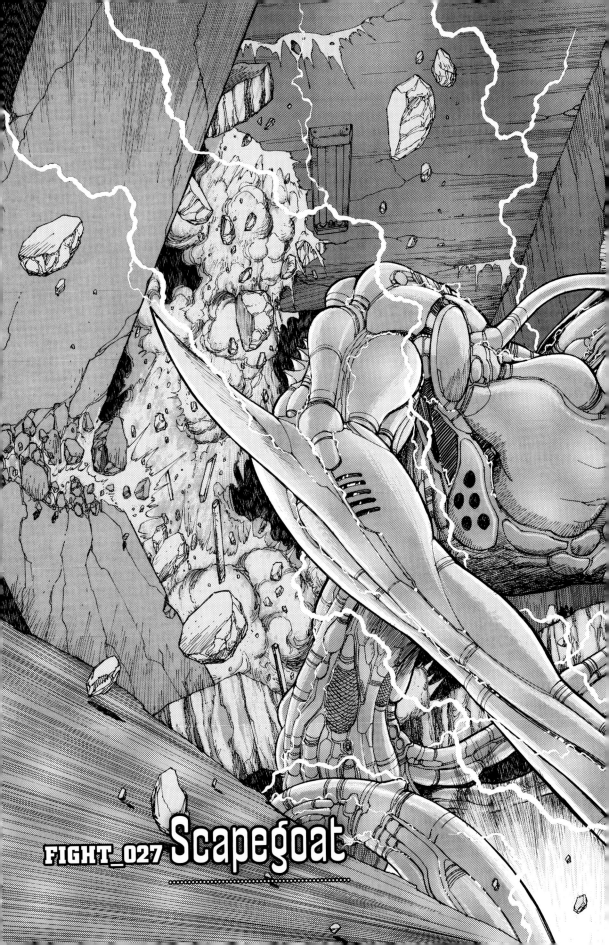

FIGHT_027 Scapegoat

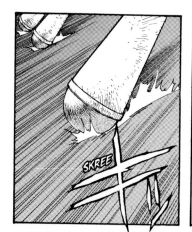

SKREE

KABOOOM トゴゴォノ！

GOOD GRIEF, WHAT'S WITH ALL THE RACKET?!

THEY DOIN' NIGHTTIME CON-STRUC-TION?!

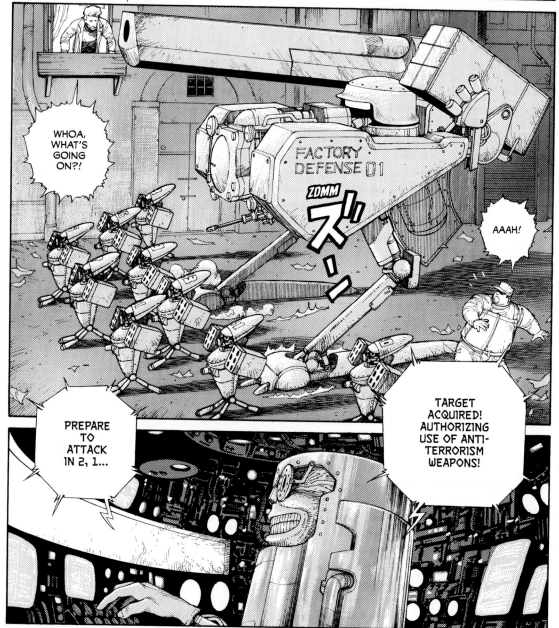

WHOA, WHAT'S GOING ON?!

FACTORY DEFENSE 01

ZDMM ズーン

AAAH!

TARGET ACQUIRED! AUTHORIZING USE OF ANTI-TERRORISM WEAPONS!

PREPARE TO ATTACK IN 2, 1...

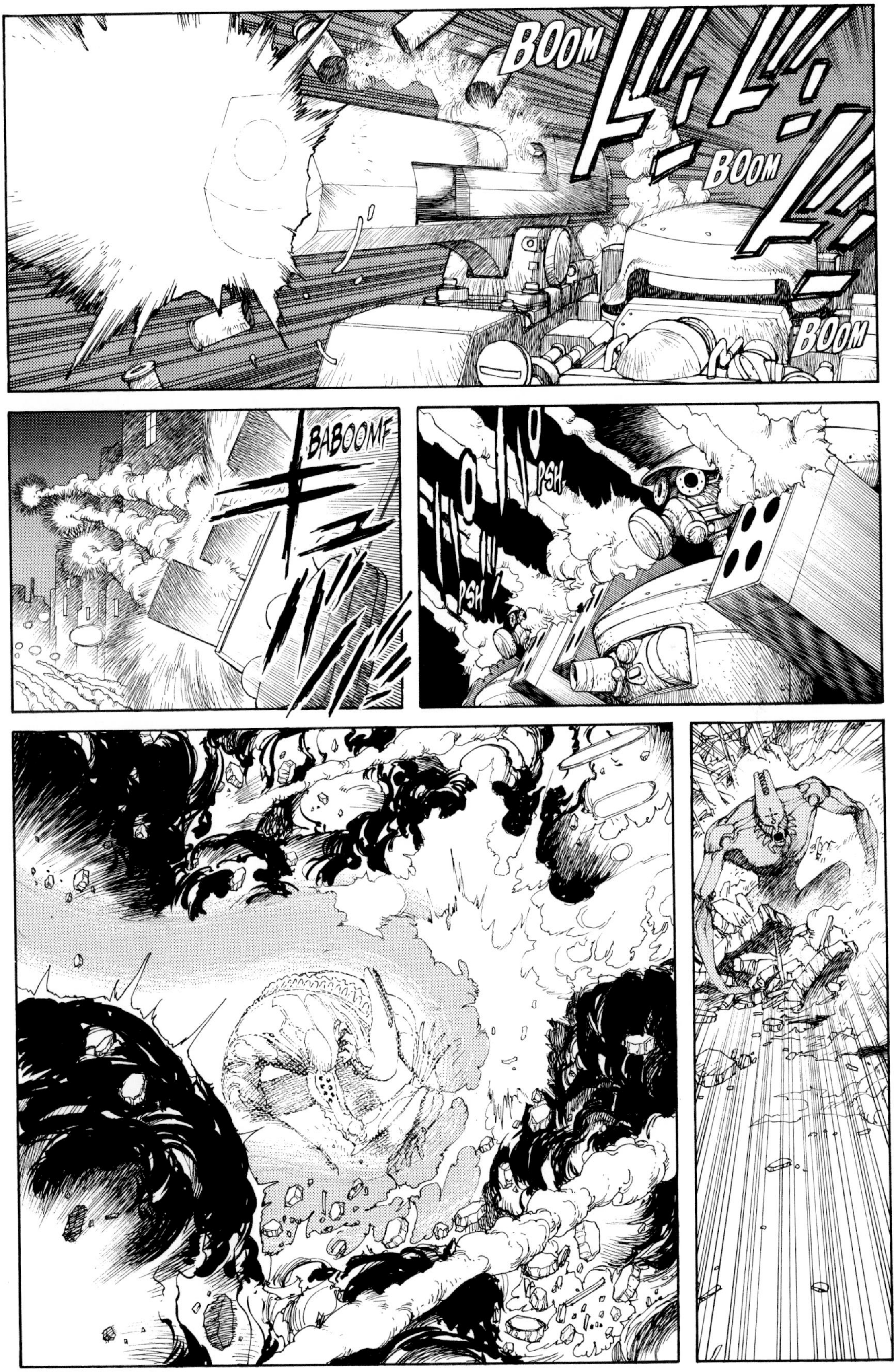
BOOM
BOOM
BOOM
PSH
PSH
BABOOMF

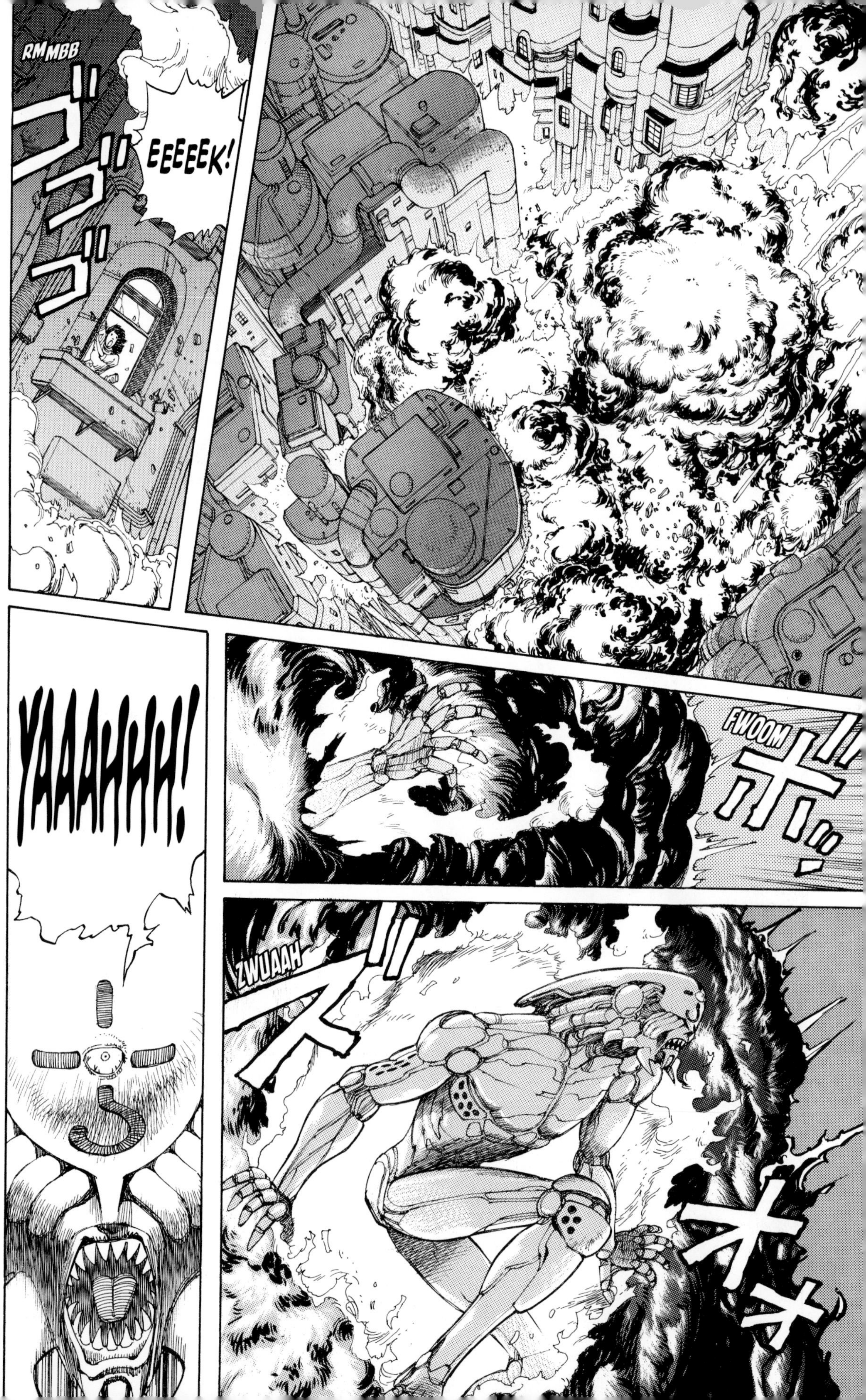
RMMBB
ゴゴゴ
EEEEEK!
FWOOM
ボッ
ZWUAAH
ズオオ
YAAAHHH!

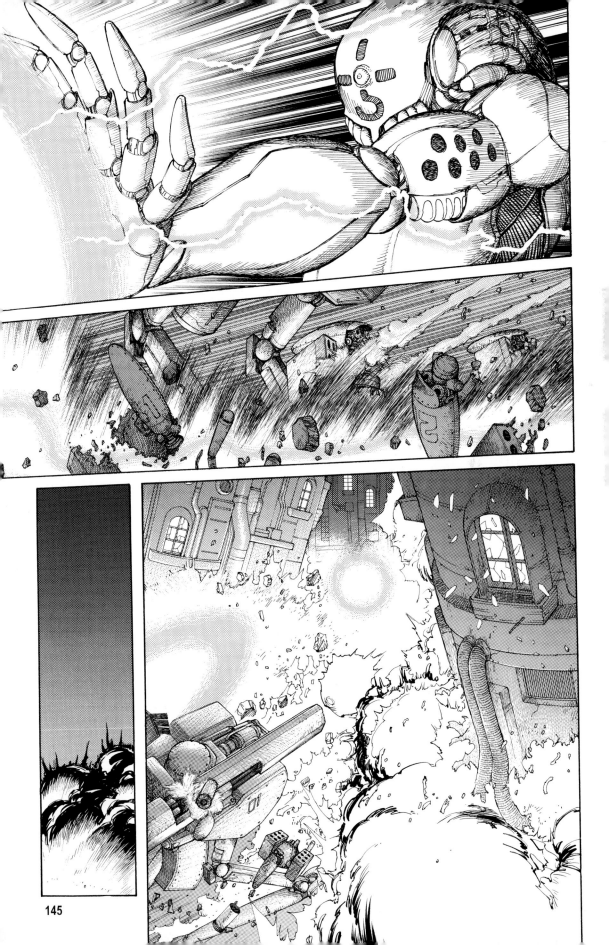

145

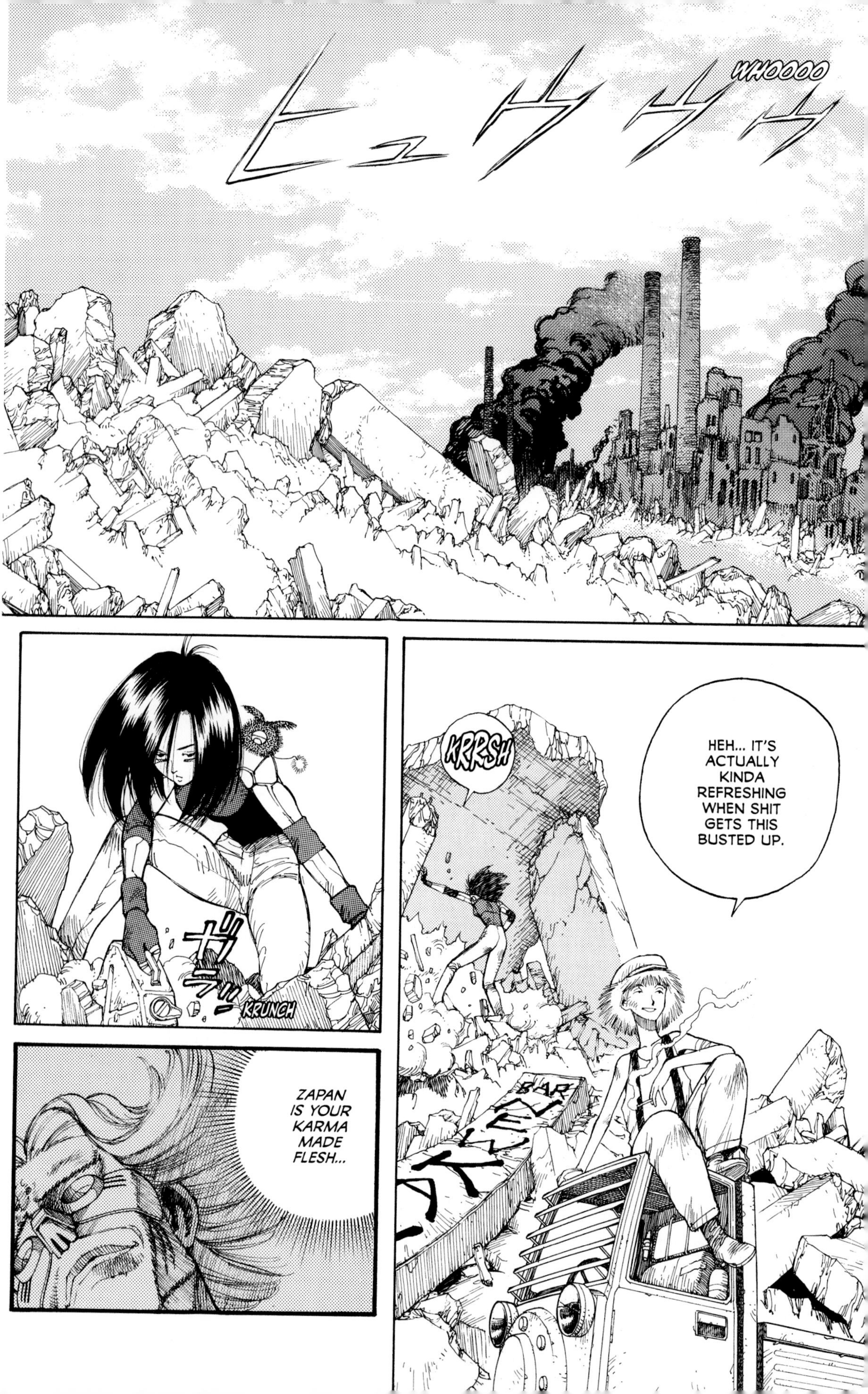
WHOOOO
KRRSH
HEH... IT'S ACTUALLY KINDA REFRESHING WHEN SHIT GETS THIS BUSTED UP.
KRUNCH
ZAPAN IS YOUR KARMA MADE FLESH...

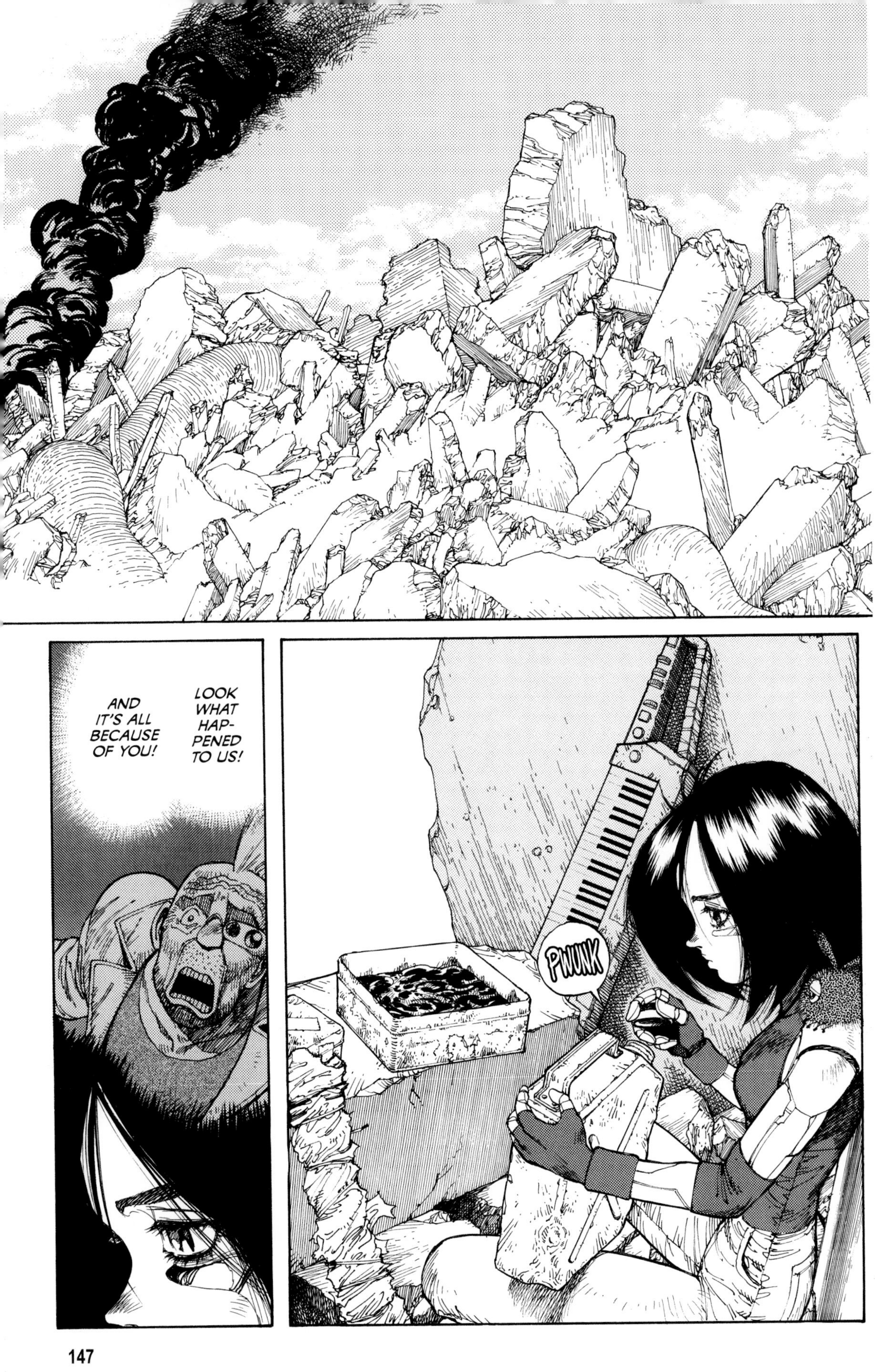
PWUNK
LOOK WHAT HAP-PENED TO US!
AND IT'S ALL BECAUSE OF YOU!

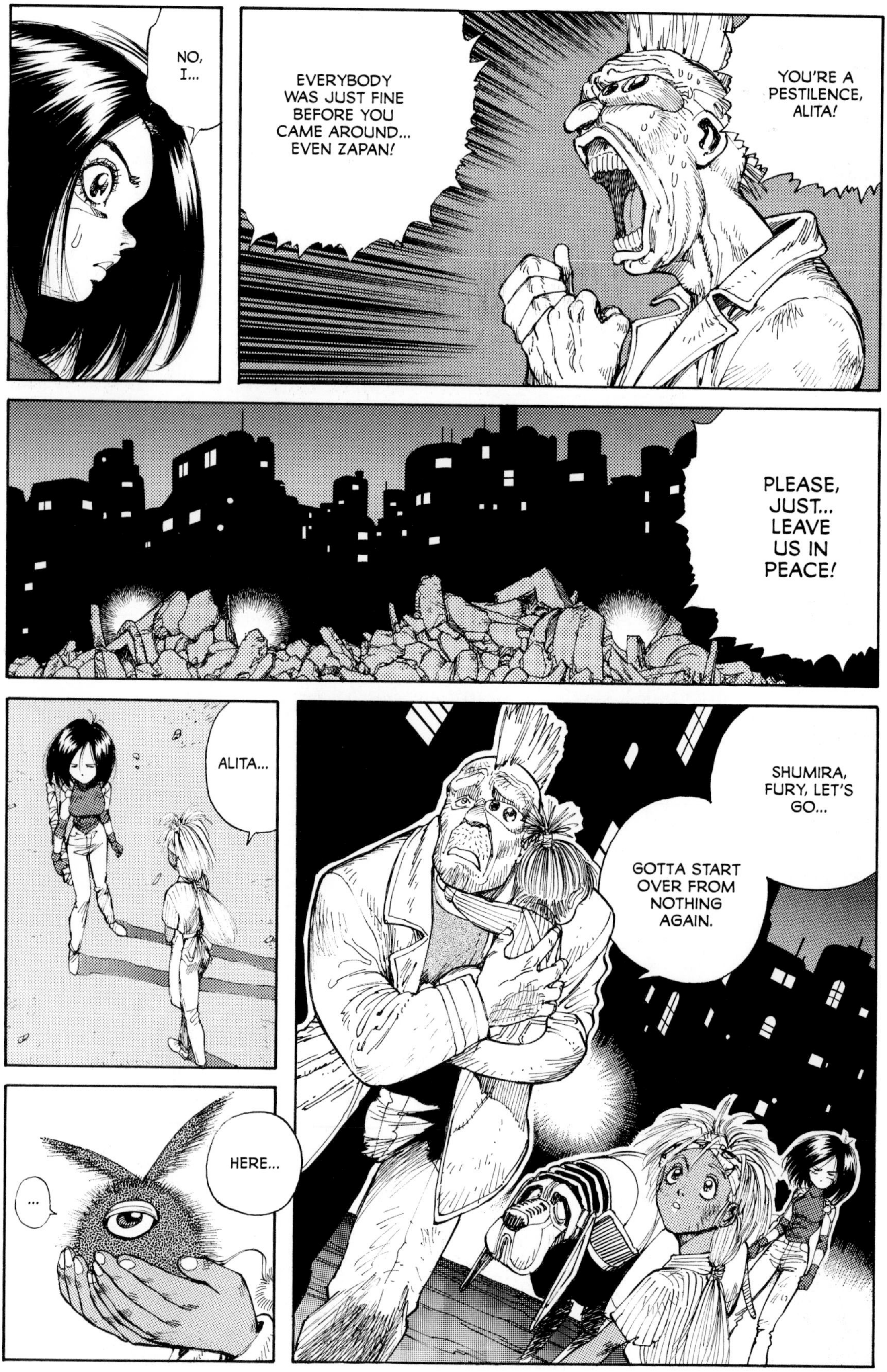
YOU'RE A PESTILENCE, ALITA!
EVERYBODY WAS JUST FINE BEFORE YOU CAME AROUND... EVEN ZAPAN!
NO, I...
PLEASE, JUST... LEAVE US IN PEACE!
SHUMIRA, FURY, LET'S GO...
GOTTA START OVER FROM NOTHING AGAIN.
ALITA...
HERE...
...

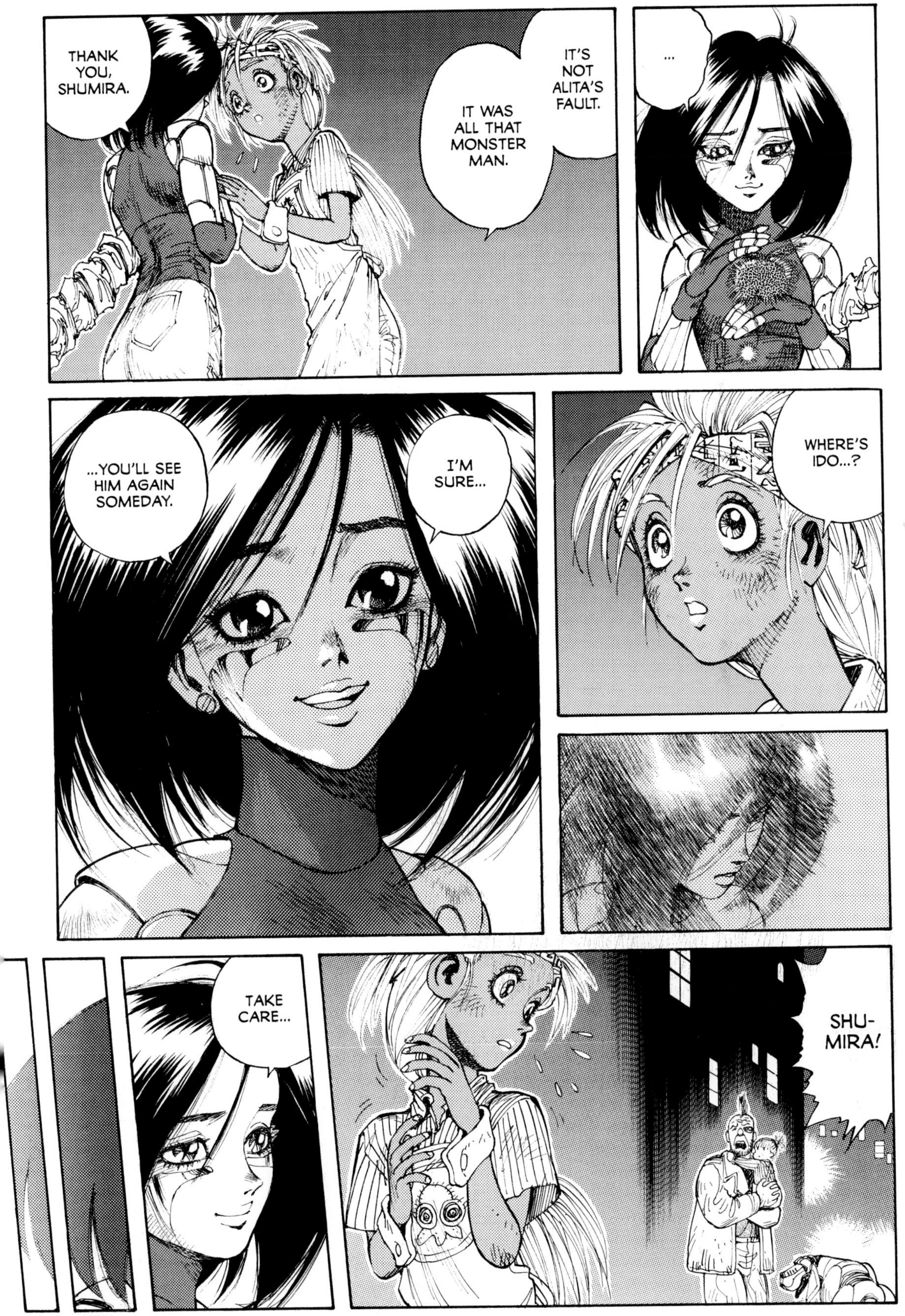
...
IT'S NOT ALITA'S FAULT.
IT WAS ALL THAT MONSTER MAN.
THANK YOU, SHUMIRA.
WHERE'S IDO...?
I'M SURE...
...YOU'LL SEE HIM AGAIN SOMEDAY.
SHU-MIRA!
TAKE CARE...

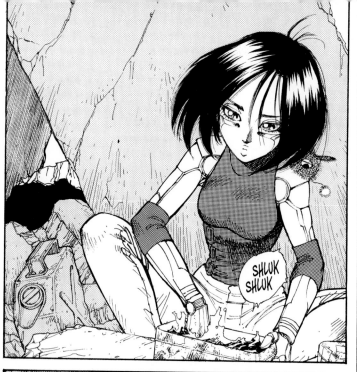

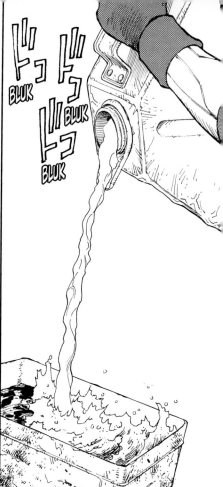

BLUK
BLUK
BLUK
SHLUK SHLUK
I'M ALL ALONE.
...
I'M REALLY ALL ALONE THIS TIME...
UP UNTIL THIS POINT, I'VE ALWAYS GIVEN MY ALL TO DO WHAT WAS RIGHT.
SO HOW DID THINGS TURN OUT SO, SO BAD...?

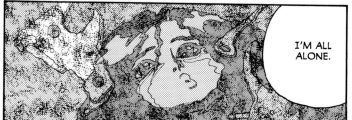

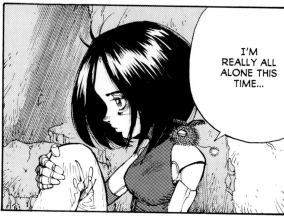

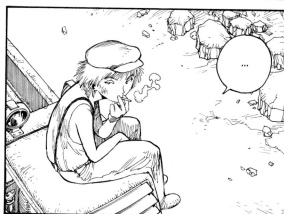

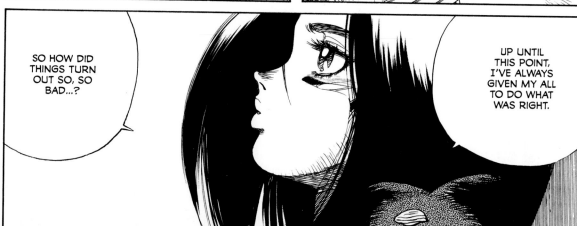

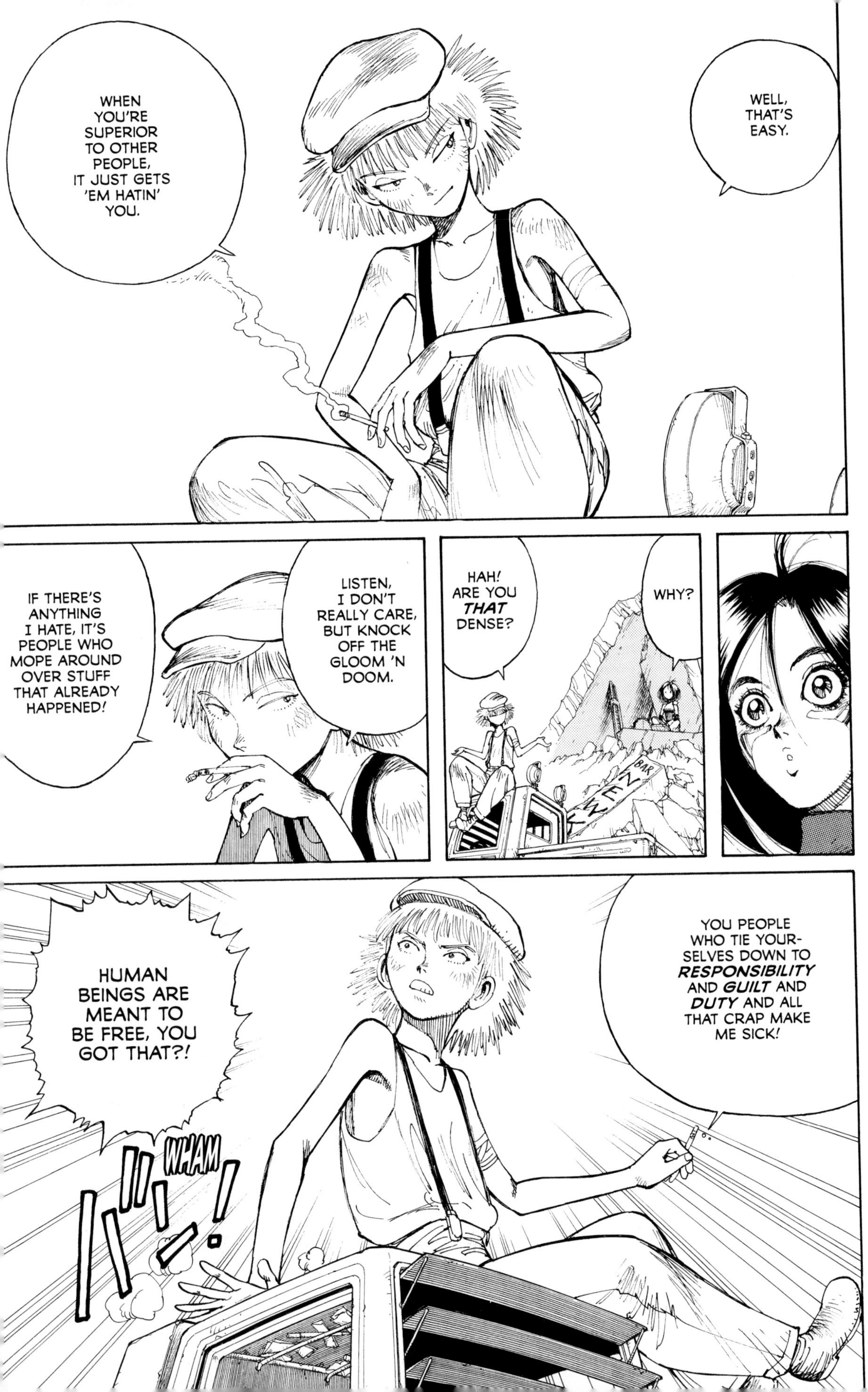
WELL, THAT'S EASY.
WHEN YOU'RE SUPERIOR TO OTHER PEOPLE, IT JUST GETS 'EM HATIN' YOU.
WHY?
HAH! ARE YOU *THAT* DENSE?
LISTEN, I DON'T REALLY CARE, BUT KNOCK OFF THE GLOOM 'N DOOM.
IF THERE'S ANYTHING I HATE, IT'S PEOPLE WHO MOPE AROUND OVER STUFF THAT ALREADY HAPPENED!
YOU PEOPLE WHO TIE YOUR-SELVES DOWN TO ***RESPONSIBILITY*** AND ***GUILT*** AND ***DUTY*** AND ALL THAT CRAP MAKE ME SICK!
HUMAN BEINGS ARE MEANT TO BE FREE, YOU GOT THAT?!
WHAM

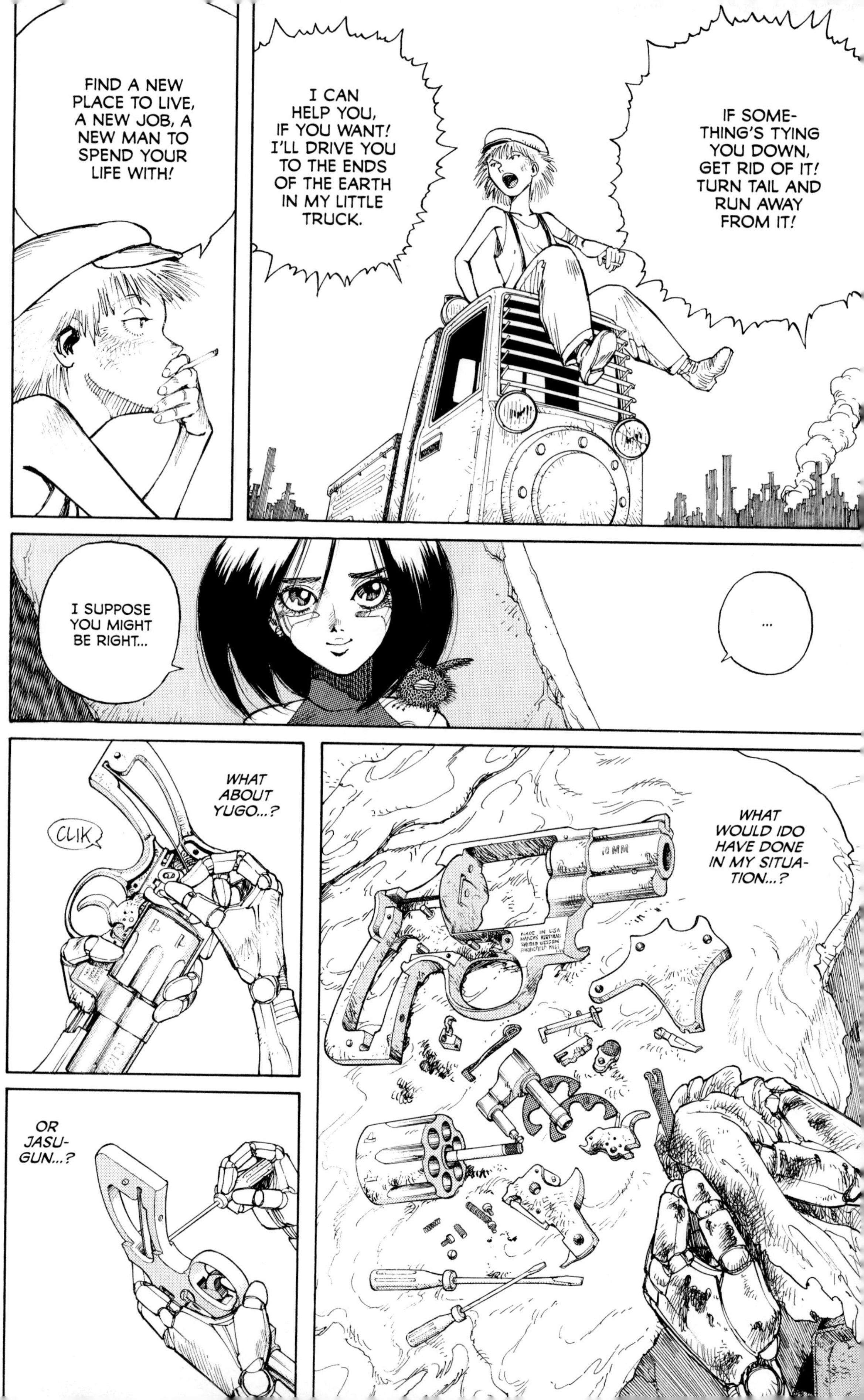
IF SOME-THING'S TYING YOU DOWN, GET RID OF IT! TURN TAIL AND RUN AWAY FROM IT!
I CAN HELP YOU, IF YOU WANT! I'LL DRIVE YOU TO THE ENDS OF THE EARTH IN MY LITTLE TRUCK.
FIND A NEW PLACE TO LIVE, A NEW JOB, A NEW MAN TO SPEND YOUR LIFE WITH!
...
I SUPPOSE YOU MIGHT BE RIGHT...
WHAT WOULD IDO HAVE DONE IN MY SITUA-TION...?
WHAT ABOUT YUGO...?
CLIK
OR JASU-GUN...?

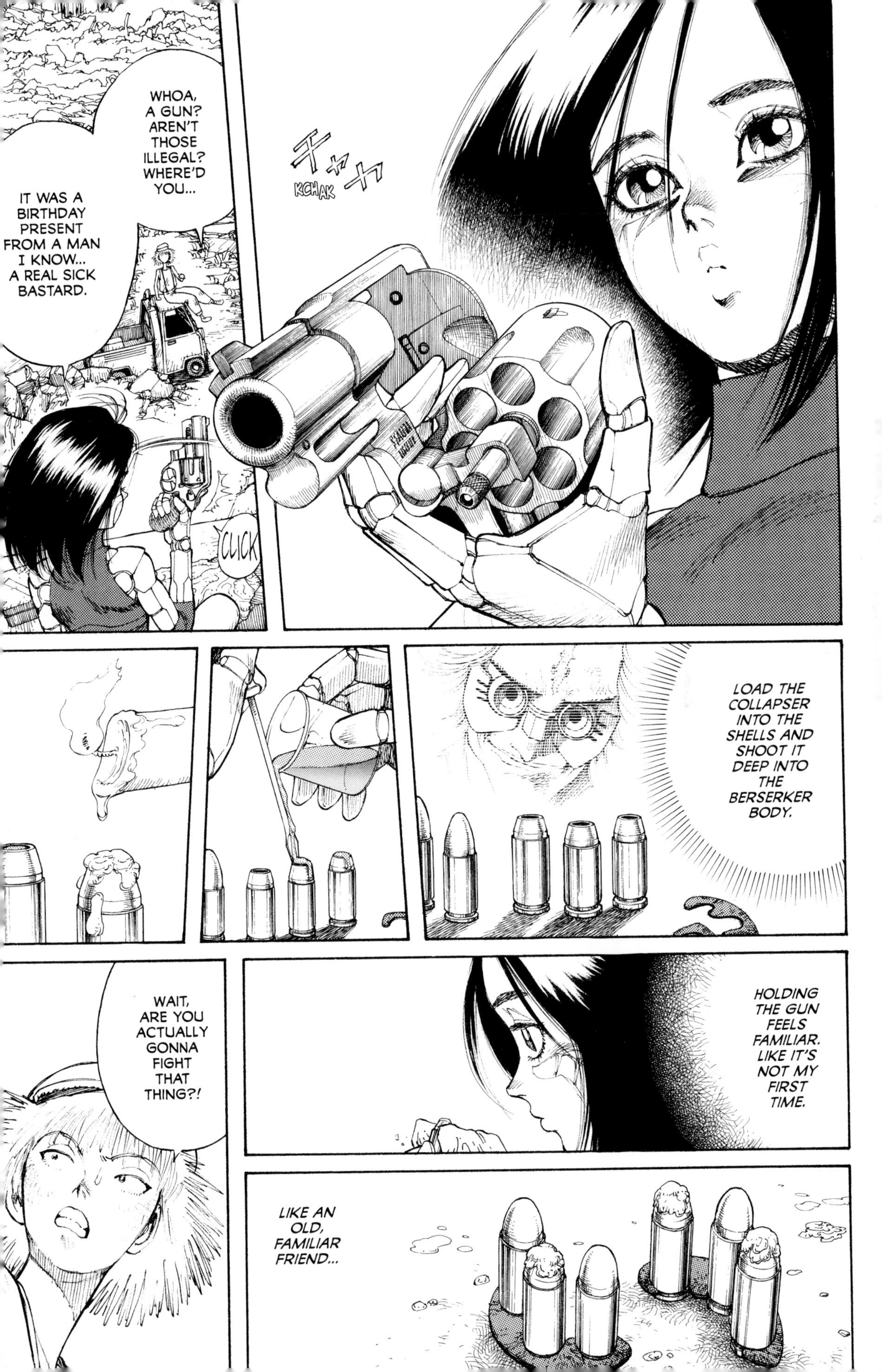
チャカ
KCHAK
WHOA, A GUN? AREN'T THOSE ILLEGAL? WHERE'D YOU...
IT WAS A BIRTHDAY PRESENT FROM A MAN I KNOW... A REAL SICK BASTARD.
CLICK
LOAD THE COLLAPSER INTO THE SHELLS AND SHOOT IT DEEP INTO THE BERSERKER BODY.
HOLDING THE GUN FEELS FAMILIAR. LIKE IT'S NOT MY FIRST TIME.
LIKE AN OLD, FAMILIAR FRIEND...
WAIT, ARE YOU ACTUALLY GONNA FIGHT THAT THING?!

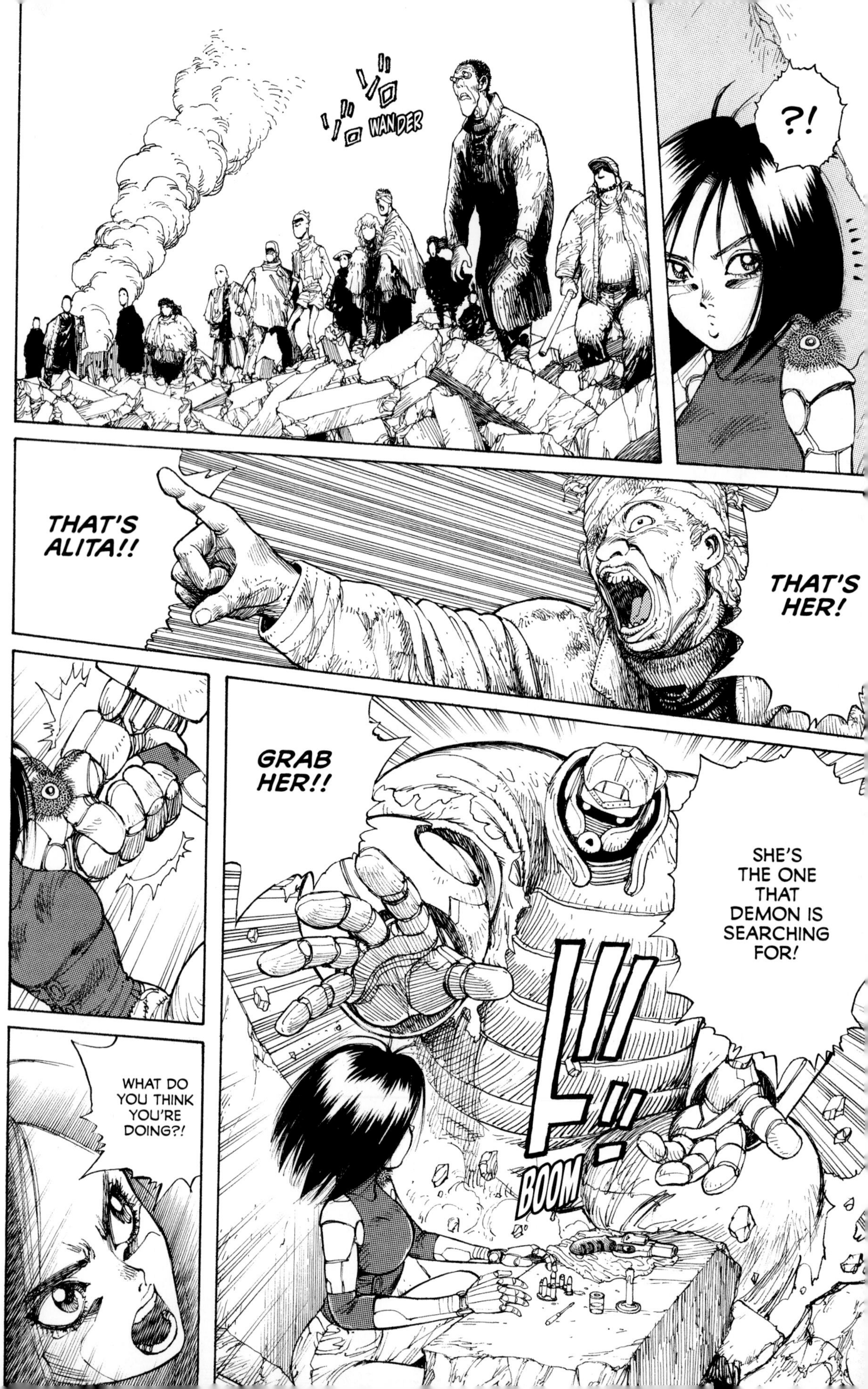
?!
WANDER
THAT'S ALITA!!
THAT'S HER!
SHE'S THE ONE THAT DEMON IS SEARCHING FOR!
GRAB HER!!
BOOM
WHAT DO YOU THINK YOU'RE DOING?!

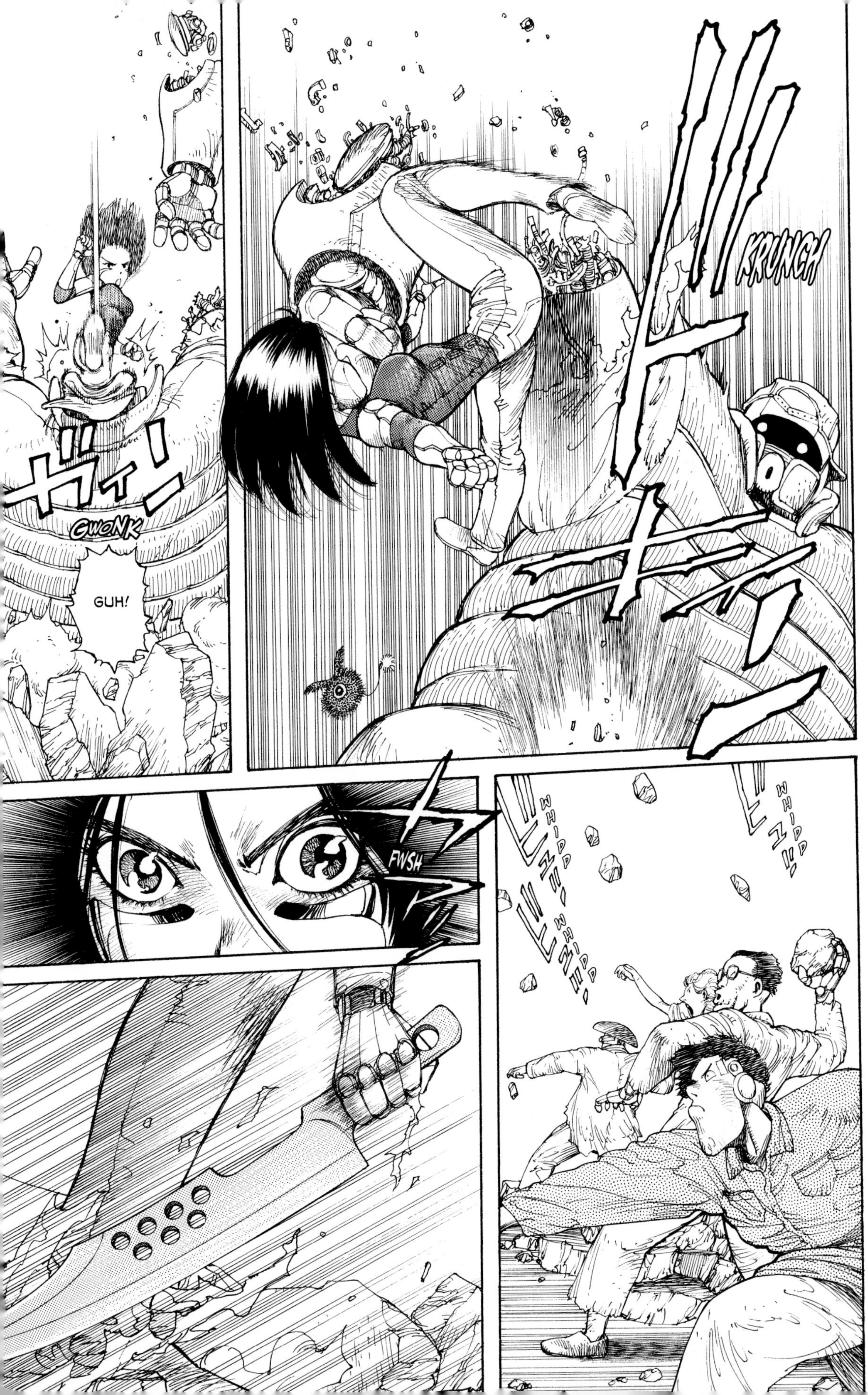
KRUNCH
ヴィー
GWONK
GUH!
WHIPP
WHIPP
WHIPP
FWSH

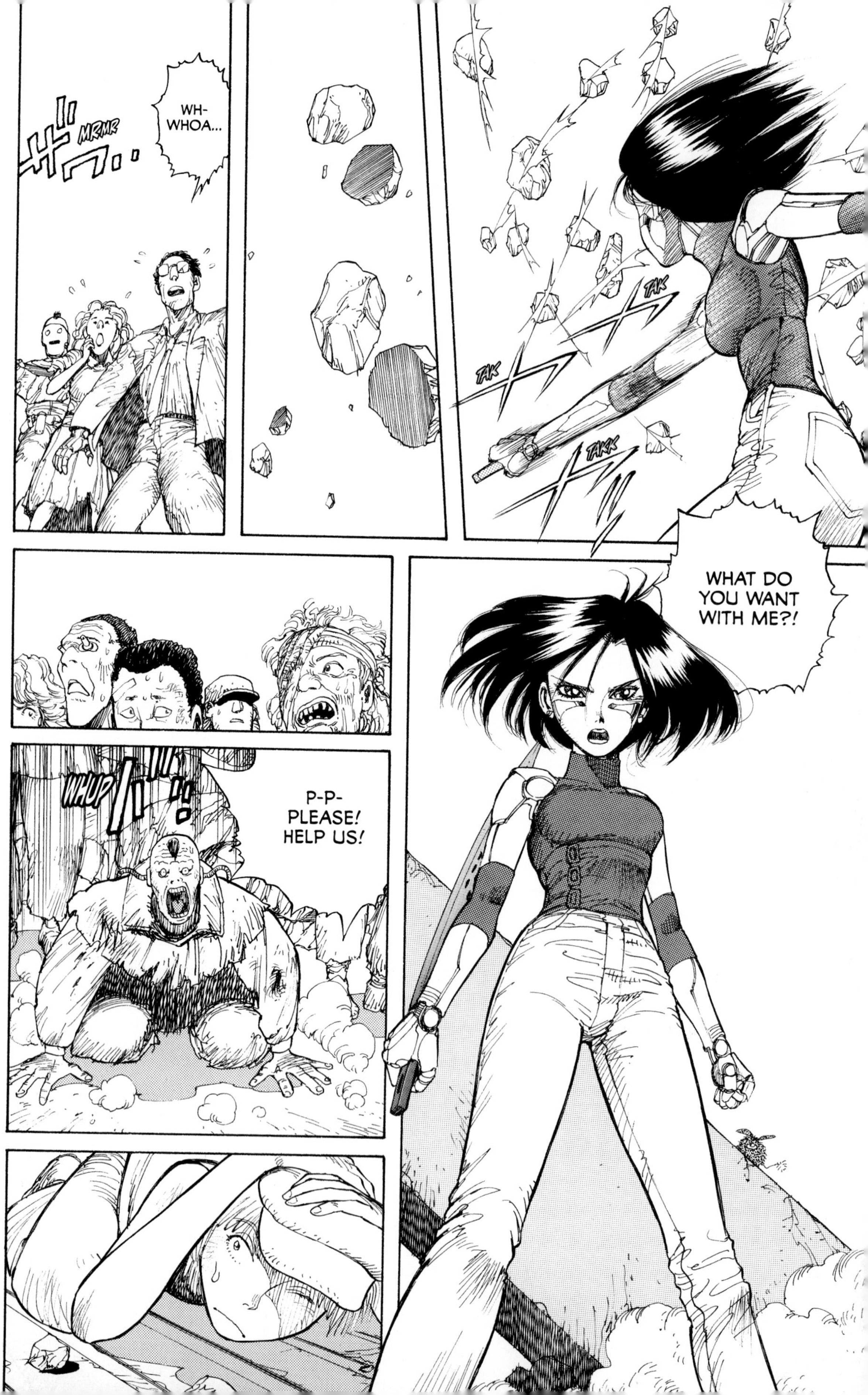
TAK
TAK
TAKK
MRMR
WH- WHOA...
WHAT DO YOU WANT WITH ME?!
WHUP
P-P- PLEASE! HELP US!

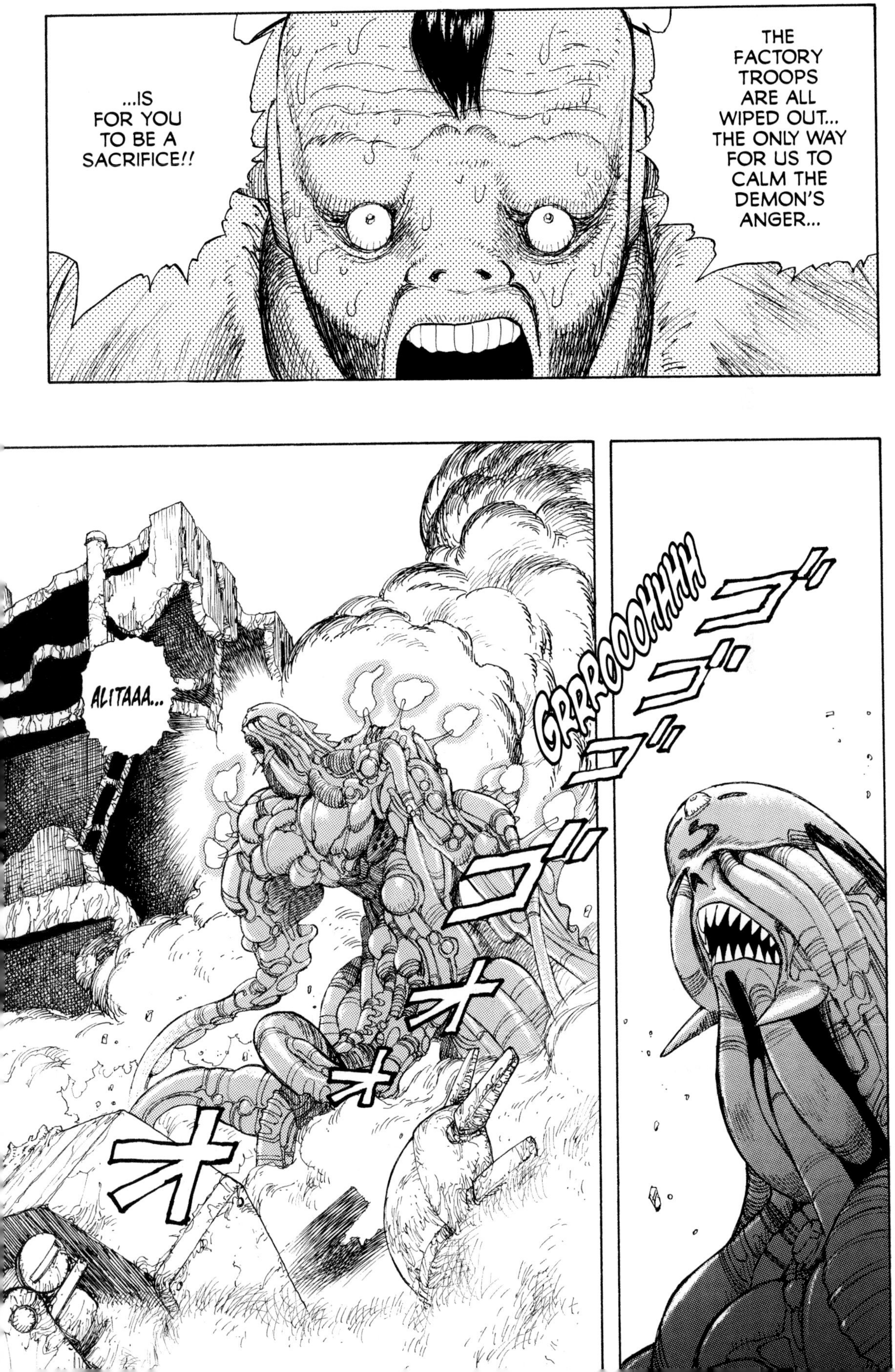
THE FACTORY TROOPS ARE ALL WIPED OUT... THE ONLY WAY FOR US TO CALM THE DEMON'S ANGER...
...IS FOR YOU TO BE A SACRIFICE!!
GRRROOOHHHH
ALITAAA...

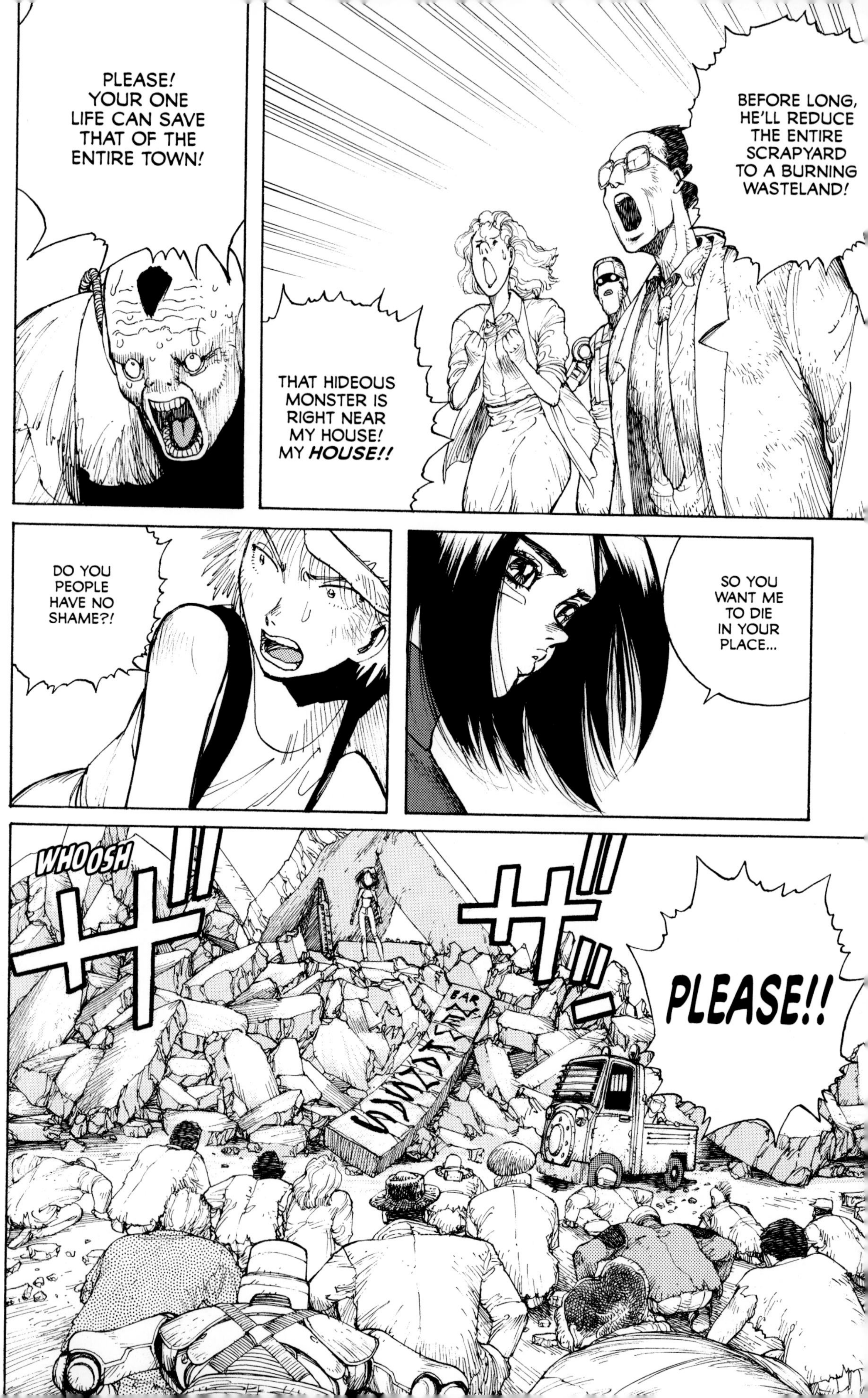
BEFORE LONG, HE'LL REDUCE THE ENTIRE SCRAPYARD TO A BURNING WASTELAND!
THAT HIDEOUS MONSTER IS RIGHT NEAR MY HOUSE! MY ***HOUSE!!***
PLEASE! YOUR ONE LIFE CAN SAVE THAT OF THE ENTIRE TOWN!
SO YOU WANT ME TO DIE IN YOUR PLACE...
DO YOU PEOPLE HAVE NO SHAME?!
PLEASE!!
WHOOSH

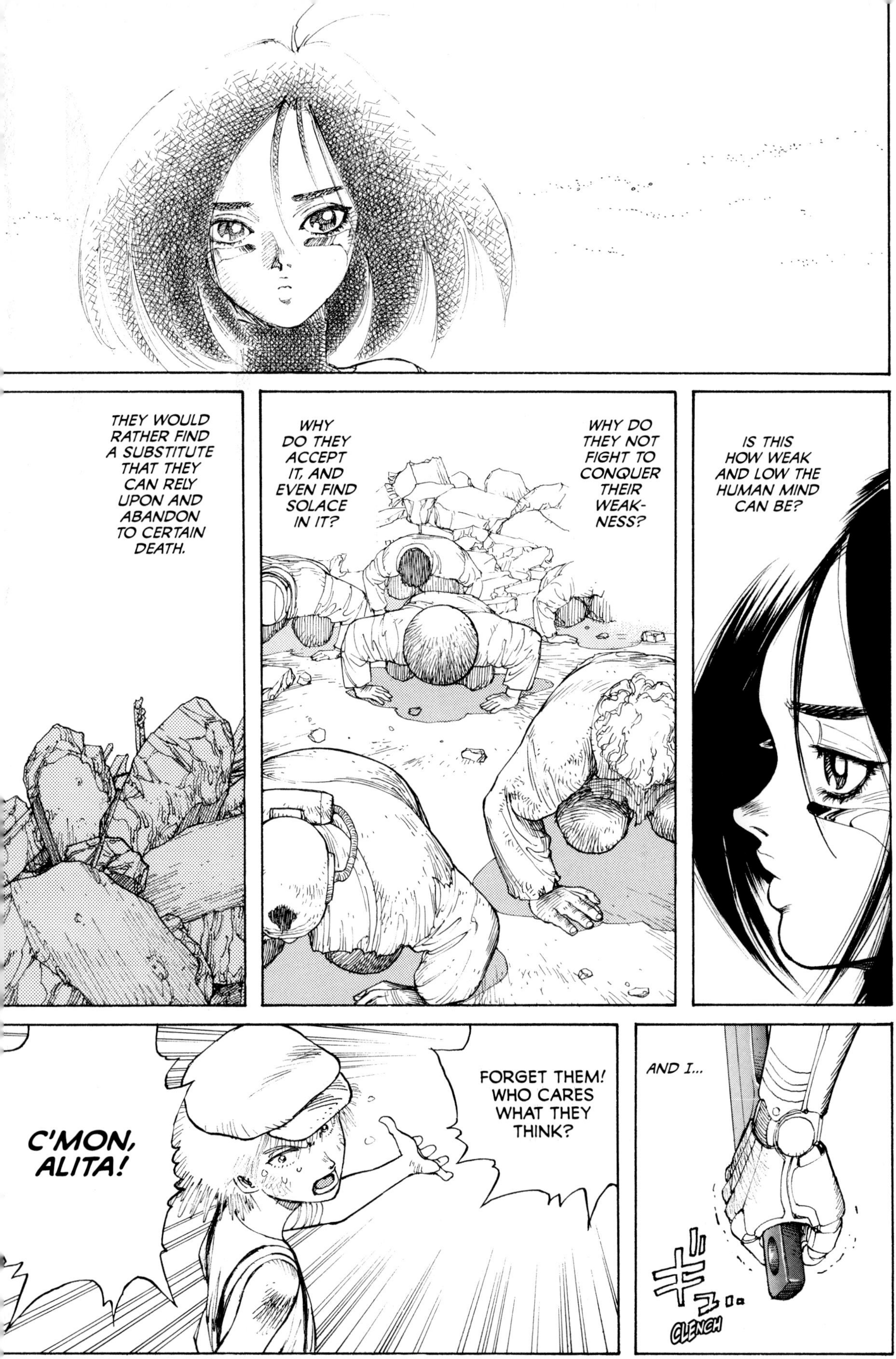
IS THIS HOW WEAK AND LOW THE HUMAN MIND CAN BE?
WHY DO THEY NOT FIGHT TO CONQUER THEIR WEAK-NESS?
WHY DO THEY ACCEPT IT, AND EVEN FIND SOLACE IN IT?
THEY WOULD RATHER FIND A SUBSTITUTE THAT THEY CAN RELY UPON AND ABANDON TO CERTAIN DEATH.
AND I...
CLENCH
FORGET THEM! WHO CARES WHAT THEY THINK?
C'MON, ALITA!

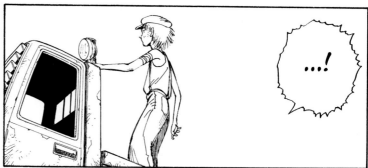

"The goat will carry on itself all their sins to a remote place; and the man shall release it in the wilderness."
-Leviticus 16:22

FIGHT_028 Face the Facts

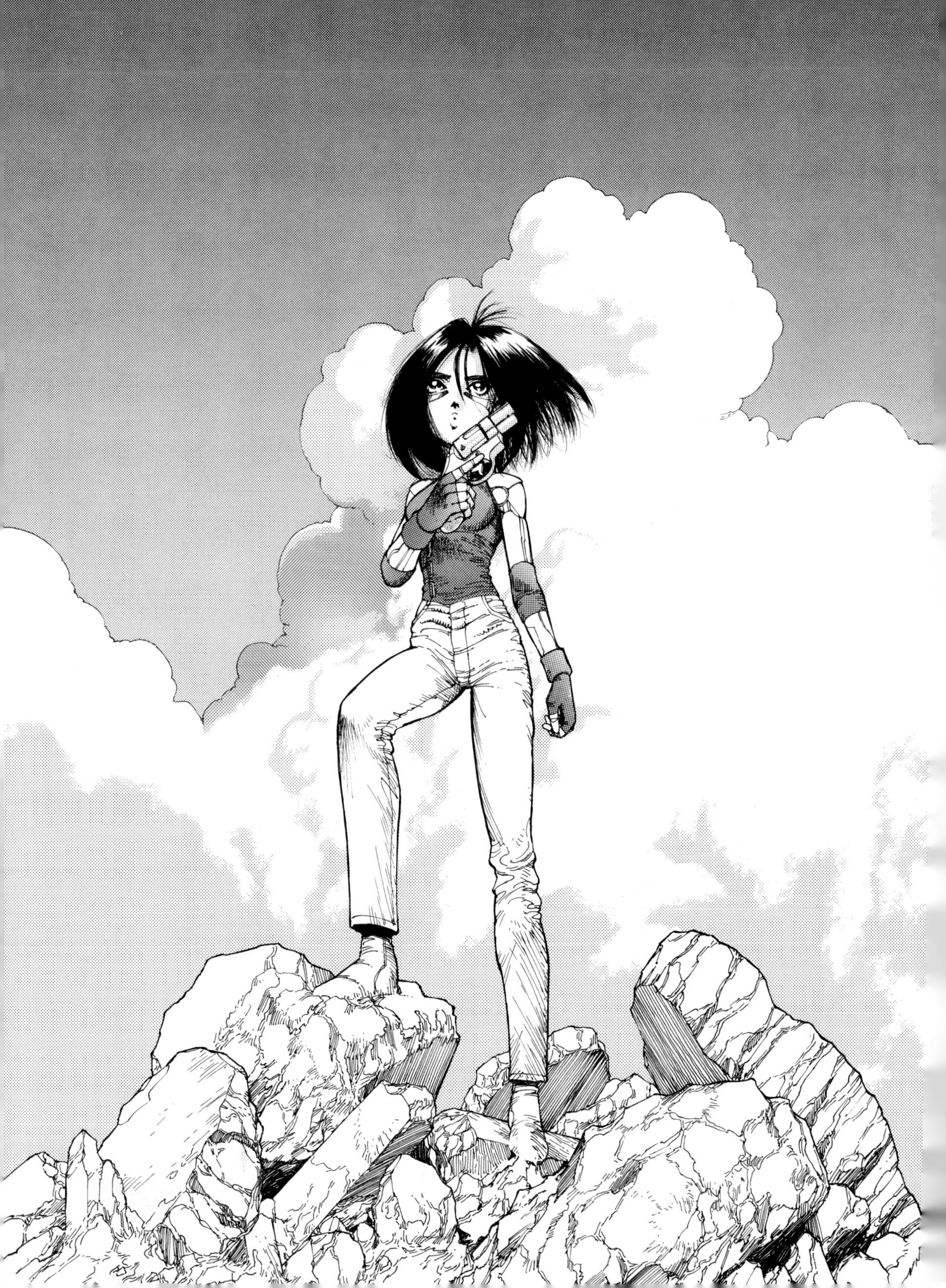

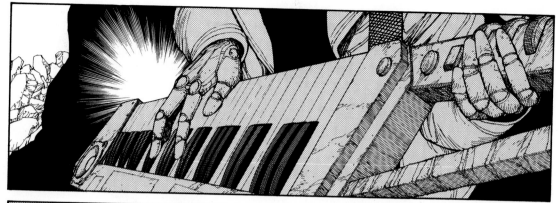

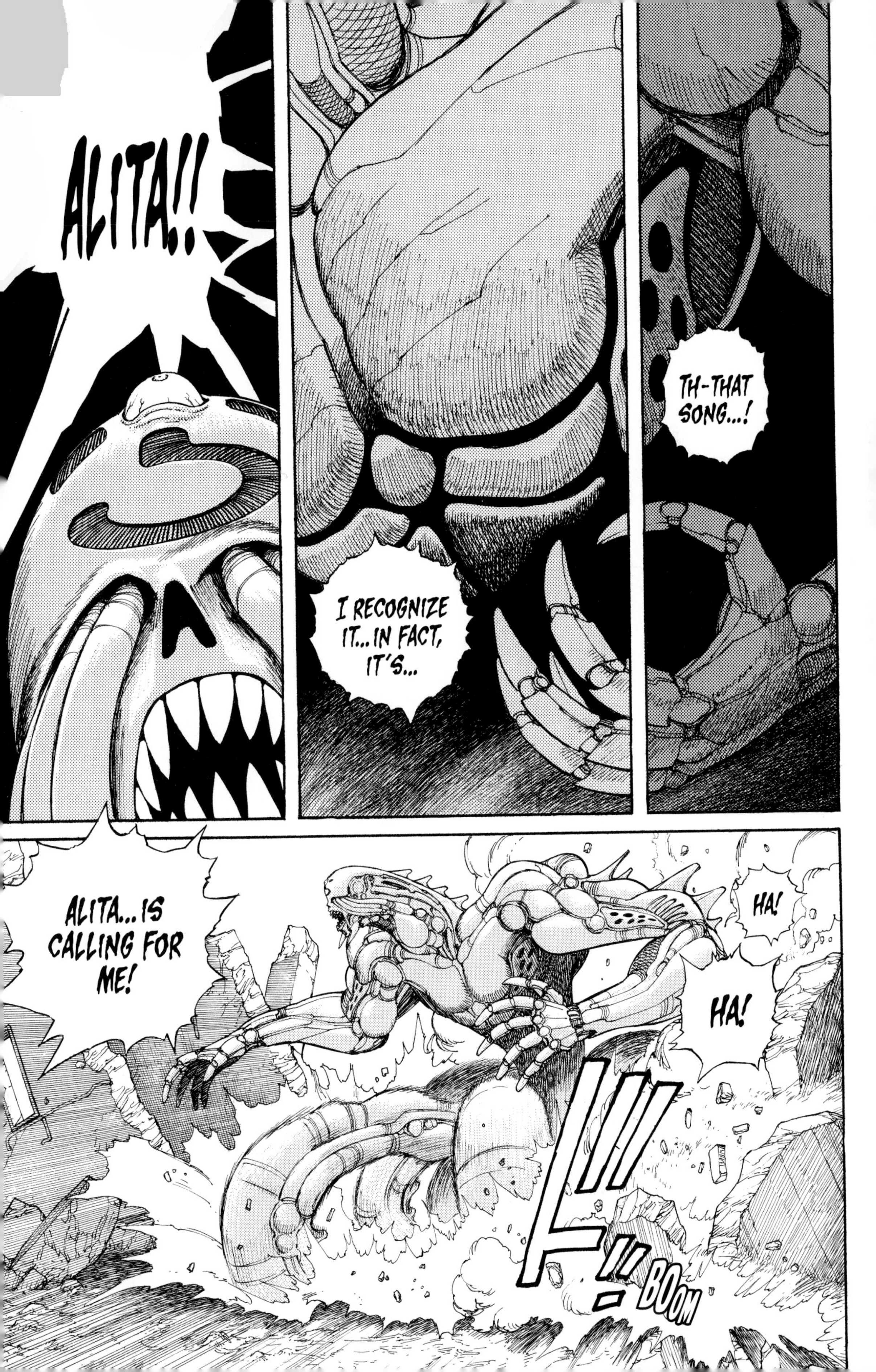
TH-THAT SONG...!
I RECOGNIZE IT... IN FACT, IT'S...
ALITA!!
HA!
HA!
ALITA... IS CALLING FOR ME!
BOOM

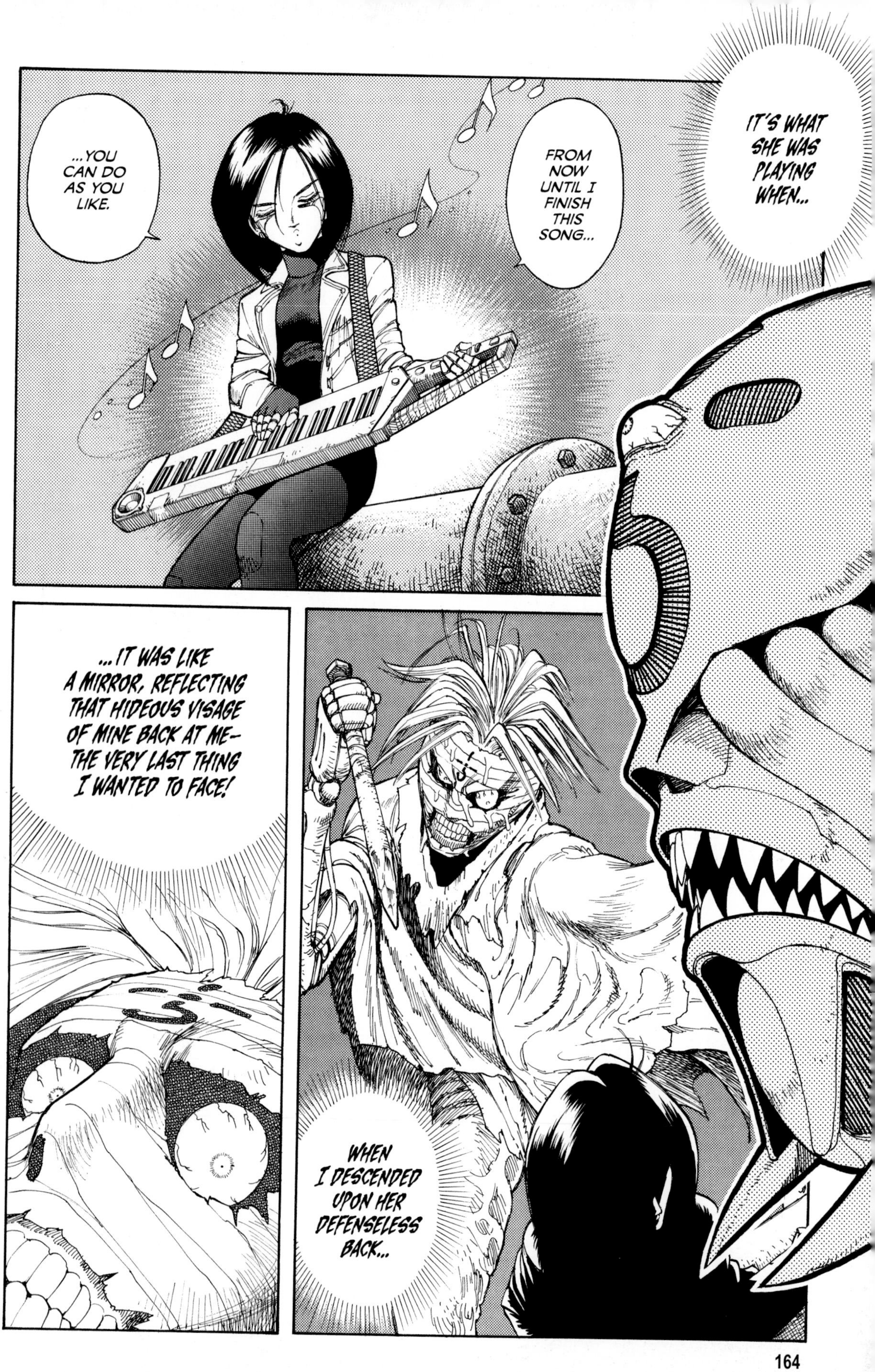
IT'S WHAT SHE WAS PLAYING WHEN...
FROM NOW UNTIL I FINISH THIS SONG...
...YOU CAN DO AS YOU LIKE.
WHEN I DESCENDED UPON HER DEFENSELESS BACK...
...IT WAS LIKE A MIRROR, REFLECTING THAT HIDEOUS VISAGE OF MINE BACK AT ME—THE VERY LAST THING I WANTED TO FACE!

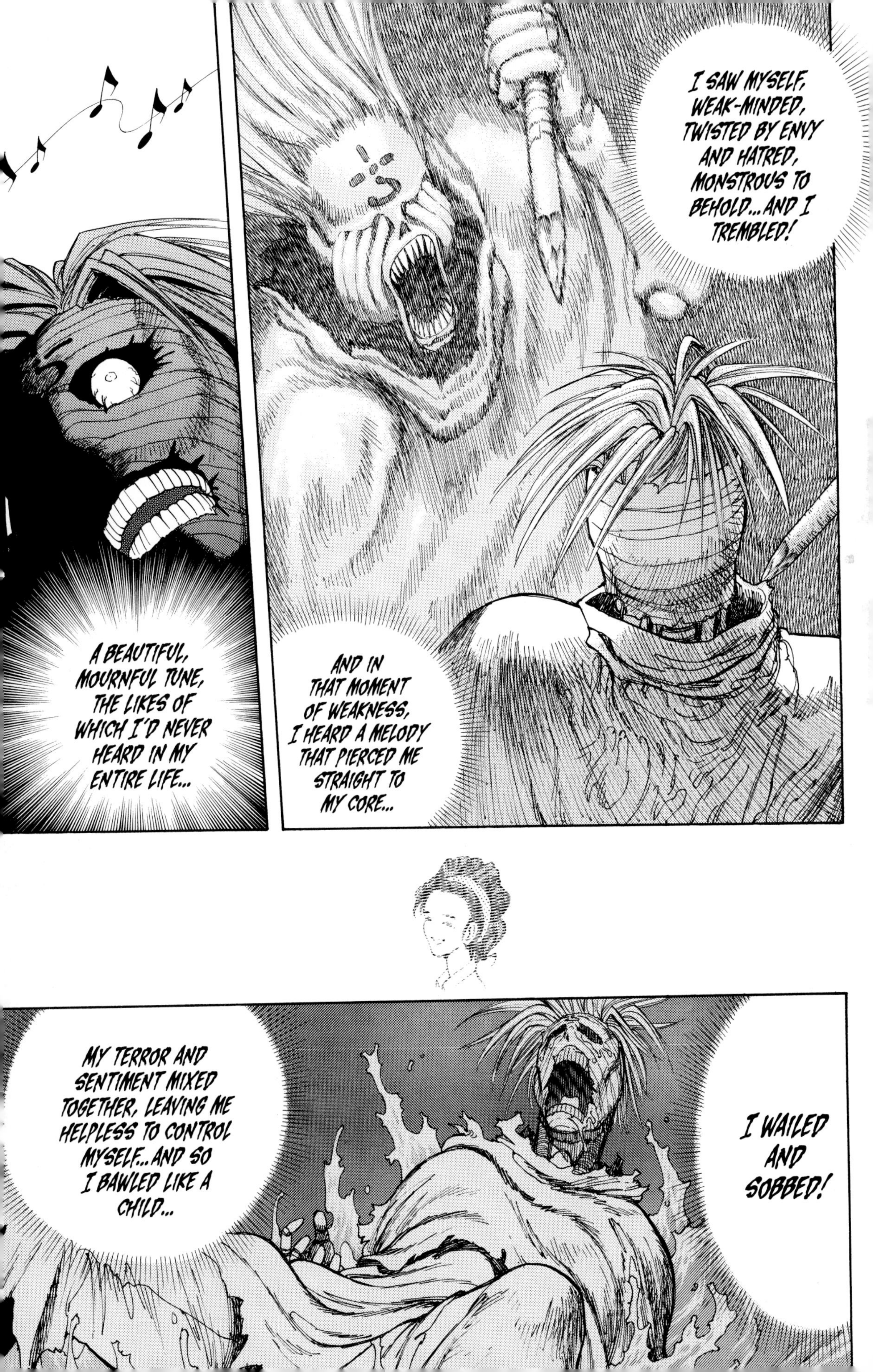
I SAW MYSELF, WEAK-MINDED, TWISTED BY ENVY AND HATRED, MONSTROUS TO BEHOLD...AND I TREMBLED!
AND IN THAT MOMENT OF WEAKNESS, I HEARD A MELODY THAT PIERCED ME STRAIGHT TO MY CORE...
A BEAUTIFUL, MOURNFUL TUNE, THE LIKES OF WHICH I'D NEVER HEARD IN MY ENTIRE LIFE...
I WAILED AND SOBBED!
MY TERROR AND SENTIMENT MIXED TOGETHER, LEAVING ME HELPLESS TO CONTROL MYSELF...AND SO I BAWLED LIKE A CHILD...

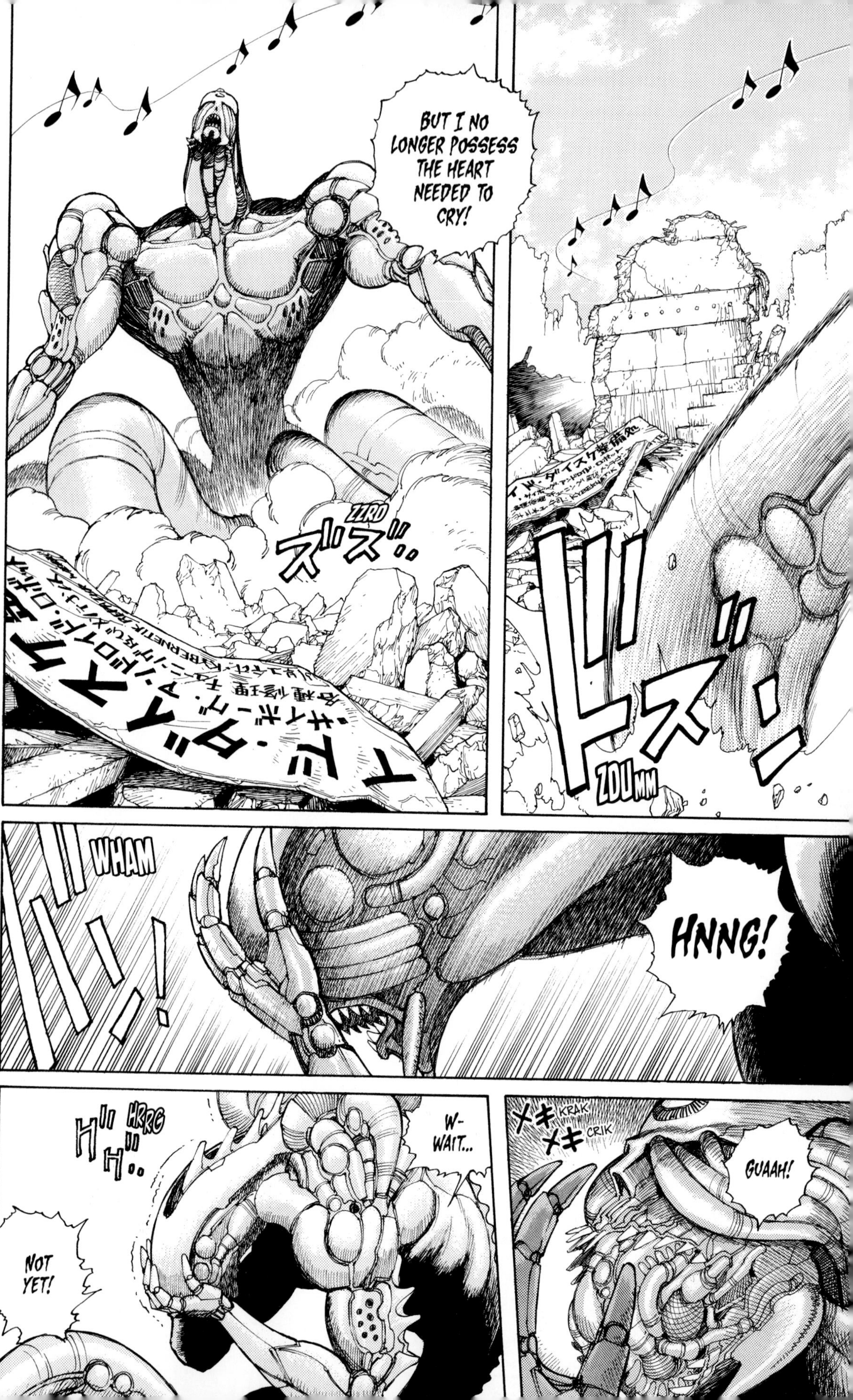
ドズン
ZOUMM
BUT I NO LONGER POSSESS THE HEART NEEDED TO CRY!
ズズ..
ZZRD
HNNG!
WHAM
メキ KRAK
メキ CRIK
GUAAH!
W-WAIT...
H H.. HRRG
NOT YET!

Sign: Daisuke Ido Repairs • Cyborgs, Androids, Robots; Repairs, Tuning & Maintenance for all models!

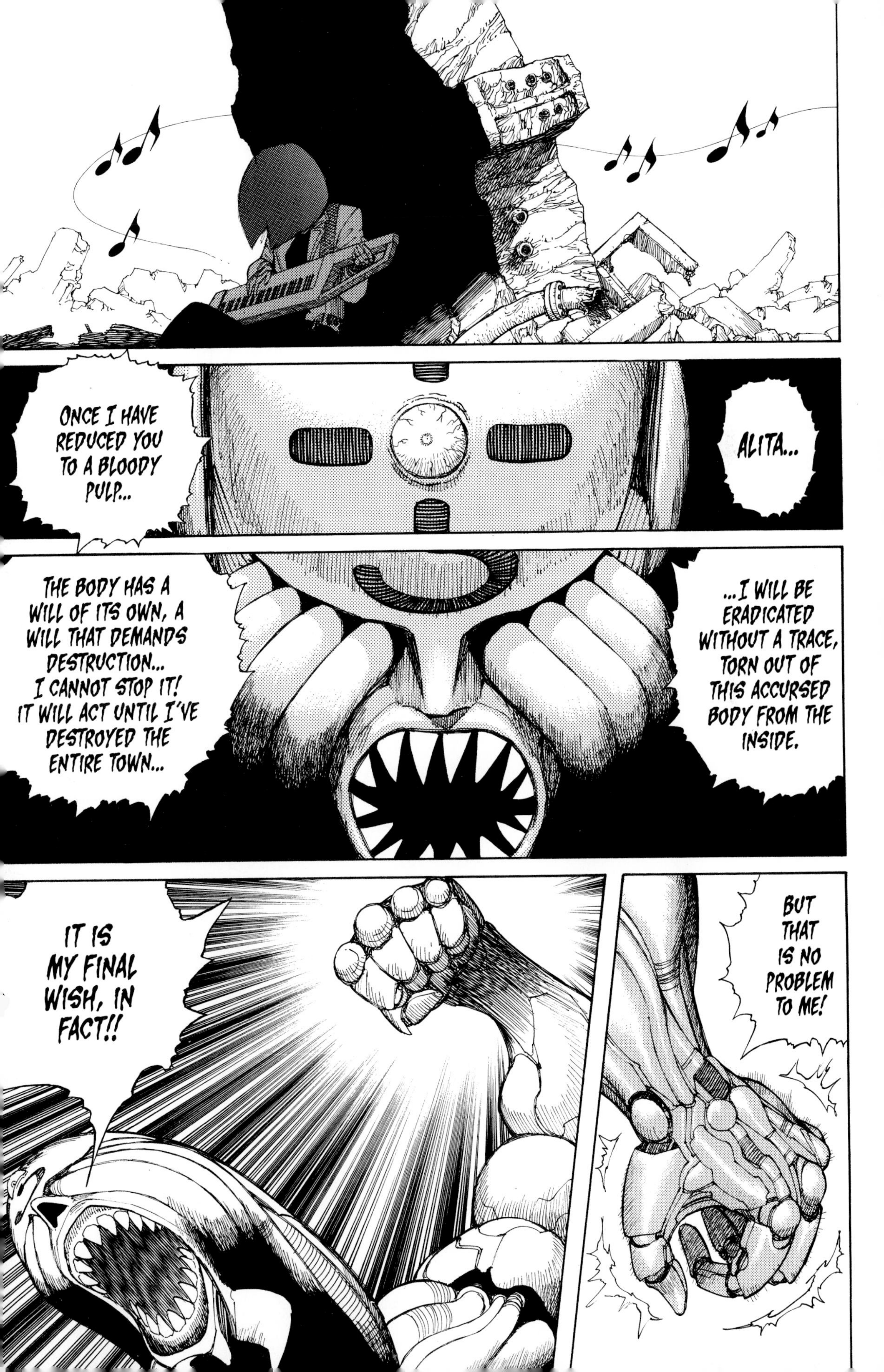
ALITA...
ONCE I HAVE REDUCED YOU TO A BLOODY PULP...
...I WILL BE ERADICATED WITHOUT A TRACE, TORN OUT OF THIS ACCURSED BODY FROM THE INSIDE.
THE BODY HAS A WILL OF ITS OWN, A WILL THAT DEMANDS DESTRUCTION... I CANNOT STOP IT! IT WILL ACT UNTIL I'VE DESTROYED THE ENTIRE TOWN...
BUT THAT IS NO PROBLEM TO ME!
IT IS MY FINAL WISH, IN FACT!!

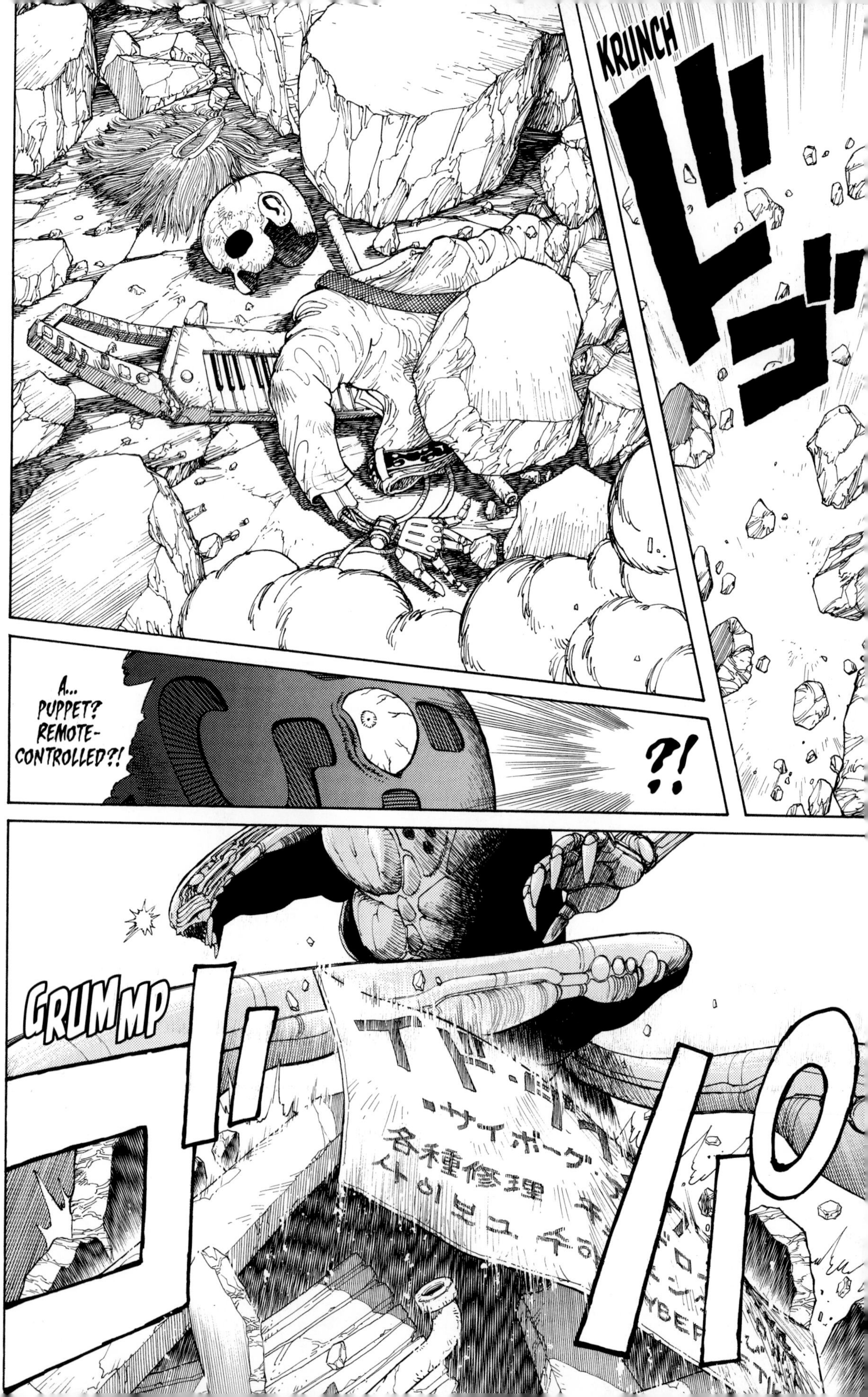
KRUNCH
?!
A... PUPPET? REMOTE-CONTROLLED?!
GRUMMP
各種修理

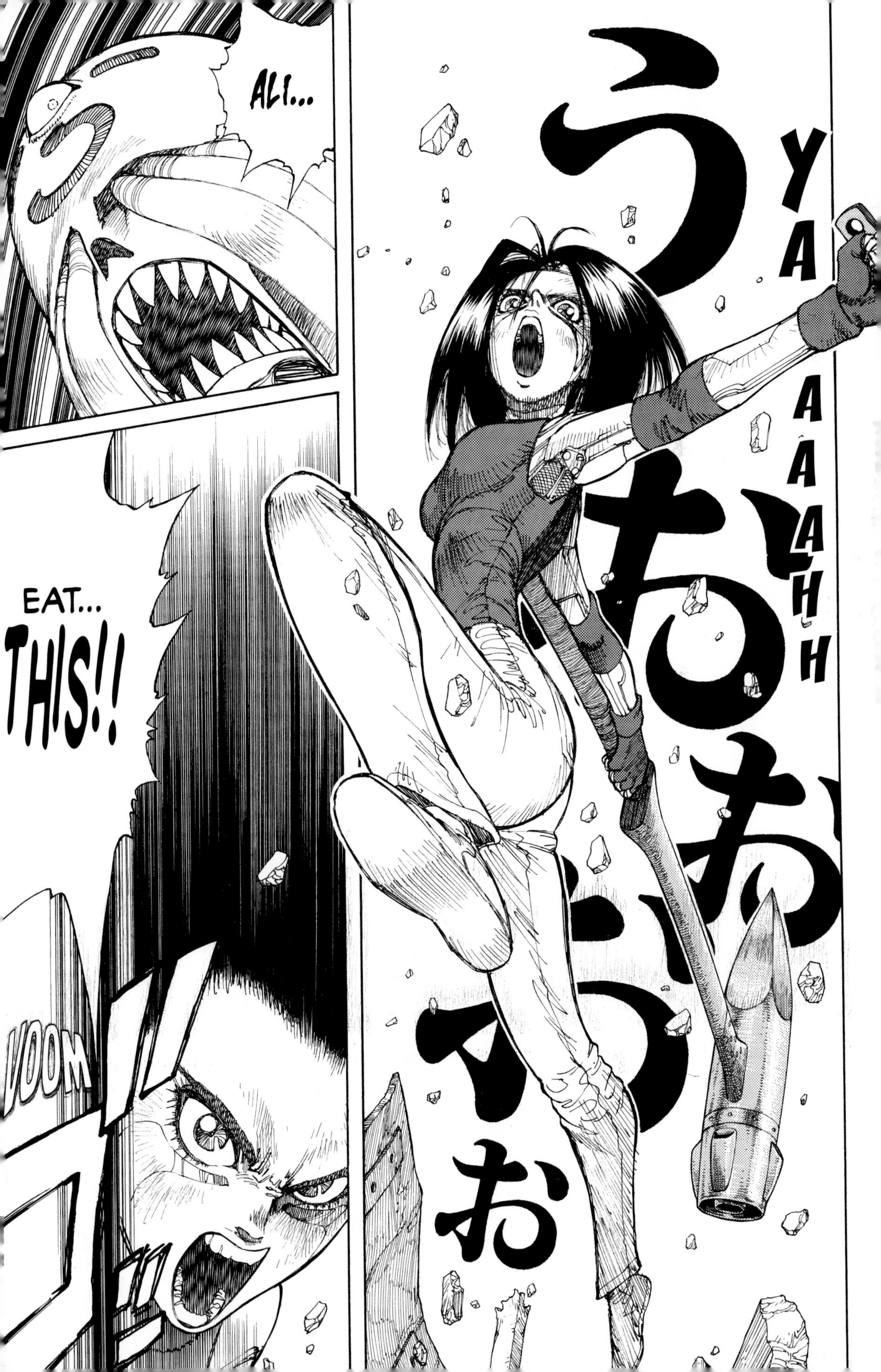
YAAAAHH
ALI...
EAT... THIS!!
VOOM

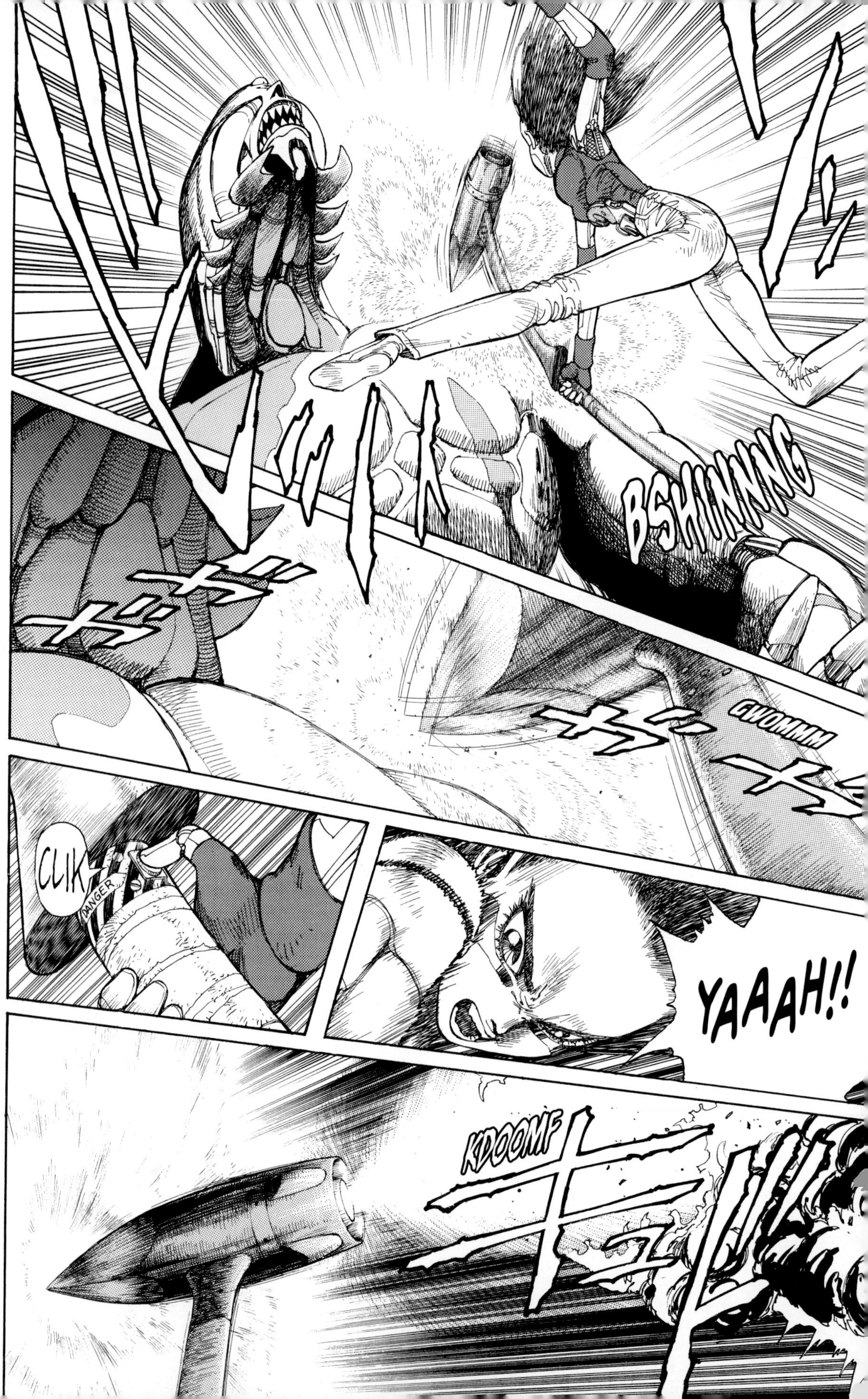
BSHINNNG
GWOMMM
YAAAH!!
CLIK
DANGER
KDOOMF

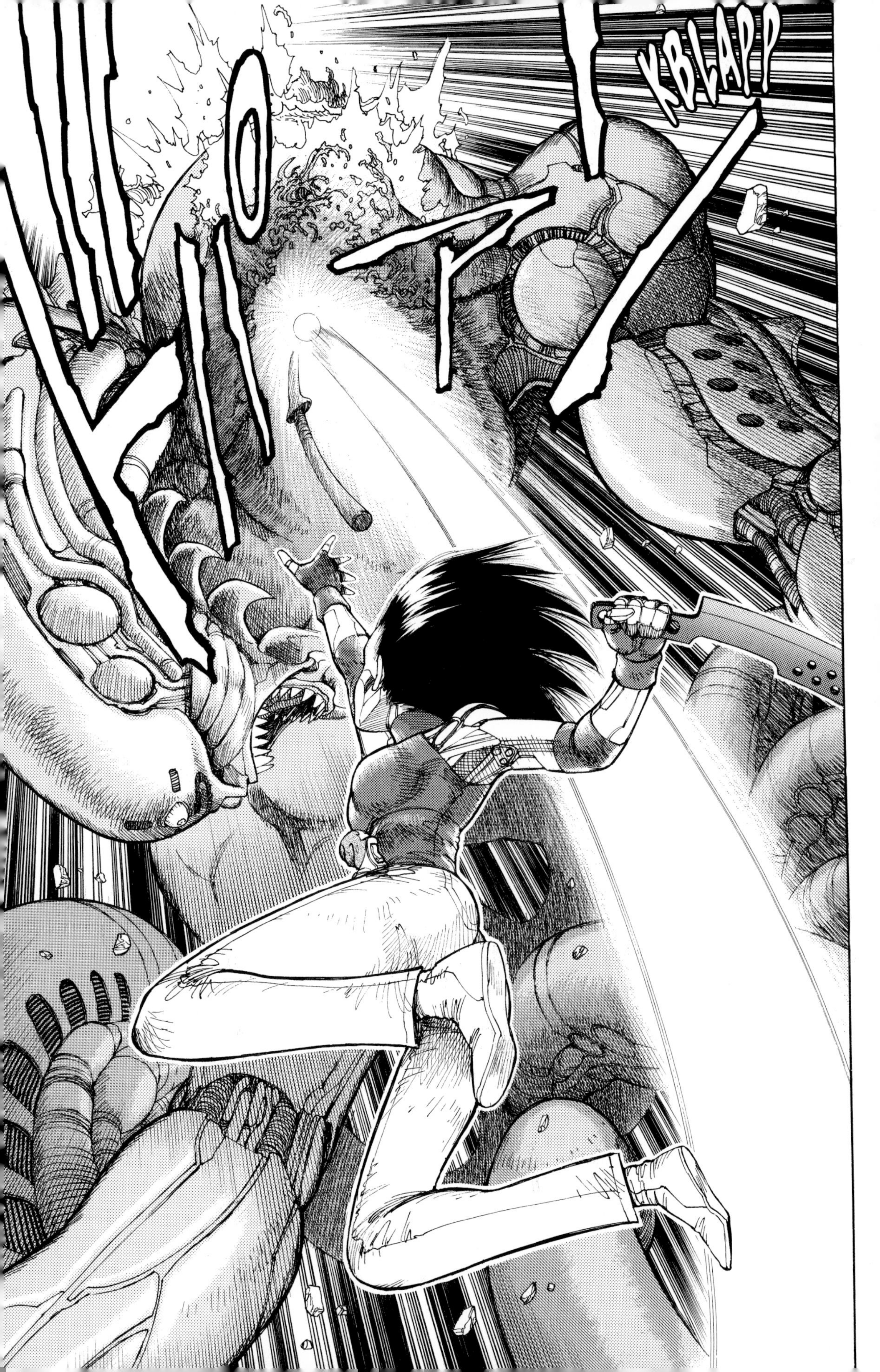
KBLAPP

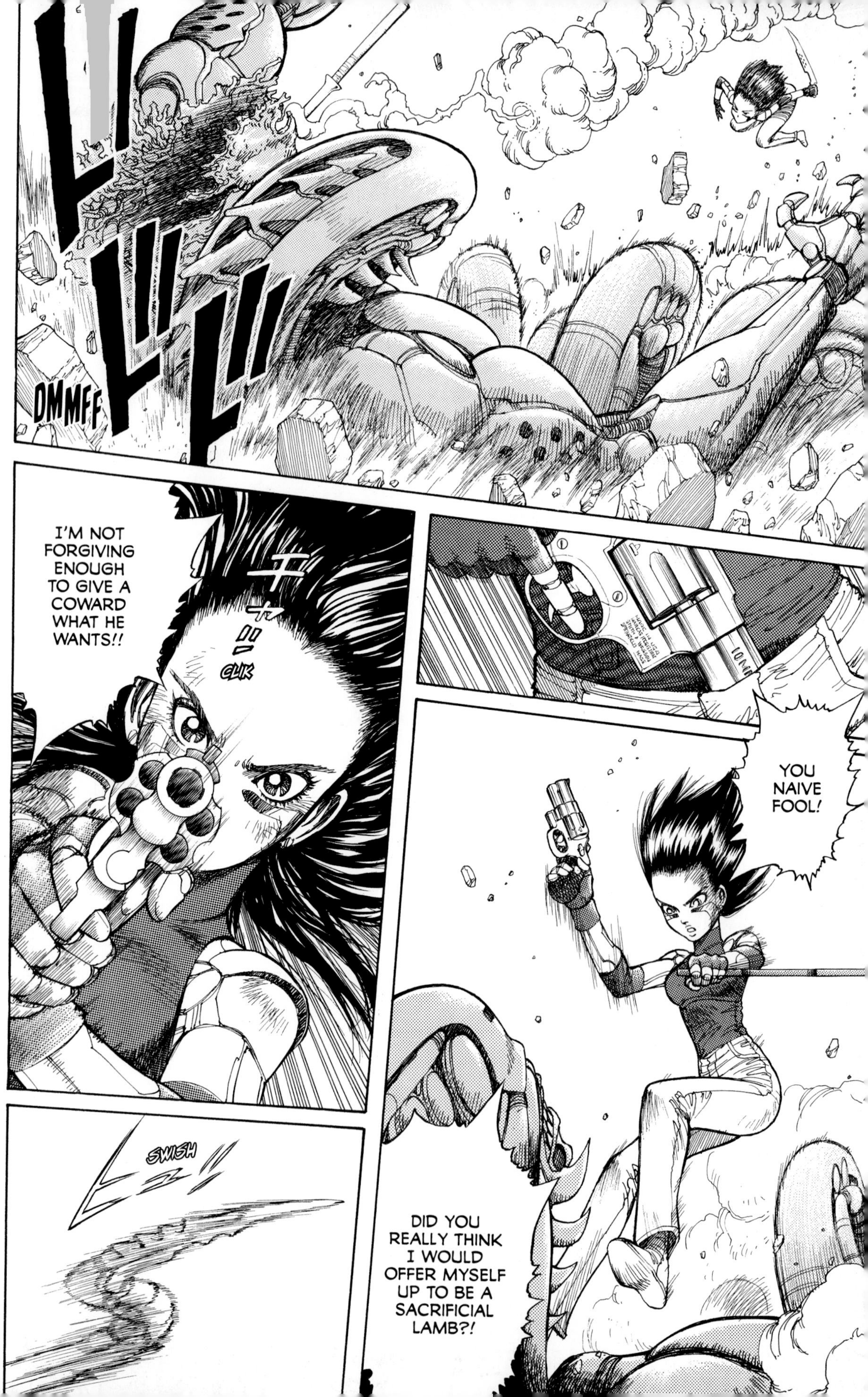
DMMFF
I'M NOT FORGIVING ENOUGH TO GIVE A COWARD WHAT HE WANTS!!
CLIK
YOU NAIVE FOOL!
DID YOU REALLY THINK I WOULD OFFER MYSELF UP TO BE A SACRIFICIAL LAMB?!
SWISH

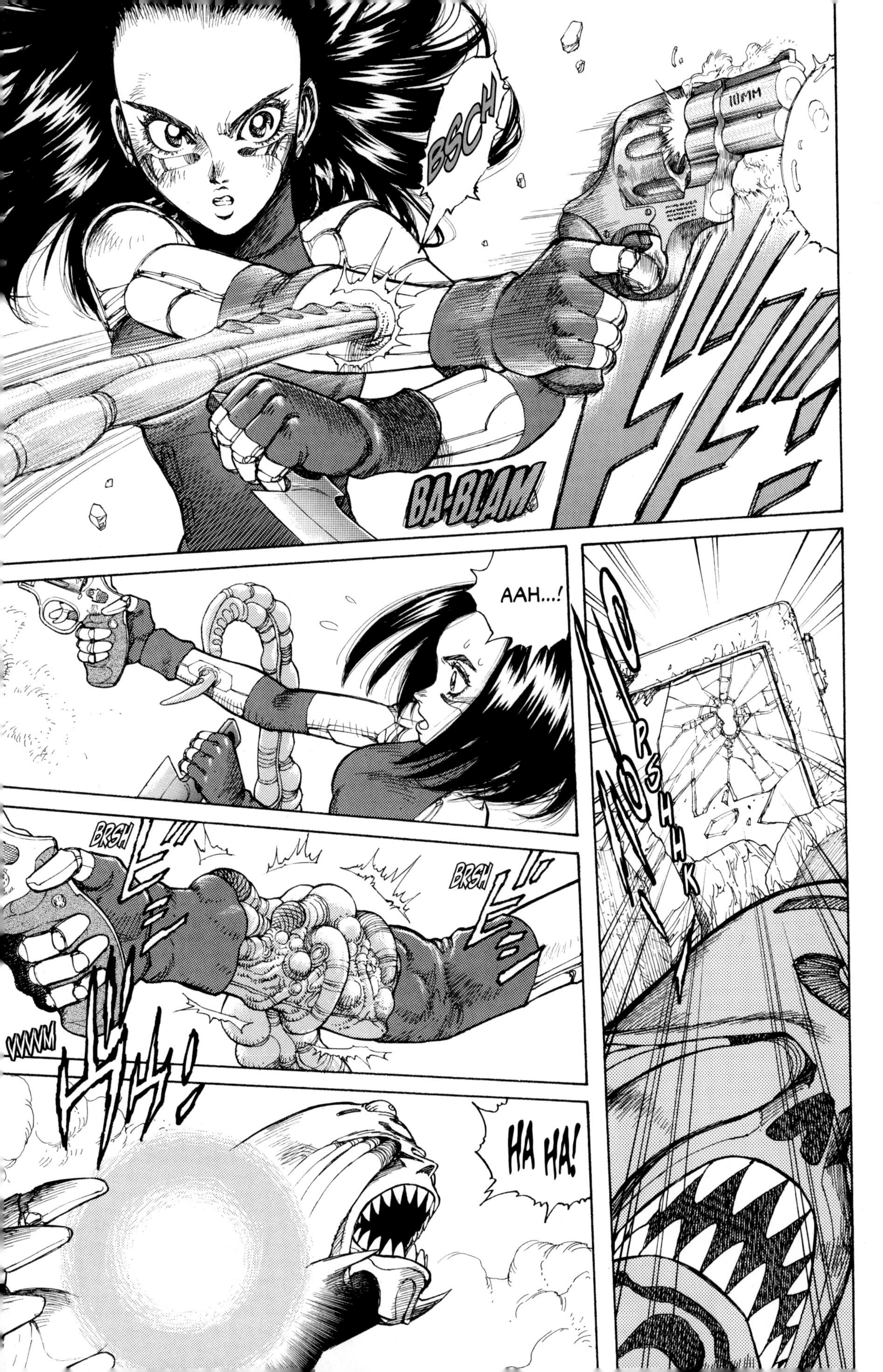
10MM
BSCH
BA-BLAM
CRSHHK
AAH...!
BRSH
BRSH
VVVM
HA HA!

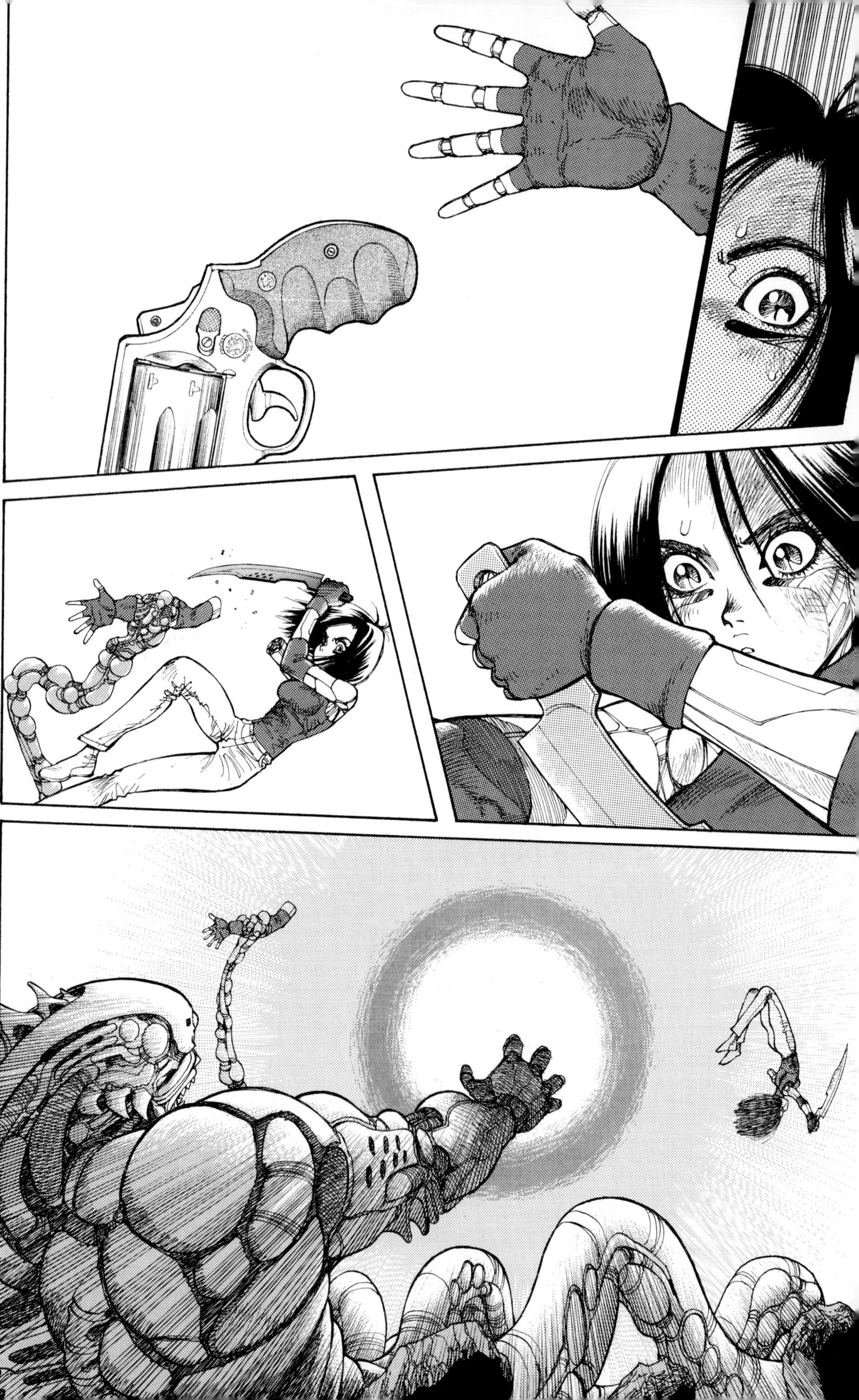

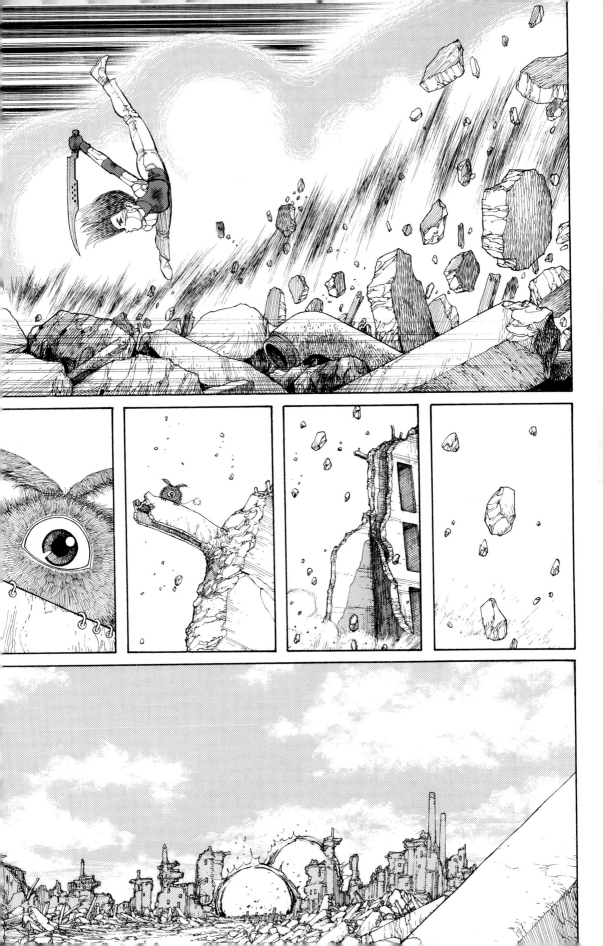

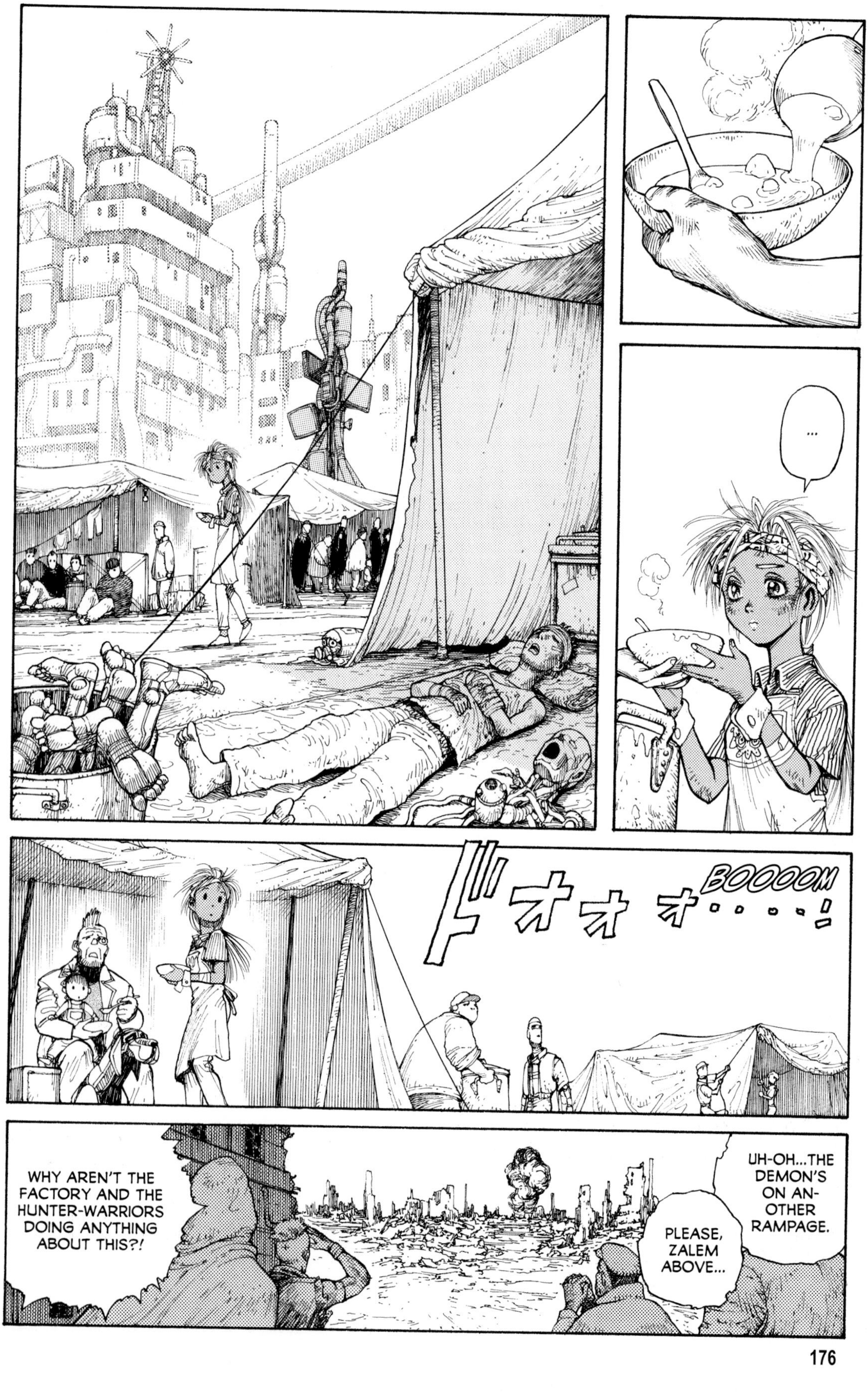
...
ドオオオ……!
BOOOOM
UH-OH...THE DEMON'S ON AN-OTHER RAMPAGE.
PLEASE, ZALEM ABOVE...
WHY AREN'T THE FACTORY AND THE HUNTER-WARRIORS DOING ANYTHING ABOUT THIS?!

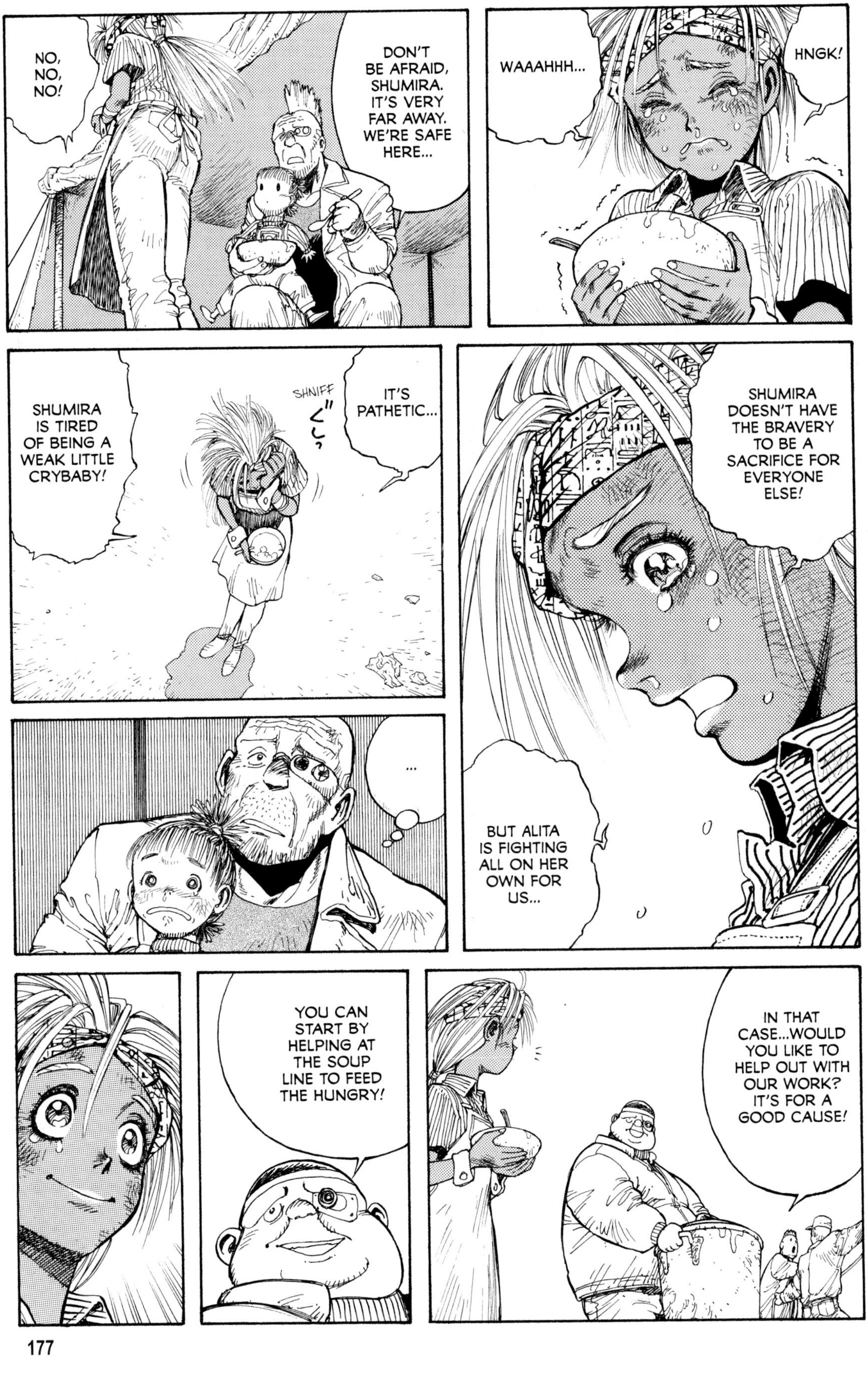

HNGK!
WAAAHHH...
DON'T BE AFRAID, SHUMIRA. IT'S VERY FAR AWAY. WE'RE SAFE HERE...
NO, NO, NO!
SHUMIRA DOESN'T HAVE THE BRAVERY TO BE A SACRIFICE FOR EVERYONE ELSE!
BUT ALITA IS FIGHTING ALL ON HER OWN FOR US...
IT'S PATHETIC...
SHNIFF
SHUMIRA IS TIRED OF BEING A WEAK LITTLE CRYBABY!
...
IN THAT CASE...WOULD YOU LIKE TO HELP OUT WITH OUR WORK? IT'S FOR A GOOD CAUSE!
YOU CAN START BY HELPING AT THE SOUP LINE TO FEED THE HUNGRY!

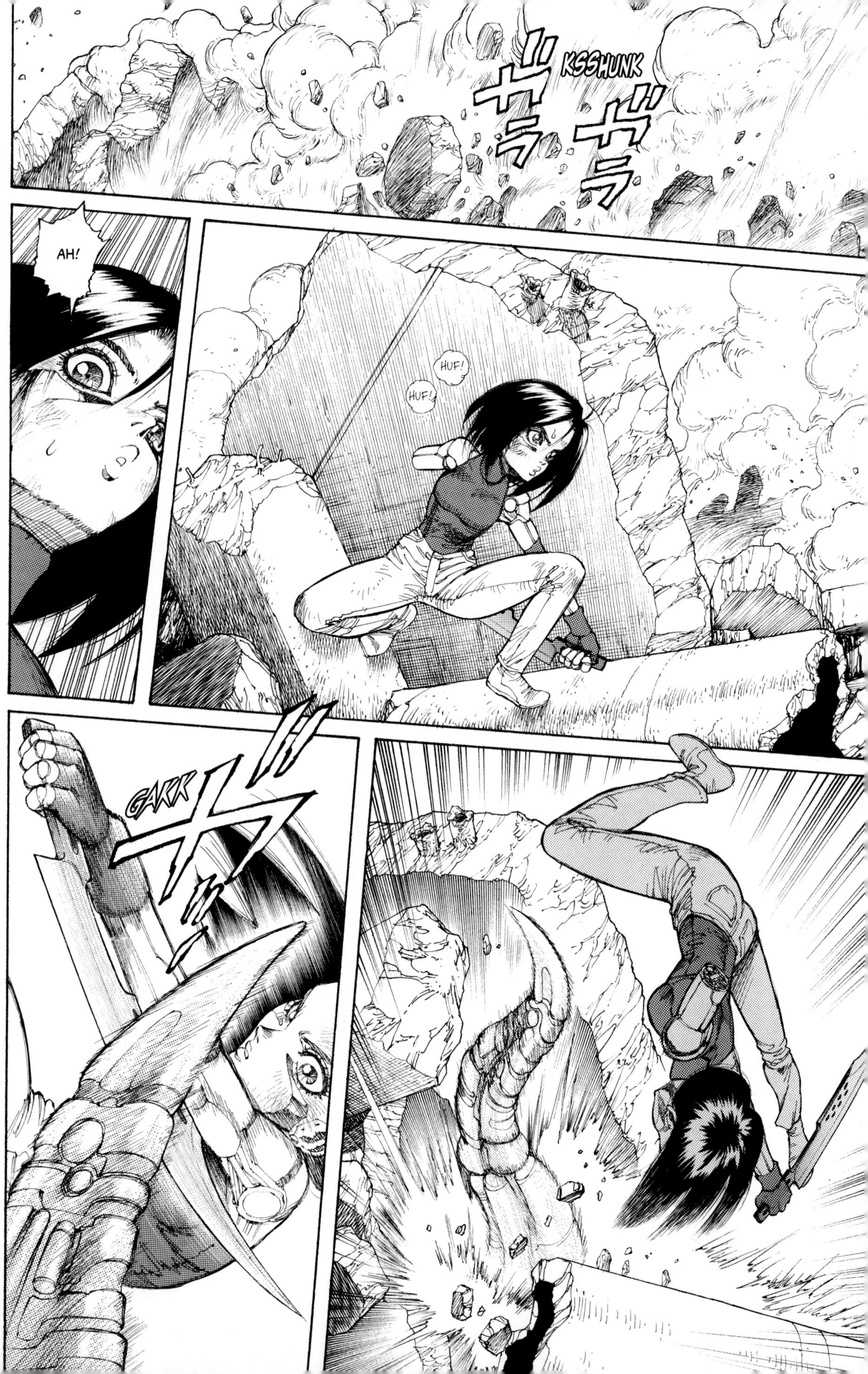
KSSHUNK
ガラガラ
HUF!
HUF!
AH!
GARK

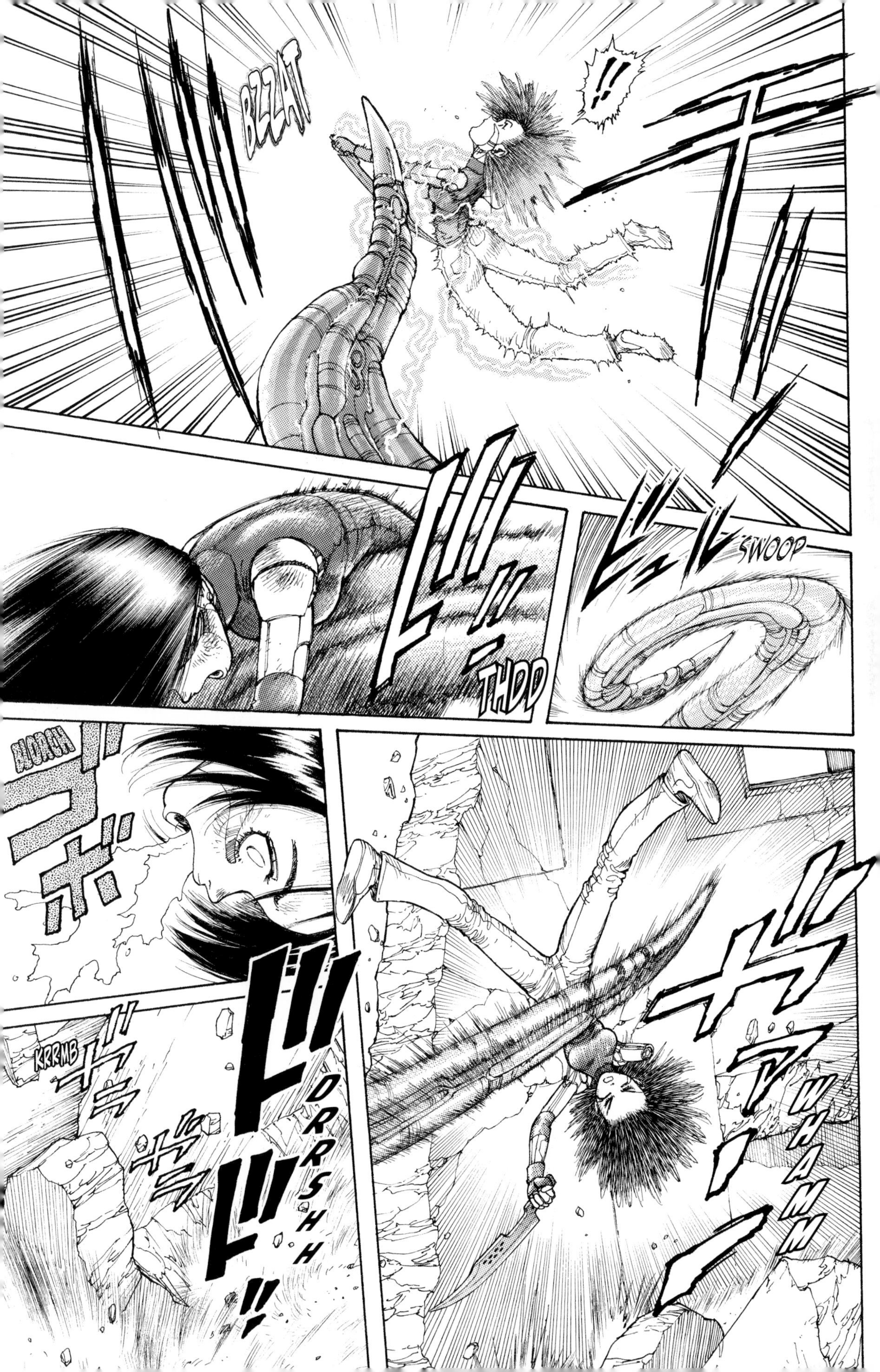
!!
BZZAT
SWOOP
THDD
WHAMMM
BLORCH
KRRMB
DRRSHH
!!

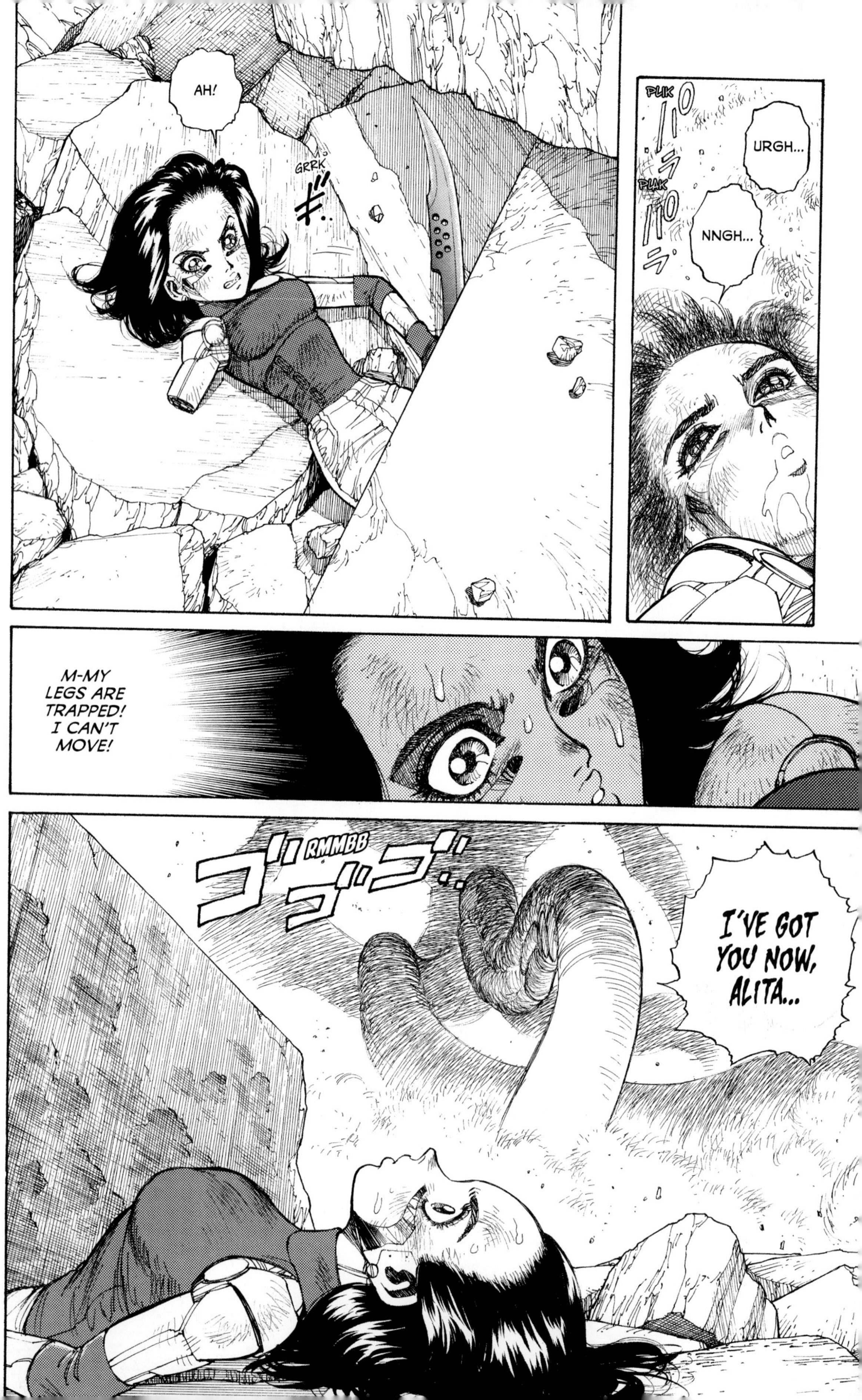
URGH...
PLIK
PLAK
NNGH...
AH!
GRRK
M-MY LEGS ARE TRAPPED! I CAN'T MOVE!
I'VE GOT YOU NOW, ALITA...
RMMBB

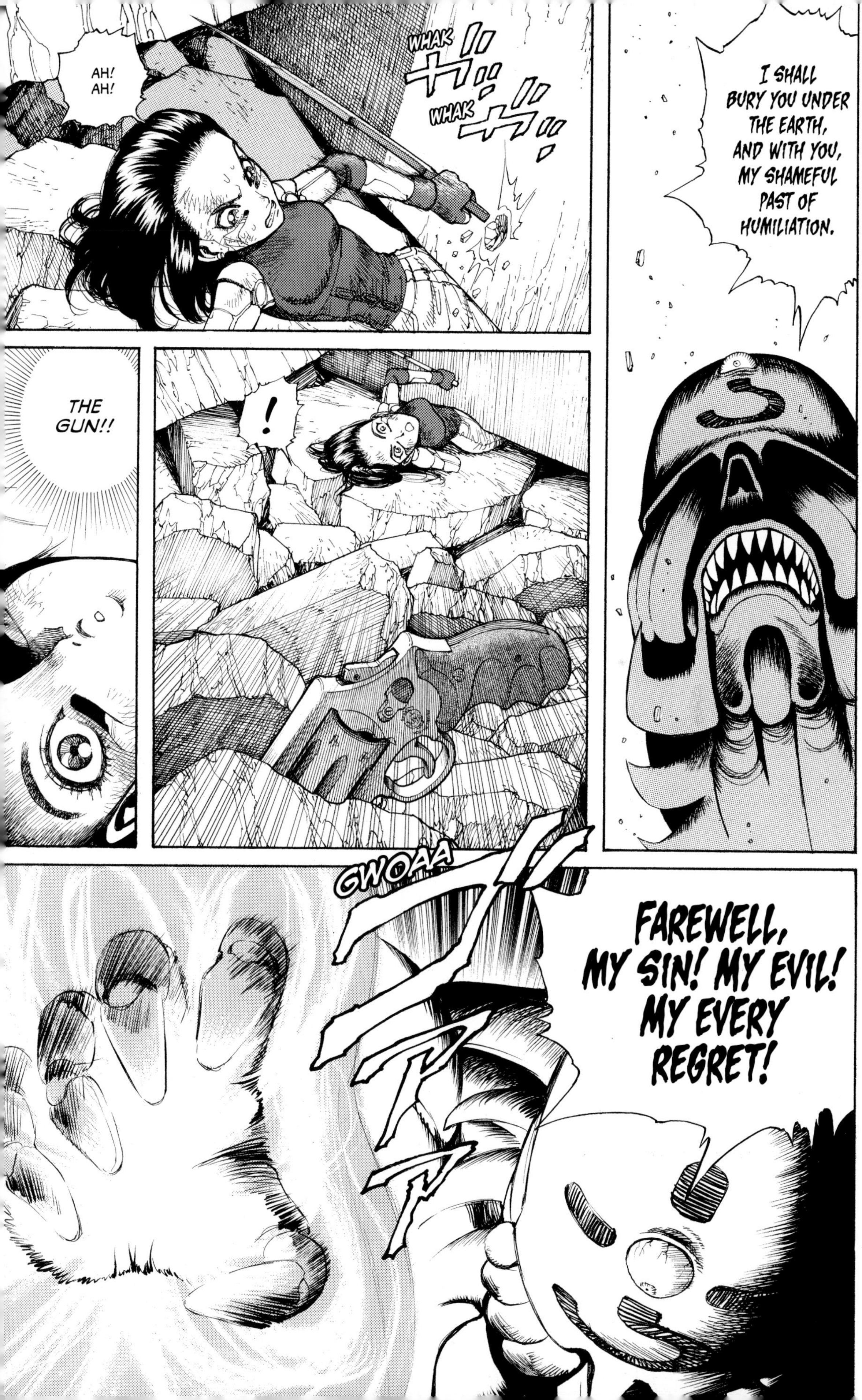
I SHALL BURY YOU UNDER THE EARTH, AND WITH YOU, MY SHAMEFUL PAST OF HUMILIATION.
WHAK
WHAK
AH! AH!
!
THE GUN!!
GWOAA
FAREWELL, MY SIN! MY EVIL! MY EVERY REGRET!

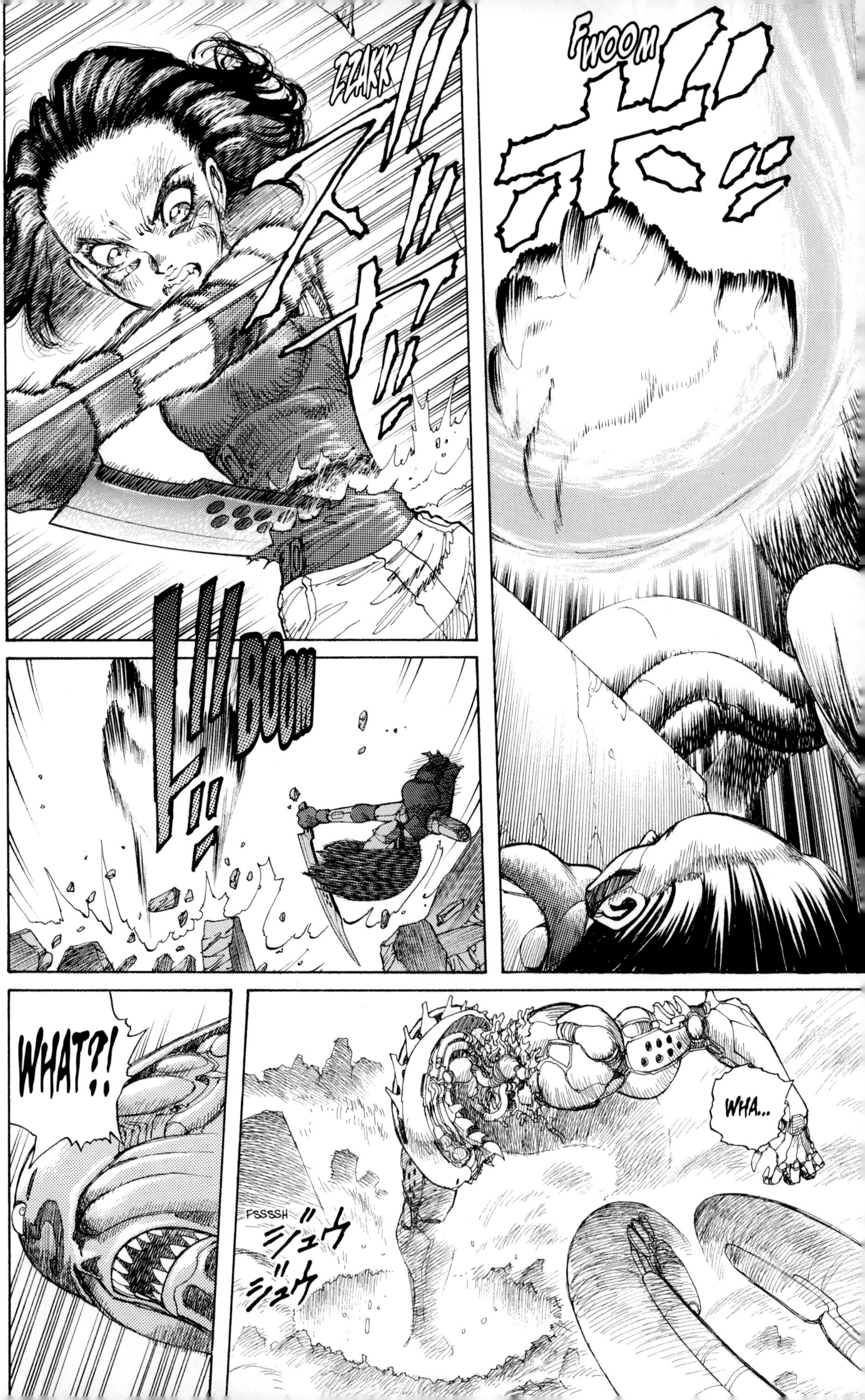
FWOOM
ボッ
ZZAKK
ズバッ!!
BOOM
ドッ!!
WHA...
FSSSSH
ジュウ
ジュウ
WHAT?!

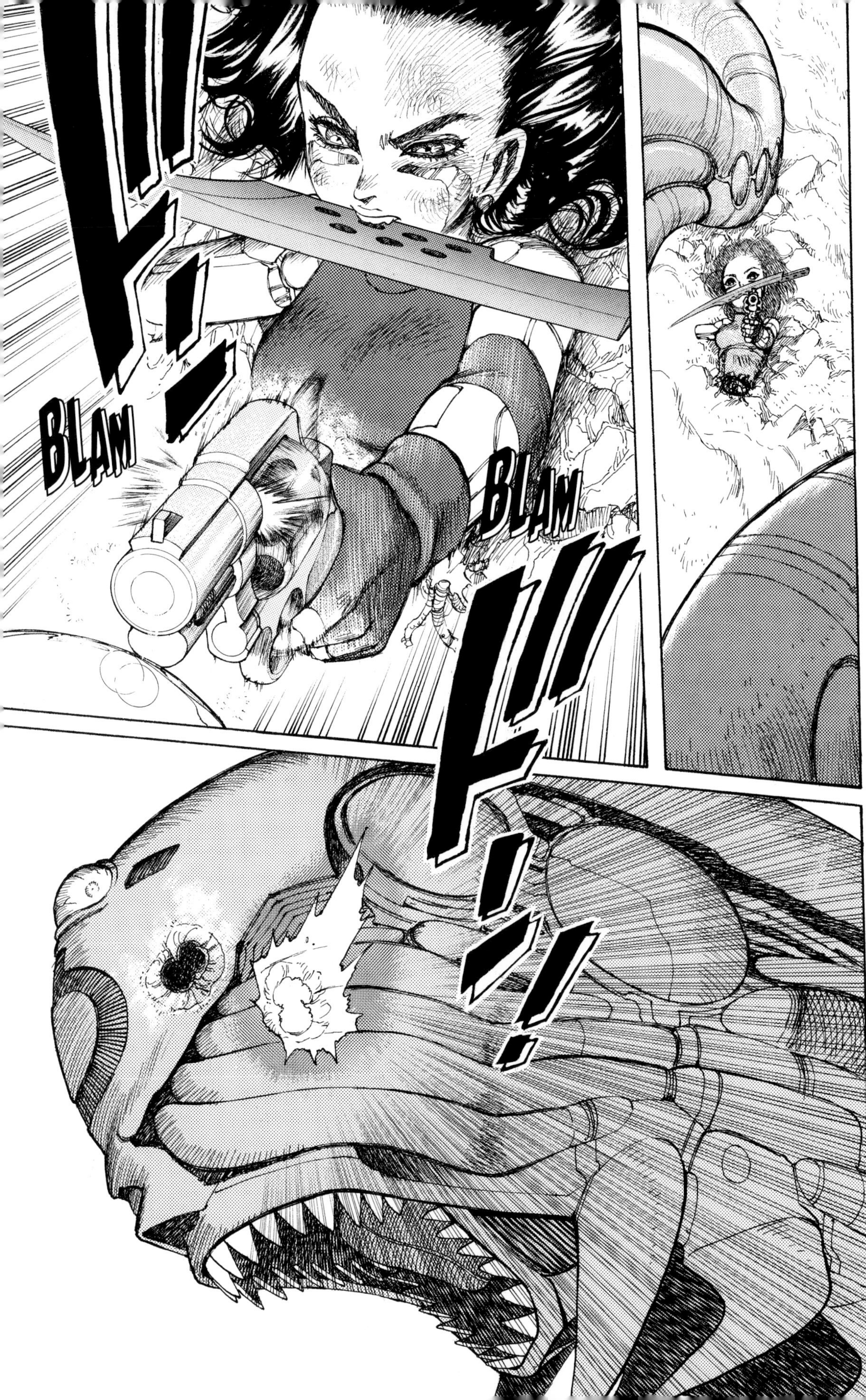
BLAM
BLAM

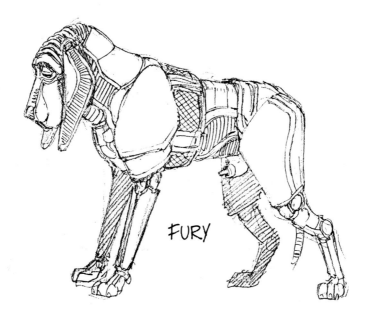

FURY

TIK
CLIK...
FFFH!
FFFH!
FIGHT_029
Lion and the Lamb

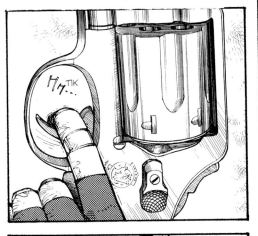

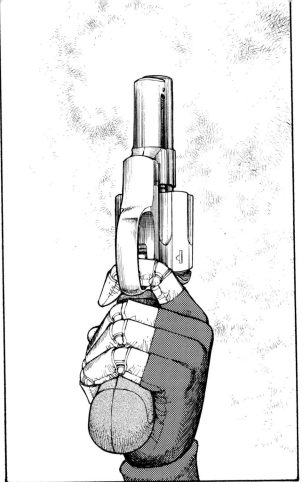

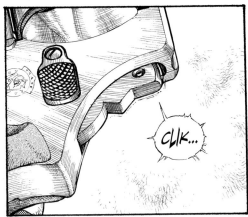

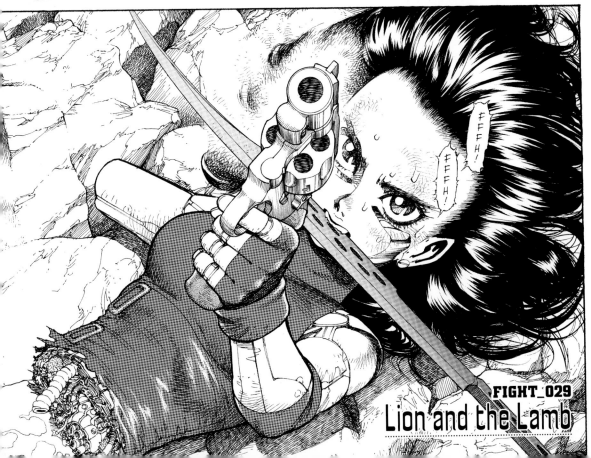

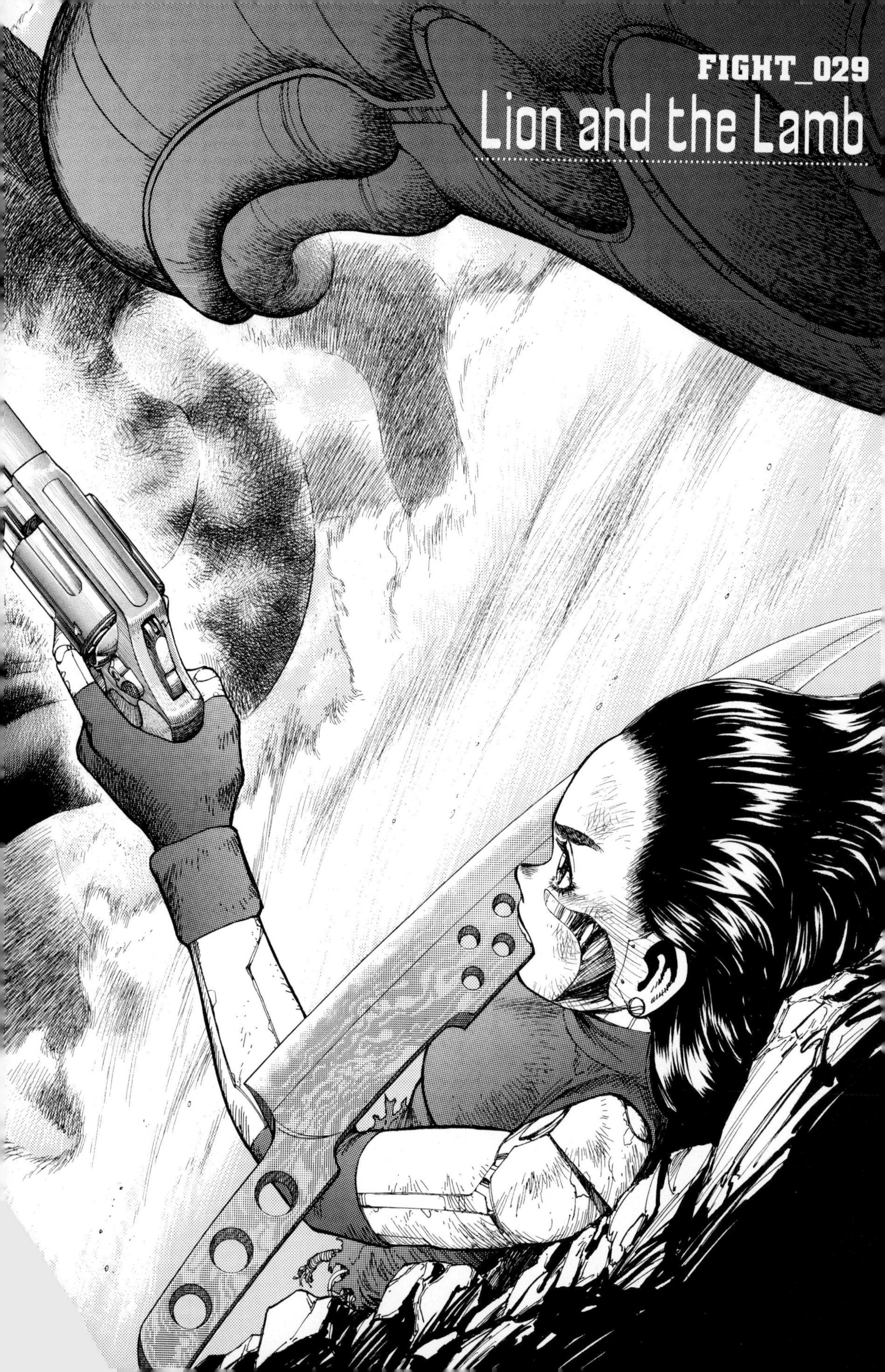
FIGHT_029
Lion and the Lamb

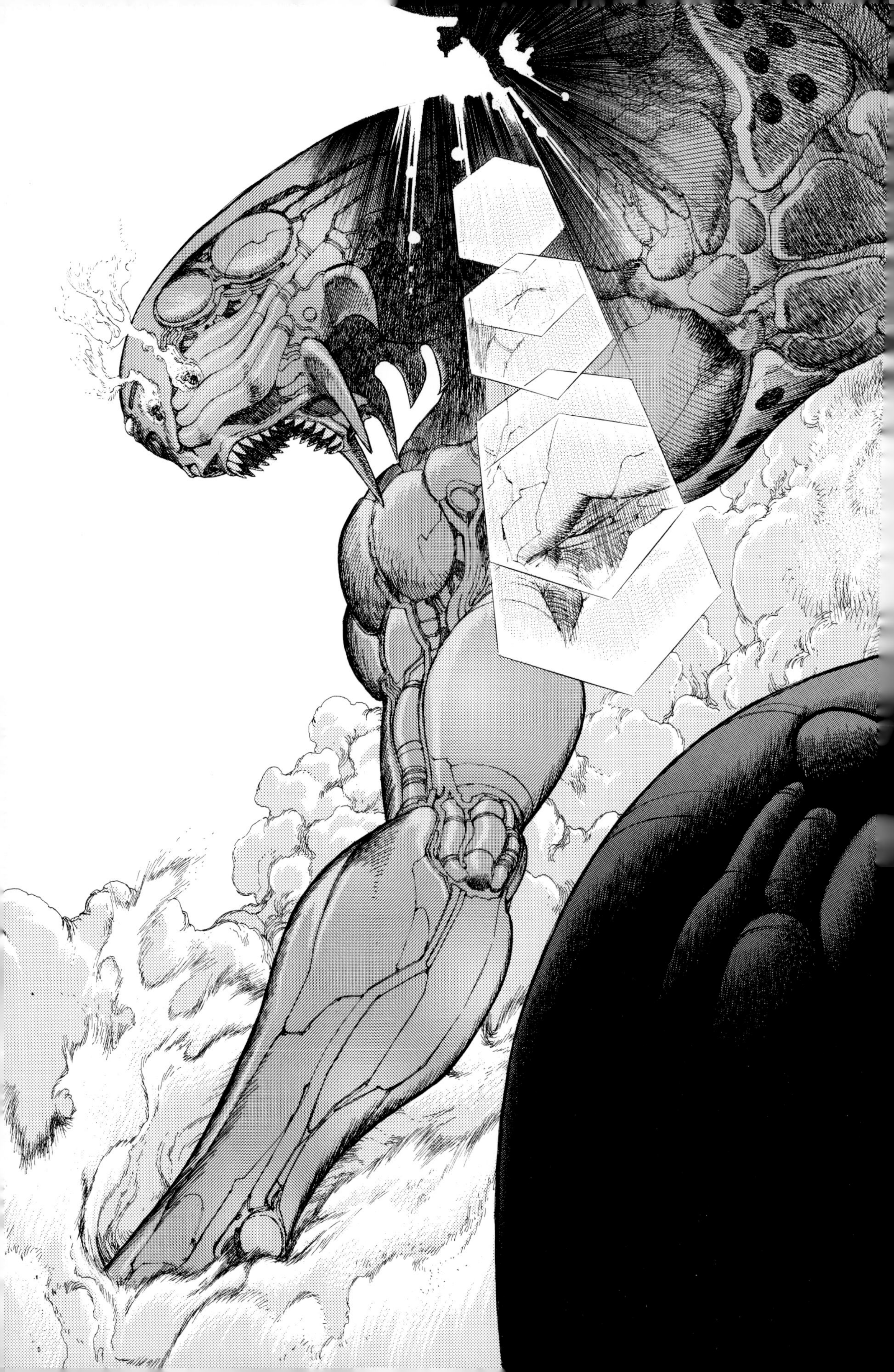

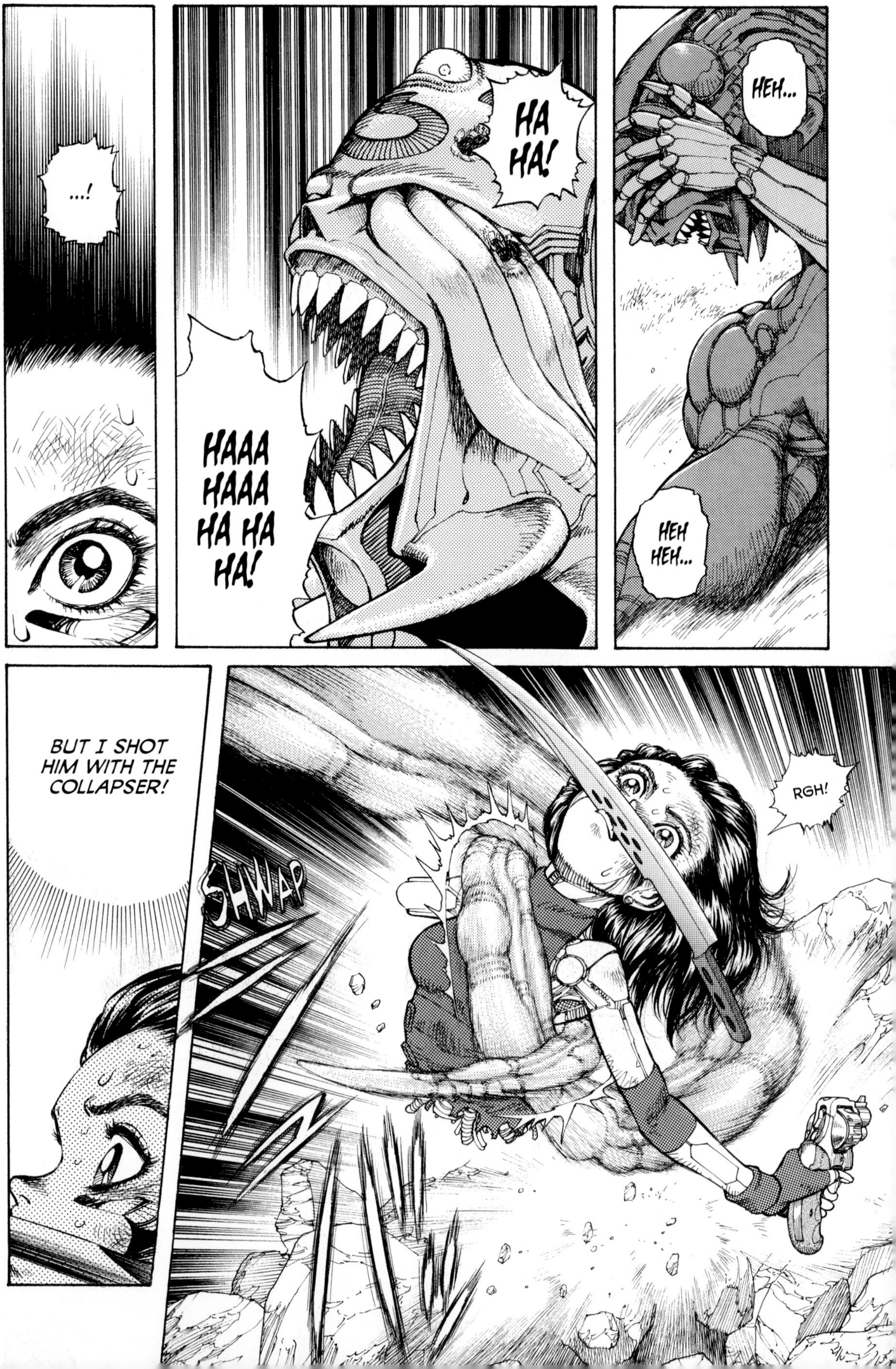
HEH...
HEH HEH...
HA HA!
HAAA HAAA HA HA HA!
...!
RGH!
SHWAP
BUT I SHOT HIM WITH THE COLLAPSER!

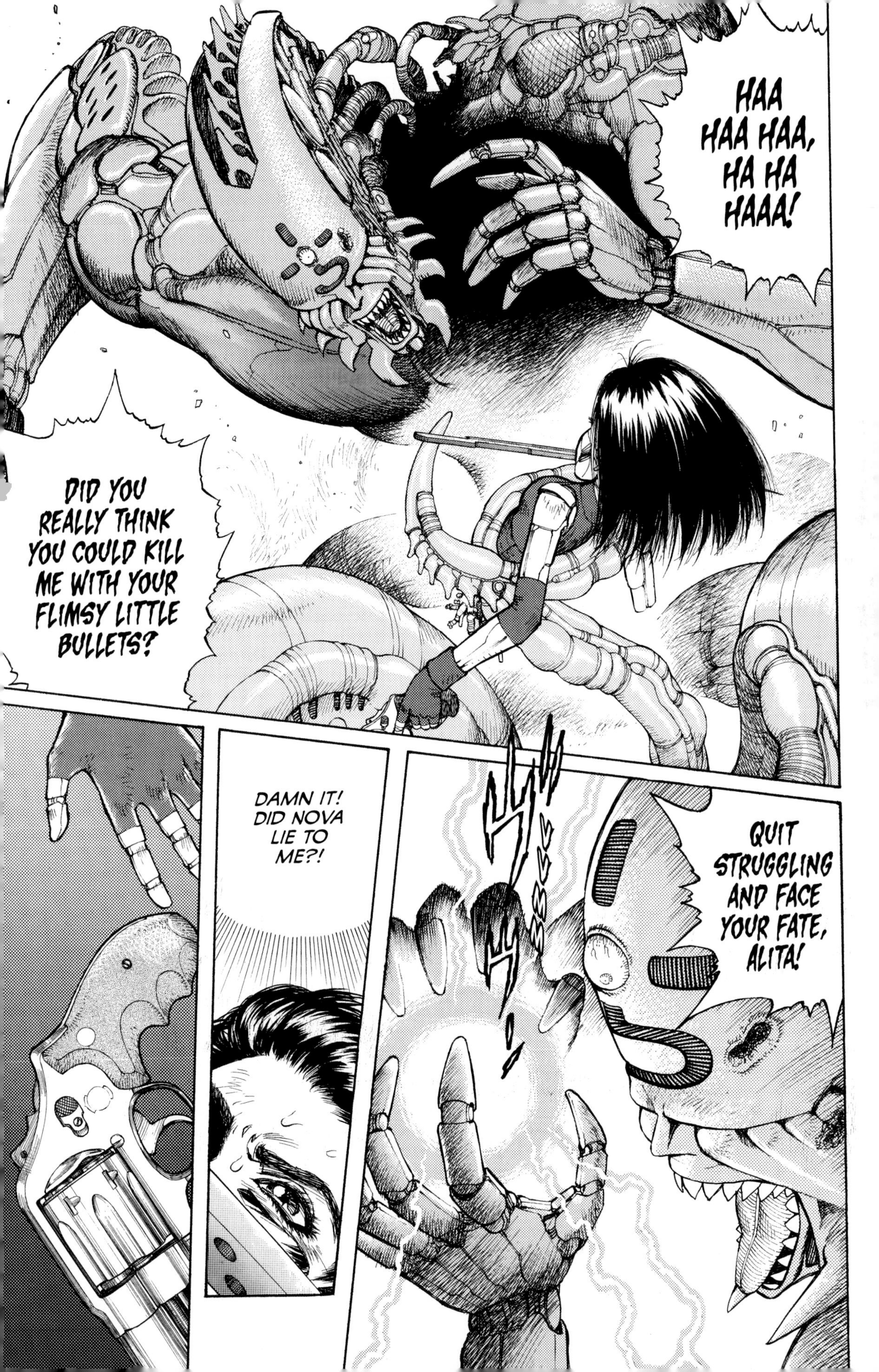
HAA HAA HAA, HA HA HAAA!
DID YOU REALLY THINK YOU COULD KILL ME WITH YOUR FLIMSY LITTLE BULLETS?
QUIT STRUGGLING AND FACE YOUR FATE, ALITA!
DAMN IT! DID NOVA LIE TO ME?!

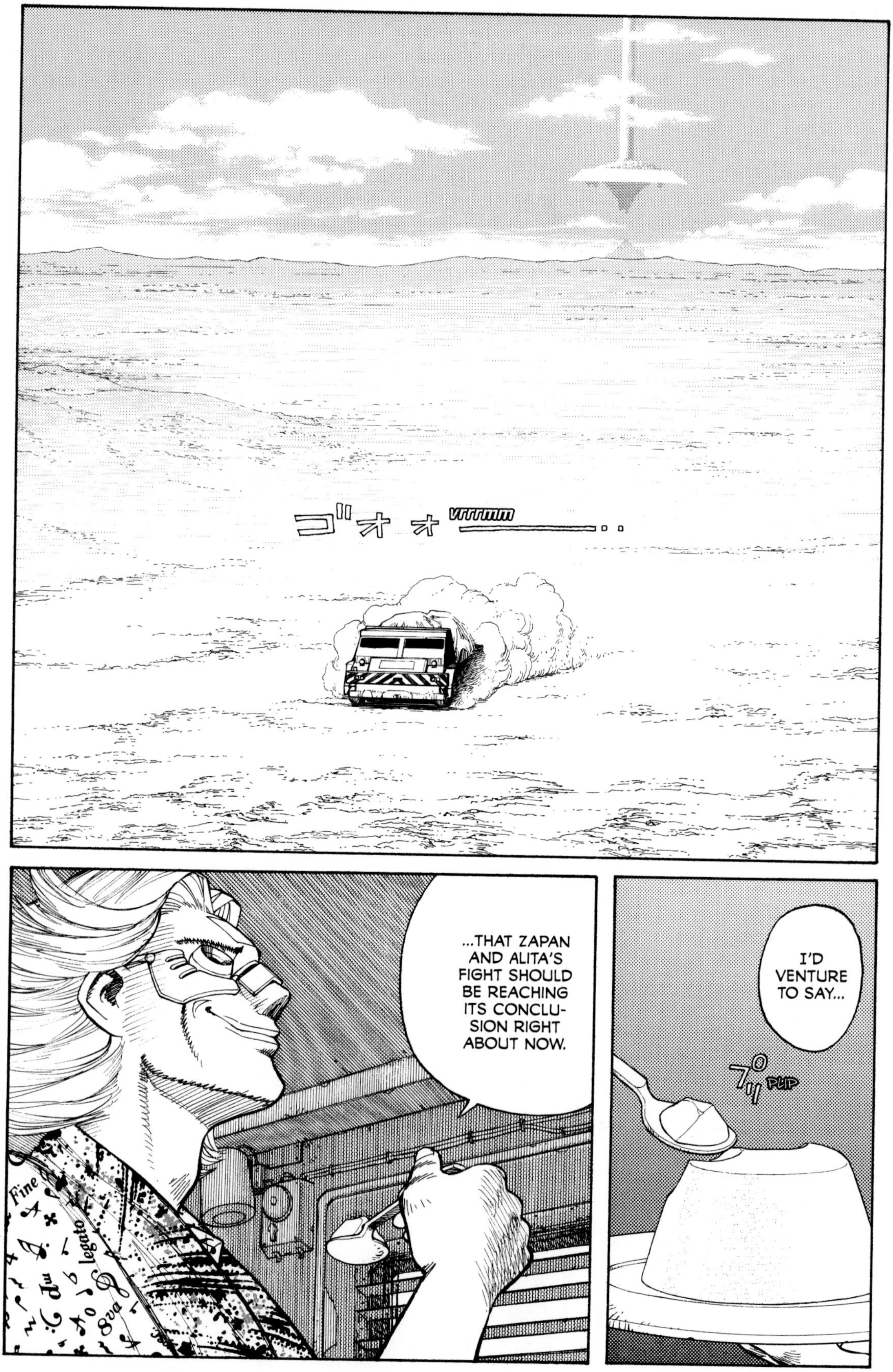
ゴオオー・・
vrrrmm
I'D VENTURE TO SAY...
PLIP
...THAT ZAPAN AND ALITA'S FIGHT SHOULD BE REACHING ITS CONCLUSION RIGHT ABOUT NOW.
Fine
legato
8va

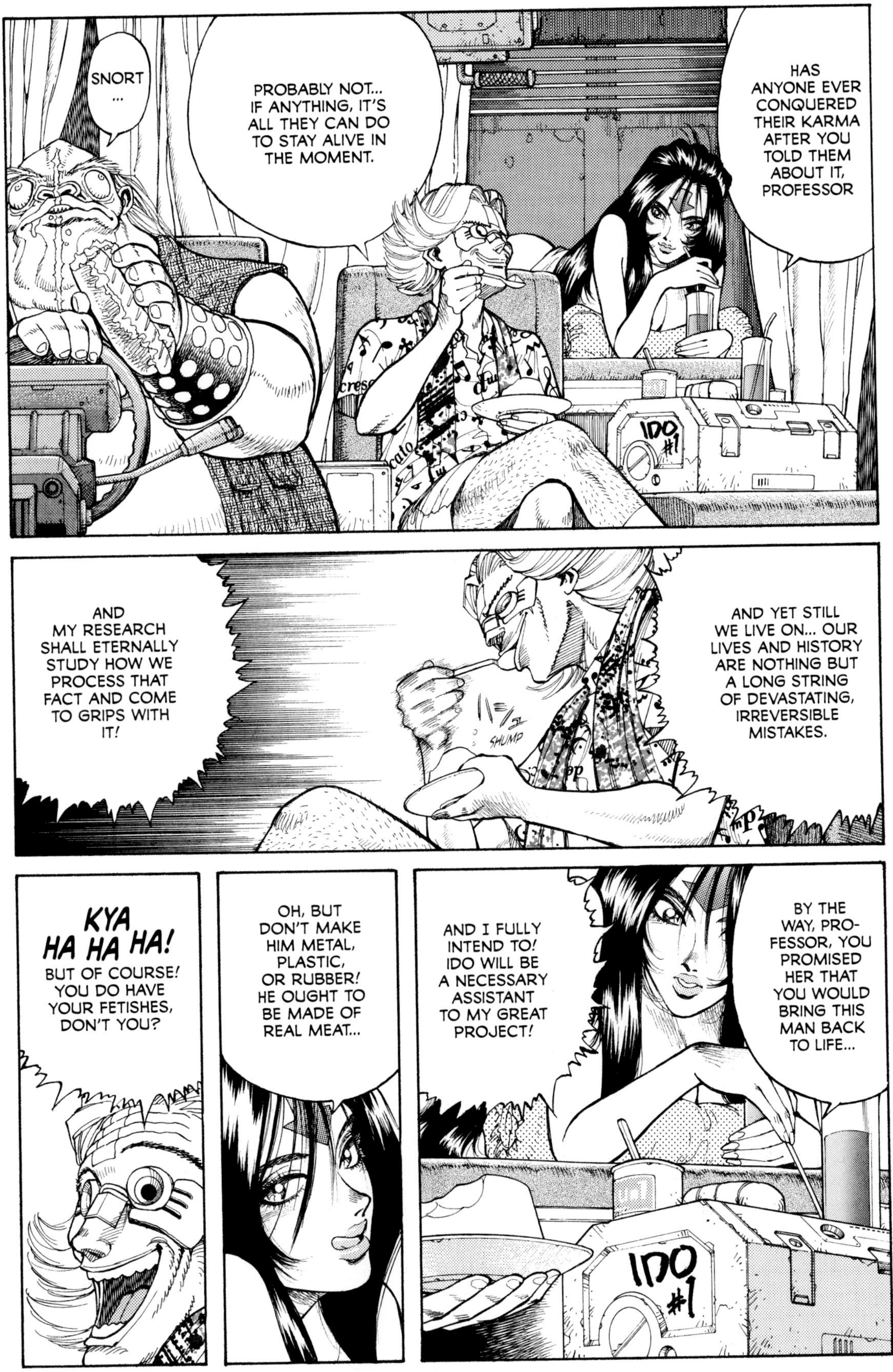
HAS ANYONE EVER CONQUERED THEIR KARMA AFTER YOU TOLD THEM ABOUT IT, PROFESSOR
PROBABLY NOT... IF ANYTHING, IT'S ALL THEY CAN DO TO STAY ALIVE IN THE MOMENT.
SNORT ...
IDO #1
AND YET STILL WE LIVE ON... OUR LIVES AND HISTORY ARE NOTHING BUT A LONG STRING OF DEVASTATING, IRREVERSIBLE MISTAKES.
SHUMP
AND MY RESEARCH SHALL ETERNALLY STUDY HOW WE PROCESS THAT FACT AND COME TO GRIPS WITH IT!
BY THE WAY, PRO-FESSOR, YOU PROMISED HER THAT YOU WOULD BRING THIS MAN BACK TO LIFE...
AND I FULLY INTEND TO! IDO WILL BE A NECESSARY ASSISTANT TO MY GREAT PROJECT!
IDO #1
OH, BUT DON'T MAKE HIM METAL, PLASTIC, OR RUBBER! HE OUGHT TO BE MADE OF REAL MEAT...
KYA HA HA HA! BUT OF COURSE! YOU DO HAVE YOUR FETISHES, DON'T YOU?

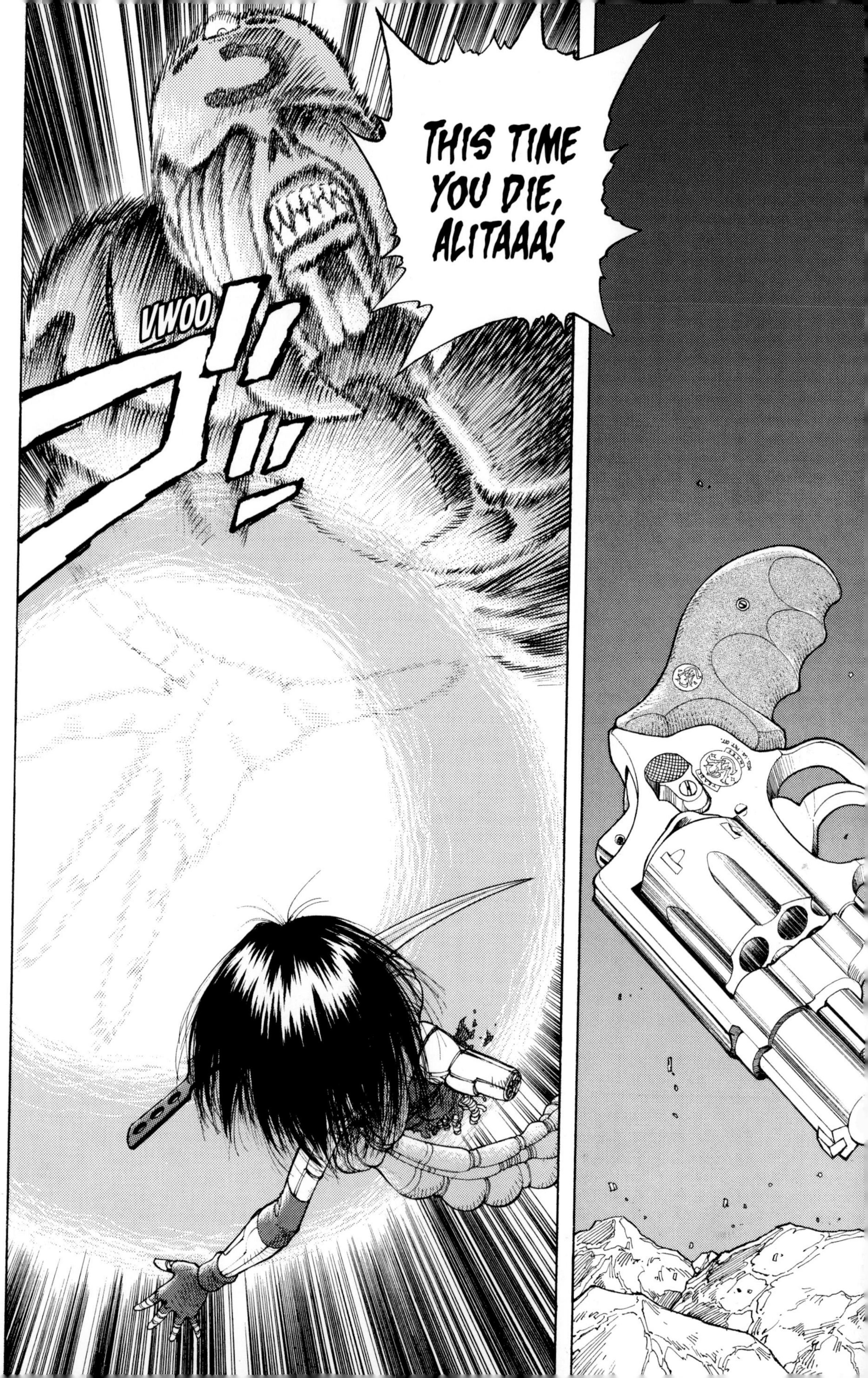
THIS TIME YOU DIE, ALITAAA!
VWOO

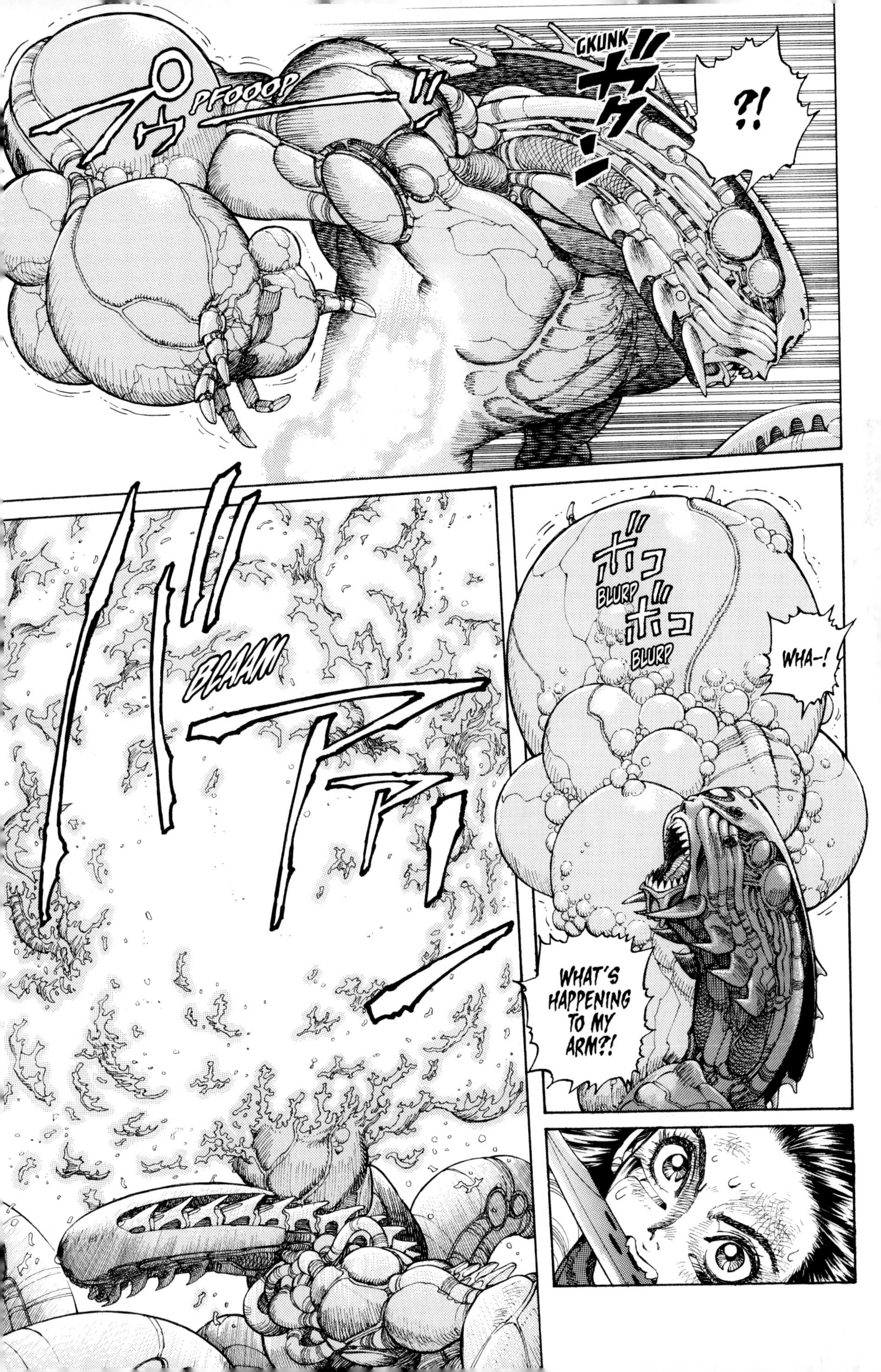
?!
GKUNK
PFOOOP
ボコ
BLURP
ボコ
BLURP
WHA–!
WHAT'S HAPPENING TO MY ARM?!
BLAAAM

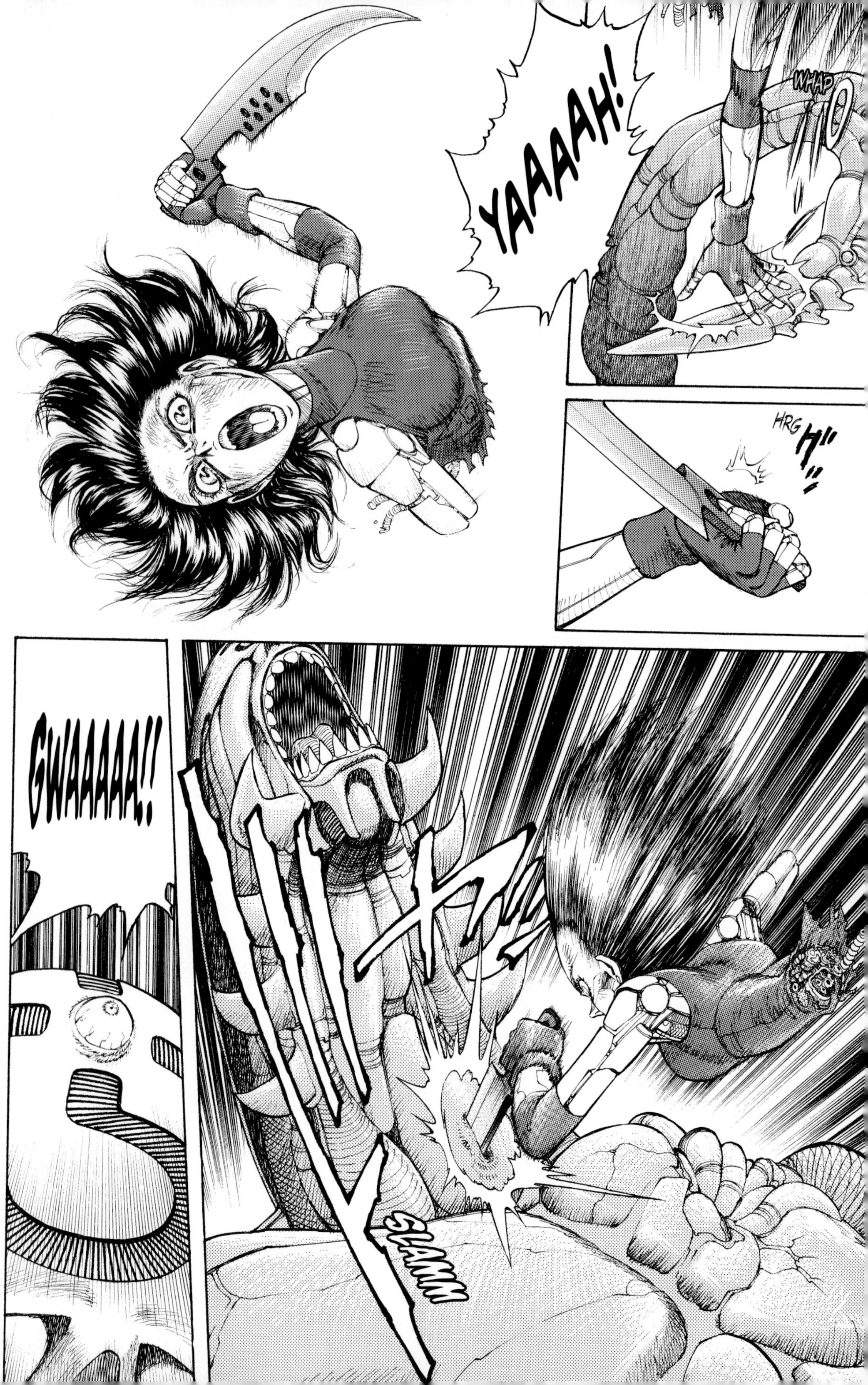
YAAAAH!
WHAP
HRG
SLAMMM
GWAAAAA!!

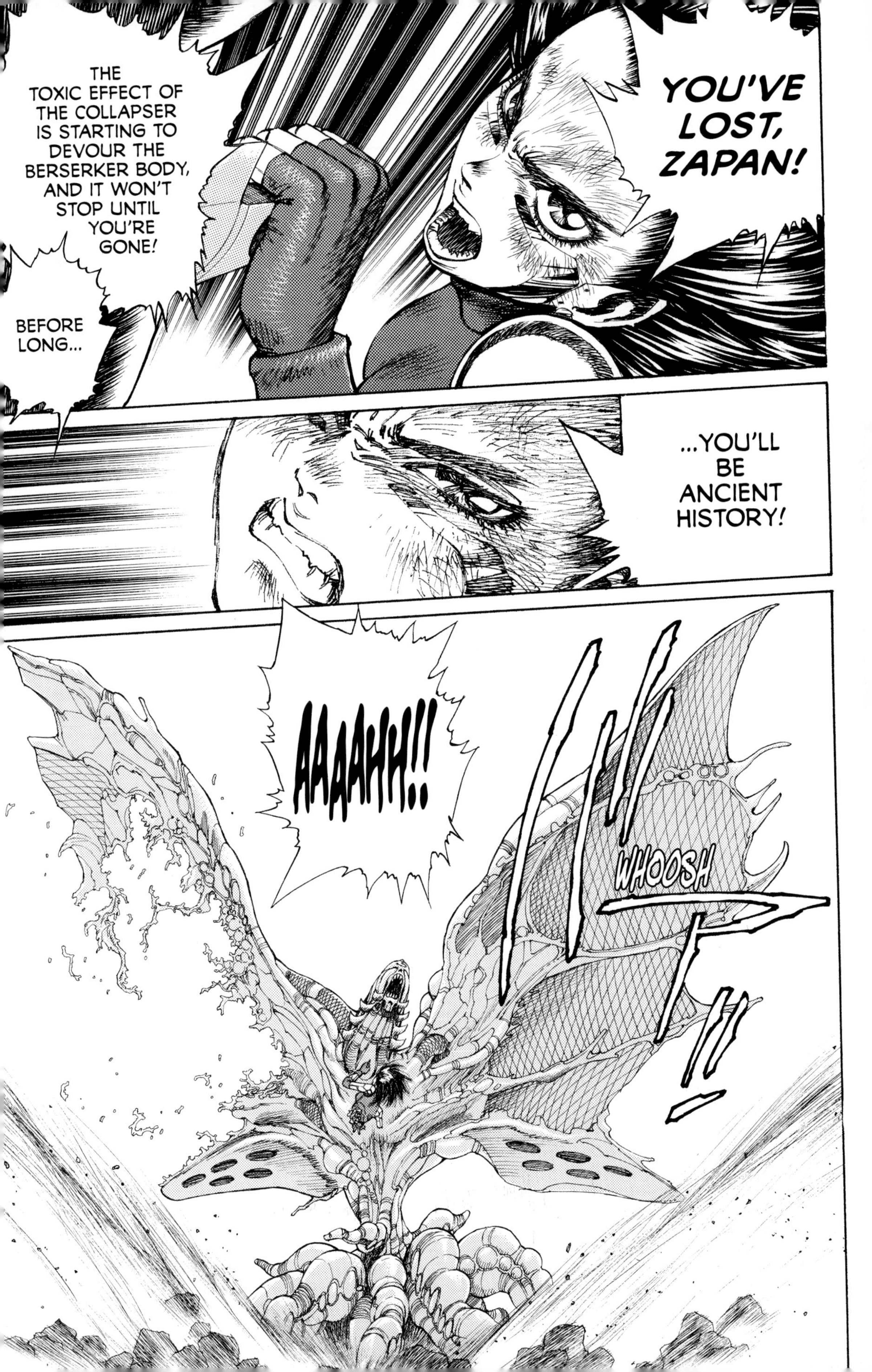
YOU'VE LOST, ZAPAN!
THE TOXIC EFFECT OF THE COLLAPSER IS STARTING TO DEVOUR THE BERSERKER BODY, AND IT WON'T STOP UNTIL YOU'RE GONE!
BEFORE LONG...
...YOU'LL BE ANCIENT HISTORY!
AAAAHH!!
WHOOSH

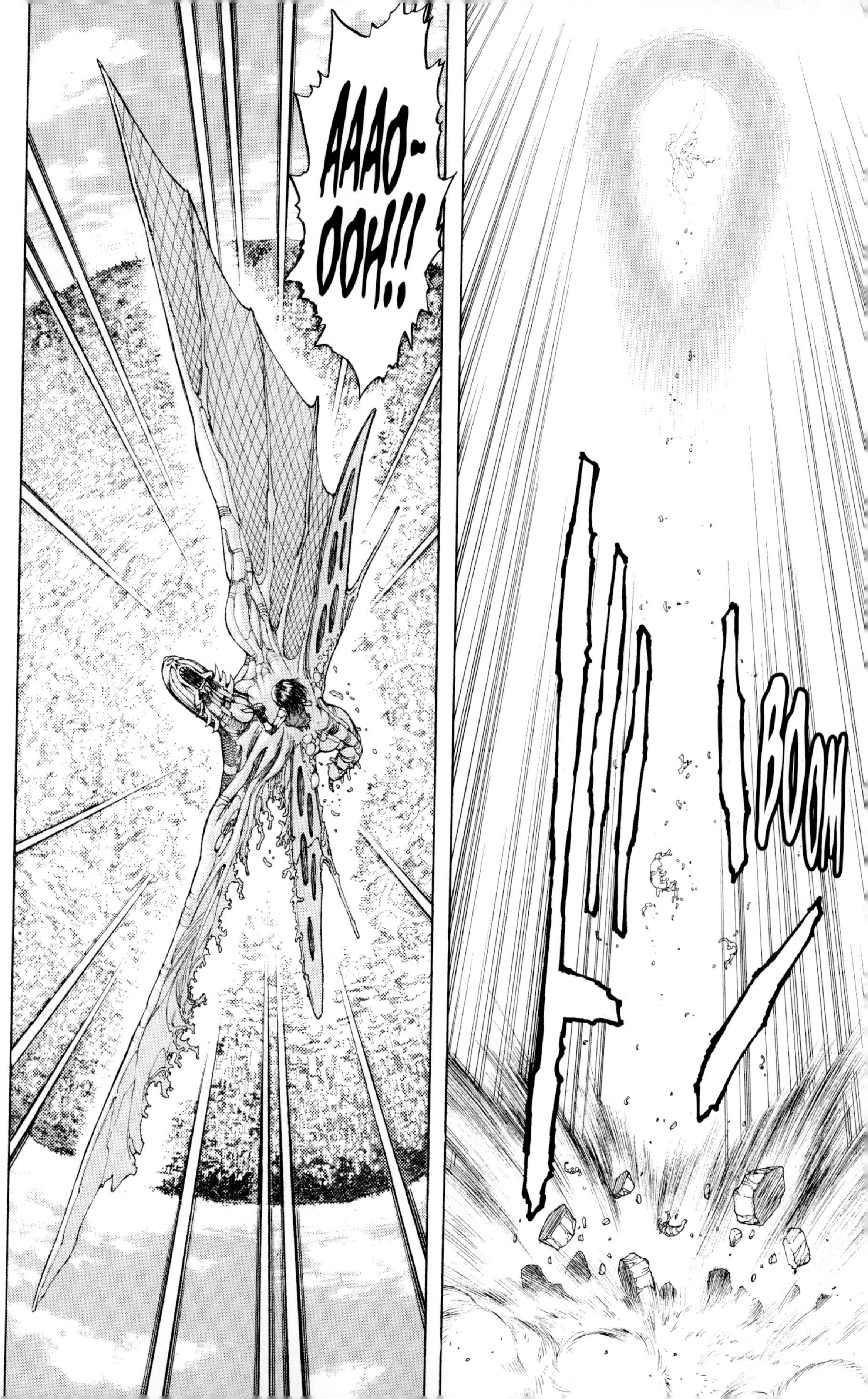
BOOM
AAAO-
OOH!!

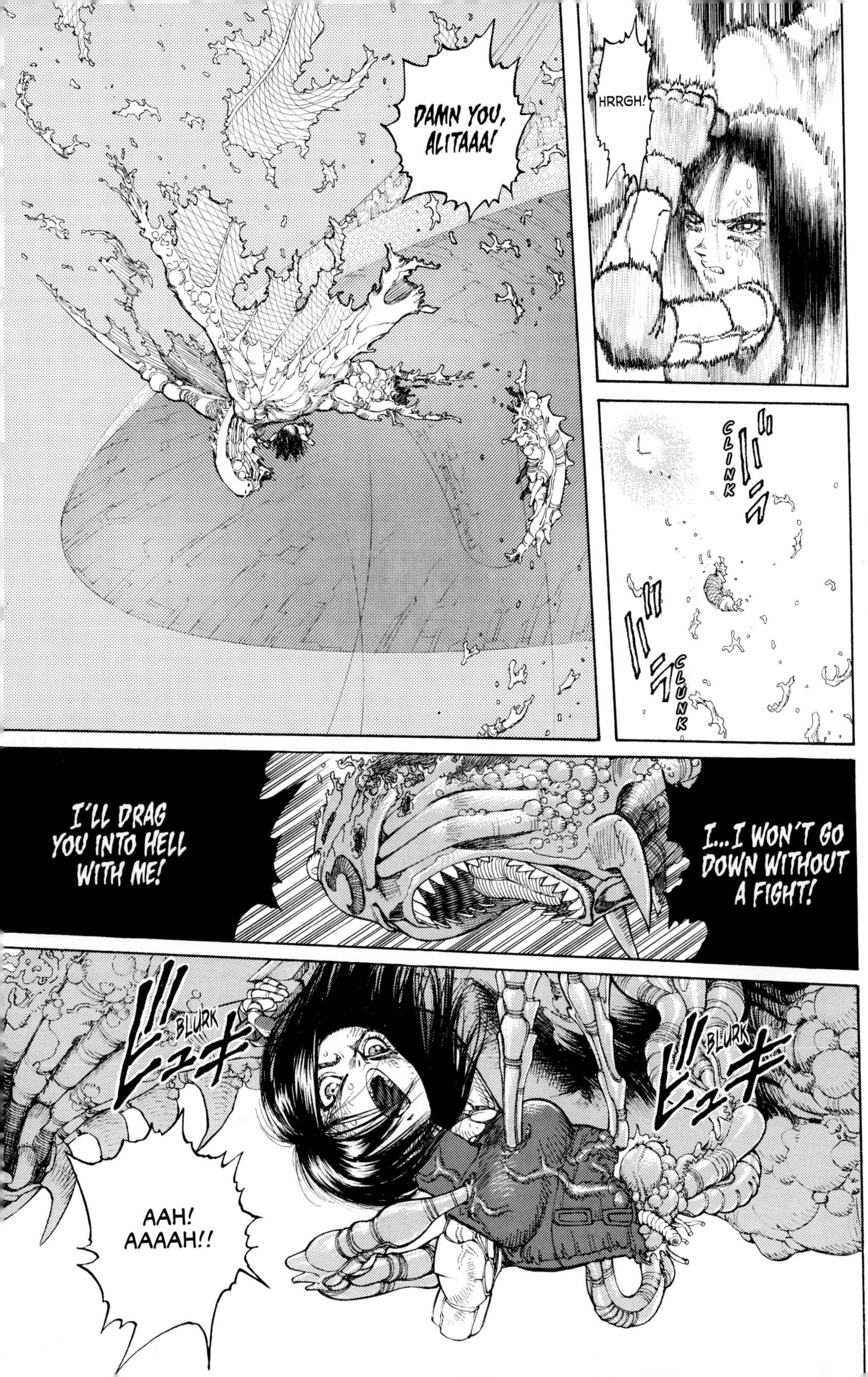
HRRGH!
CLINK
CLUNK
DAMN YOU, ALITAAA!
I...I WON'T GO DOWN WITHOUT A FIGHT!
I'LL DRAG YOU INTO HELL WITH ME!
BLURK
BLURK
AAH! AAAAH!!

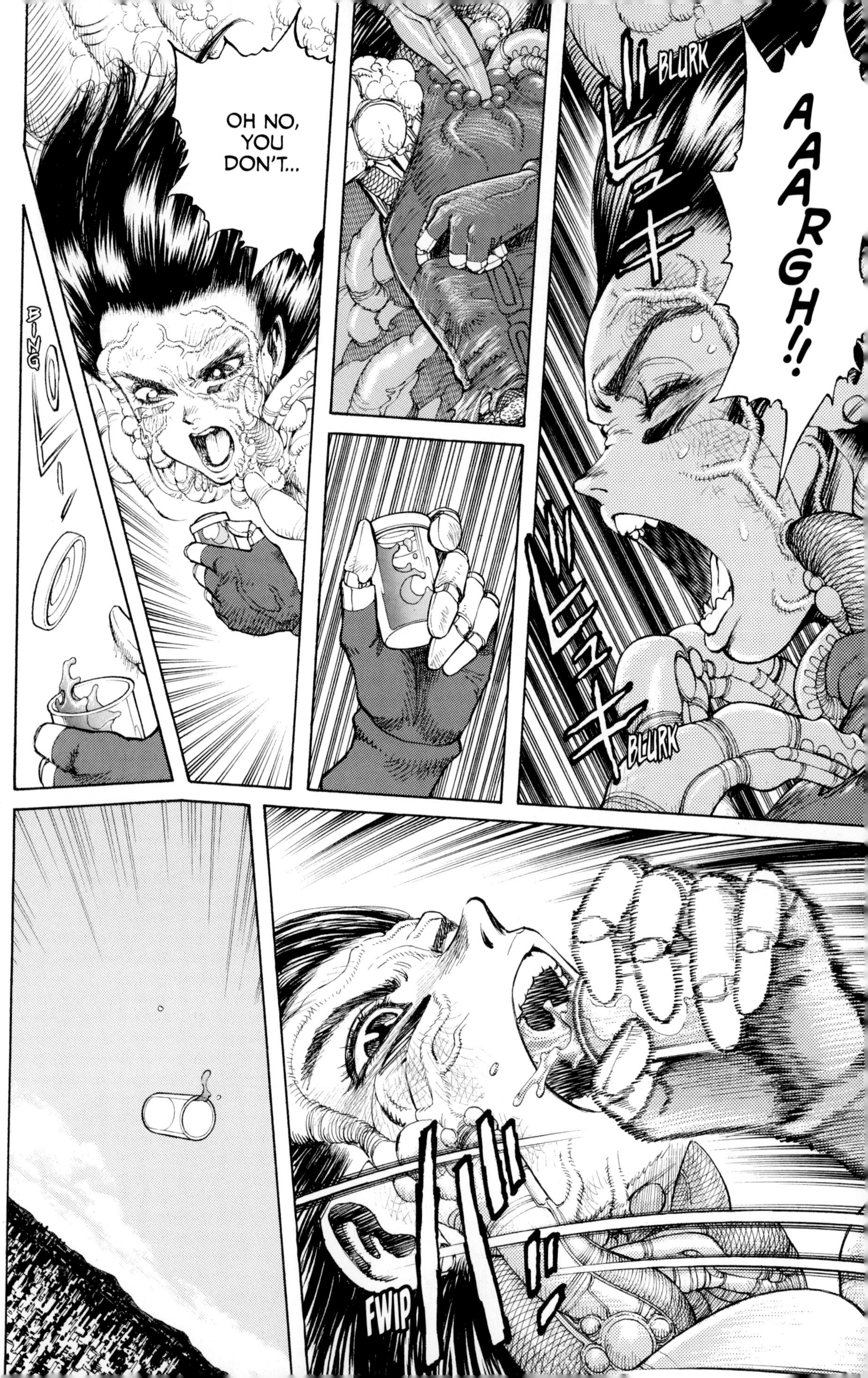
BLURK
AAARGH!!
BLURK
OH NO, YOU DON'T...
BING
FWIP

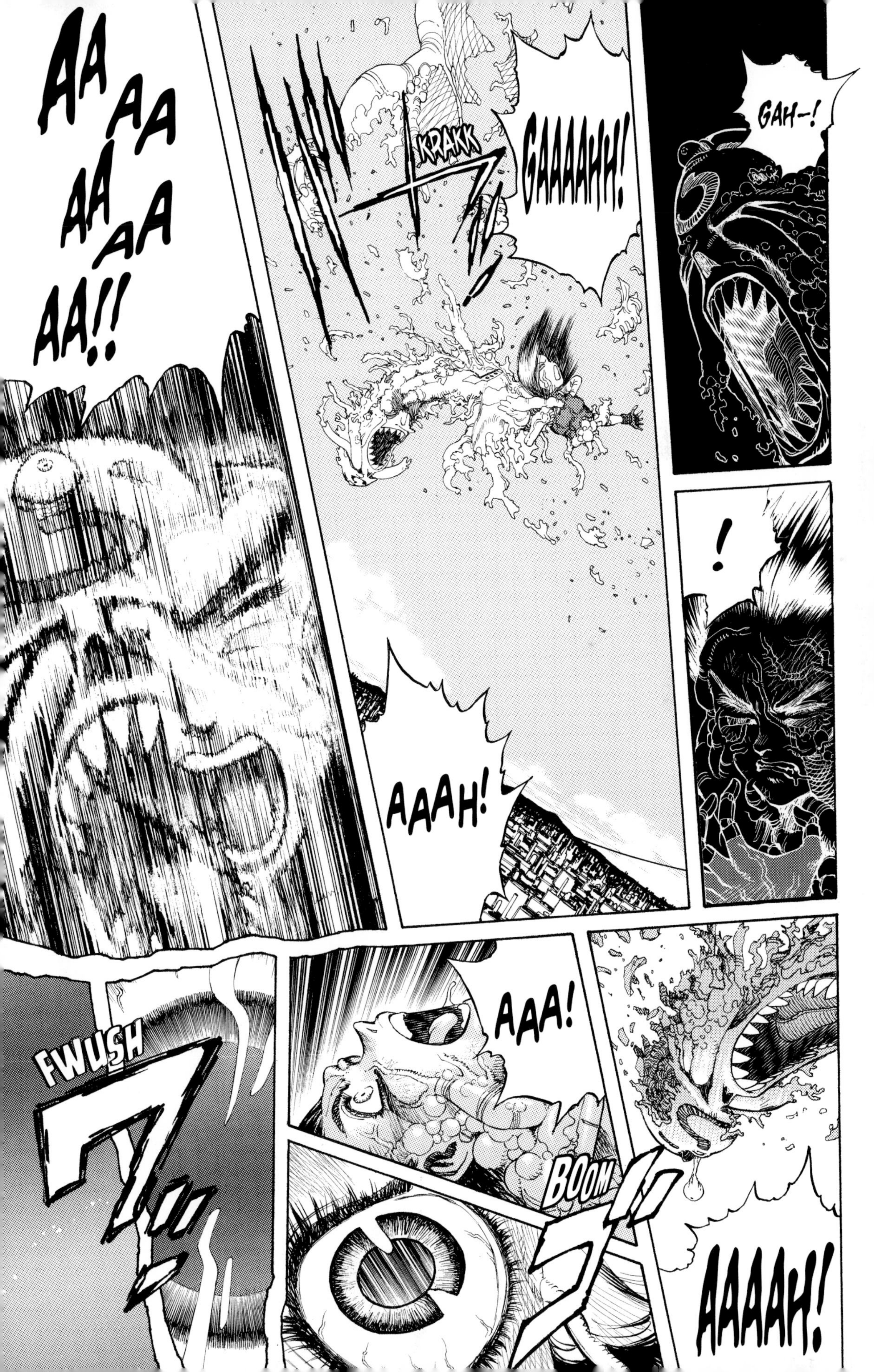
GAH-!
!
GAAAAHH!
KRAKK
AAAH!
AA
AA
AA
AA
AA
AA!!
AAAAH!
BOOM
AAA!
FWUSH

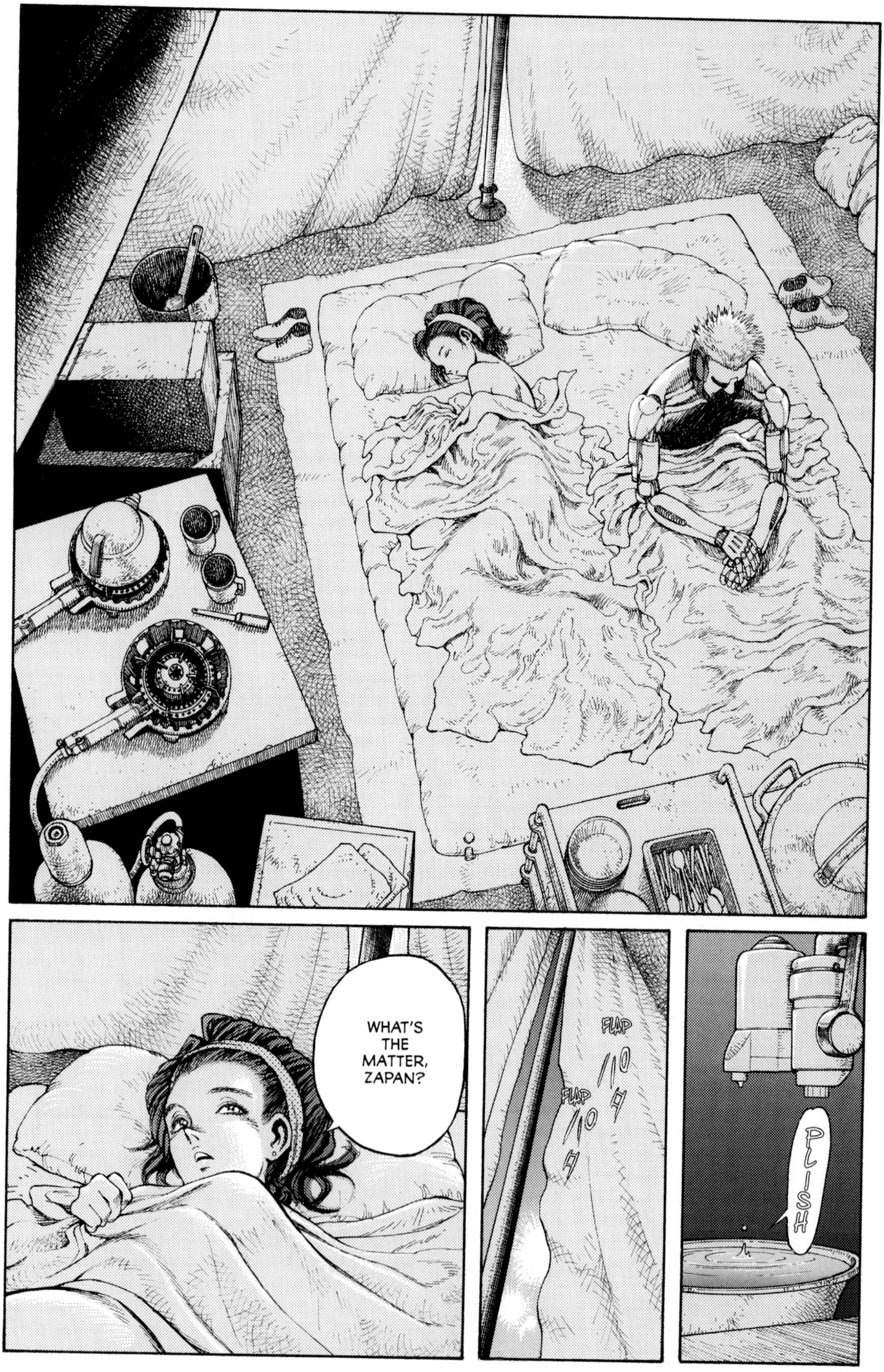
PLISH
FLAP
FLAP
WHAT'S THE MATTER, ZAPAN?

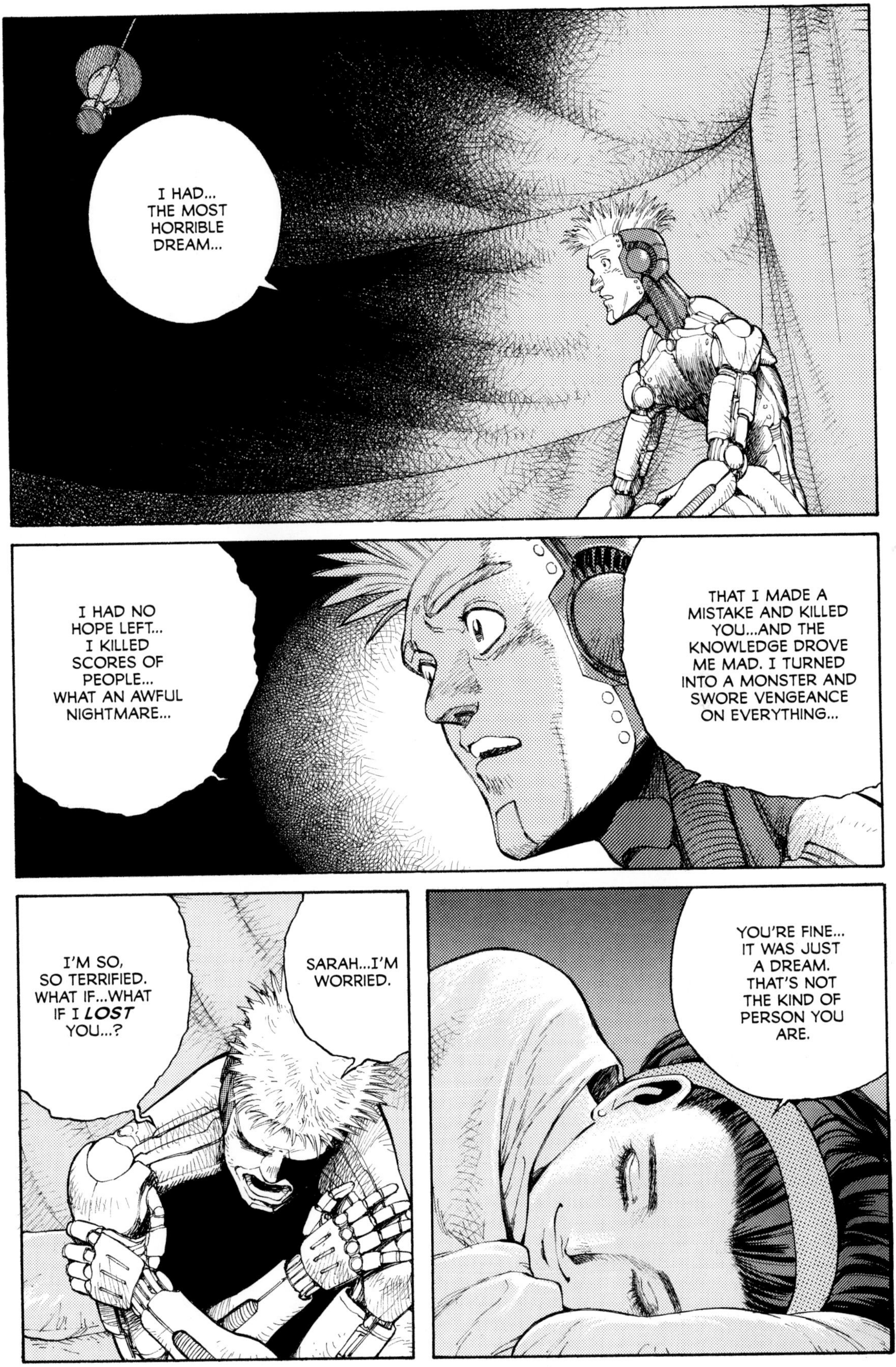
I HAD... THE MOST HORRIBLE DREAM...
THAT I MADE A MISTAKE AND KILLED YOU...AND THE KNOWLEDGE DROVE ME MAD. I TURNED INTO A MONSTER AND SWORE VENGEANCE ON EVERYTHING...
I HAD NO HOPE LEFT... I KILLED SCORES OF PEOPLE... WHAT AN AWFUL NIGHTMARE...
YOU'RE FINE... IT WAS JUST A DREAM. THAT'S NOT THE KIND OF PERSON YOU ARE.
SARAH...I'M WORRIED.
I'M SO, SO TERRIFIED. WHAT IF...WHAT IF I ***LOST*** YOU...?

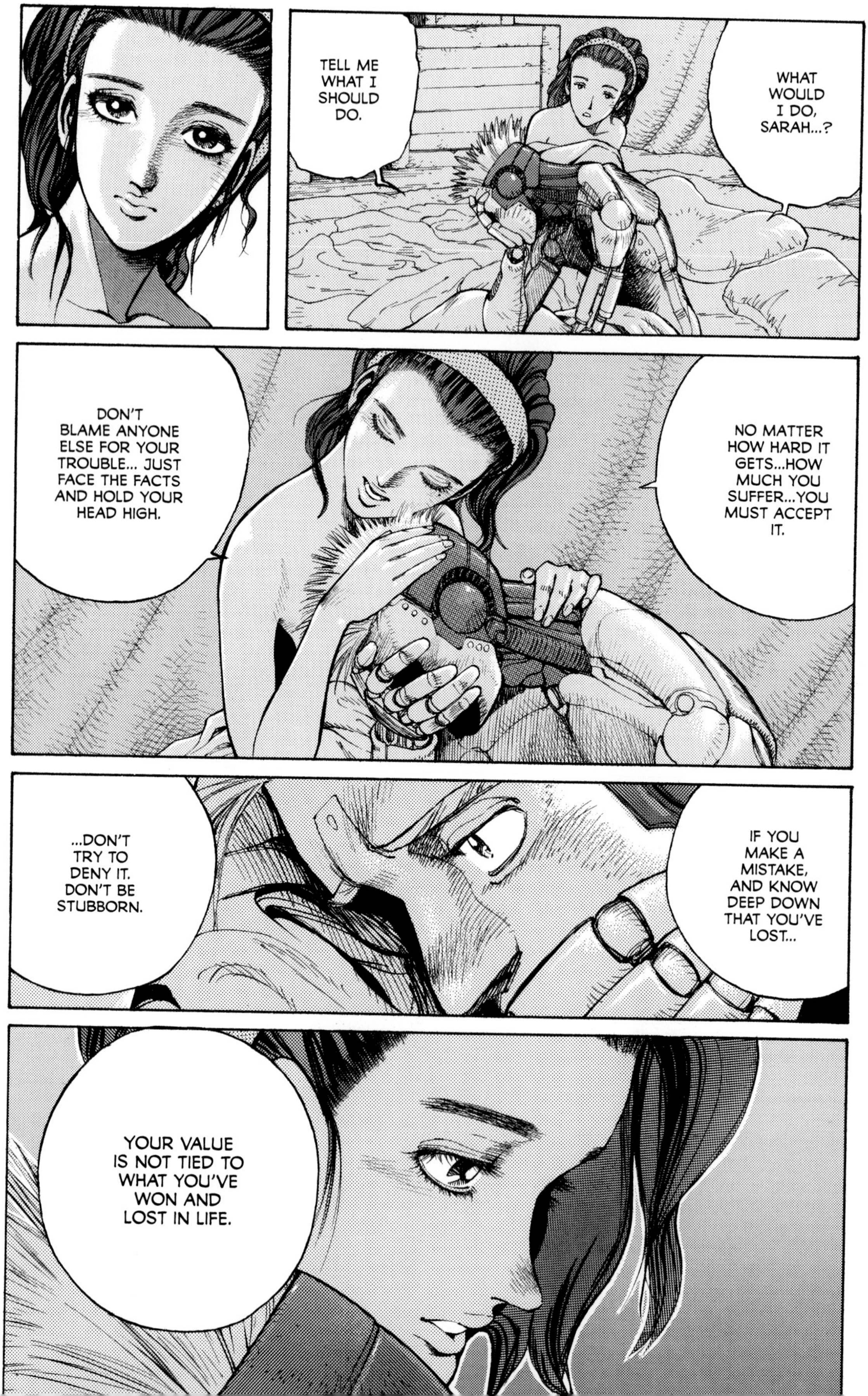
WHAT WOULD I DO, SARAH...?
TELL ME WHAT I SHOULD DO.
NO MATTER HOW HARD IT GETS...HOW MUCH YOU SUFFER...YOU MUST ACCEPT IT.
DON'T BLAME ANYONE ELSE FOR YOUR TROUBLE... JUST FACE THE FACTS AND HOLD YOUR HEAD HIGH.
IF YOU MAKE A MISTAKE, AND KNOW DEEP DOWN THAT YOU'VE LOST...
...DON'T TRY TO DENY IT. DON'T BE STUBBORN.
YOUR VALUE IS NOT TIED TO WHAT YOU'VE WON AND LOST IN LIFE.

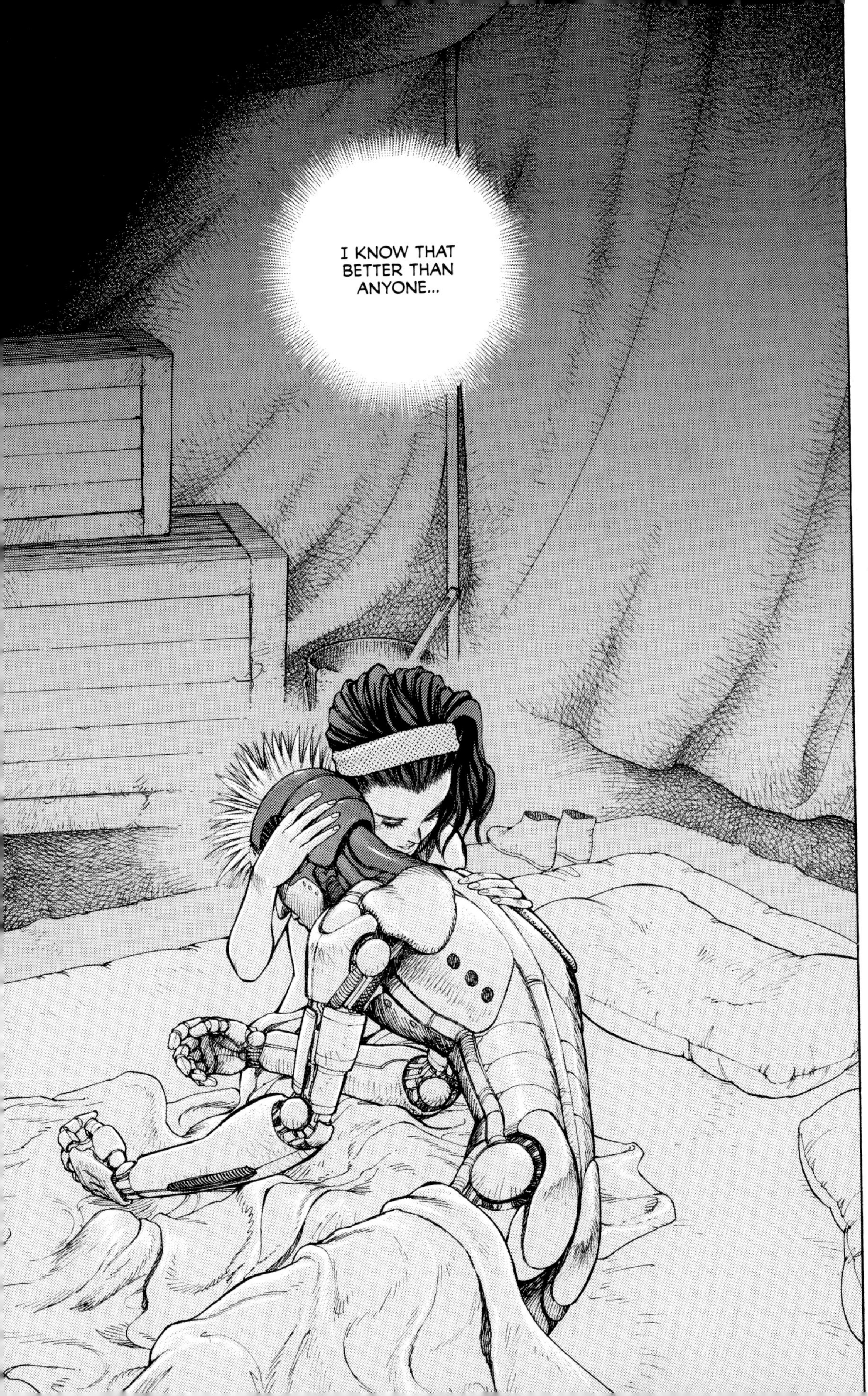
I KNOW THAT BETTER THAN ANYONE...

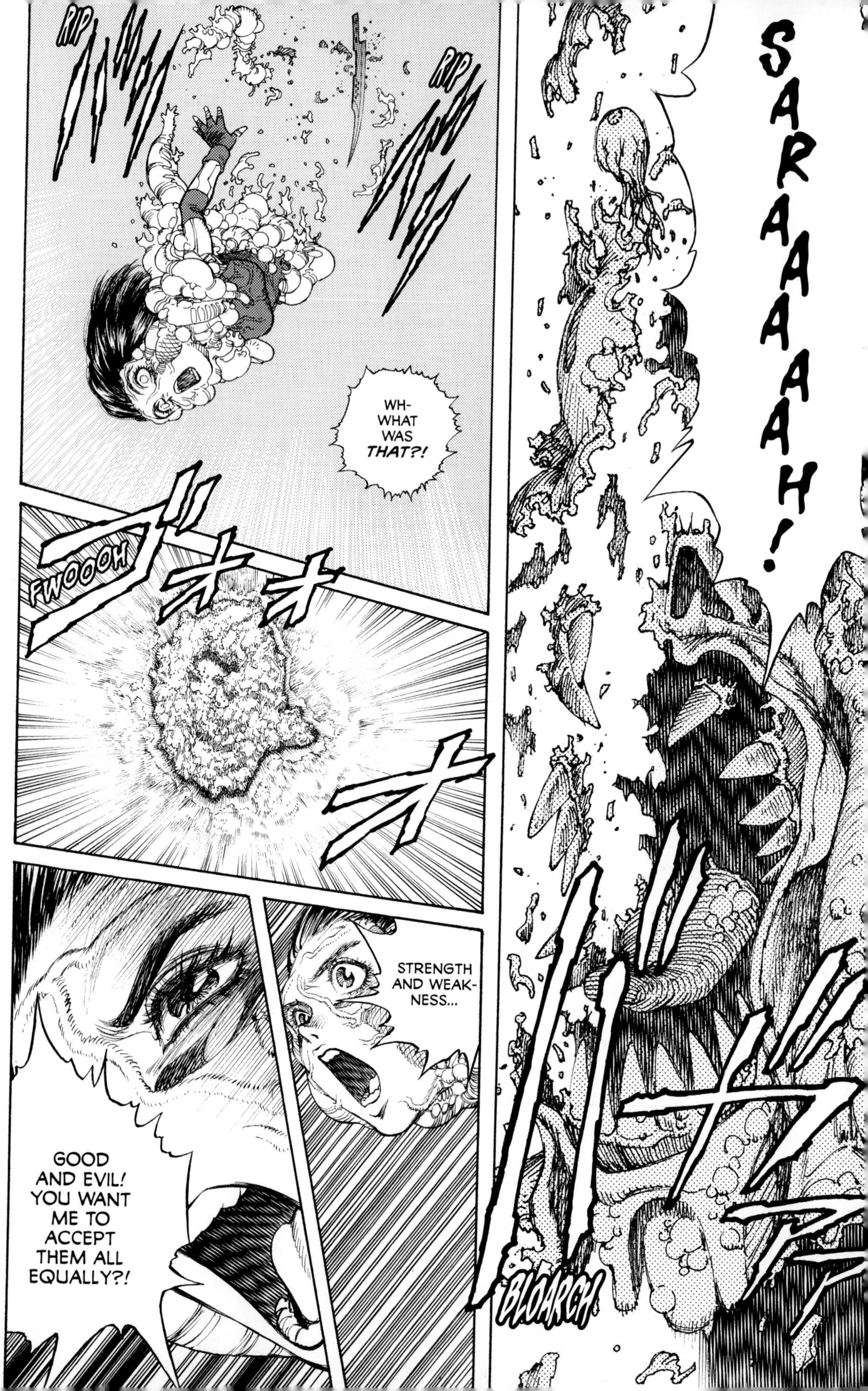
SARAAAAAH!
BLOARCH
RIP
RIP
WH- WHAT WAS *THAT*?!
FWOOOH
STRENGTH AND WEAK-NESS...
GOOD AND EVIL! YOU WANT ME TO ACCEPT THEM ALL EQUALLY?!

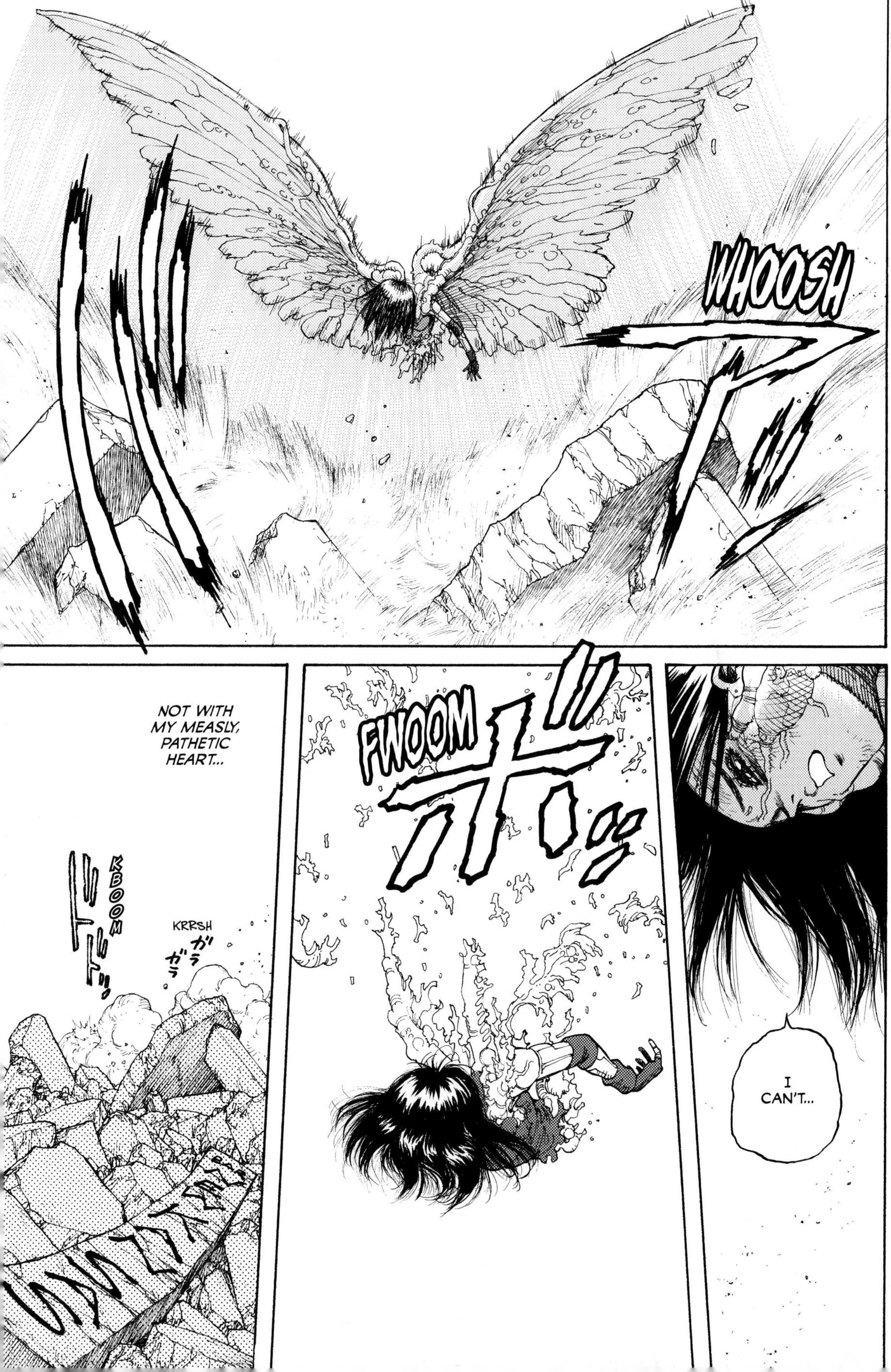
WHOOSH
I CAN'T...
FWOOM
NOT WITH MY MEASLY, PATHETIC HEART...
KBOOM
KRRSH
ガラ ガラ

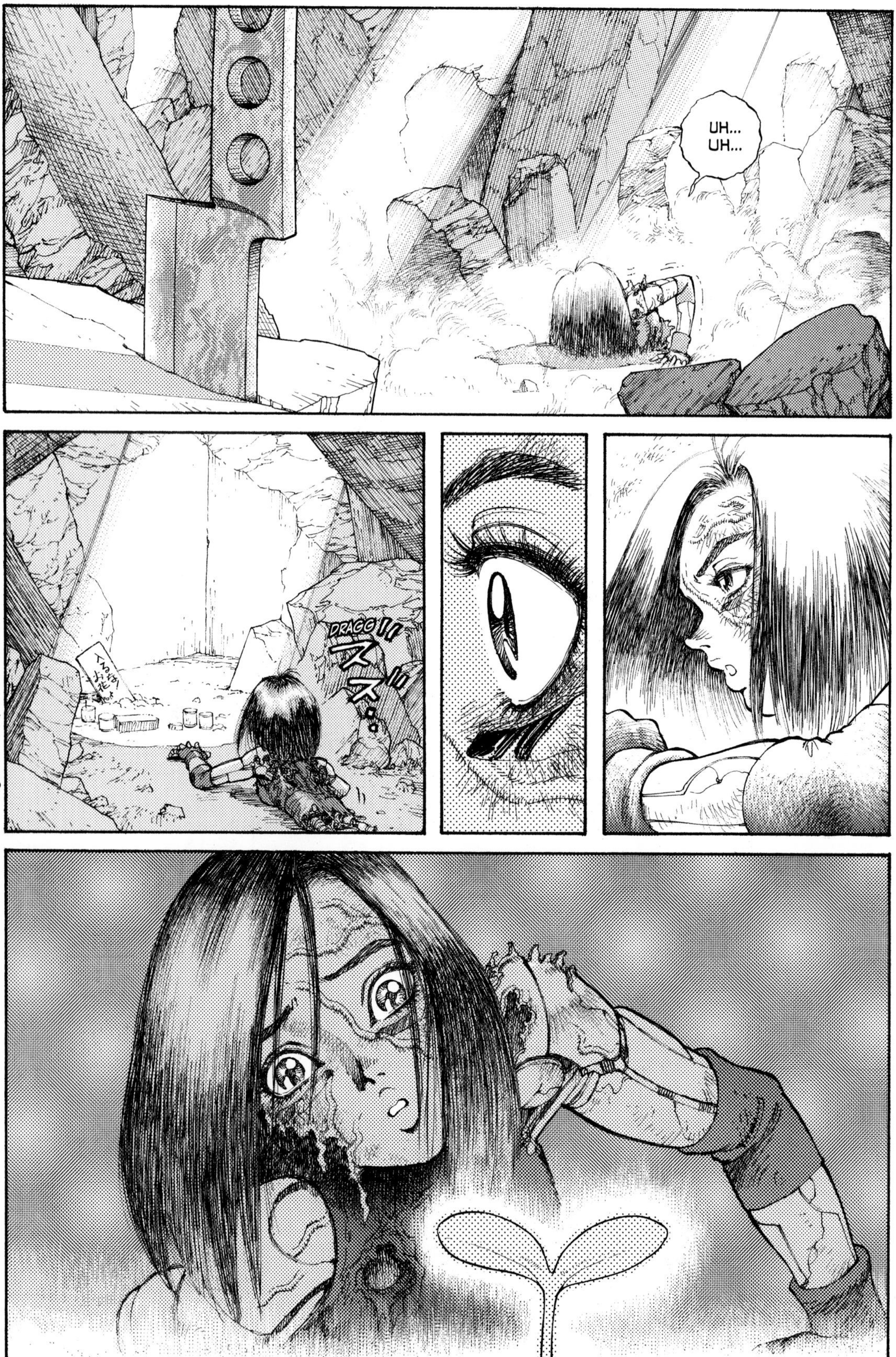
UH...
UH...
DRAGG!!

Sign: Don't step on the flowers!

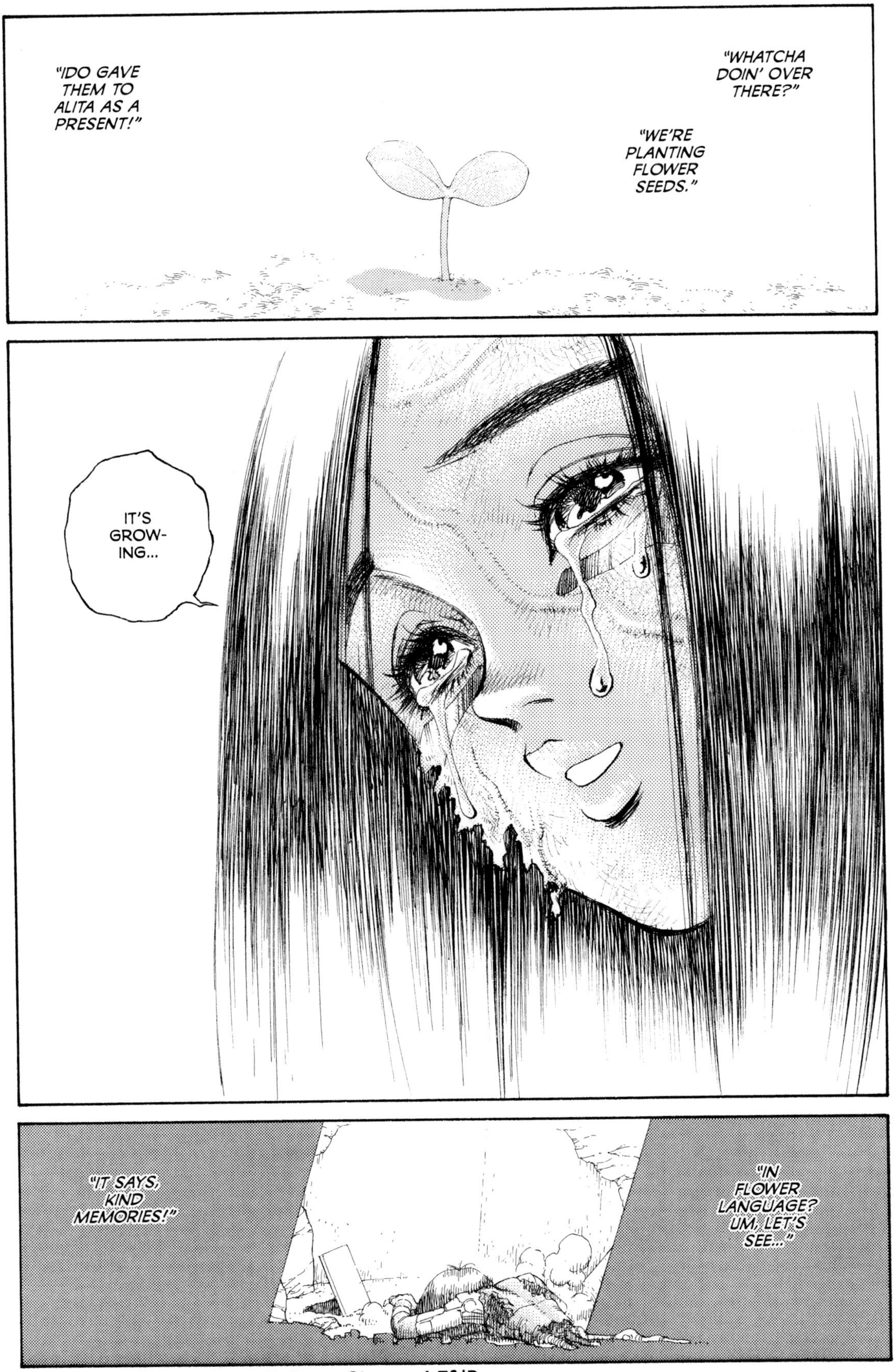
"WHATCHA DOIN' OVER THERE?"
"WE'RE PLANTING FLOWER SEEDS."
"IDO GAVE THEM TO ALITA AS A PRESENT!"
IT'S GROW-ING...
"IN FLOWER LANGUAGE? UM, LET'S SEE..."
"IT SAYS, KIND MEMORIES!"

Battle Angel Alita Part 5: Lost Sheep / END

Nanotechnology

EXPLAINED!

ONE NANOMETER IS 10^{-9} METERS, OR 1/1,000,000,000TH OF A METER. "NANO" COMES FROM THE GREEK ROOT NANOS, MEANING "DWARF." INCIDENTALLY, THE KANJI CORRESPONDING TO ONE NANO IS JIN, MEANING "DUST."

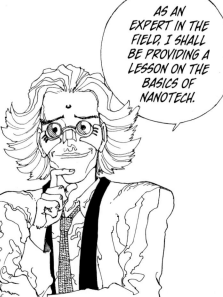

AS AN EXPERT IN THE FIELD, I SHALL BE PROVIDING A LESSON ON THE BASICS OF NANOTECH.

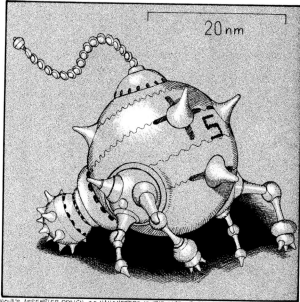

A NANOMACHINE IS A MICROSCOPIC ROBOT CONSISTING OF GEARS, BEARINGS AND MOTORS CONSTRUCTED AT THE INDIVIDUAL MOLECULAR LEVEL. IT'S POWERED BY STATIC ELECTRICITY, AND DUE TO THE PROPERTIES OF MOLECULAR BONDS, IS VERY HARDY. IT RUNS OFF OF PRELOADED PROGRAMMING. THESE MOLECULAR ROBOTS ARE CALLED "ASSEMBLERS."

20nm
S
NOVA'S ASSEMBLER DESIGN. 20 NANOMETERS IS THE SIZE OF THE WORLD'S SMALLEST VIRUSES.

AN ASSEMBLER CAN GRAB AND PLACE MOLECULES AND ATOMS AT A SPEED OF A MILLION PER SECOND, MEANING THAT IT CAN CREATE A PERFECT REPLICA OF ITSELF IN ABOUT FIFTEEN MINUTES.

WHEN EACH COPY THEN REPEATS THE REPLICATION PROCESS, THEIR NUMBERS GROW EXPONENTIALLY. WITHIN TEN HOURS YOU'D HAVE 68 BILLION NANOMACHINES. IN LESS THAN A DAY, THEY'D WEIGH AN ACTUAL TON. BY THE END OF TWO DAYS, THEY COULD WEIGH MORE THAN THE ACTUAL EARTH. NATURALLY, THERE WILL BE MULTIPLE LAYERS OF PROGRAMMING AND FAILSAFE MECHANISMS DESIGNED TO AVOID SUCH A DISASTER.

THE ROOTS OF NANOTECHNOLOGY

1942: THE FIRST PIECE OF SCI-FI WRITING INVOLVING NANOTECH: ROBERT A. HEINLEIN'S SHORT STORY "WALDO."

1959: RICHARD FEYNMAN GIVES A LECTURE TITLED "THERE'S PLENTY OF ROOM AT THE BOTTOM."

1976: ERIC DREXLER FIRST PROPOSES THE CONCEPT OF THE "ASSEMBLER."

1981: THE STM (SCANNING TUNNELING MICRO SCOPE) IS DEVELOPED BY DRS. ROHRER AND BINNIG AT IBM ZURICH RESEARCH LABORATORY.

1986: ERIC DREXLER'S *BIBLE OF NANOTECHNOLOGY: ENGINES OF CREATION.*

1990: IBM SCIENTISTS USE THEIR STM TO CREATE THE IBM LOGO USING ATOMS (VISUALIZED BELOW).

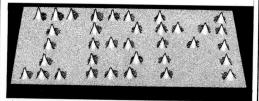

5 nm
SPELLED USING 35 XENON ATOMS.

IN THEORY, ASSEMBLERS CAN ESSENTIALLY CREATE ANYTHING THAT IS PHYSICALLY POSSIBLE TO EXIST. THEIR INDUSTRIAL POWER IS BASICALLY LIMITLESS.

IN PRACTICE

- BRAIN RECONSTRUCTION........(BRAIN AUGMENTATION)
- BERSERKER BODY..........................(MECHANICAL LIFE)
- ARTIFICIAL SPINE..............(ARTIFICIAL STRUCTURES)
- RESTORERS..(IMMORTALITY)

(OTHER USES)

- SYTHESIZING FOOD FROM INORGANIC MATTER
- AUTO-GROWTH/COMPLETION OF ALL KINDS OF MECHANICAL DEVICES
- DEVELOPMENT OF NEW MATERIALS
- MOLECULAR COMPUTING
- PLANET TERRAFORMING
- ETC.

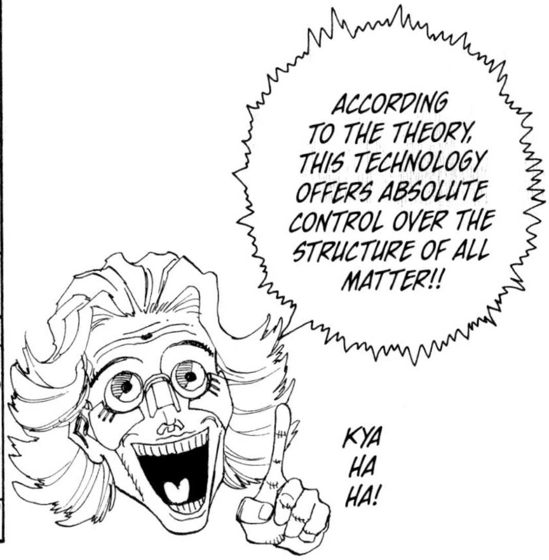
ACCORDING TO THE THEORY, THIS TECHNOLOGY OFFERS ABSOLUTE CONTROL OVER THE STRUCTURE OF ALL MATTER!!
KYA HA HA!

THE CREATION OF FLAN!

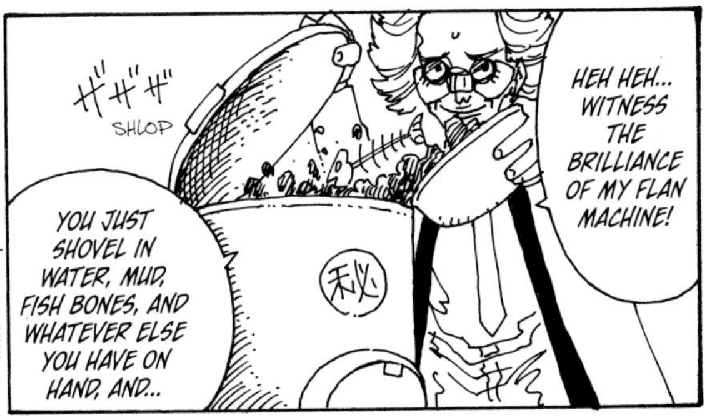
HEH HEH... WITNESS THE BRILLIANCE OF MY FLAN MACHINE!
ザザザ
SHLOP
秘
YOU JUST SHOVEL IN WATER, MUD, FISH BONES, AND WHATEVER ELSE YOU HAVE ON HAND, AND...

Machine: Top Secret

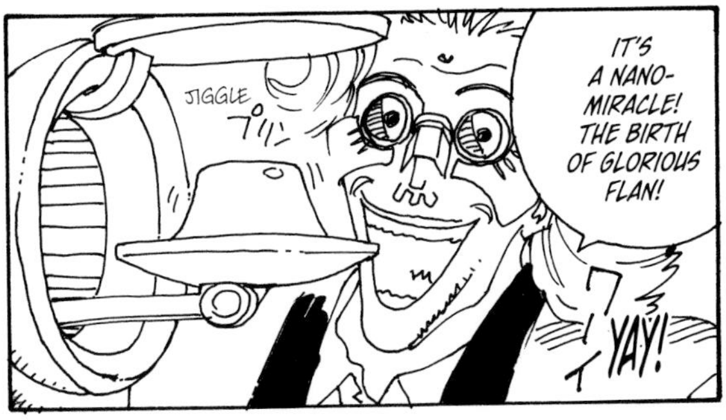
IT'S A NANO-MIRACLE! THE BIRTH OF GLORIOUS FLAN!
ワーイ
YAY!
プリン
JIGGLE

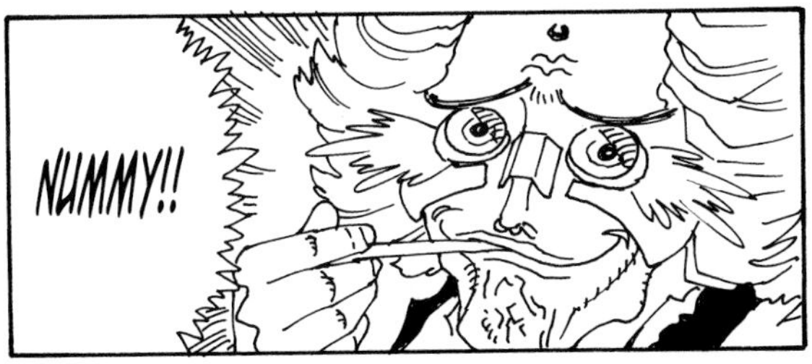
NUMMY!!

THEN THE MACHINE WENT ON THE FRITZ.

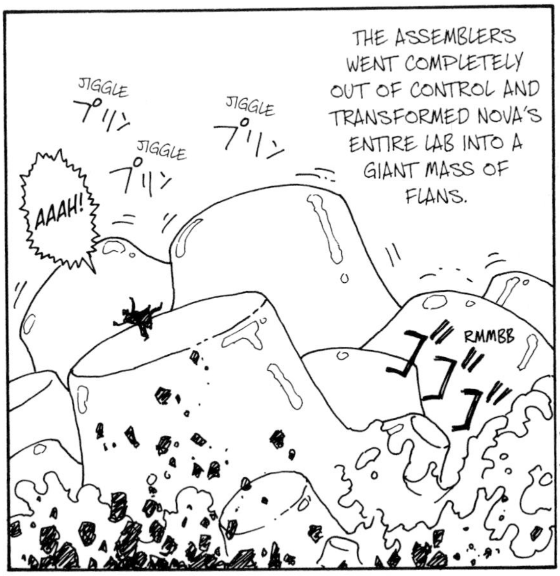
THE ASSEMBLERS WENT COMPLETELY OUT OF CONTROL AND TRANSFORMED NOVA'S ENTIRE LAB INTO A GIANT MASS OF FLANS.
プリン
JIGGLE
プリン
JIGGLE
プリン
JIGGLE
AAAH!
ゴゴゴ
RMMBB

THE END.

YUKITO.
1993. 8. 12.

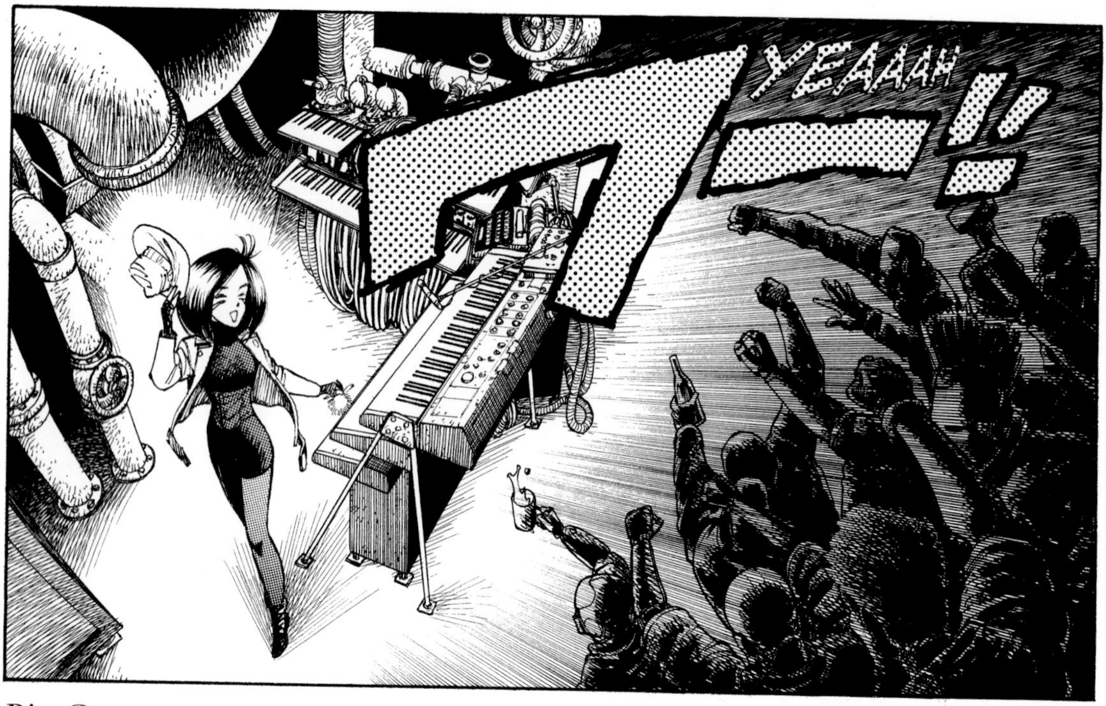
ワー!!
YEAAAH

Big Generator, page 15

The lyrics to Alita's song in this scene come from the original English adaptation of the Battle Angel Alita manga by Fred Burke and Toshifumi Yoshida for Viz Media in 1998, and are printed as such in the latest edition of the manga in Japan. However, in the initial 1993 Japanese release, she was singing the lyrics (with proper attribution) to the Yes song "Big Generator." Some remnants of this can be seen in the crowd chants, which are left in their untouched state like all of the sound effects in this edition.

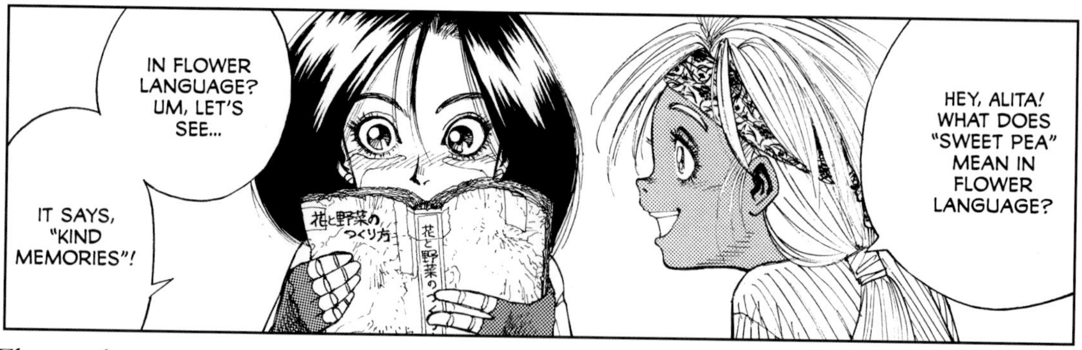
HEY, ALITA! WHAT DOES "SWEET PEA" MEAN IN FLOWER LANGUAGE?
IN FLOWER LANGUAGE? UM, LET'S SEE...
IT SAYS, "KIND MEMORIES"!
花と野菜のつくり方

Flower language, page 71

Originally called *hanakotoba* in Japanese, flower language is a way to communicate meaning through flowers. In the West, this can be called "the language of flowers" or "florigraphy." In Japan, *hanakotoba* as a concept is fairly common, so it often comes up in media like manga and anime.

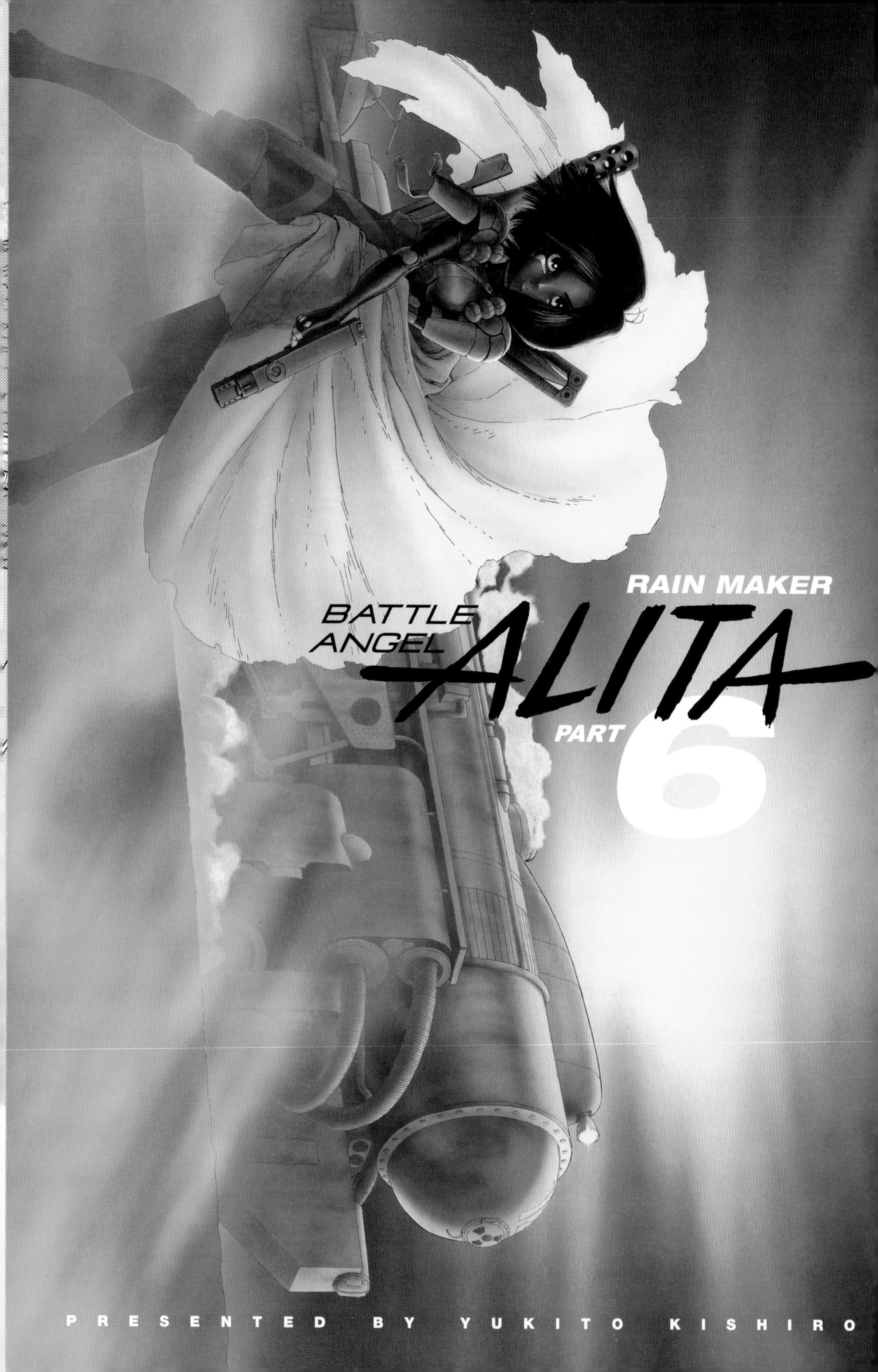
RAIN MAKER
BATTLE
ANGEL
ALITA
PART 6
PRESENTED BY YUKITO KISHIRO

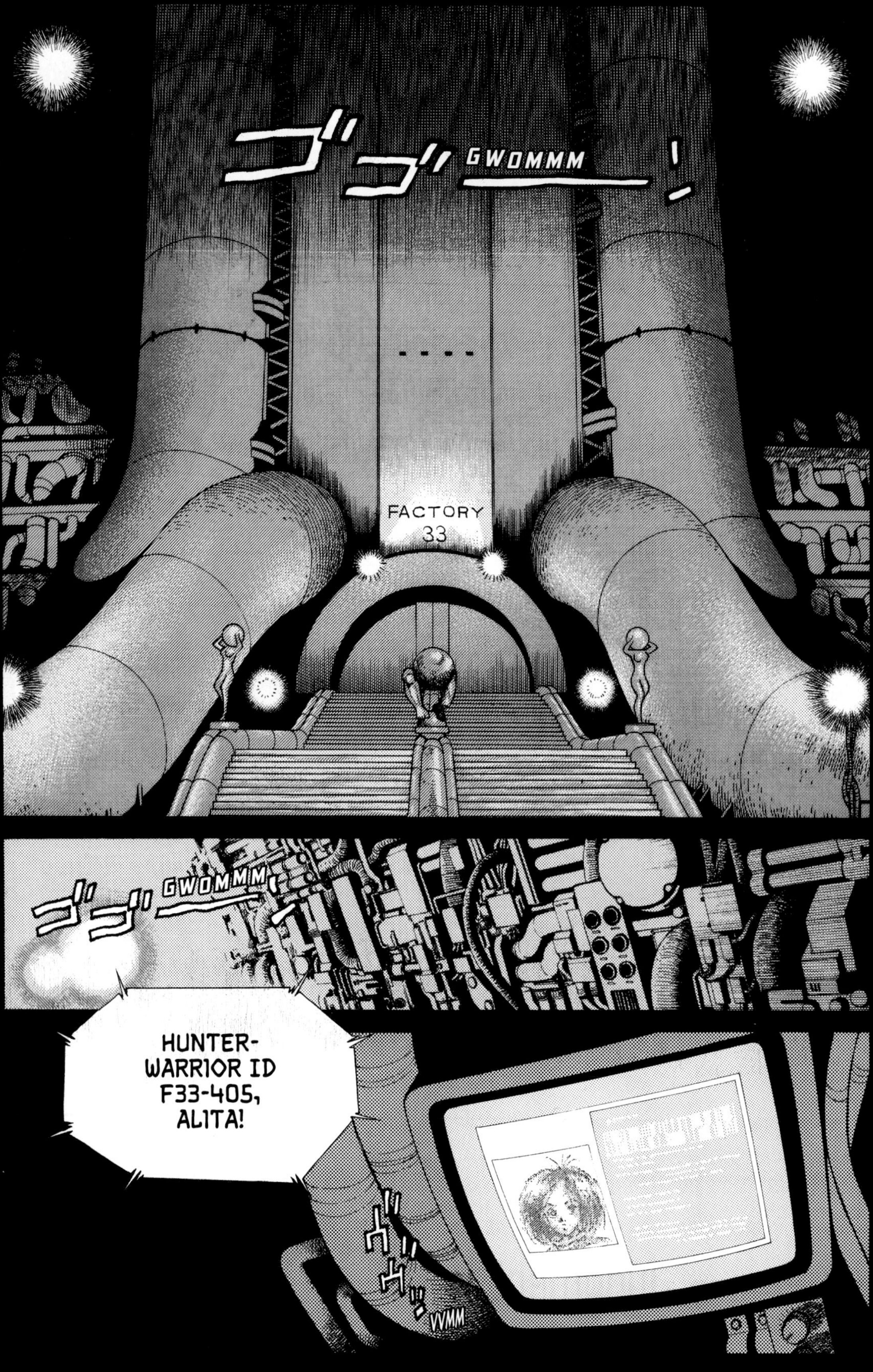
ゴゴ GWOMMM
....
FACTORY 33
ゴゴ GWOMMM
HUNTER-WARRIOR ID F33-405, ALITA!
VVMM

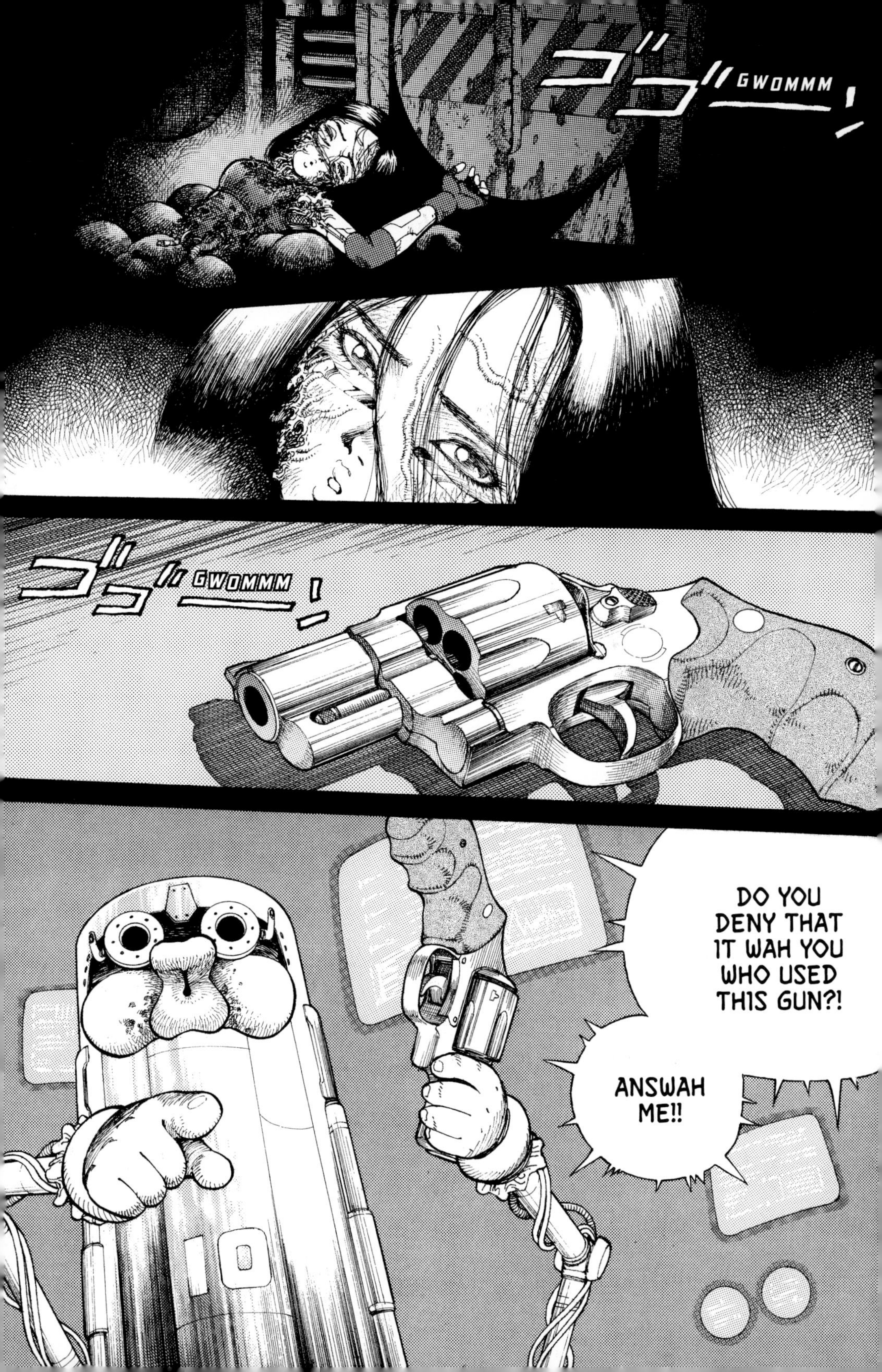
GWOMMM
GWOMMM
DO YOU DENY THAT IT WAH YOU WHO USED THIS GUN?!
ANSWAH ME!!

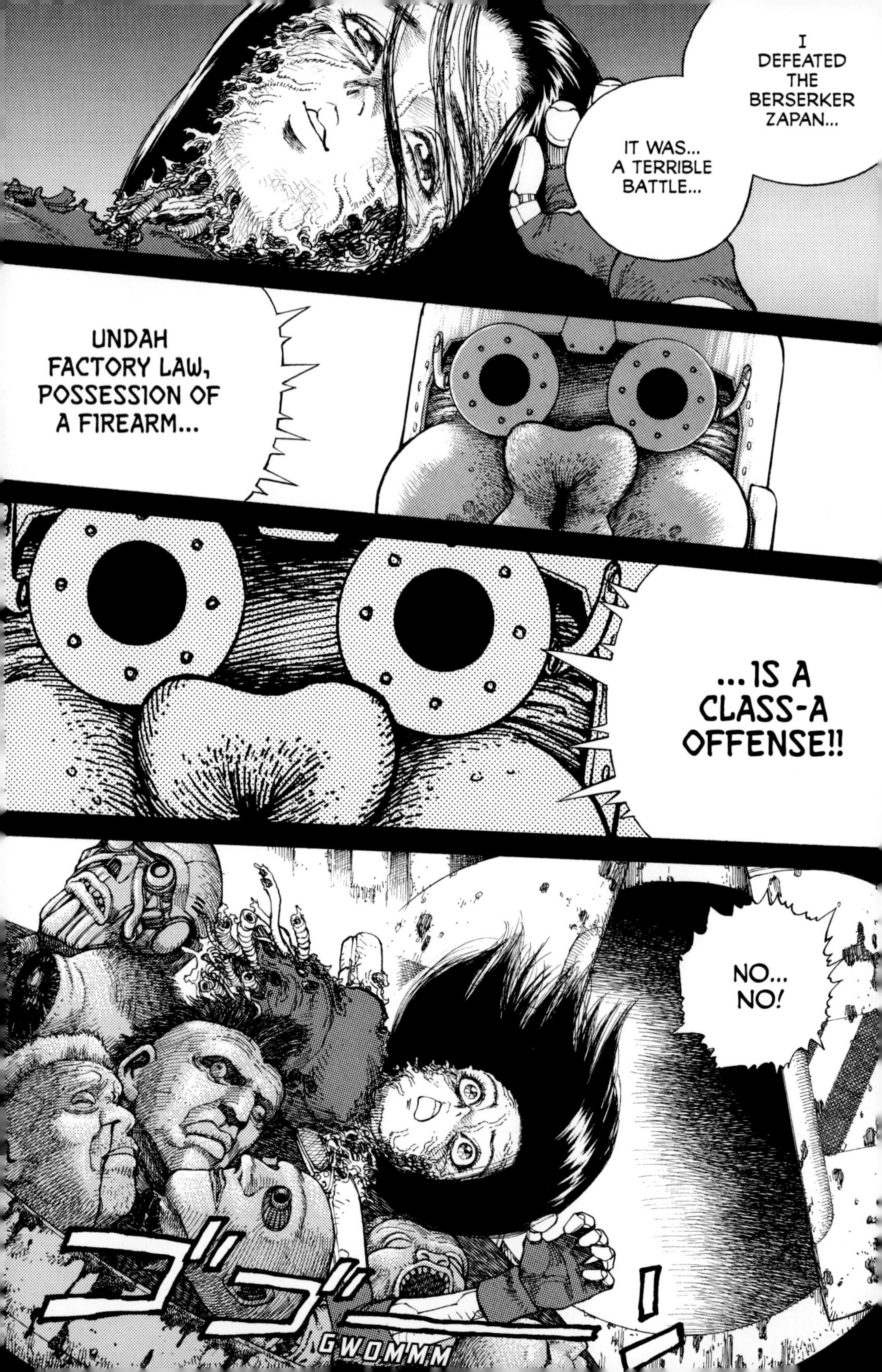
I DEFEATED THE BERSERKER ZAPAN...
IT WAS... A TERRIBLE BATTLE...
UNDAH FACTORY LAW, POSSESSION OF A FIREARM...
...IS A CLASS-A OFFENSE!!
NO... NO!
GWOMMM

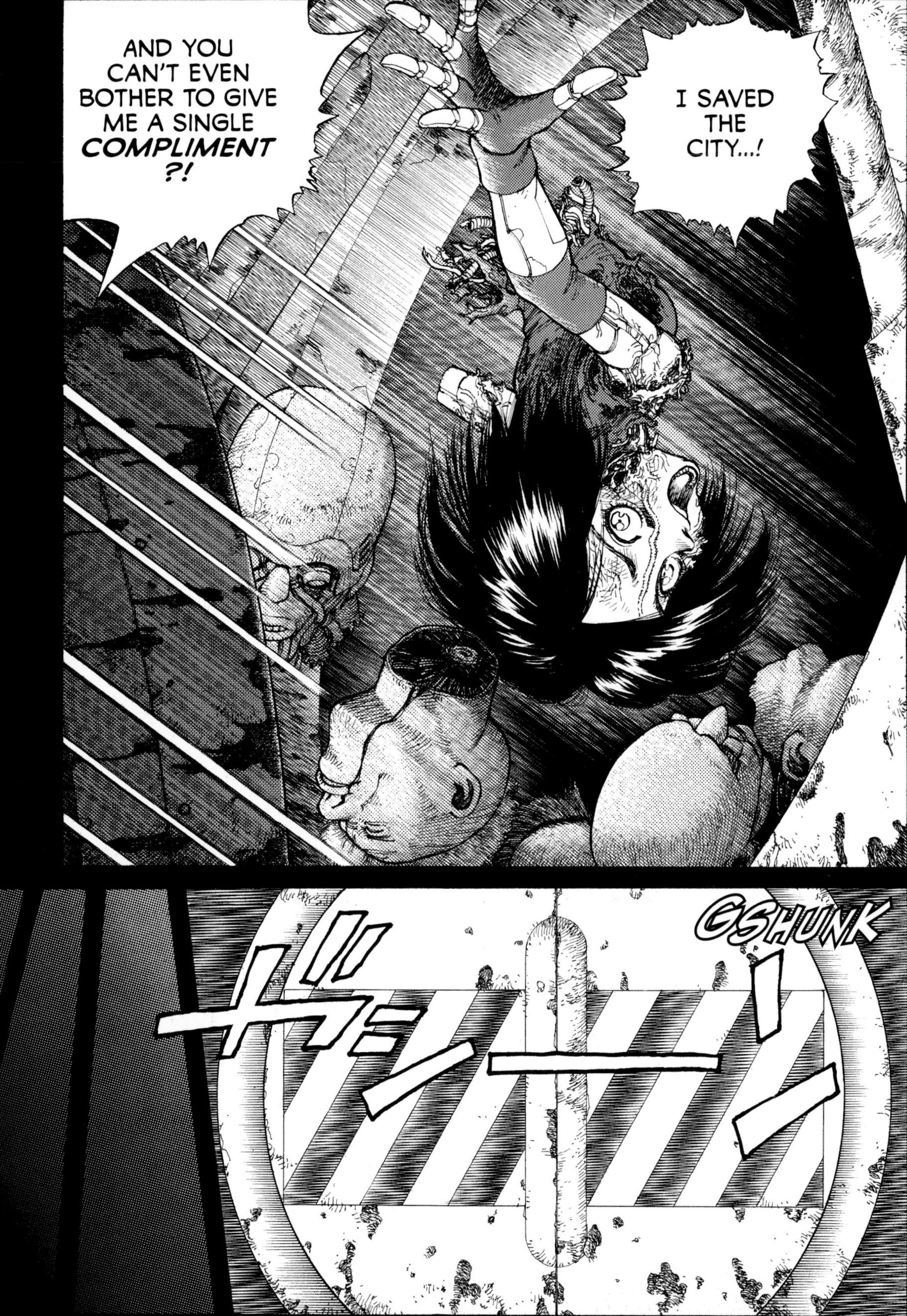
I SAVED THE CITY...!
AND YOU CAN'T EVEN BOTHER TO GIVE ME A SINGLE *COMPLIMENT* ?!
GSHUNK

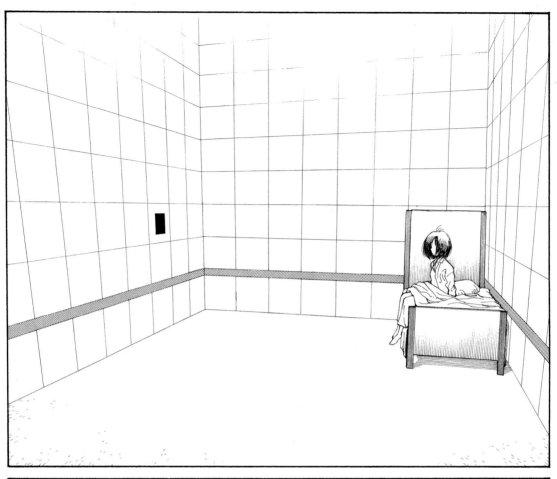

HUH...?

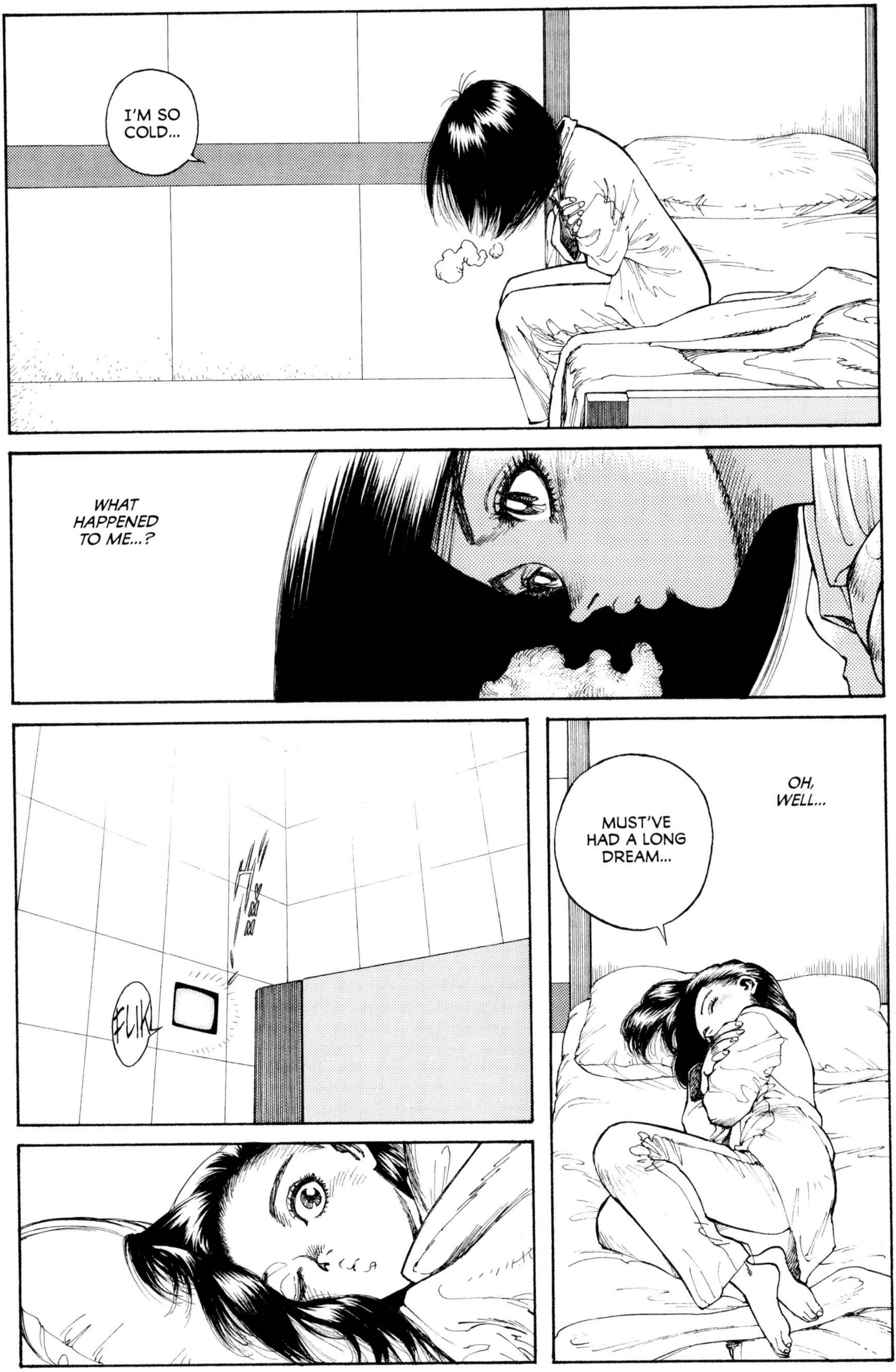
I'M SO COLD...
WHAT HAPPENED TO ME...?
OH, WELL...
MUST'VE HAD A LONG DREAM...
FLIK

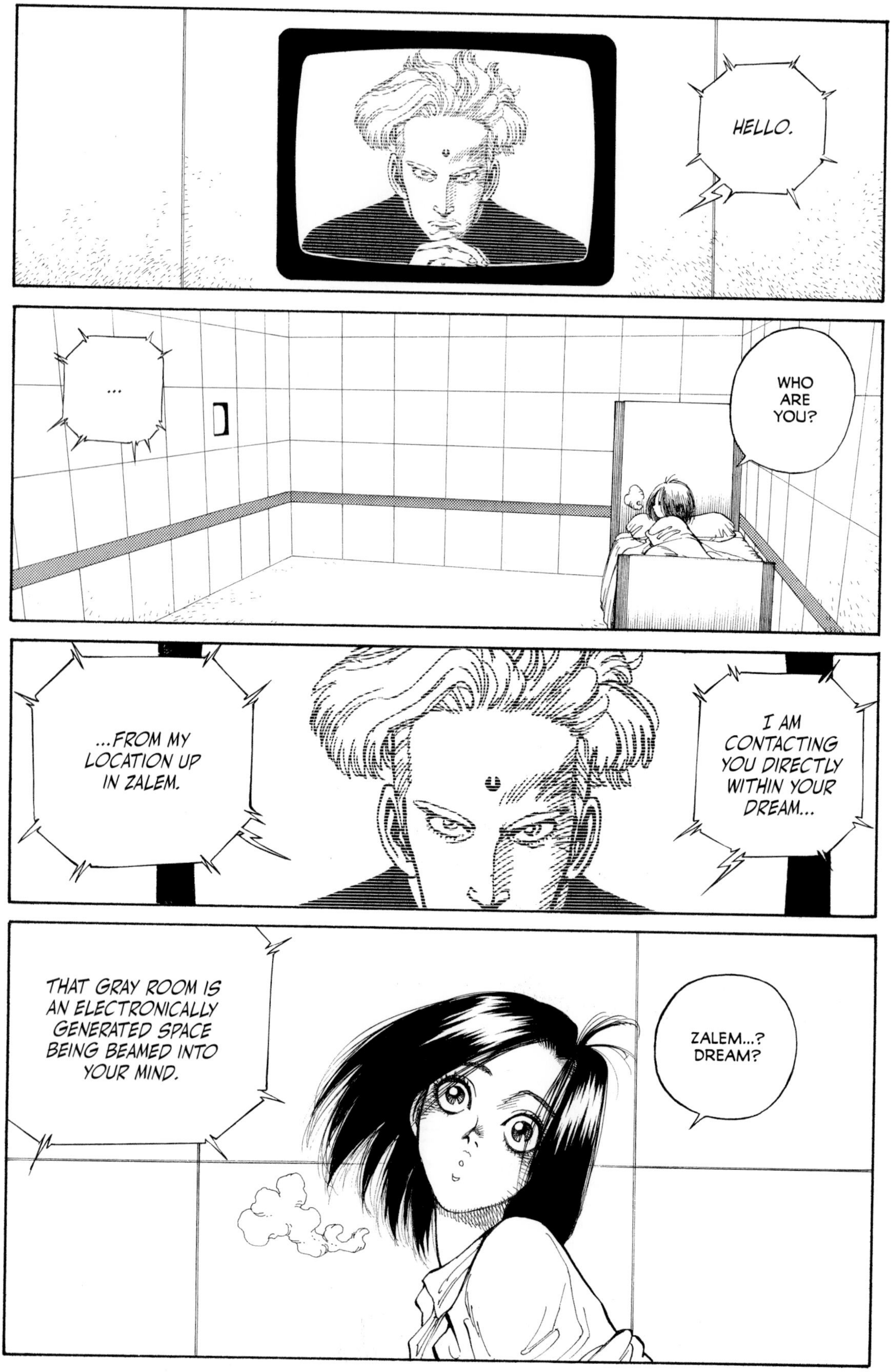
HELLO.
WHO ARE YOU?
...
I AM CONTACTING YOU DIRECTLY WITHIN YOUR DREAM...
...FROM MY LOCATION UP IN ZALEM.
ZALEM...? DREAM?
THAT GRAY ROOM IS AN ELECTRONICALLY GENERATED SPACE BEING BEAMED INTO YOUR MIND.

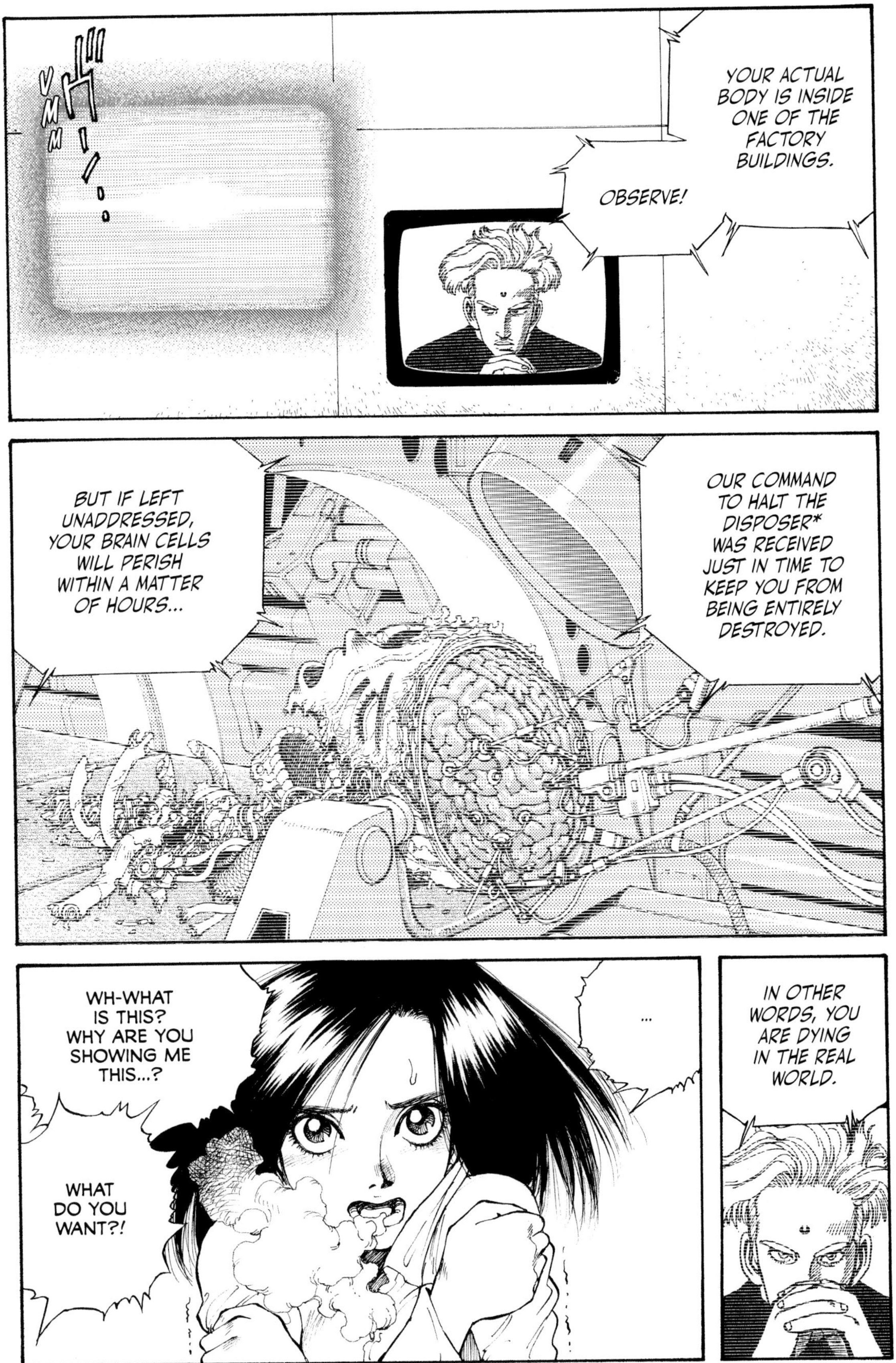
YOUR ACTUAL BODY IS INSIDE ONE OF THE FACTORY BUILDINGS.
OBSERVE!
VMMM
OUR COMMAND TO HALT THE DISPOSER* WAS RECEIVED JUST IN TIME TO KEEP YOU FROM BEING ENTIRELY DESTROYED.
BUT IF LEFT UNADDRESSED, YOUR BRAIN CELLS WILL PERISH WITHIN A MATTER OF HOURS...
IN OTHER WORDS, YOU ARE DYING IN THE REAL WORLD.
...
WH-WHAT IS THIS? WHY ARE YOU SHOWING ME THIS...?
WHAT DO YOU WANT?!

***Disposer:** An electric waste-disposal machine that crushes garbage and flushes it into the sewers.

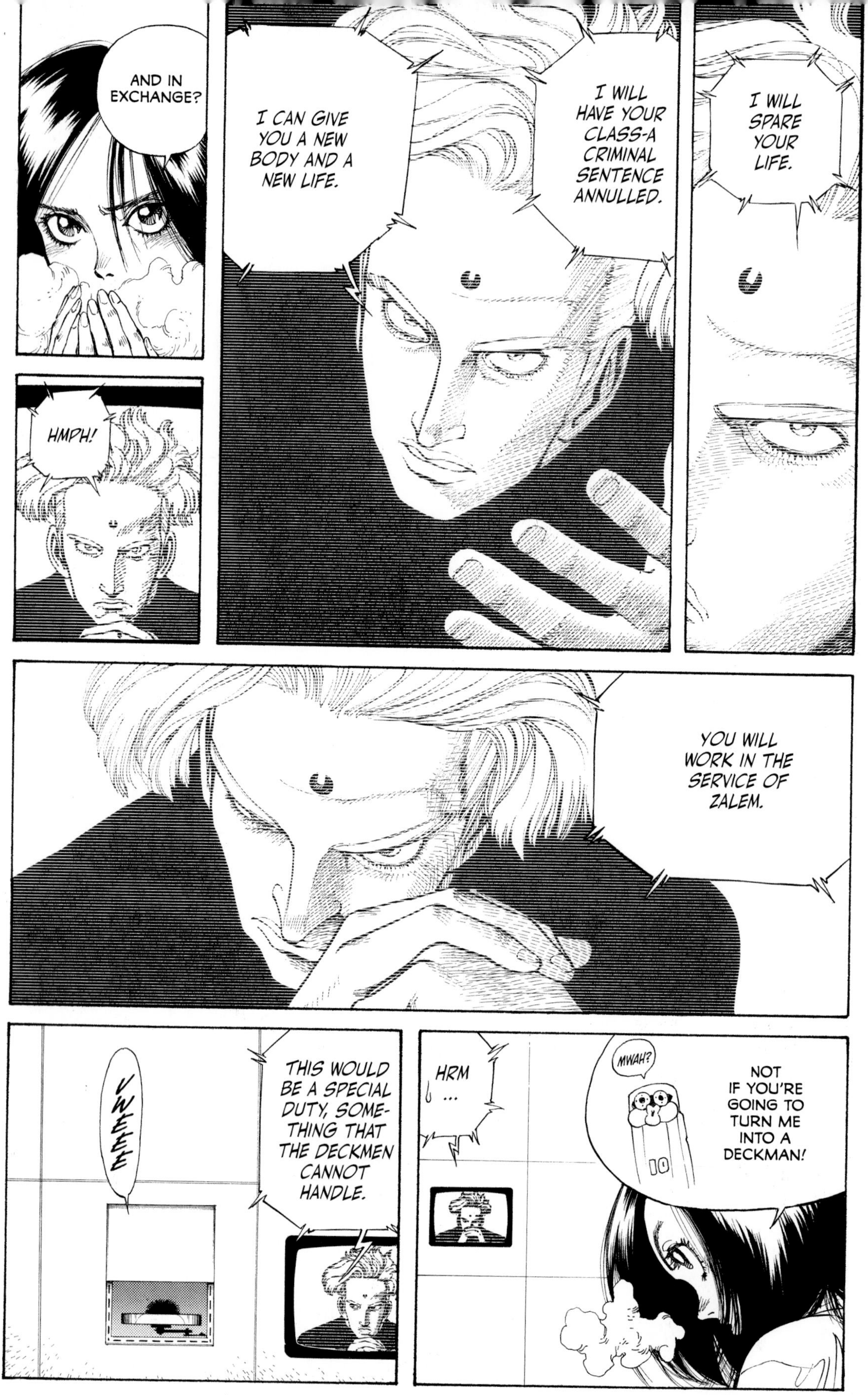
I WILL SPARE YOUR LIFE.
I WILL HAVE YOUR CLASS-A CRIMINAL SENTENCE ANNULLED.
I CAN GIVE YOU A NEW BODY AND A NEW LIFE.
AND IN EXCHANGE?
HMPH!
YOU WILL WORK IN THE SERVICE OF ZALEM.
NOT IF YOU'RE GOING TO TURN ME INTO A DECKMAN!
MWAH?
HRM ...
THIS WOULD BE A SPECIAL DUTY, SOME-THING THAT THE DECKMEN CANNOT HANDLE.
VWEEEE

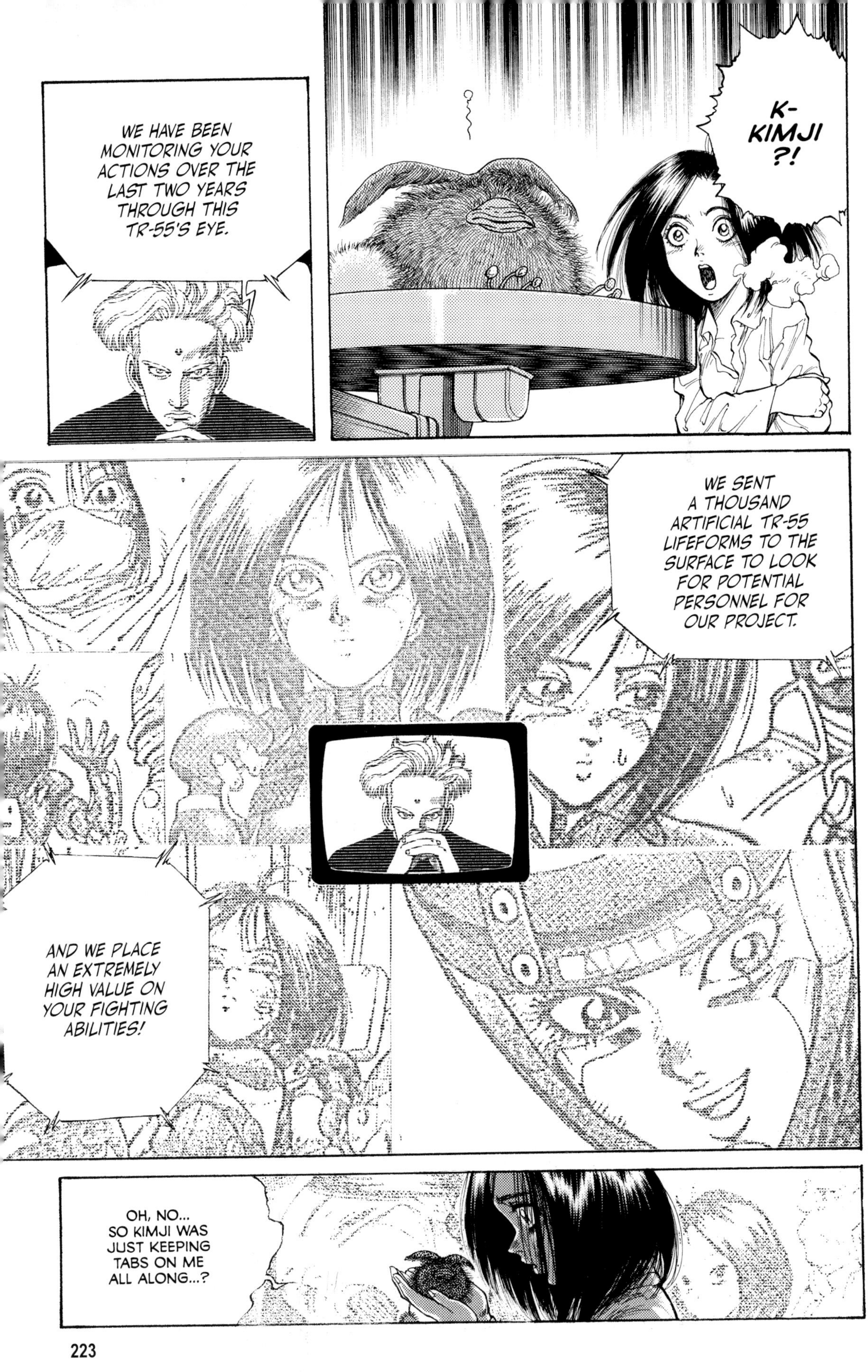
K-KIMJI?!
WE HAVE BEEN MONITORING YOUR ACTIONS OVER THE LAST TWO YEARS THROUGH THIS TR-55'S EYE.
WE SENT A THOUSAND ARTIFICIAL TR-55 LIFEFORMS TO THE SURFACE TO LOOK FOR POTENTIAL PERSONNEL FOR OUR PROJECT.
AND WE PLACE AN EXTREMELY HIGH VALUE ON YOUR FIGHTING ABILITIES!
OH, NO... SO KIMJI WAS JUST KEEPING TABS ON ME ALL ALONG...?

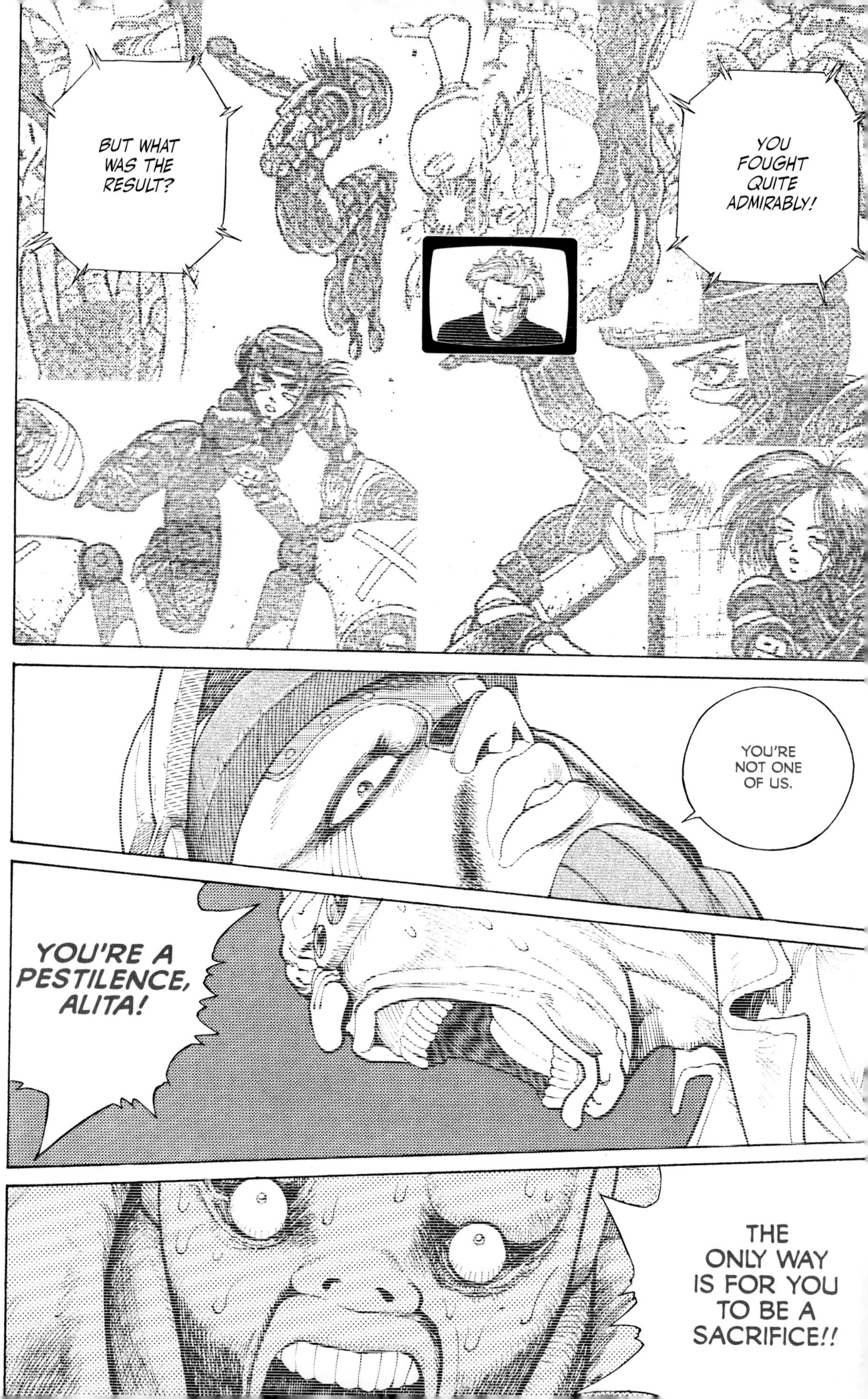
YOU FOUGHT QUITE ADMIRABLY!
BUT WHAT WAS THE RESULT?
YOU'RE NOT ONE OF US.
YOU'RE A PESTILENCE, ALITA!
THE ONLY WAY IS FOR YOU TO BE A SACRIFICE!!

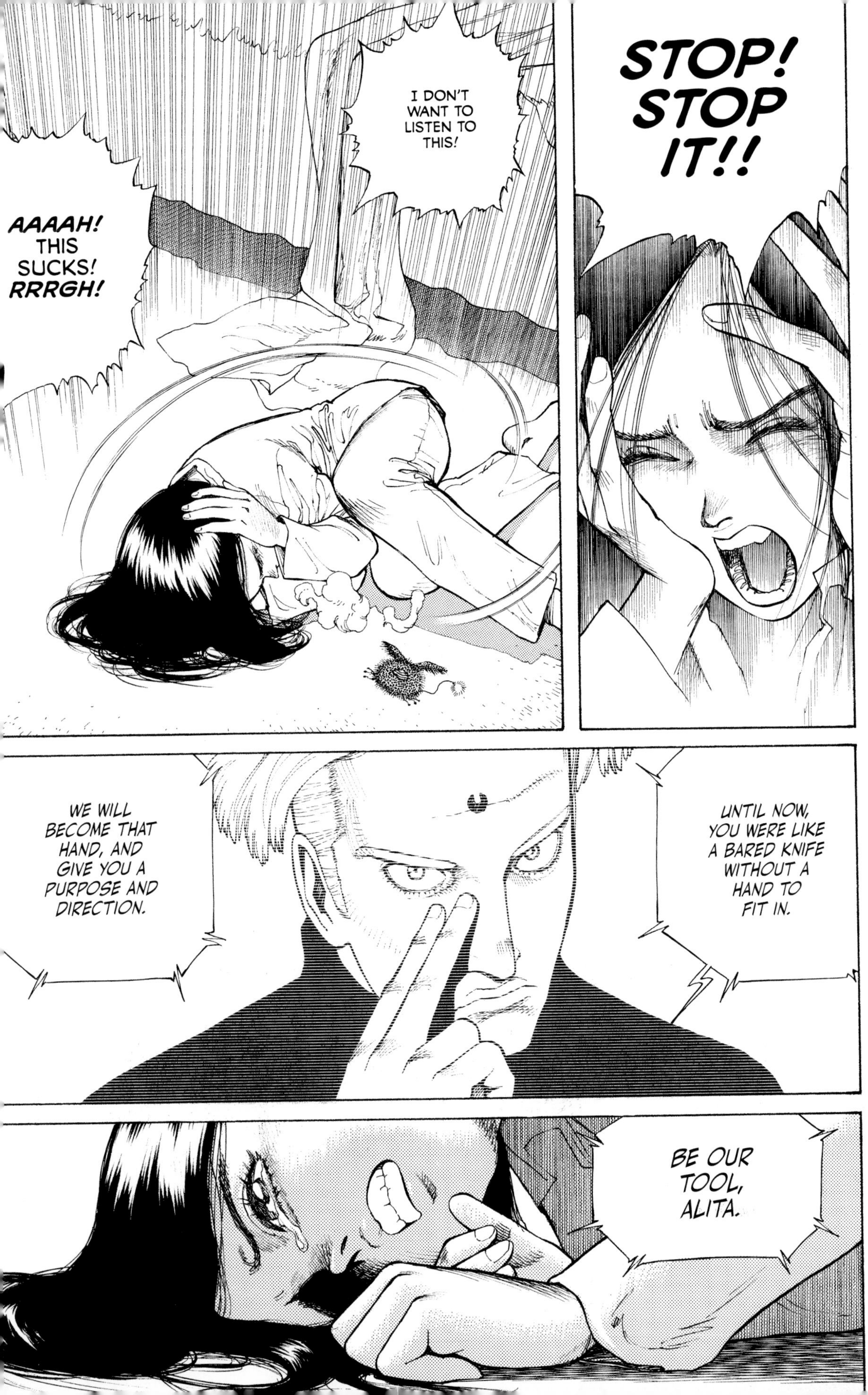
STOP! STOP IT!!
I DON'T WANT TO LISTEN TO THIS!
AAAAH! THIS SUCKS! RRRGH!
UNTIL NOW, YOU WERE LIKE A BARED KNIFE WITHOUT A HAND TO FIT IN.
WE WILL BECOME THAT HAND, AND GIVE YOU A PURPOSE AND DIRECTION.
BE OUR TOOL, ALITA.

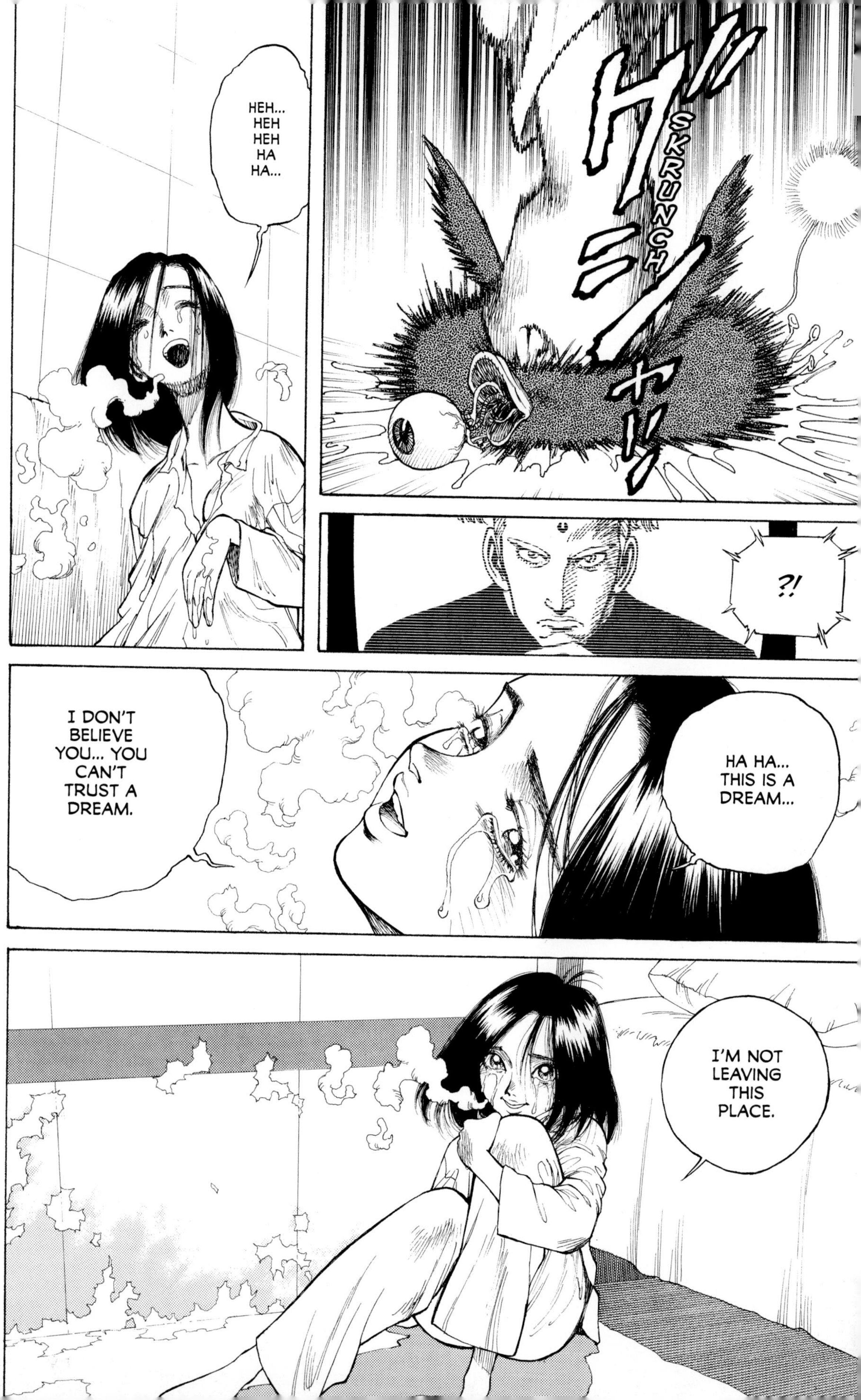
SKRUNCH
?!
HEH... HEH HEH HA HA...
HA HA... THIS IS A DREAM...
I DON'T BELIEVE YOU... YOU CAN'T TRUST A DREAM.
I'M NOT LEAVING THIS PLACE.

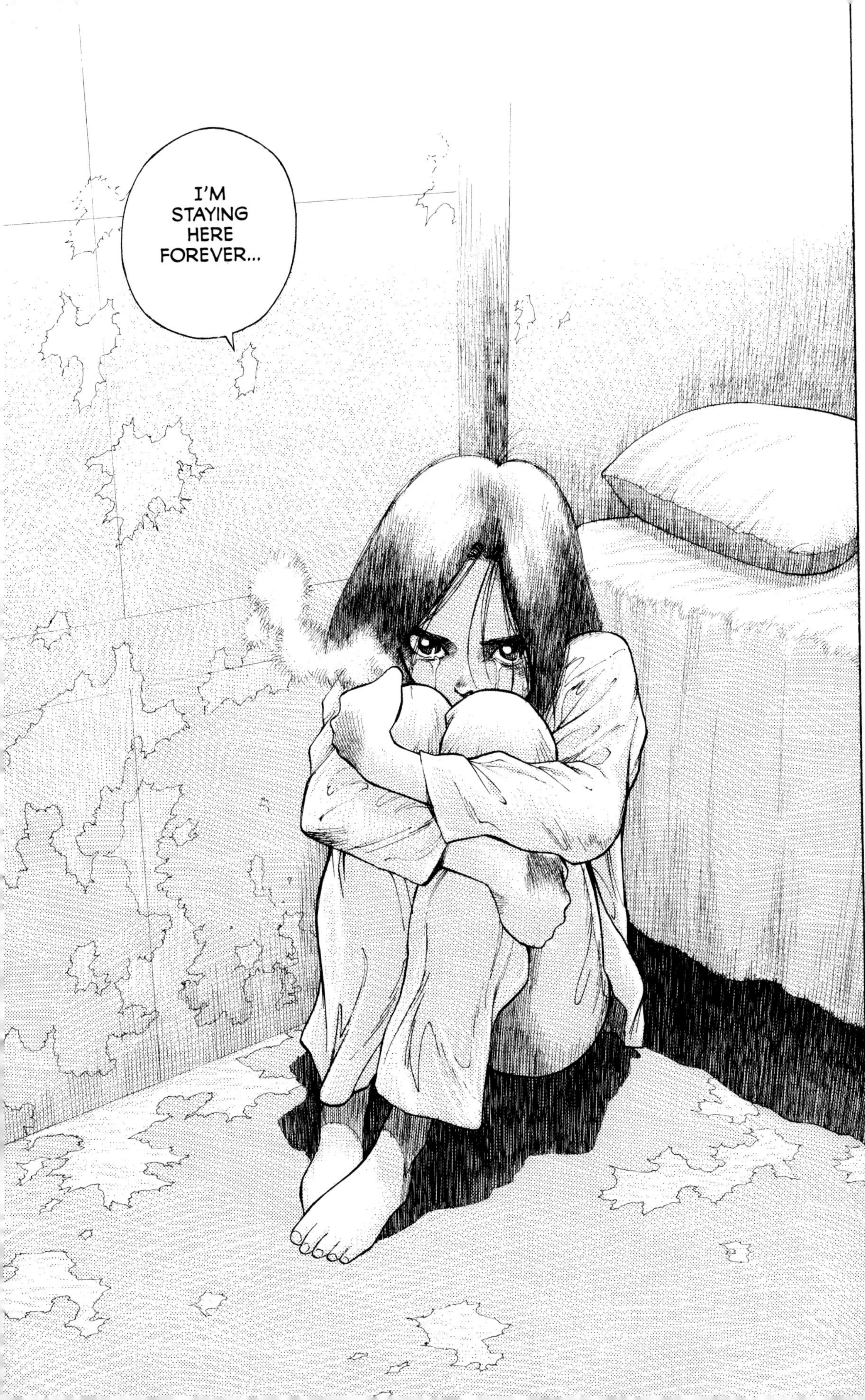
I'M STAYING HERE FOREVER...

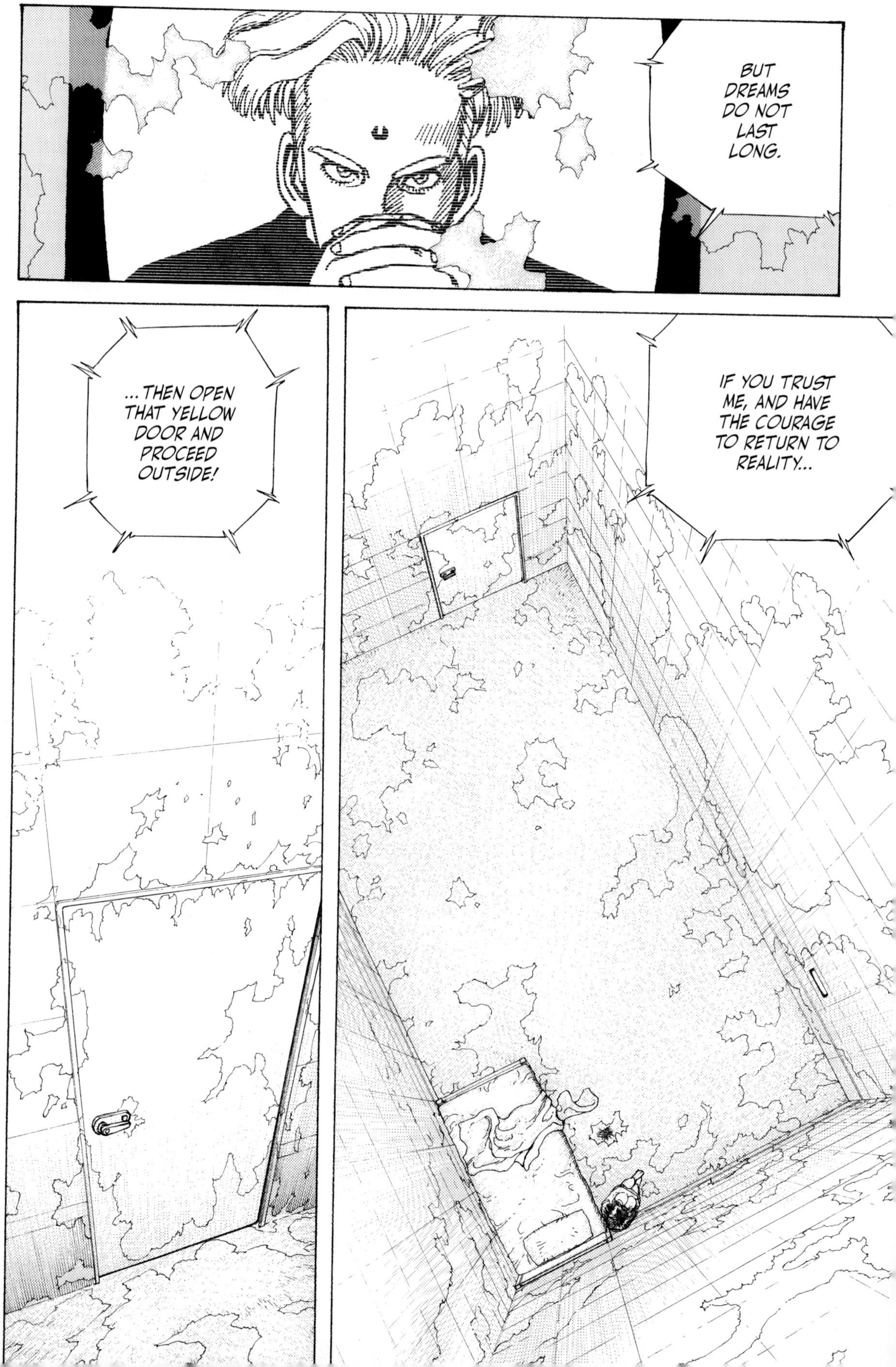
BUT DREAMS DO NOT LAST LONG.
IF YOU TRUST ME, AND HAVE THE COURAGE TO RETURN TO REALITY...
...THEN OPEN THAT YELLOW DOOR AND PROCEED OUTSIDE!

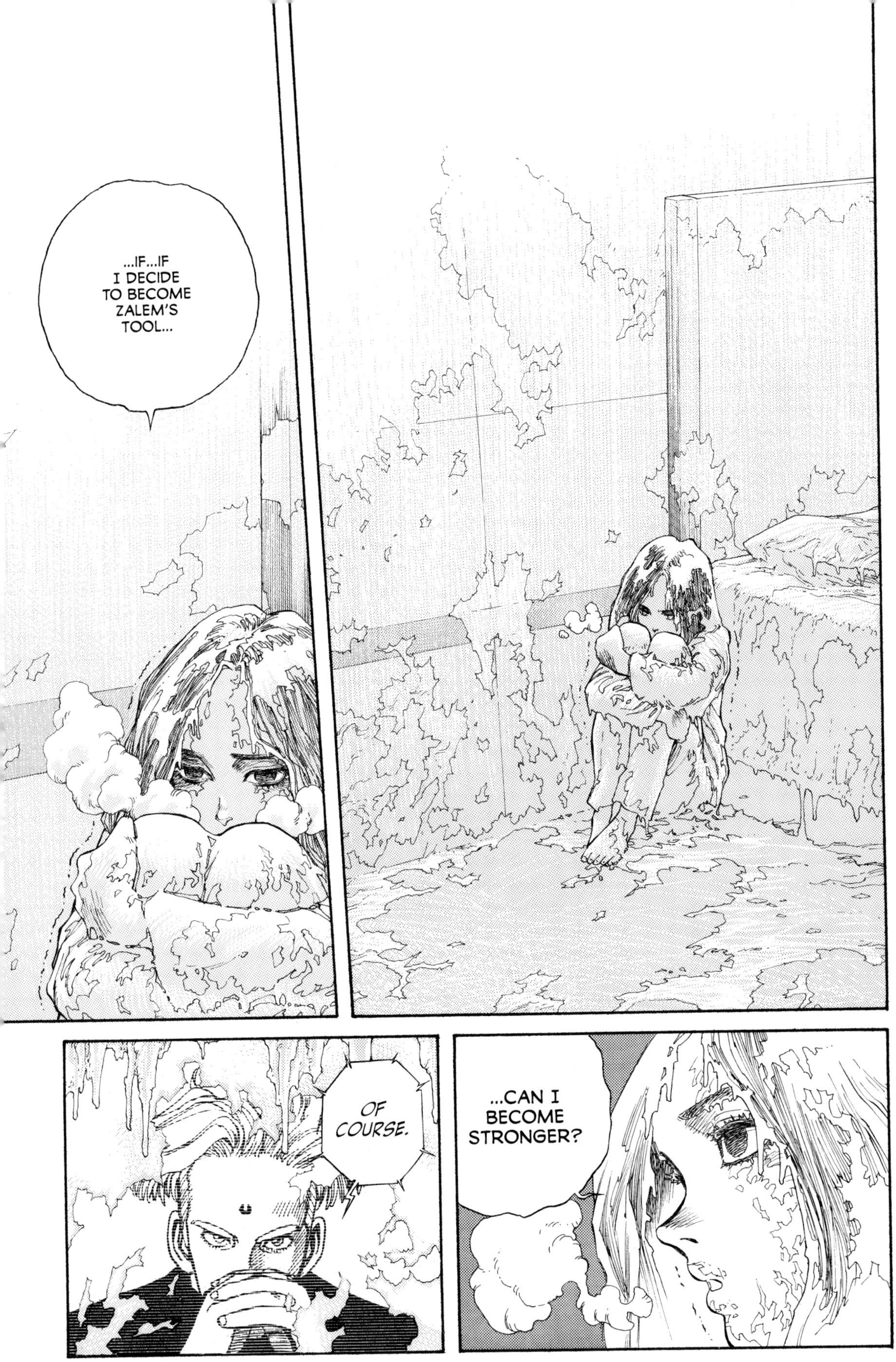

...IF...IF I DECIDE TO BECOME ZALEM'S TOOL...
...CAN I BECOME STRONGER?
OF COURSE.

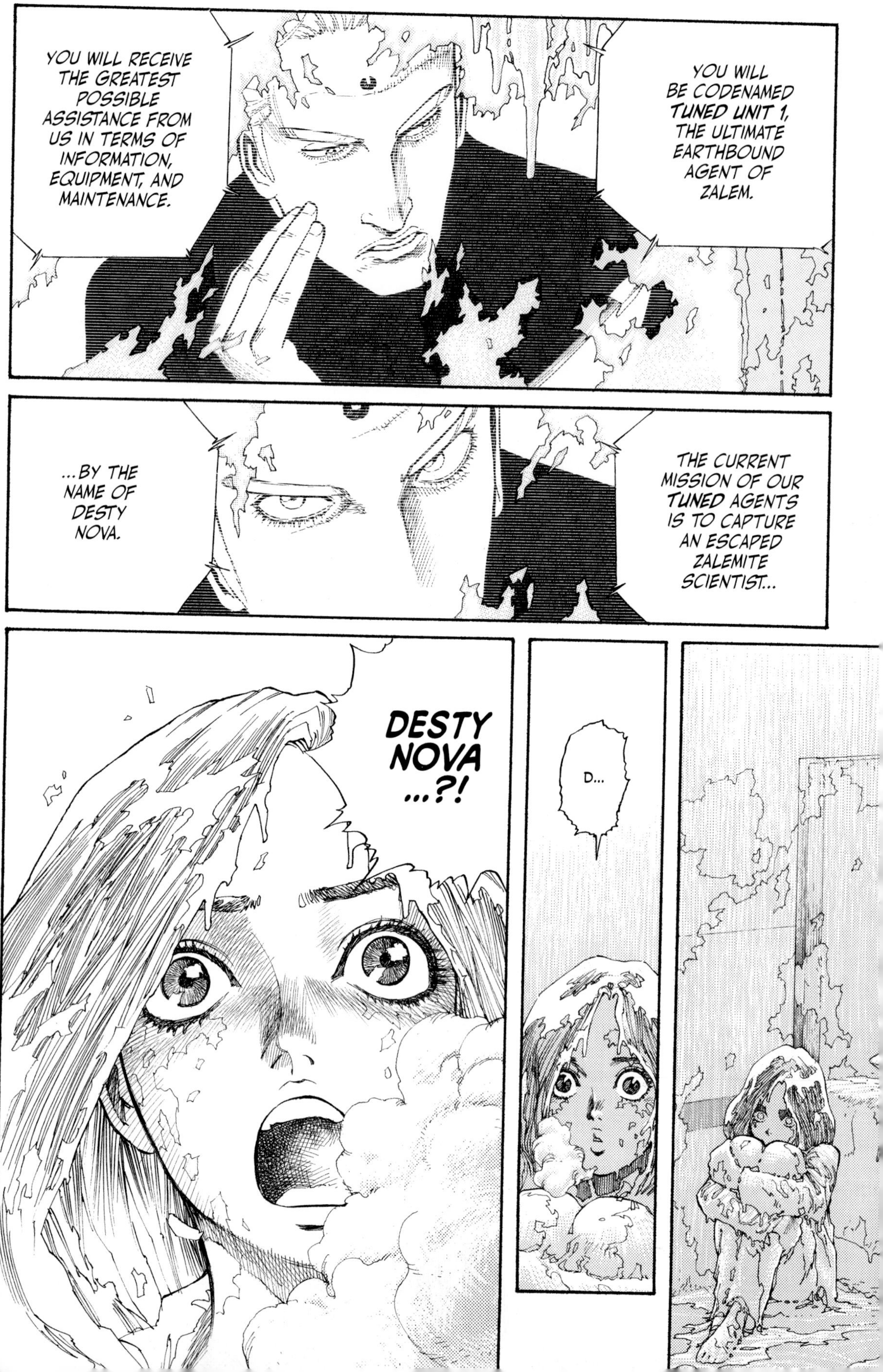
YOU WILL BE CODENAMED **TUNED UNIT 1**, THE ULTIMATE EARTHBOUND AGENT OF ZALEM.
YOU WILL RECEIVE THE GREATEST POSSIBLE ASSISTANCE FROM US IN TERMS OF INFORMATION, EQUIPMENT, AND MAINTENANCE.
THE CURRENT MISSION OF OUR **TUNED** AGENTS IS TO CAPTURE AN ESCAPED ZALEMITE SCIENTIST...
...BY THE NAME OF DESTY NOVA.
D...
DESTY NOVA ...?!

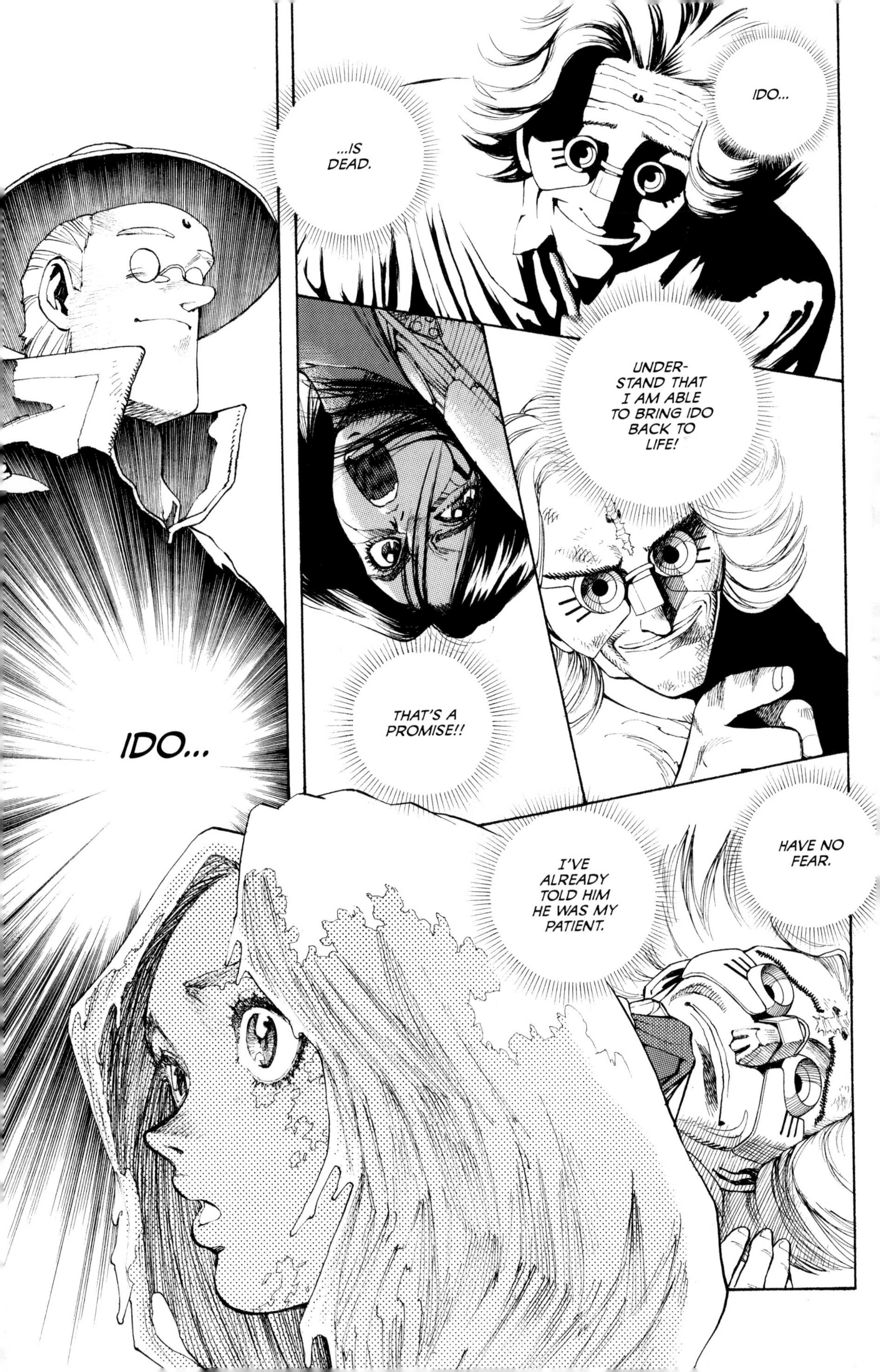
IDO...
...IS DEAD.
UNDER-STAND THAT I AM ABLE TO BRING IDO BACK TO LIFE!
THAT'S A PROMISE!!
HAVE NO FEAR.
I'VE ALREADY TOLD HIM HE WAS MY PATIENT.
IDO...

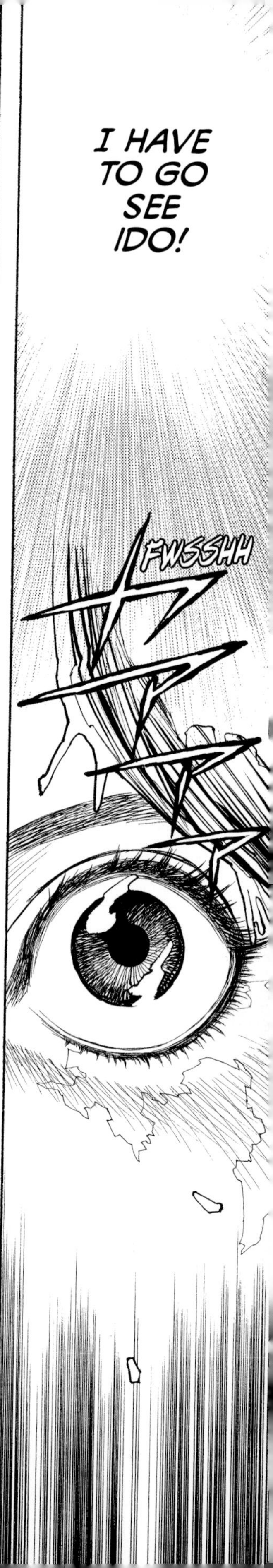
I HAVE TO GO SEE IDO!
FWSSHH
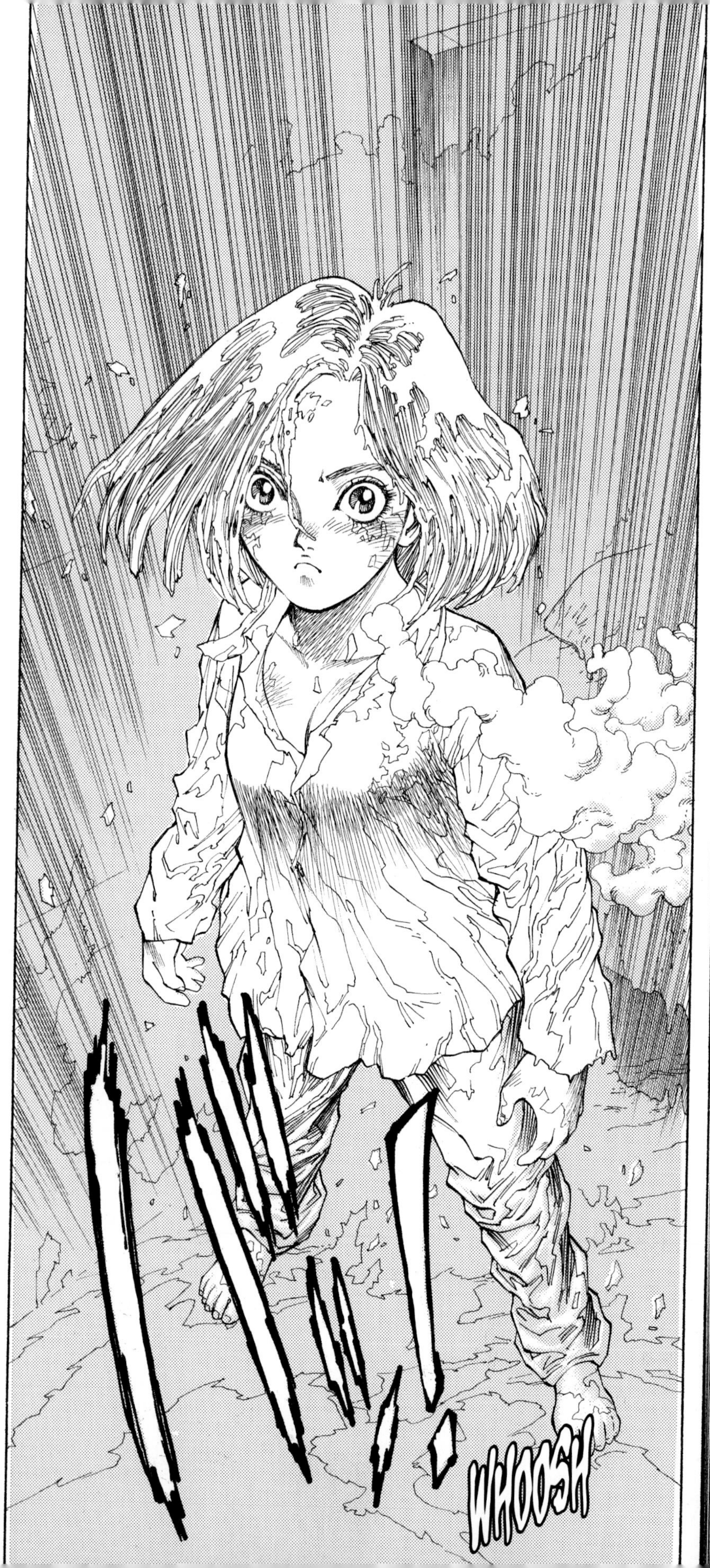
WHOOSH

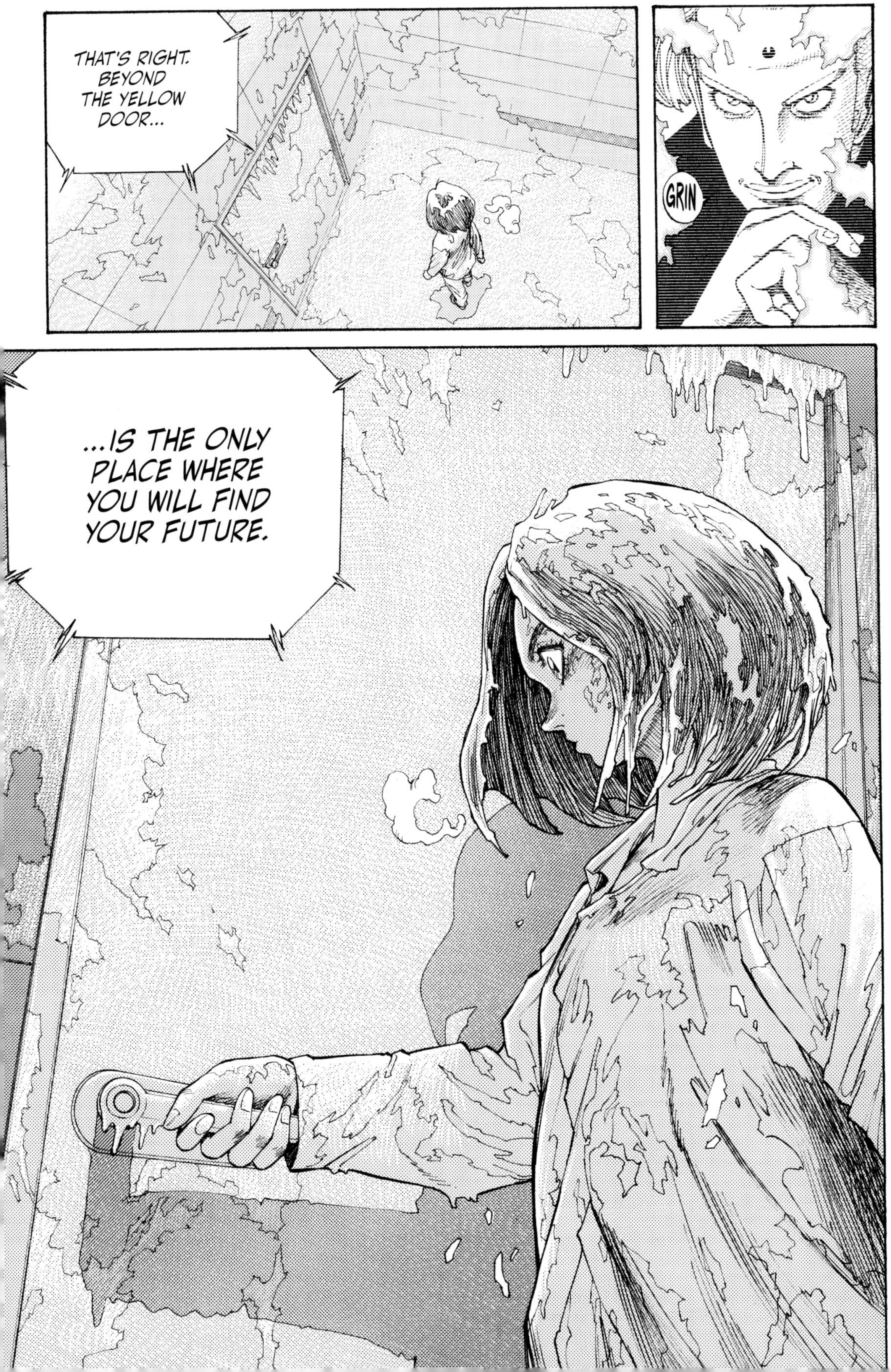
GRIN
THAT'S RIGHT. BEYOND THE YELLOW DOOR...
...IS THE ONLY PLACE WHERE YOU WILL FIND YOUR FUTURE.

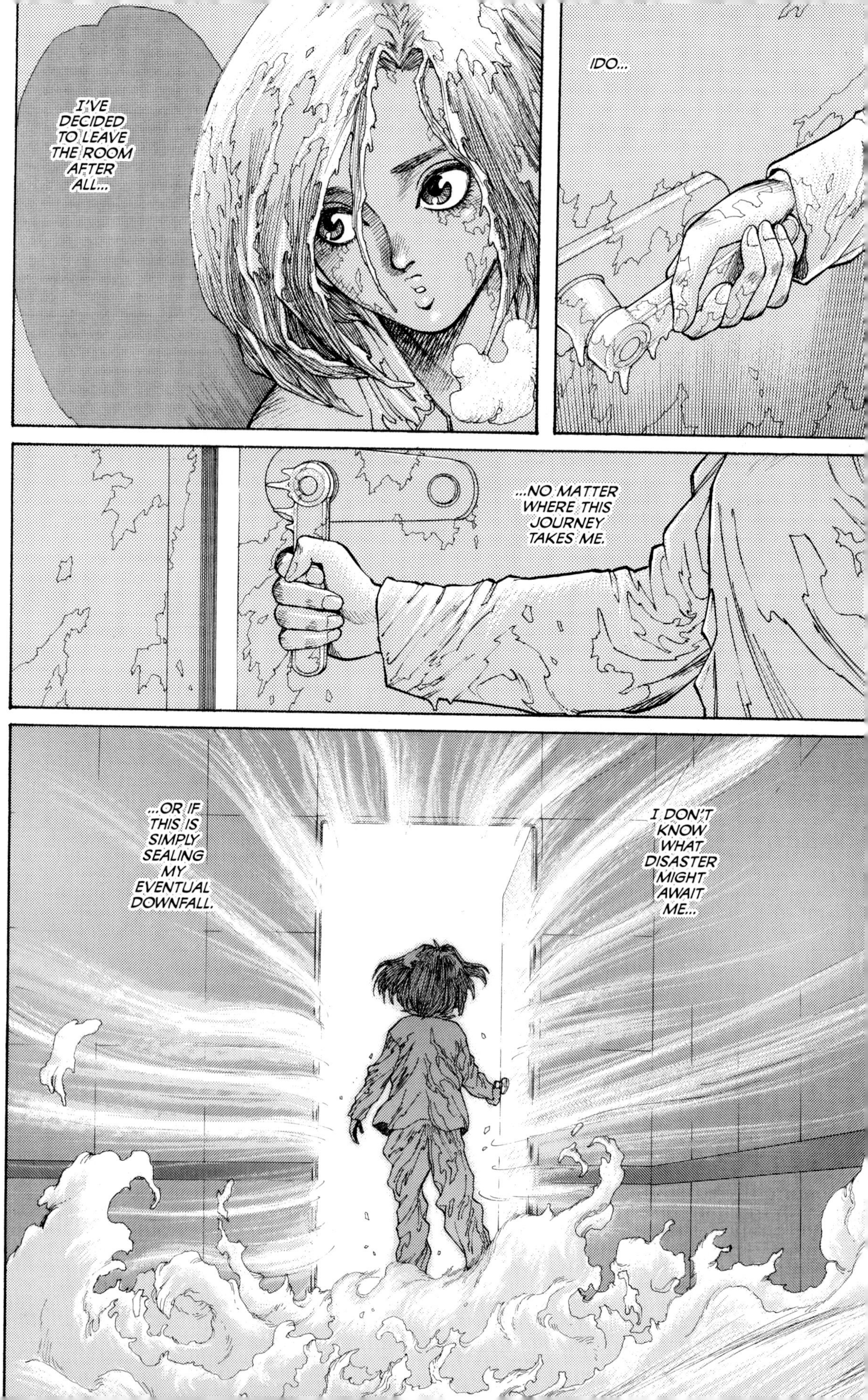
IDO...
I'VE DECIDED TO LEAVE THE ROOM AFTER ALL...
...NO MATTER WHERE THIS JOURNEY TAKES ME.
I DON'T KNOW WHAT DISASTER MIGHT AWAIT ME...
...OR IF THIS IS SIMPLY SEALING MY EVENTUAL DOWNFALL.

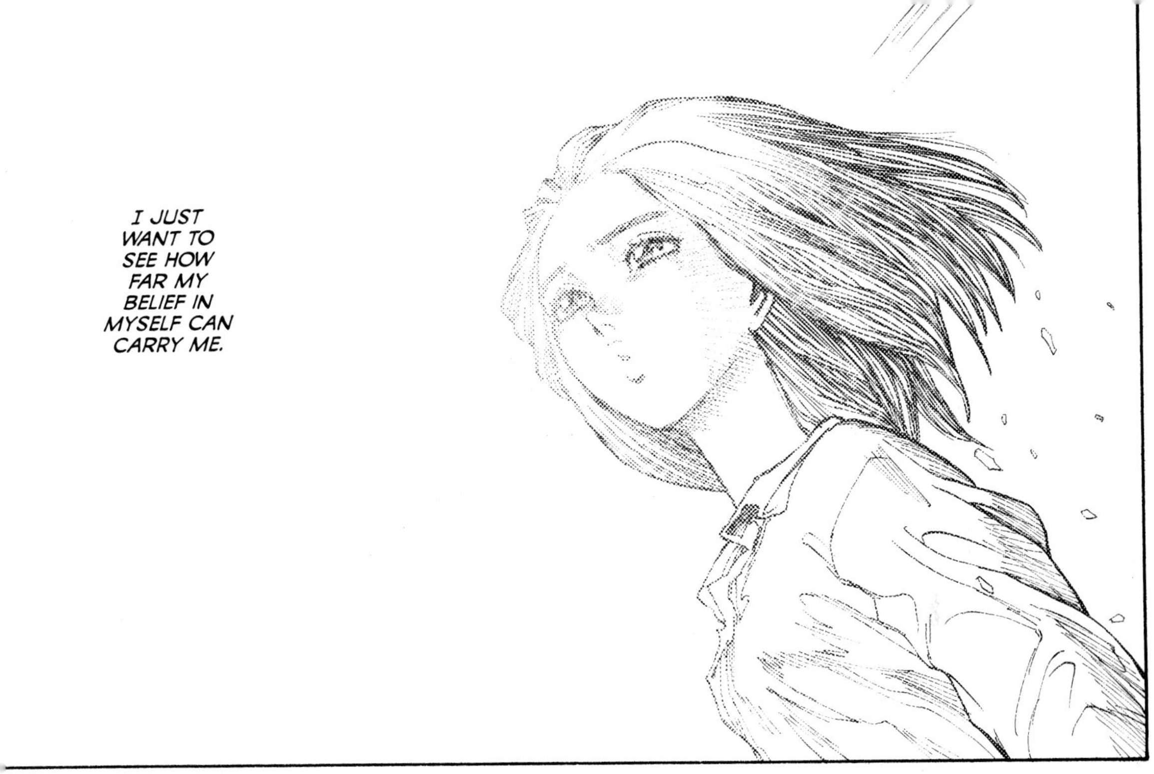
I JUST WANT TO SEE HOW FAR MY BELIEF IN MYSELF CAN CARRY ME.
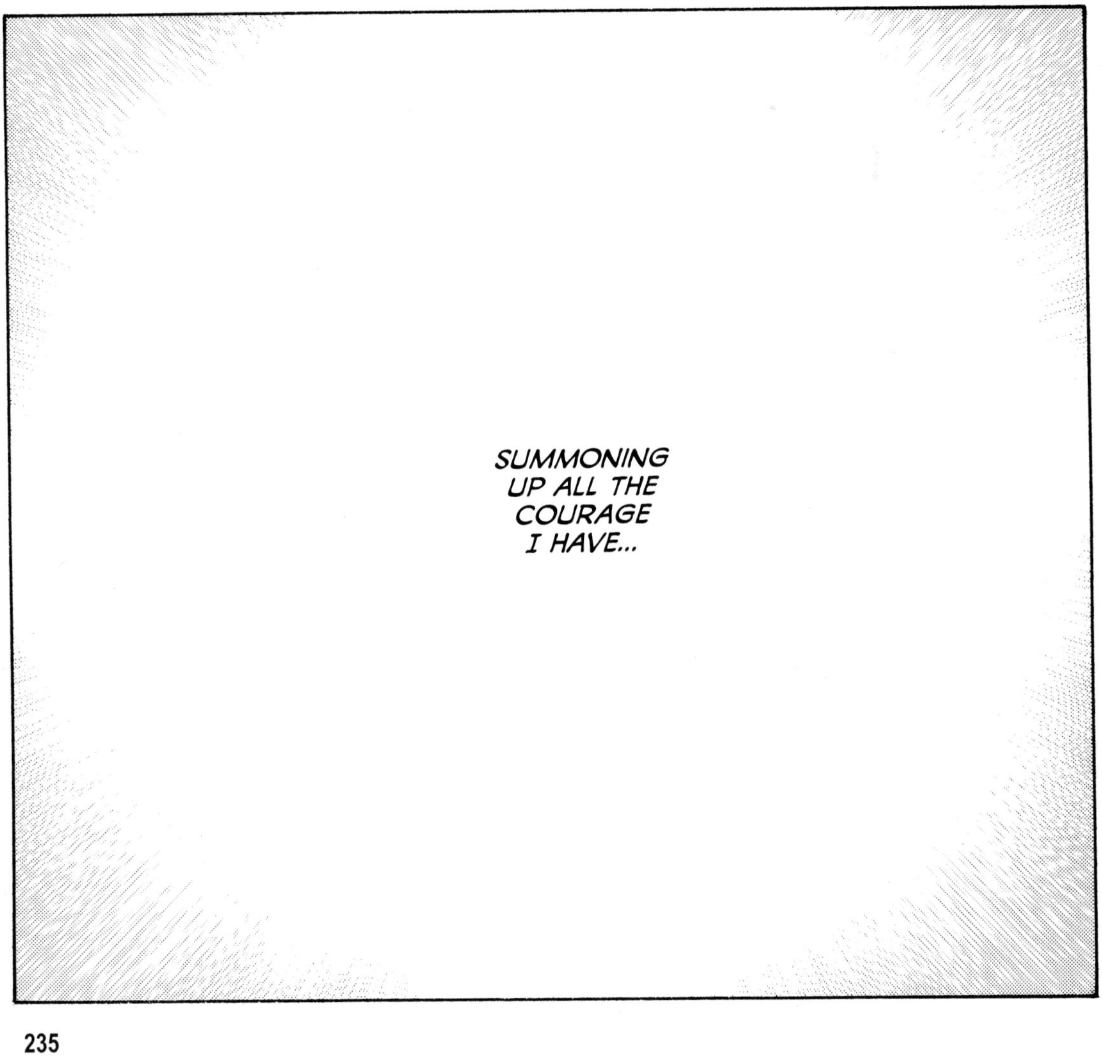
SUMMONING UP ALL THE COURAGE I HAVE...

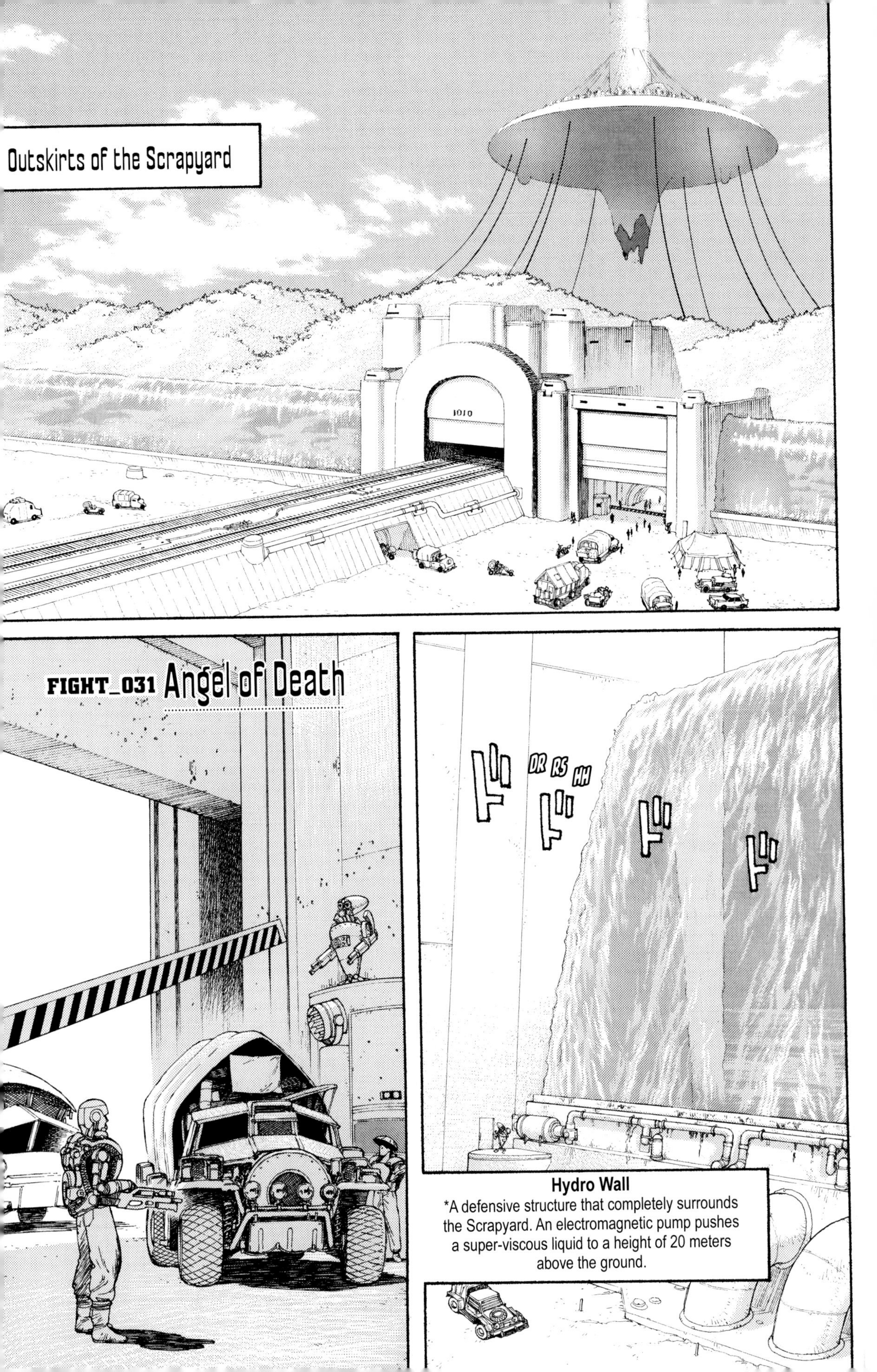
Outskirts of the Scrapyard
1010
ドドドド
DR RS HH
Hydro Wall
*A defensive structure that completely surrounds the Scrapyard. An electromagnetic pump pushes a super-viscous liquid to a height of 20 meters above the ground.
FIGHT_031 Angel of Death

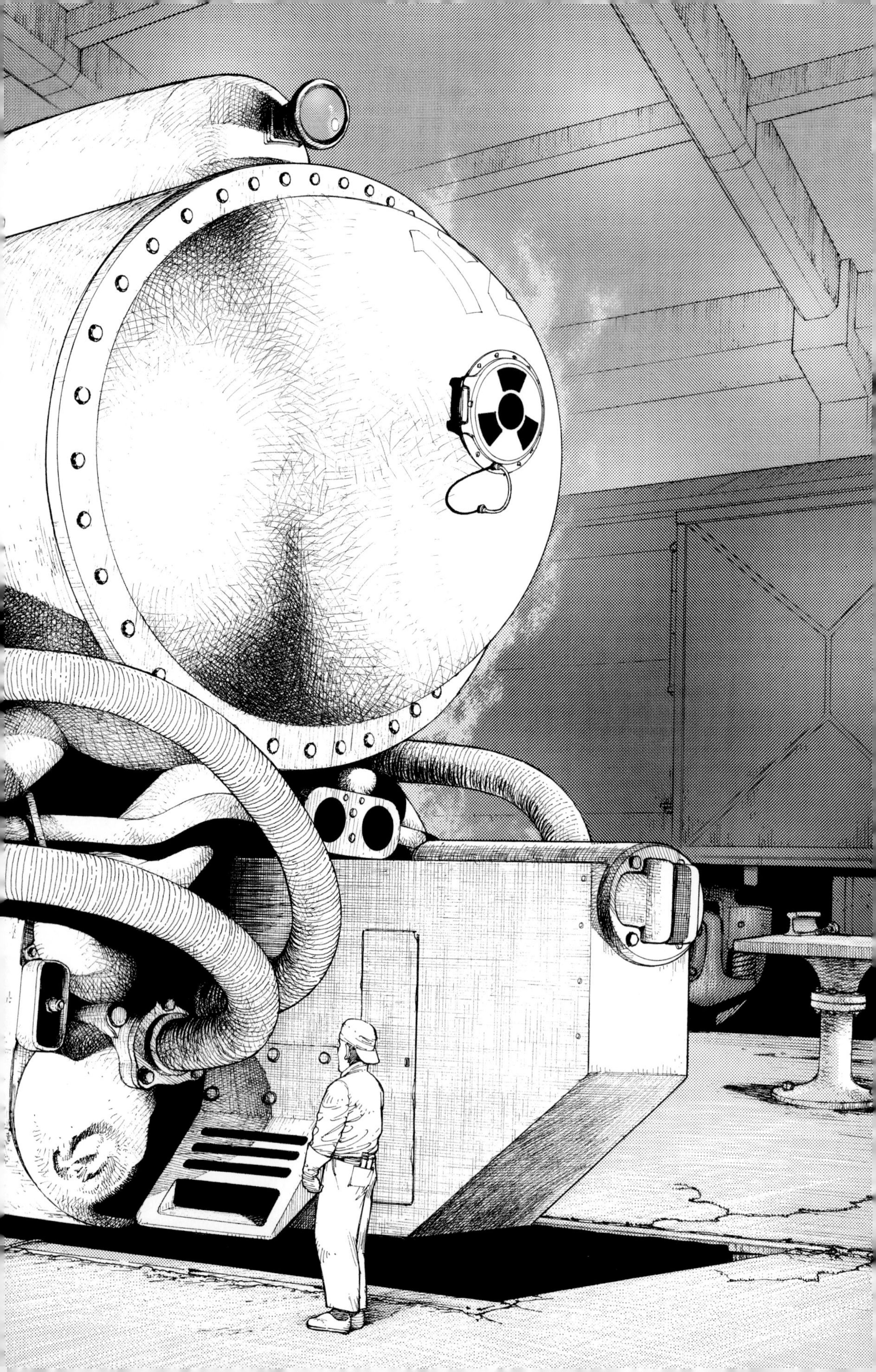

FIGHT_031 Angel of Death

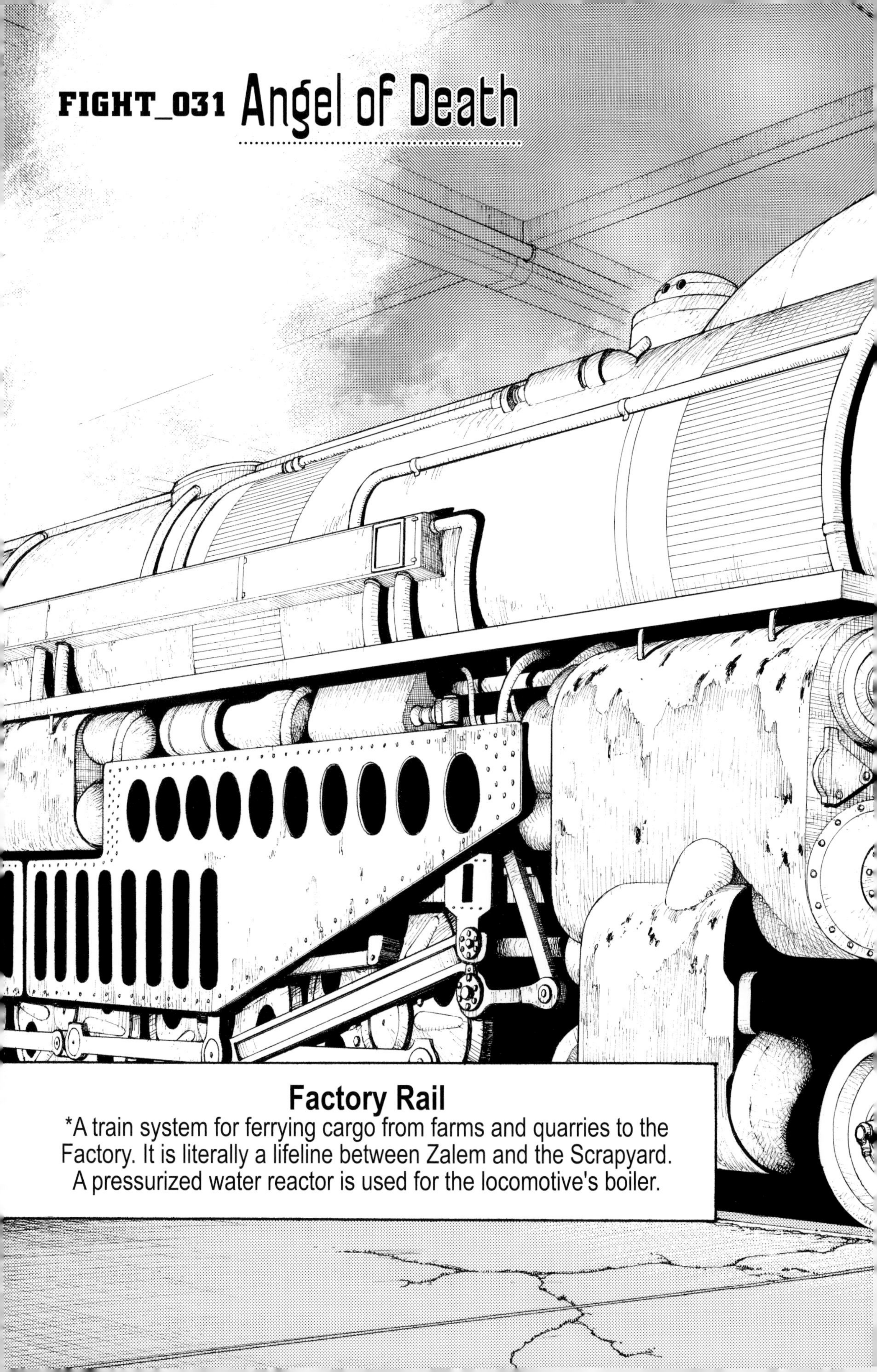

Factory Rail

*A train system for ferrying cargo from farms and quarries to the Factory. It is literally a lifeline between Zalem and the Scrapyard. A pressurized water reactor is used for the locomotive's boiler.

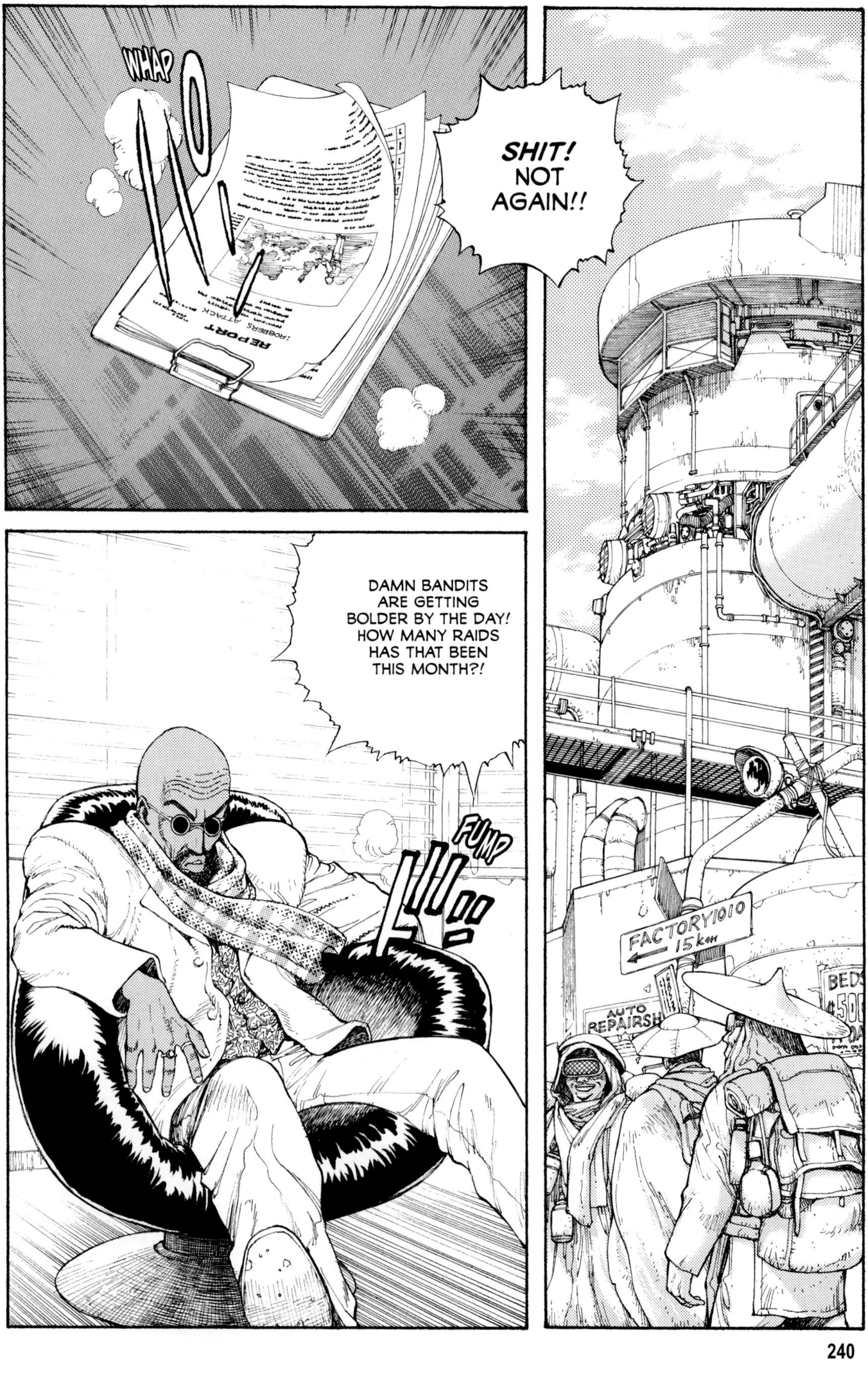
SHIT! NOT AGAIN!!
FACTORY 1010
15 km
AUTO REPAIRSH
BEDS
WHAP
REPORT
ROBBERS ATTACK
DAMN BANDITS ARE GETTING BOLDER BY THE DAY! HOW MANY RAIDS HAS THAT BEEN THIS MONTH?!
FUMP

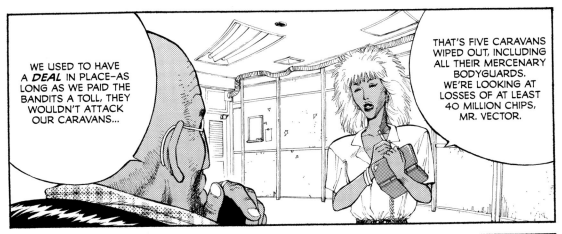

THAT'S FIVE CARAVANS WIPED OUT, INCLUDING ALL THEIR MERCENARY BODYGUARDS. WE'RE LOOKING AT LOSSES OF AT LEAST 40 MILLION CHIPS, MR. VECTOR.
WE USED TO HAVE A *DEAL* IN PLACE–AS LONG AS WE PAID THE BANDITS A TOLL, THEY WOULDN'T ATTACK OUR CARAVANS...
...BUT EVER SINCE THOSE BARJACK MOBILE BANDITS SHOWED UP FIVE YEARS AGO, THEY'VE BEEN EXPANDING THEIR REACH AND MESSIN' UP MY ARRANGEMENT!
THEY'RE NO JOKE... IN THE SOUTHERN SECTOR, THEY EVEN STOLE AN ENTIRE FACTORY TRAIN!!
I CAN'T BELIEVE THEY'RE TRYING TO SCREW WITH THE FACTORY ITSELF! IF I DON'T GET A HANDLE ON THIS, THEY COULD MUSCLE ME OUTTA THE BROKERING MARKET.
THE ONLY THING WE KNOW ABOUT THE LEADER OF BARJACK IS THE NAME *DEN*.

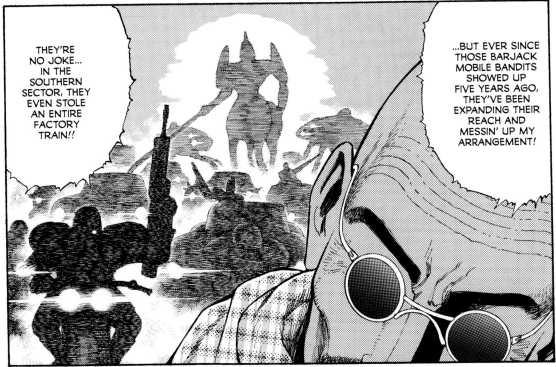

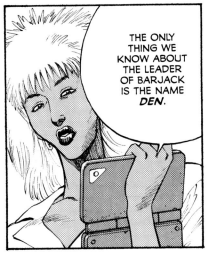

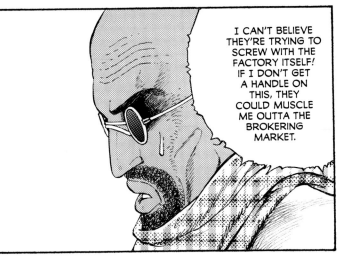

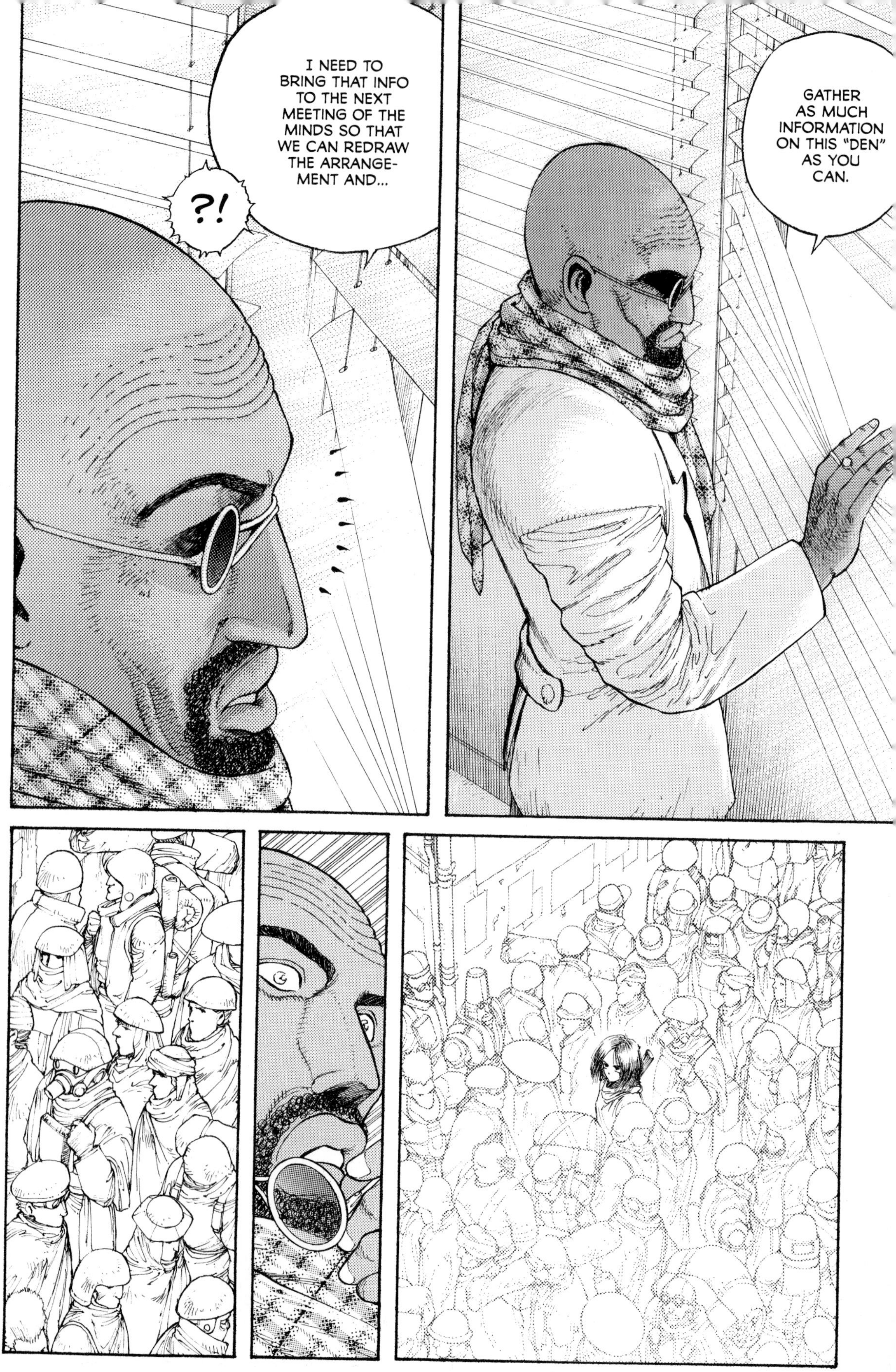
GATHER AS MUCH INFORMATION ON THIS "DEN" AS YOU CAN.
I NEED TO BRING THAT INFO TO THE NEXT MEETING OF THE MINDS SO THAT WE CAN REDRAW THE ARRANGE-MENT AND...
?!

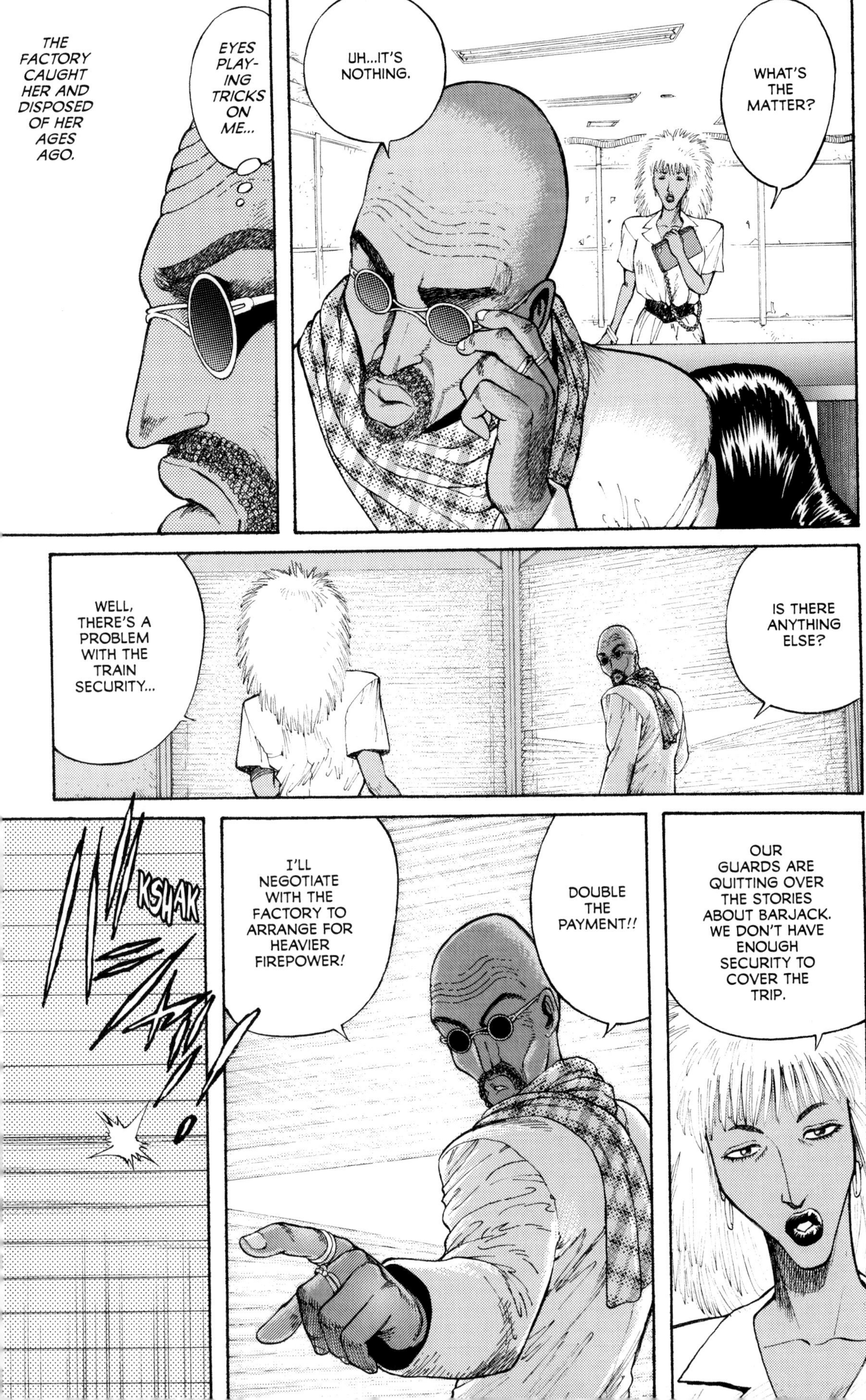
WHAT'S THE MATTER?
UH...IT'S NOTHING.
EYES PLAYING-ING TRICKS ON ME...
THE FACTORY CAUGHT HER AND DISPOSED OF HER AGES AGO.
IS THERE ANYTHING ELSE?
WELL, THERE'S A PROBLEM WITH THE TRAIN SECURITY...
OUR GUARDS ARE QUITTING OVER THE STORIES ABOUT BARJACK. WE DON'T HAVE ENOUGH SECURITY TO COVER THE TRIP.
DOUBLE THE PAYMENT!!
I'LL NEGOTIATE WITH THE FACTORY TO ARRANGE FOR HEAVIER FIREPOWER!
KSHAK

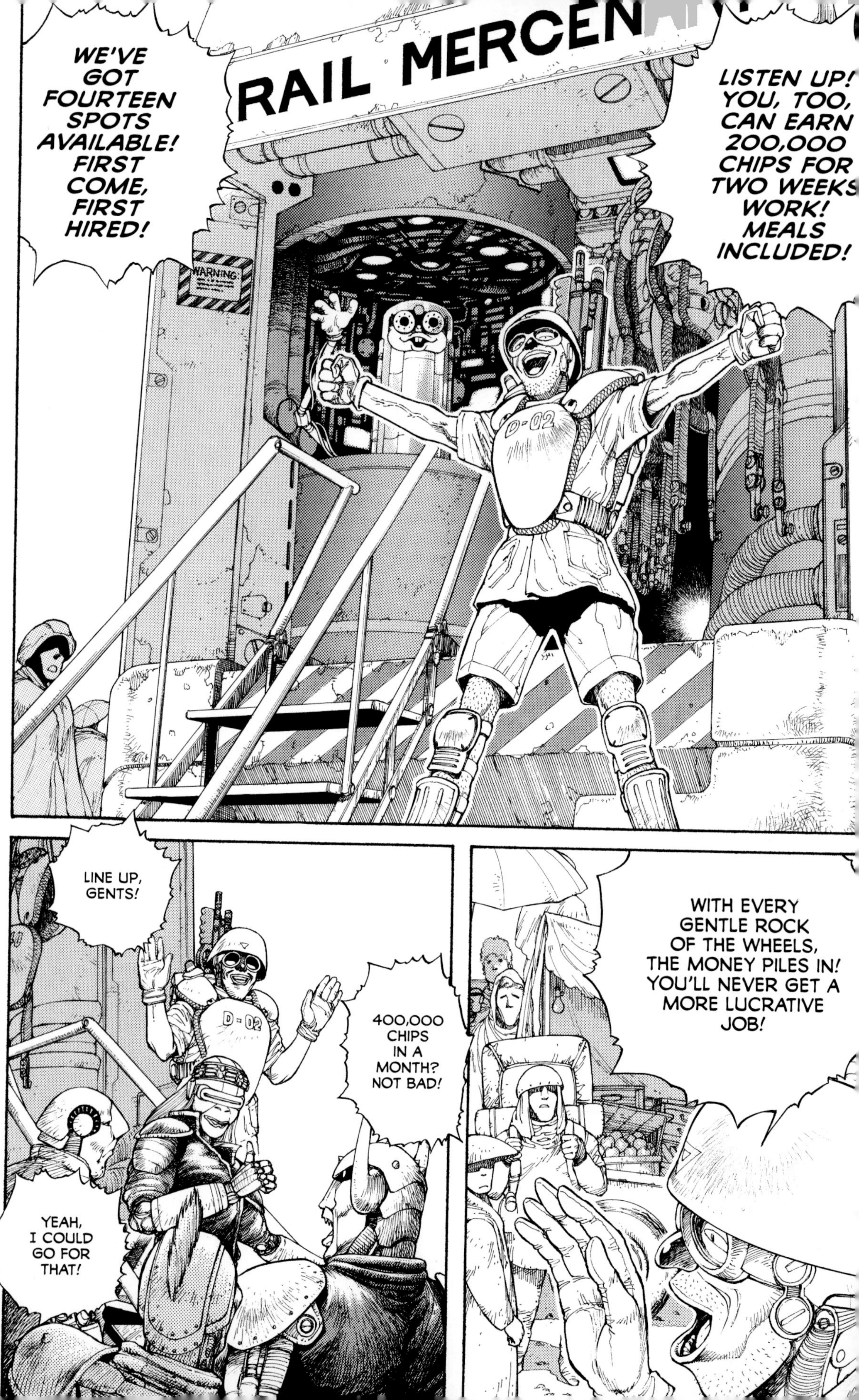
RAIL MERCEN
LISTEN UP! YOU, TOO, CAN EARN 200,000 CHIPS FOR TWO WEEKS WORK! MEALS INCLUDED!
WE'VE GOT FOURTEEN SPOTS AVAILABLE! FIRST COME, FIRST HIRED!
WARNING
D-02
WITH EVERY GENTLE ROCK OF THE WHEELS, THE MONEY PILES IN! YOU'LL NEVER GET A MORE LUCRATIVE JOB!
LINE UP, GENTS!
D-02
400,000 CHIPS IN A MONTH? NOT BAD!
YEAH, I COULD GO FOR THAT!

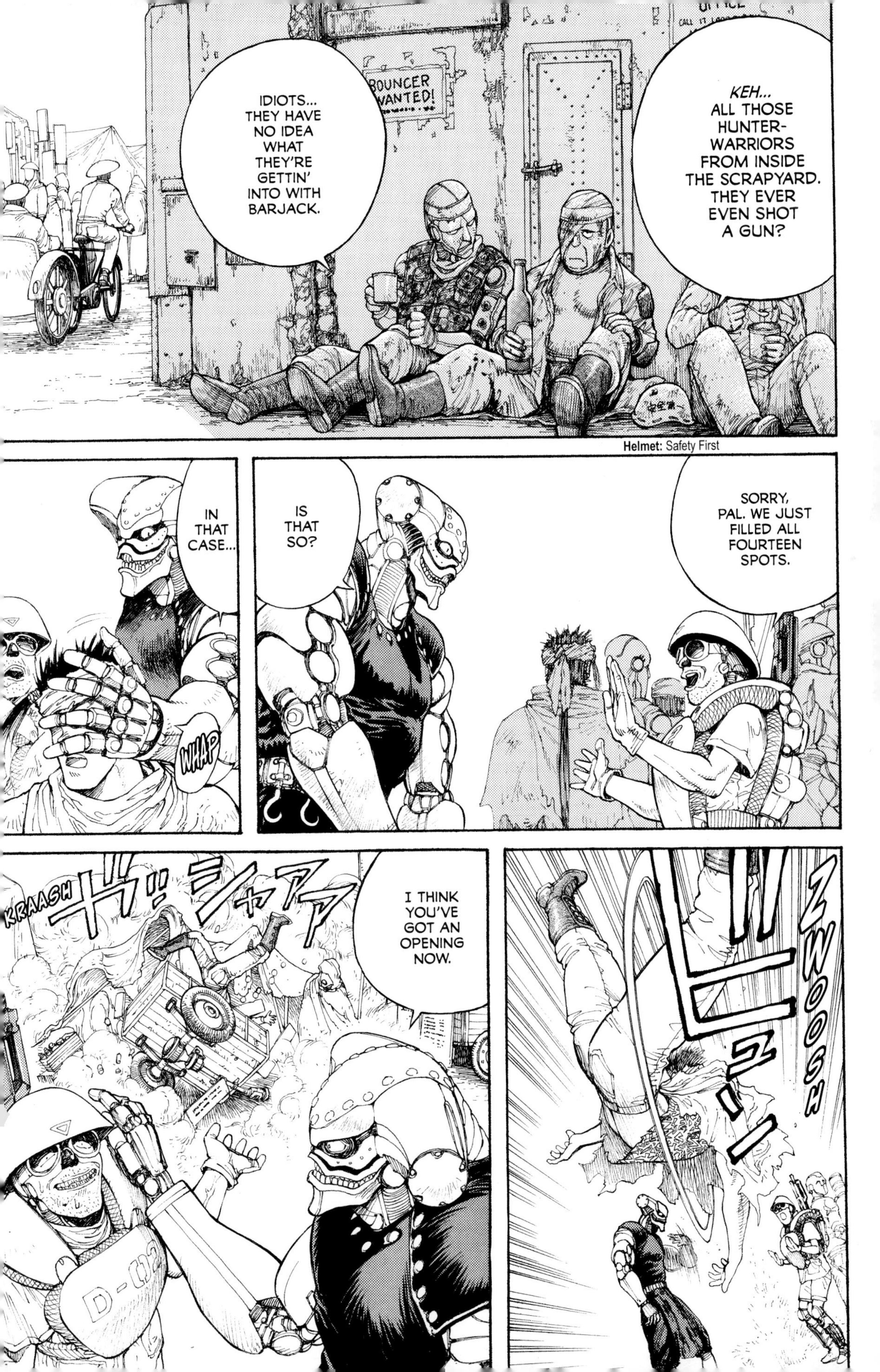
BOUNCER WANTED!
KEH... ALL THOSE HUNTER-WARRIORS FROM INSIDE THE SCRAPYARD. THEY EVER EVEN SHOT A GUN?
IDIOTS... THEY HAVE NO IDEA WHAT THEY'RE GETTIN' INTO WITH BARJACK.
Helmet: Safety First
SORRY, PAL. WE JUST FILLED ALL FOURTEEN SPOTS.
IS THAT SO?
IN THAT CASE...
WHAP
ZWOOOSH
I THINK YOU'VE GOT AN OPENING NOW.
KRAASH

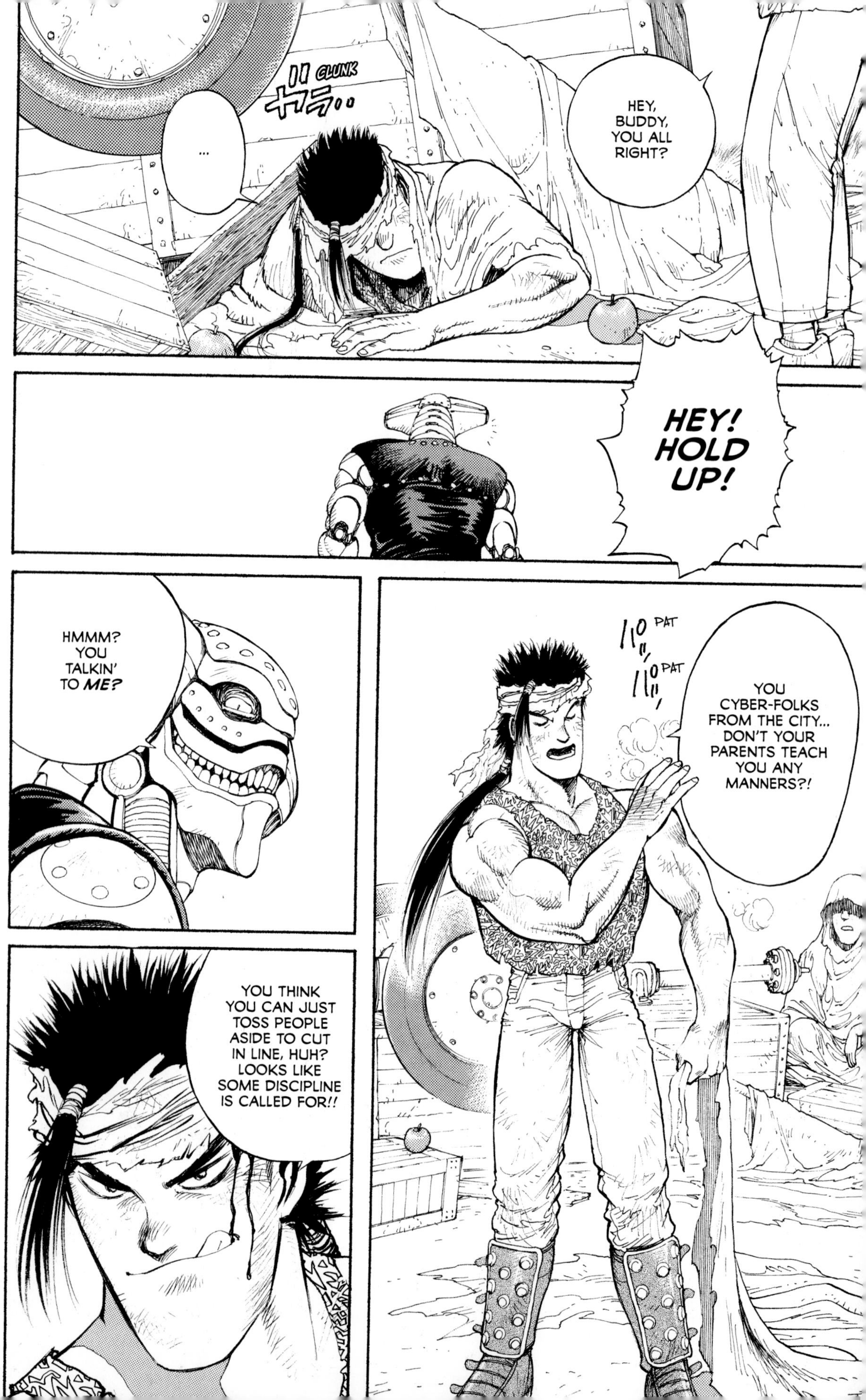
HEY, BUDDY, YOU ALL RIGHT?
CLUNK
...
HEY! HOLD UP!
PAT
PAT
YOU CYBER-FOLKS FROM THE CITY... DON'T YOUR PARENTS TEACH YOU ANY MANNERS?!
HMMM? YOU TALKIN' TO *ME?*
YOU THINK YOU CAN JUST TOSS PEOPLE ASIDE TO CUT IN LINE, HUH? LOOKS LIKE SOME DISCIPLINE IS CALLED FOR!!

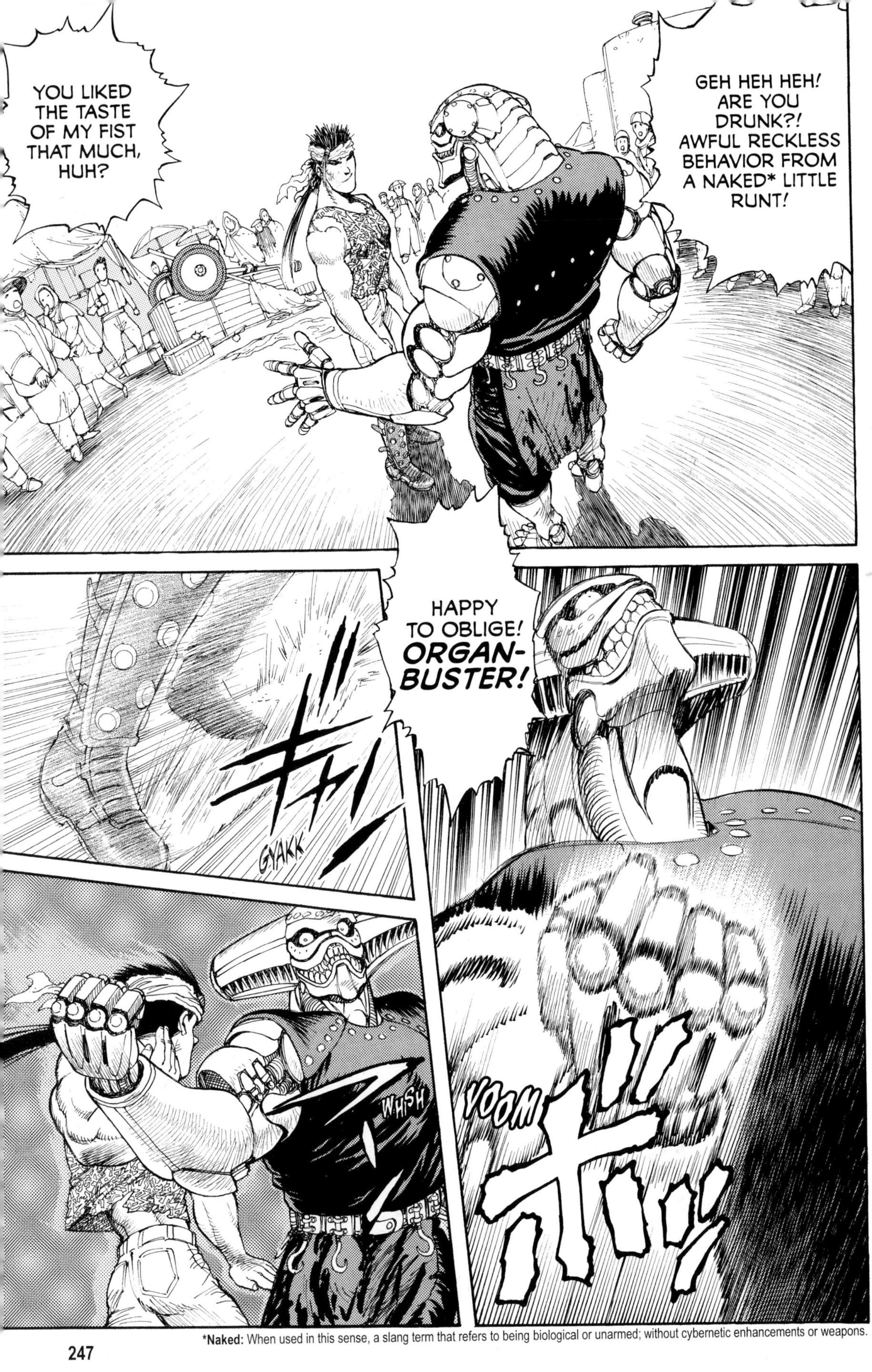
GEH HEH HEH! ARE YOU DRUNK?! AWFUL RECKLESS BEHAVIOR FROM A NAKED* LITTLE RUNT!
YOU LIKED THE TASTE OF MY FIST THAT MUCH, HUH?
HAPPY TO OBLIGE! ORGAN-BUSTER!
VOOM
GYAKK
WHISH

***Naked:** When used in this sense, a slang term that refers to being biological or unarmed; without cybernetic enhancements or weapons.

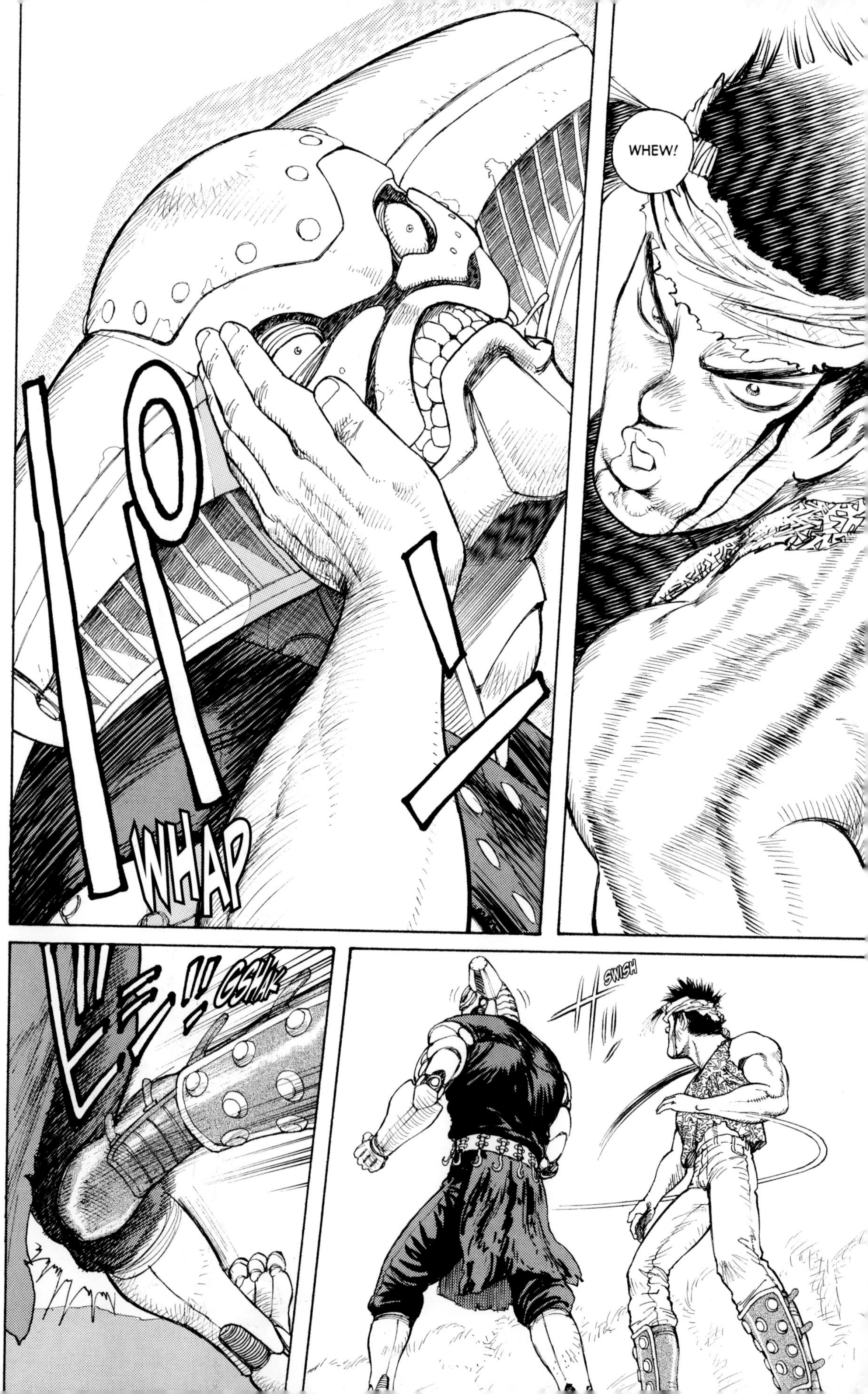
WHEW!
WHAP
SWISH
GSHAK

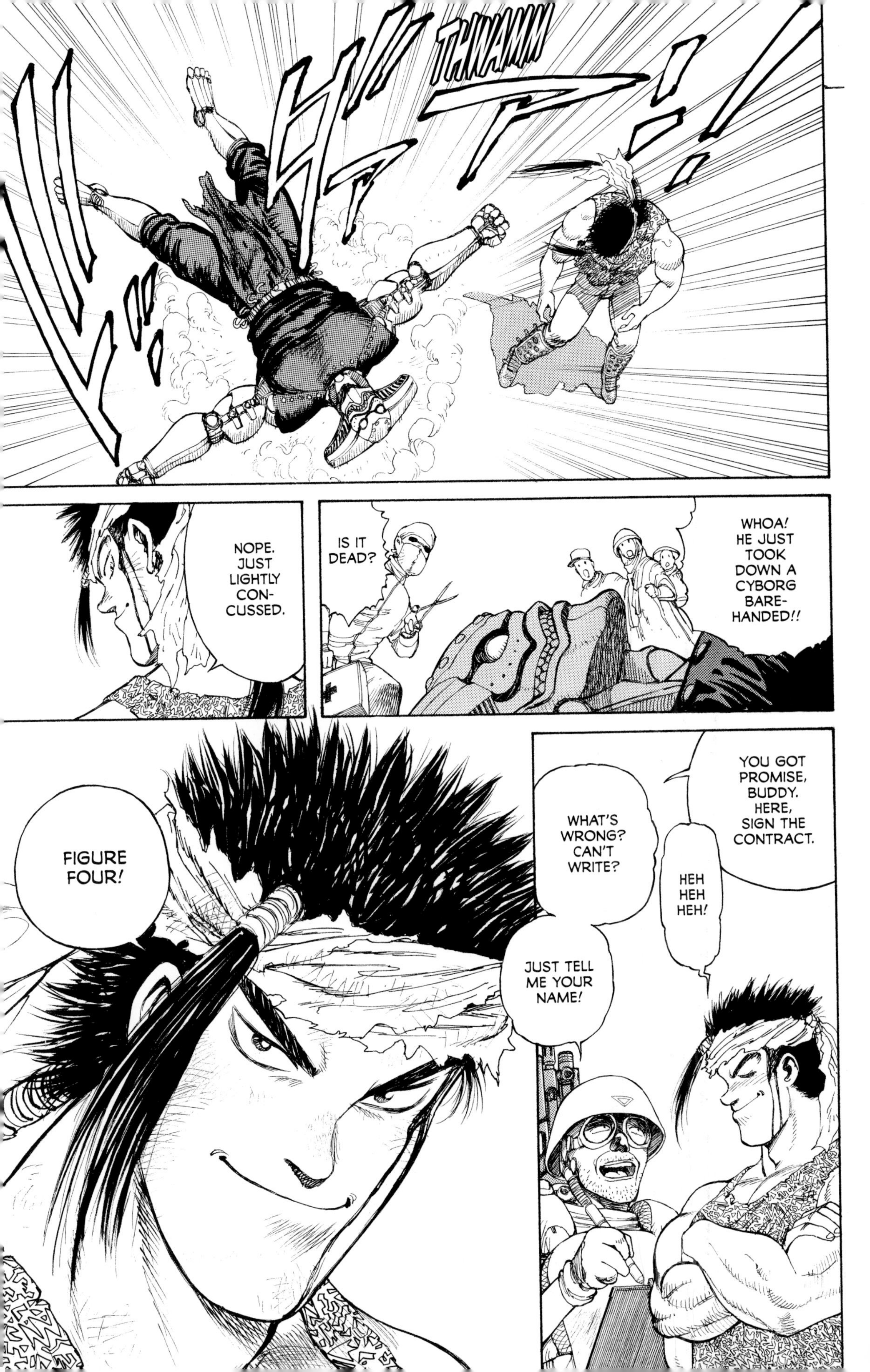
THWAMM
WHOA! HE JUST TOOK DOWN A CYBORG BARE-HANDED!!
IS IT DEAD?
NOPE. JUST LIGHTLY CON-CUSSED.
YOU GOT PROMISE, BUDDY. HERE, SIGN THE CONTRACT.
HEH HEH HEH!
WHAT'S WRONG? CAN'T WRITE?
JUST TELL ME YOUR NAME!
FIGURE FOUR!

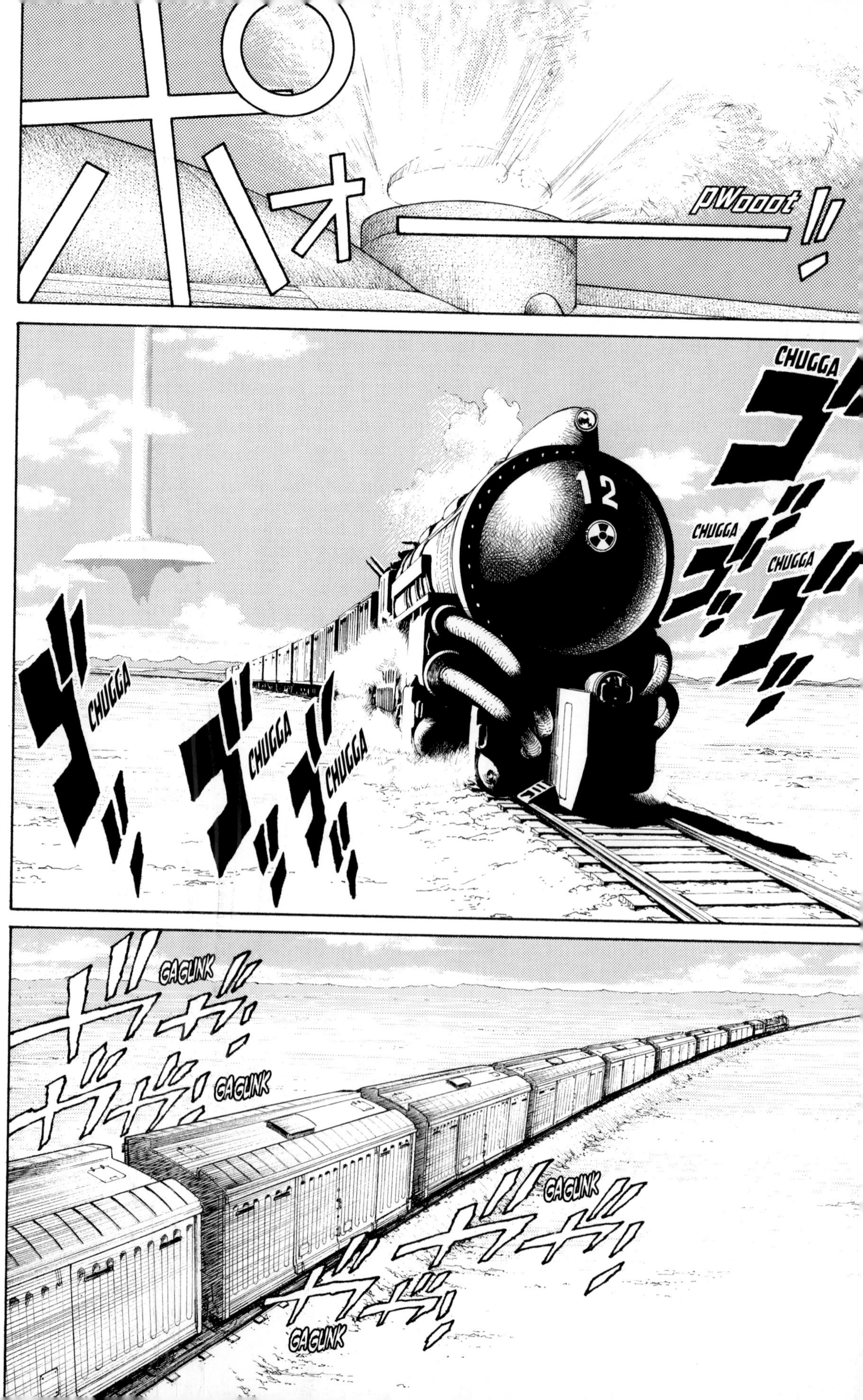
pWooot!!
CHUGGA
CHUGGA
CHUGGA
CHUGGA
CHUGGA
CHUGGA
GAGUNK
GAGUNK
GAGUNK
GAGUNK

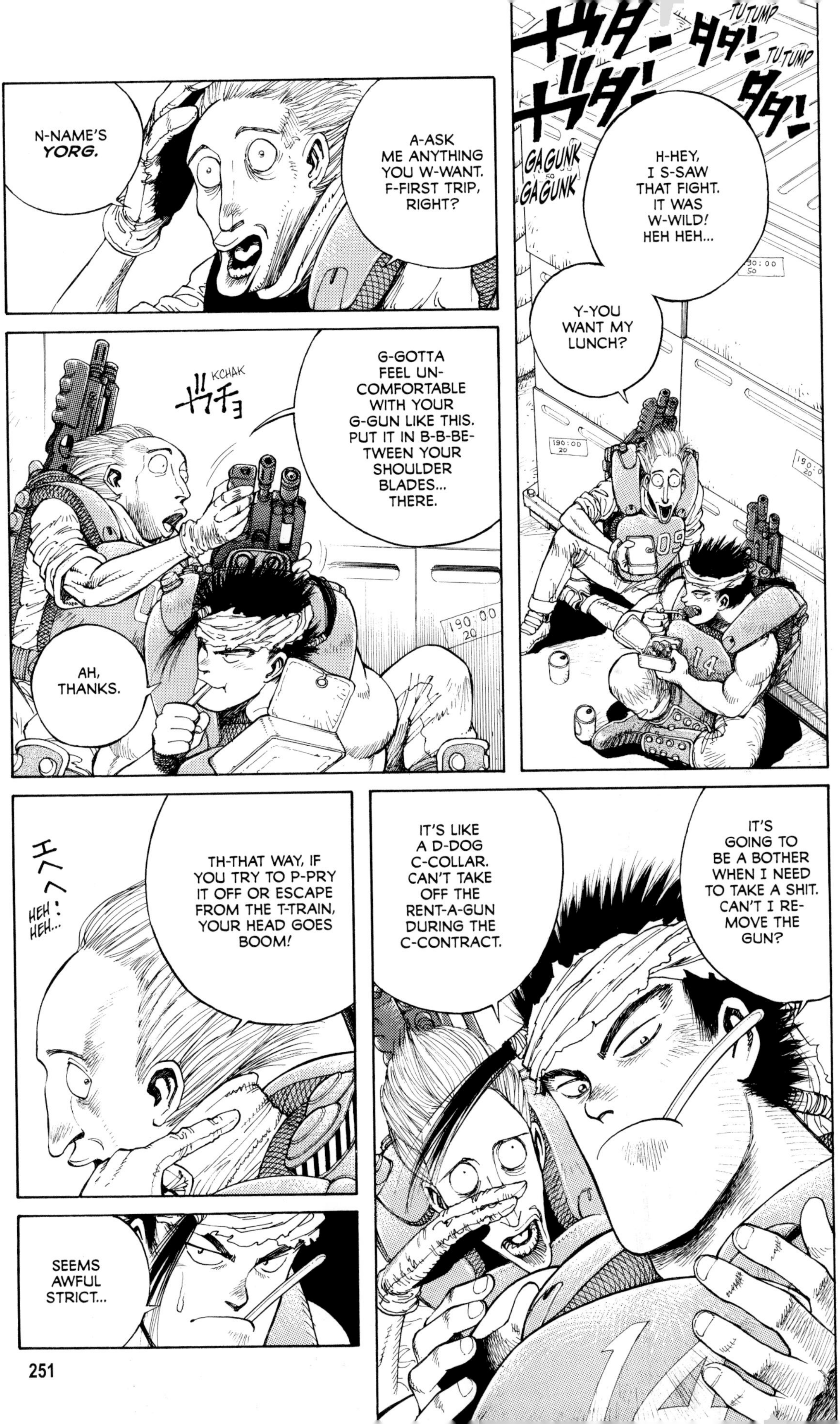
TUTUMP
TUTUMP
GAGUNK GAGUNK
H-HEY, I S-SAW THAT FIGHT. IT WAS W-WILD! HEH HEH...
Y-YOU WANT MY LUNCH?
A-ASK ME ANYTHING YOU W-WANT. F-FIRST TRIP, RIGHT?
N-NAME'S *YORG.*
KCHAK
G-GOTTA FEEL UN-COMFORTABLE WITH YOUR G-GUN LIKE THIS. PUT IT IN B-B-BE-TWEEN YOUR SHOULDER BLADES... THERE.
AH, THANKS.
IT'S GOING TO BE A BOTHER WHEN I NEED TO TAKE A SHIT. CAN'T I RE-MOVE THE GUN?
IT'S LIKE A D-DOG C-COLLAR. CAN'T TAKE OFF THE RENT-A-GUN DURING THE C-CONTRACT.
TH-THAT WAY, IF YOU TRY TO P-PRY IT OFF OR ESCAPE FROM THE T-TRAIN, YOUR HEAD GOES BOOM!
HEH HEH...
SEEMS AWFUL STRICT...

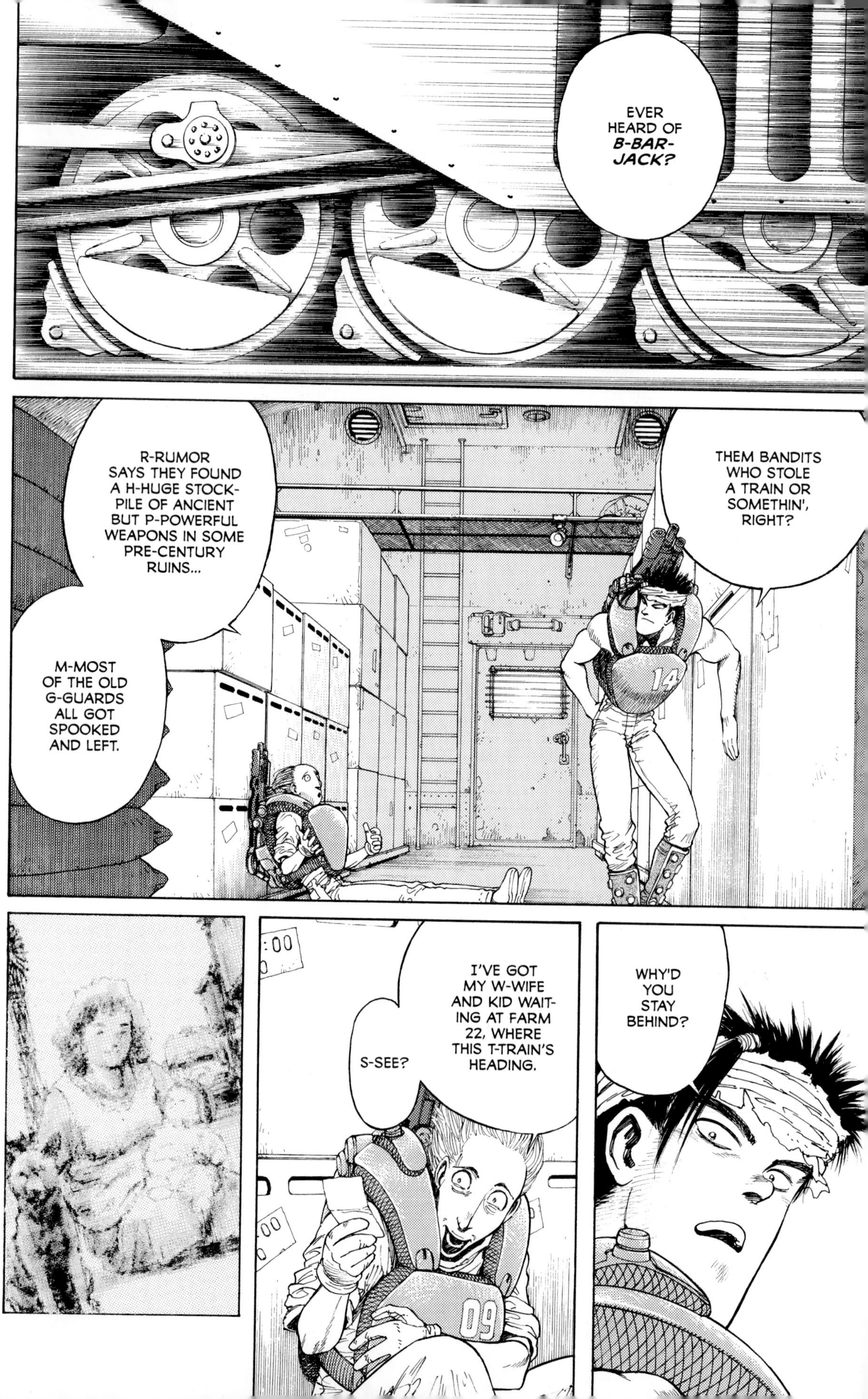
EVER HEARD OF B-BAR-JACK?
THEM BANDITS WHO STOLE A TRAIN OR SOMETHIN', RIGHT?
R-RUMOR SAYS THEY FOUND A H-HUGE STOCK-PILE OF ANCIENT BUT P-POWERFUL WEAPONS IN SOME PRE-CENTURY RUINS...
M-MOST OF THE OLD G-GUARDS ALL GOT SPOOKED AND LEFT.
WHY'D YOU STAY BEHIND?
I'VE GOT MY W-WIFE AND KID WAIT-ING AT FARM 22, WHERE THIS T-TRAIN'S HEADING.
S-SEE?

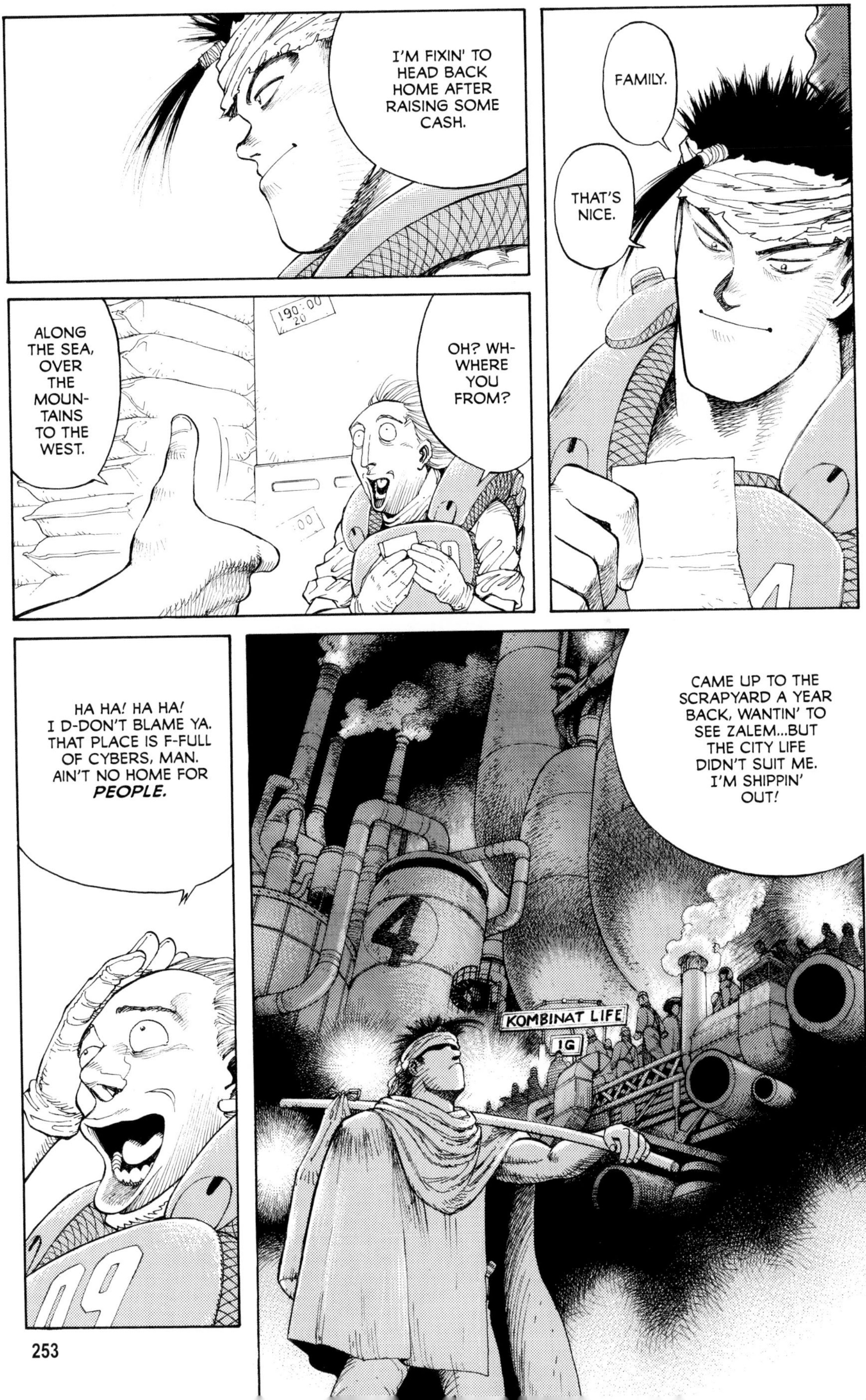
FAMILY.
THAT'S NICE.
I'M FIXIN' TO HEAD BACK HOME AFTER RAISING SOME CASH.
OH? WH-WHERE YOU FROM?
ALONG THE SEA, OVER THE MOUN-TAINS TO THE WEST.
CAME UP TO THE SCRAPYARD A YEAR BACK, WANTIN' TO SEE ZALEM...BUT THE CITY LIFE DIDN'T SUIT ME. I'M SHIPPIN' OUT!
KOMBINAT LIFE
1G
HA HA! HA HA! I D-DON'T BLAME YA. THAT PLACE IS F-FULL OF CYBERS, MAN. AIN'T NO HOME FOR ***PEOPLE.***

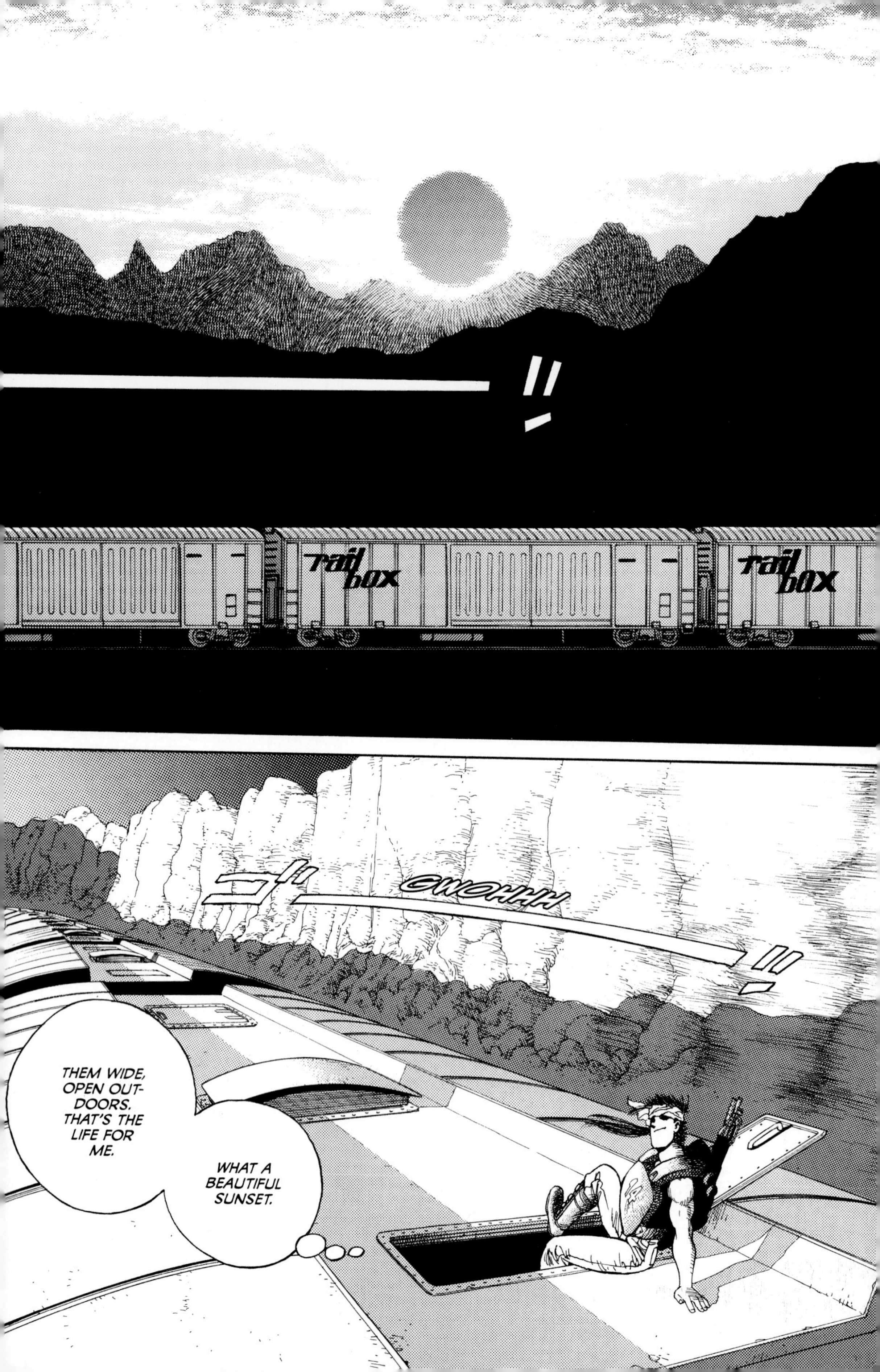
GWOHHH
WHAT A BEAUTIFUL SUNSET.
THEM WIDE, OPEN OUT-DOORS. THAT'S THE LIFE FOR ME.

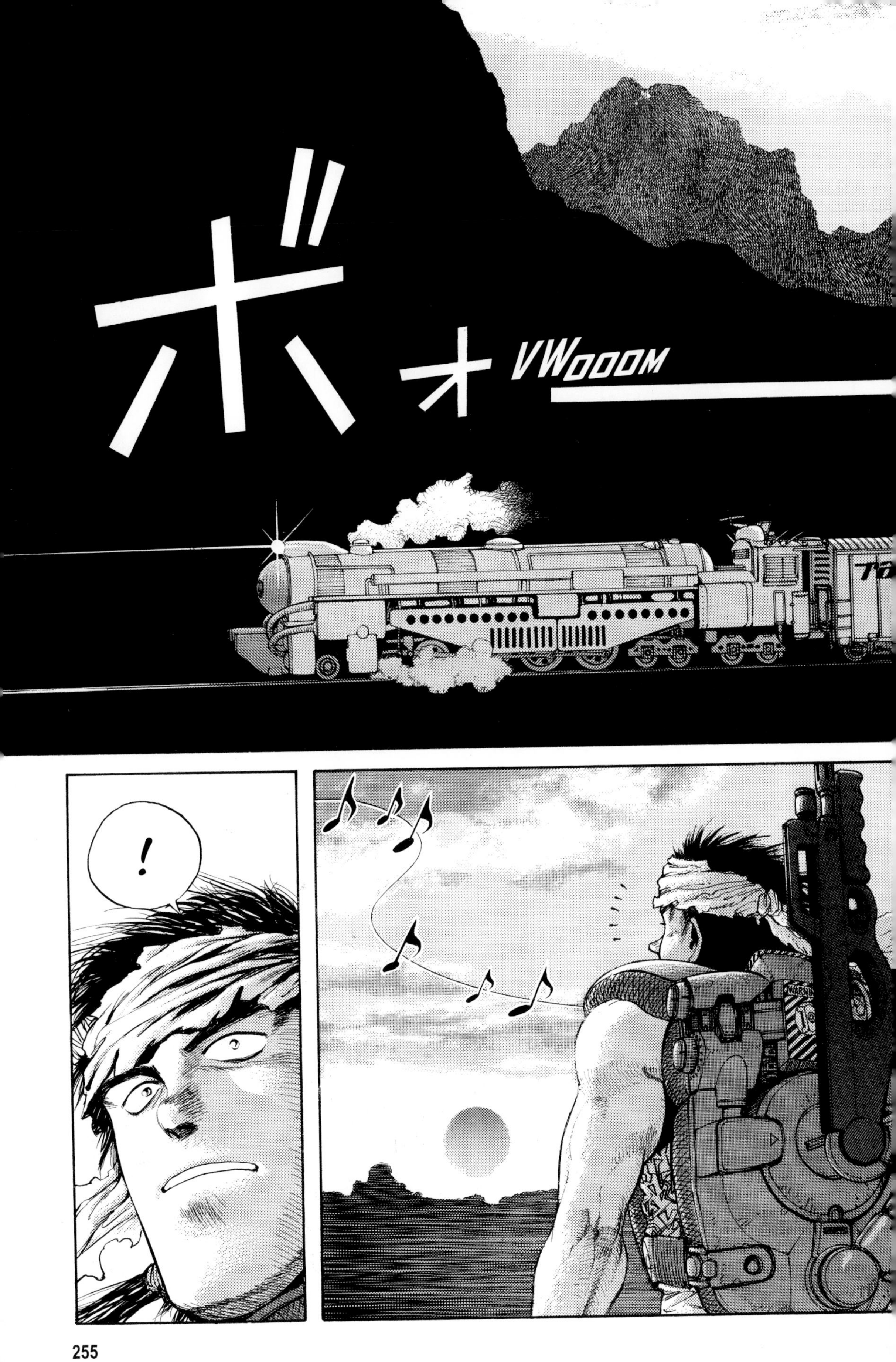
ボォ
VWoooM
!

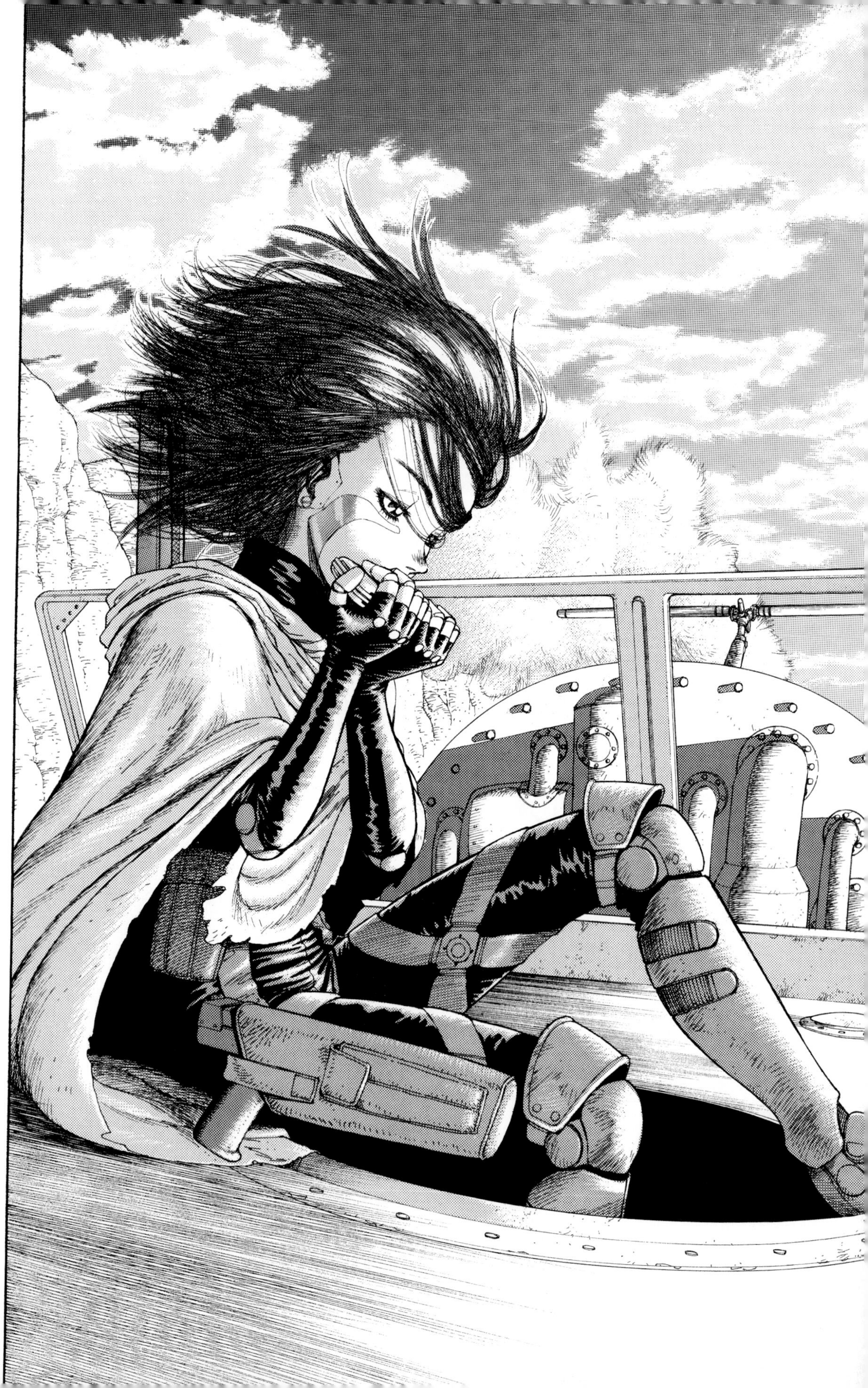

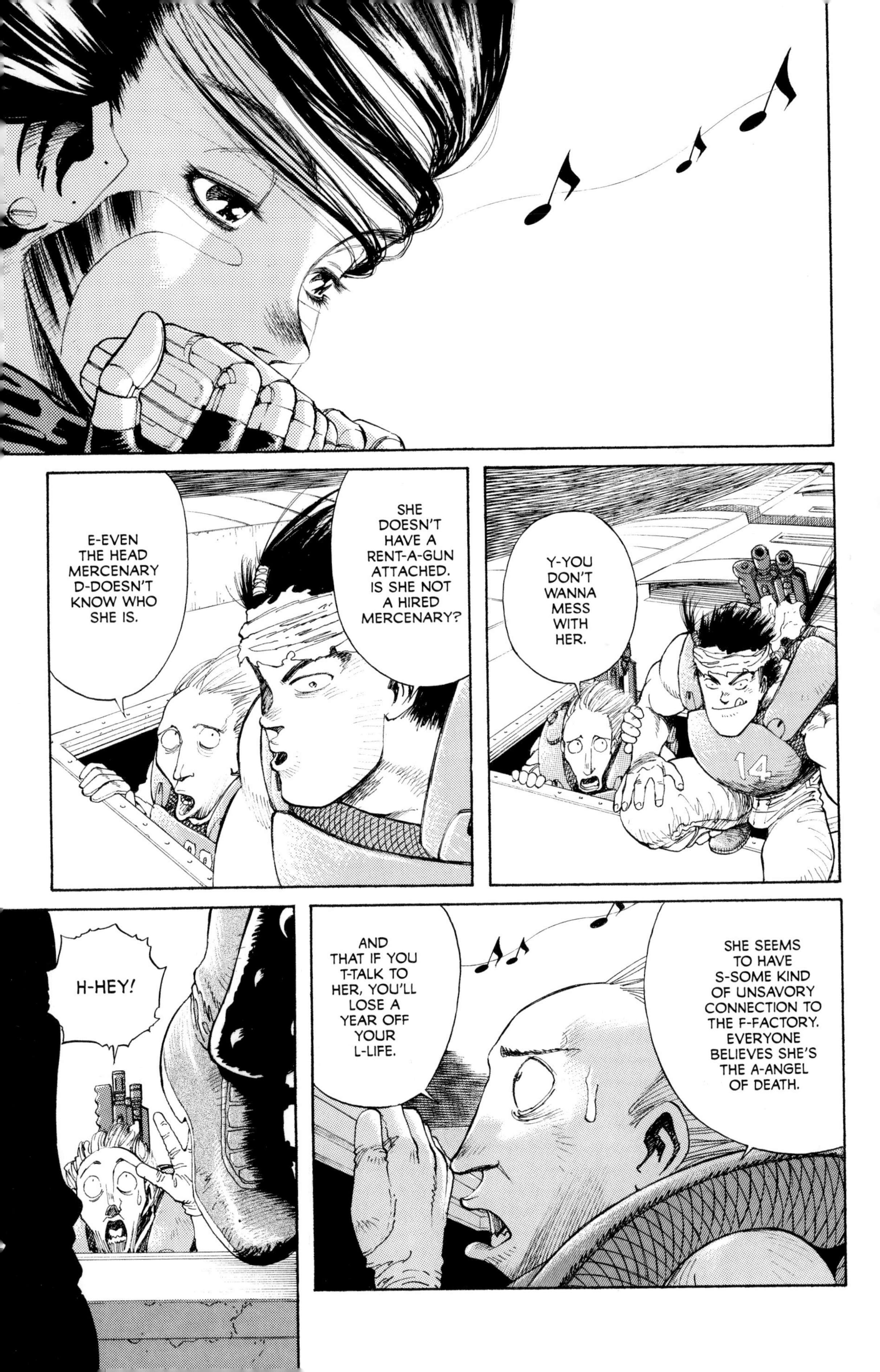
Y-YOU DON'T WANNA MESS WITH HER.
SHE DOESN'T HAVE A RENT-A-GUN ATTACHED. IS SHE NOT A HIRED MERCENARY?
E-EVEN THE HEAD MERCENARY D-DOESN'T KNOW WHO SHE IS.
SHE SEEMS TO HAVE S-SOME KIND OF UNSAVORY CONNECTION TO THE F-FACTORY. EVERYONE BELIEVES SHE'S THE A-ANGEL OF DEATH.
AND THAT IF YOU T-TALK TO HER, YOU'LL LOSE A YEAR OFF YOUR L-LIFE.
H-HEY!

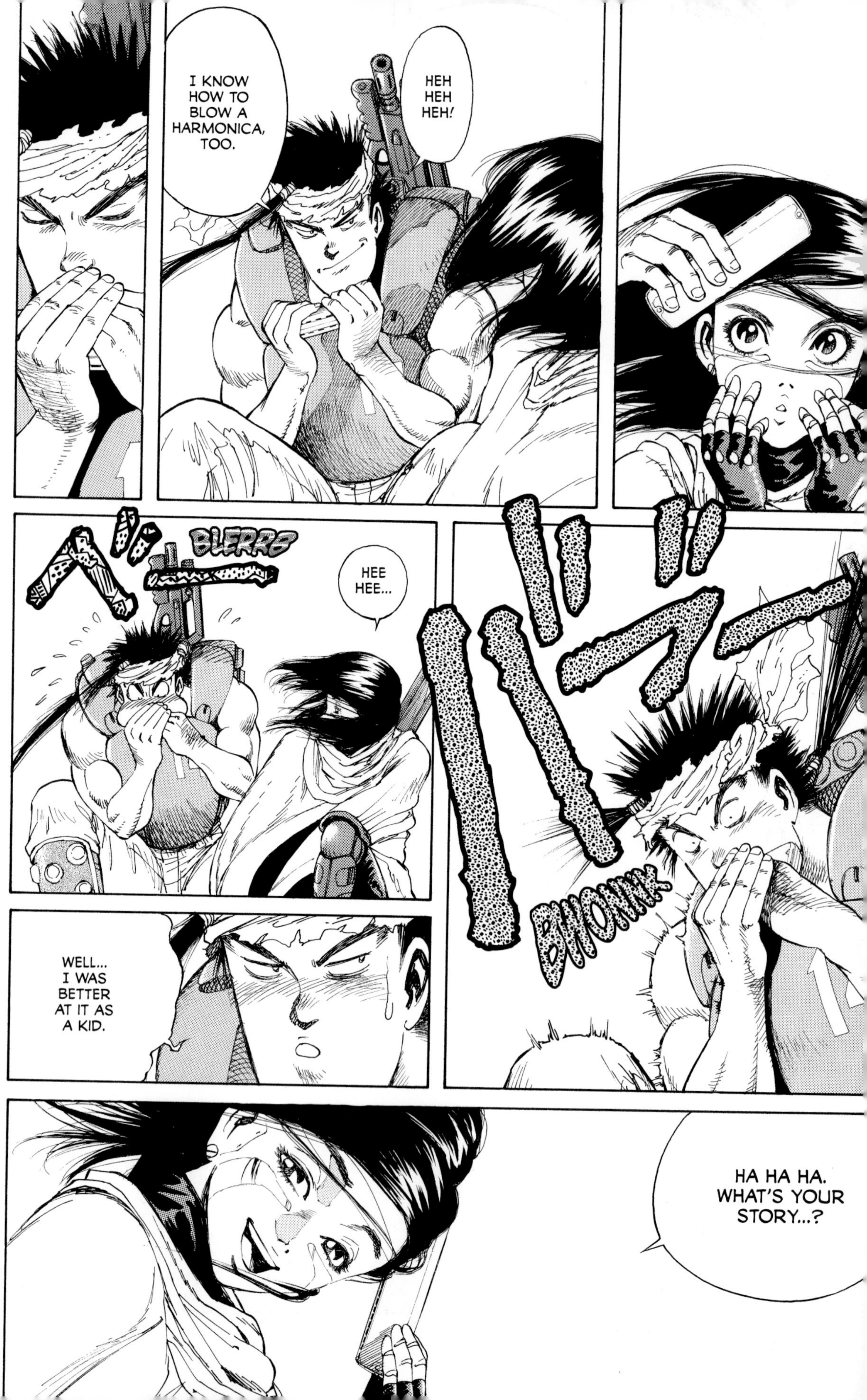
HEH HEH HEH!
I KNOW HOW TO BLOW A HARMONICA, TOO.
BWONNK
BLERRB
HEE HEE...
WELL... I WAS BETTER AT IT AS A KID.
HA HA HA. WHAT'S YOUR STORY...?

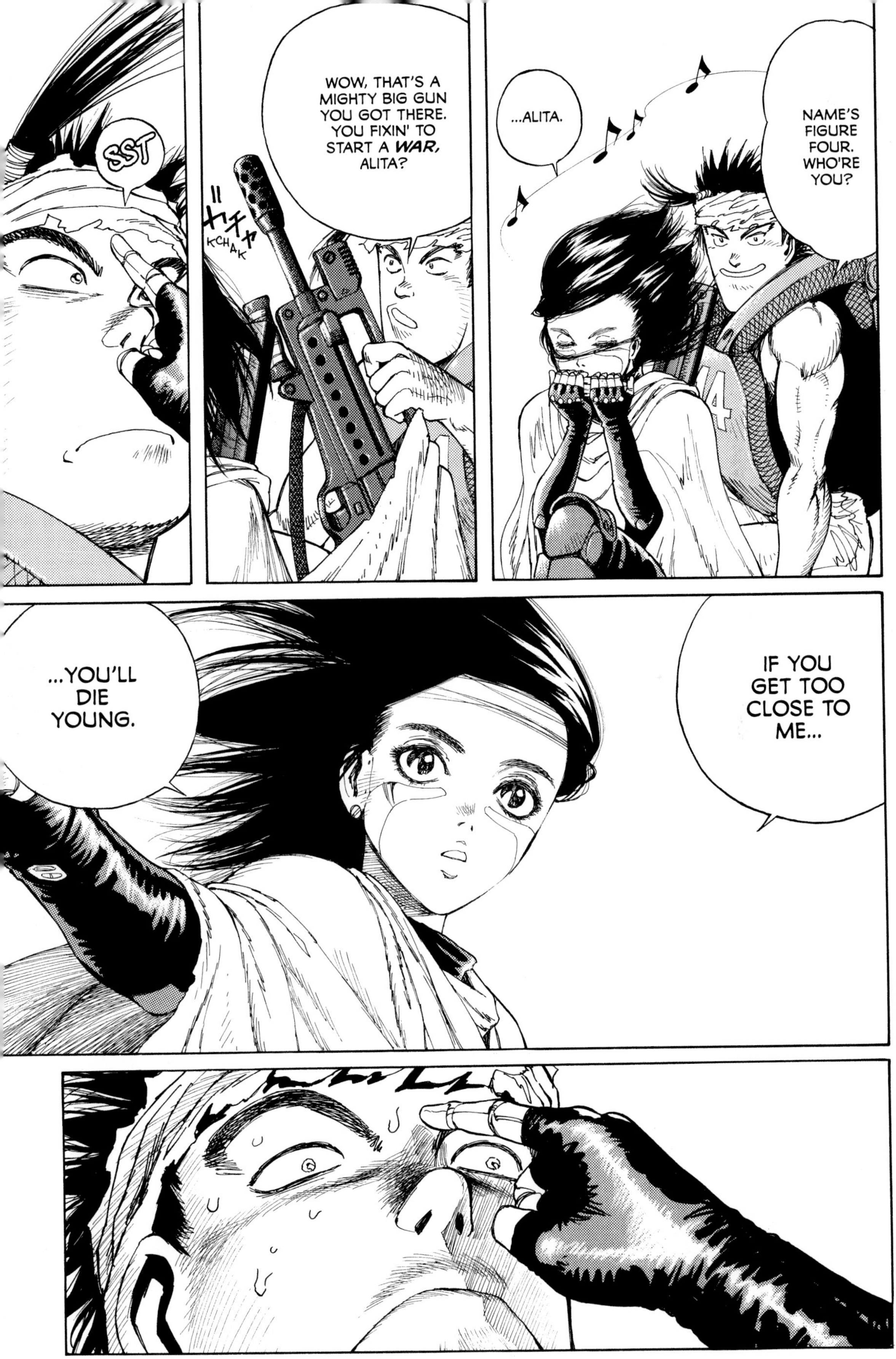
NAME'S FIGURE FOUR. WHO'RE YOU?
...ALITA.
WOW, THAT'S A MIGHTY BIG GUN YOU GOT THERE. YOU FIXIN' TO START A *WAR,* ALITA?
KCHAK
SST
IF YOU GET TOO CLOSE TO ME...
...YOU'LL DIE YOUNG.

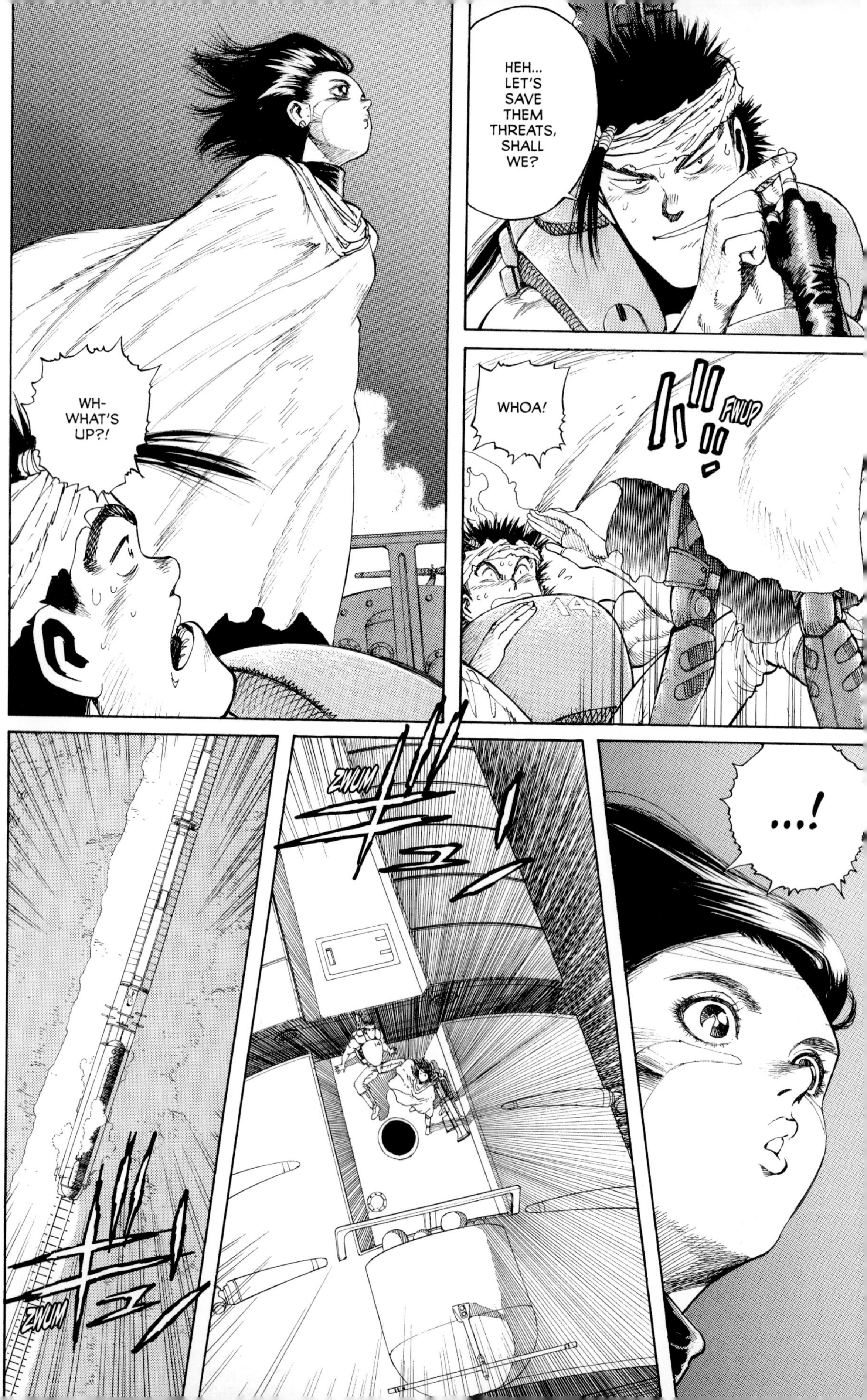
HEH... LET'S SAVE THEM THREATS, SHALL WE?
WHOA!
FWUP
WH- WHAT'S UP?!
...!
ZWUM
ZWUM

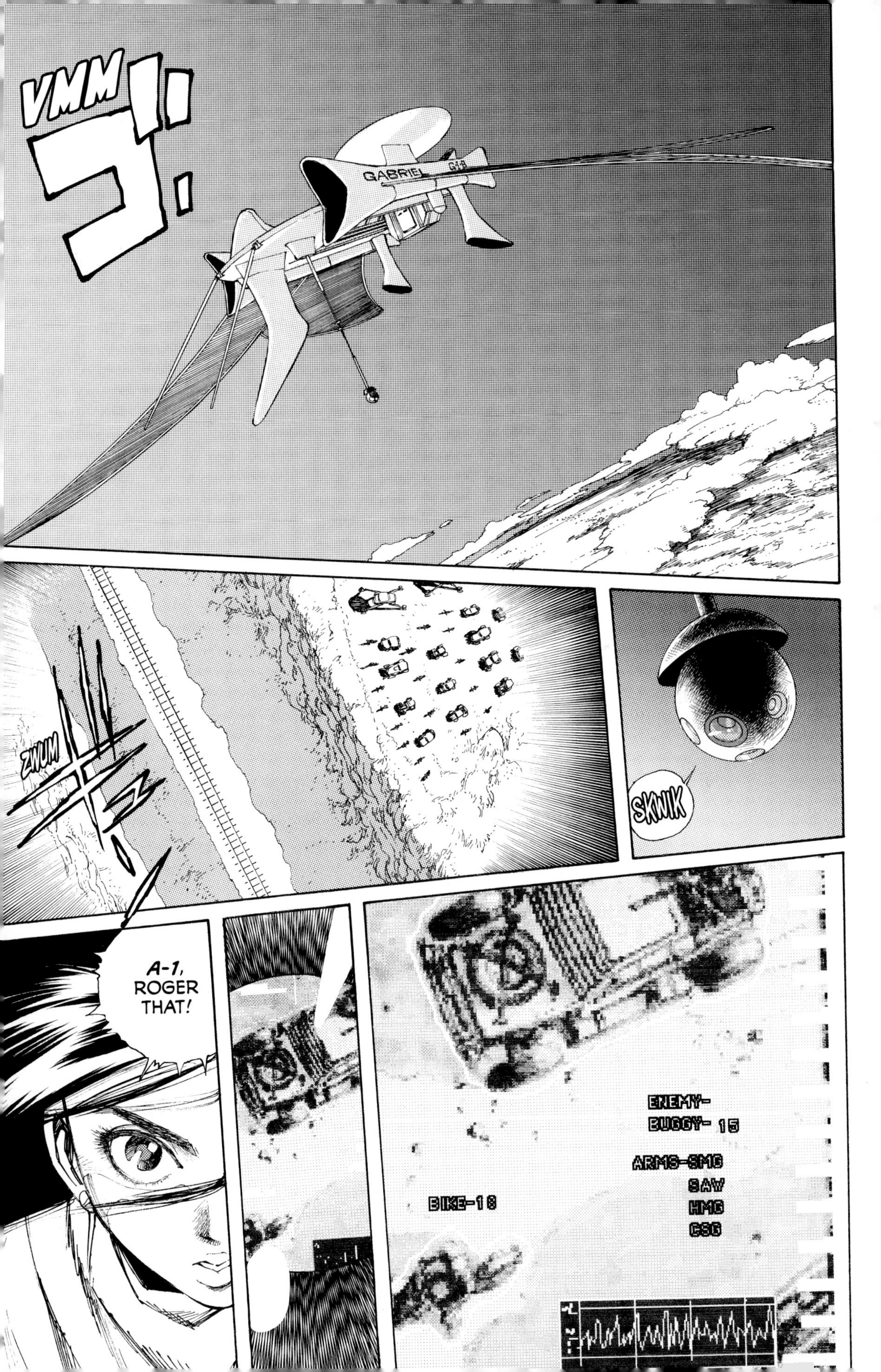
VMM
ゴ!!
GABRIEL
SKWIK
ZWUM
ENEMY-
BUGGY- 15
ARMS-SMG
SAW
HMG
CSG
BIKE-18
A-1, ROGER THAT!

WHAT? WHAT IS IT?!
WHOOSH
HEY, CHIEF! WE GOT COMPANY— GO ON BATTLE ALERT!
HUH?! BUT THE MONITORS SHOW NOTHING...
WHATCHA GOT, NUMBER 5?
NO REESPONSE ON PERSONNEL OR INFRARED RADARS.
THERE, YOU HEAR THAT? SMOOTH SAILING.
YANK

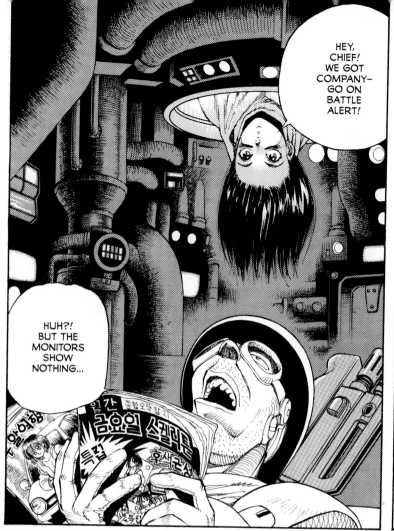

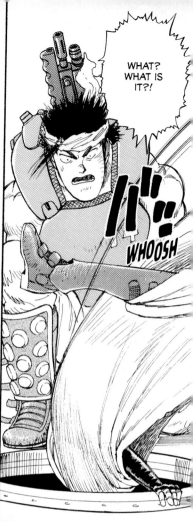

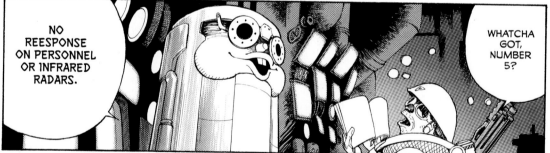

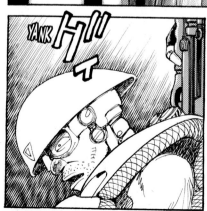

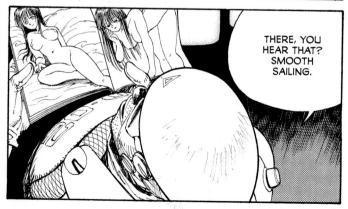

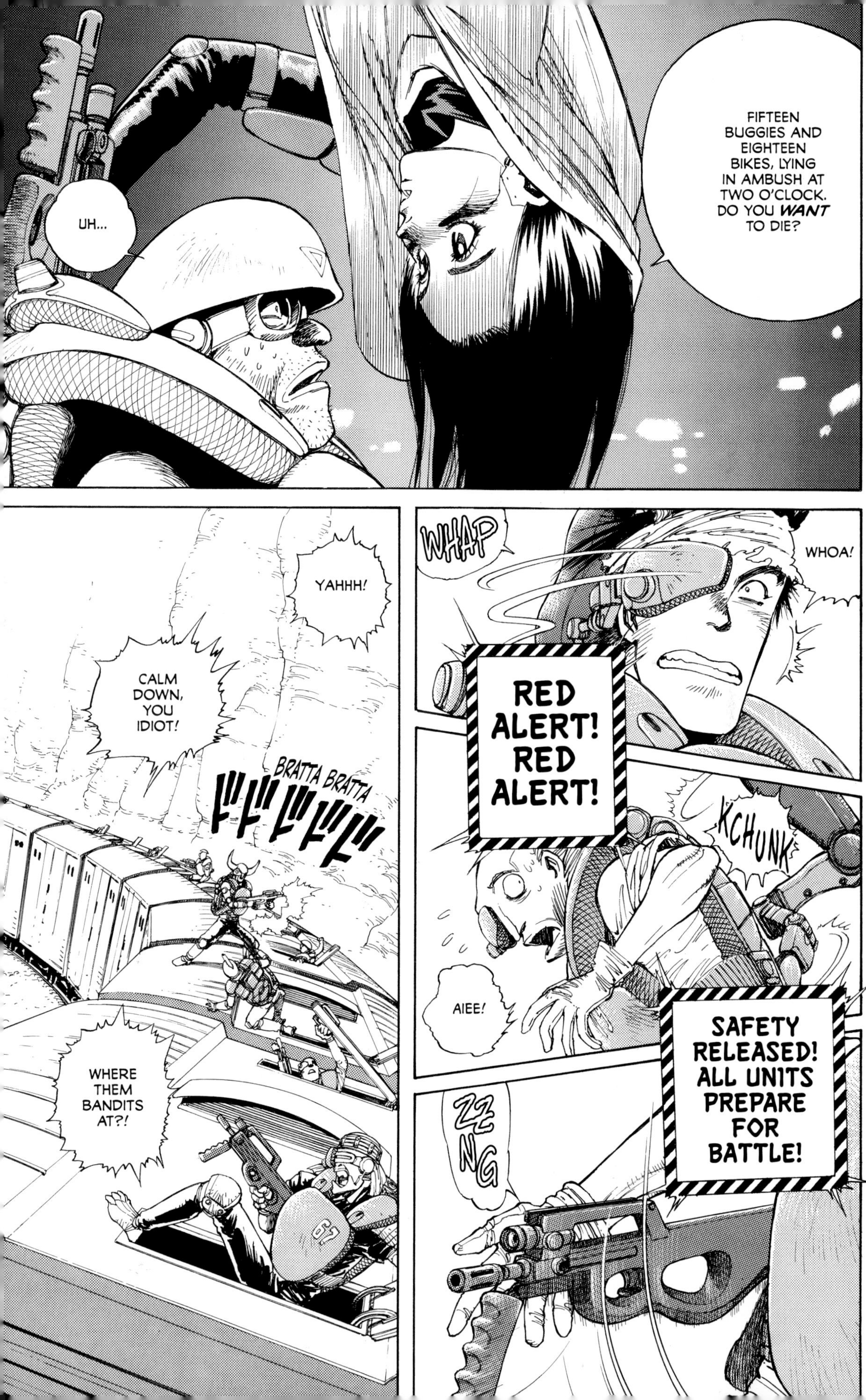
FIFTEEN BUGGIES AND EIGHTEEN BIKES, LYING IN AMBUSH AT TWO O'CLOCK. DO YOU *WANT* TO DIE?
UH...
WHAP
WHOA!
RED ALERT! RED ALERT!
KCHUNK
AIEE!
SAFETY RELEASED! ALL UNITS PREPARE FOR BATTLE!
ZZNG
YAHHH!
CALM DOWN, YOU IDIOT!
BRATTA BRATTA
WHERE THEM BANDITS AT?!

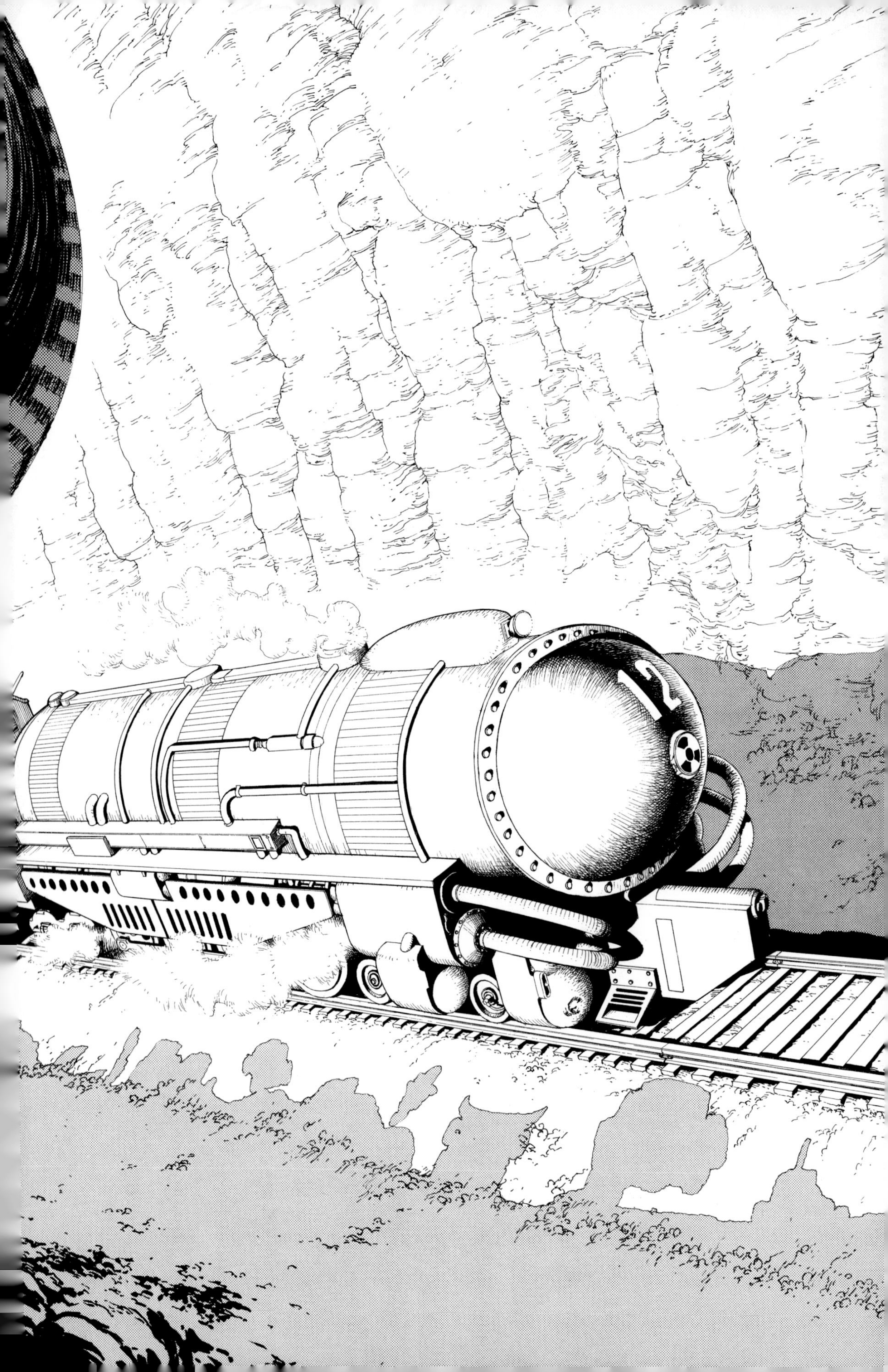
12

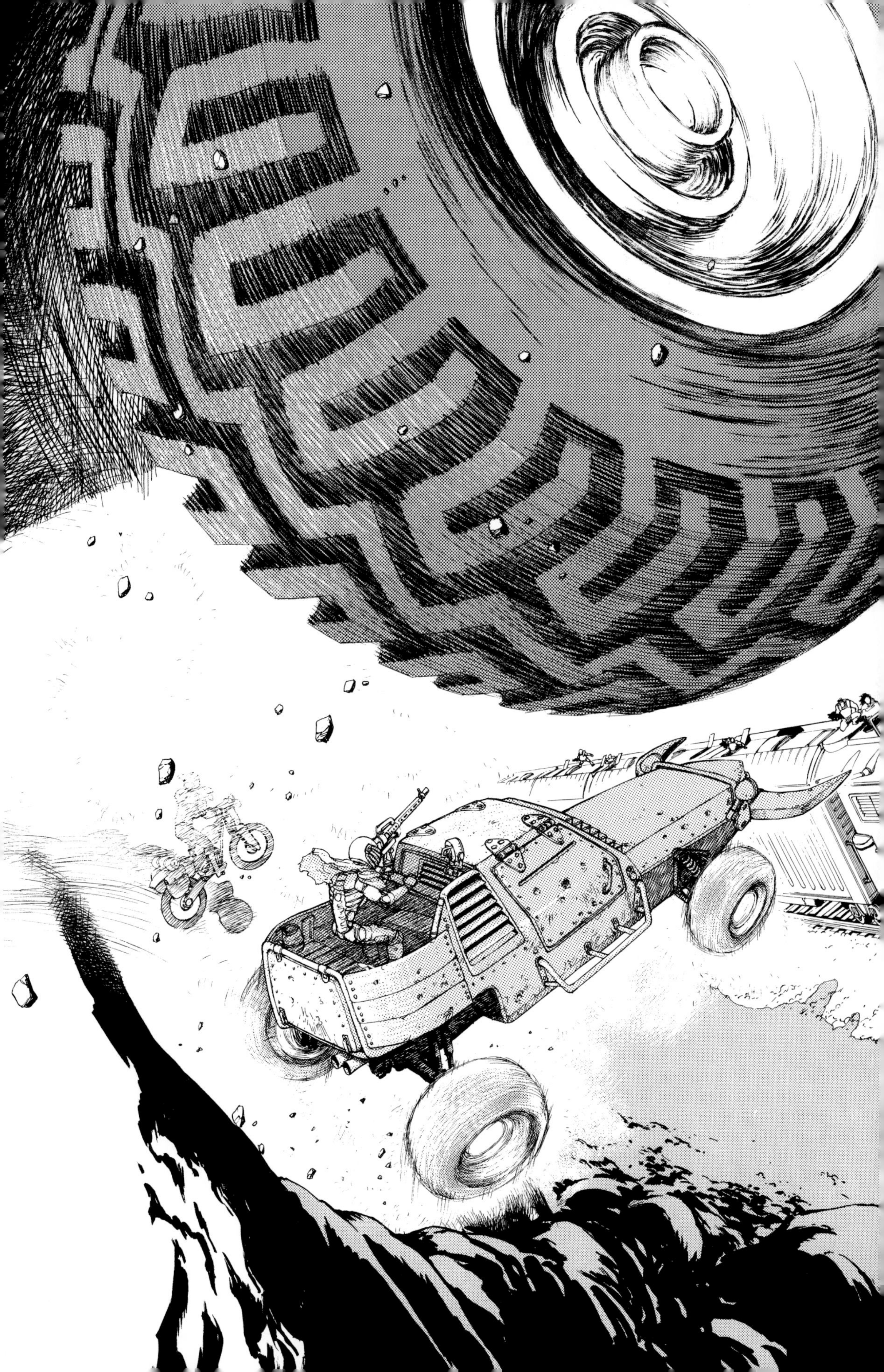

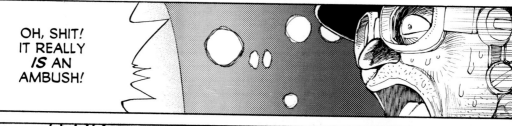

OH, SHIT! IT REALLY *IS* AN AMBUSH!

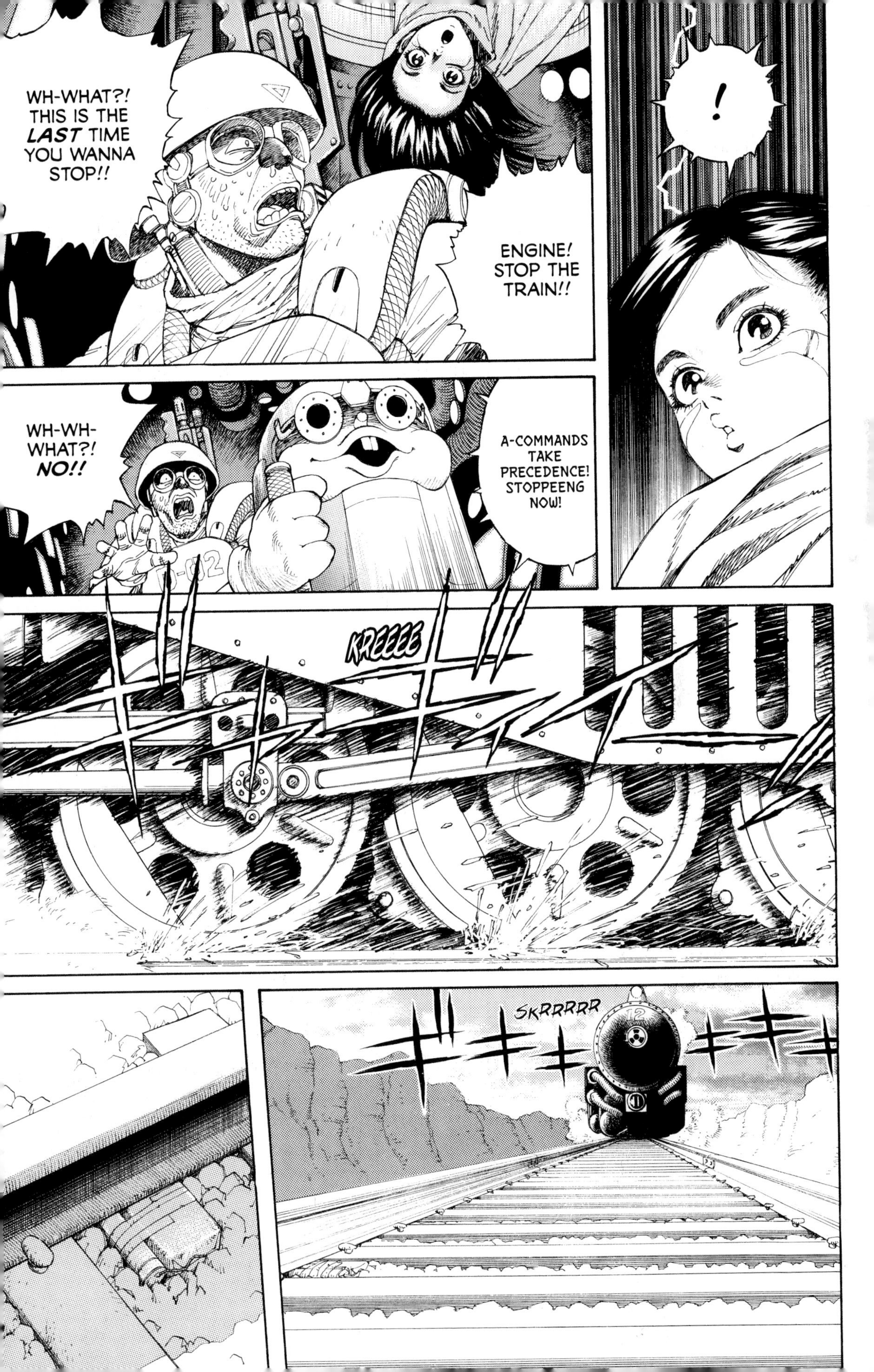
!
ENGINE! STOP THE TRAIN!!
WH-WHAT?! THIS IS THE *LAST* TIME YOU WANNA STOP!!
A-COMMANDS TAKE PRECEDENCE! STOPPEENG NOW!
WH-WH-WHAT?! *NO!!*
KREEEEE
SKRRRRR

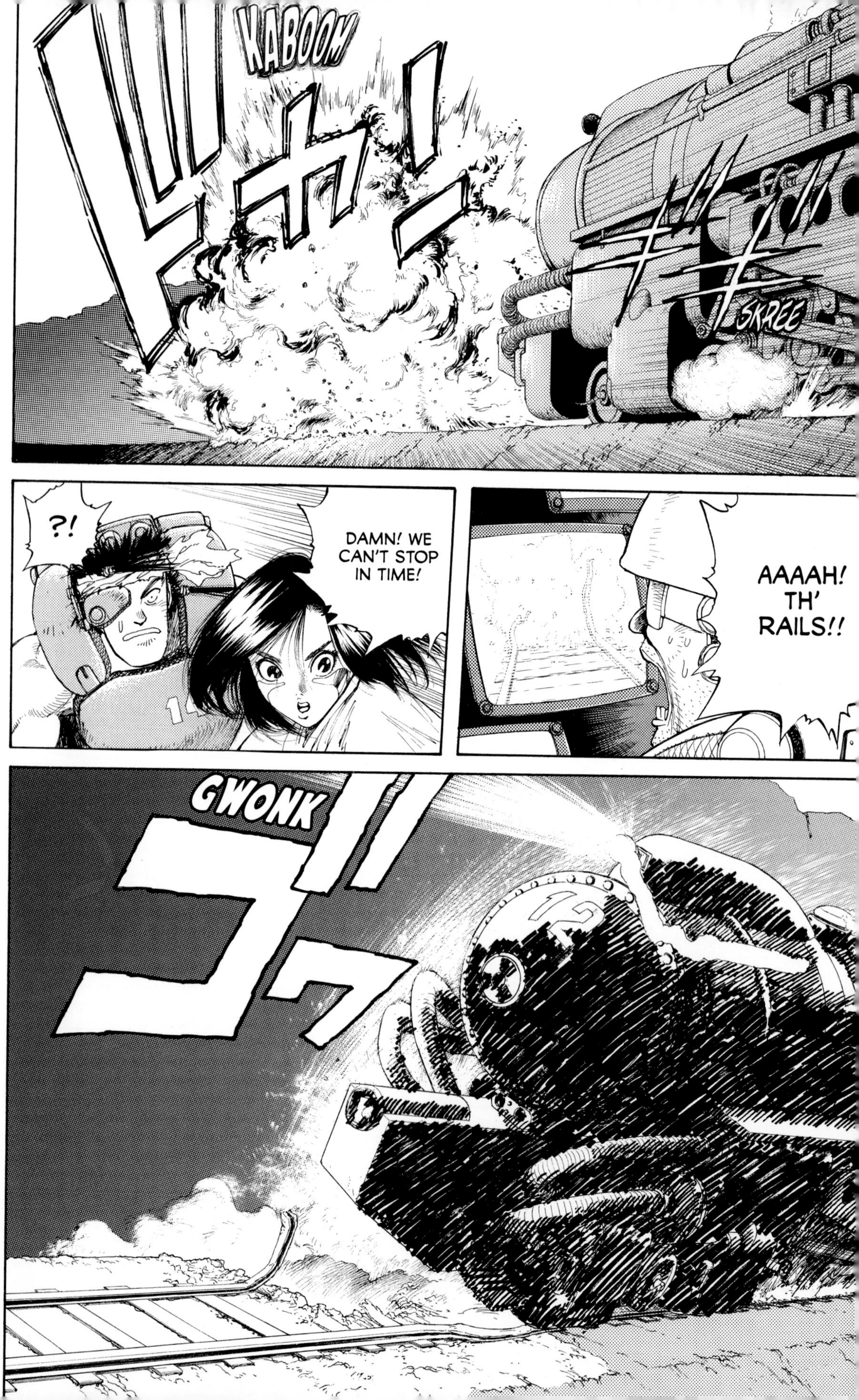
KABOOM
SKREE
AAAAH! TH' RAILS!!
?!
DAMN! WE CAN'T STOP IN TIME!
GWONK

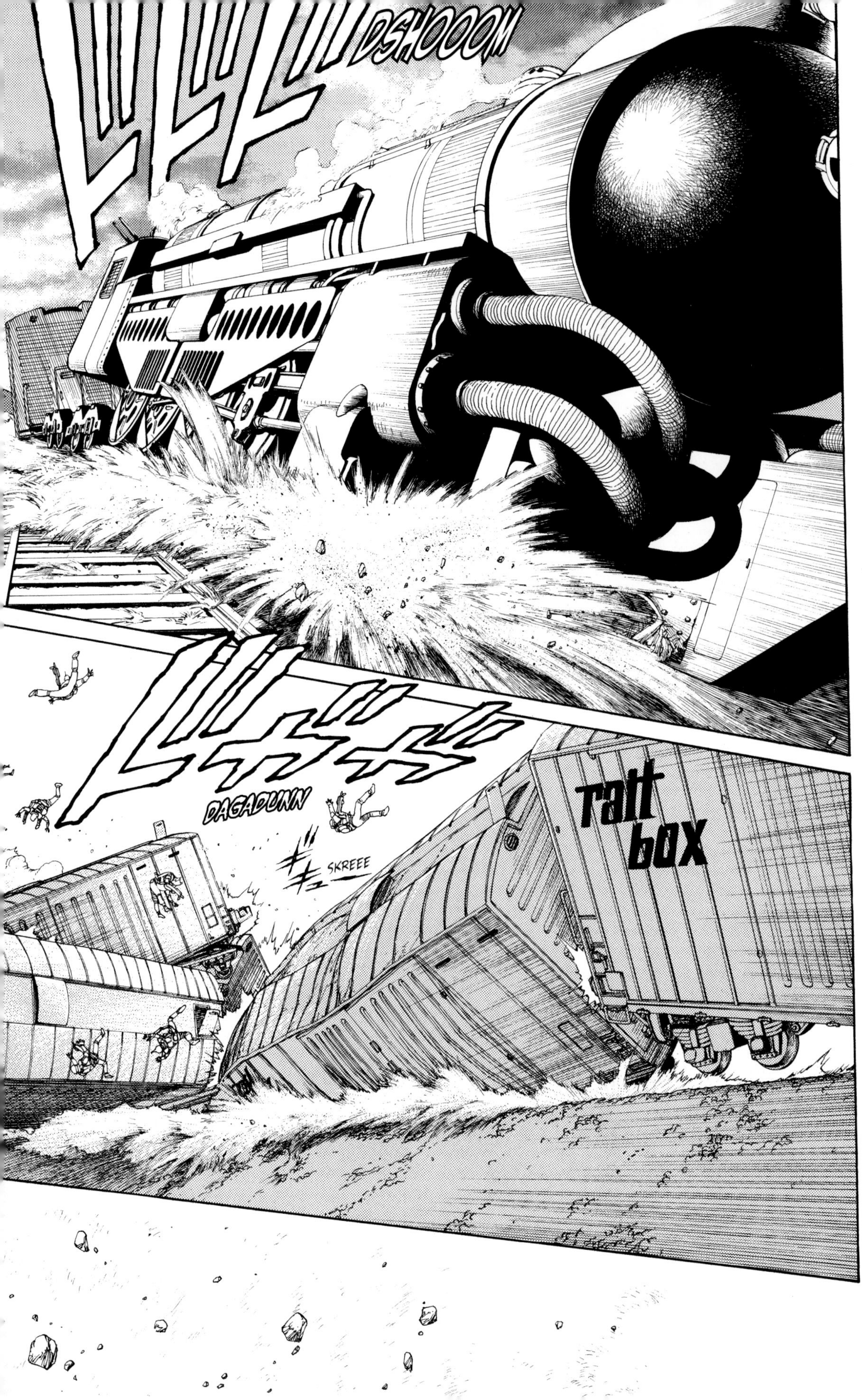
DSHOOOM
DAGADUNN
SKREEE
rail box

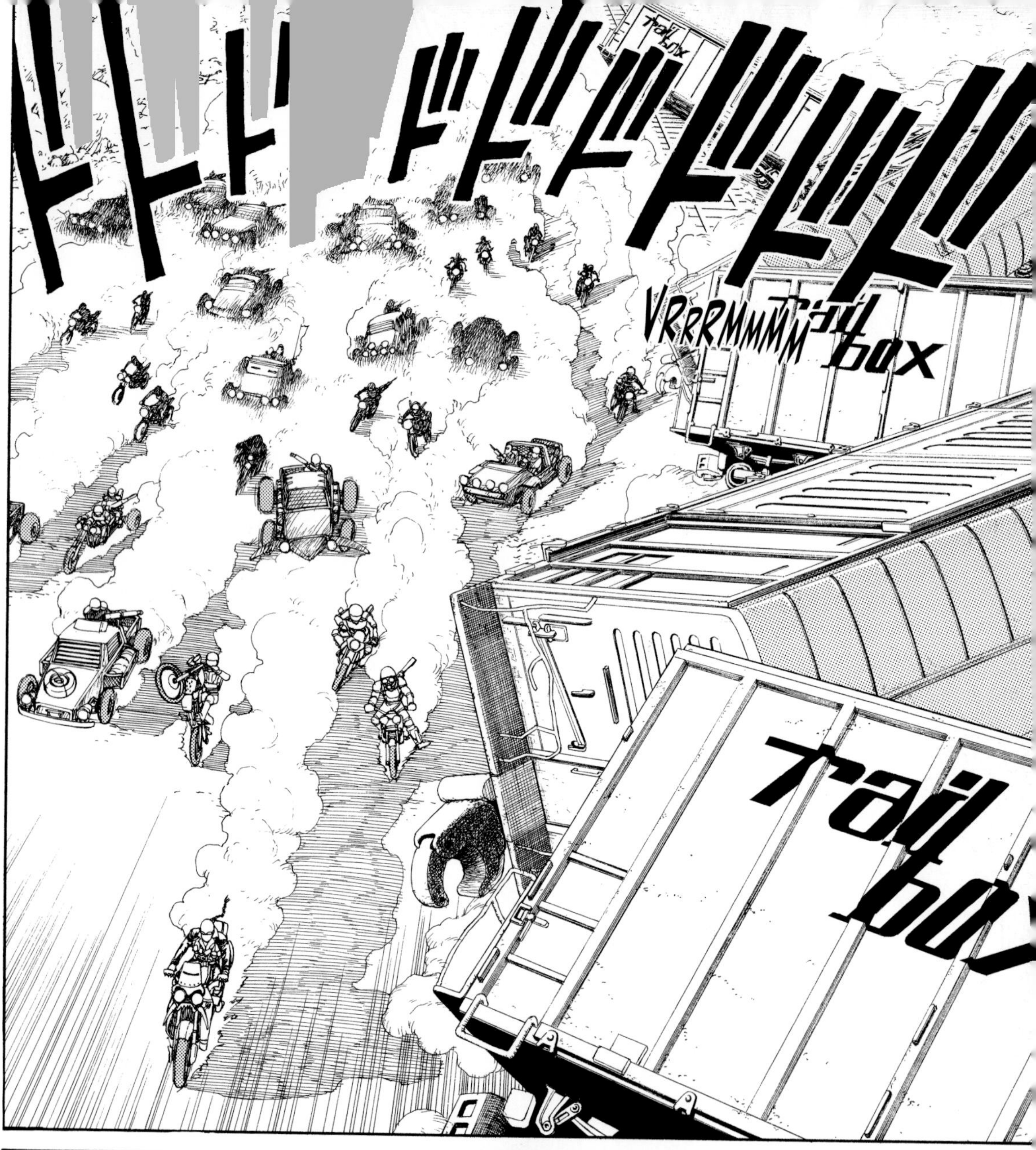
VRRRMMMM
trail box
trail box
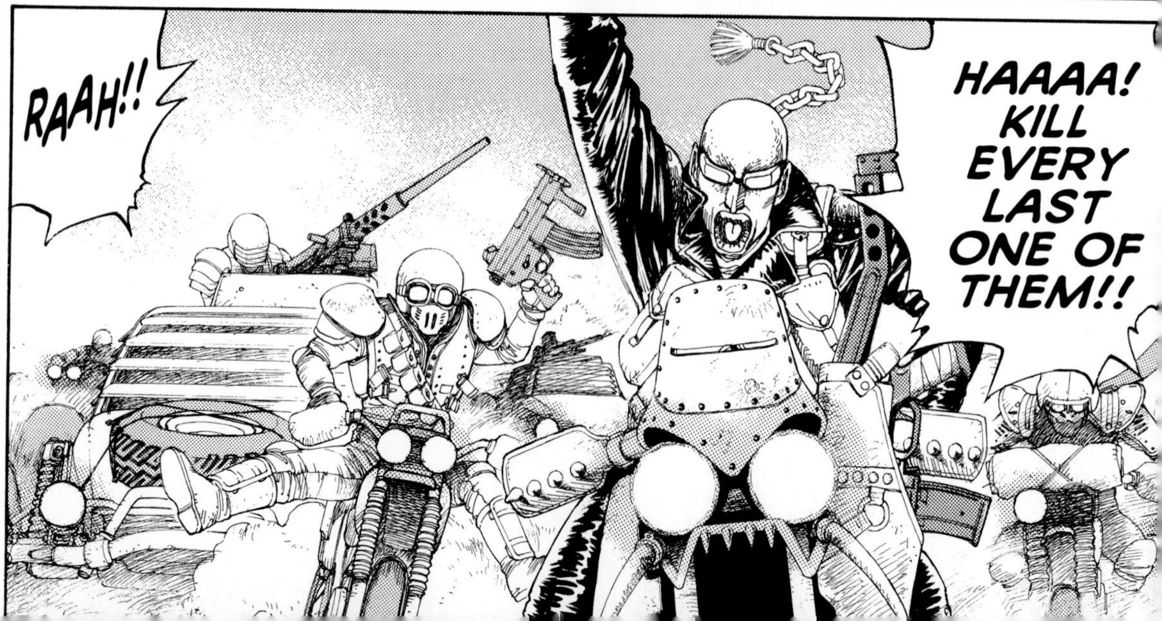
HAAAA! KILL EVERY LAST ONE OF THEM!!
RAAH!!

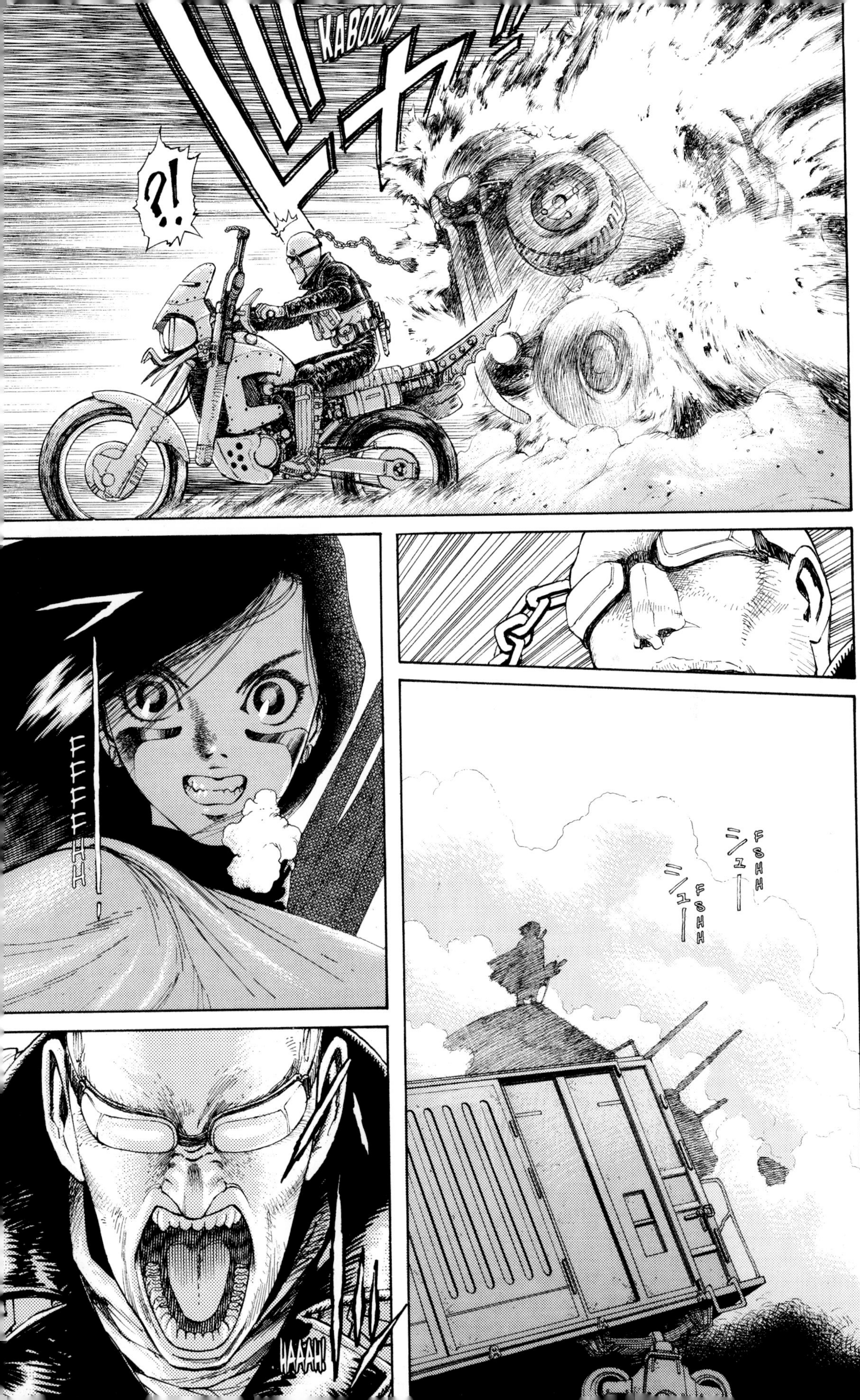
KABOOM
?!
FSHH
FSHH
FFFFHH
HAAAH!

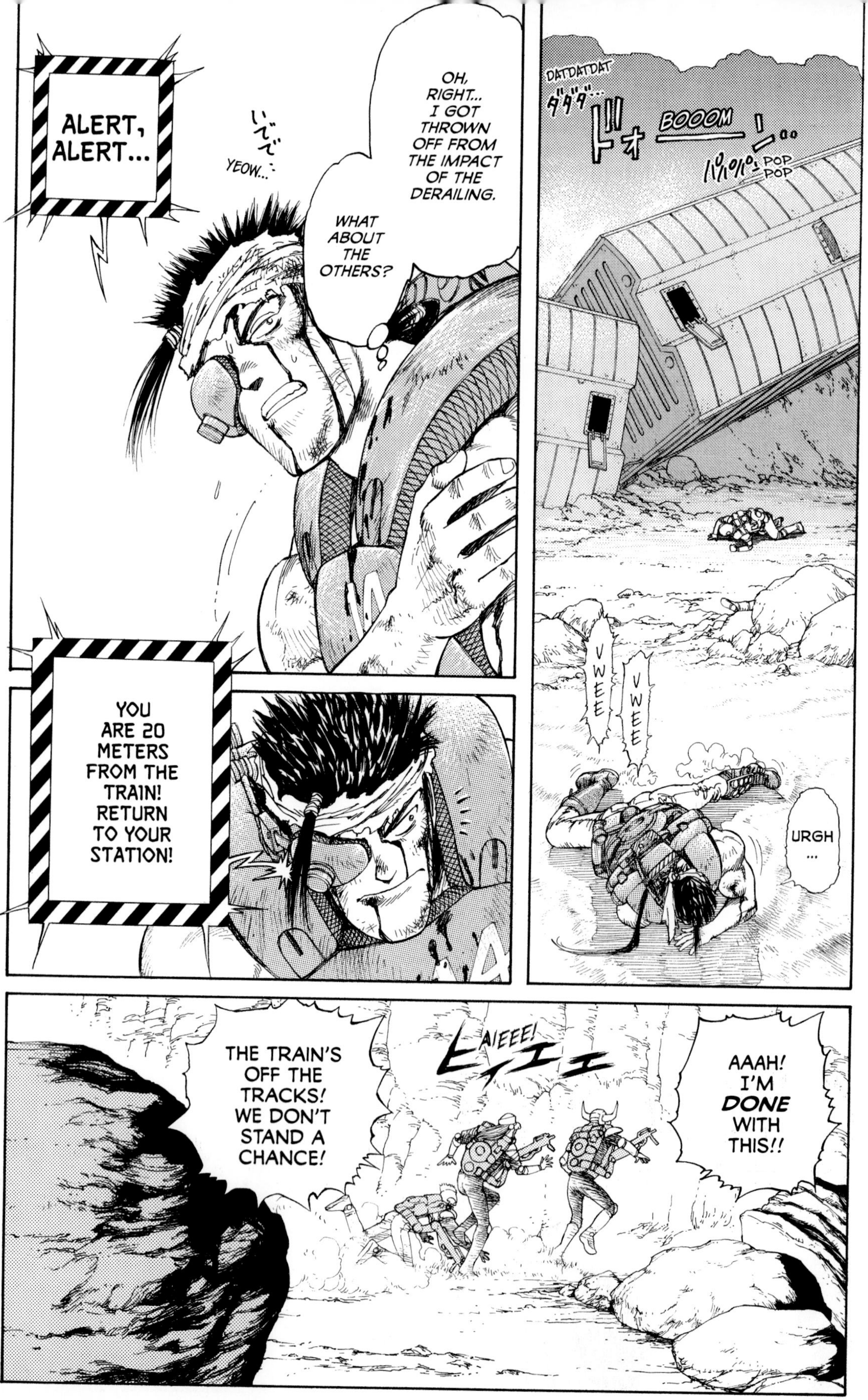
ダダダ…
DATDATDAT
ドォ
BOOOM
パパパ
POP POP
VWEE
VWEE
URGH...
OH, RIGHT... I GOT THROWN OFF FROM THE IMPACT OF THE DERAILING.
WHAT ABOUT THE OTHERS?
いでで
YEOW...
ALERT, ALERT...
YOU ARE 20 METERS FROM THE TRAIN! RETURN TO YOUR STATION!
AAAH! I'M DONE WITH THIS!!
ヒィエエ
AIEEE!
THE TRAIN'S OFF THE TRACKS! WE DON'T STAND A CHANCE!

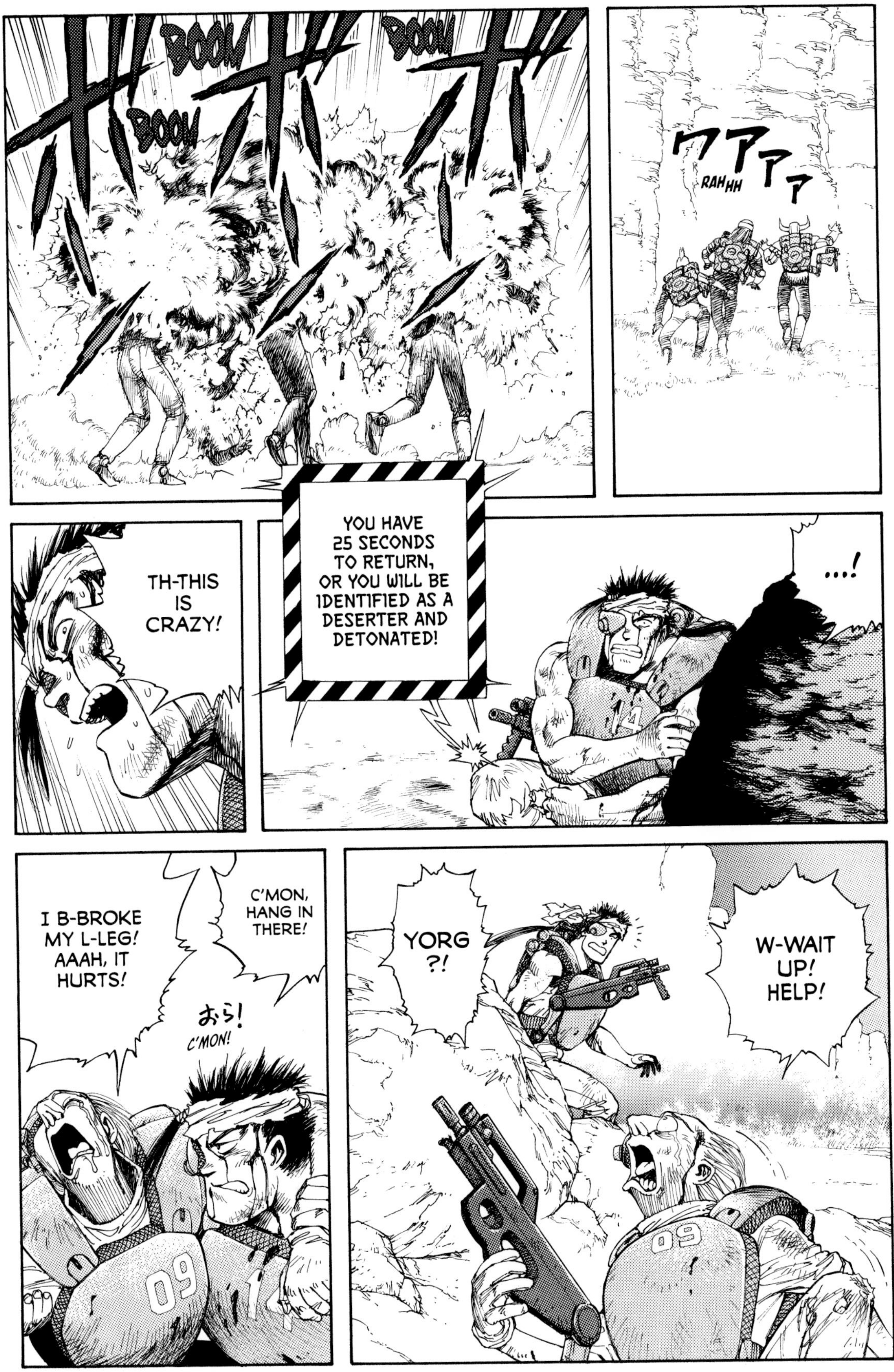
ワアアア
RAHHH
ボボボ
BOOM
BOOM
BOOM
...!
YOU HAVE 25 SECONDS TO RETURN, OR YOU WILL BE IDENTIFIED AS A DESERTER AND DETONATED!
TH-THIS IS CRAZY!
W-WAIT UP! HELP!
YORG ?!
C'MON, HANG IN THERE!
I B-BROKE MY L-LEG! AAAH, IT HURTS!
おら!
C'MON!

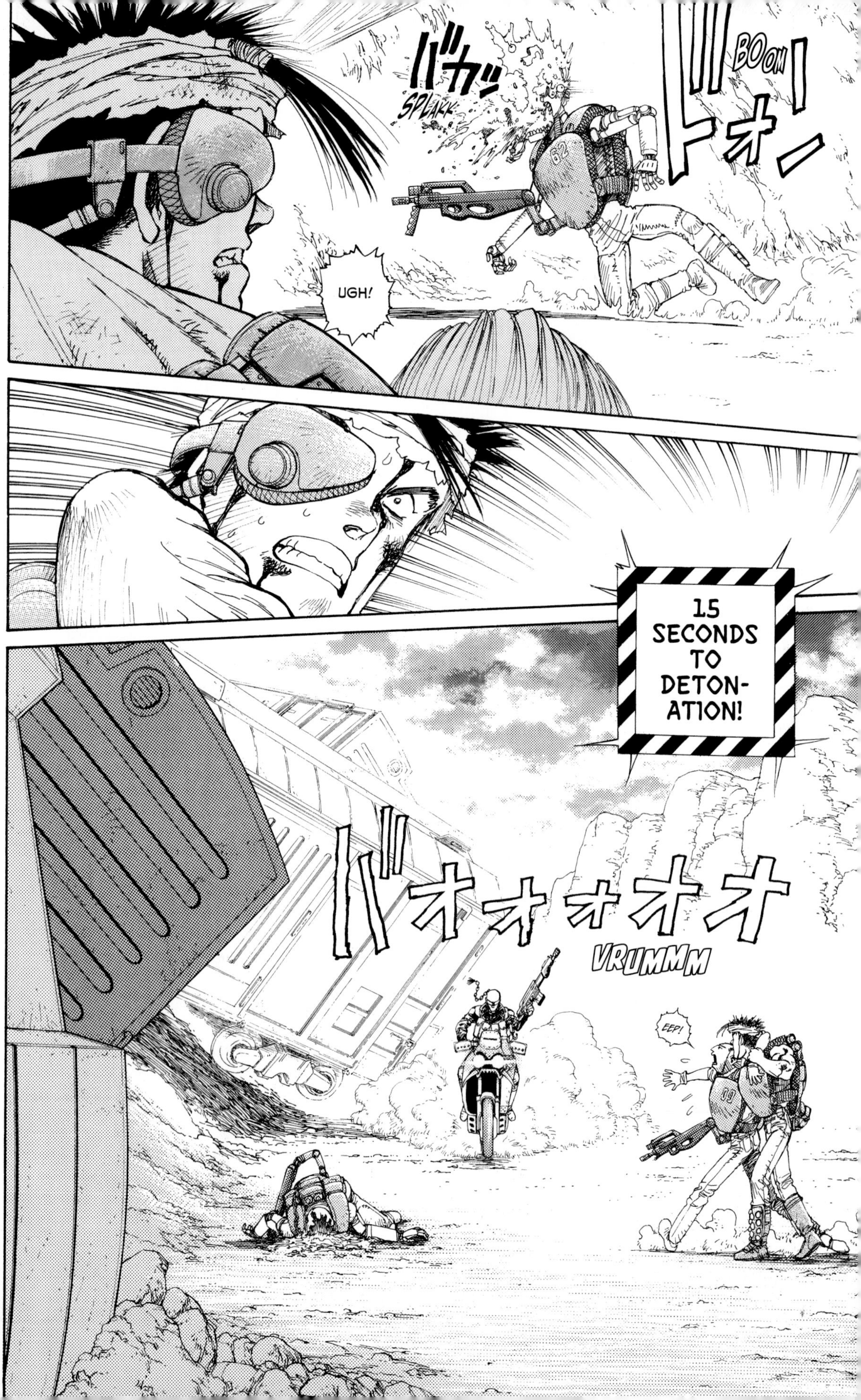
ドオー
BOOM
バガッ
SPLAKK
UGH!
15 SECONDS TO DETON-ATION!
ドオォォオオ
VRUMMM
EEP!

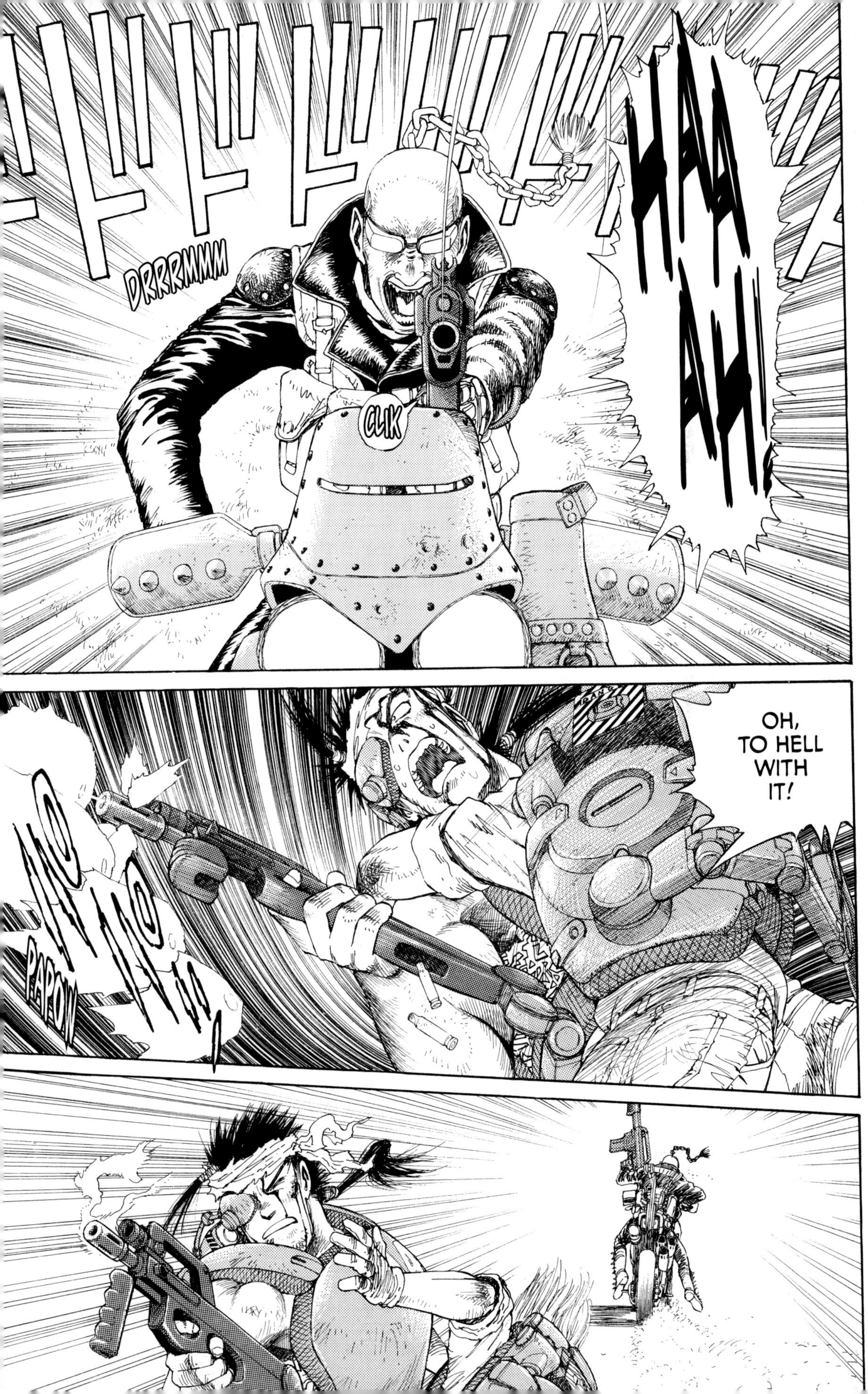
DRRRMMM
CLIK
HAAAH!
OH, TO HELL WITH IT!
PAPOW

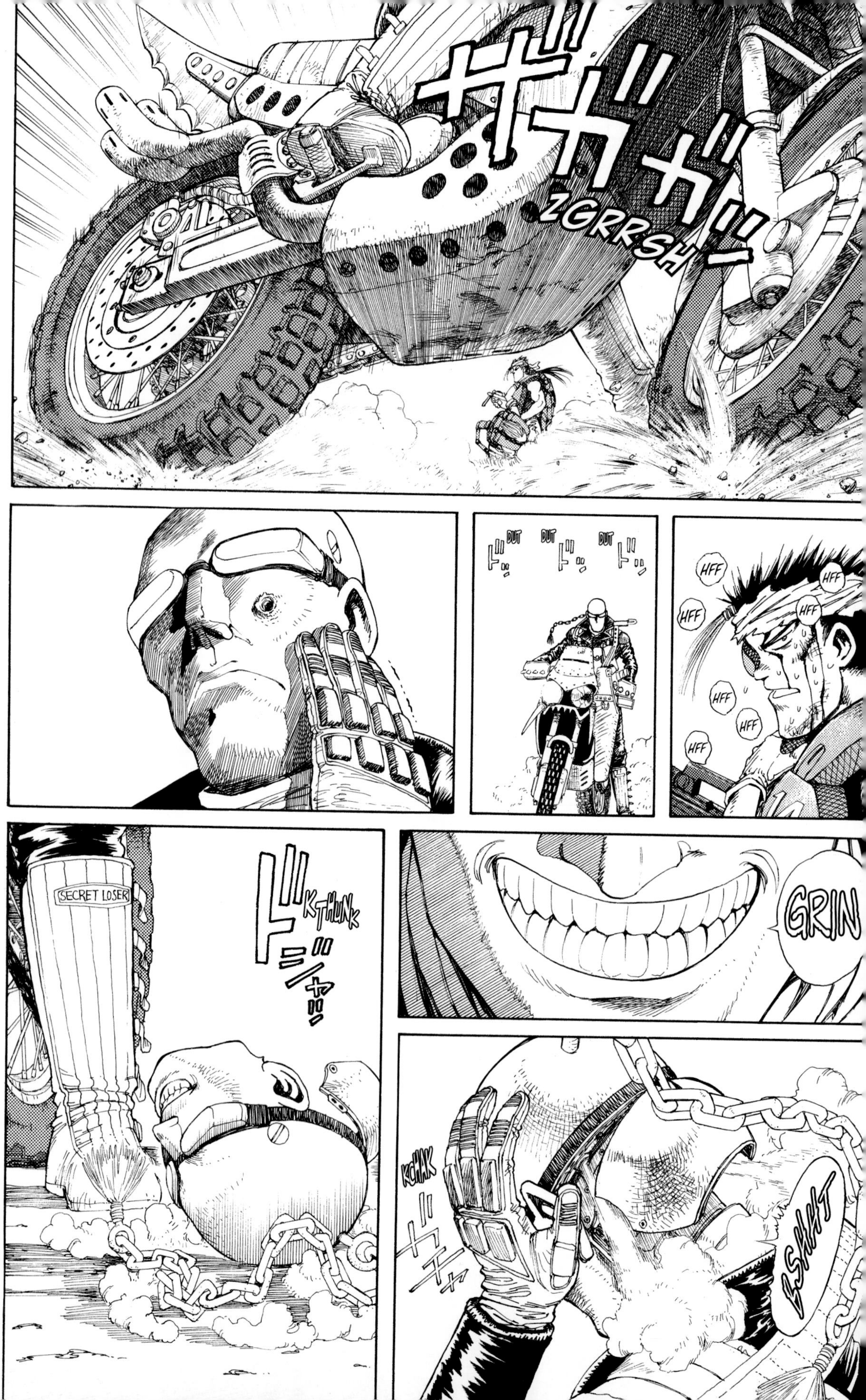
ガガガ!!!
ZGRRSH
ドッ DUT
ドッ DUT
ドッ DUT
HFF
HFF
HFF
HFF
HFF
HFF
HFF
GRIN
ガチャ
KCHAK
SHHT
ドッシャ!!
KTHUNK
SECRET LOSER

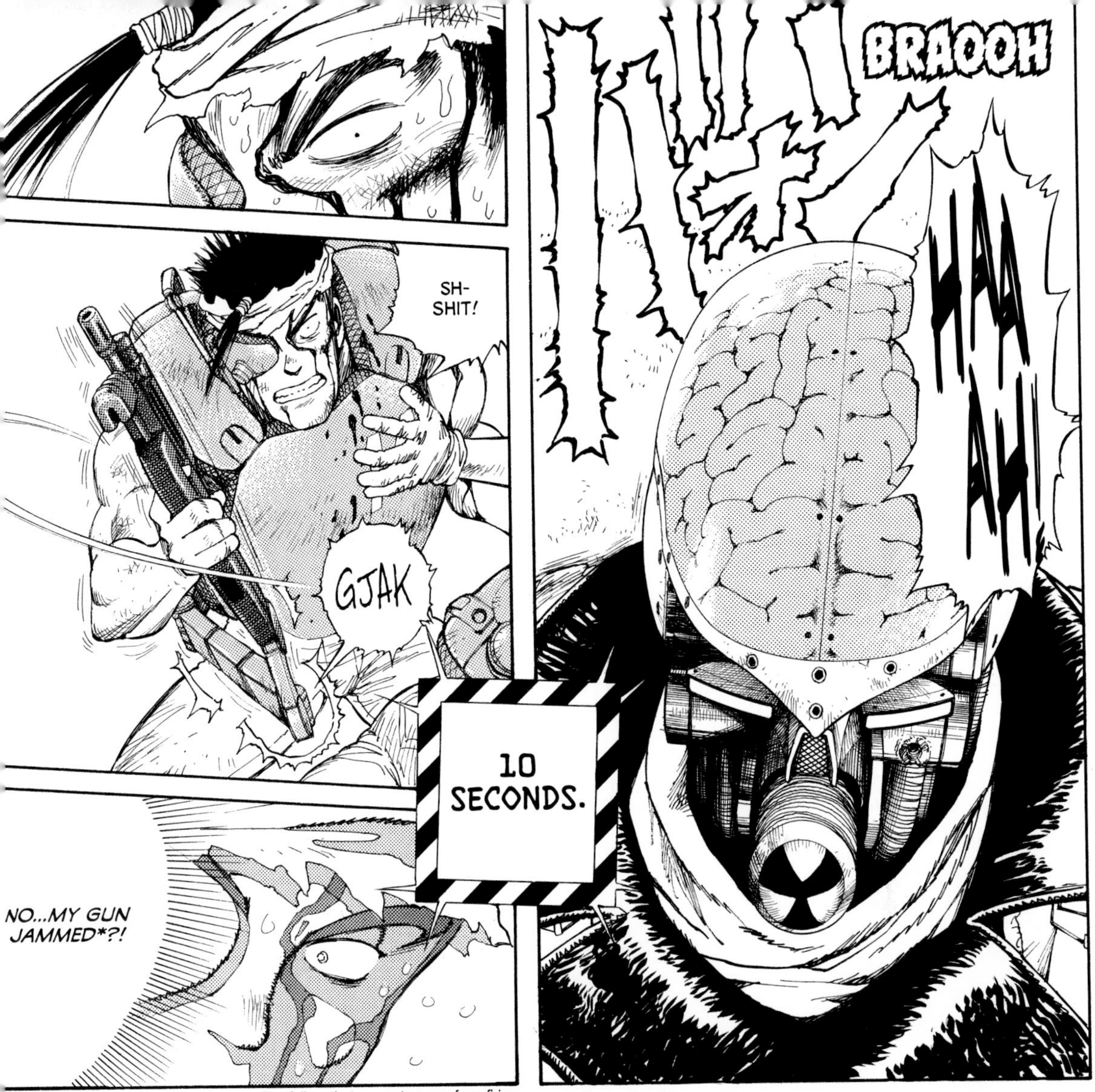
BRAOOH
HAA AH!
10 SECONDS.
SH-SHIT!
GJAK
NO...MY GUN JAMMED*?!

***Jam:** An operation failure that prevents a gun from firing.

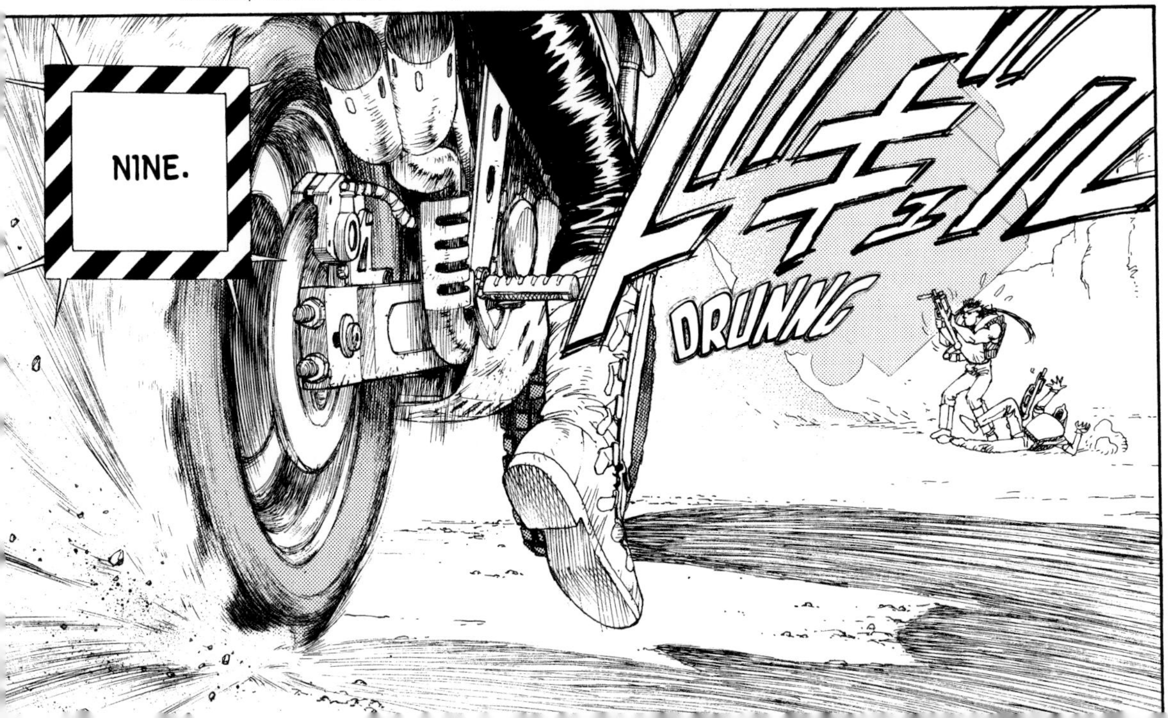
NINE.
DRUNNG

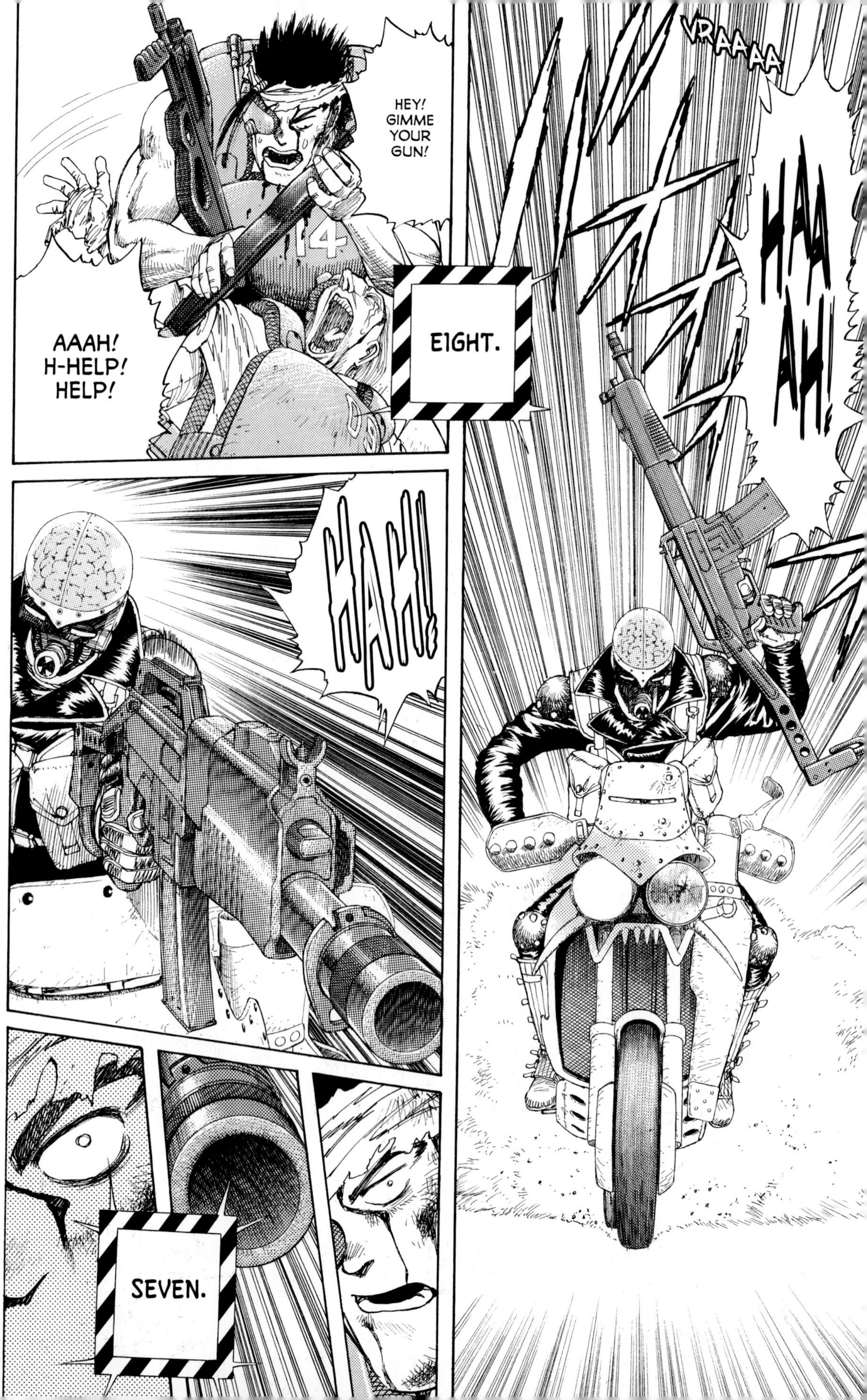
VRAAAA
HAAAAH!
EIGHT.
HEY! GIMME YOUR GUN!
AAAH! H-HELP! HELP!
HAH!
SEVEN.

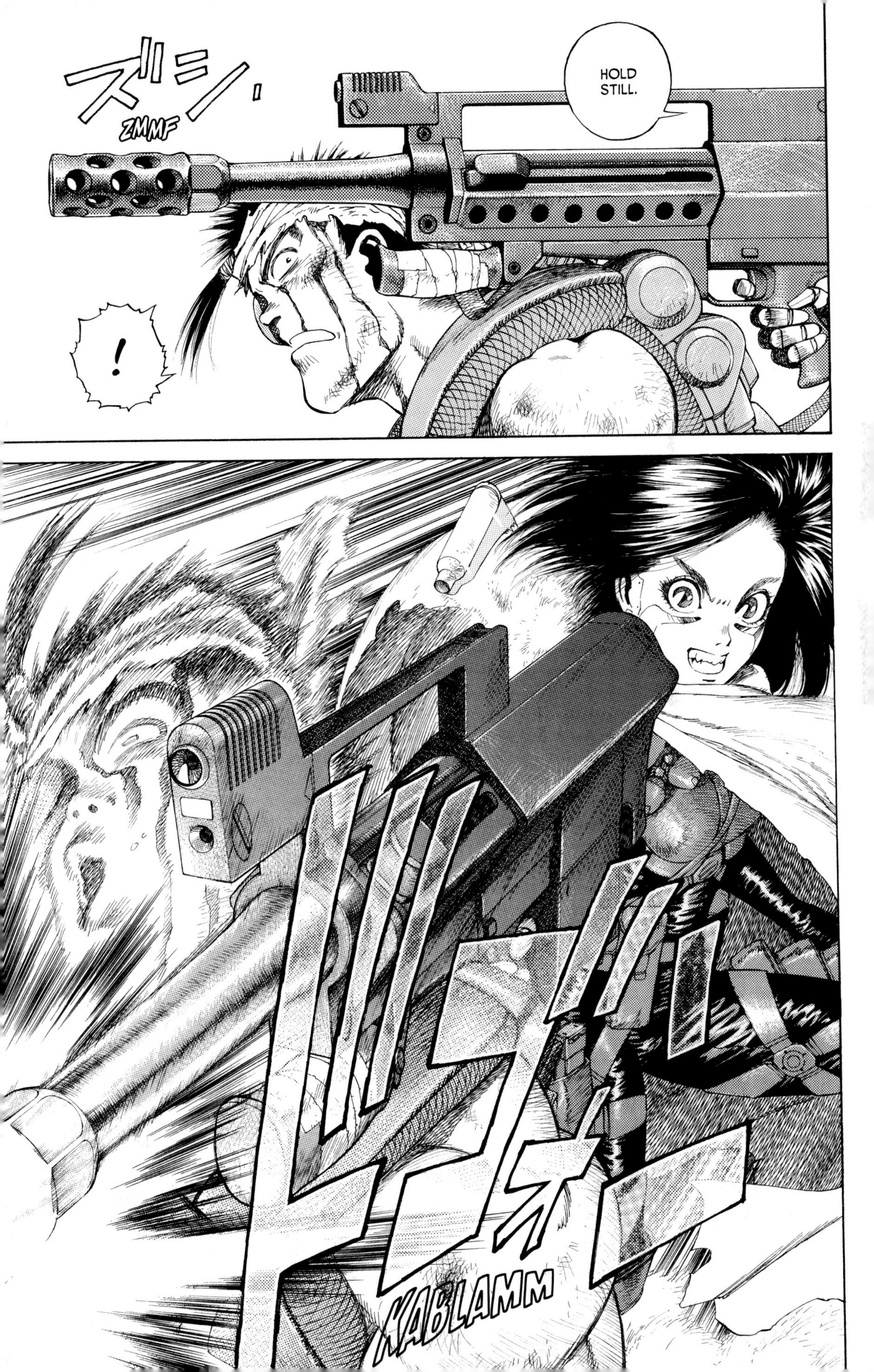
HOLD STILL.
ZMMF
!
KABLAMM

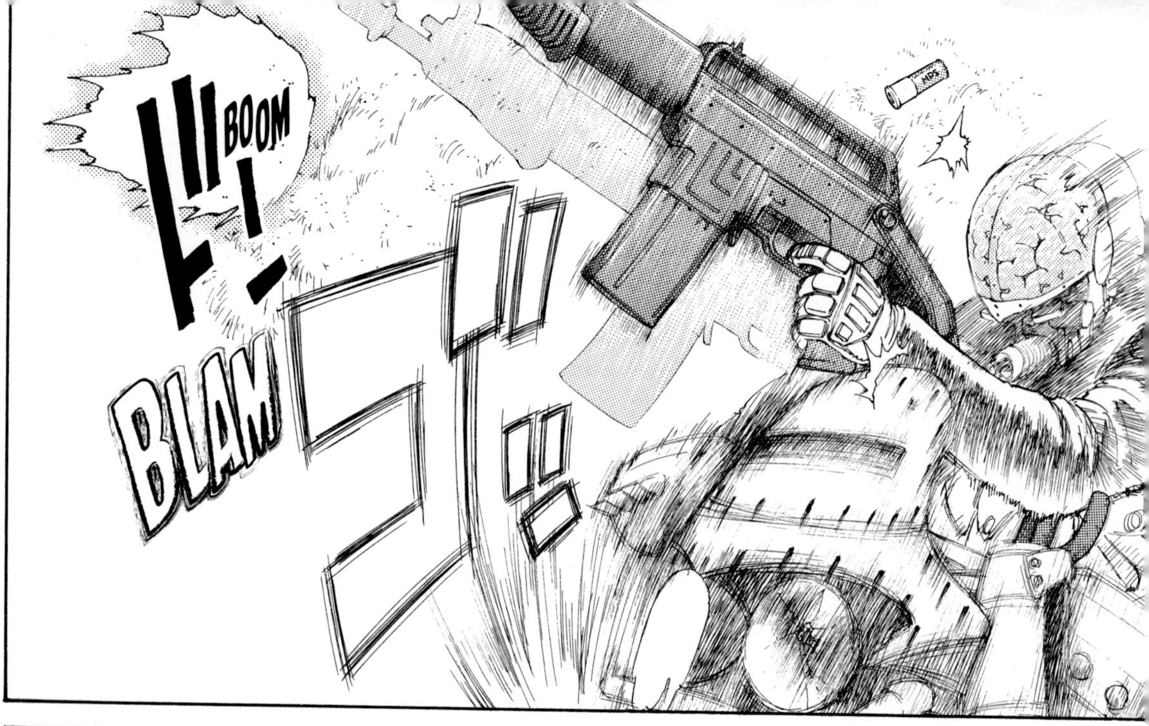
BOOM
BLAM
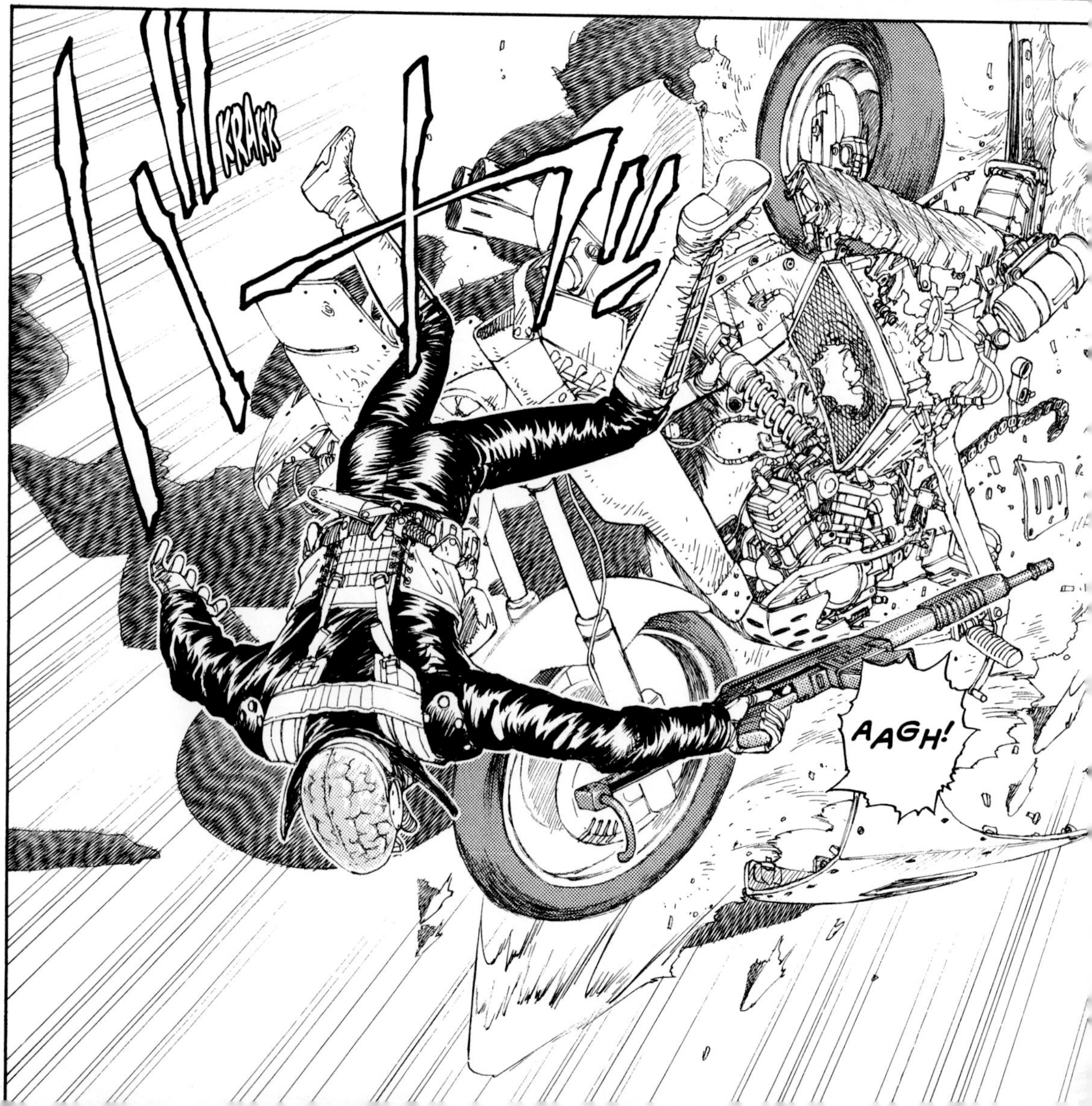
KRAKK
AAGH!

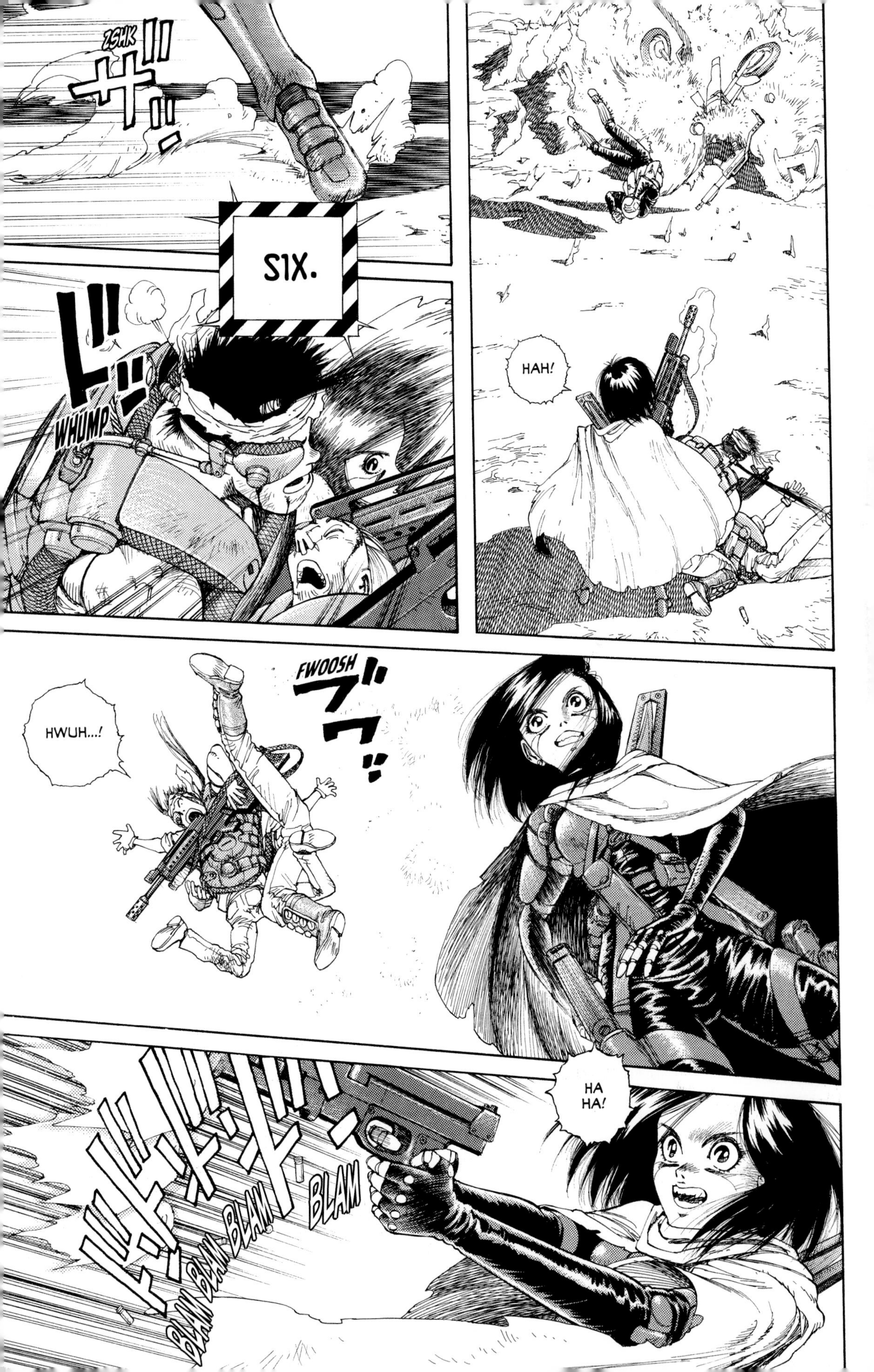
HAH!
ZSHK
SIX.
WHUMP
FWOOSH
HWUH...!
HA HA!
BLAM
BLAM
BLAM
BLAM

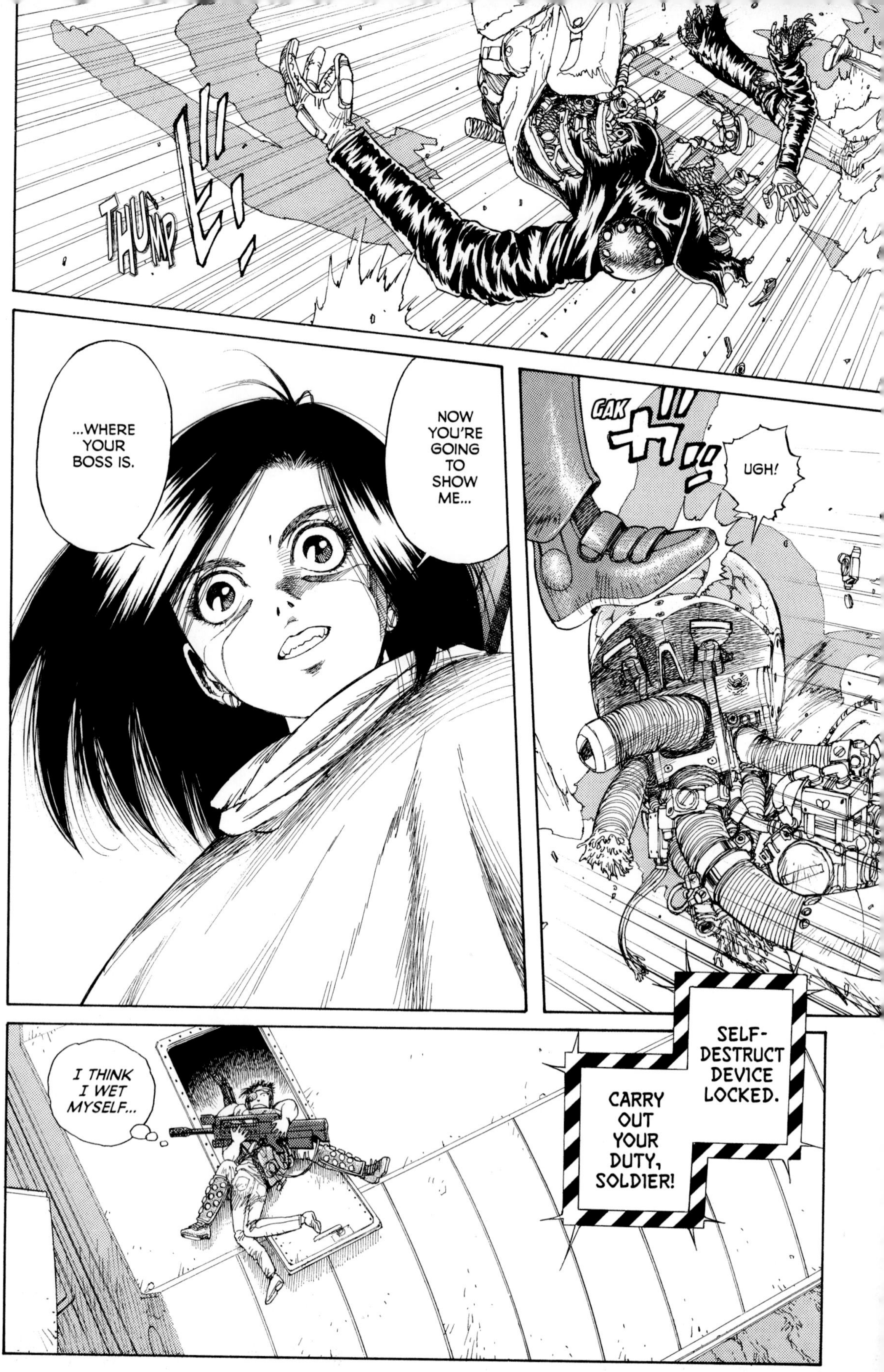
THUMP
GAK
UGH!
NOW YOU'RE GOING TO SHOW ME...
...WHERE YOUR BOSS IS.
SELF-DESTRUCT DEVICE LOCKED.
CARRY OUT YOUR DUTY, SOLDIER!
I THINK I WET MYSELF...

FIGHT_032 Wild West Heroes

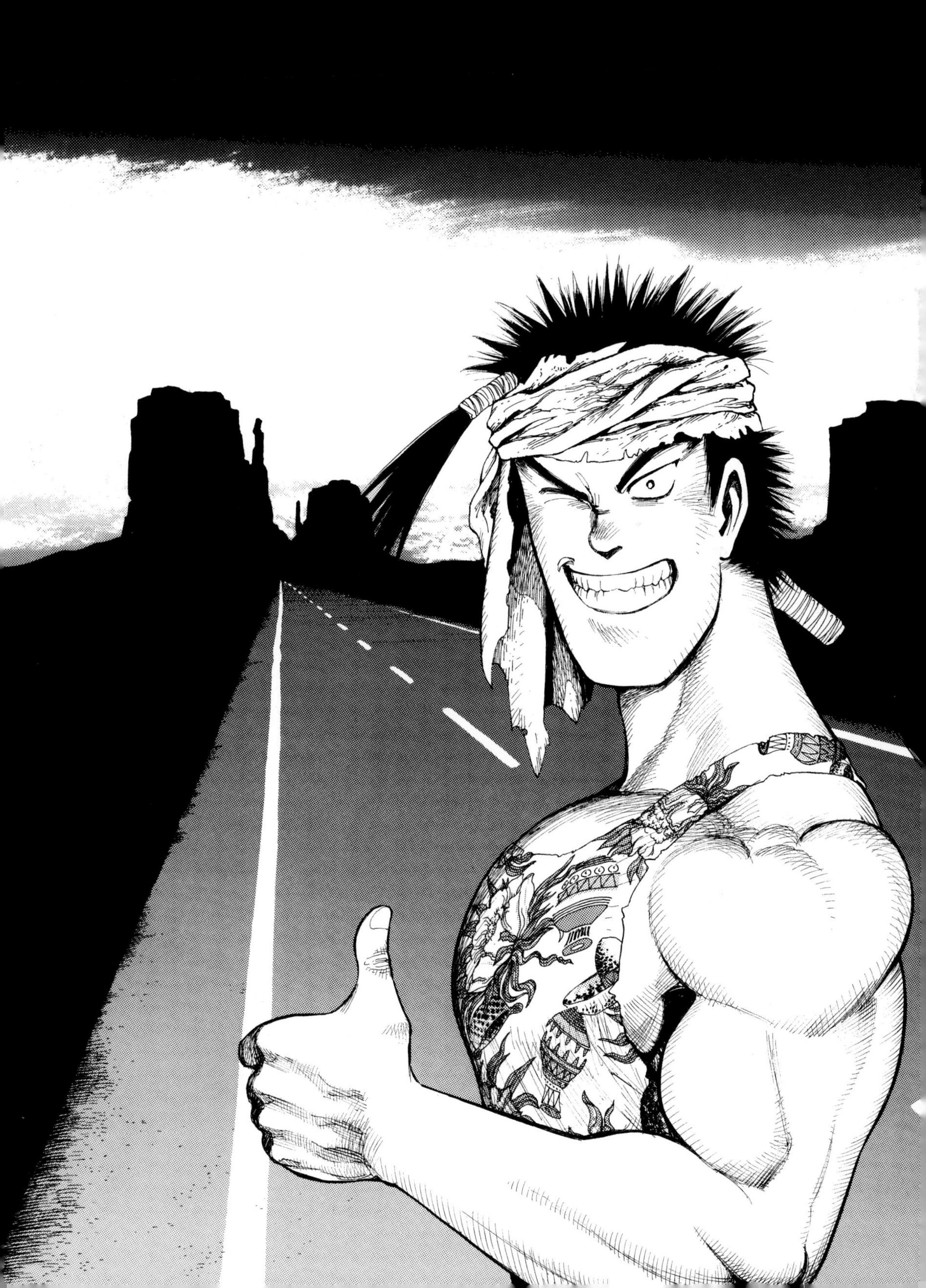

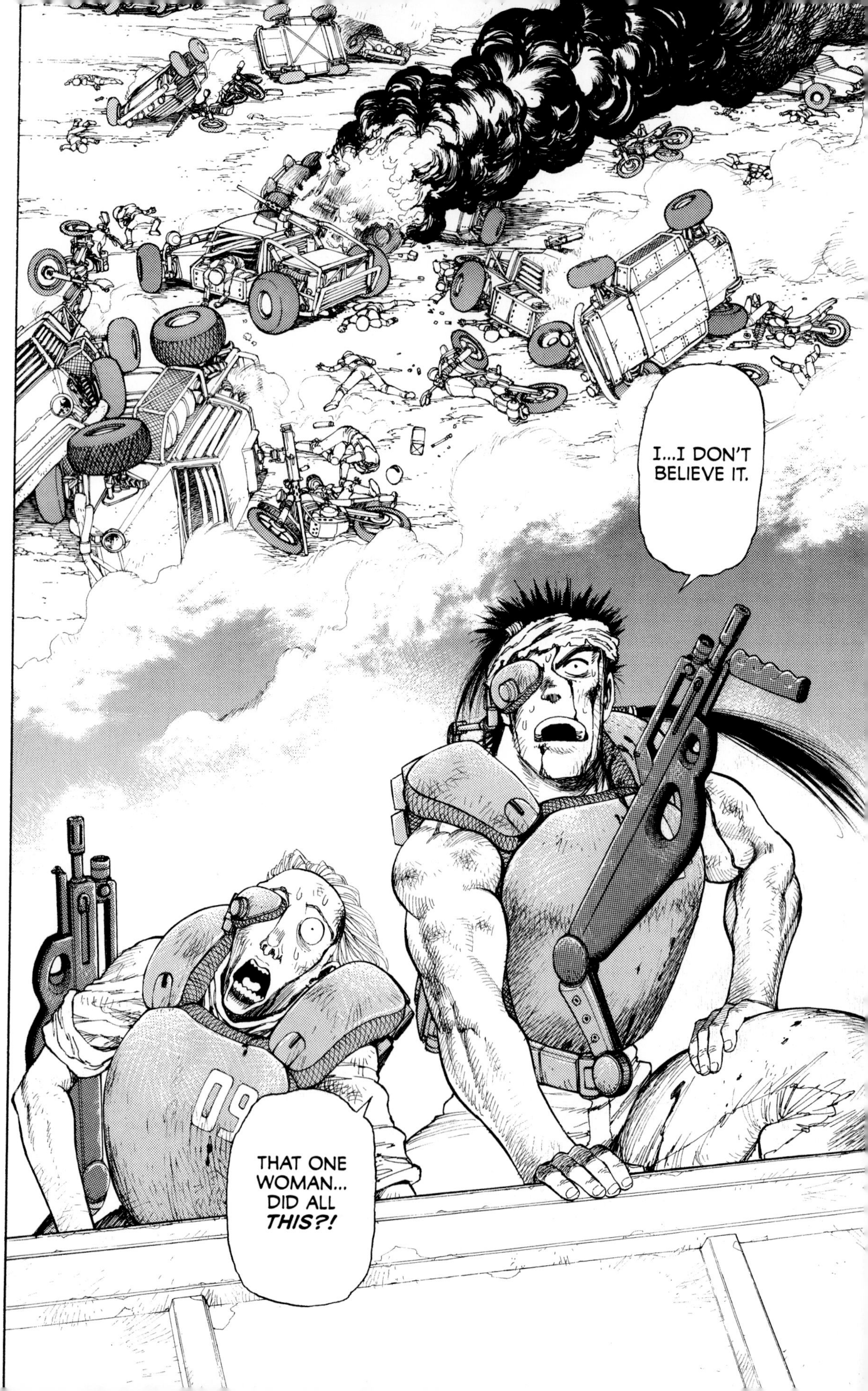
I...I DON'T BELIEVE IT.
THAT ONE WOMAN... DID ALL *THIS?!*

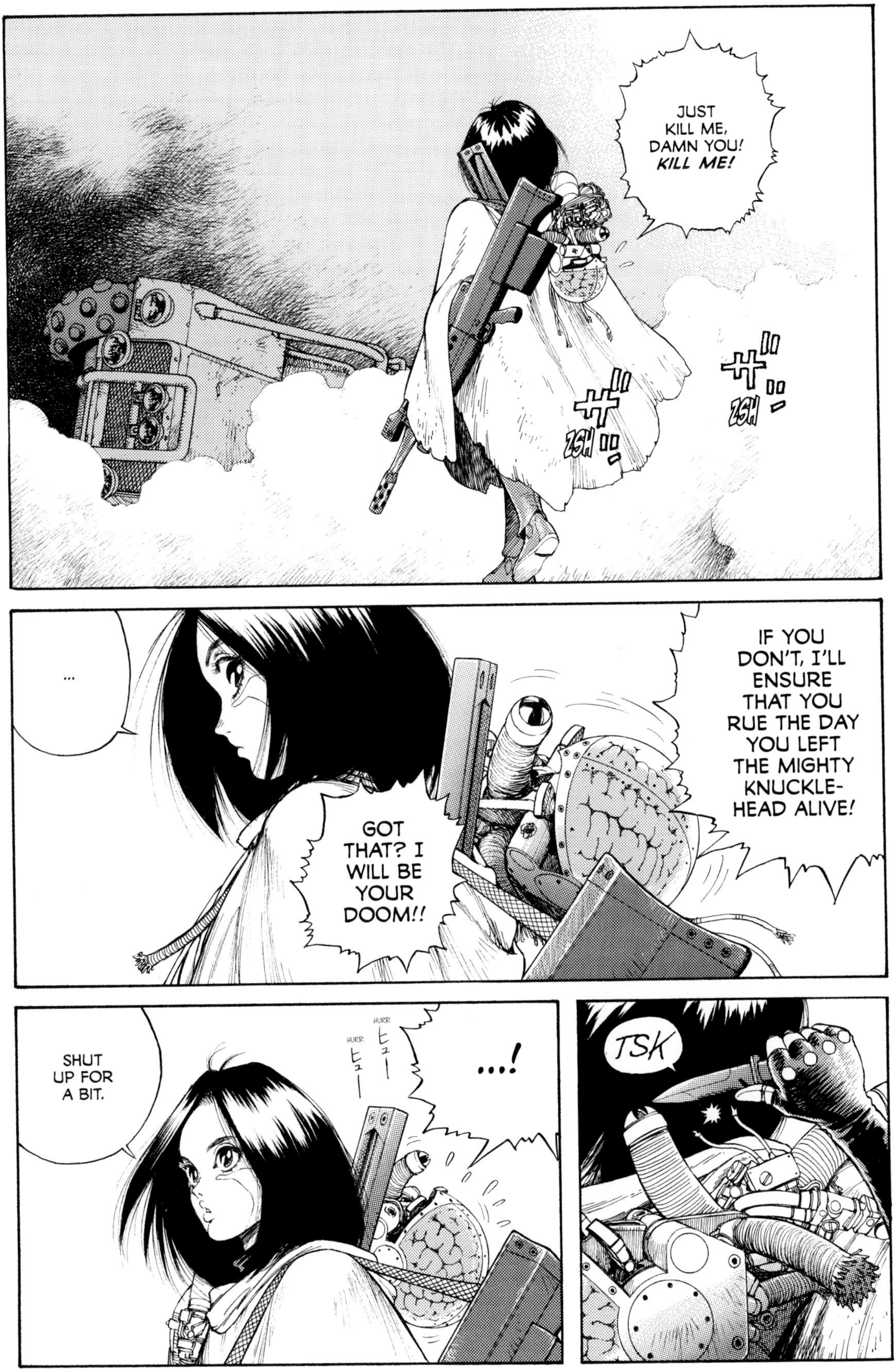
JUST KILL ME, DAMN YOU! KILL ME!
ZSH
ZSH
IF YOU DON'T, I'LL ENSURE THAT YOU RUE THE DAY YOU LEFT THE MIGHTY KNUCKLE-HEAD ALIVE!
GOT THAT? I WILL BE YOUR DOOM!!
...
TSK
...!
HURR
HURR
SHUT UP FOR A BIT.

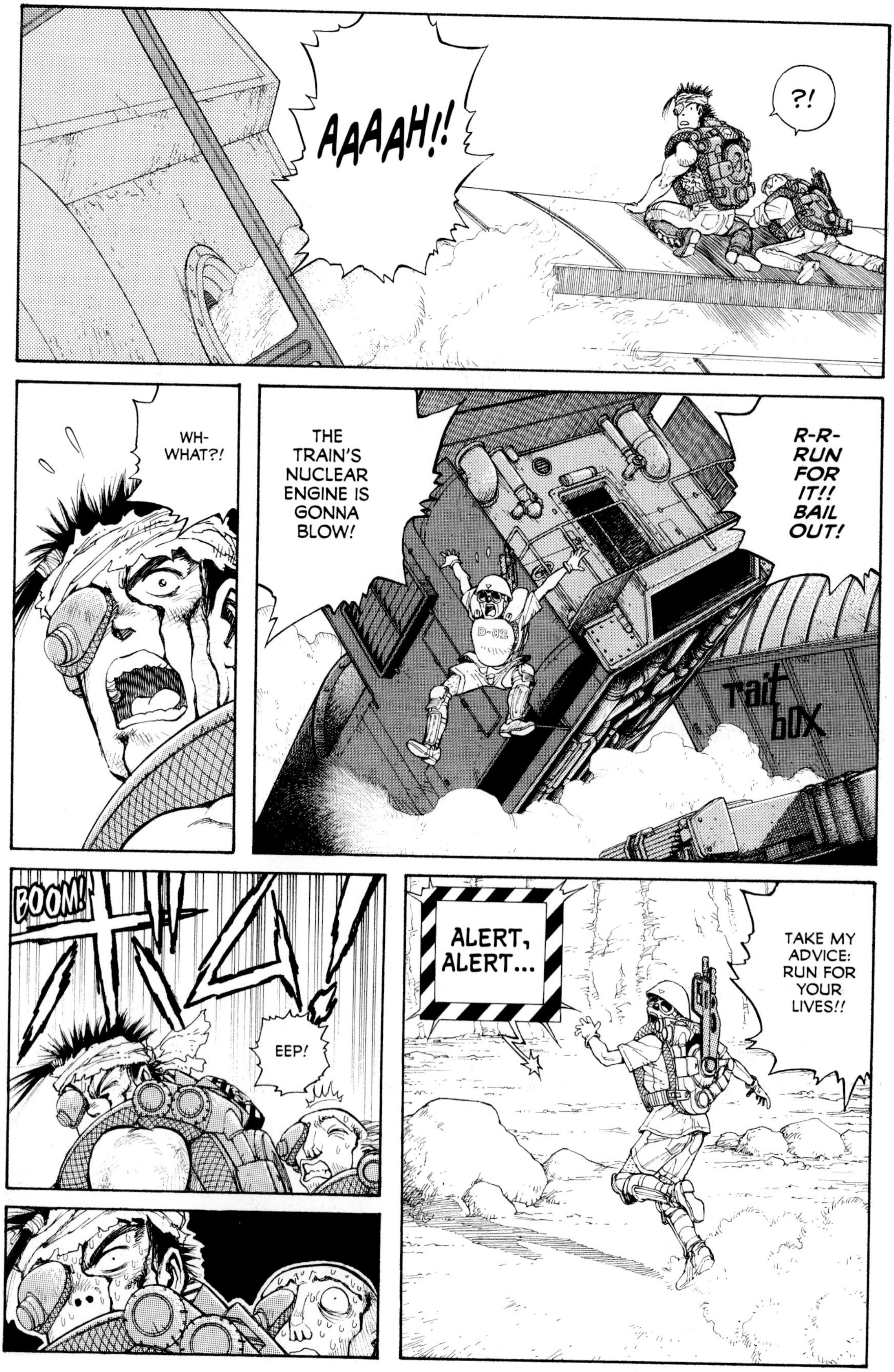
?!
AAAAH!!
R-R-RUN FOR IT!! BAIL OUT!
THE TRAIN'S NUCLEAR ENGINE IS GONNA BLOW!
D-02
WH-WHAT?!
TAKE MY ADVICE: RUN FOR YOUR LIVES!!
ALERT, ALERT...
BOOM!
EEP!

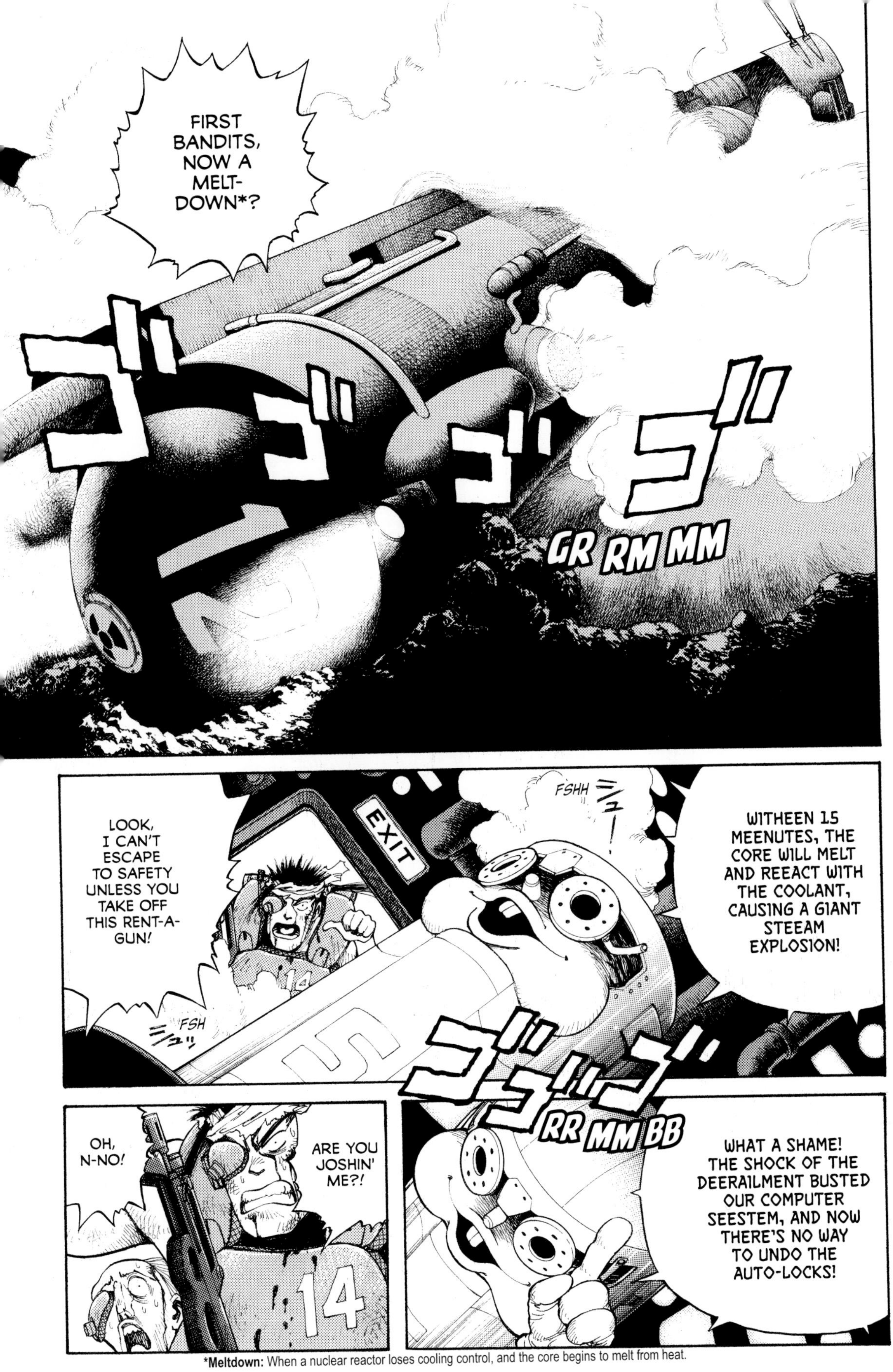
FIRST BANDITS, NOW A MELT-DOWN*?
GR RM MM
WITHEEN 15 MEENUTES, THE CORE WILL MELT AND REEACT WITH THE COOLANT, CAUSING A GIANT STEEAM EXPLOSION!
FSHH
EXIT
LOOK, I CAN'T ESCAPE TO SAFETY UNLESS YOU TAKE OFF THIS RENT-A-GUN!
FSH
RR MM BB
WHAT A SHAME! THE SHOCK OF THE DEERAILMENT BUSTED OUR COMPUTER SEESTEM, AND NOW THERE'S NO WAY TO UNDO THE AUTO-LOCKS!
ARE YOU JOSHIN' ME?!
OH, N-NO!

***Meltdown:** When a nuclear reactor loses cooling control, and the core begins to melt from heat.

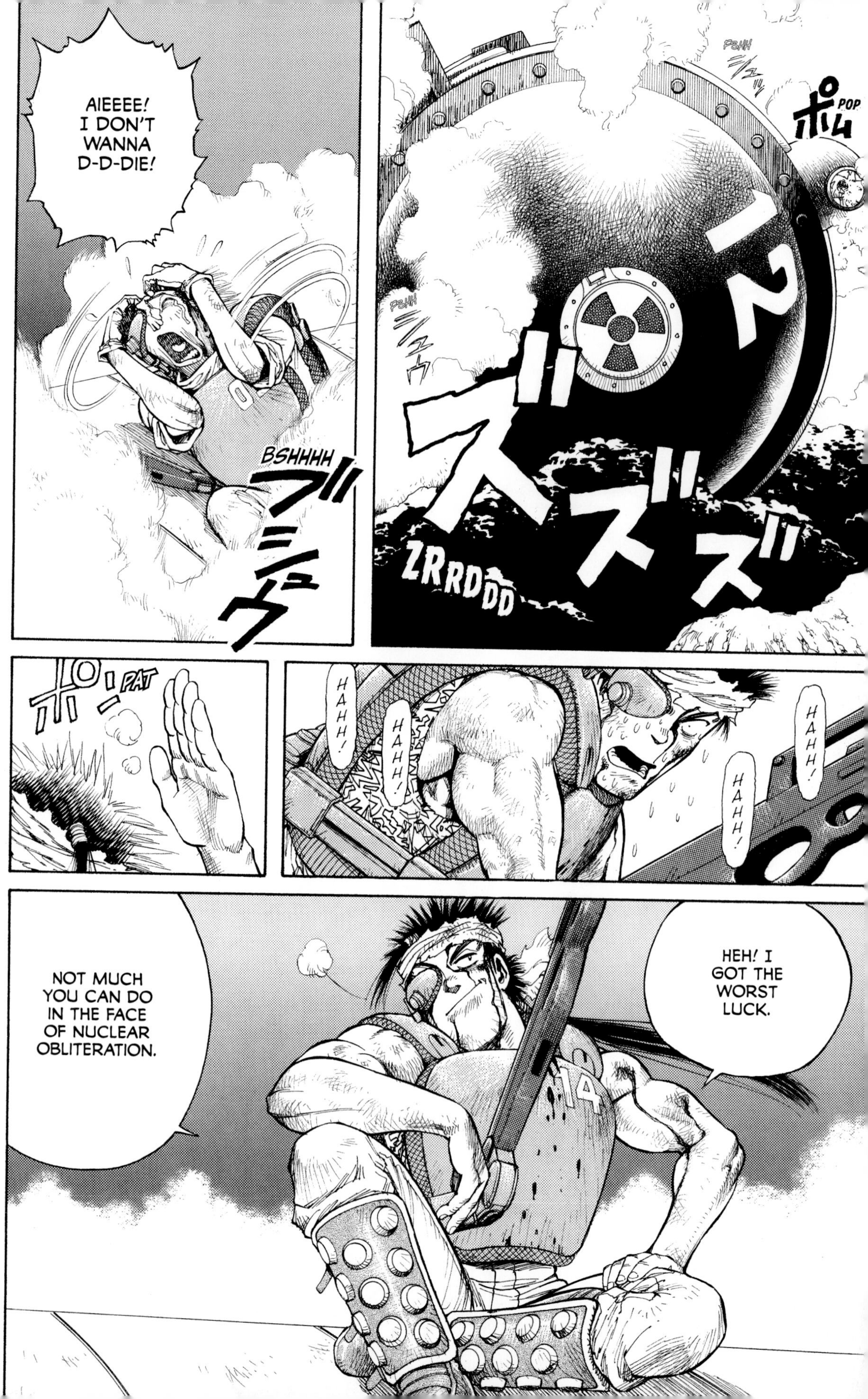
PSHH
POP
12
PSHH
ZRRDDD
AIEEEE! I DON'T WANNA D-D-DIE!
BSHHHH
HAHH! HAHH!
HAHH! HAHH!
PAT
HEH! I GOT THE WORST LUCK.
NOT MUCH YOU CAN DO IN THE FACE OF NUCLEAR OBLITERATION.
14

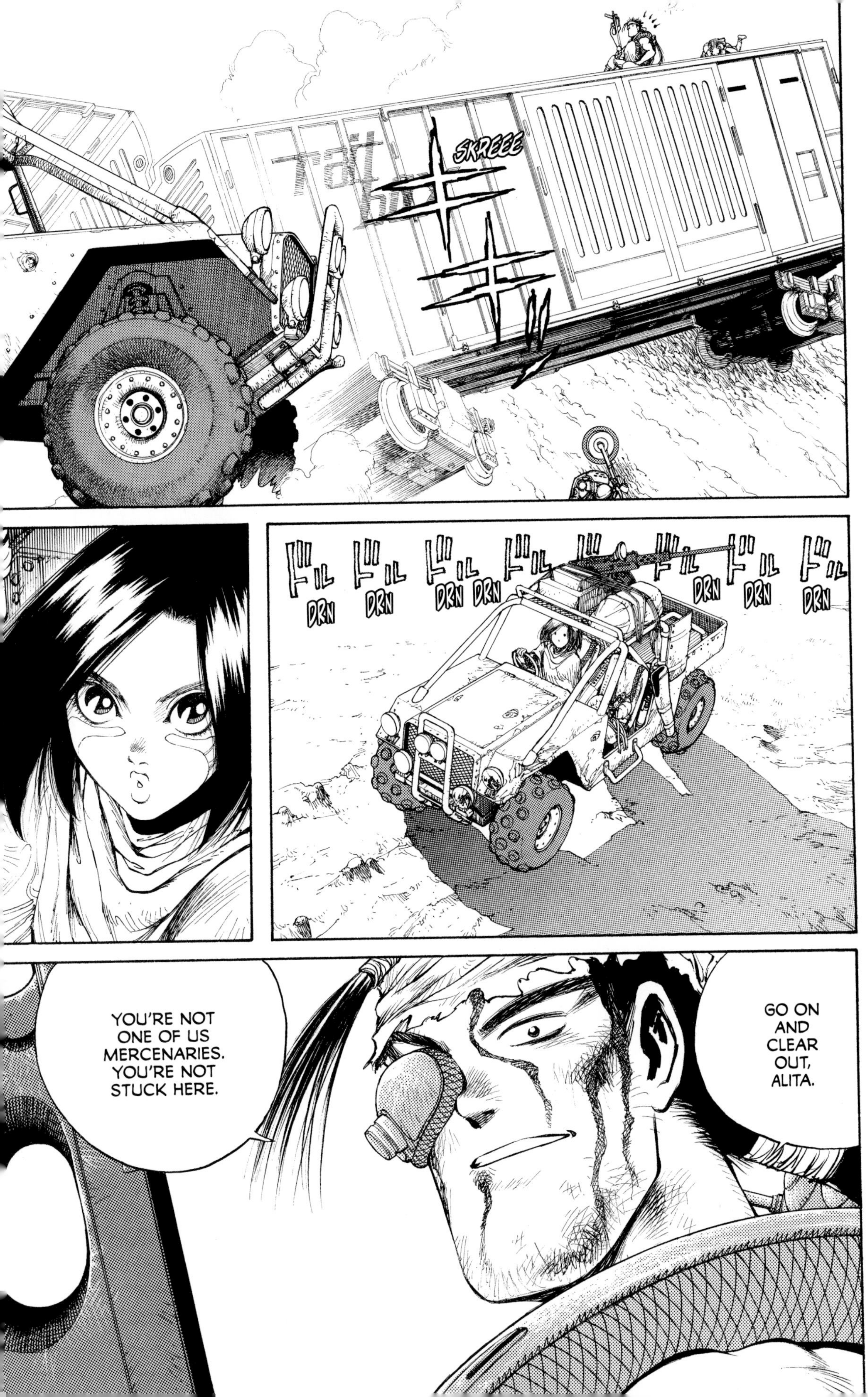
SKREEE
DRN DRN DRN DRN DRN DRN DRN DRN
GO ON AND CLEAR OUT, ALITA.
YOU'RE NOT ONE OF US MERCENARIES. YOU'RE NOT STUCK HERE.

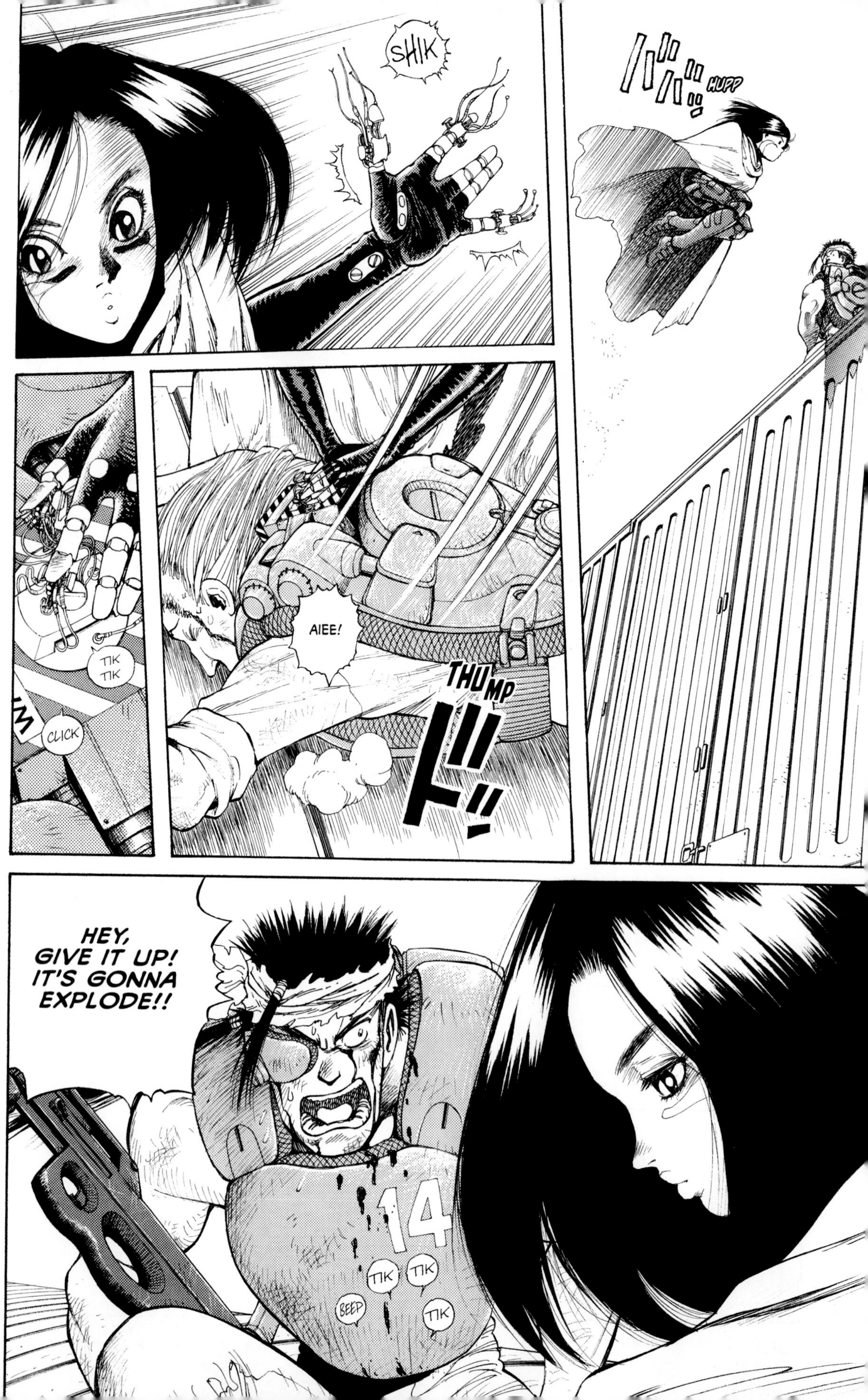
HUPP
SHIK
AIEE!
THUMP
TIK TIK
CLICK
HEY, GIVE IT UP! IT'S GONNA EXPLODE!!
14
TIK
TIK
BEEP
TIK

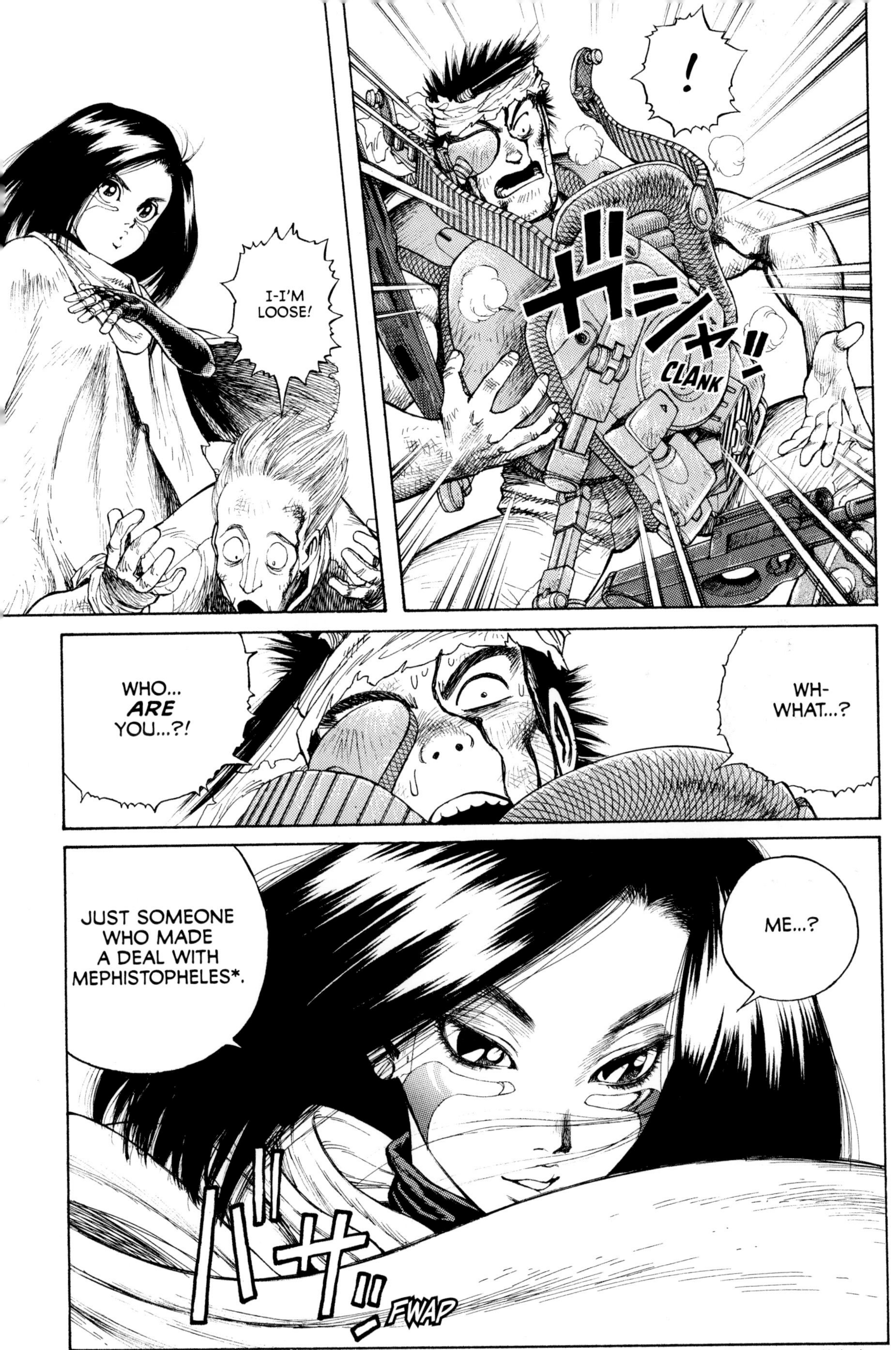
!
CLANK
I-I'M LOOSE!
WH- WHAT...?
WHO... ARE YOU...?!
ME...?
JUST SOMEONE WHO MADE A DEAL WITH MEPHISTOPHELES*.
FWAP

***Mephistopheles:** A capricious demon from Goethe's Faust. By making a deal with the demon, Dr. Faust gains youth and the ability to travel throughout time on a grand adventure.

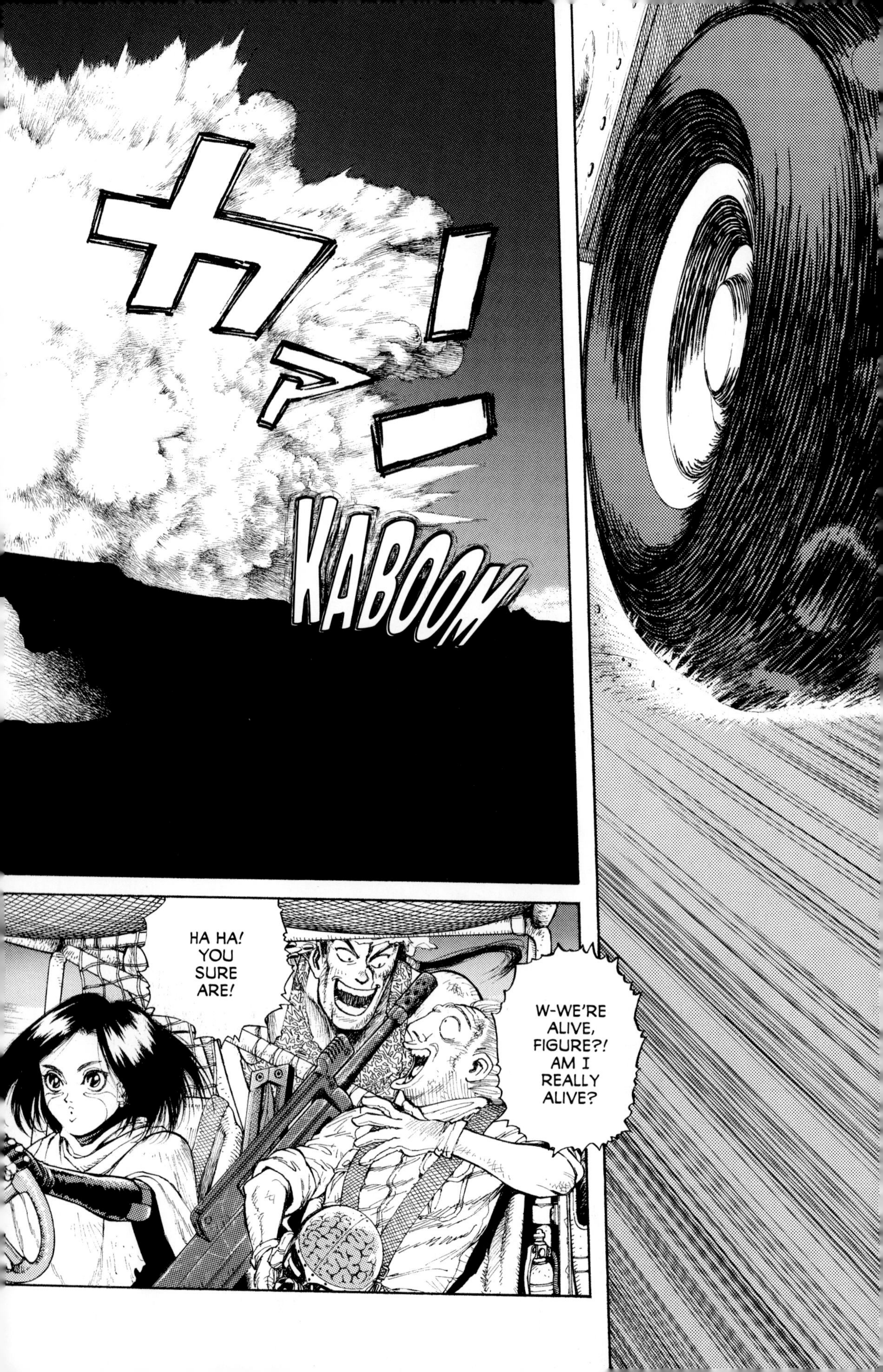
KABOOM
W-WE'RE ALIVE, FIGURE?! AM I REALLY ALIVE?
HA HA! YOU SURE ARE!

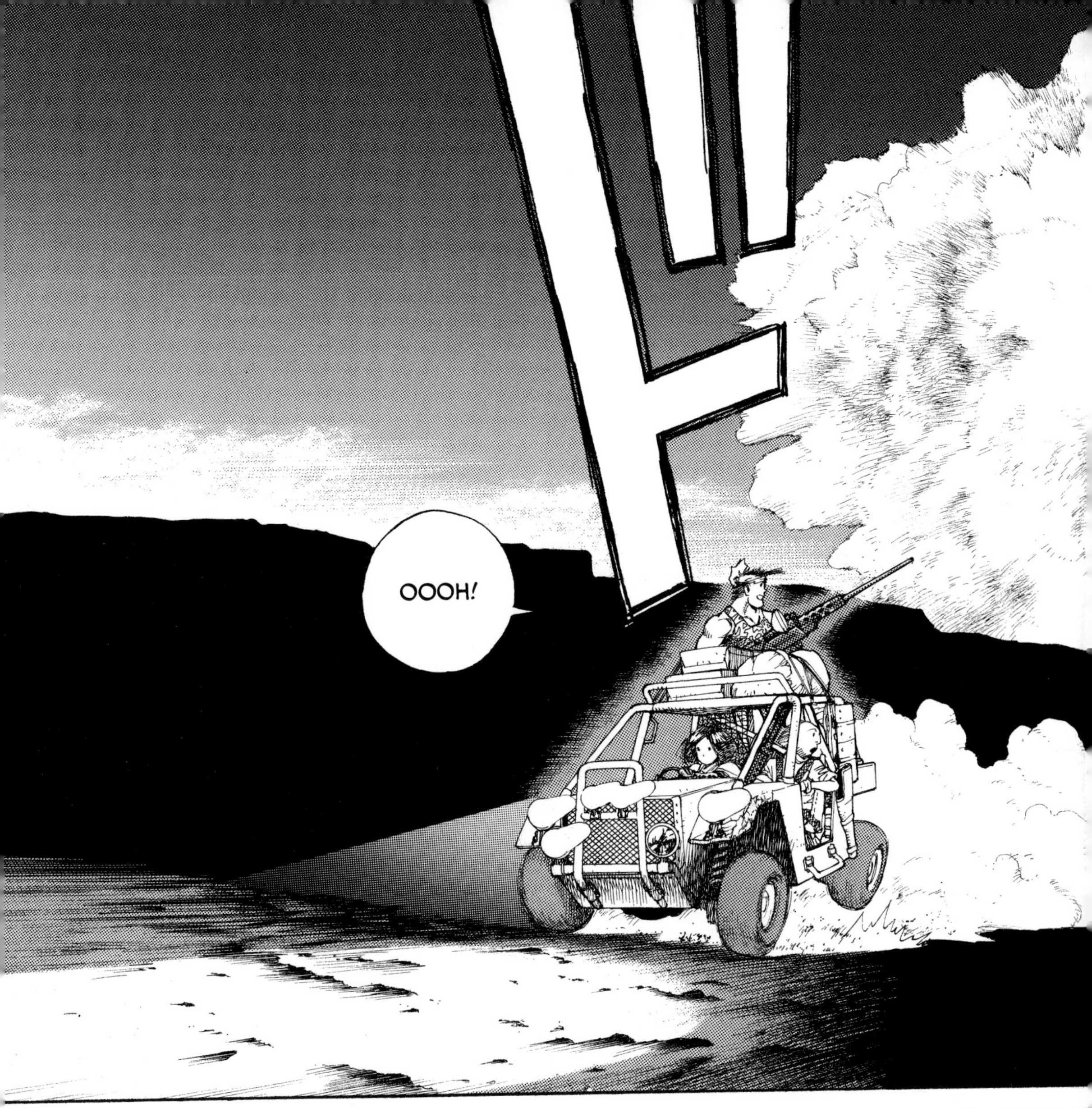
ド
OOOH!

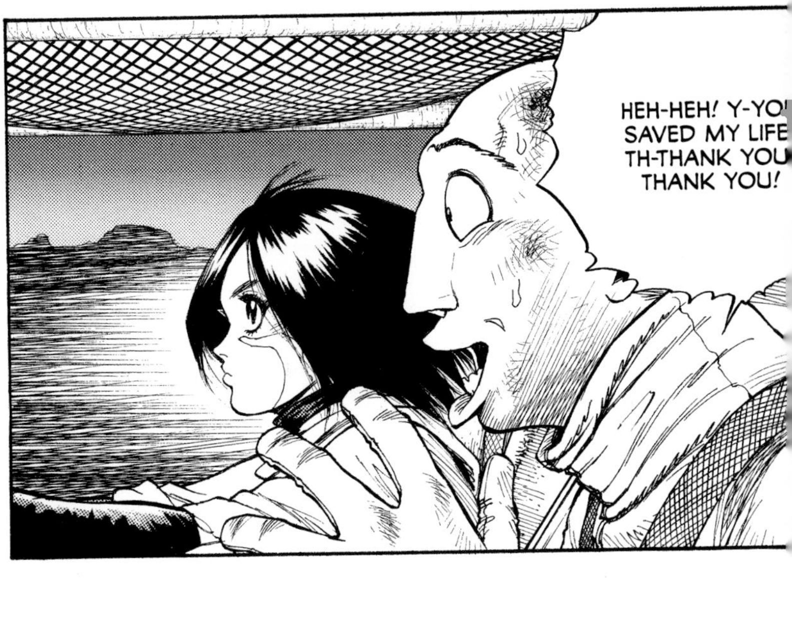
HEH-HEH! Y-YOU SAVED MY LIFE TH-THANK YOU THANK YOU!

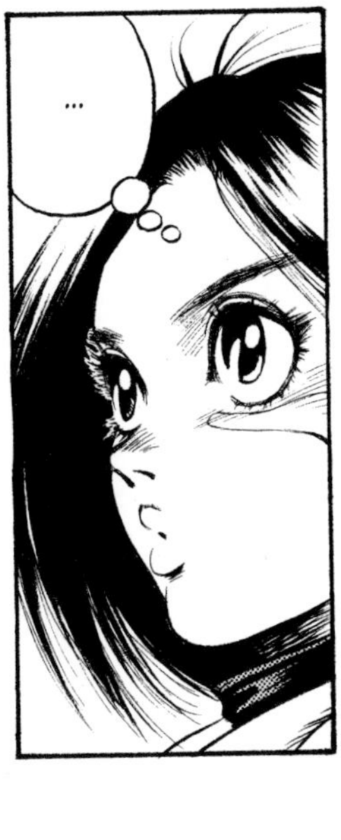
...

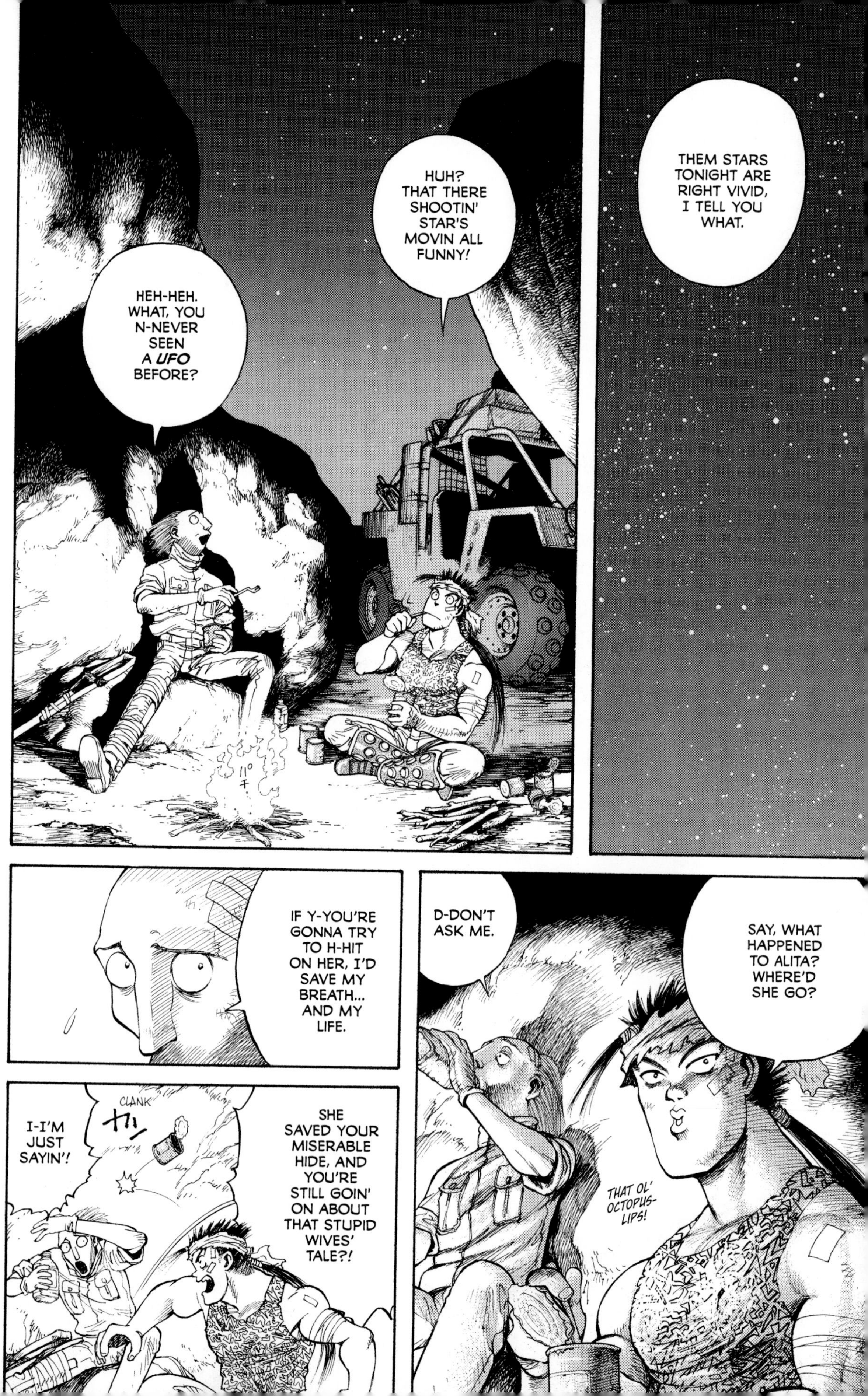
THEM STARS TONIGHT ARE RIGHT VIVID, I TELL YOU WHAT.
HUH? THAT THERE SHOOTIN' STAR'S MOVIN ALL FUNNY!
HEH-HEH. WHAT, YOU N-NEVER SEEN A *UFO* BEFORE?
SAY, WHAT HAPPENED TO ALITA? WHERE'D SHE GO?
D-DON'T ASK ME.
THAT OL' OCTOPUS-LIPS!
IF Y-YOU'RE GONNA TRY TO H-HIT ON HER, I'D SAVE MY BREATH... AND MY LIFE.
SHE SAVED YOUR MISERABLE HIDE, AND YOU'RE STILL GOIN' ON ABOUT THAT STUPID WIVES' TALE?!
CLANK
I-I'M JUST SAYIN'!

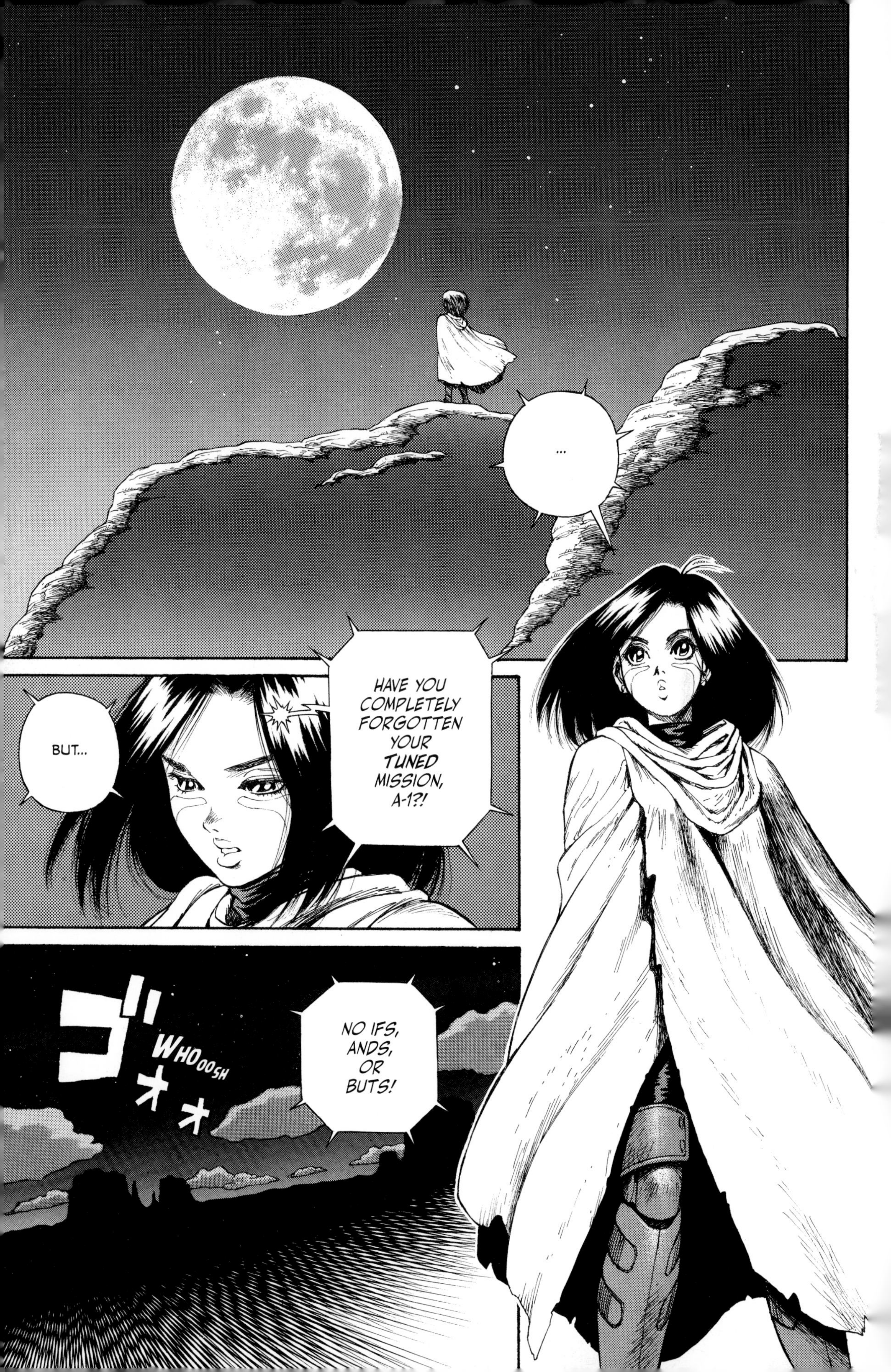
...
HAVE YOU COMPLETELY FORGOTTEN YOUR TUNED MISSION, A-1?!
BUT...
NO IFS, ANDS, OR BUTS!
ゴオオ
WHOOOSH

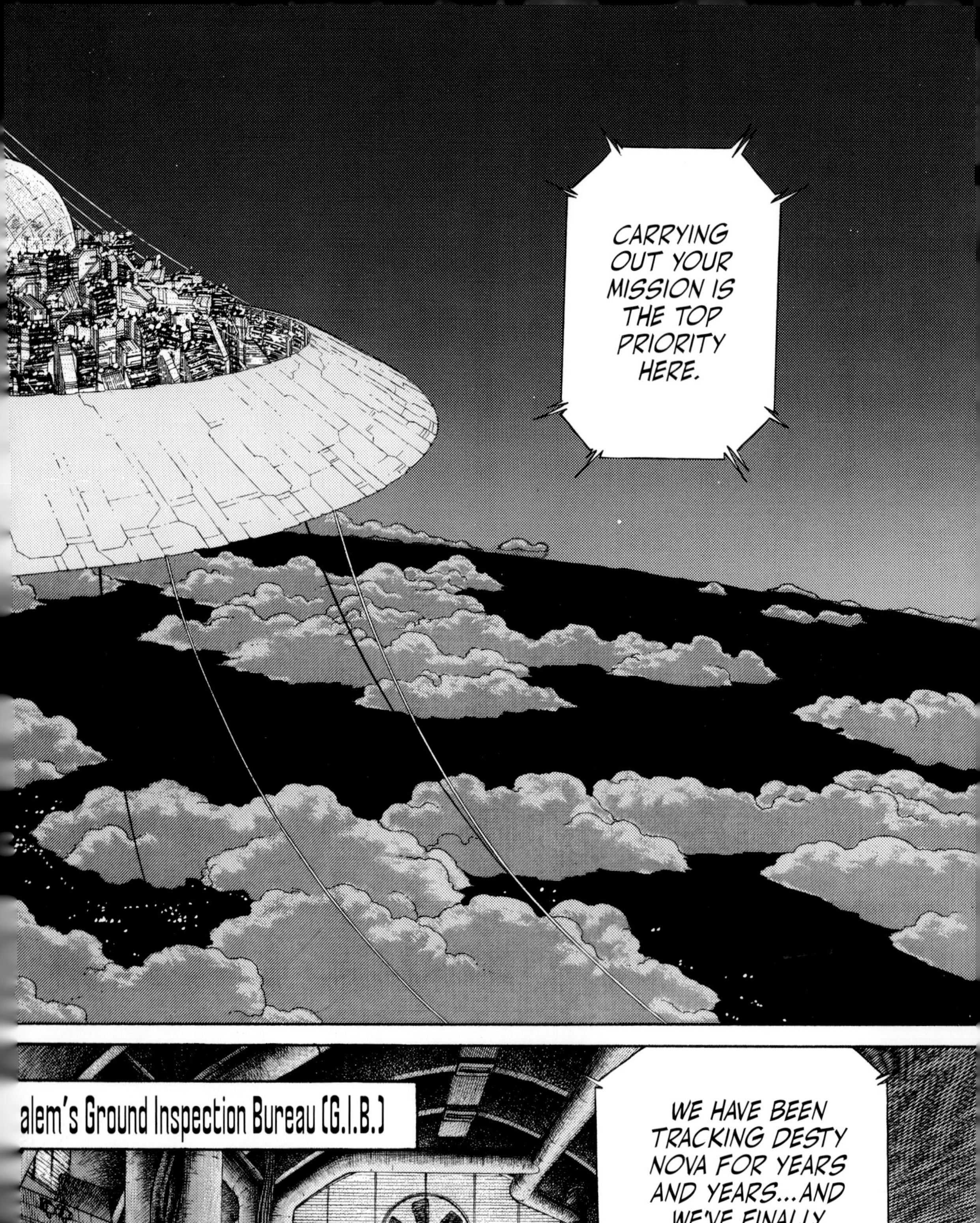
CARRYING OUT YOUR MISSION IS THE TOP PRIORITY HERE.
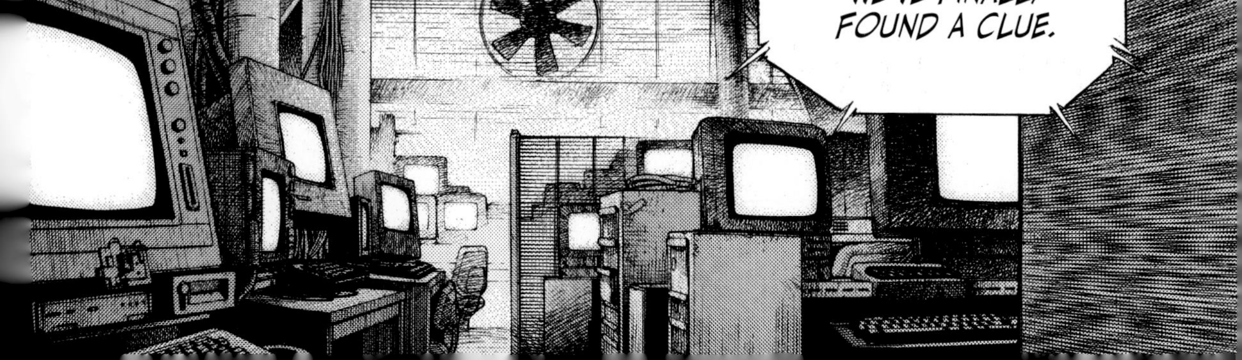
WE HAVE BEEN TRACKING DESTY NOVA FOR YEARS AND YEARS...AND WE'VE FINALLY FOUND A CLUE.
alem's Ground Inspection Bureau (G.I.B.)

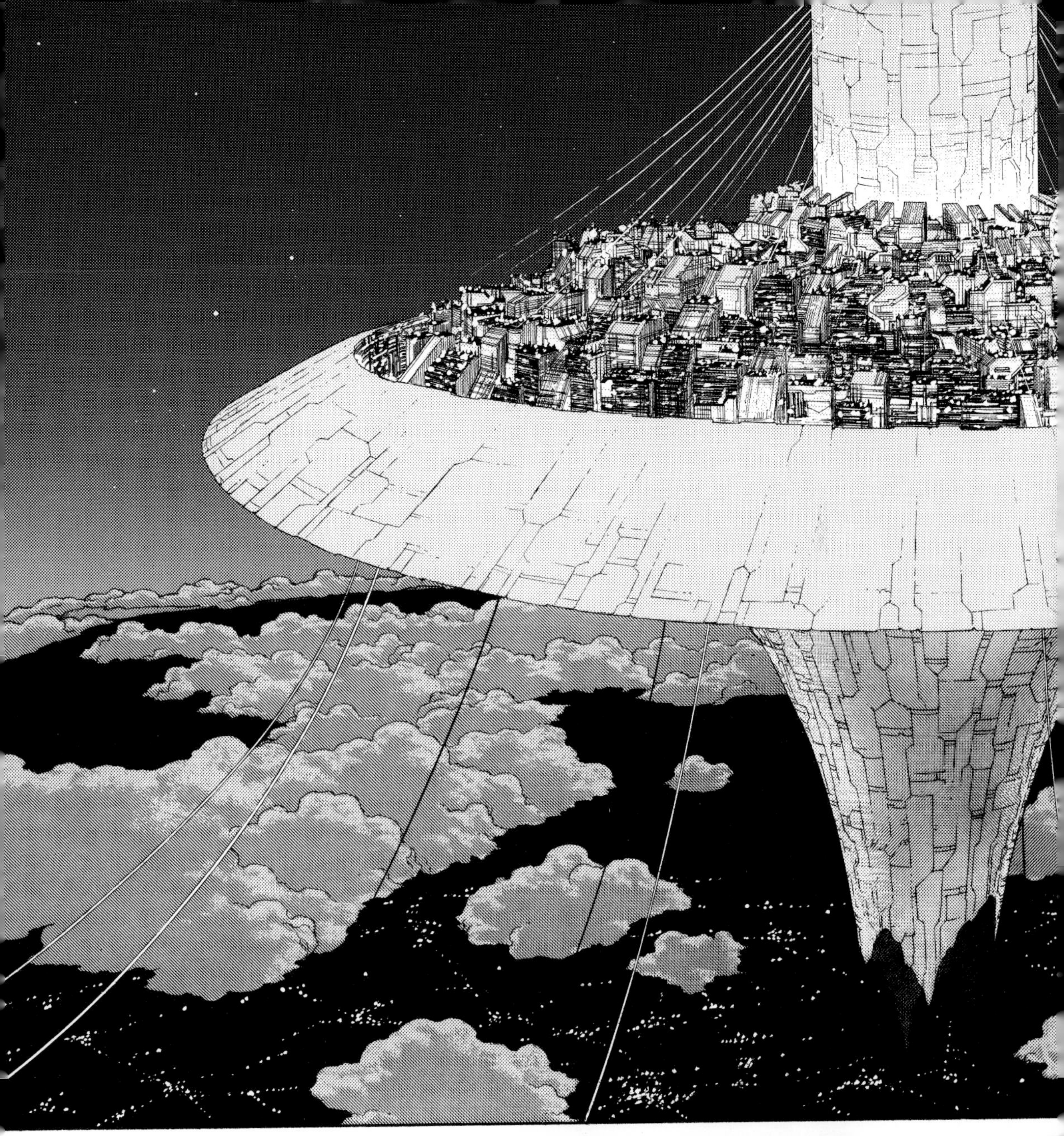

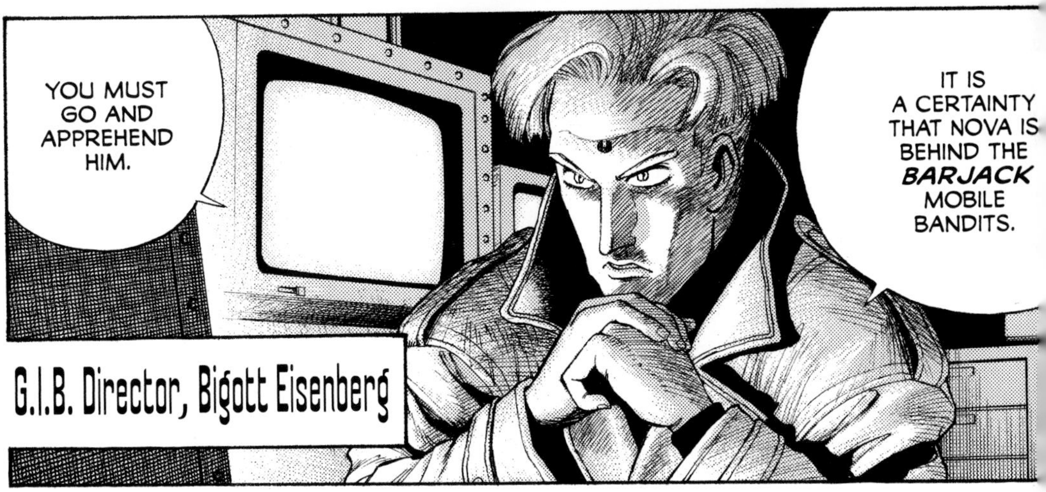
IT IS A CERTAINTY THAT NOVA IS BEHIND THE *BARJACK* MOBILE BANDITS.
YOU MUST GO AND APPREHEND HIM.
G.I.B. Director, Bigott Eisenberg

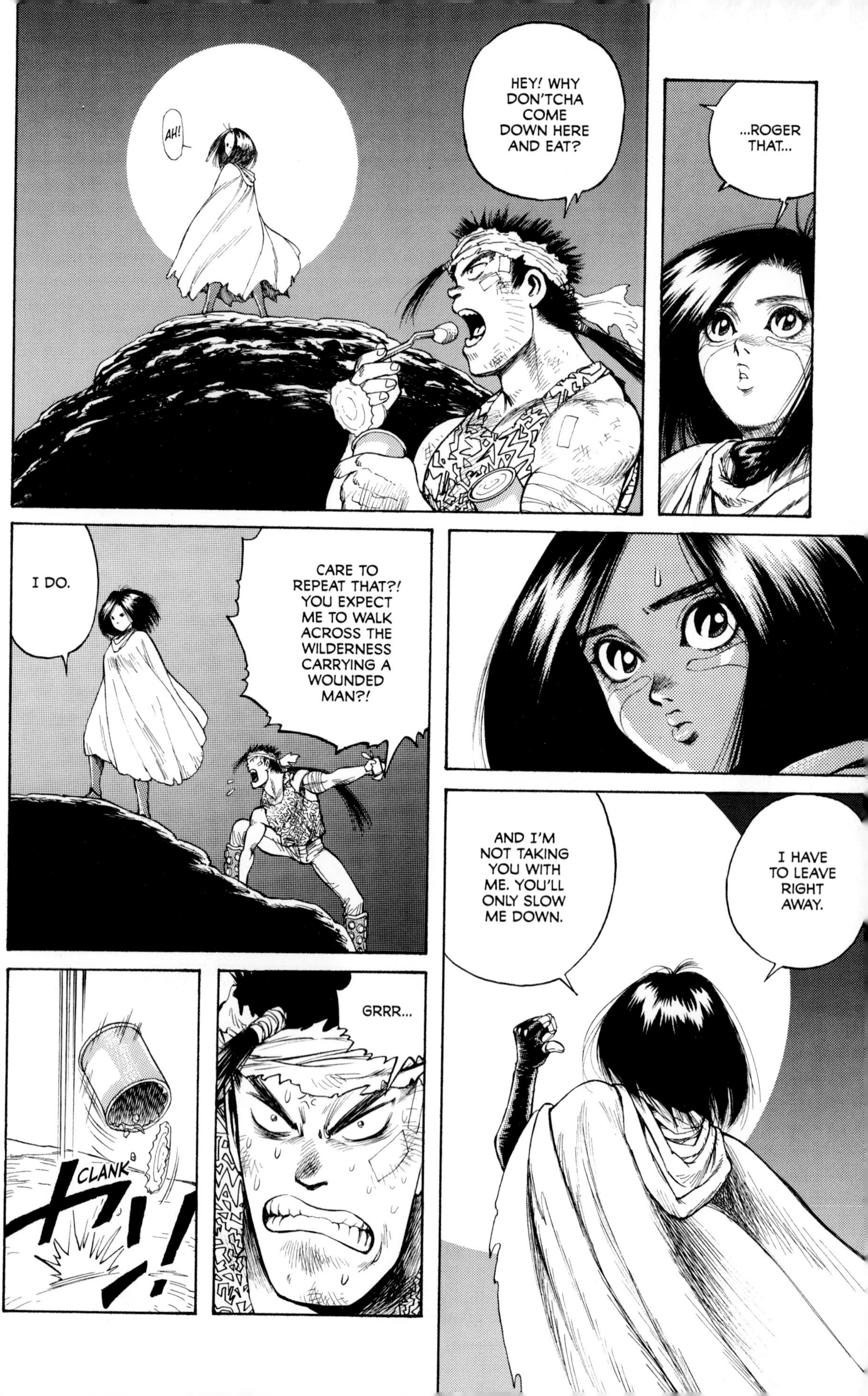
HEY! WHY DON'TCHA COME DOWN HERE AND EAT?
AH!
...ROGER THAT...
I HAVE TO LEAVE RIGHT AWAY.
AND I'M NOT TAKING YOU WITH ME. YOU'LL ONLY SLOW ME DOWN.
CARE TO REPEAT THAT?! YOU EXPECT ME TO WALK ACROSS THE WILDERNESS CARRYING A WOUNDED MAN?!
I DO.
GRRR...
CLANK

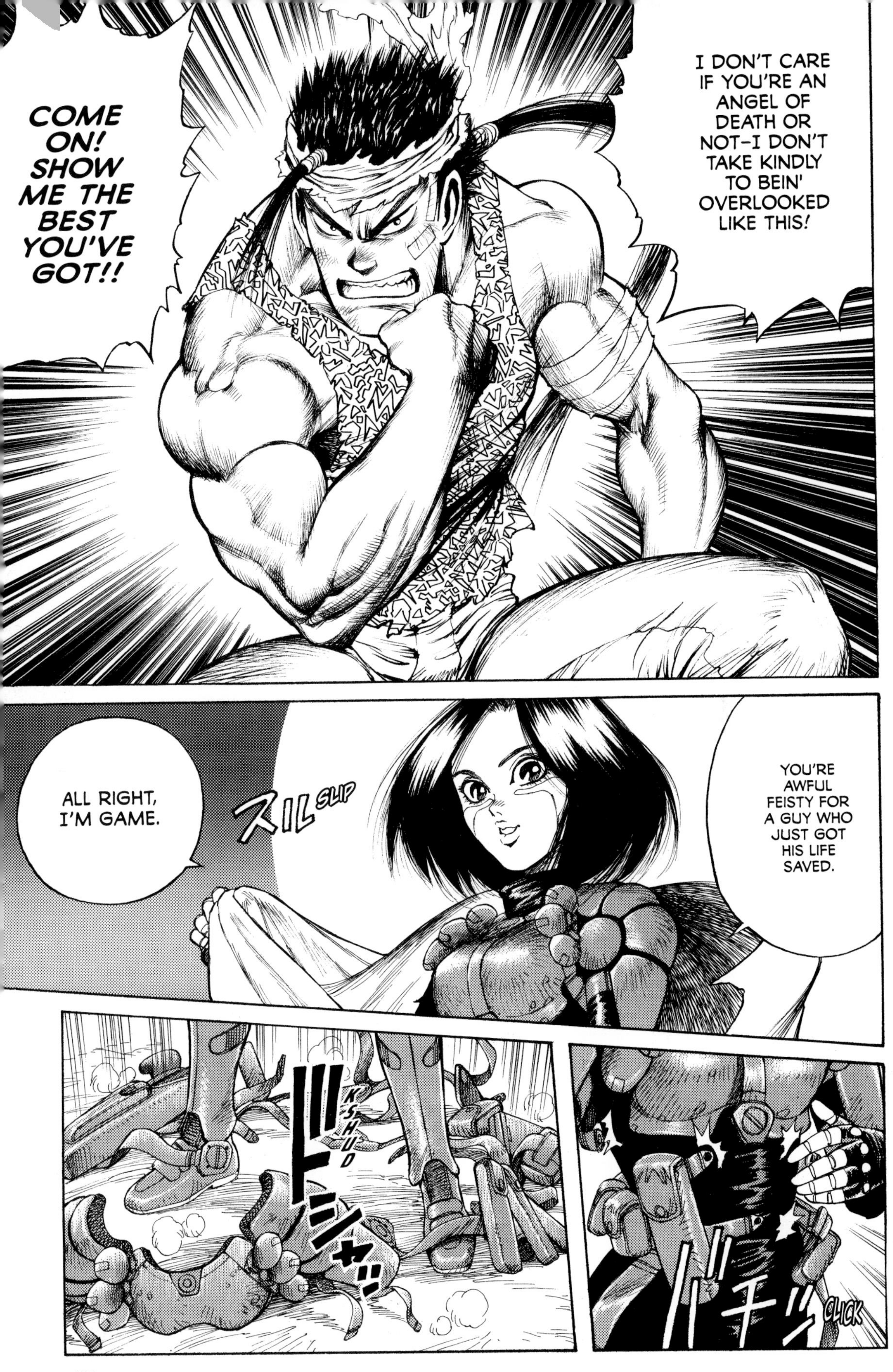
I DON'T CARE IF YOU'RE AN ANGEL OF DEATH OR NOT–I DON'T TAKE KINDLY TO BEIN' OVERLOOKED LIKE THIS!
COME ON! SHOW ME THE BEST YOU'VE GOT!!
YOU'RE AWFUL FEISTY FOR A GUY WHO JUST GOT HIS LIFE SAVED.
スル SLIP
ALL RIGHT, I'M GAME.
ドチッ CLICK
ドシャッ KSHUD

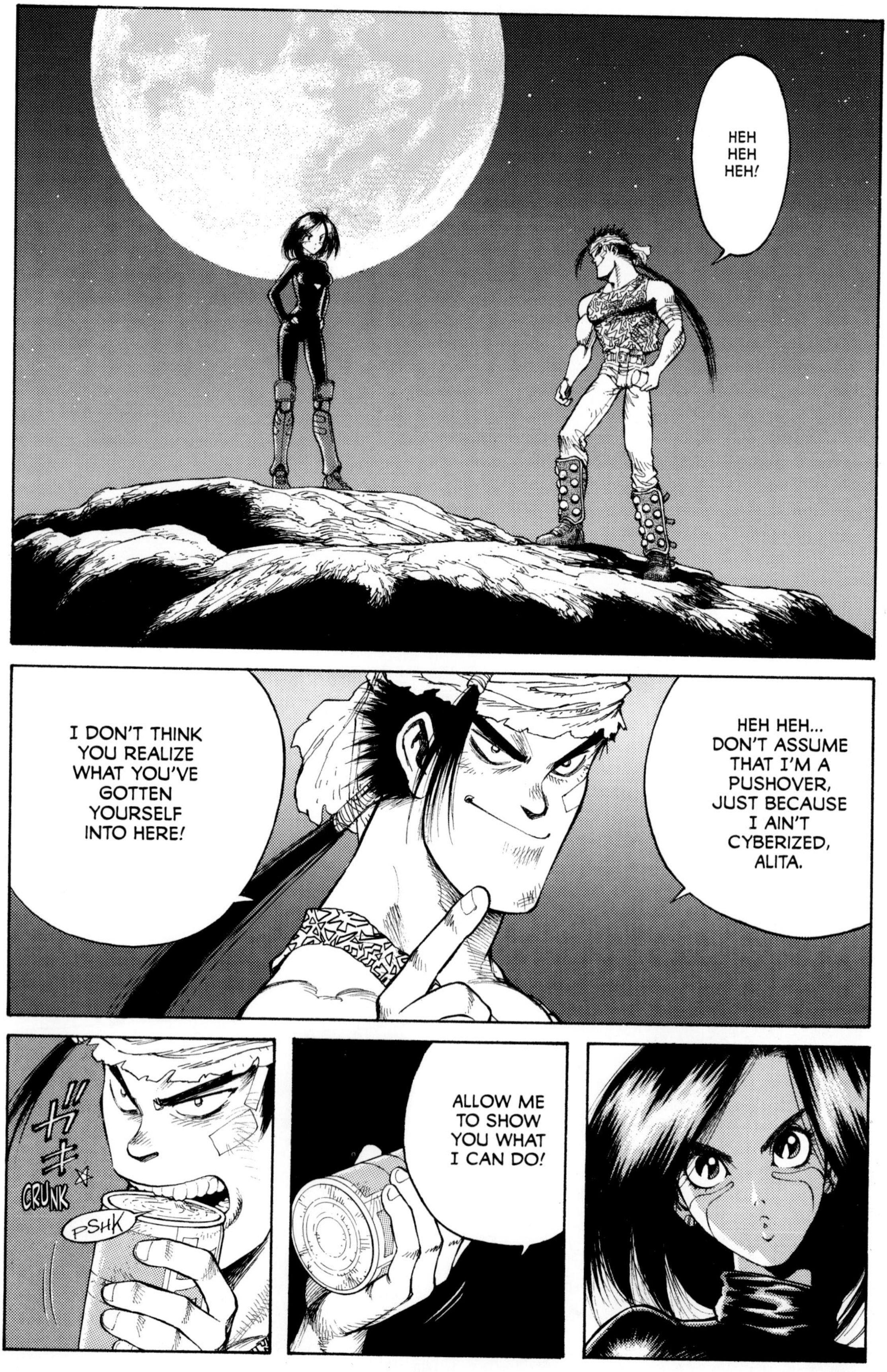
HEH HEH HEH!
HEH HEH... DON'T ASSUME THAT I'M A PUSHOVER, JUST BECAUSE I AIN'T CYBERIZED, ALITA.
I DON'T THINK YOU REALIZE WHAT YOU'VE GOTTEN YOURSELF INTO HERE!
ALLOW ME TO SHOW YOU WHAT I CAN DO!
CRUNK
PSHK

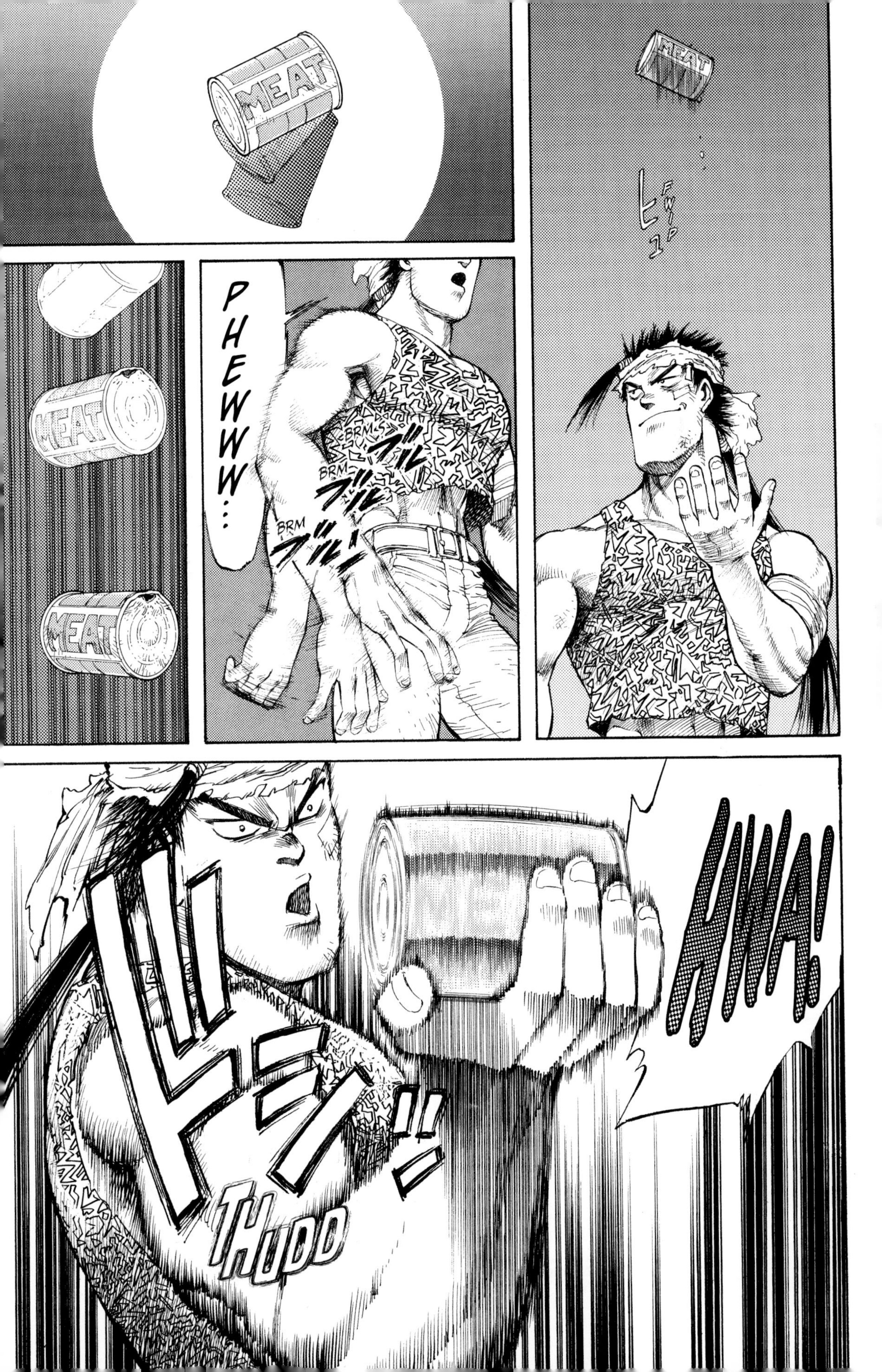

MEAT
FWIP
MEAT
PHEWWWW...
BRM
BRM
BRM
MEAT
MEAT
HWA!
THUDD

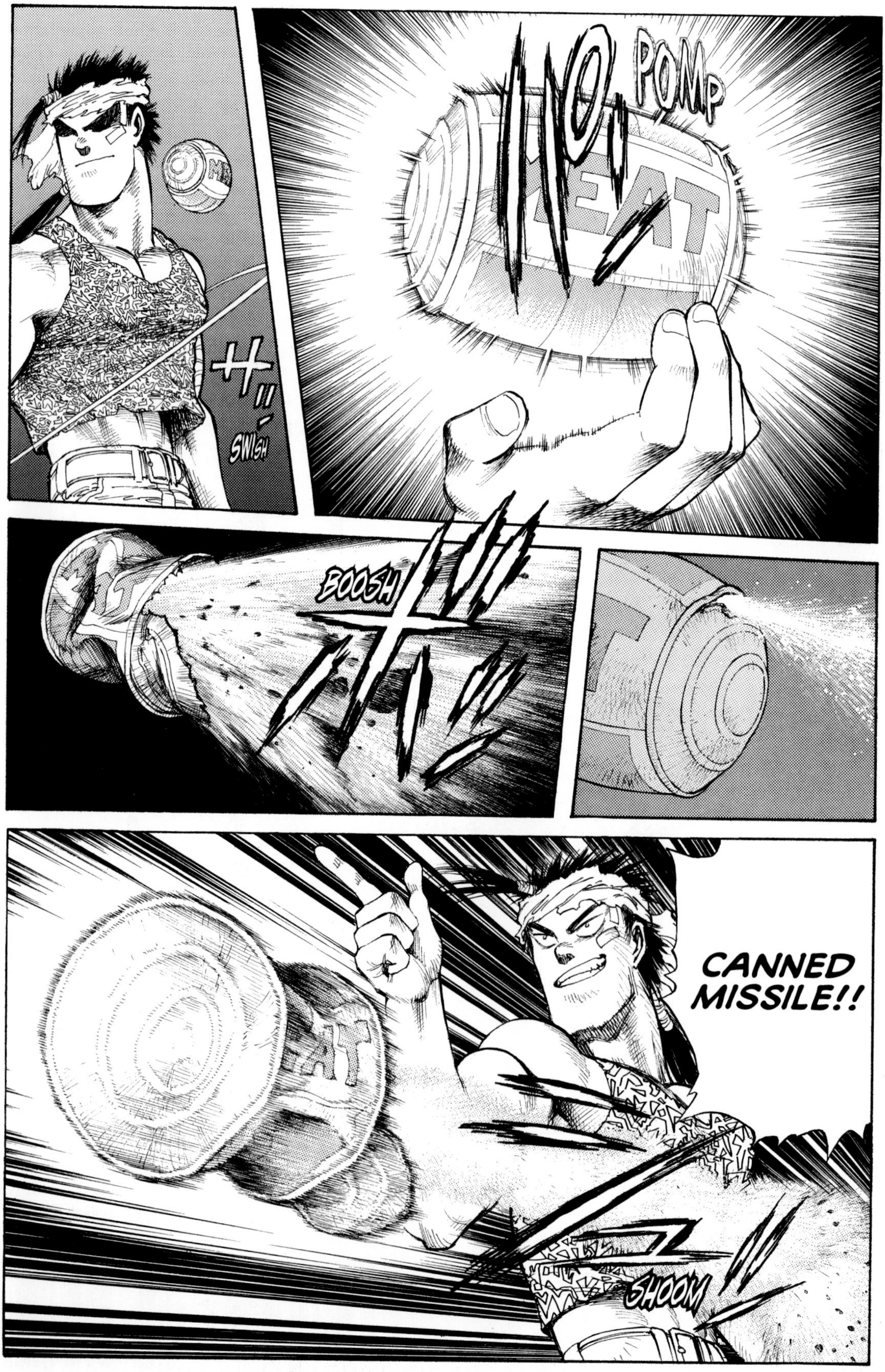
POMP
SWISH
BOOSH
CANNED MISSILE!!
SHOOM

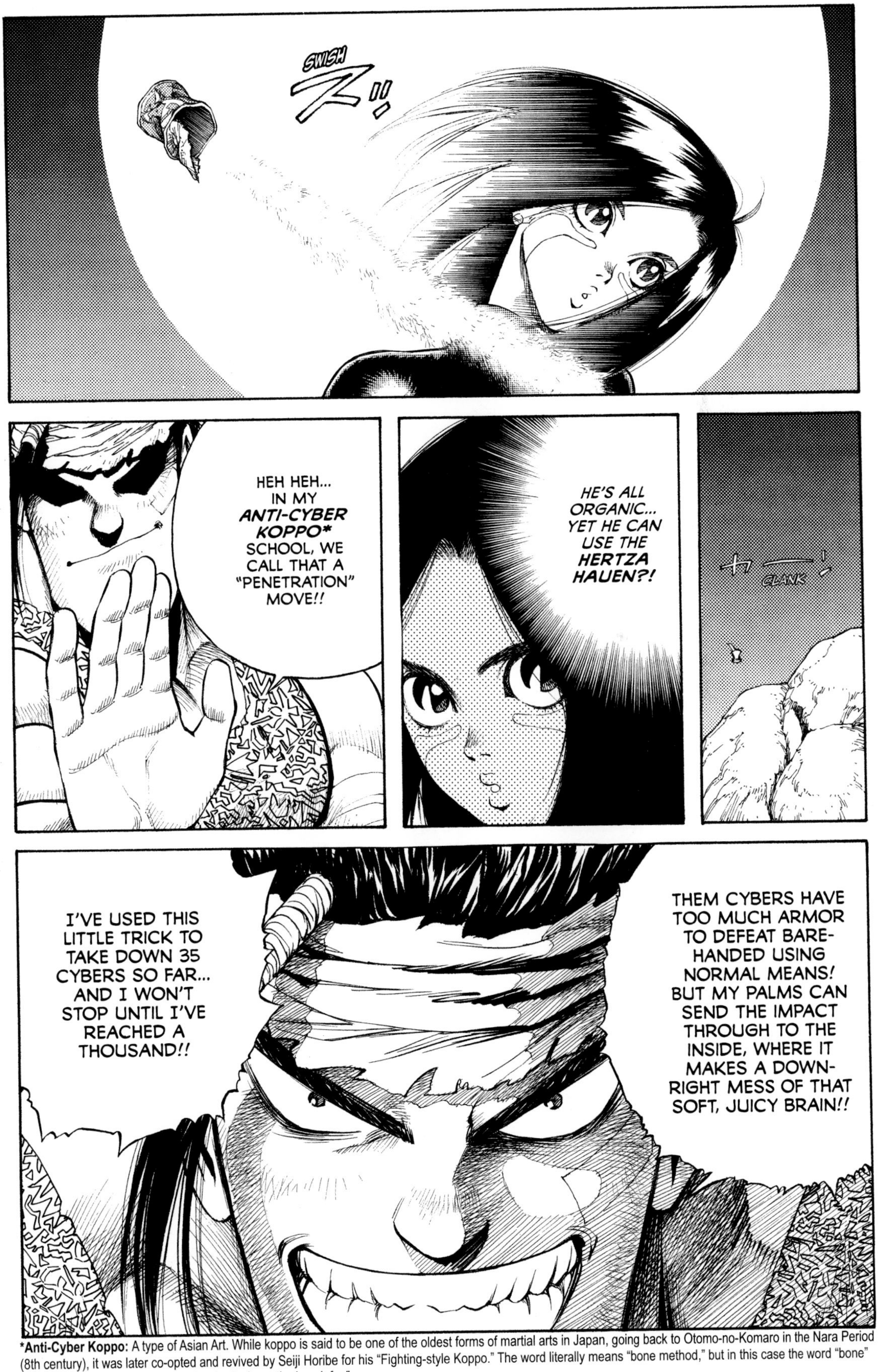
SWISH
CLANK
HE'S ALL ORGANIC... YET HE CAN USE THE *HERTZA HAUEN*?!
HEH HEH... IN MY *ANTI-CYBER KOPPO** SCHOOL, WE CALL THAT A "PENETRATION" MOVE!!
THEM CYBERS HAVE TOO MUCH ARMOR TO DEFEAT BARE-HANDED USING NORMAL MEANS! BUT MY PALMS CAN SEND THE IMPACT THROUGH TO THE INSIDE, WHERE IT MAKES A DOWN-RIGHT MESS OF THAT SOFT, JUICY BRAIN!!
I'VE USED THIS LITTLE TRICK TO TAKE DOWN 35 CYBERS SO FAR... AND I WON'T STOP UNTIL I'VE REACHED A THOUSAND!!

***Anti-Cyber Koppo:** A type of Asian Art. While koppo is said to be one of the oldest forms of martial arts in Japan, going back to Otomo-no-Komaro in the Nara Period (8th century), it was later co-opted and revived by Seiji Horibe for his "Fighting-style Koppo." The word literally means "bone method," but in this case the word "bone" means more like "trick" or "knack," as in, "to have the knack for."

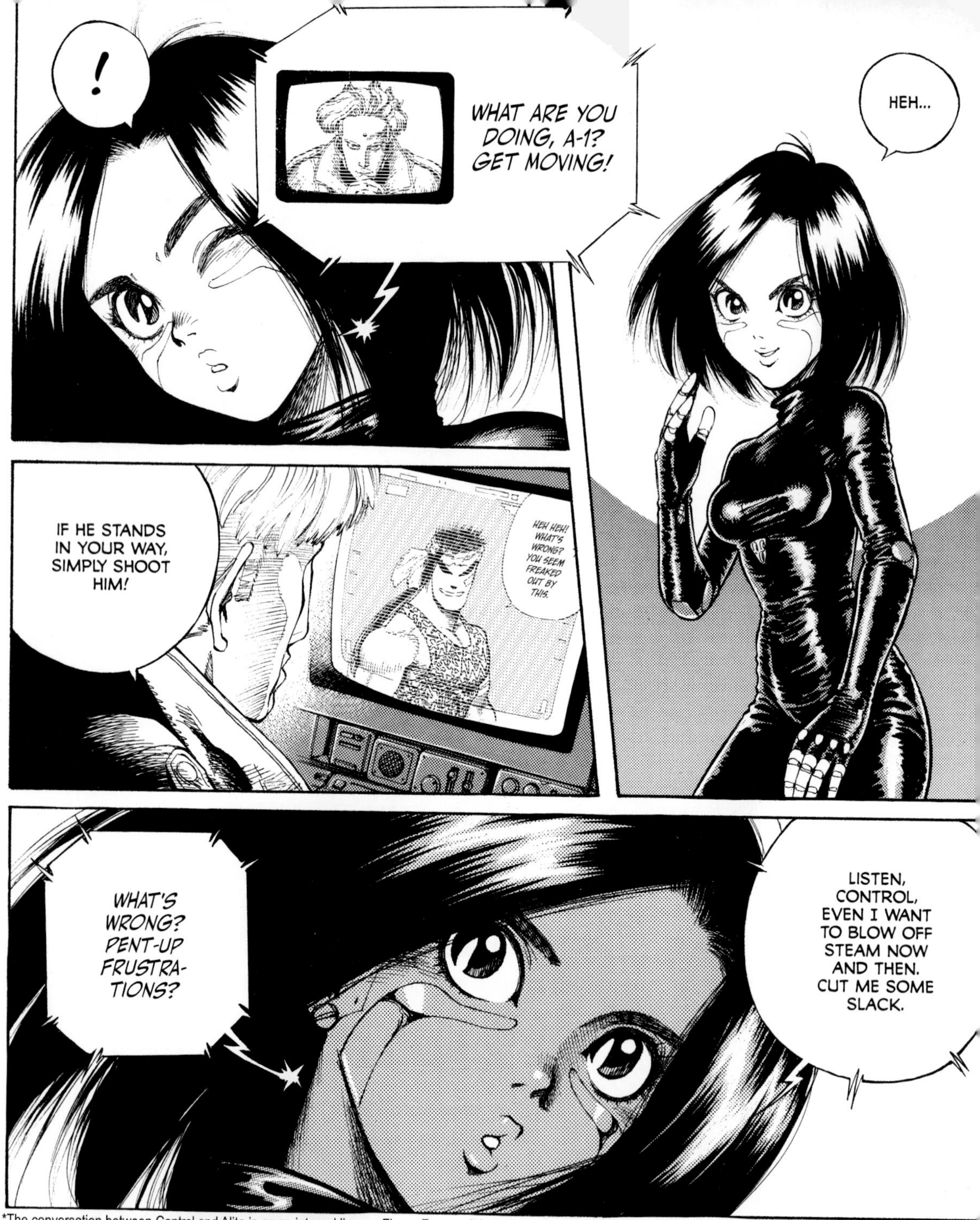
HEH...
WHAT ARE YOU DOING, A-1? GET MOVING!
!
HEH HEH! WHAT'S WRONG? YOU SEEM FREAKED OUT BY THIS.
IF HE STANDS IN YOUR WAY, SIMPLY SHOOT HIM!
LISTEN, CONTROL, EVEN I WANT TO BLOW OFF STEAM NOW AND THEN. CUT ME SOME SLACK.
WHAT'S WRONG? PENT-UP FRUSTRATIONS?

*The conversation between Control and Alita is on an internal line, so Figure Four can't hear them.

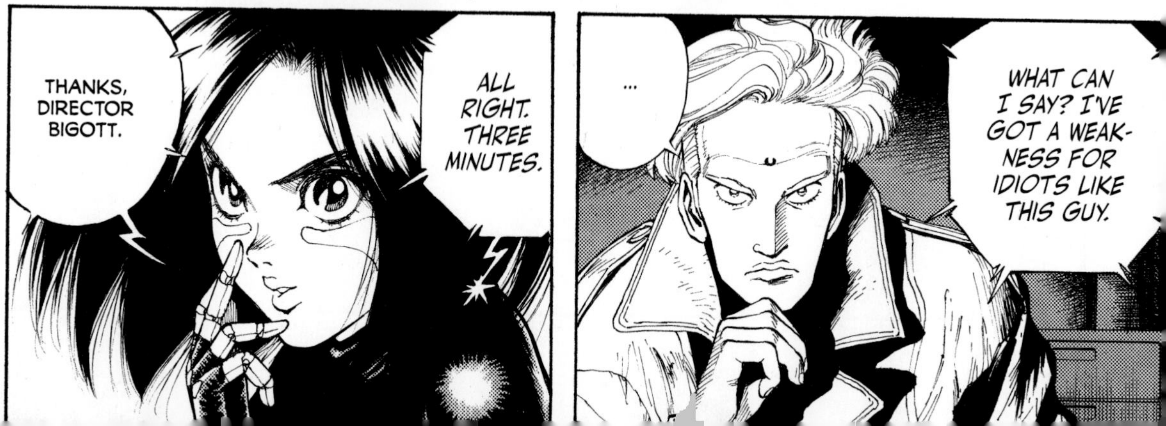
WHAT CAN I SAY? I'VE GOT A WEAKNESS FOR IDIOTS LIKE THIS GUY.
...
ALL RIGHT. THREE MINUTES.
THANKS, DIRECTOR BIGOTT.

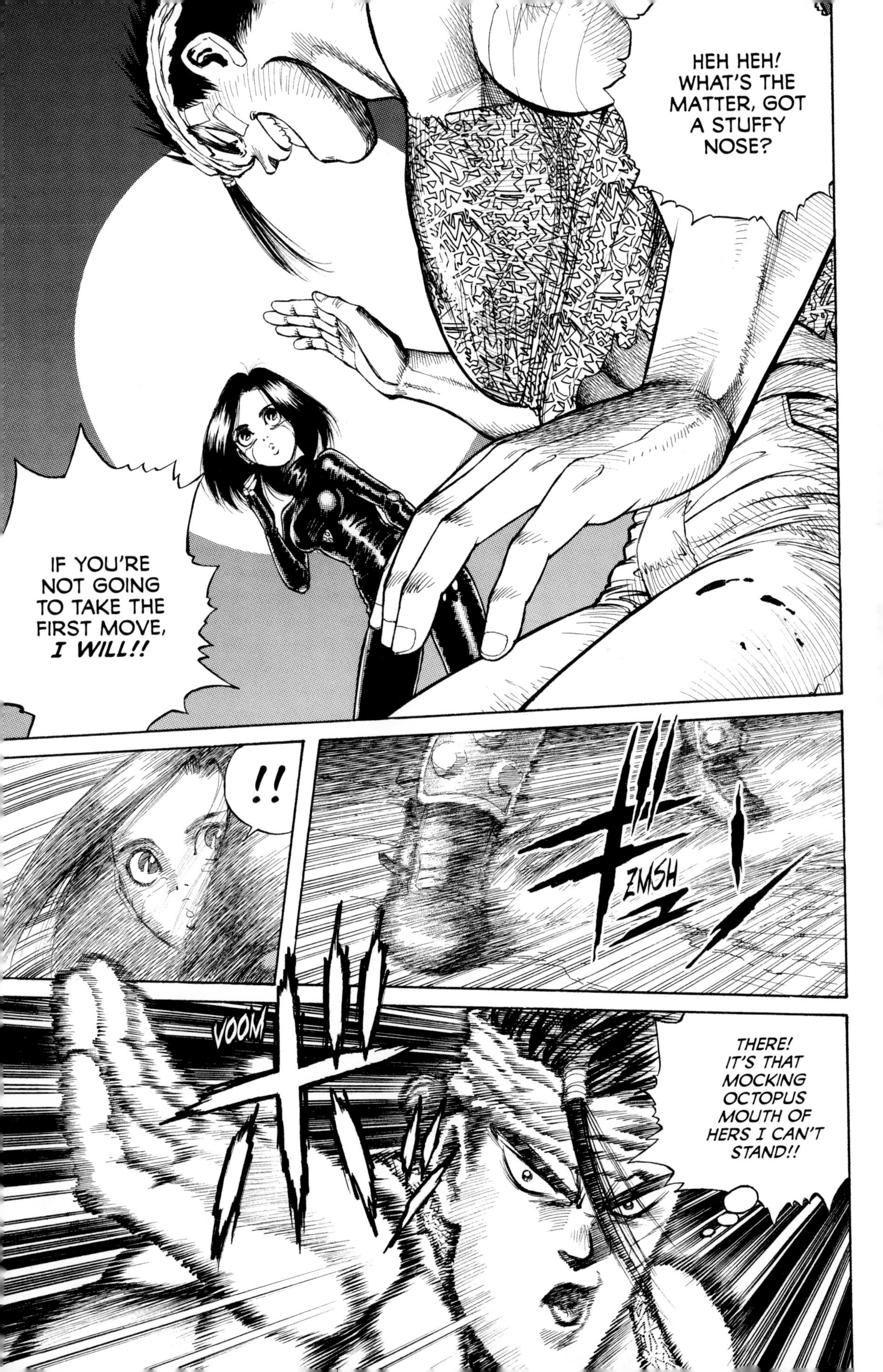
HEH HEH! WHAT'S THE MATTER, GOT A STUFFY NOSE?
IF YOU'RE NOT GOING TO TAKE THE FIRST MOVE, ***I WILL!!***
ZMSH
!!
THERE! IT'S THAT MOCKING OCTOPUS MOUTH OF HERS I CAN'T STAND!!
VOOM

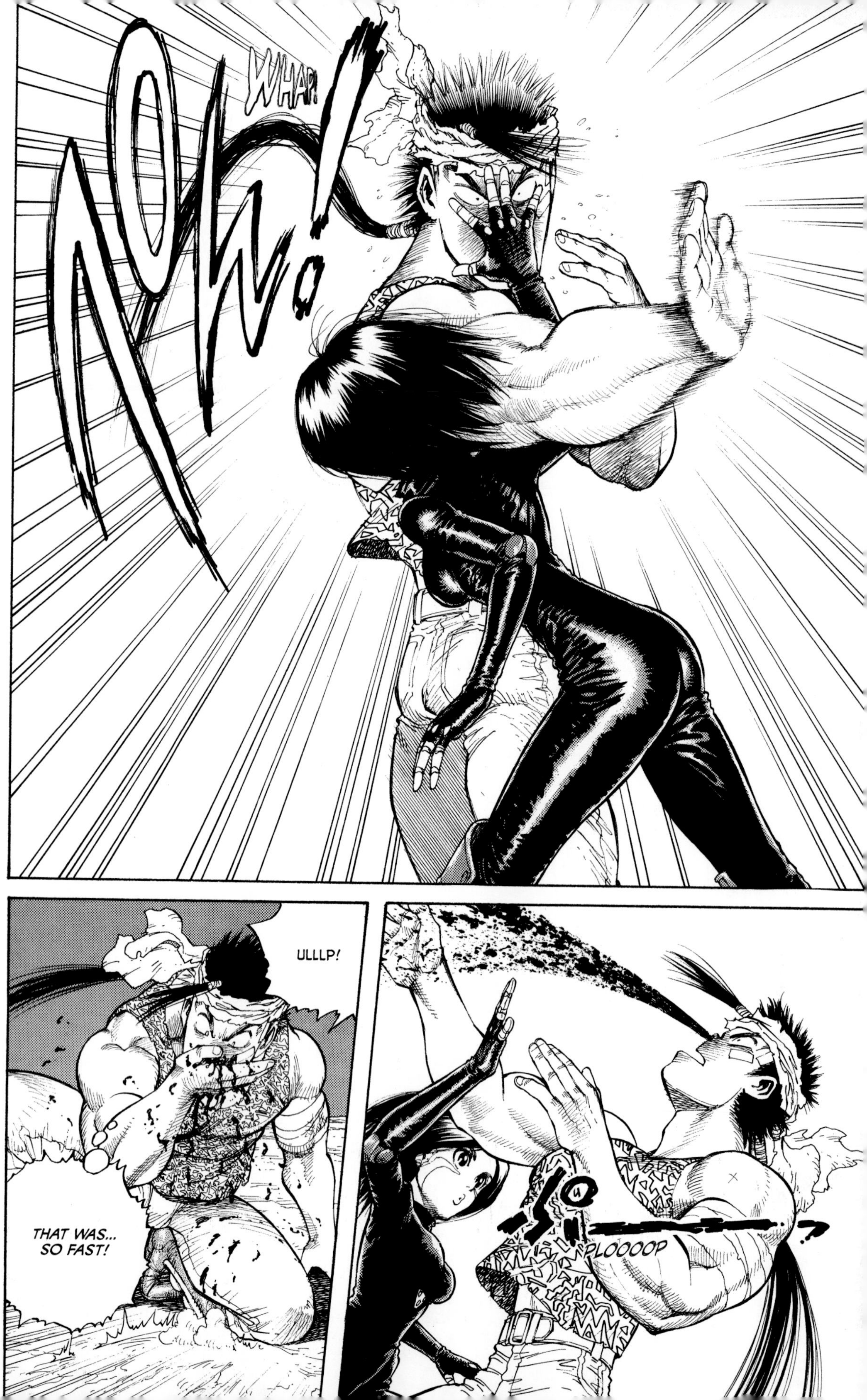
WHAP!
PLOOOOP
ULLLP!
THAT WAS... SO FAST!

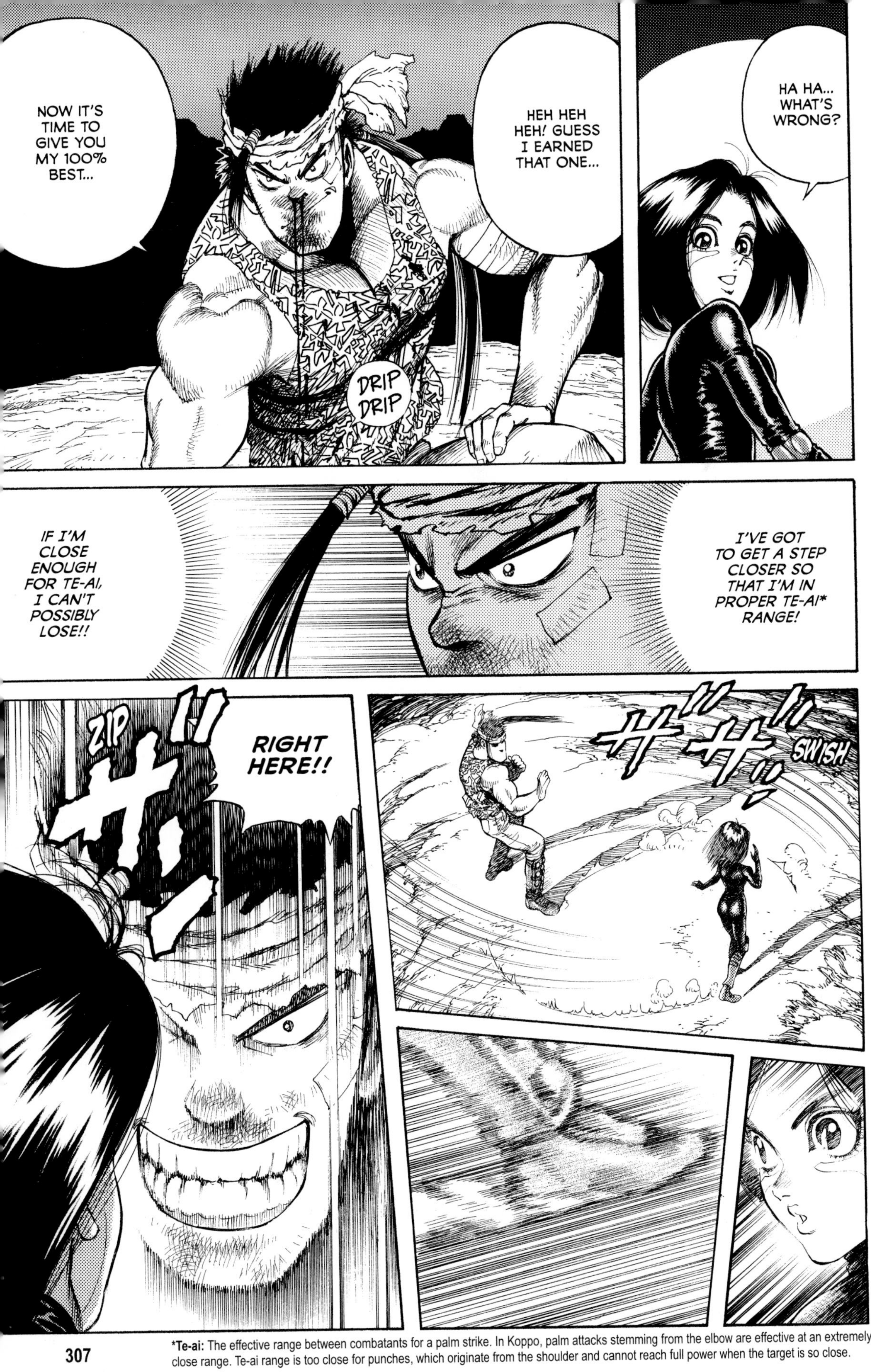
HA HA... WHAT'S WRONG?
HEH HEH HEH! GUESS I EARNED THAT ONE...
NOW IT'S TIME TO GIVE YOU MY 100% BEST...
DRIP DRIP
I'VE GOT TO GET A STEP CLOSER SO THAT I'M IN PROPER TE-AI* RANGE!
IF I'M CLOSE ENOUGH FOR TE-AI, I CAN'T POSSIBLY LOSE!!
SWISH
RIGHT HERE!!
ZIP

*Te-ai: The effective range between combatants for a palm strike. In Koppo, palm attacks stemming from the elbow are effective at an extremely close range. Te-ai range is too close for punches, which originate from the shoulder and cannot reach full power when the target is so close.

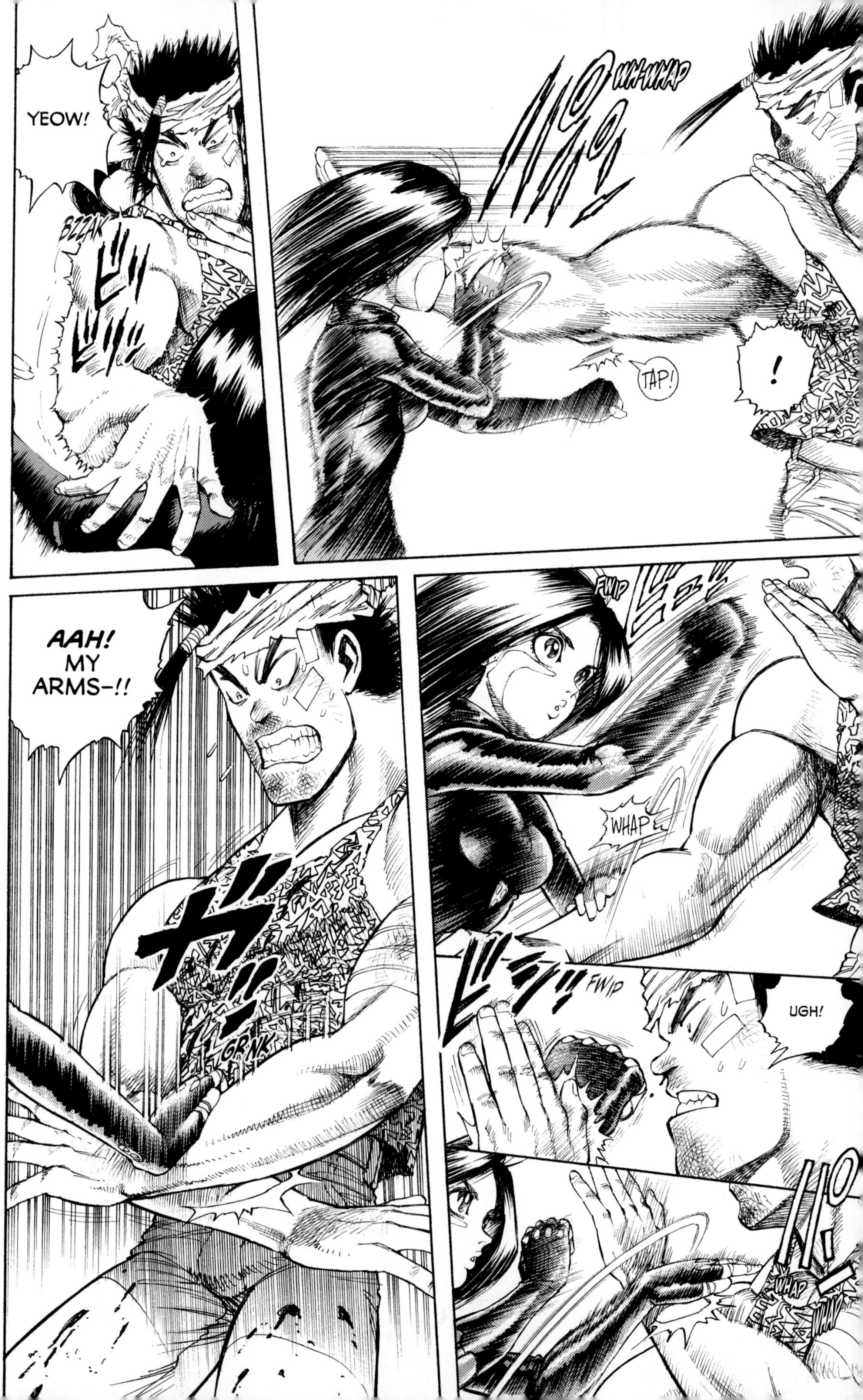
WH-WHAP
TAP!
!
YEOW!
BZZAK
FWIP
WHAP
FWIP
UGH!
WHAP
AAH! MY ARMS-!!
GRNK

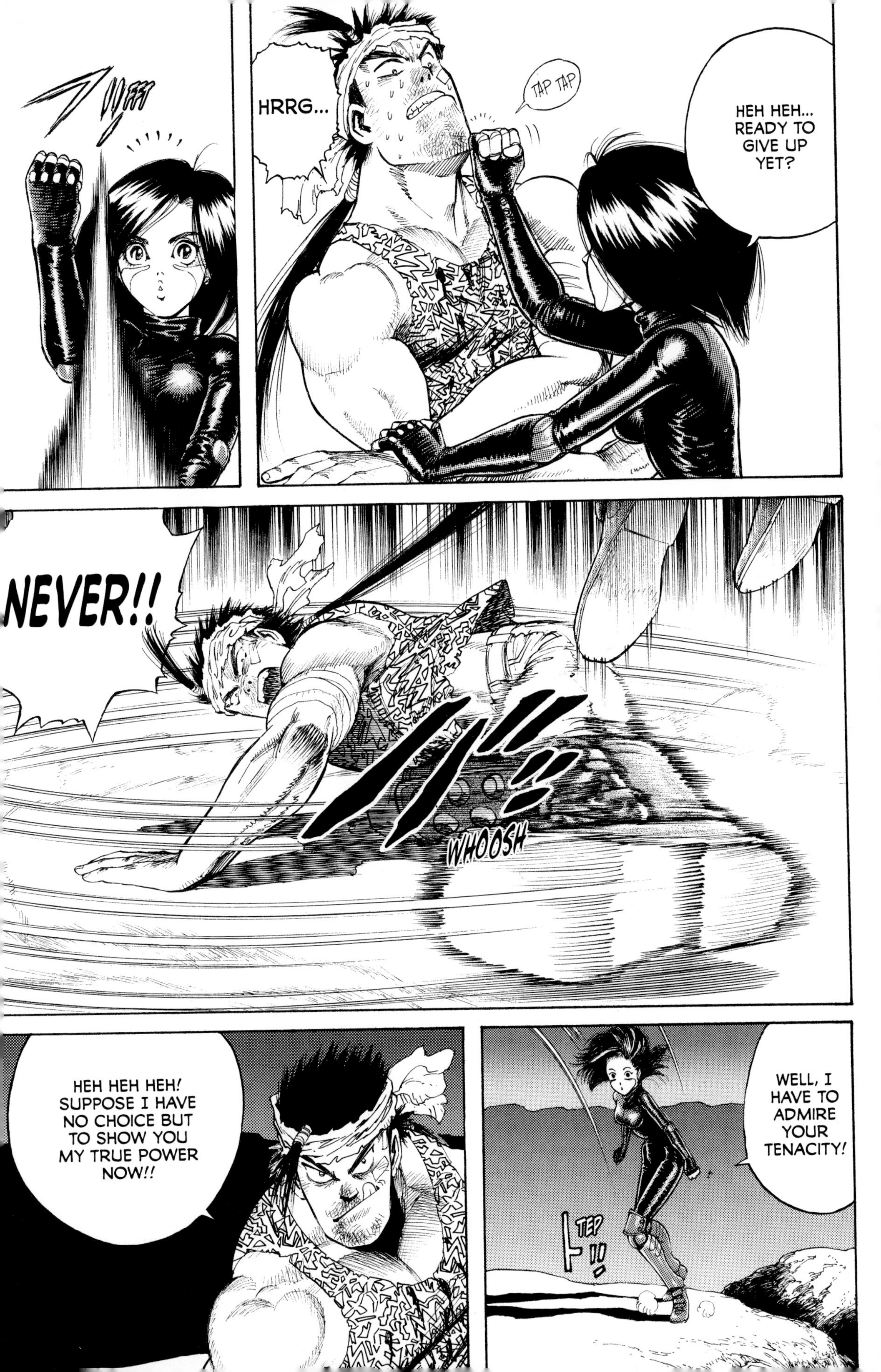
HEH HEH... READY TO GIVE UP YET?
TAP TAP
HRRG...
NEVER!!
WHOOSH
WELL, I HAVE TO ADMIRE YOUR TENACITY!
TEP!!
HEH HEH HEH! SUPPOSE I HAVE NO CHOICE BUT TO SHOW YOU MY TRUE POWER NOW!!

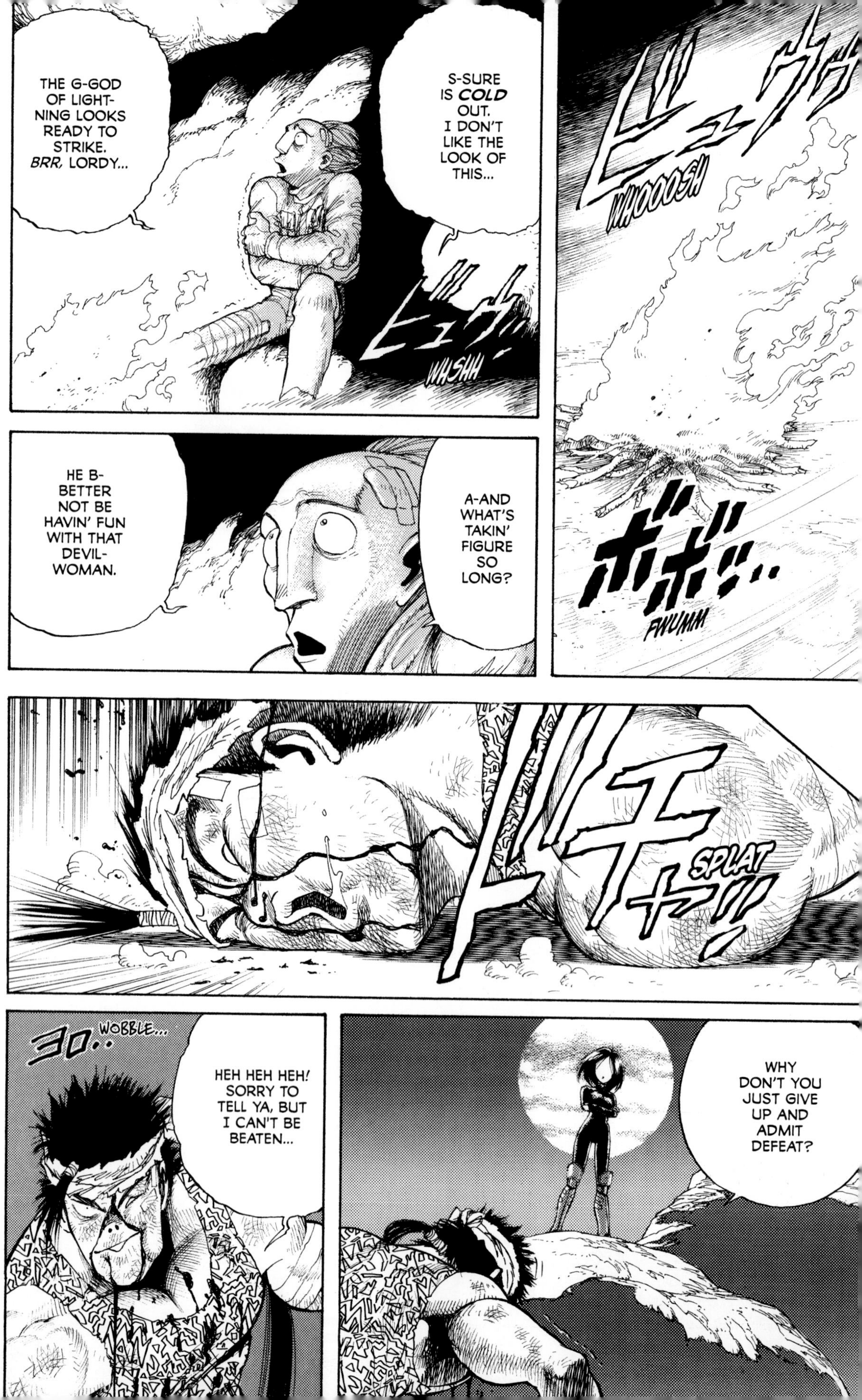
WHOOOSH
FWUMM
S-SURE IS *COLD* OUT. I DON'T LIKE THE LOOK OF THIS...
THE G-GOD OF LIGHTNING LOOKS READY TO STRIKE. *BRR,* LORDY...
WHSHH
A-AND WHAT'S TAKIN' FIGURE SO LONG?
HE B-BETTER NOT BE HAVIN' FUN WITH THAT DEVIL-WOMAN.
SPLAT
WHY DON'T YOU JUST GIVE UP AND ADMIT DEFEAT?
WOBBLE...
HEH HEH HEH! SORRY TO TELL YA, BUT I CAN'T BE BEATEN...

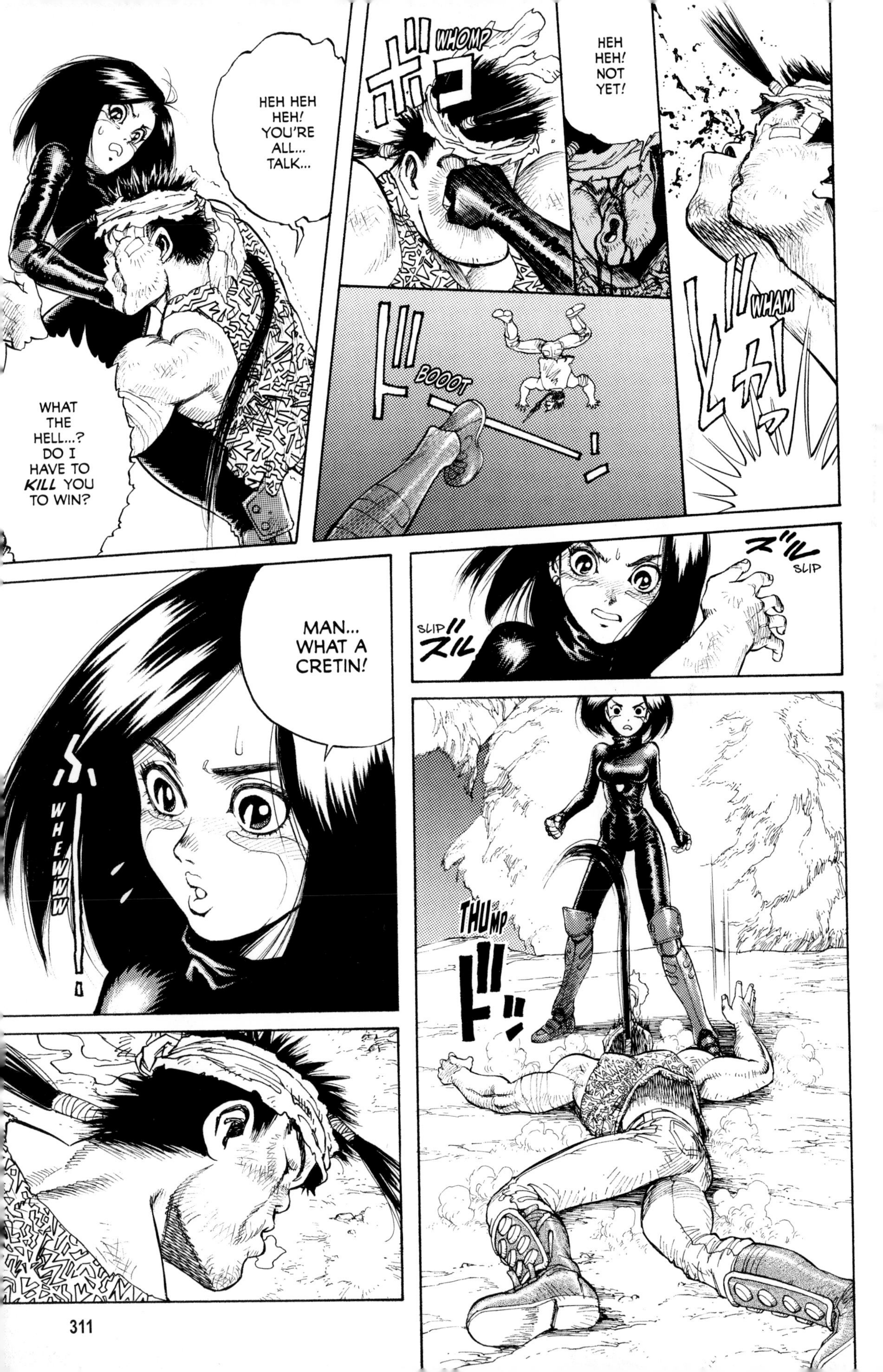
WHAM
HEH HEH! NOT YET!
WHOMP
ボコ
BOOOT
ド
HEH HEH HEH! YOU'RE ALL... TALK...
WHAT THE HELL...? DO I HAVE TO *KILL* YOU TO WIN?
ズル SLIP
SLIP ズル
THUMP
MAN... WHAT A CRETIN!
WHEWWW

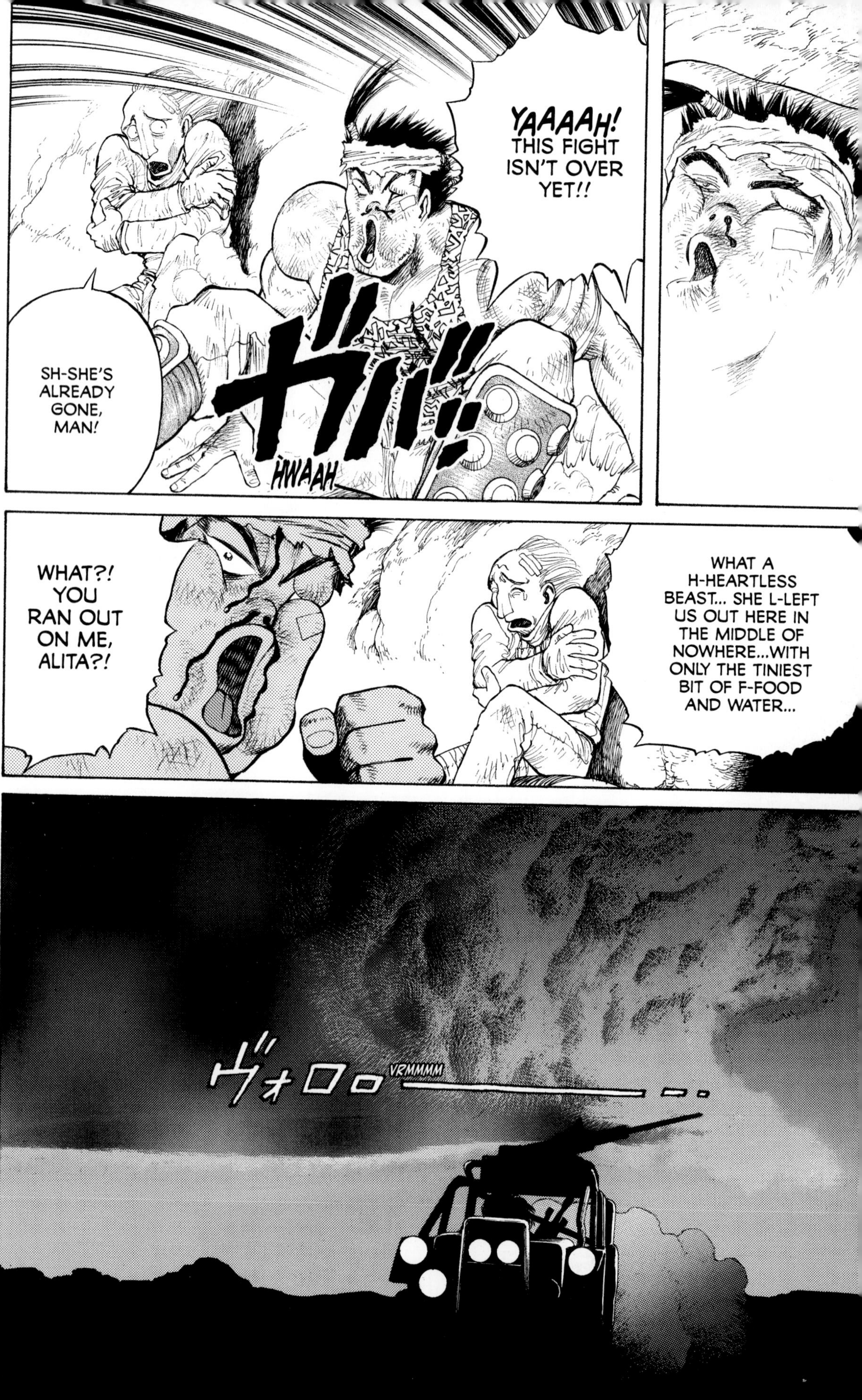
YAAAAH! THIS FIGHT ISN'T OVER YET!!
ガバッ
HWAAH
SH-SHE'S ALREADY GONE, MAN!
WHAT A H-HEARTLESS BEAST... SHE L-LEFT US OUT HERE IN THE MIDDLE OF NOWHERE...WITH ONLY THE TINIEST BIT OF F-FOOD AND WATER...
WHAT?! YOU RAN OUT ON ME, ALITA?!
ヴォロロ
VRMMMM

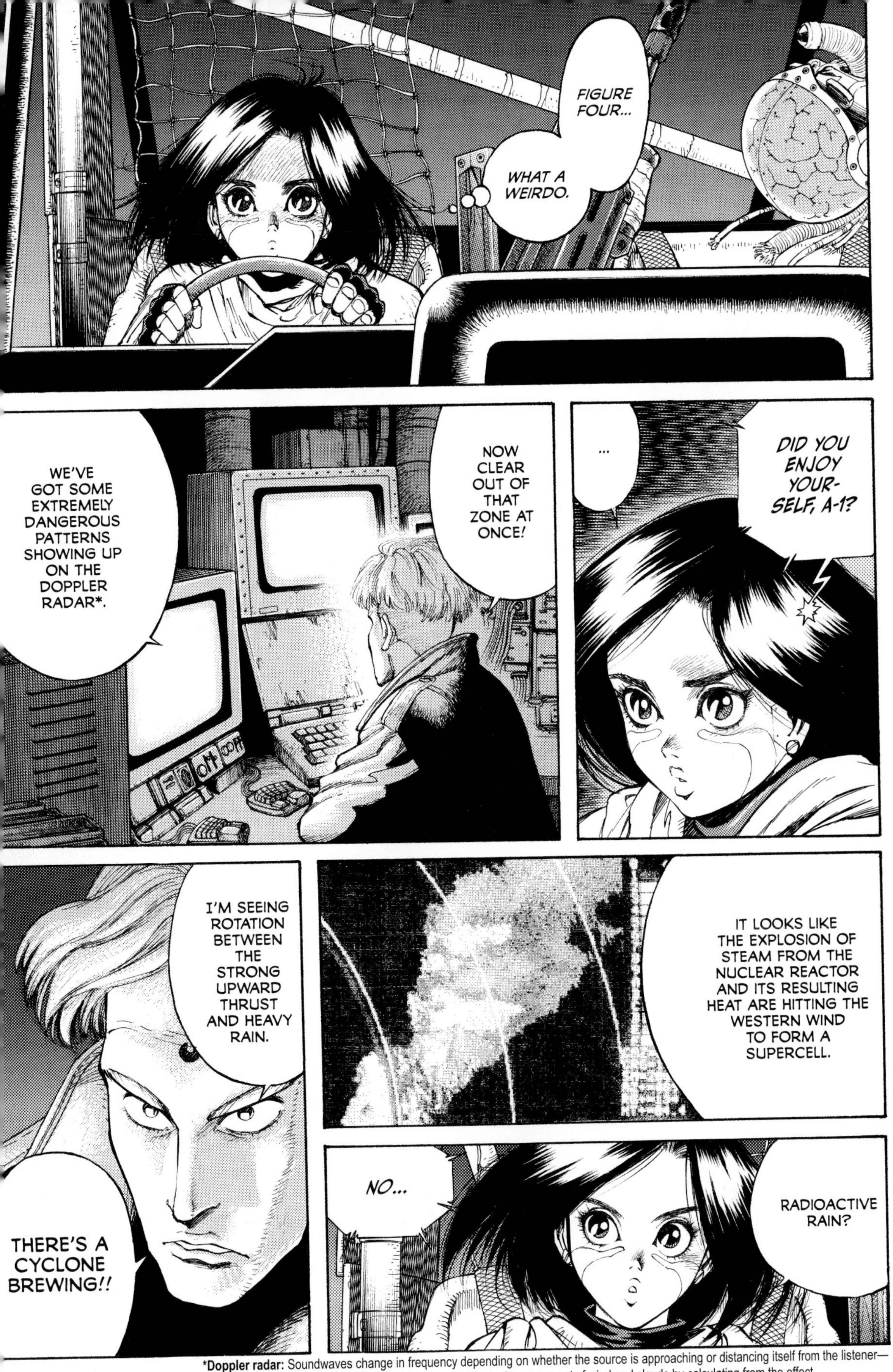
FIGURE FOUR...
WHAT A WEIRDO.
DID YOU ENJOY YOUR-SELF, A-1?
...
NOW CLEAR OUT OF THAT ZONE AT ONCE!
WE'VE GOT SOME EXTREMELY DANGEROUS PATTERNS SHOWING UP ON THE DOPPLER RADAR*.
IT LOOKS LIKE THE EXPLOSION OF STEAM FROM THE NUCLEAR REACTOR AND ITS RESULTING HEAT ARE HITTING THE WESTERN WIND TO FORM A SUPERCELL.
RADIOACTIVE RAIN?
NO...
I'M SEEING ROTATION BETWEEN THE STRONG UPWARD THRUST AND HEAVY RAIN.
THERE'S A CYCLONE BREWING!!

***Doppler radar:** Soundwaves change in frequency depending on whether the source is approaching or distancing itself from the listener—this is called the "Doppler effect." A Doppler radar interprets the movement of wind and clouds by calculating from the effect.

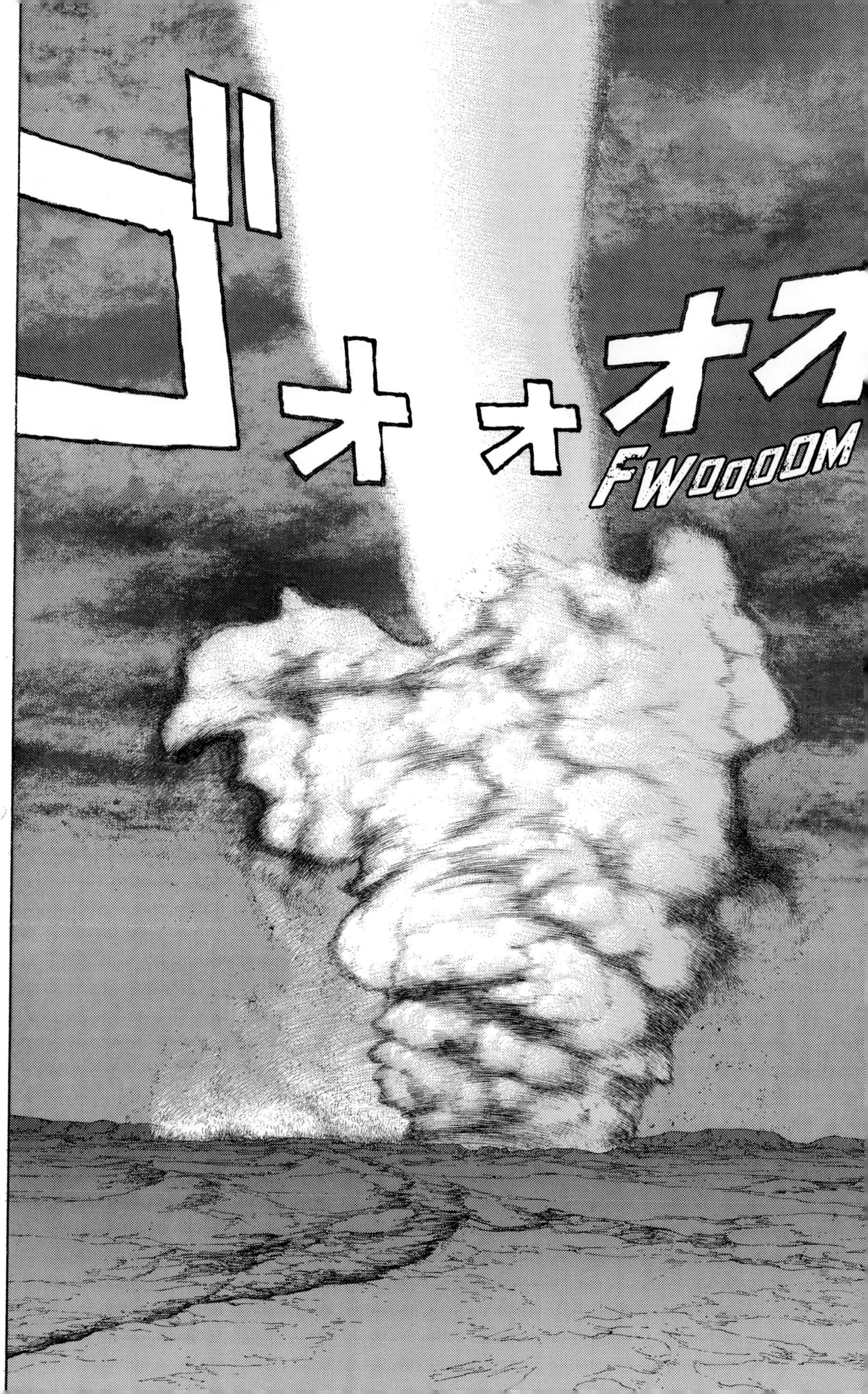
ゴォォオオ
FWOOOOOM

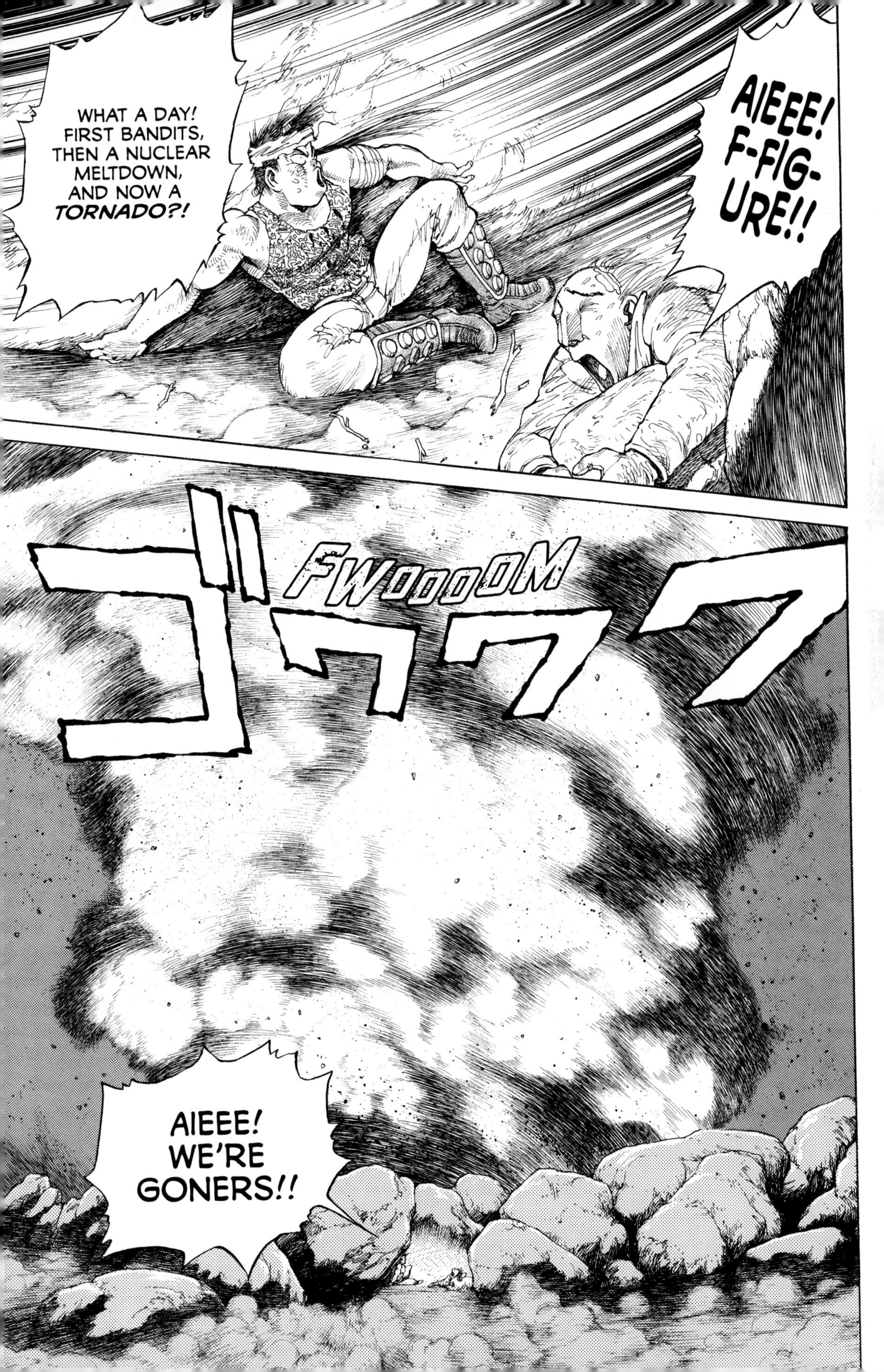
AIEEE! F-FIG-URE!!
WHAT A DAY! FIRST BANDITS, THEN A NUCLEAR MELTDOWN, AND NOW A *TORNADO?!*
FWOOOOOM
AIEEE! WE'RE GONERS!!

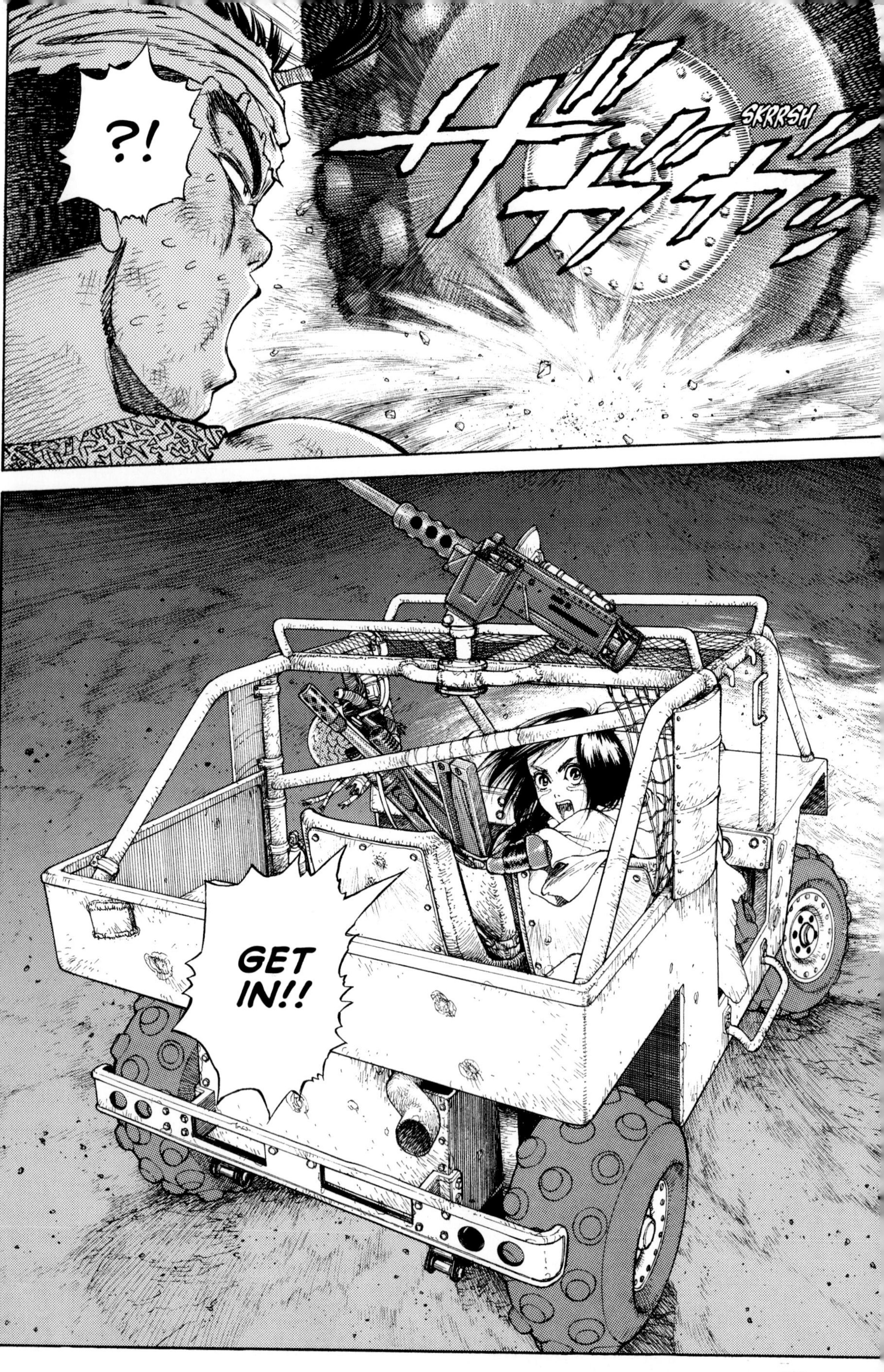
?!
SKRRSH
GET IN!!

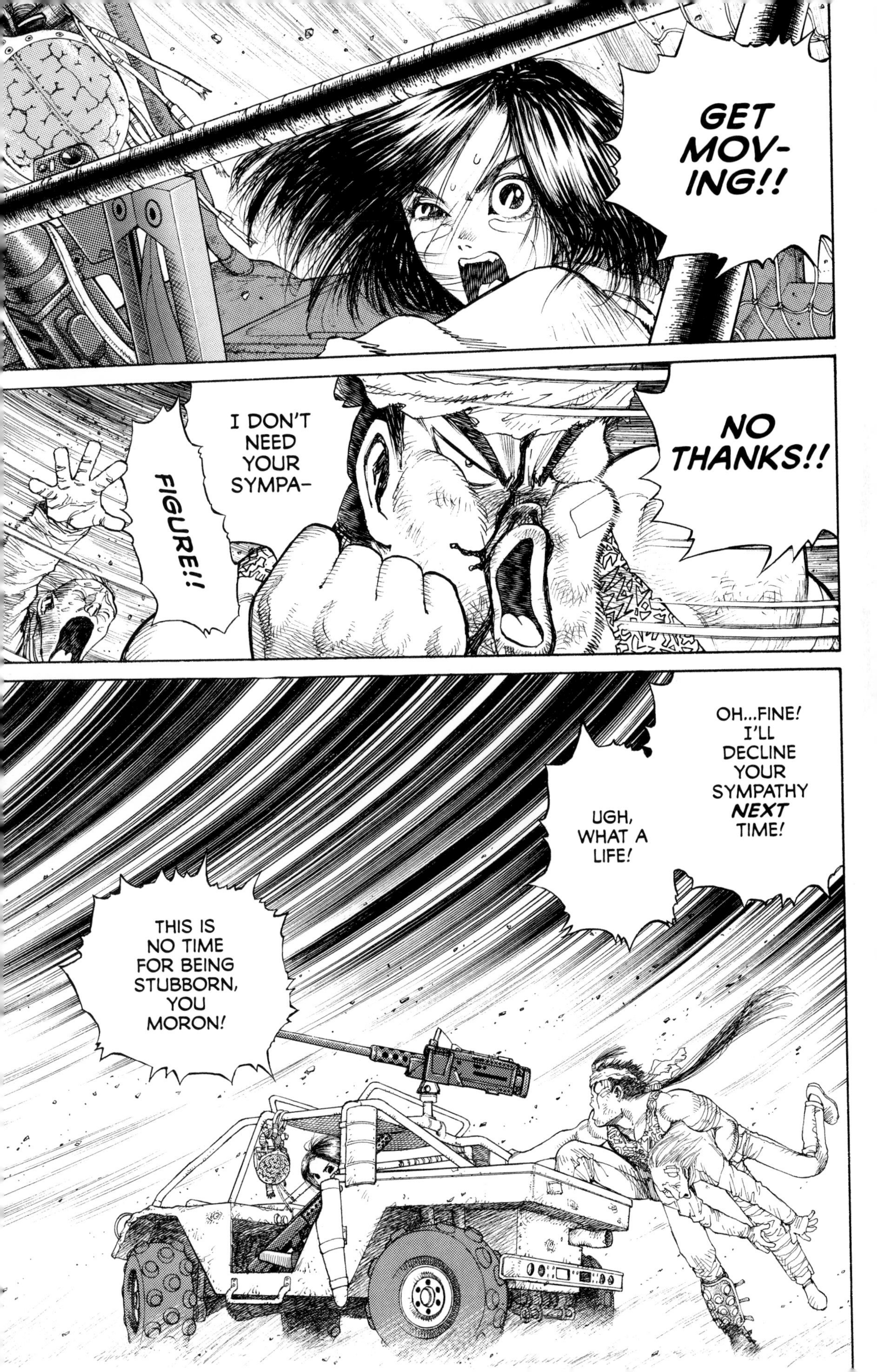
GET MOVING!!
NO THANKS!!
I DON'T NEED YOUR SYMPA-
FIGURE!!
OH...FINE! I'LL DECLINE YOUR SYMPATHY *NEXT* TIME!
UGH, WHAT A LIFE!
THIS IS NO TIME FOR BEING STUBBORN, YOU MORON!

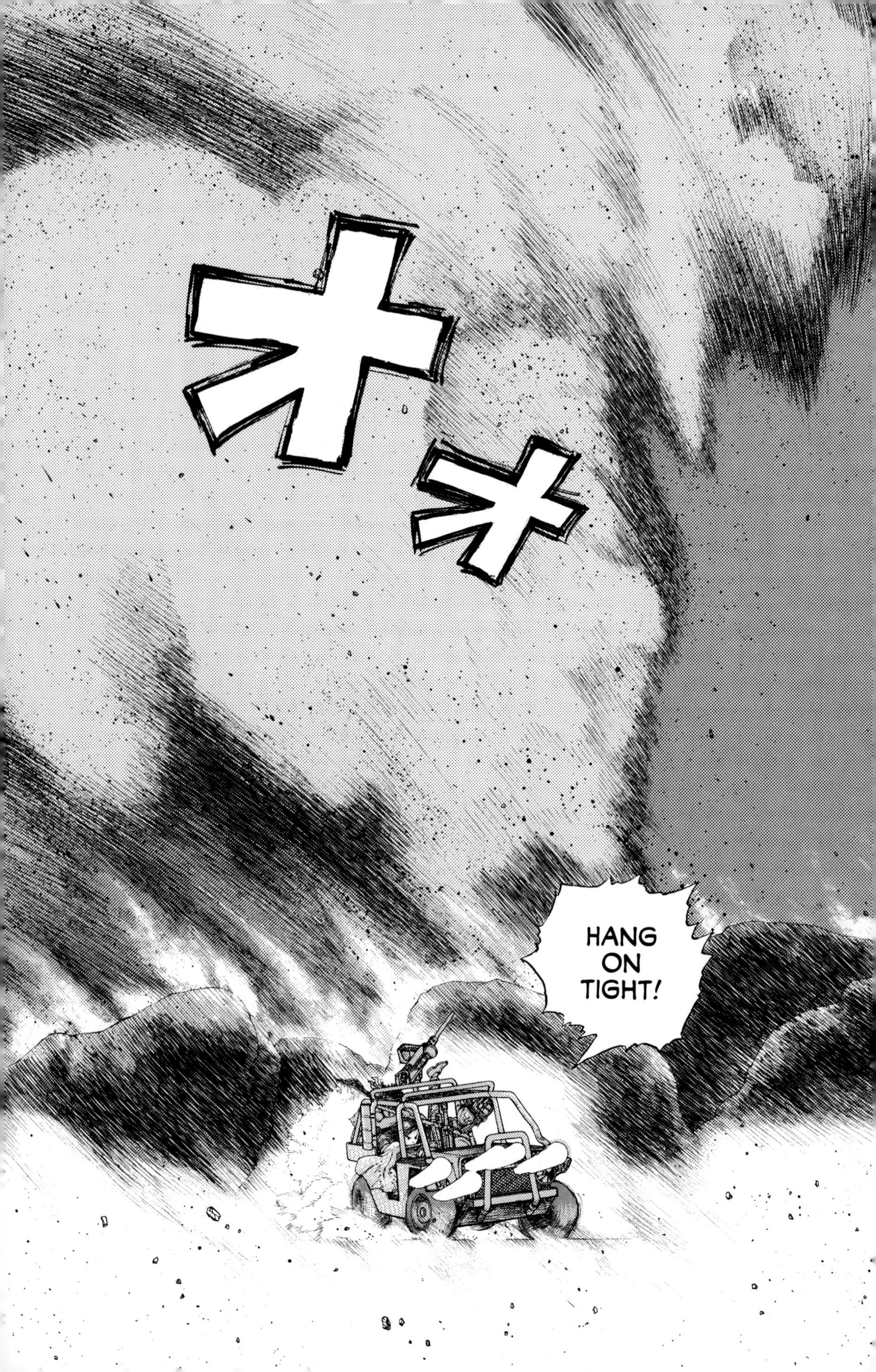
オォ
HANG ON TIGHT!

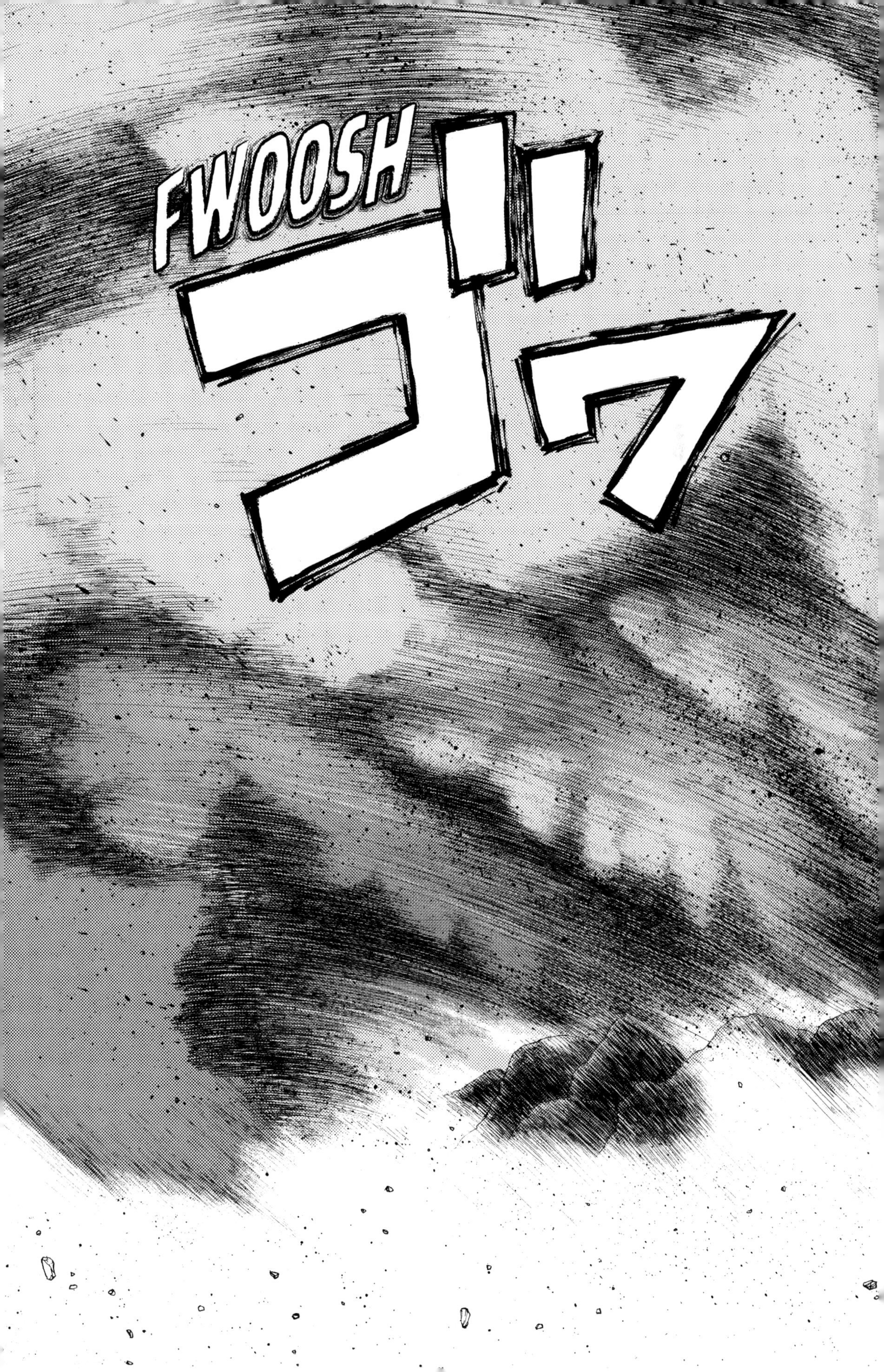
FWOOSH
ゴワ

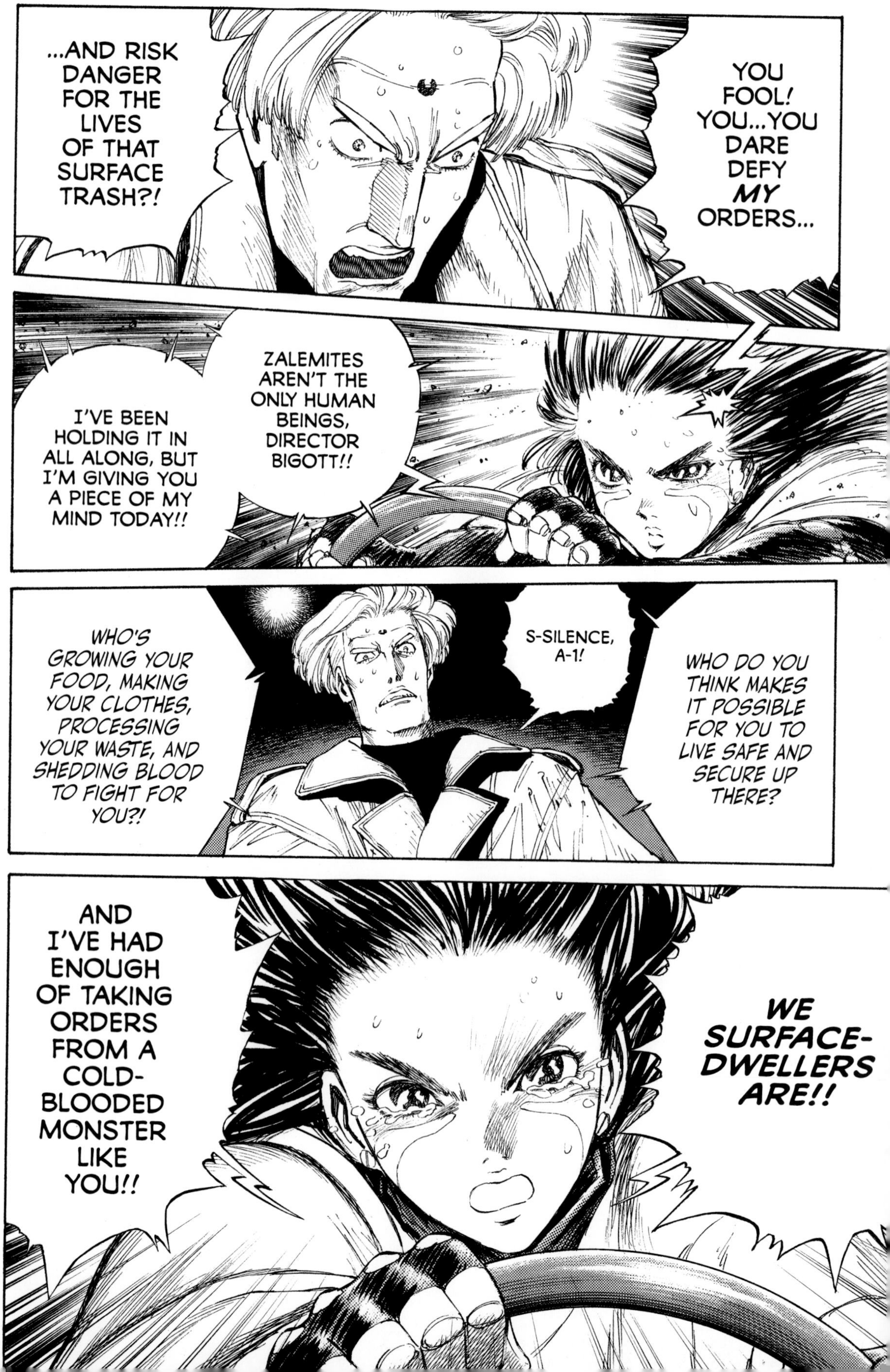
YOU FOOL! YOU...YOU DARE DEFY *MY* ORDERS...
...AND RISK DANGER FOR THE LIVES OF THAT SURFACE TRASH?!
ZALEMITES AREN'T THE ONLY HUMAN BEINGS, DIRECTOR BIGOTT!!
I'VE BEEN HOLDING IT IN ALL ALONG, BUT I'M GIVING YOU A PIECE OF MY MIND TODAY!!
WHO DO YOU THINK MAKES IT POSSIBLE FOR YOU TO LIVE SAFE AND SECURE UP THERE?
S-SILENCE, A-1!
WHO'S GROWING YOUR FOOD, MAKING YOUR CLOTHES, PROCESSING YOUR WASTE, AND SHEDDING BLOOD TO FIGHT FOR YOU?!
WE SURFACE-DWELLERS ARE!!
AND I'VE HAD ENOUGH OF TAKING ORDERS FROM A COLD-BLOODED MONSTER LIKE YOU!!

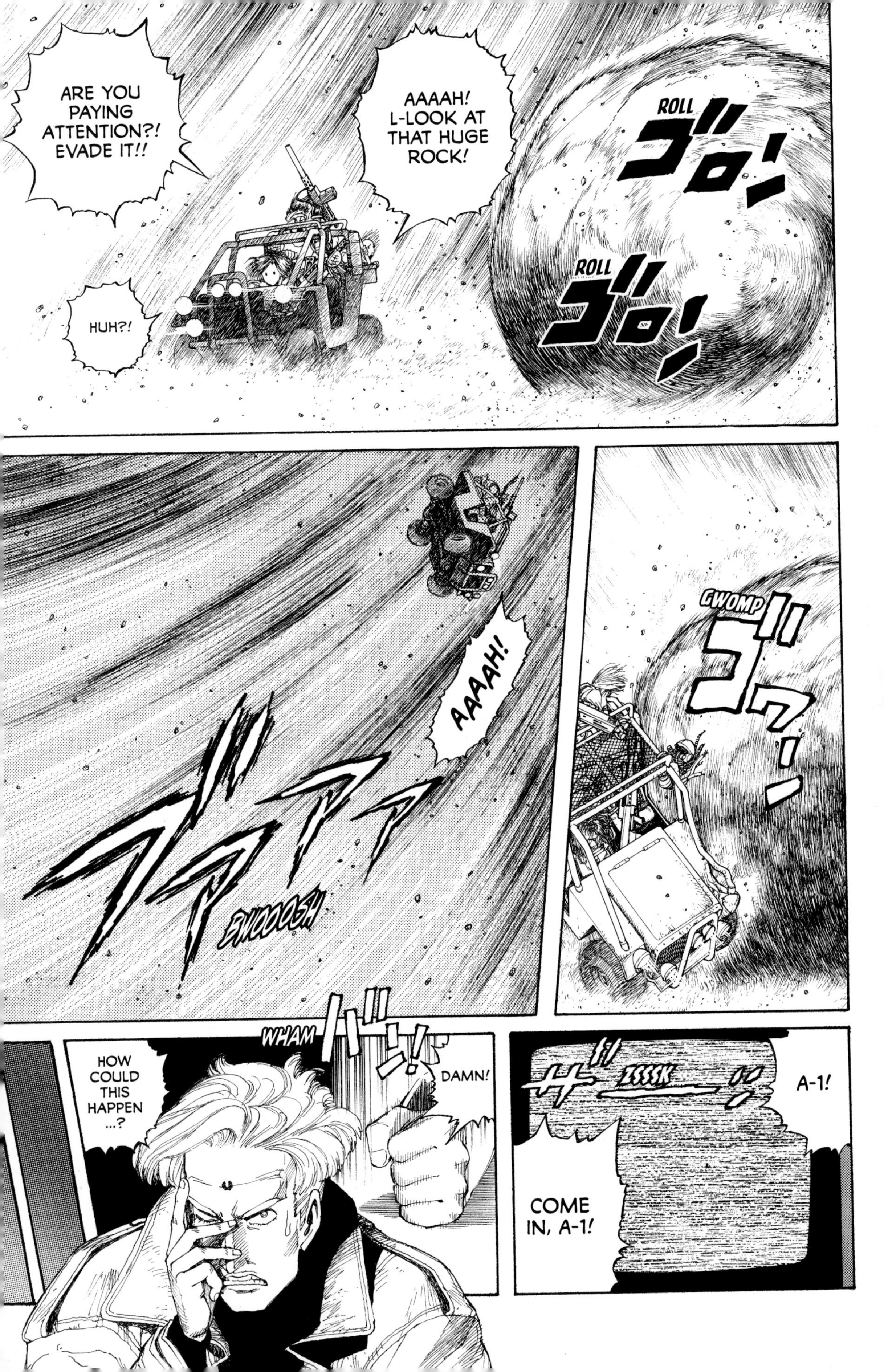
ROLL
AAAAH! L-LOOK AT THAT HUGE ROCK!
ARE YOU PAYING ATTENTION?! EVADE IT!!
ROLL
HUH?!
GWOMP
AAAAH!
SWOOOSH
ZSSSK
A-1!
COME IN, A-1!
WHAM
DAMN!
HOW COULD THIS HAPPEN ...?

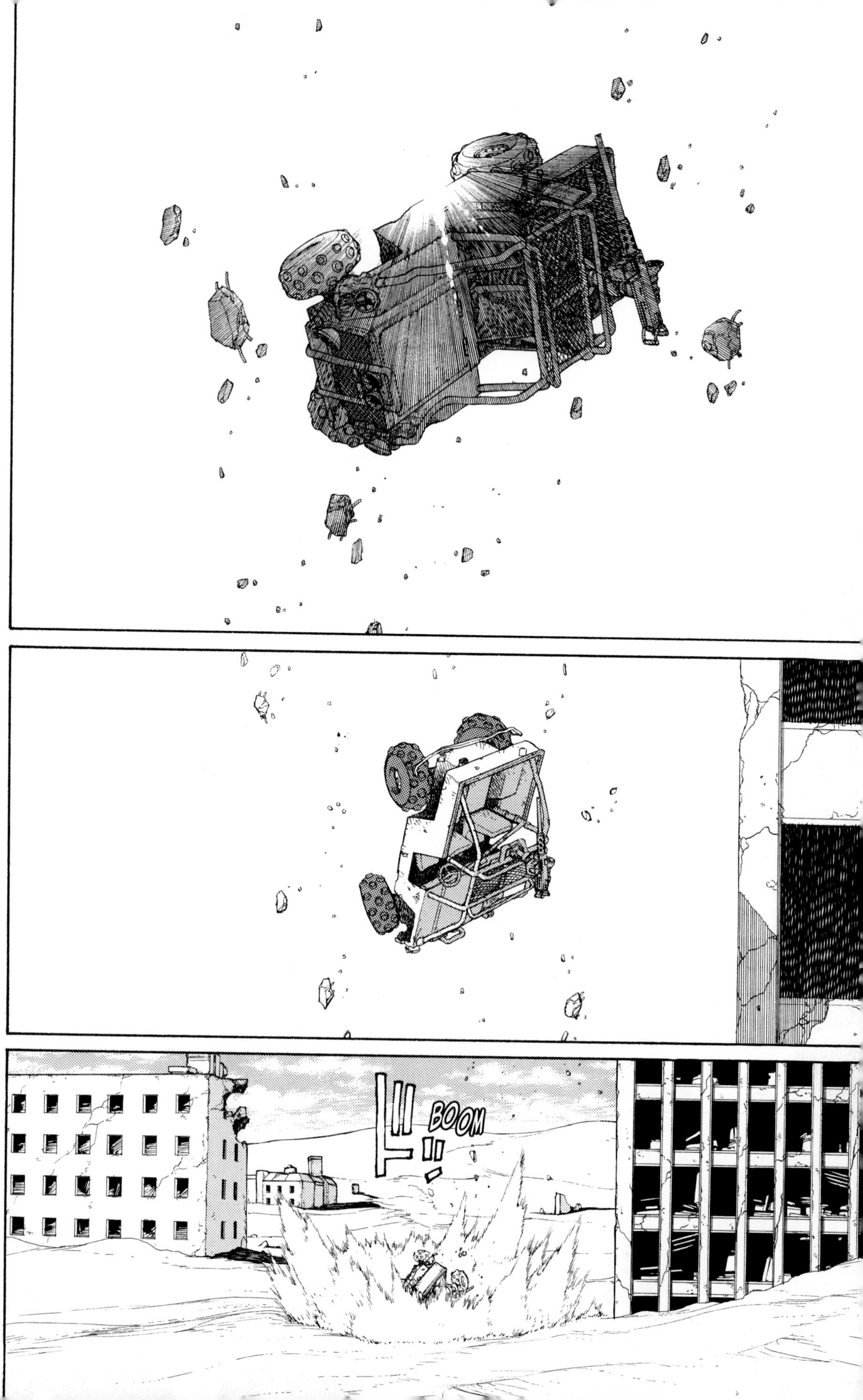
BOOM

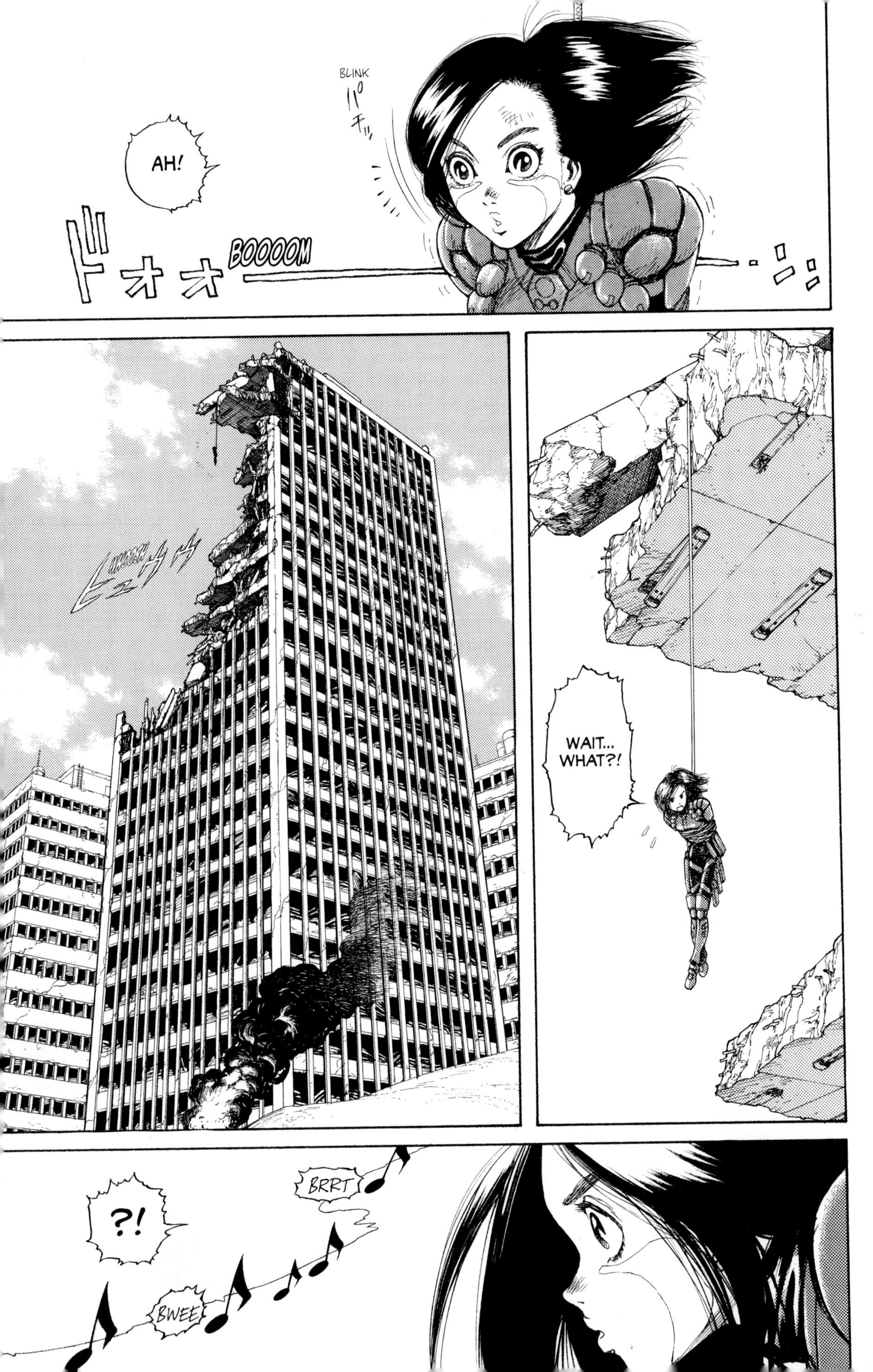
BLINK
パチッ
AH!
ドオオ
BOOOOM
WAIT... WHAT?!
WHOOSH
BRRT
?!
BWEE

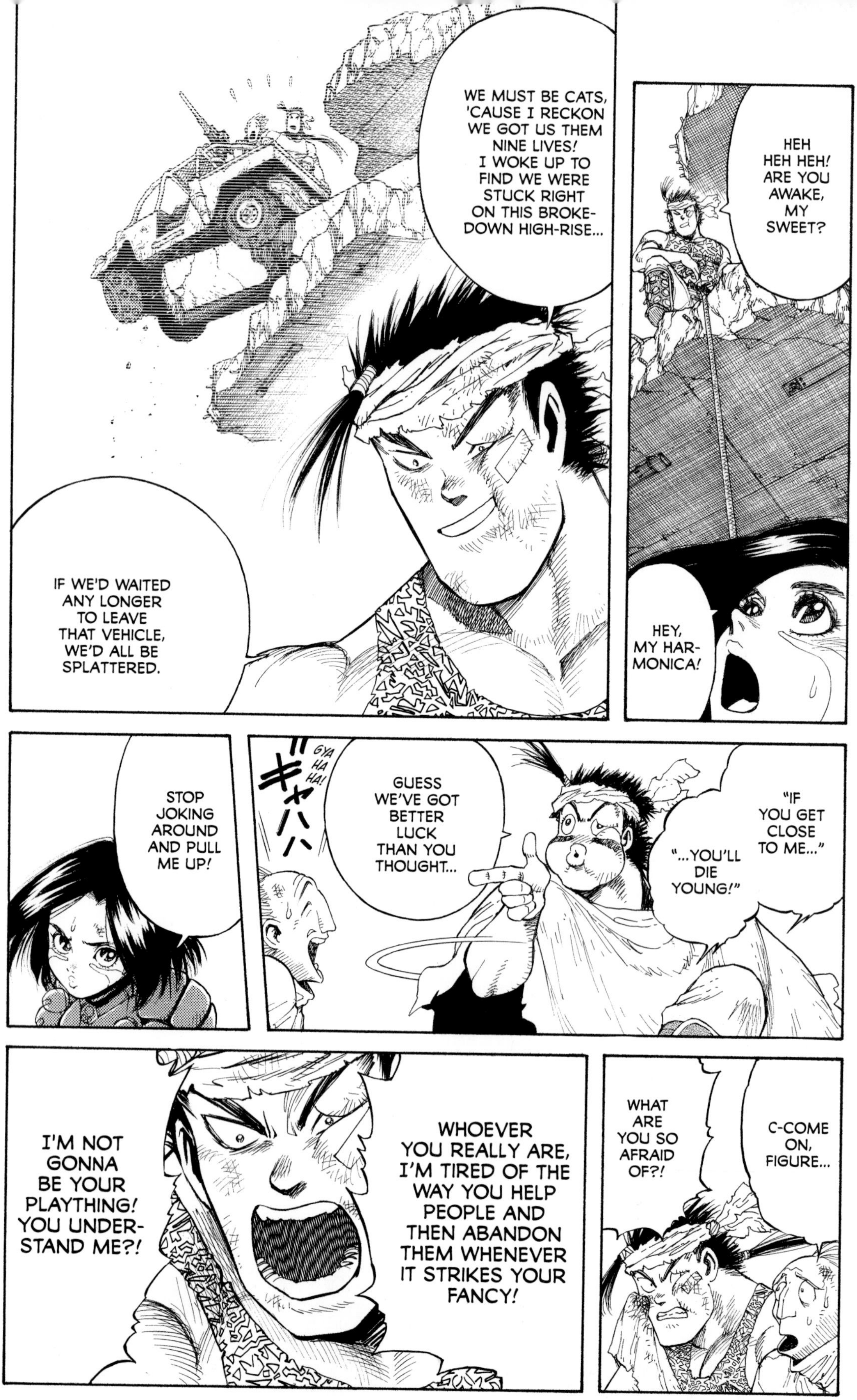
HEH HEH HEH! ARE YOU AWAKE, MY SWEET?
HEY, MY HAR-MONICA!
WE MUST BE CATS, 'CAUSE I RECKON WE GOT US THEM NINE LIVES! I WOKE UP TO FIND WE WERE STUCK RIGHT ON THIS BROKE-DOWN HIGH-RISE...
IF WE'D WAITED ANY LONGER TO LEAVE THAT VEHICLE, WE'D ALL BE SPLATTERED.
"IF YOU GET CLOSE TO ME..."
"...YOU'LL DIE YOUNG!"
GUESS WE'VE GOT BETTER LUCK THAN YOU THOUGHT...
GYA HA HA!
STOP JOKING AROUND AND PULL ME UP!
C-COME ON, FIGURE...
WHAT ARE YOU SO AFRAID OF?!
WHOEVER YOU REALLY ARE, I'M TIRED OF THE WAY YOU HELP PEOPLE AND THEN ABANDON THEM WHENEVER IT STRIKES YOUR FANCY!
I'M NOT GONNA BE YOUR PLAYTHING! YOU UNDER-STAND ME?!

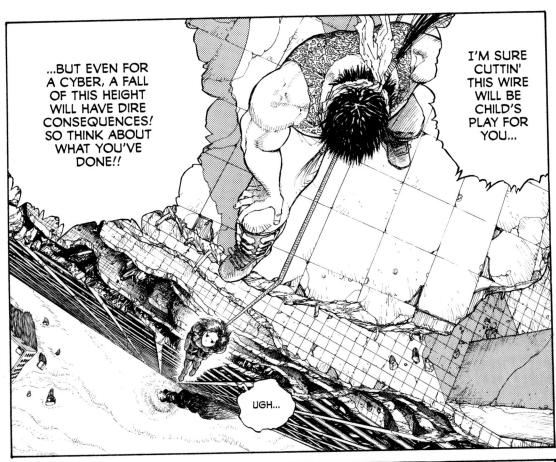

I'M SURE CUTTIN' THIS WIRE WILL BE CHILD'S PLAY FOR YOU...
...BUT EVEN FOR A CYBER, A FALL OF THIS HEIGHT WILL HAVE DIRE CONSEQUENCES! SO THINK ABOUT WHAT YOU'VE DONE!!
UGH...
UNGRATEFUL PUNK... HE HAS NO IDEA WHAT I JUST DID FOR HIM!
CONTROL! COME IN, CONTROL!
DAMN, NO SIGNAL...
HEY! IS ***KNUCKLEHEAD***, THE LEADER OF THOSE BANDITS, STILL INTACT?!
HMM? NOW THAT YOU MENTION IT...
H-HE WASN'T IN THE CAR.
TOO BAD! LOOKS LIKE HIS BRAIN MUST HAVE FALLEN OUT AT SOME POINT!

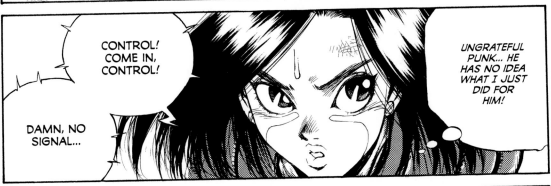

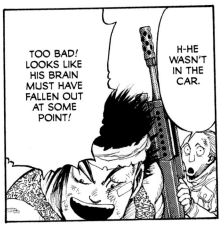

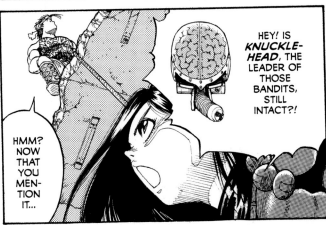

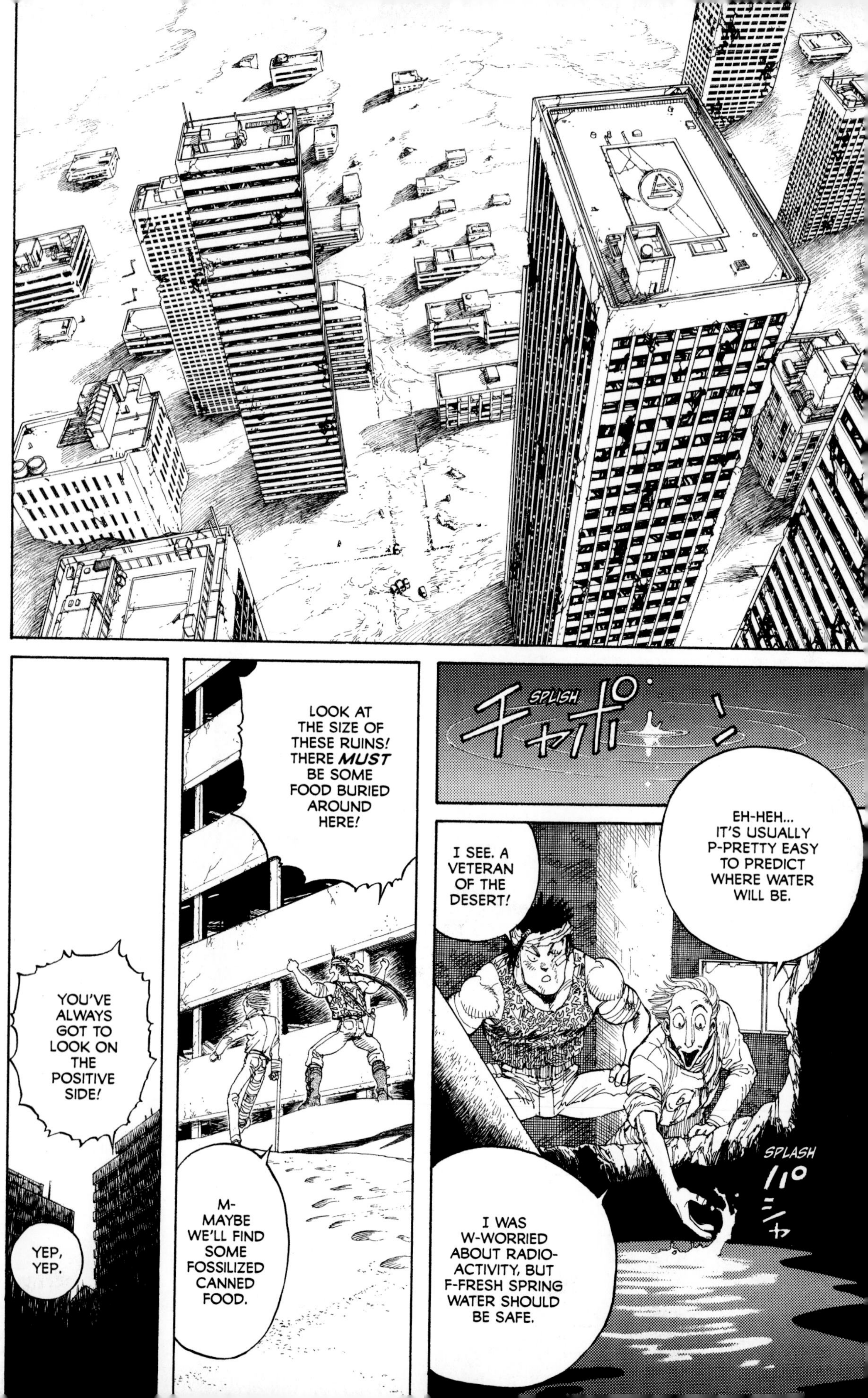
SPLISH
チャポン
EH-HEH... IT'S USUALLY P-PRETTY EASY TO PREDICT WHERE WATER WILL BE.
I SEE. A VETERAN OF THE DESERT!
SPLASH
パシャ
I WAS W-WORRIED ABOUT RADIO-ACTIVITY, BUT F-FRESH SPRING WATER SHOULD BE SAFE.
LOOK AT THE SIZE OF THESE RUINS! THERE MUST BE SOME FOOD BURIED AROUND HERE!
M-MAYBE WE'LL FIND SOME FOSSILIZED CANNED FOOD.
YOU'VE ALWAYS GOT TO LOOK ON THE POSITIVE SIDE!
YEP, YEP.

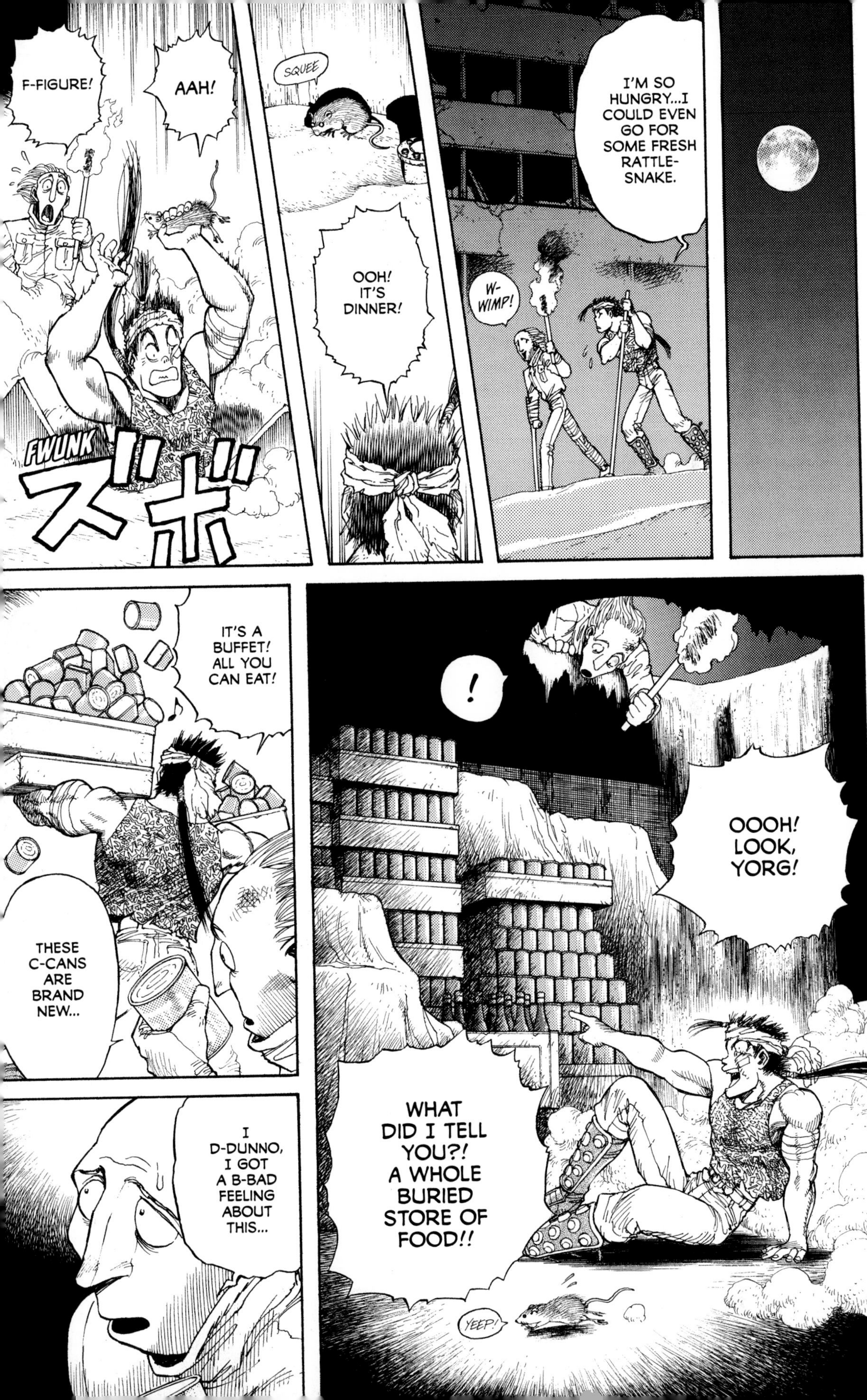
I'M SO HUNGRY...I COULD EVEN GO FOR SOME FRESH RATTLE-SNAKE.
W-WIMP!
SQUEE
OOH! IT'S DINNER!
AAH!
F-FIGURE!
FWUNK
ズボ
!
OOOH! LOOK, YORG!
WHAT DID I TELL YOU?! A WHOLE BURIED STORE OF FOOD!!
YEEP!
IT'S A BUFFET! ALL YOU CAN EAT!
THESE C-CANS ARE BRAND NEW...
I D-DUNNO, I GOT A B-BAD FEELING ABOUT THIS...

プラン
PLONG

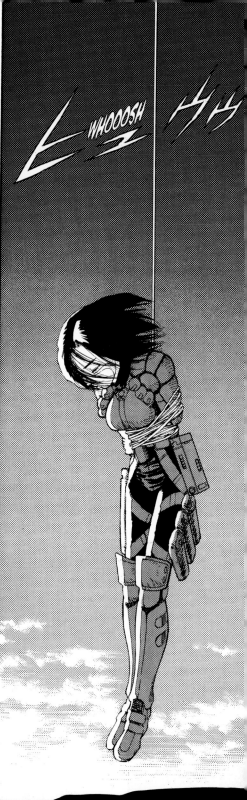

WHOOOSH

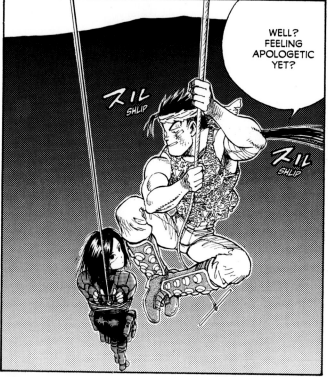

WELL? FEELING APOLOGETIC YET?

ズル
SHLIP

ズル
SHLIP

EVEN A CYBER'S GOTTA GET HUNGRY, RIGHT?

HERE, GOT SOME YUMMY CORNED BEEF FOR YA.

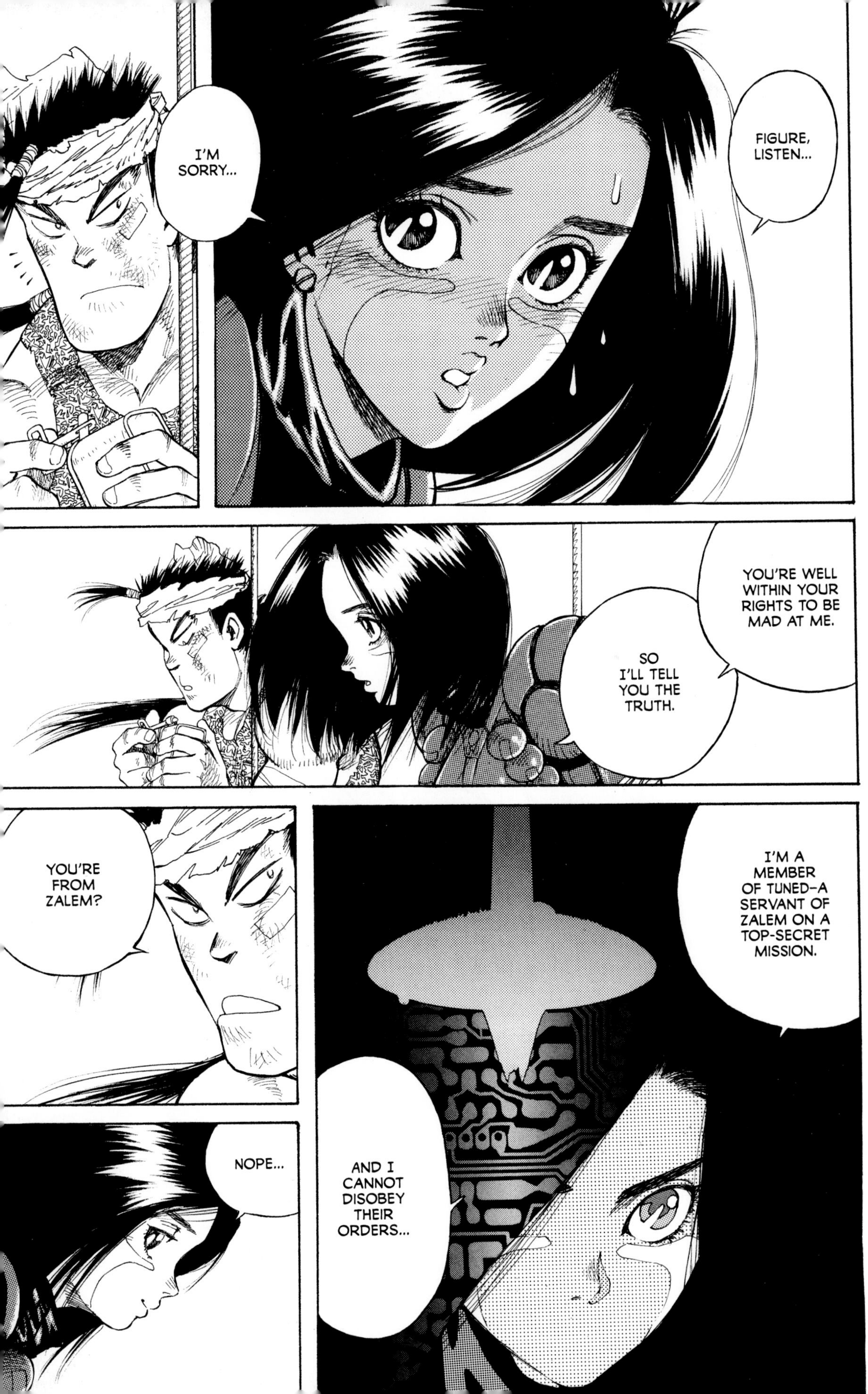
FIGURE, LISTEN...
I'M SORRY...
YOU'RE WELL WITHIN YOUR RIGHTS TO BE MAD AT ME.
SO I'LL TELL YOU THE TRUTH.
I'M A MEMBER OF TUNED–A SERVANT OF ZALEM ON A TOP-SECRET MISSION.
AND I CANNOT DISOBEY THEIR ORDERS...
YOU'RE FROM ZALEM?
NOPE...

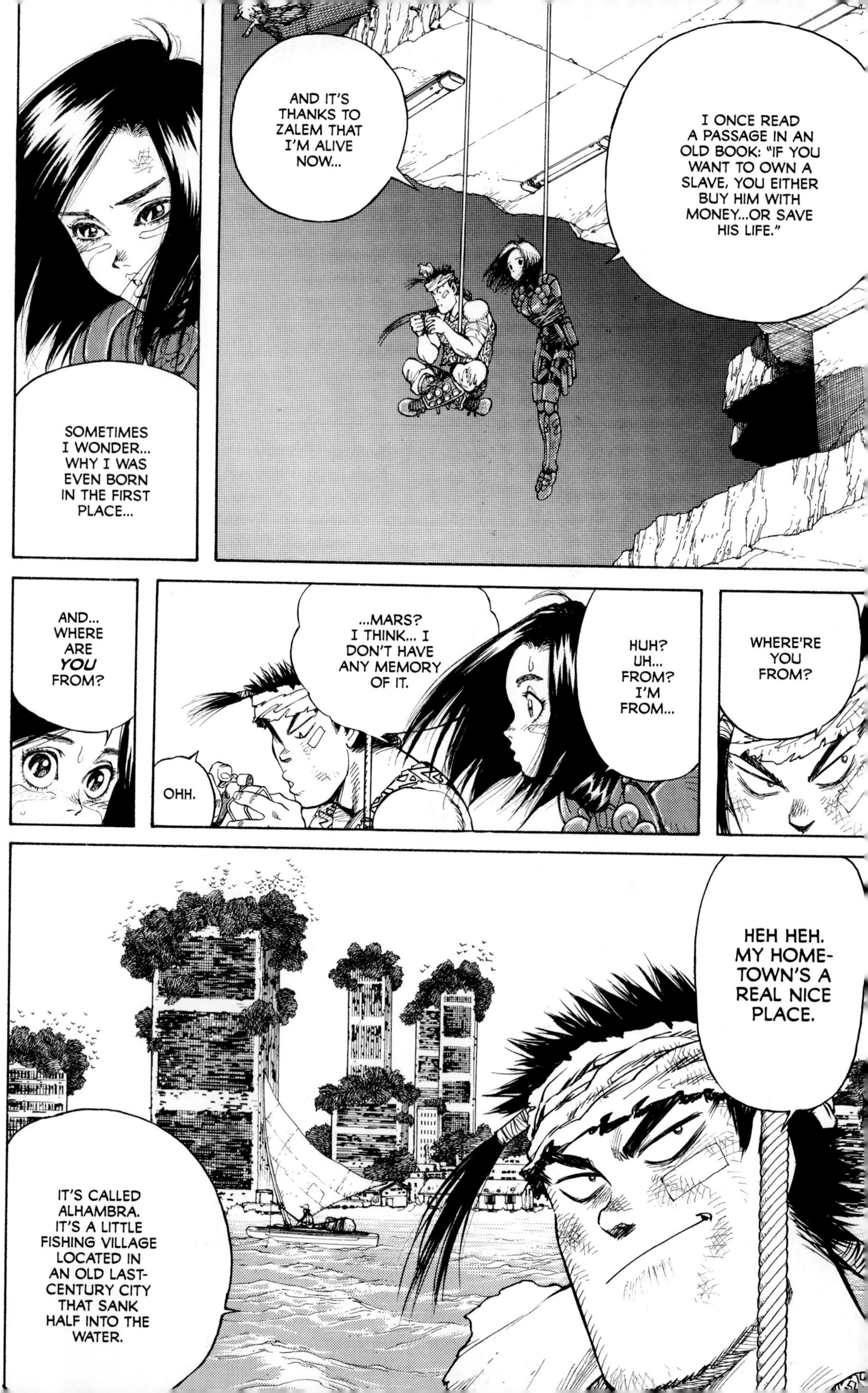
I ONCE READ A PASSAGE IN AN OLD BOOK: "IF YOU WANT TO OWN A SLAVE, YOU EITHER BUY HIM WITH MONEY...OR SAVE HIS LIFE."
AND IT'S THANKS TO ZALEM THAT I'M ALIVE NOW...
SOMETIMES I WONDER... WHY I WAS EVEN BORN IN THE FIRST PLACE...
WHERE'RE YOU FROM?
HUH? UH... FROM? I'M FROM...
...MARS? I THINK... I DON'T HAVE ANY MEMORY OF IT.
OHH.
AND... WHERE ARE *YOU* FROM?
HEH HEH. MY HOME-TOWN'S A REAL NICE PLACE.
IT'S CALLED ALHAMBRA. IT'S A LITTLE FISHING VILLAGE LOCATED IN AN OLD LAST-CENTURY CITY THAT SANK HALF INTO THE WATER.

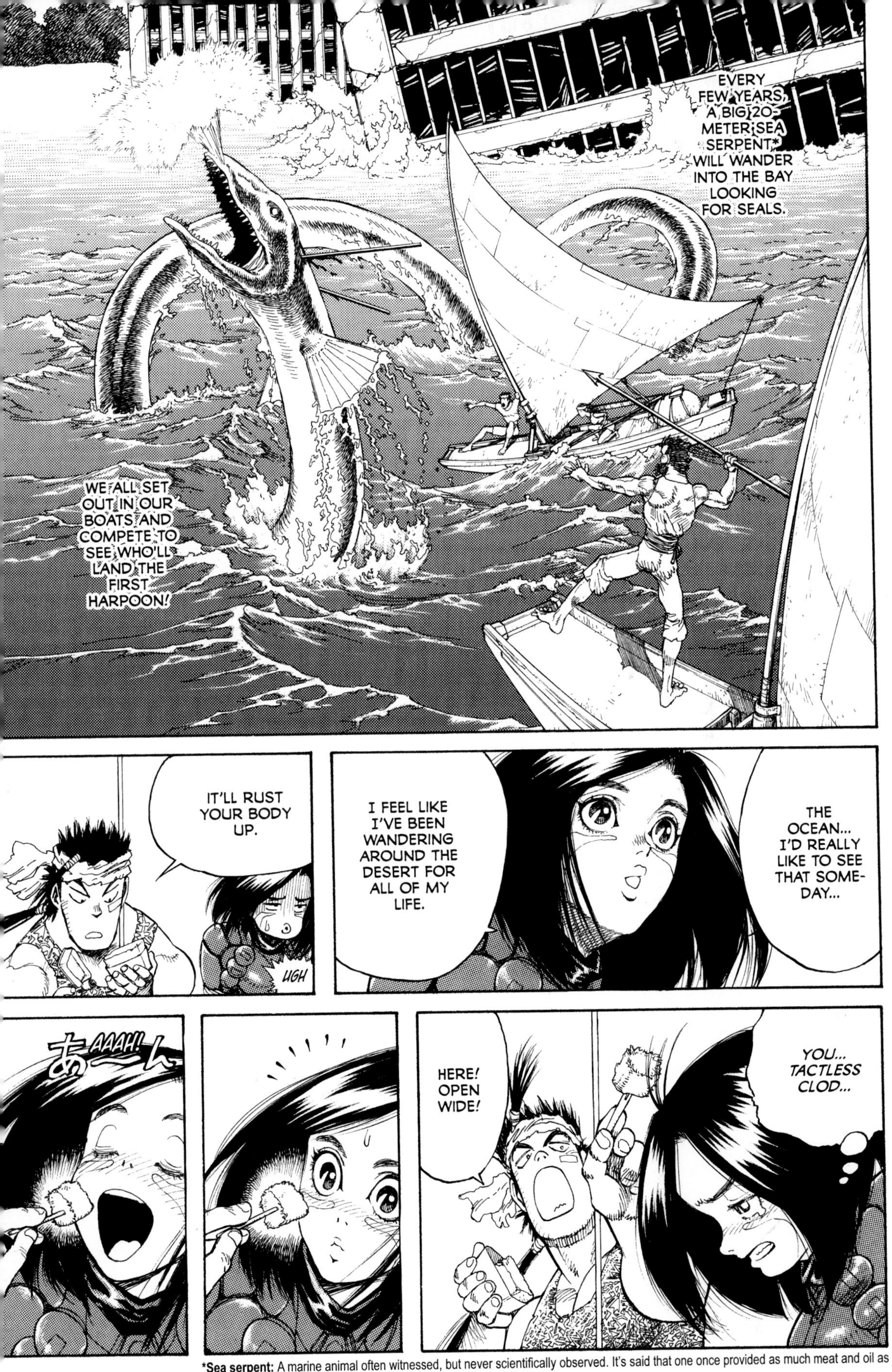
EVERY FEW YEARS, A BIG 20-METER SEA SERPENT* WILL WANDER INTO THE BAY LOOKING FOR SEALS.
WE ALL SET OUT IN OUR BOATS AND COMPETE TO SEE WHO'LL LAND THE FIRST HARPOON!
THE OCEAN... I'D REALLY LIKE TO SEE THAT SOMEDAY...
I FEEL LIKE I'VE BEEN WANDERING AROUND THE DESERT FOR ALL OF MY LIFE.
IT'LL RUST YOUR BODY UP.
UGH
YOU... TACTLESS CLOD...
HERE! OPEN WIDE!
AAAH!
あ〜ん

***Sea serpent:** A marine animal often witnessed, but never scientifically observed. It's said that one once provided as much meat and oil as an entire whale.

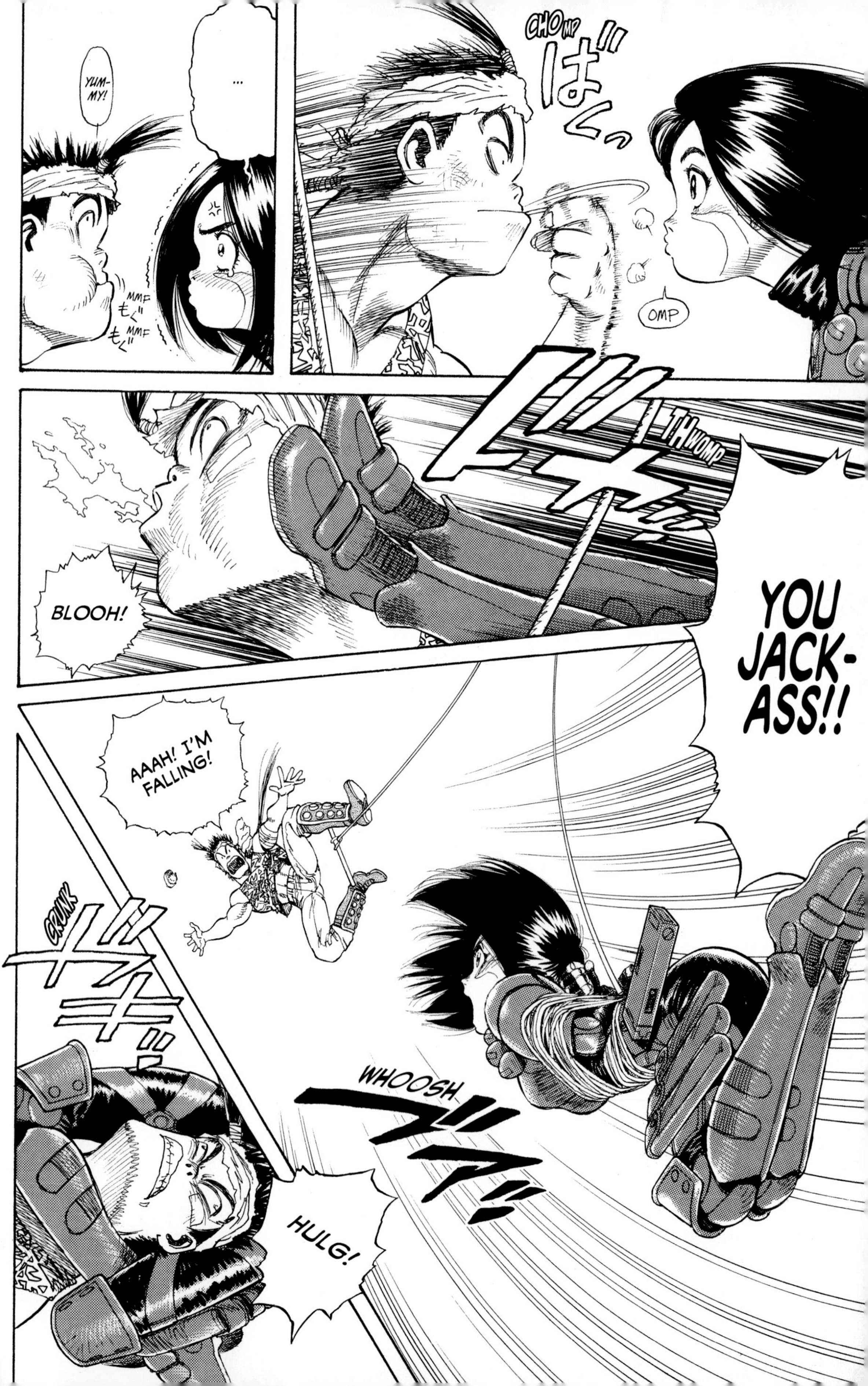
CHOMP
ばくっ
OMP
YUMMY!
...
MMF もぐ
MMF もぐ
THWOMP
BLOOH!
YOU JACKASS!!
AAAH! I'M FALLING!
CRUNK
WHOOSH
HULG!

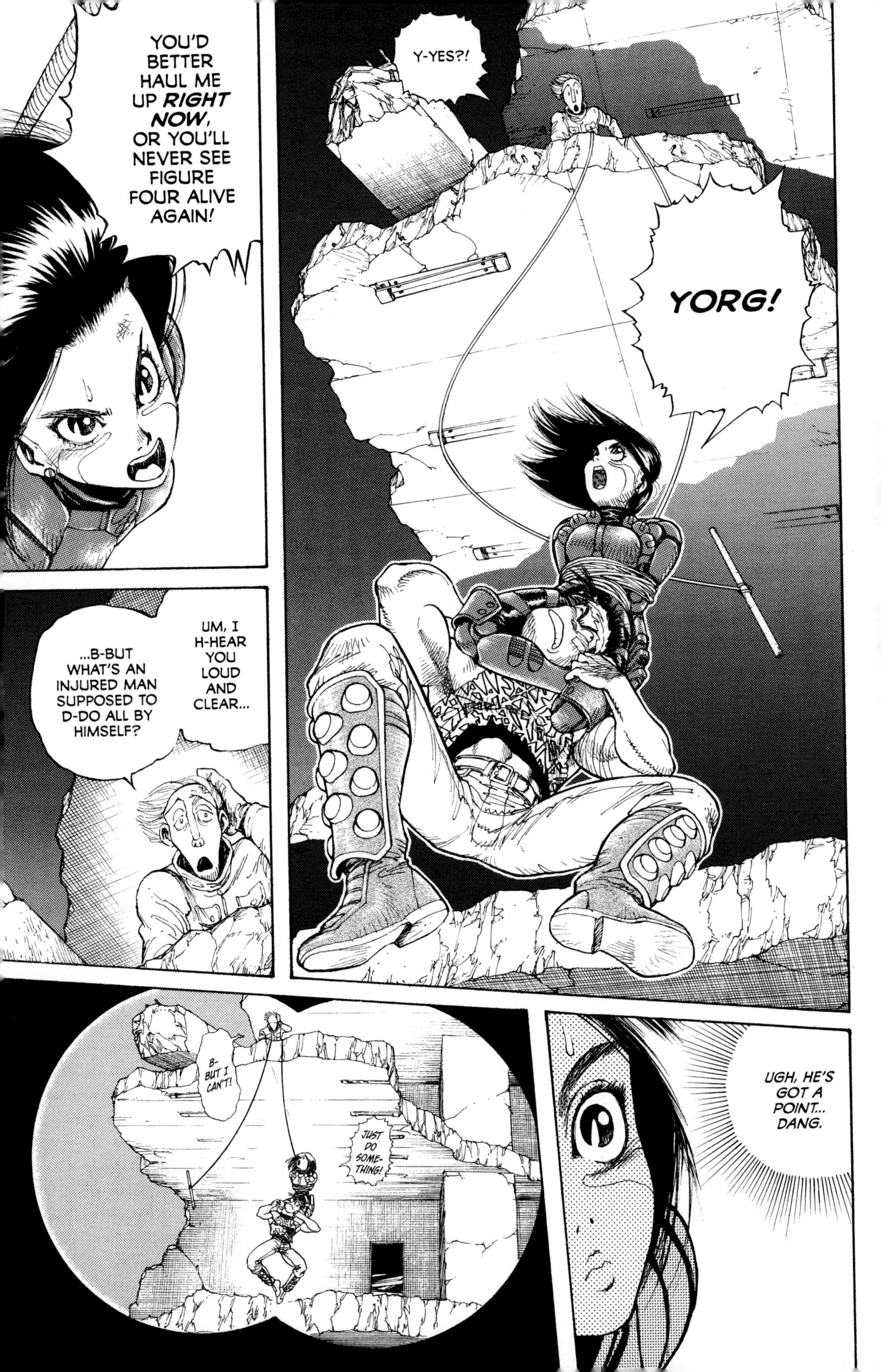
YORG!
Y-YES?!
YOU'D BETTER HAUL ME UP RIGHT NOW, OR YOU'LL NEVER SEE FIGURE FOUR ALIVE AGAIN!
UM, I H-HEAR YOU LOUD AND CLEAR...
...B-BUT WHAT'S AN INJURED MAN SUPPOSED TO D-DO ALL BY HIMSELF?
UGH, HE'S GOT A POINT... DANG.
B-BUT I CAN'T!
JUST DO SOME-THING!

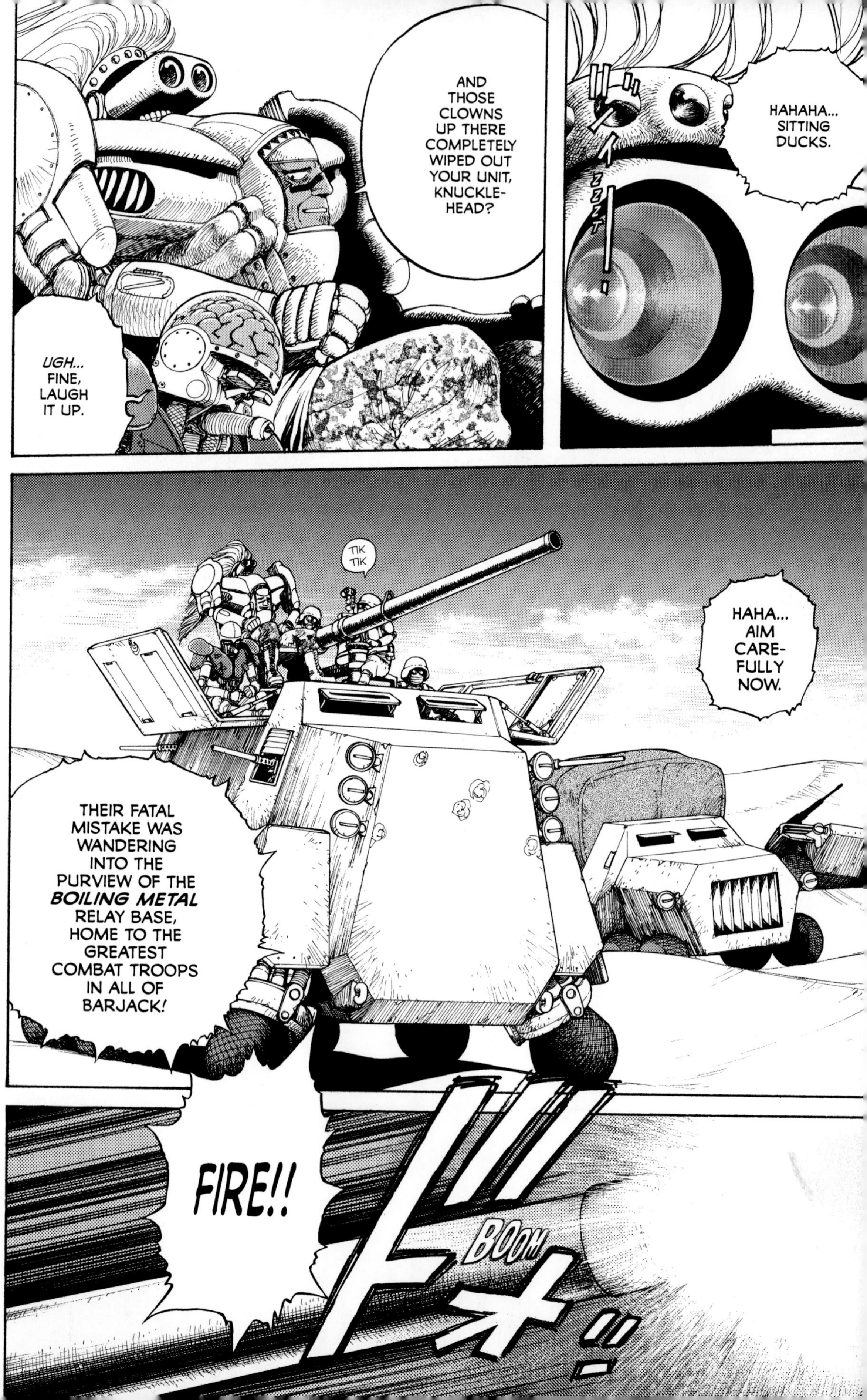
ZZZT
HAHAHA... SITTING DUCKS.
AND THOSE CLOWNS UP THERE COMPLETELY WIPED OUT YOUR UNIT, KNUCKLE-HEAD?
UGH... FINE, LAUGH IT UP.
HAHA... AIM CARE-FULLY NOW.
TIK TIK
THEIR FATAL MISTAKE WAS WANDERING INTO THE PURVIEW OF THE ***BOILING METAL*** RELAY BASE, HOME TO THE GREATEST COMBAT TROOPS IN ALL OF BARJACK!
BOOM
FIRE!!

FIGHT_033 Dog Eat Dog

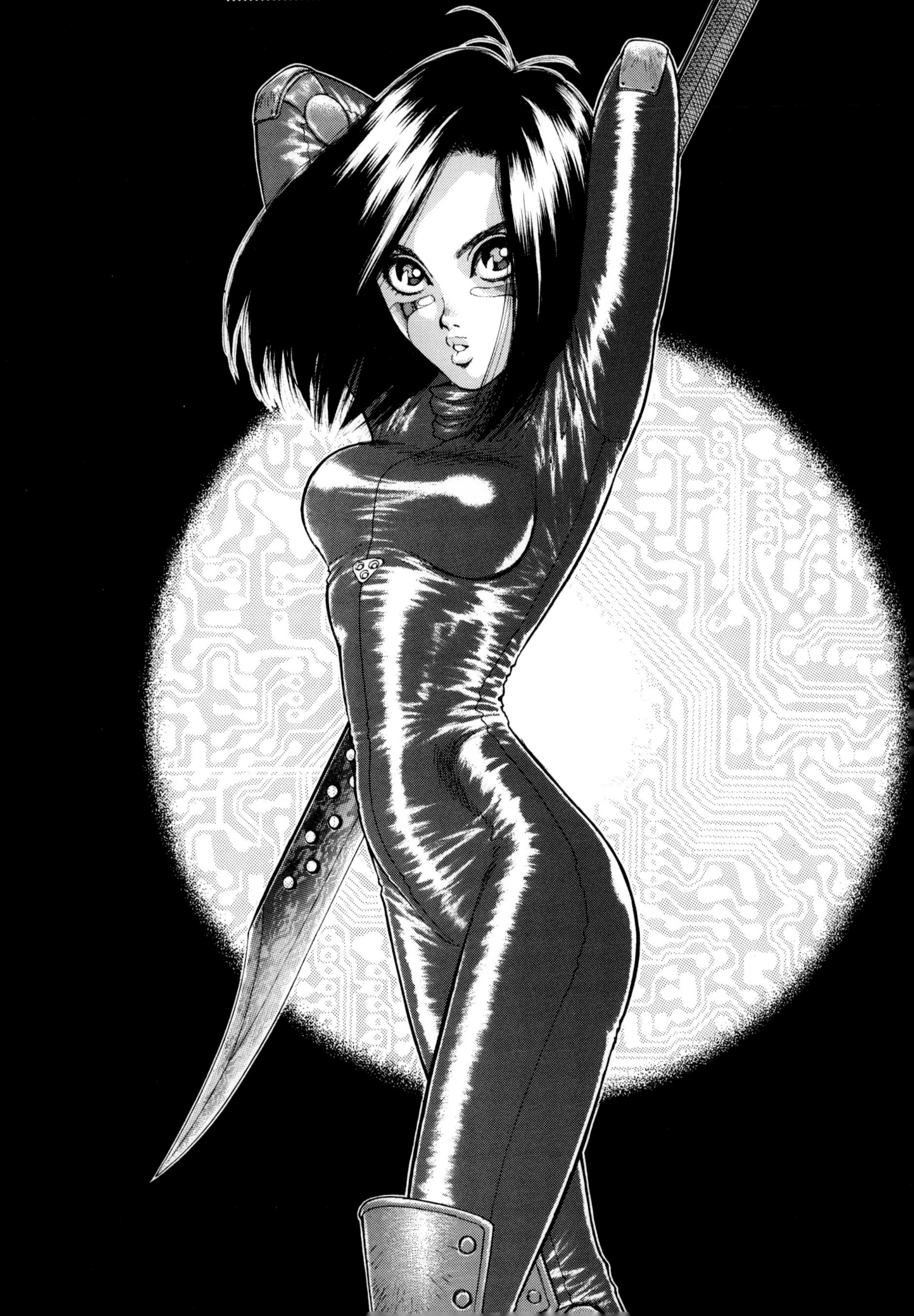

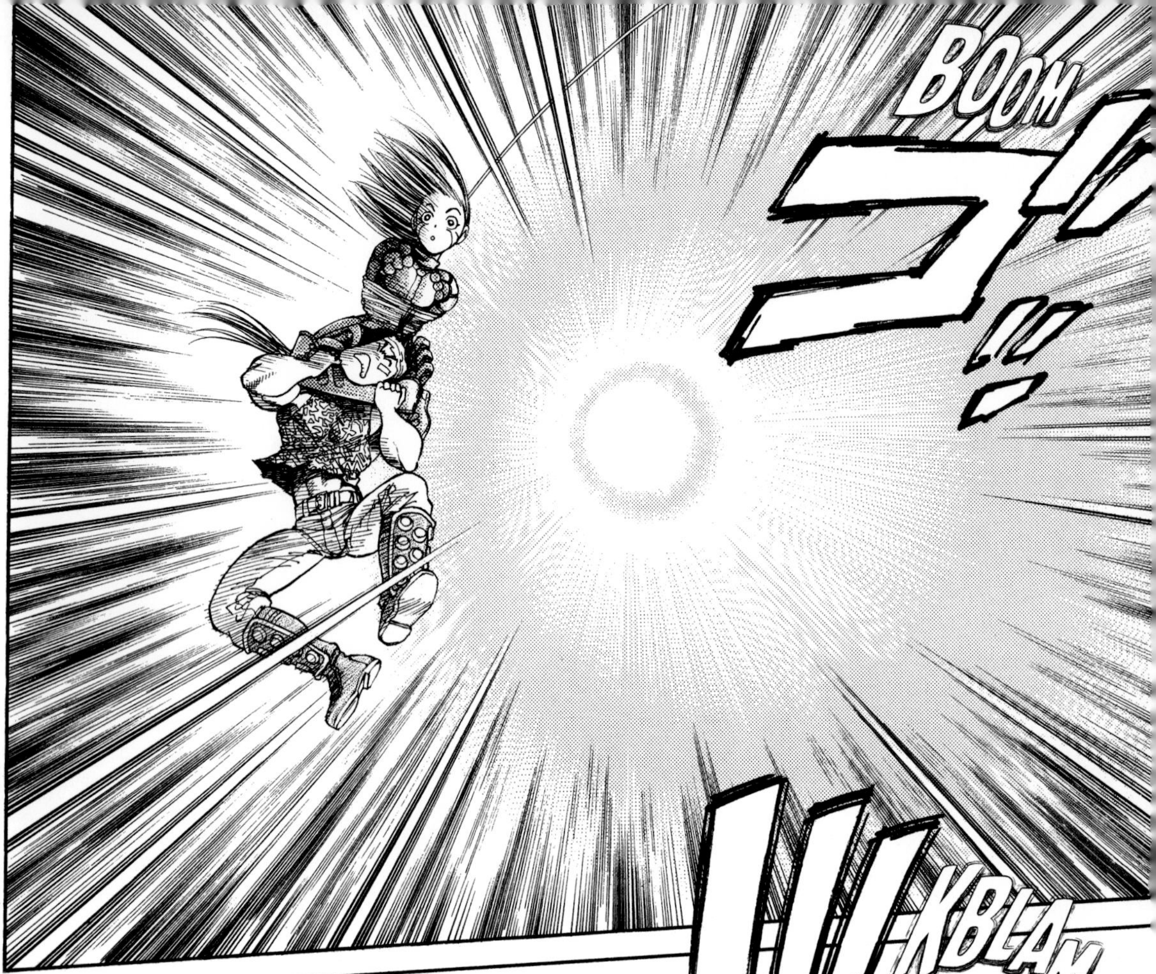
BOOM

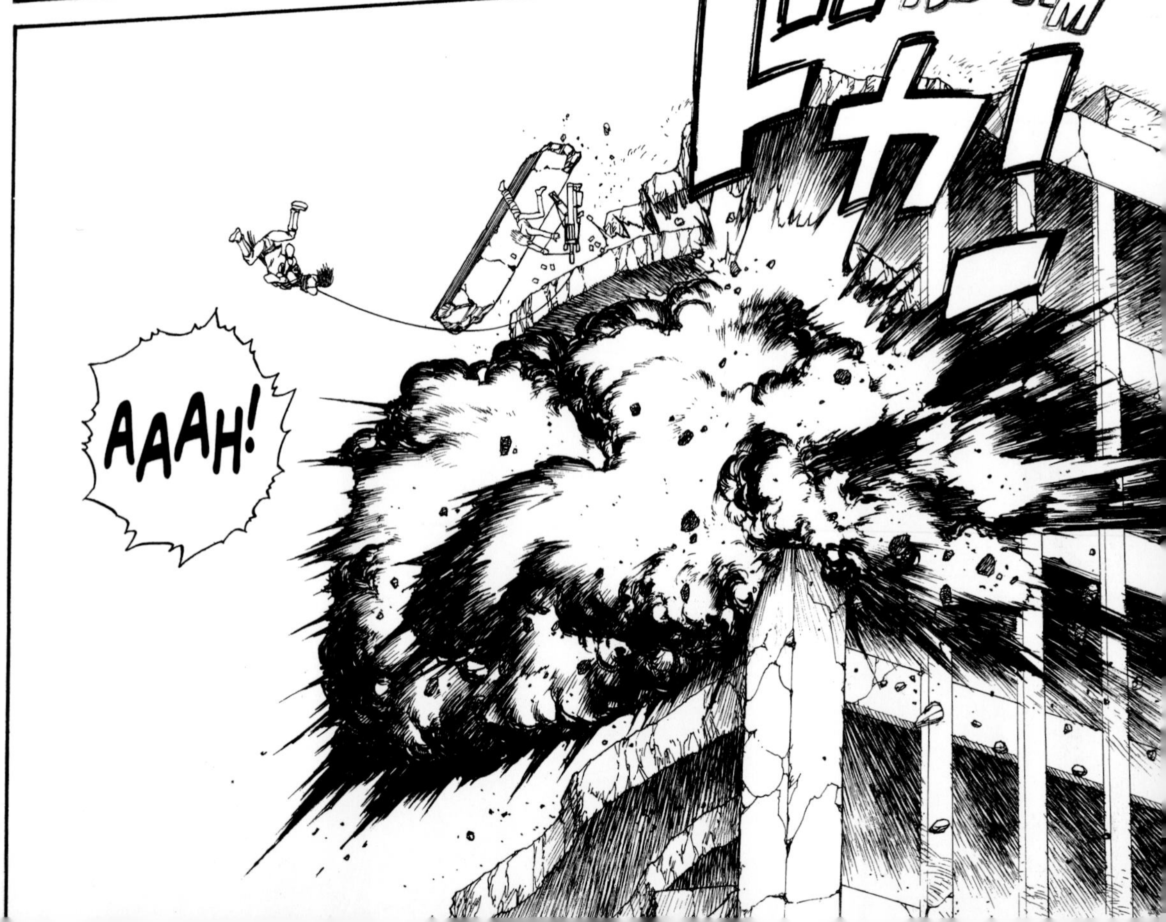
KBLAM
AAAH!

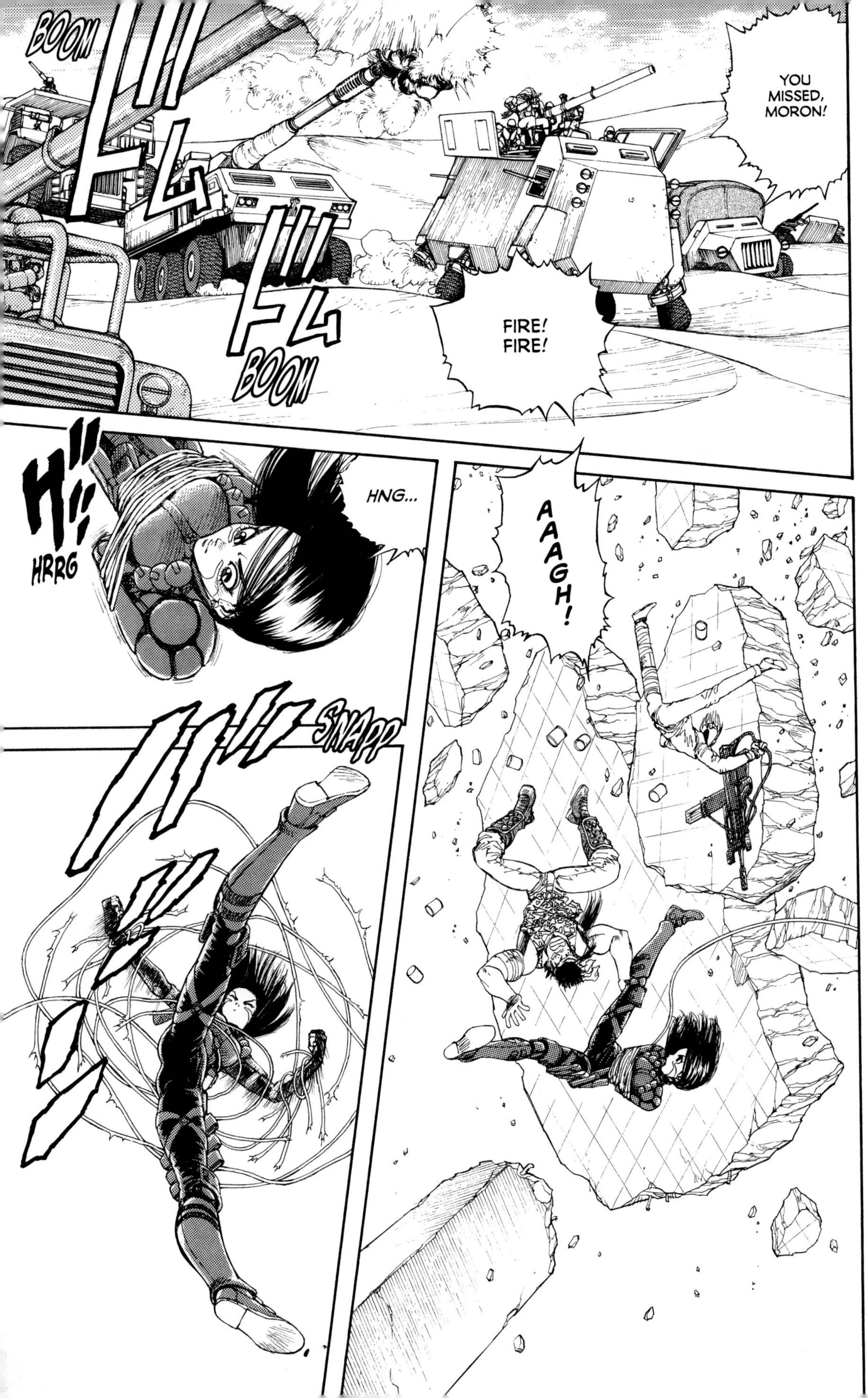
YOU MISSED, MORON!
BOOM
FIRE! FIRE!
BOOM
AAAAGH!
HNG...
HRRG
SNAPP

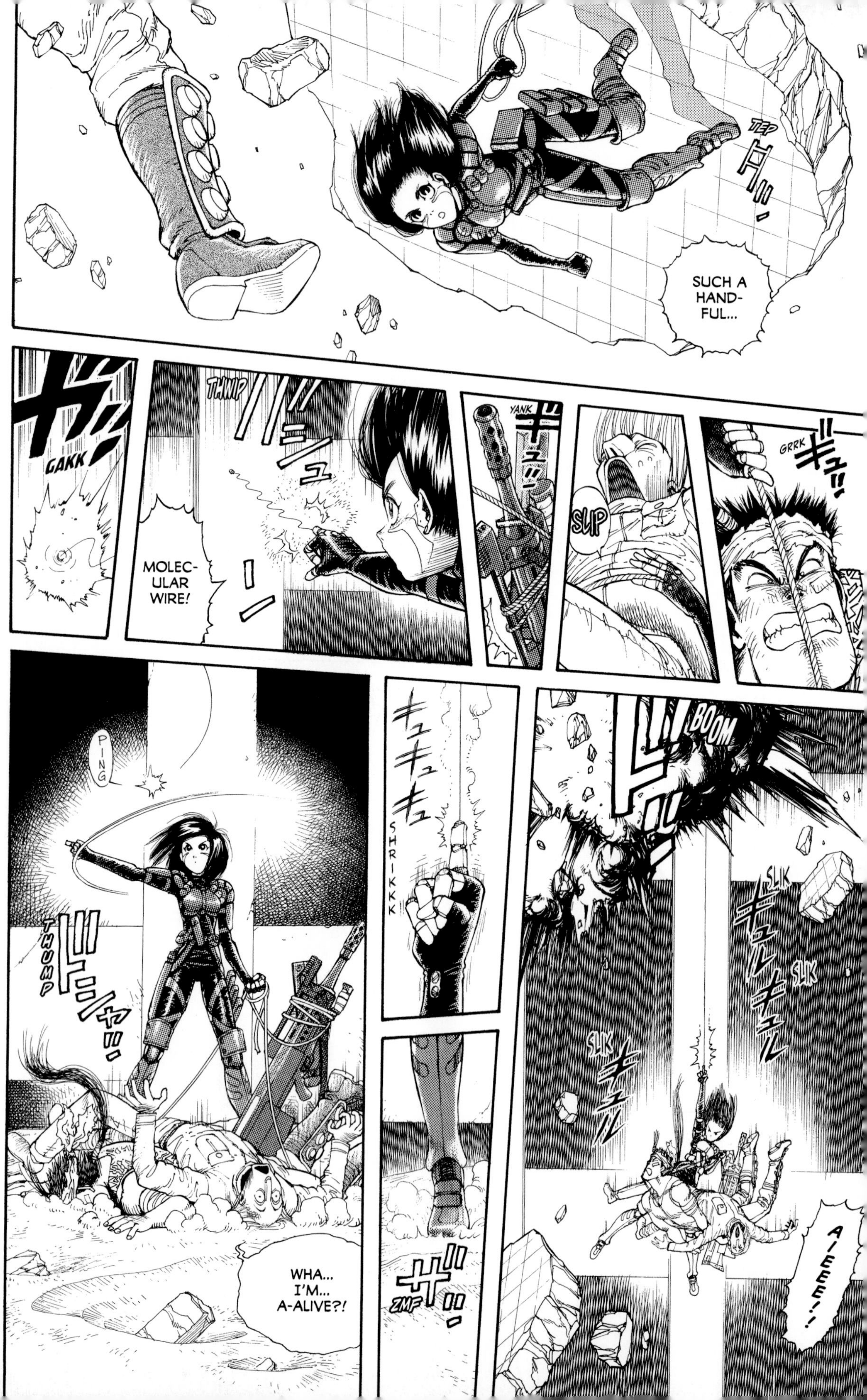
TEP
SUCH A HANDFUL...
GRRK
SLIP
YANK
THWIP
MOLECULAR WIRE!
GAKK
BOOM
SLIK
SLIK
SLIK
AIEEEE!!
SHRIKKK
ZMF
PING
THUMP
WHA... I'M... A-ALIVE?!

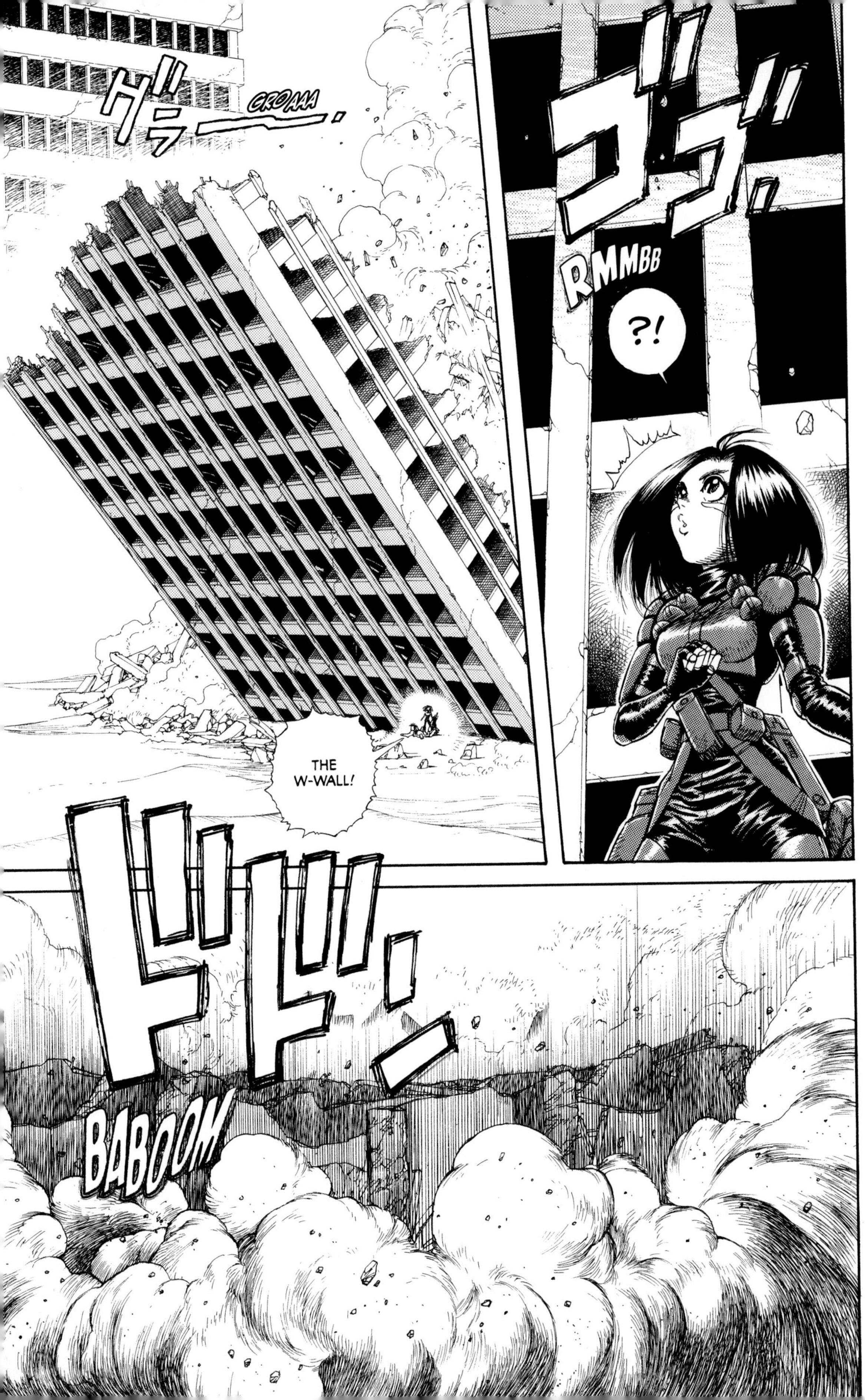
ゴゴ
RMMBB
?!
ガラー
CROAAA
THE W-WALL!
ドドン
BABOOM

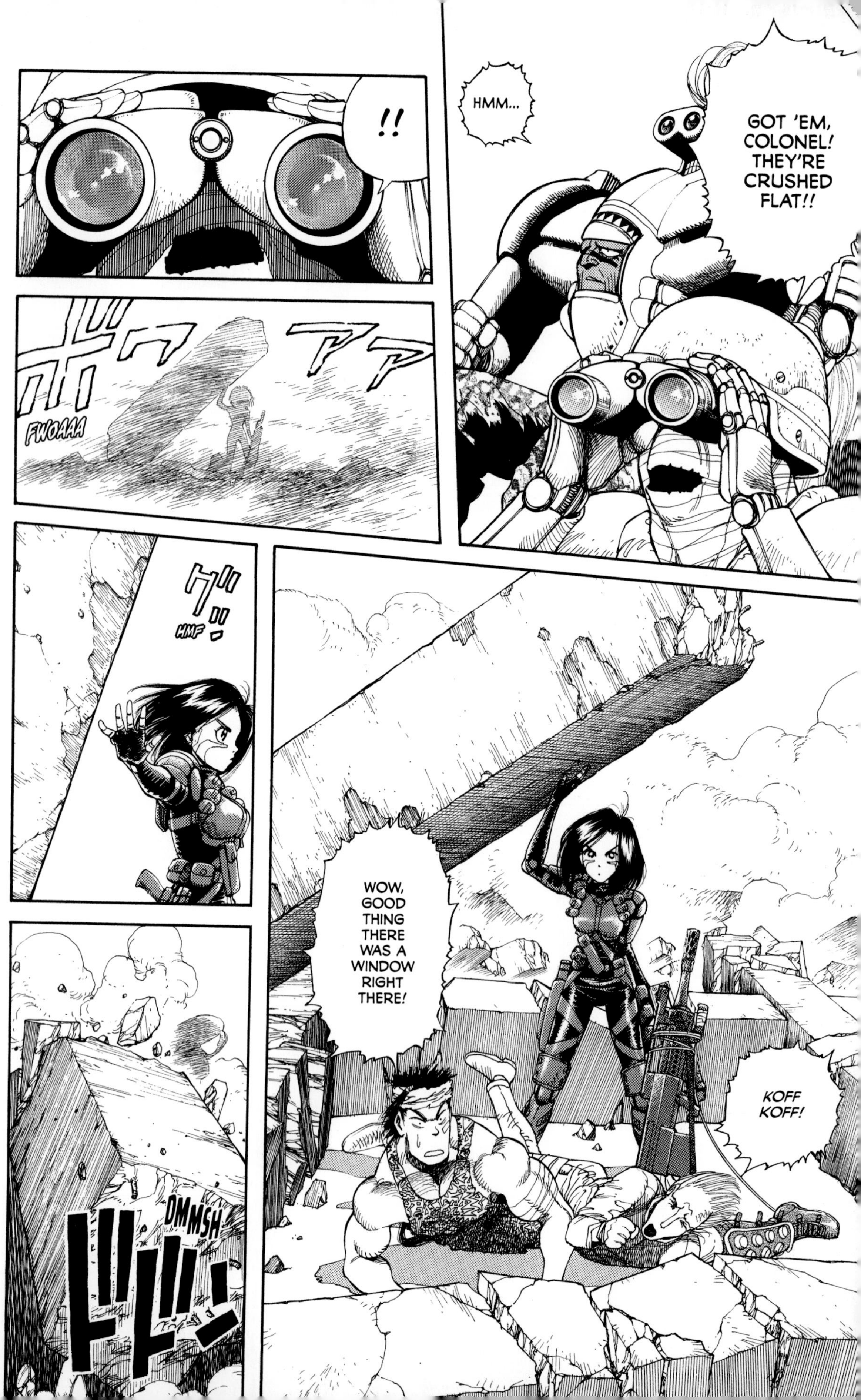
GOT 'EM, COLONEL! THEY'RE CRUSHED FLAT!!
HMM...
!!
ボワアア
FWOAAA
WOW, GOOD THING THERE WAS A WINDOW RIGHT THERE!
KOFF KOFF!
グッ
HMF
DMMSH

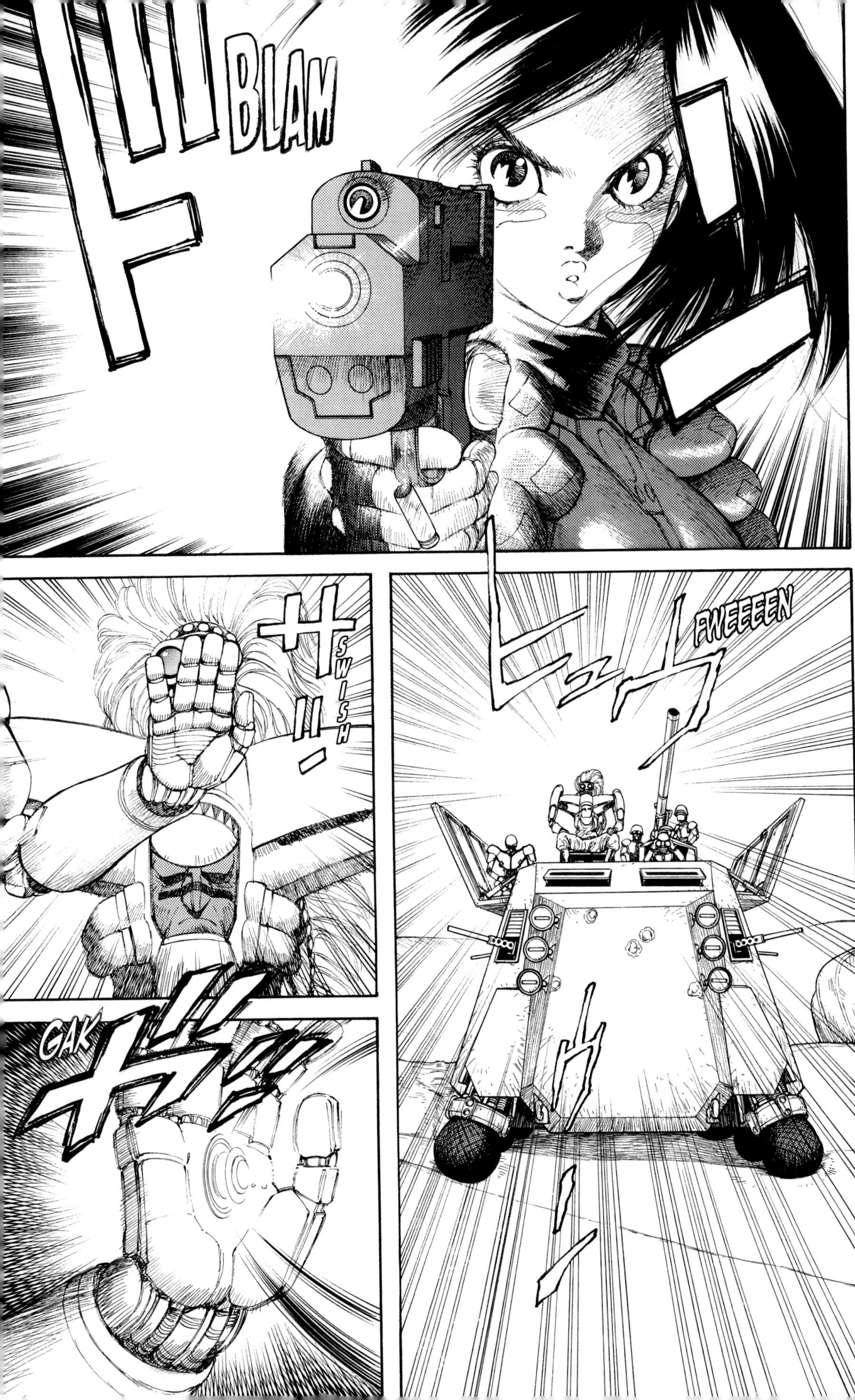
BLAM
FWEEEEN
SWISH
GAK

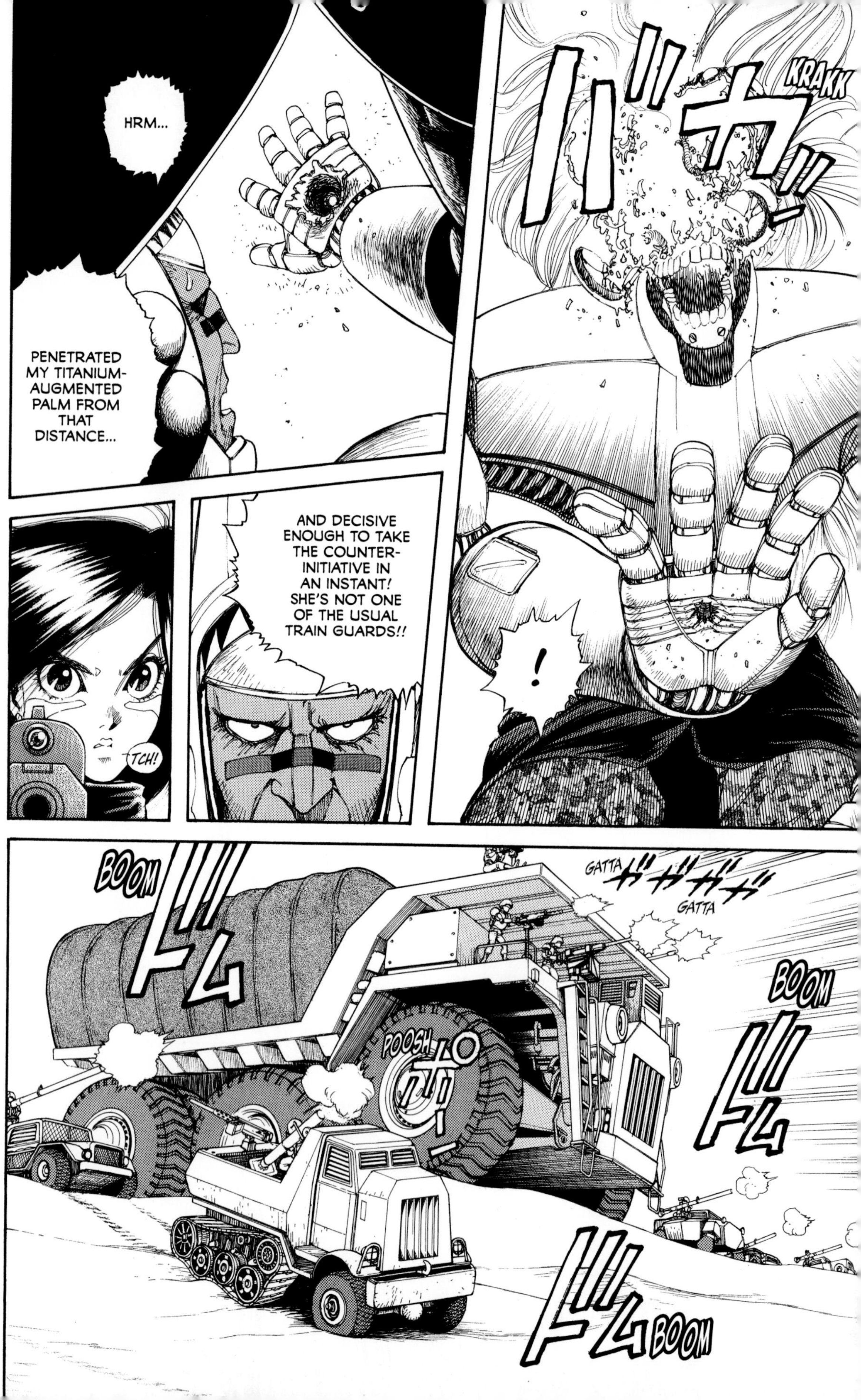
KRAKK
!
HRM...
PENETRATED MY TITANIUM-AUGMENTED PALM FROM THAT DISTANCE...
AND DECISIVE ENOUGH TO TAKE THE COUNTER-INITIATIVE IN AN INSTANT! SHE'S NOT ONE OF THE USUAL TRAIN GUARDS!!
TCH!
GATTA
GATTA
BOOM
BOOM
POOSH
BOOM

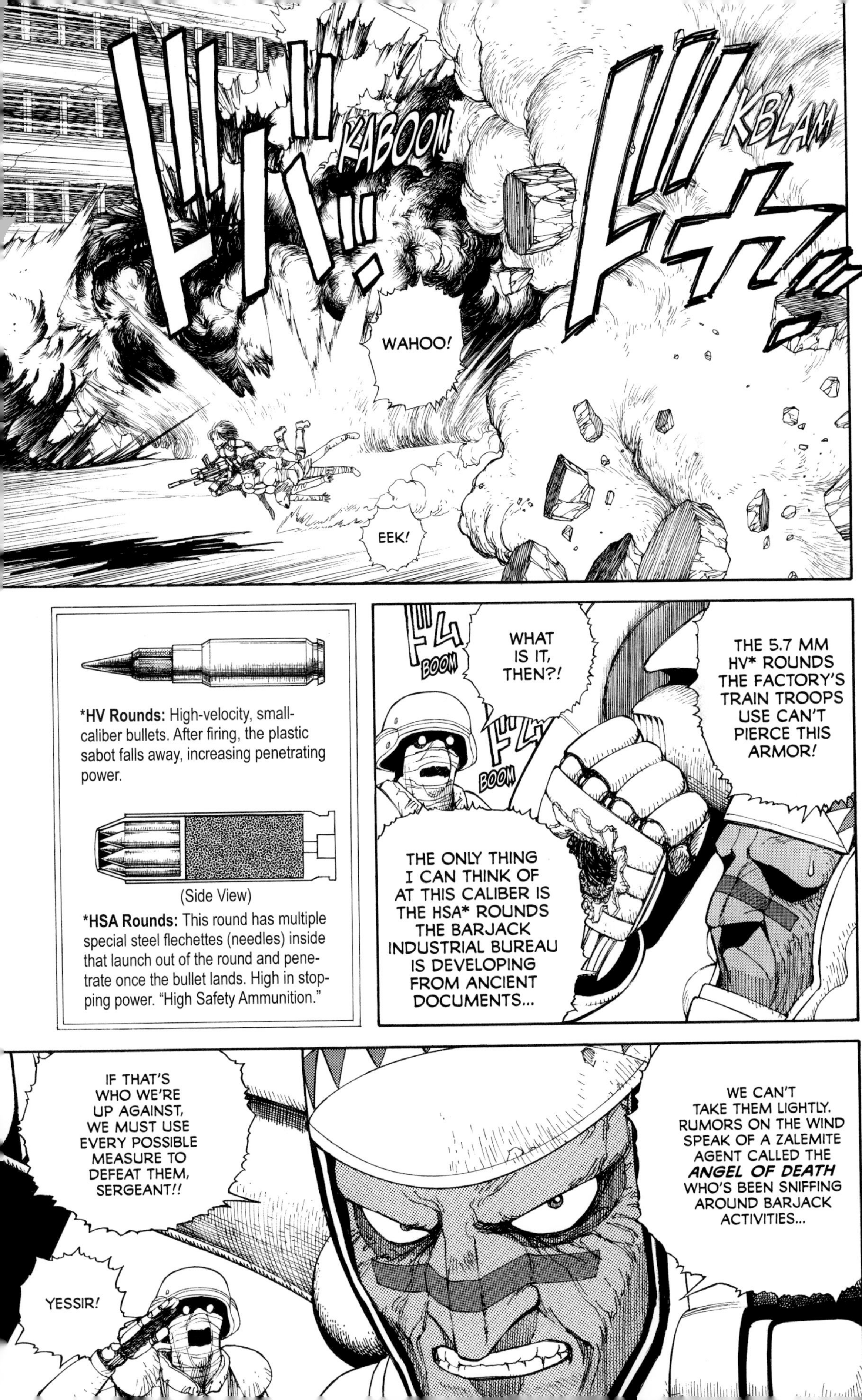
KBLAM
KABOOM
WAHOO!
EEK!
THE 5.7 MM HV* ROUNDS THE FACTORY'S TRAIN TROOPS USE CAN'T PIERCE THIS ARMOR!
WHAT IS IT, THEN?!
BOOM
BOOM
THE ONLY THING I CAN THINK OF AT THIS CALIBER IS THE HSA* ROUNDS THE BARJACK INDUSTRIAL BUREAU IS DEVELOPING FROM ANCIENT DOCUMENTS...
*HV Rounds: High-velocity, small-caliber bullets. After firing, the plastic sabot falls away, increasing penetrating power.
(Side View)
*HSA Rounds: This round has multiple special steel flechettes (needles) inside that launch out of the round and penetrate once the bullet lands. High in stopping power. "High Safety Ammunition."
WE CAN'T TAKE THEM LIGHTLY. RUMORS ON THE WIND SPEAK OF A ZALEMITE AGENT CALLED THE ANGEL OF DEATH WHO'S BEEN SNIFFING AROUND BARJACK ACTIVITIES...
IF THAT'S WHO WE'RE UP AGAINST, WE MUST USE EVERY POSSIBLE MEASURE TO DEFEAT THEM, SERGEANT!!
YESSIR!

YOU'RE UP, CHUMPS!!
I'M HUMAN SCUM!
RAHHH!
MAMA! MAMA!
I CAN'T DO THIS! I CAN'T!
AAAAH...
VWEEE
INJECT ADRENALIZER!
PSSSST
SHHHK
GRIK
ACK
OH!
OH!
ACK
OH!
GWEEEE

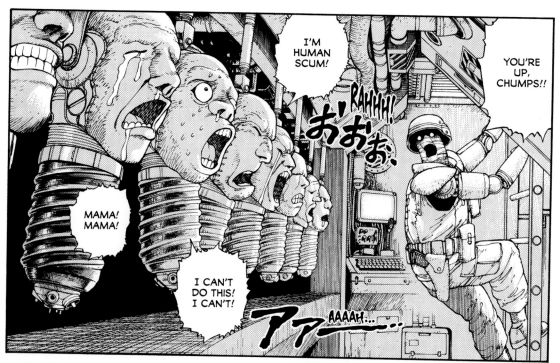

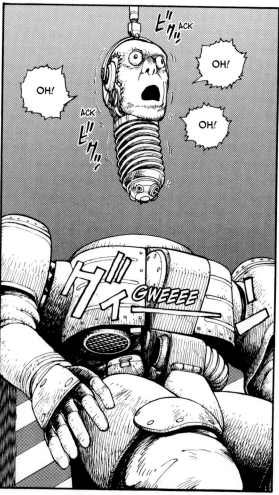

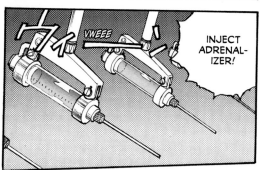

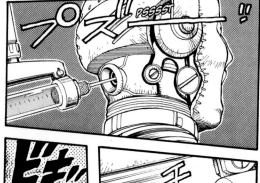

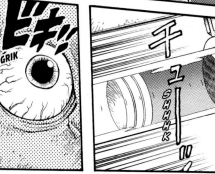

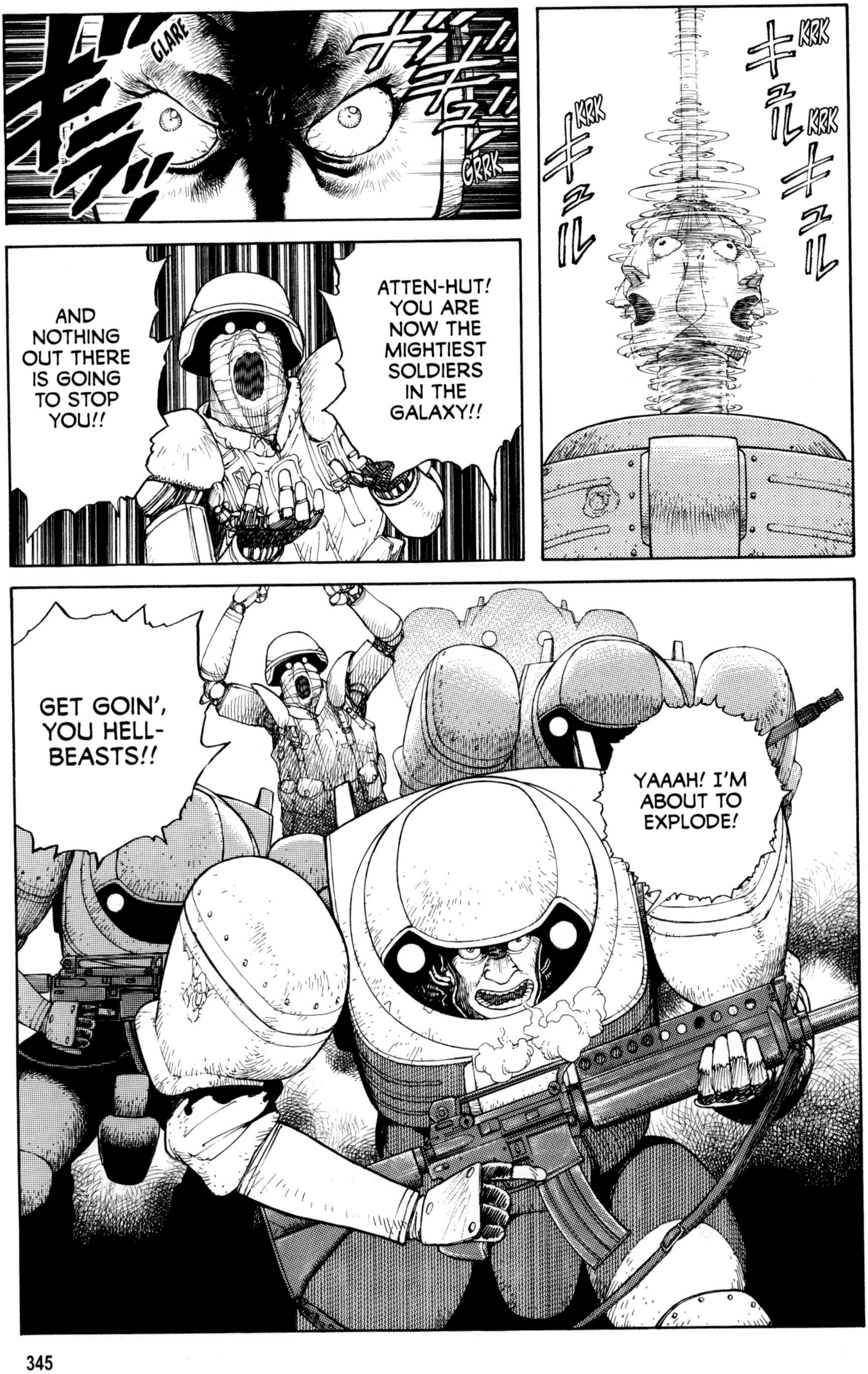
KRK
キュル
KRK
キュル
KRK
キュル
GLARE
GRRK
ATTEN-HUT! YOU ARE NOW THE MIGHTIEST SOLDIERS IN THE GALAXY!!
AND NOTHING OUT THERE IS GOING TO STOP YOU!!
YAAAH! I'M ABOUT TO EXPLODE!
GET GOIN', YOU HELL-BEASTS!!

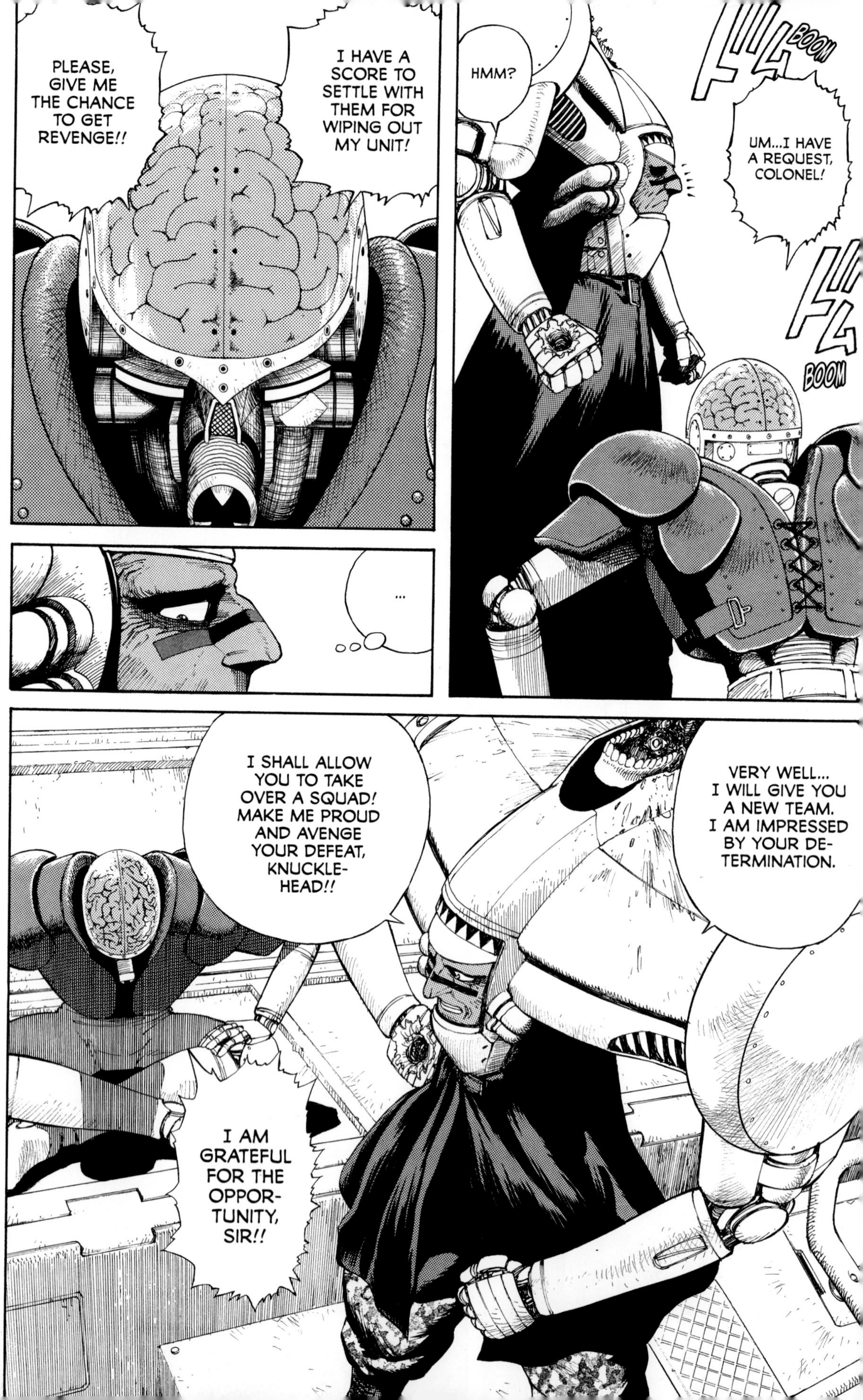
BOOM
UM...I HAVE A REQUEST, COLONEL!
BOOM
HMM?
I HAVE A SCORE TO SETTLE WITH THEM FOR WIPING OUT MY UNIT!
PLEASE, GIVE ME THE CHANCE TO GET REVENGE!!
...
VERY WELL... I WILL GIVE YOU A NEW TEAM. I AM IMPRESSED BY YOUR DE-TERMINATION.
I SHALL ALLOW YOU TO TAKE OVER A SQUAD! MAKE ME PROUD AND AVENGE YOUR DEFEAT, KNUCKLE-HEAD!!
I AM GRATEFUL FOR THE OPPOR-TUNITY, SIR!!

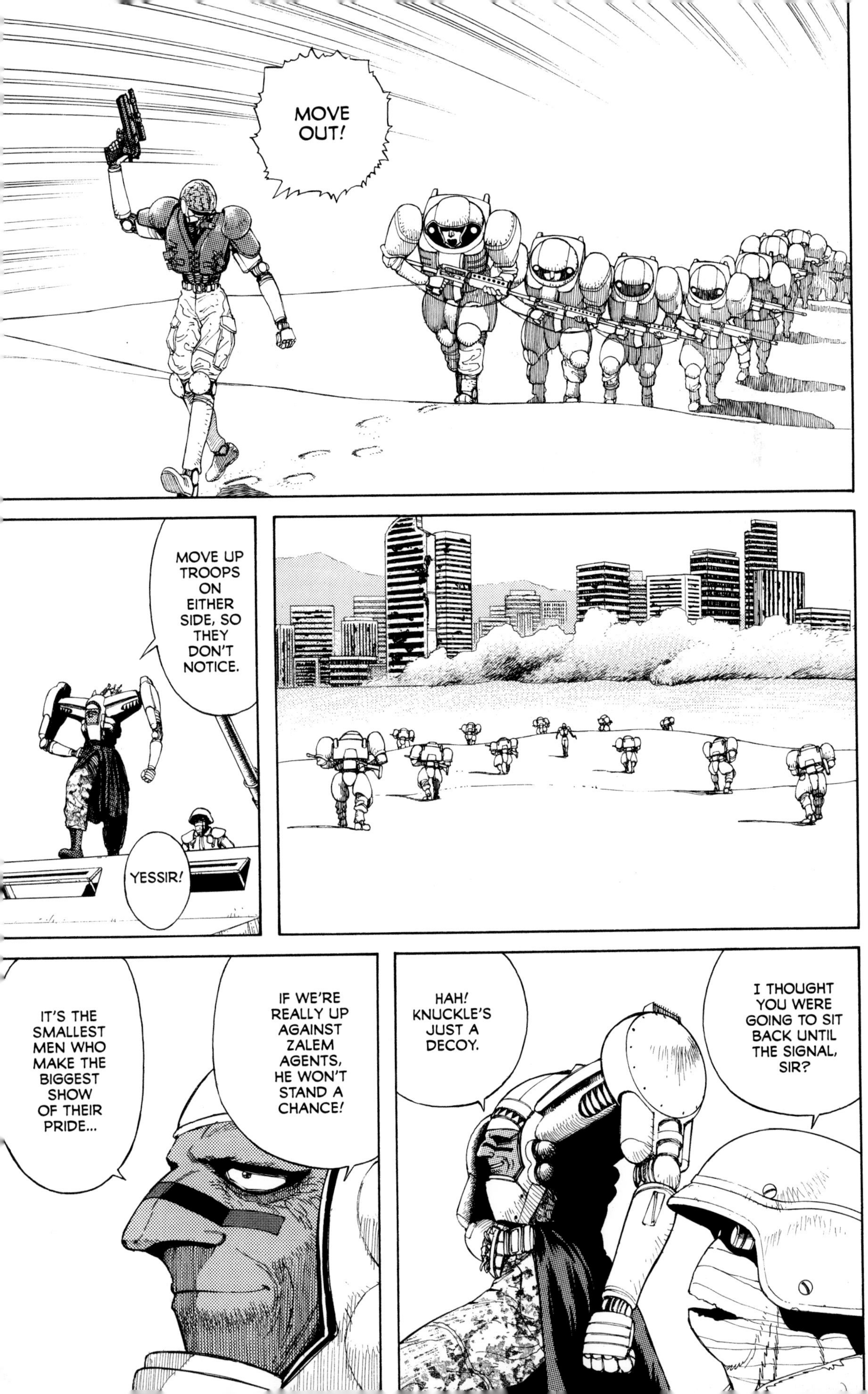
MOVE OUT!
MOVE UP TROOPS ON EITHER SIDE, SO THEY DON'T NOTICE.
YESSIR!
I THOUGHT YOU WERE GOING TO SIT BACK UNTIL THE SIGNAL, SIR?
HAH! KNUCKLE'S JUST A DECOY.
IF WE'RE REALLY UP AGAINST ZALEM AGENTS, HE WON'T STAND A CHANCE!
IT'S THE SMALLEST MEN WHO MAKE THE BIGGEST SHOW OF THEIR PRIDE...

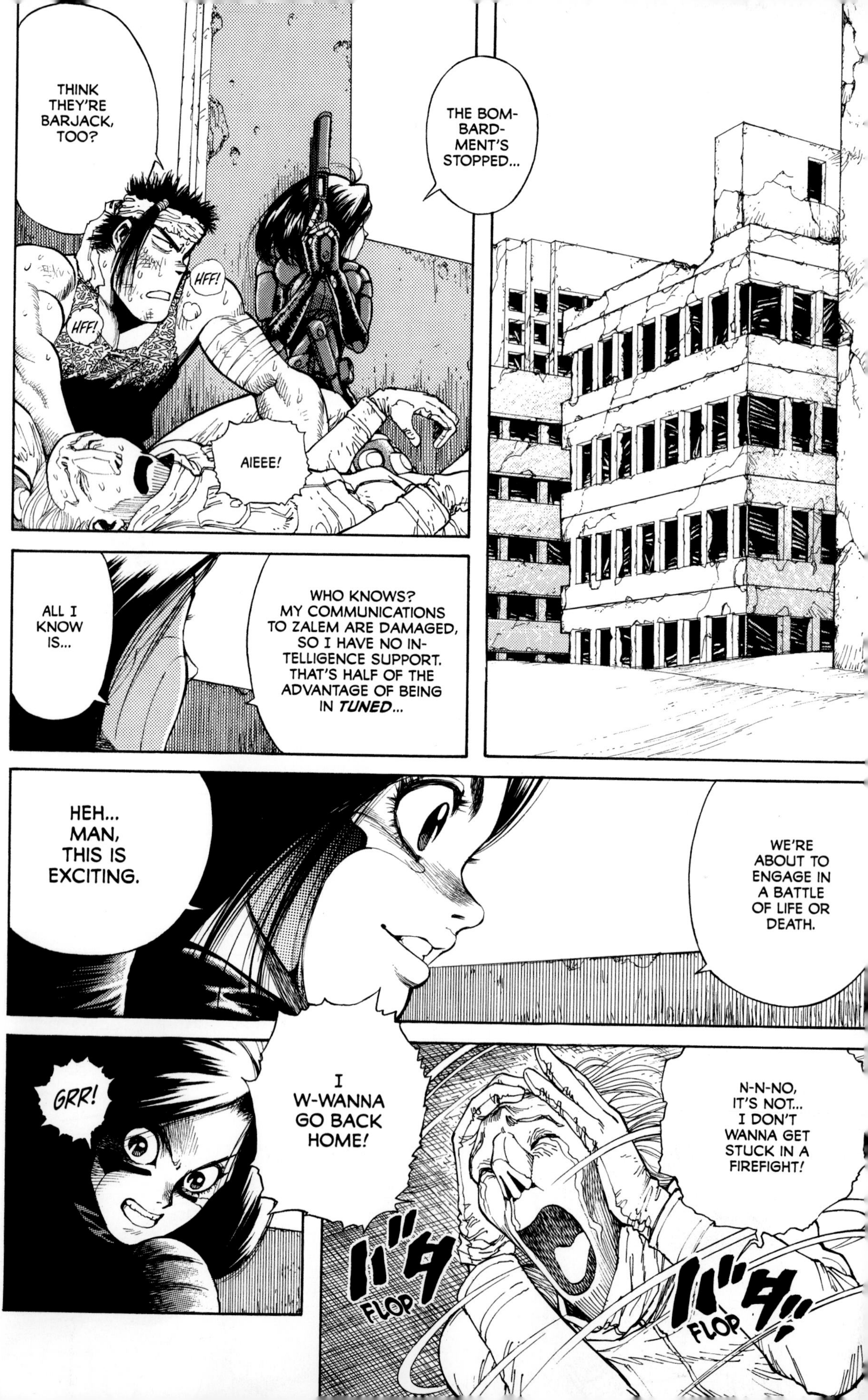
THE BOM-BARD-MENT'S STOPPED...
THINK THEY'RE BARJACK, TOO?
HFF!
HFF!
AIEEE!
WHO KNOWS? MY COMMUNICATIONS TO ZALEM ARE DAMAGED, SO I HAVE NO IN-TELLIGENCE SUPPORT. THAT'S HALF OF THE ADVANTAGE OF BEING IN *TUNED*...
ALL I KNOW IS...
WE'RE ABOUT TO ENGAGE IN A BATTLE OF LIFE OR DEATH.
HEH... MAN, THIS IS EXCITING.
N-N-NO, IT'S NOT... I DON'T WANNA GET STUCK IN A FIREFIGHT!
I W-WANNA GO BACK HOME!
バタッ!! FLOP
バタ FLOP
GRR!

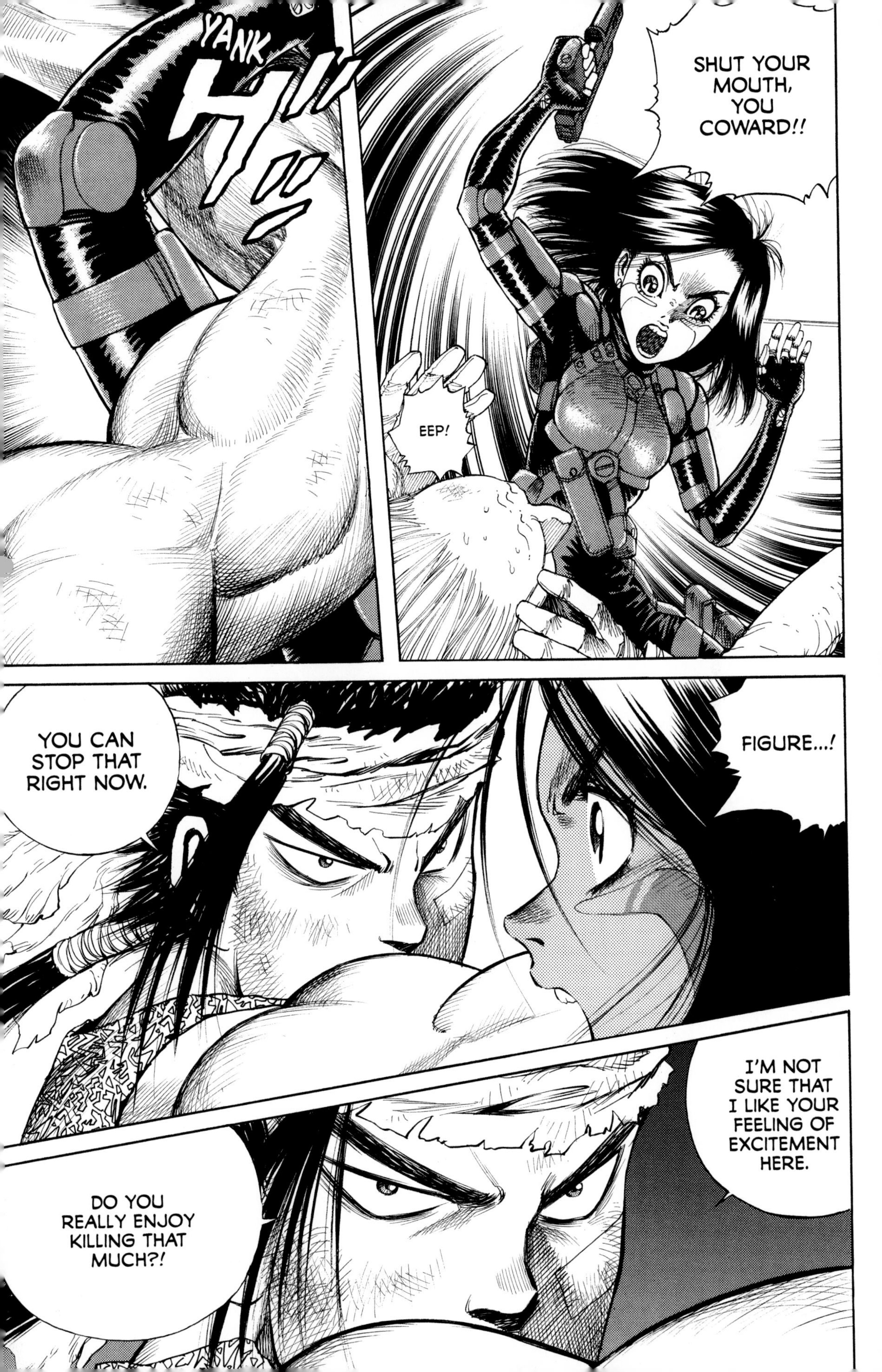
SHUT YOUR MOUTH, YOU COWARD!!
EEP!
YANK
FIGURE...!
YOU CAN STOP THAT RIGHT NOW.
I'M NOT SURE THAT I LIKE YOUR FEELING OF EXCITEMENT HERE.
DO YOU REALLY ENJOY KILLING THAT MUCH?!

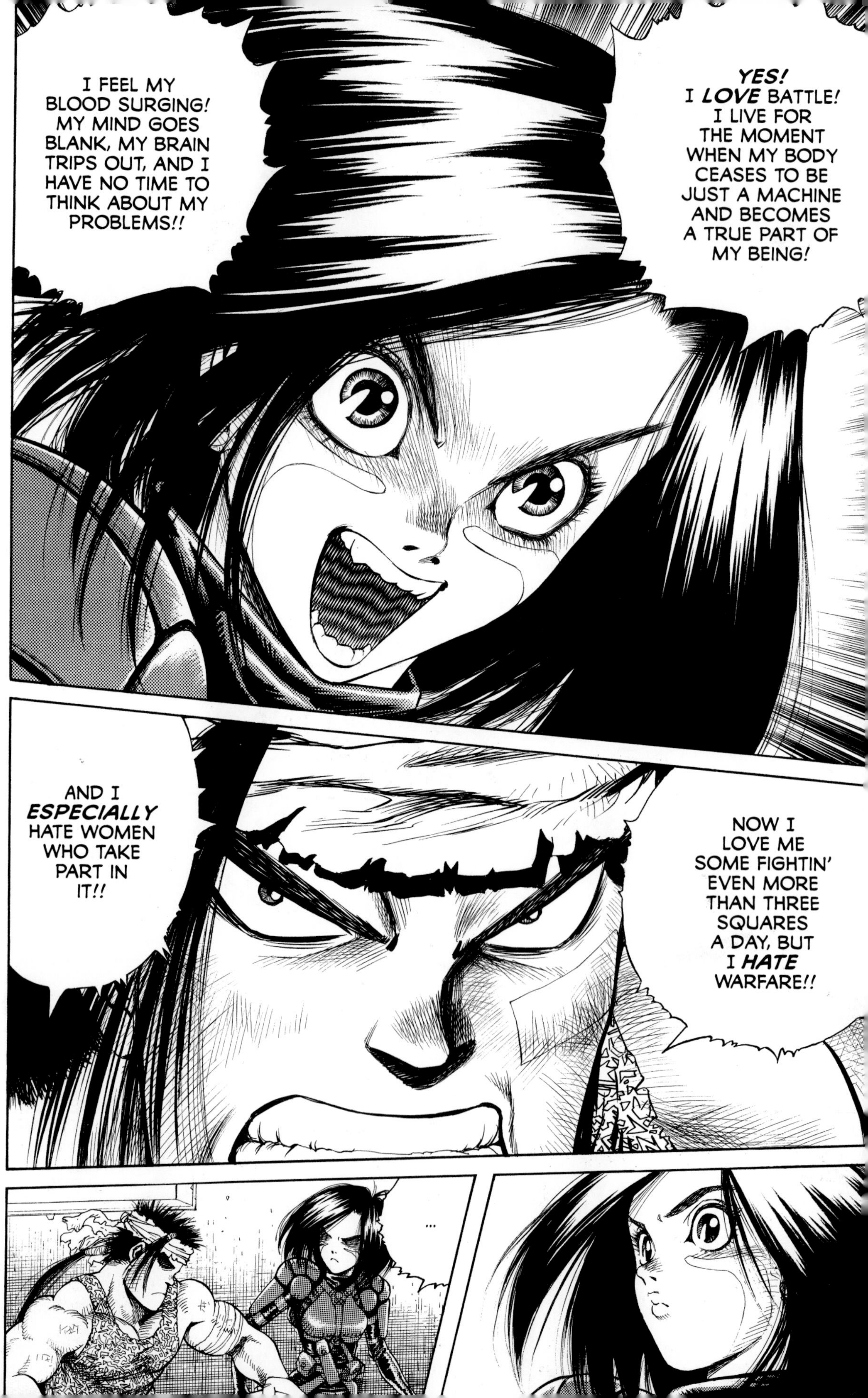
YES! I LOVE BATTLE! I LIVE FOR THE MOMENT WHEN MY BODY CEASES TO BE JUST A MACHINE AND BECOMES A TRUE PART OF MY BEING!
I FEEL MY BLOOD SURGING! MY MIND GOES BLANK, MY BRAIN TRIPS OUT, AND I HAVE NO TIME TO THINK ABOUT MY PROBLEMS!!
NOW I LOVE ME SOME FIGHTIN' EVEN MORE THAN THREE SQUARES A DAY, BUT I HATE WARFARE!!
AND I ESPECIALLY HATE WOMEN WHO TAKE PART IN IT!!
...

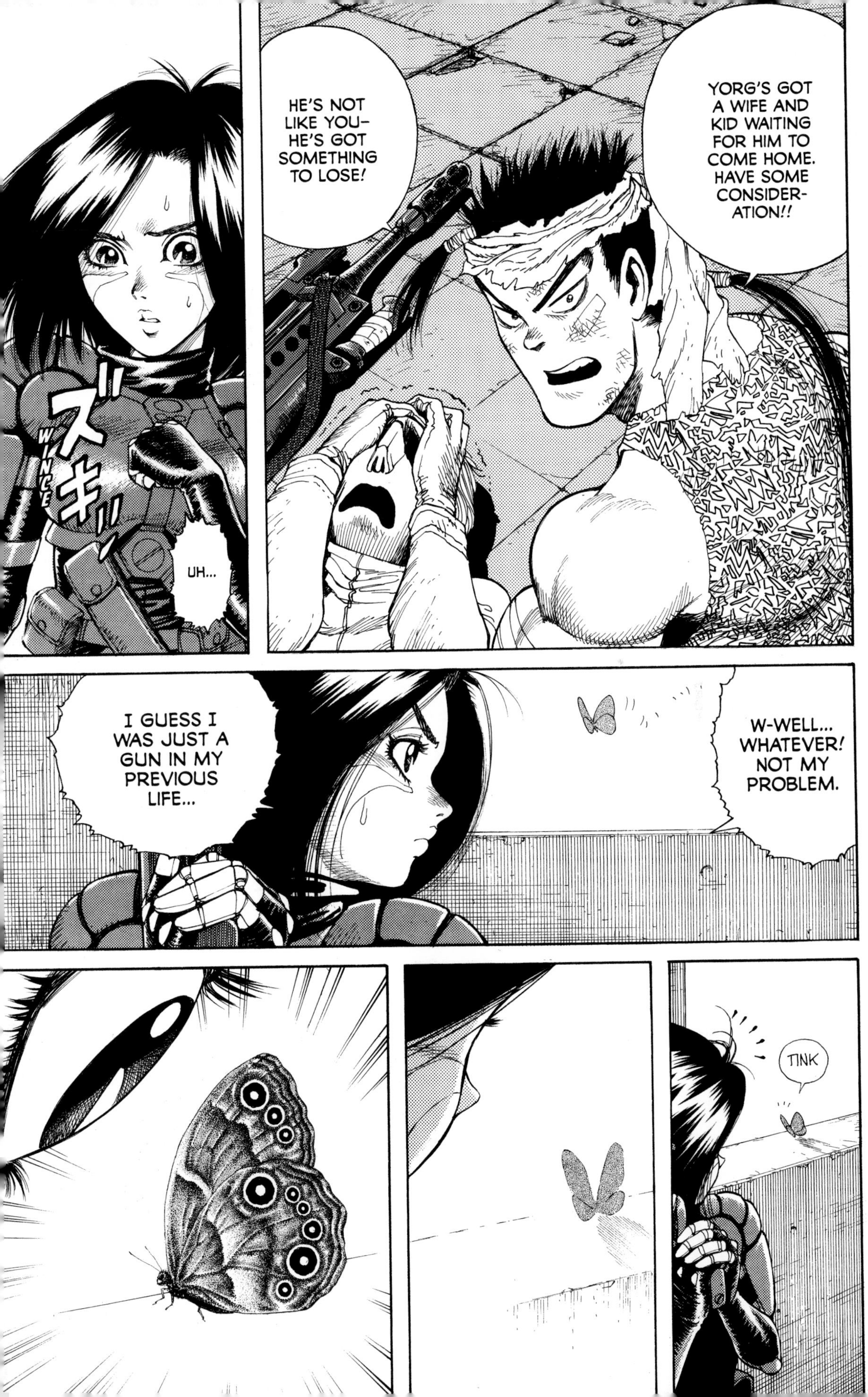
YORG'S GOT A WIFE AND KID WAITING FOR HIM TO COME HOME. HAVE SOME CONSIDER-ATION!!
HE'S NOT LIKE YOU—HE'S GOT SOMETHING TO LOSE!
ズキッ
WINCE
UH...
W-WELL... WHATEVER! NOT MY PROBLEM.
I GUESS I WAS JUST A GUN IN MY PREVIOUS LIFE...
TINK

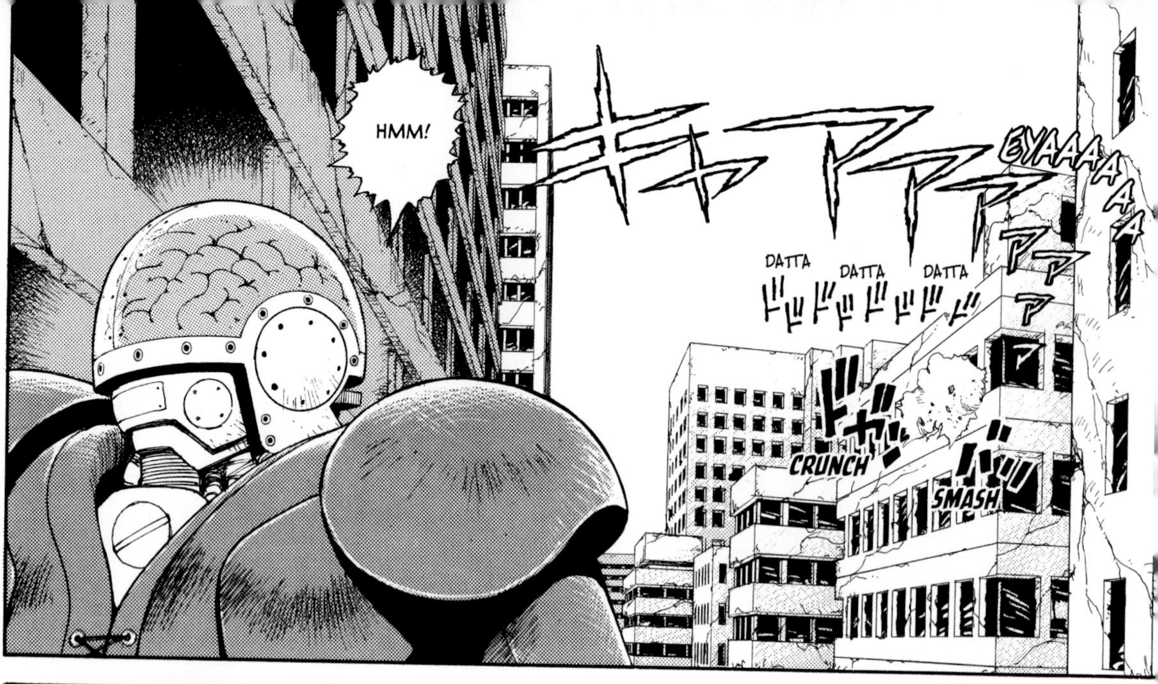
EYAAAAAAA
DATTA DATTA DATTA
CRUNCH
SMASH
HMM!

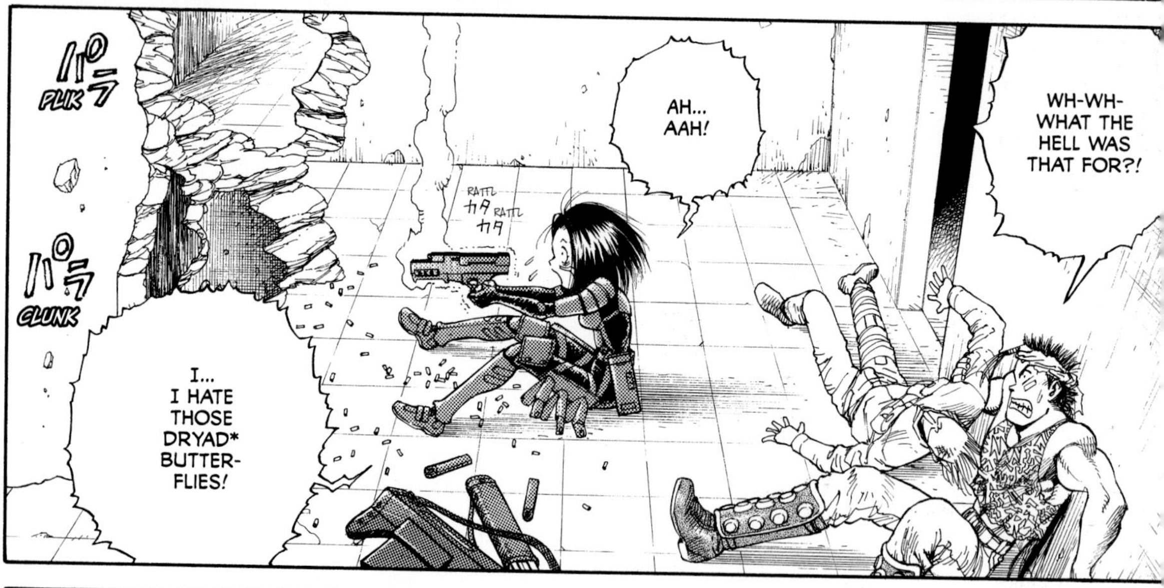
WH-WH-WHAT THE HELL WAS THAT FOR?!
AH... AAH!
RATTL RATTL
PLIK
CLUNK
I... I HATE THOSE DRYAD* BUTTERFLIES!

***Dryad Butterfly (Minois dryas):**
A brown butterfly with eyelets on its wings. It's in the family of four-legged butterflies, and there are about 2,500 such varieties in the world. The author also finds them extremely disturbing.

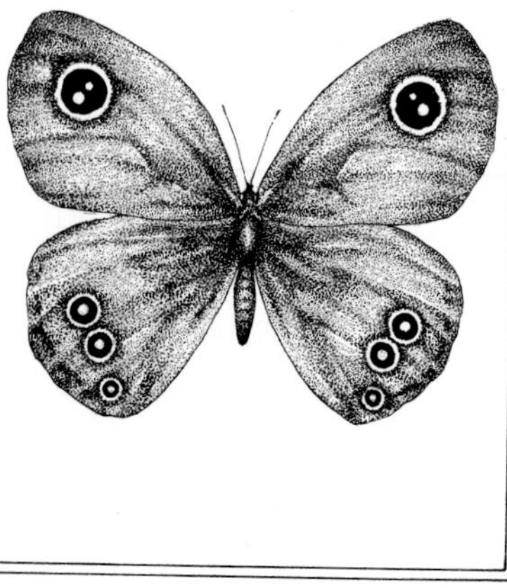

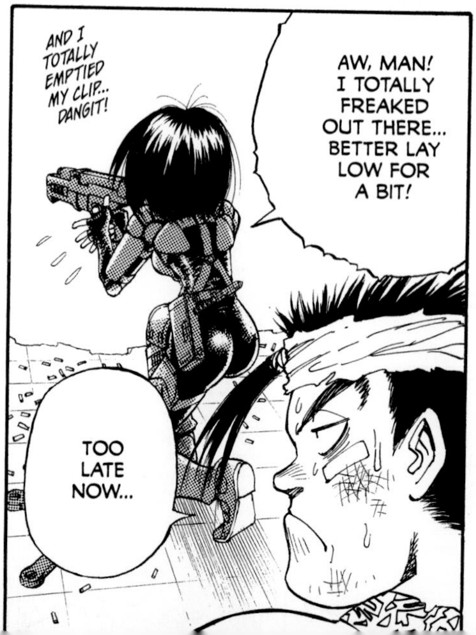
AW, MAN! I TOTALLY FREAKED OUT THERE... BETTER LAY LOW FOR A BIT!
AND I TOTALLY EMPTIED MY CLIP... DANGIT!
TOO LATE NOW...

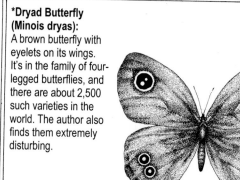

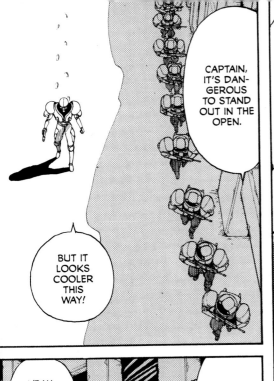

HAH! WHAT IDIOTS! THEY GAVE AWAY THEIR POSITION!
I GUESS THEY REALLY DO WANT ME TO KILL THEM! WELL, I AIM TO PLEASE!
ZSH
ZSH
CAPTAIN, IT'S DANGEROUS TO STAND OUT IN THE OPEN.
BUT IT LOOKS COOLER THIS WAY!
PSH! AMATEUR... FORGET HIM.
YEAH, LET'S GO.
HEY! I DIDN'T GIVE YOU THOSE ORDERS!!
SWISH
IGNORE HIM.
FWIP
BOOM

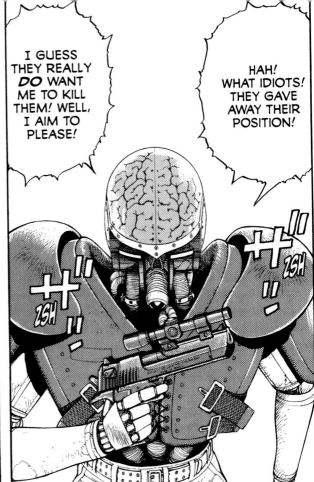

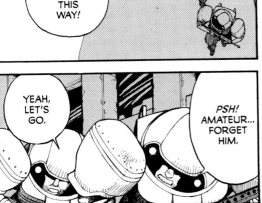

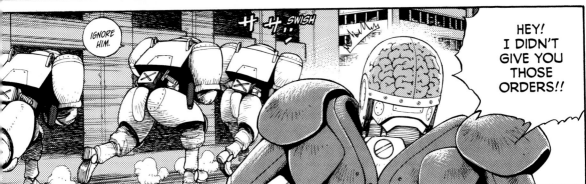

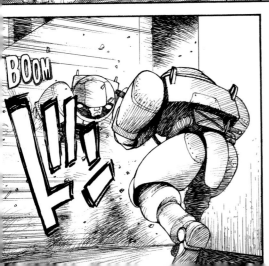

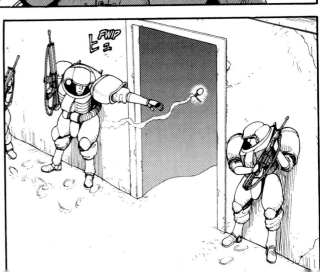

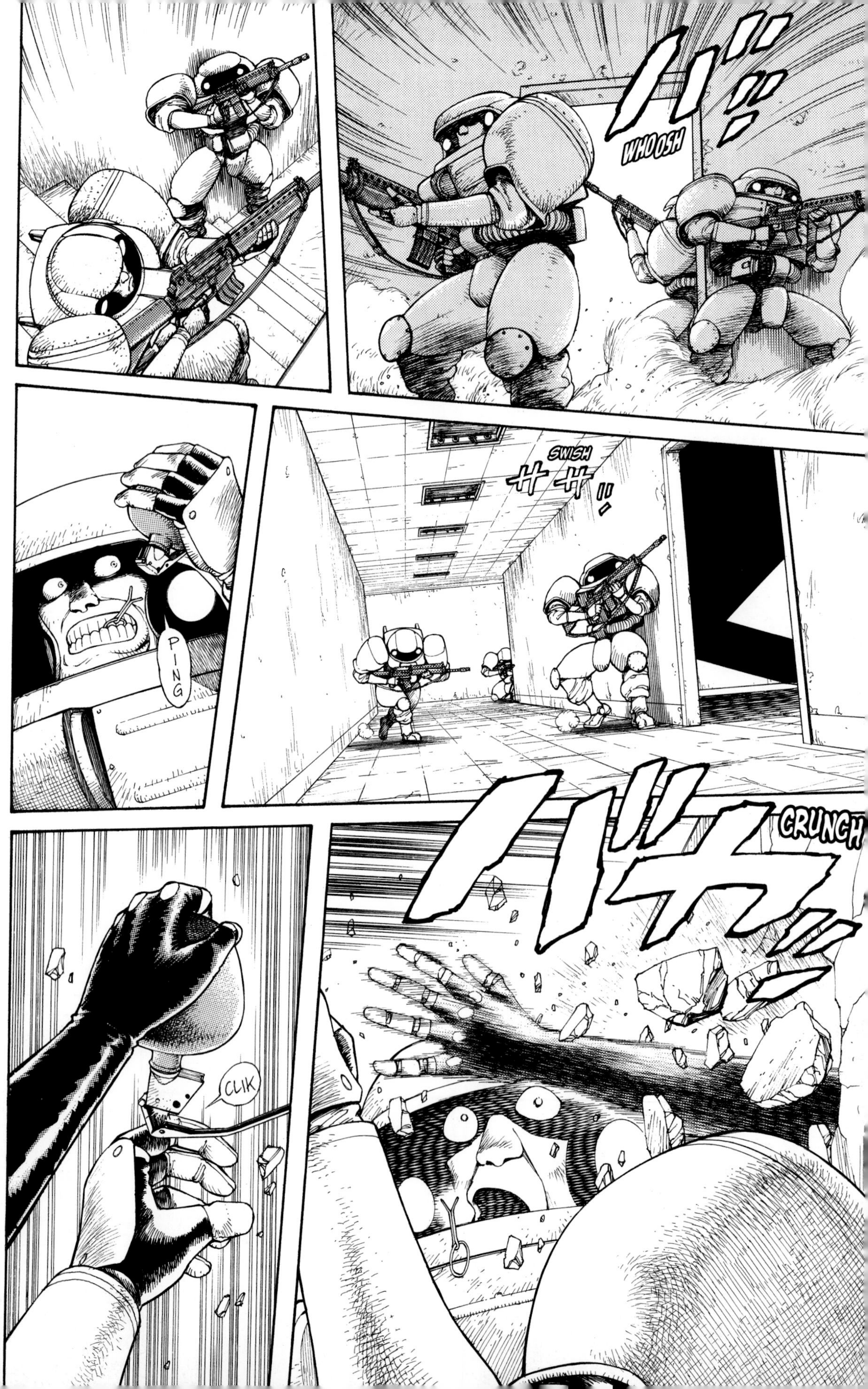
WHOOSH
SWISH
PING
CRUNCH
CLIK

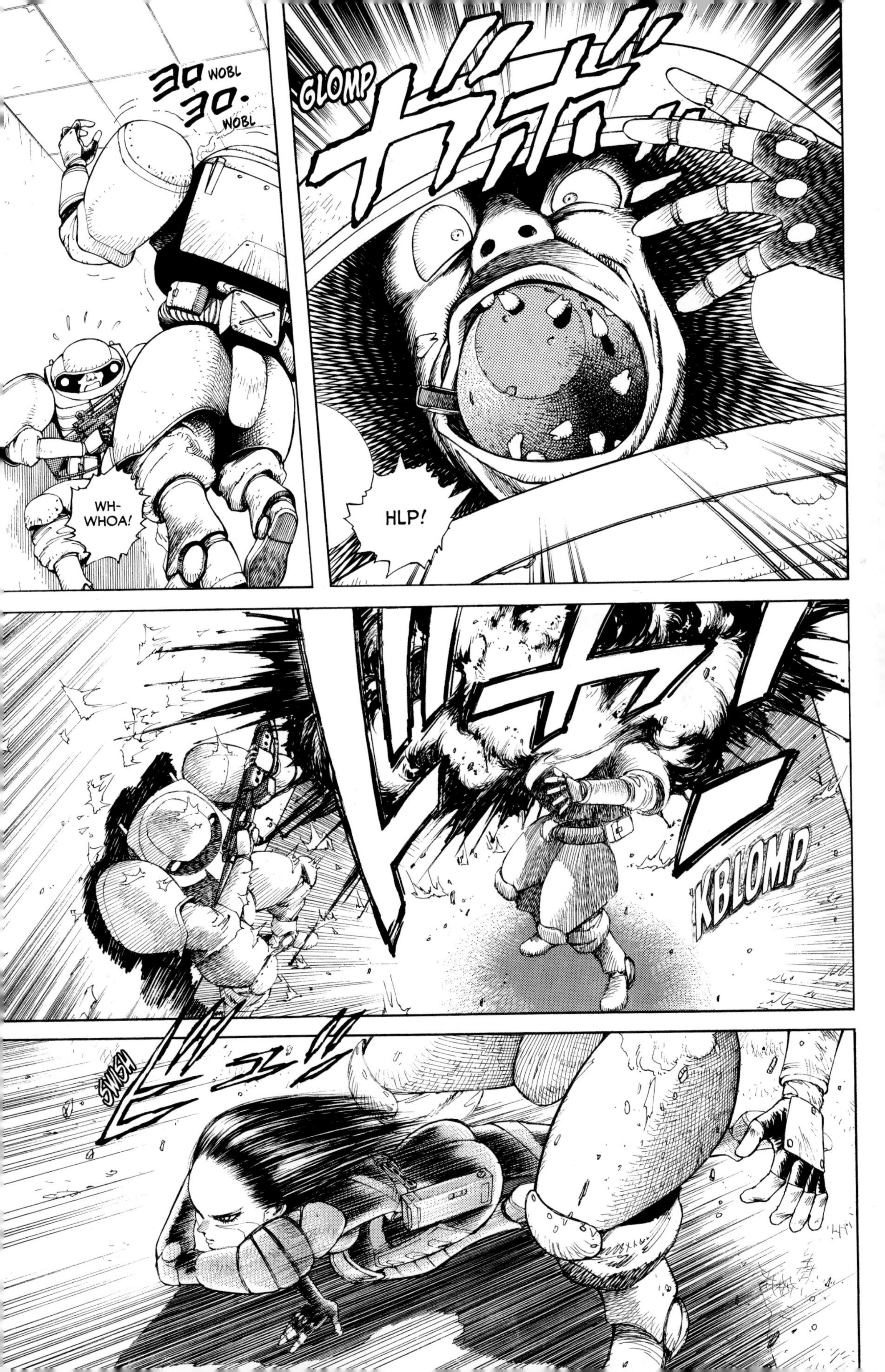
GLOMP
HLP!
WOBL
WOBL
WH-WHOA!
KBLOMP
SWISH

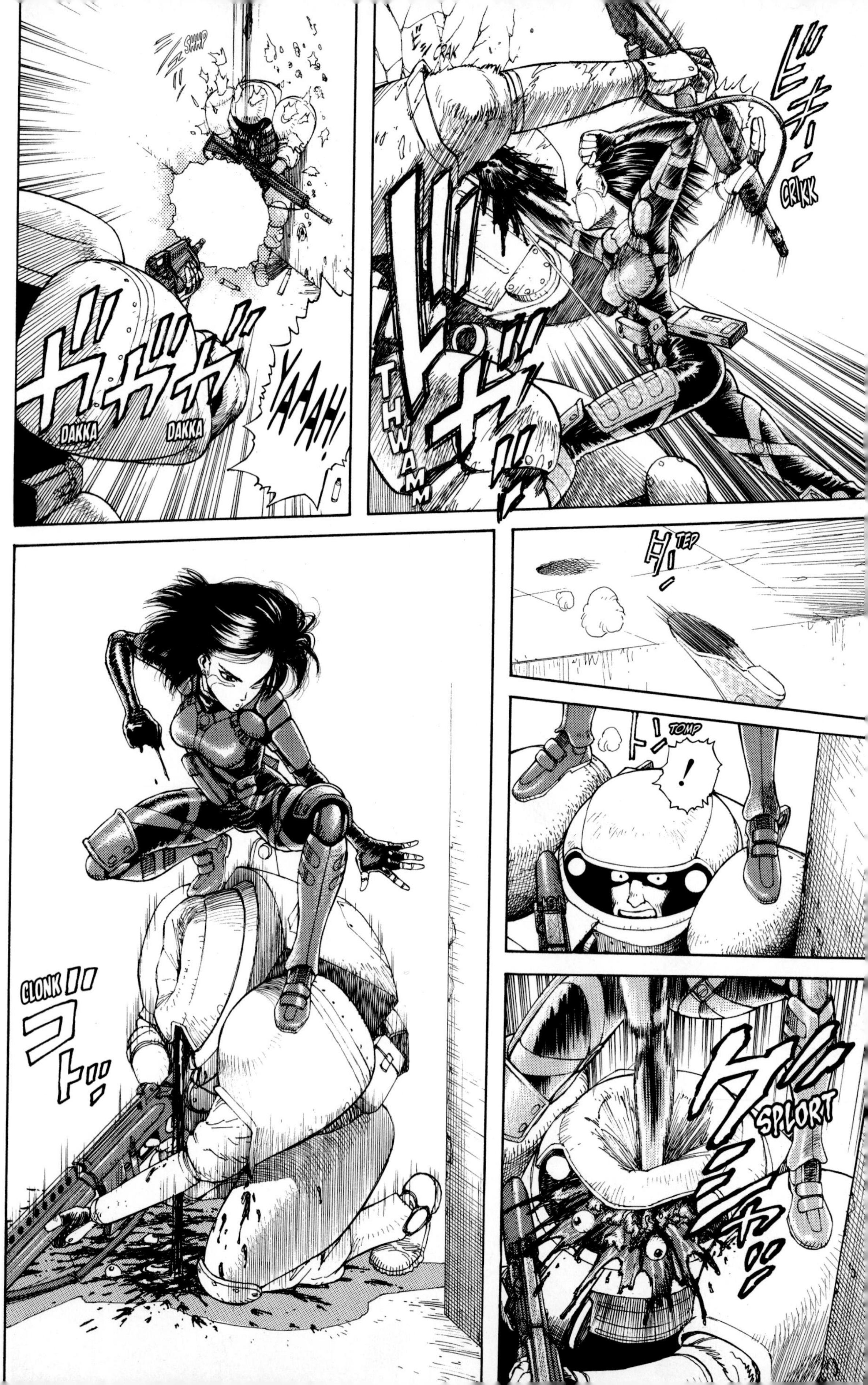

CRAK
CRIKK
THWAMM
SHWIP
DAKKA
DAKKA
YAAAH!
TEP
TOMP
!
SPLORT
CLONK

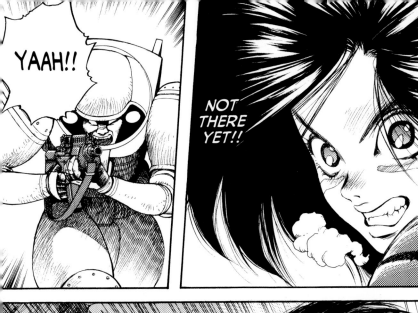

YAAH!!

NOT THERE YET!!

MORE! UNTIL EVERY-THING IS BLANK!!

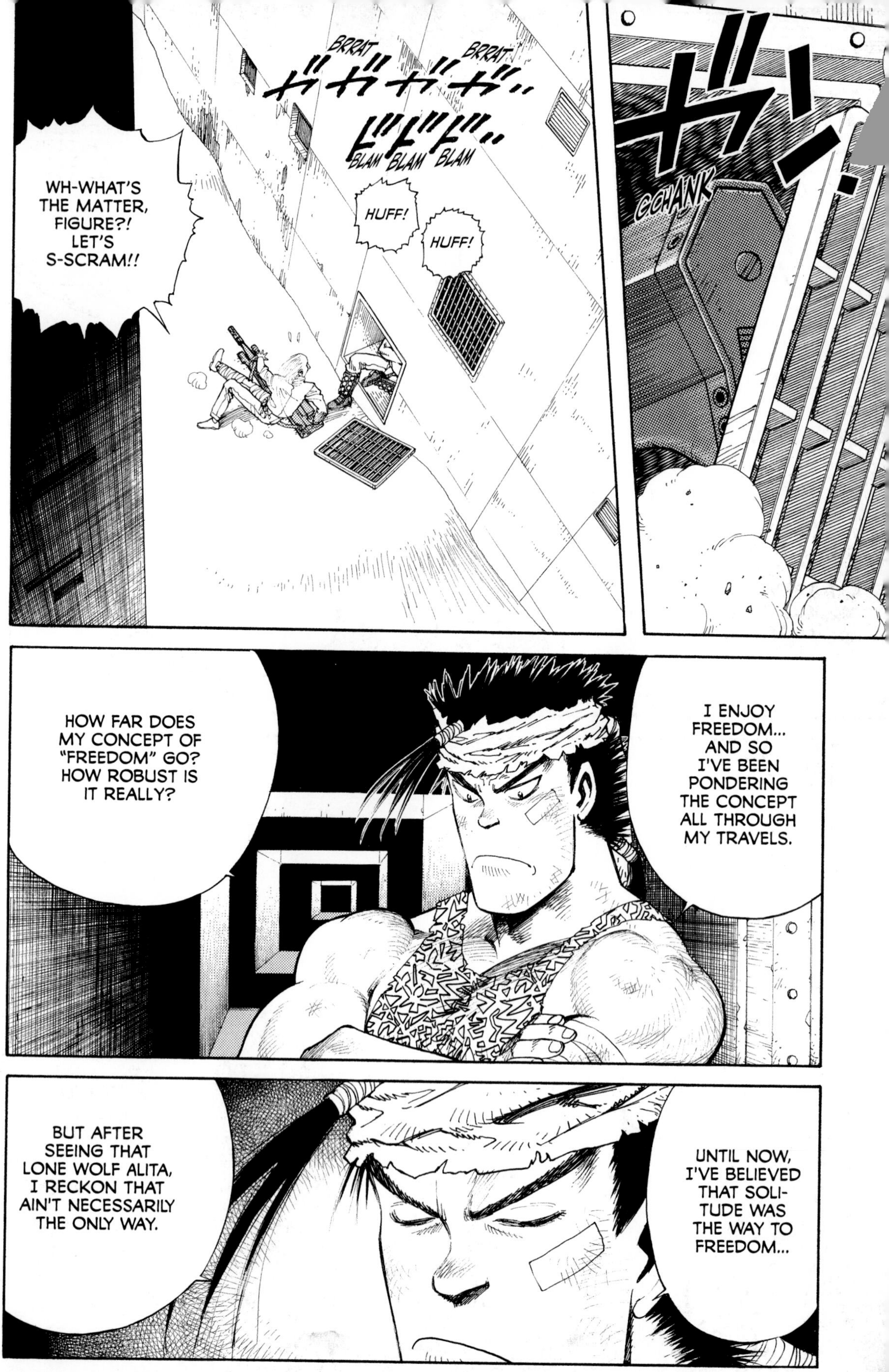
CHANK
BRRAT
BRRAT
BLAM BLAM BLAM
HUFF!
HUFF!
WH-WHAT'S THE MATTER, FIGURE?! LET'S S-SCRAM!!
I ENJOY FREEDOM... AND SO I'VE BEEN PONDERING THE CONCEPT ALL THROUGH MY TRAVELS.
HOW FAR DOES MY CONCEPT OF "FREEDOM" GO? HOW ROBUST IS IT REALLY?
UNTIL NOW, I'VE BELIEVED THAT SOLI-TUDE WAS THE WAY TO FREEDOM...
BUT AFTER SEEING THAT LONE WOLF ALITA, I RECKON THAT AIN'T NECESSARILY THE ONLY WAY.

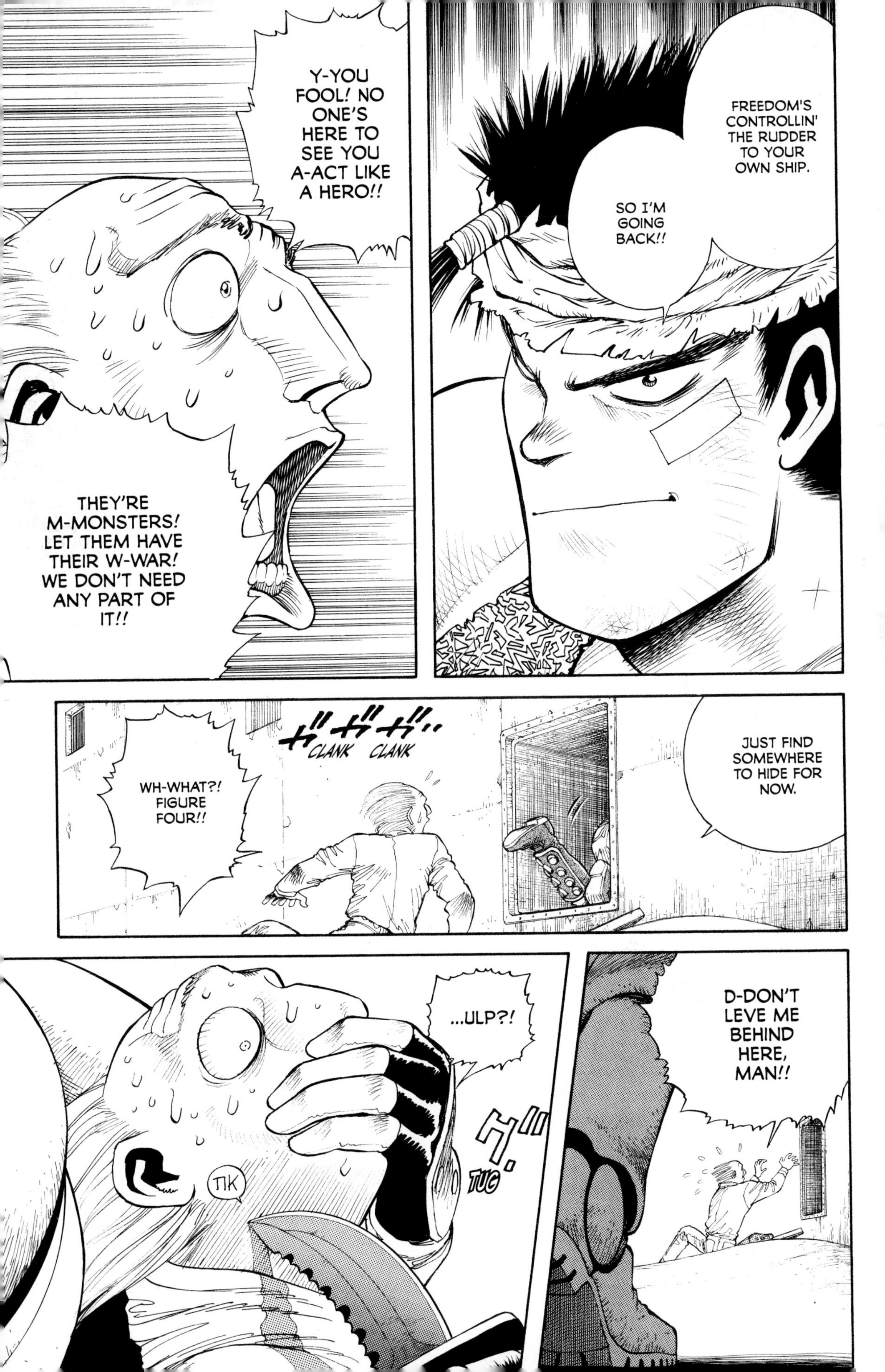
FREEDOM'S CONTROLLIN' THE RUDDER TO YOUR OWN SHIP.
SO I'M GOING BACK!!
Y-YOU FOOL! NO ONE'S HERE TO SEE YOU A-ACT LIKE A HERO!!
THEY'RE M-MONSTERS! LET THEM HAVE THEIR W-WAR! WE DON'T NEED ANY PART OF IT!!
JUST FIND SOMEWHERE TO HIDE FOR NOW.
ガガガ
CLANK CLANK
WH-WHAT?! FIGURE FOUR!!
D-DON'T LEVE ME BEHIND HERE, MAN!!
...ULP?!
グッ
TUG
TIK

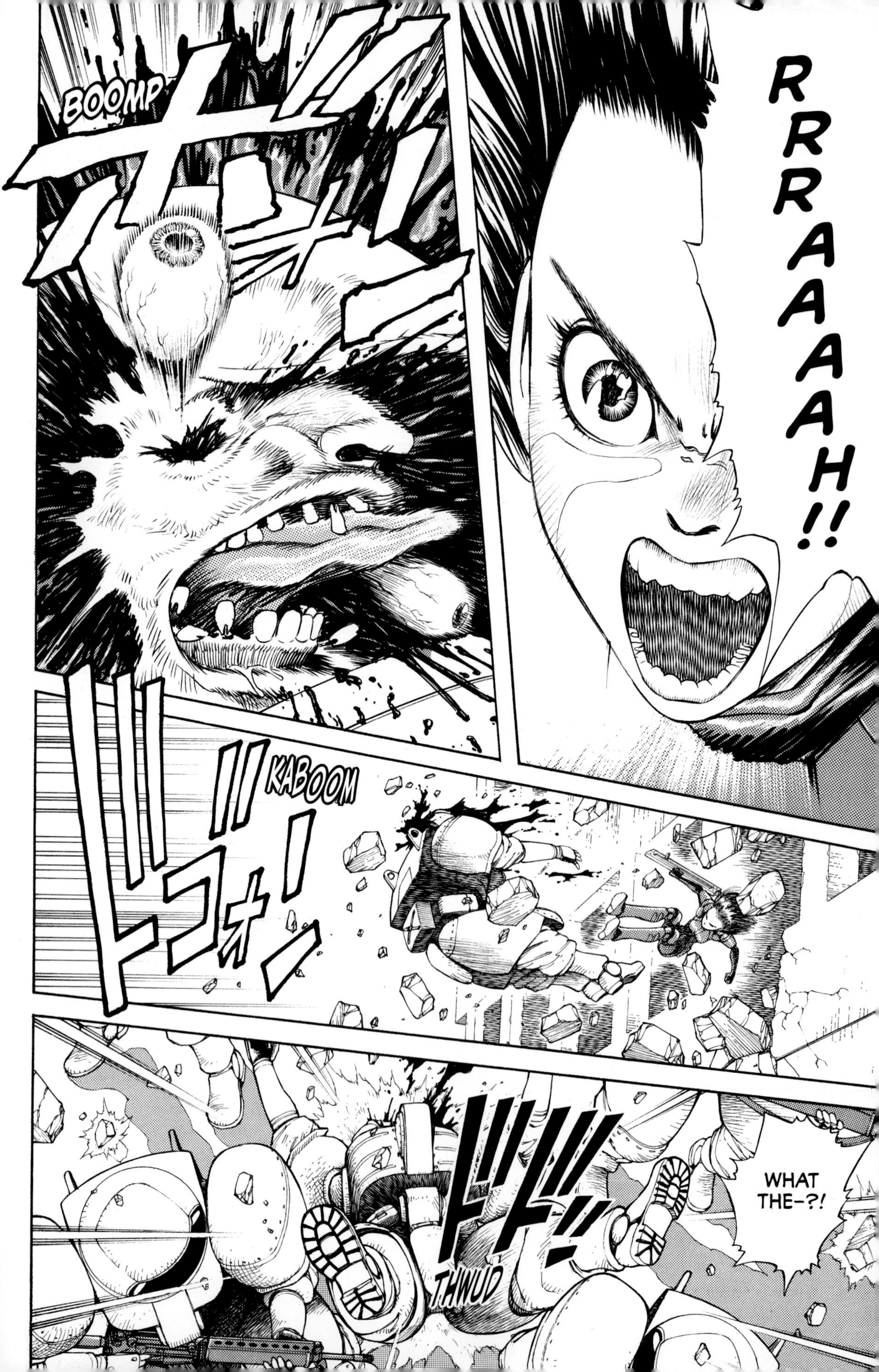
RRRAAAAAH!!
BOOMP
KABOOM
WHAT THE-?!
THWUD

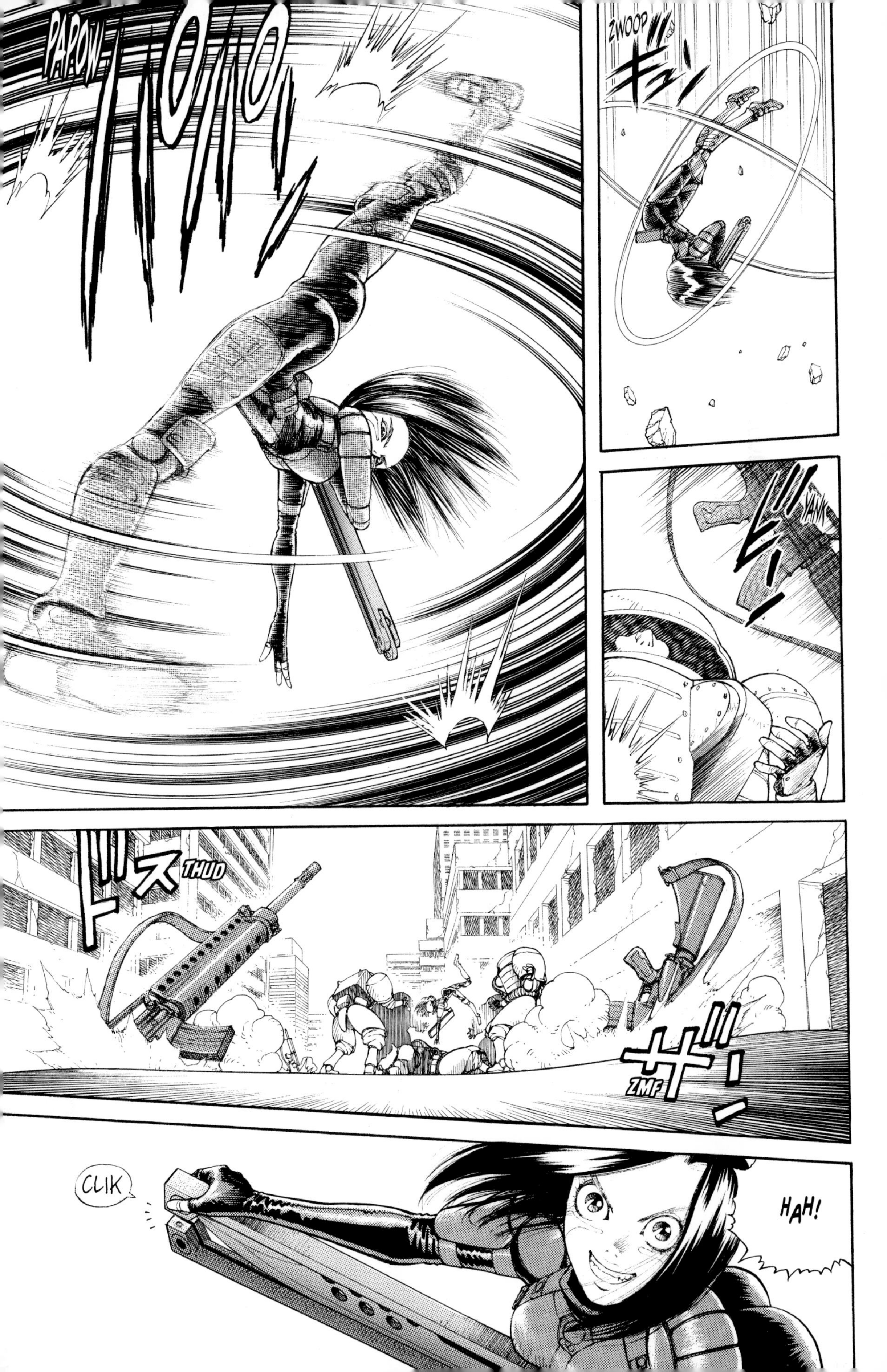

ZWOOP
YANK
PAPOW
THUD
ZMF
HAH!
CLIK

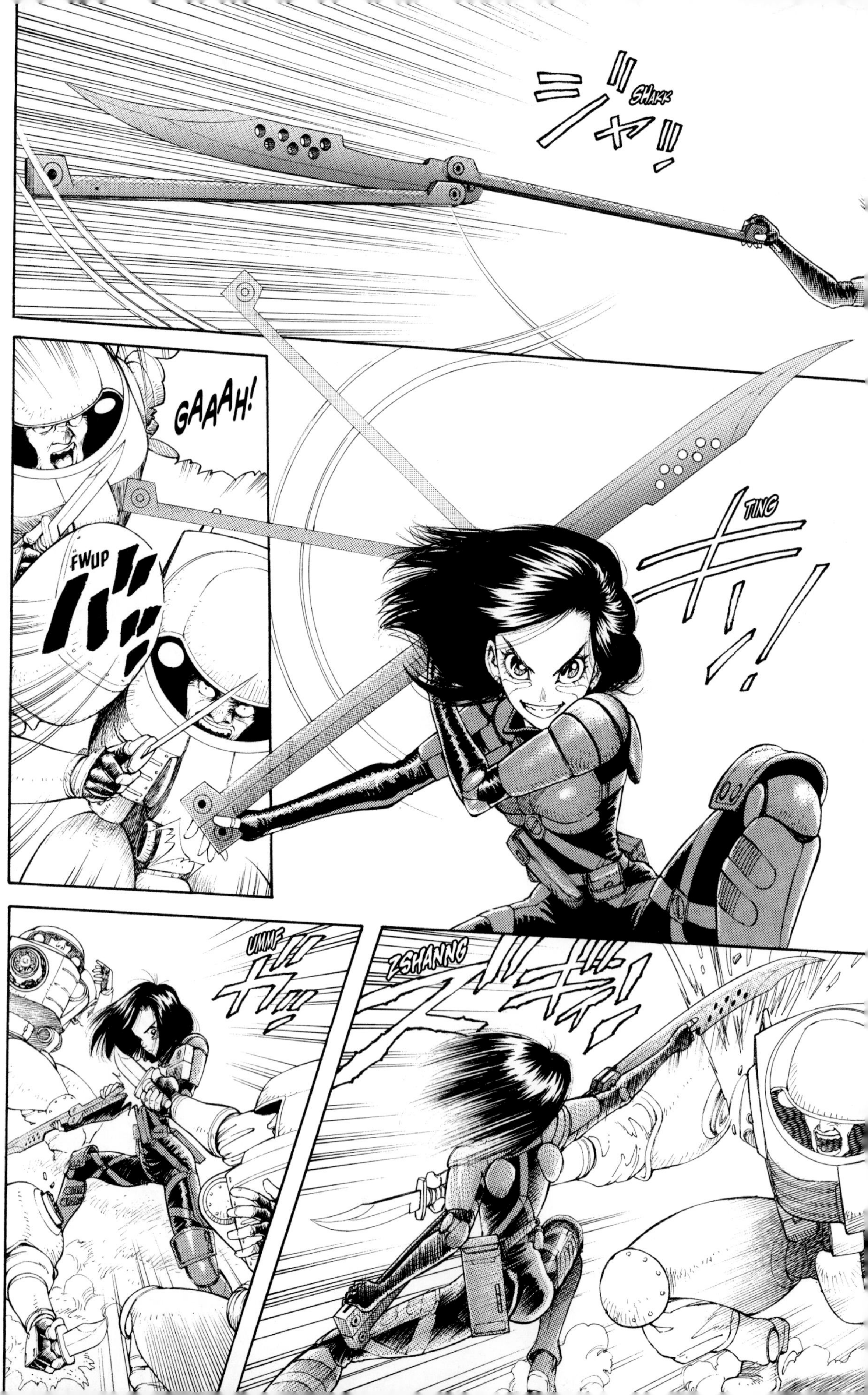

SHAKK
ジャ!!
TING
キン!
GAAAH!
FWUP
バッ
ZSHANNG
ズギン!
UMMF
ヤッ

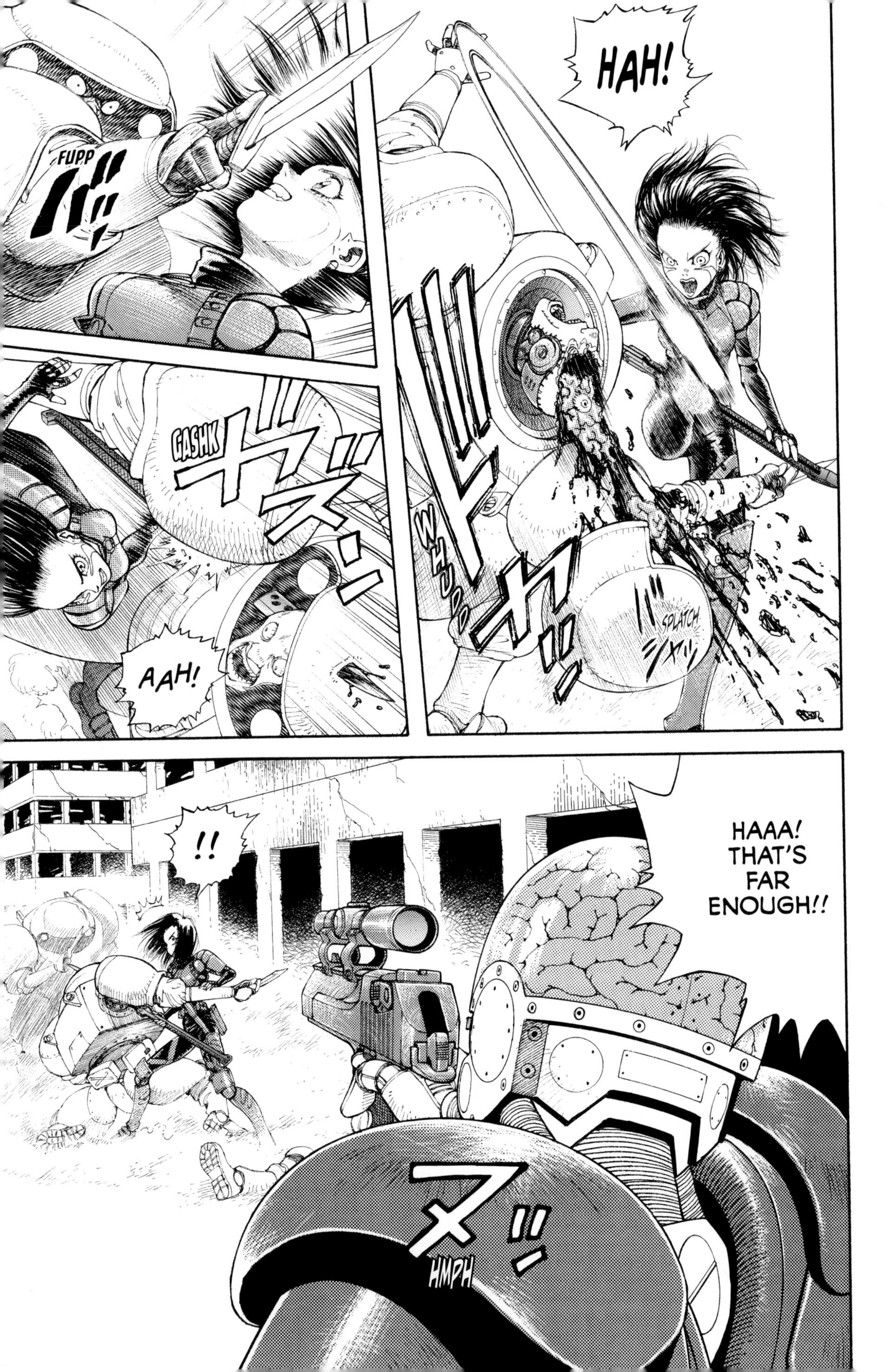
HAH!
WHUDD
SPLATCH
FUPP
GASHK
AAH!
HAAA! THAT'S FAR ENOUGH!!
!!
HMPH

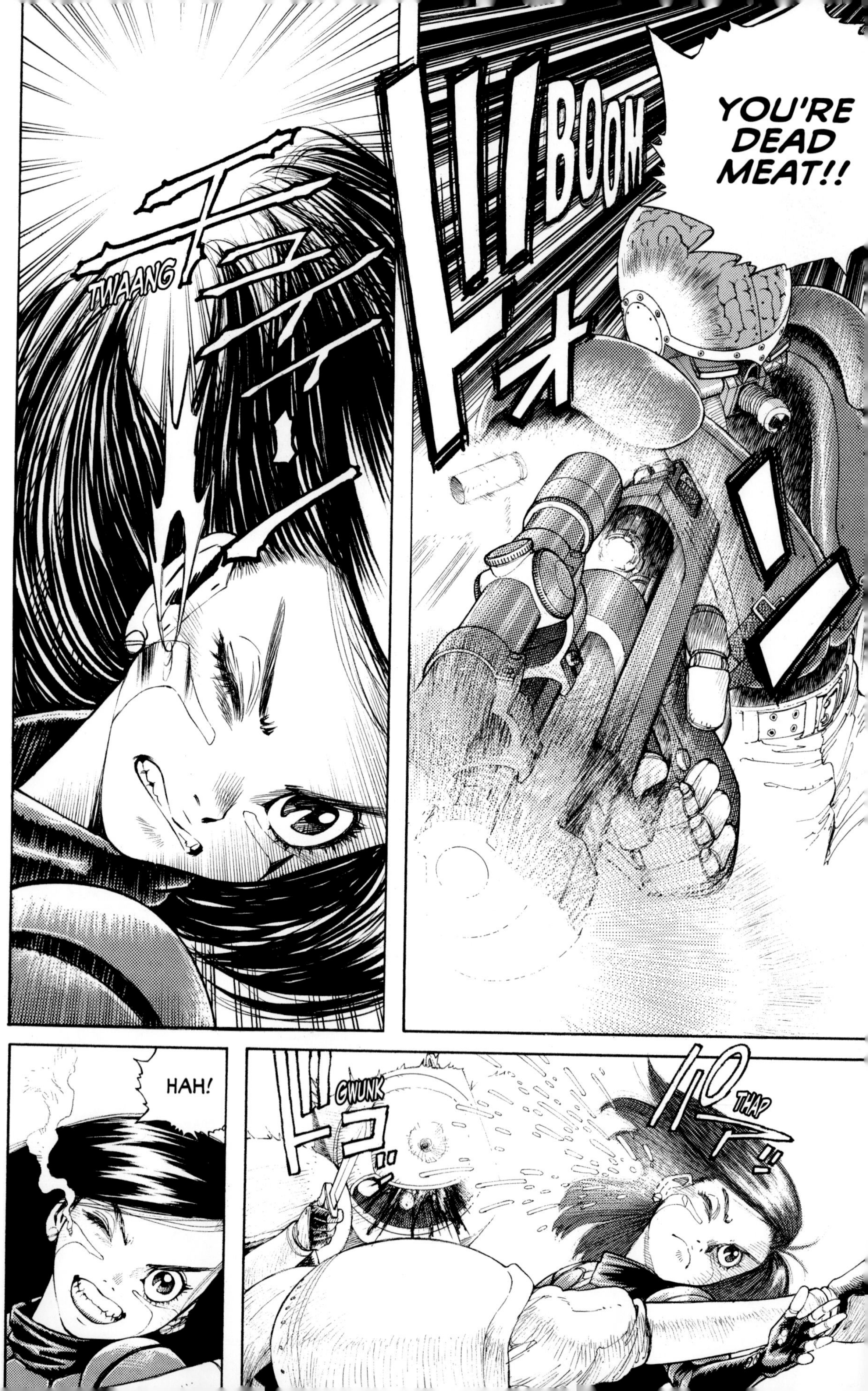
YOU'RE DEAD MEAT!!
BOOM
TWAANG
THAP
CWUNK
HAH!

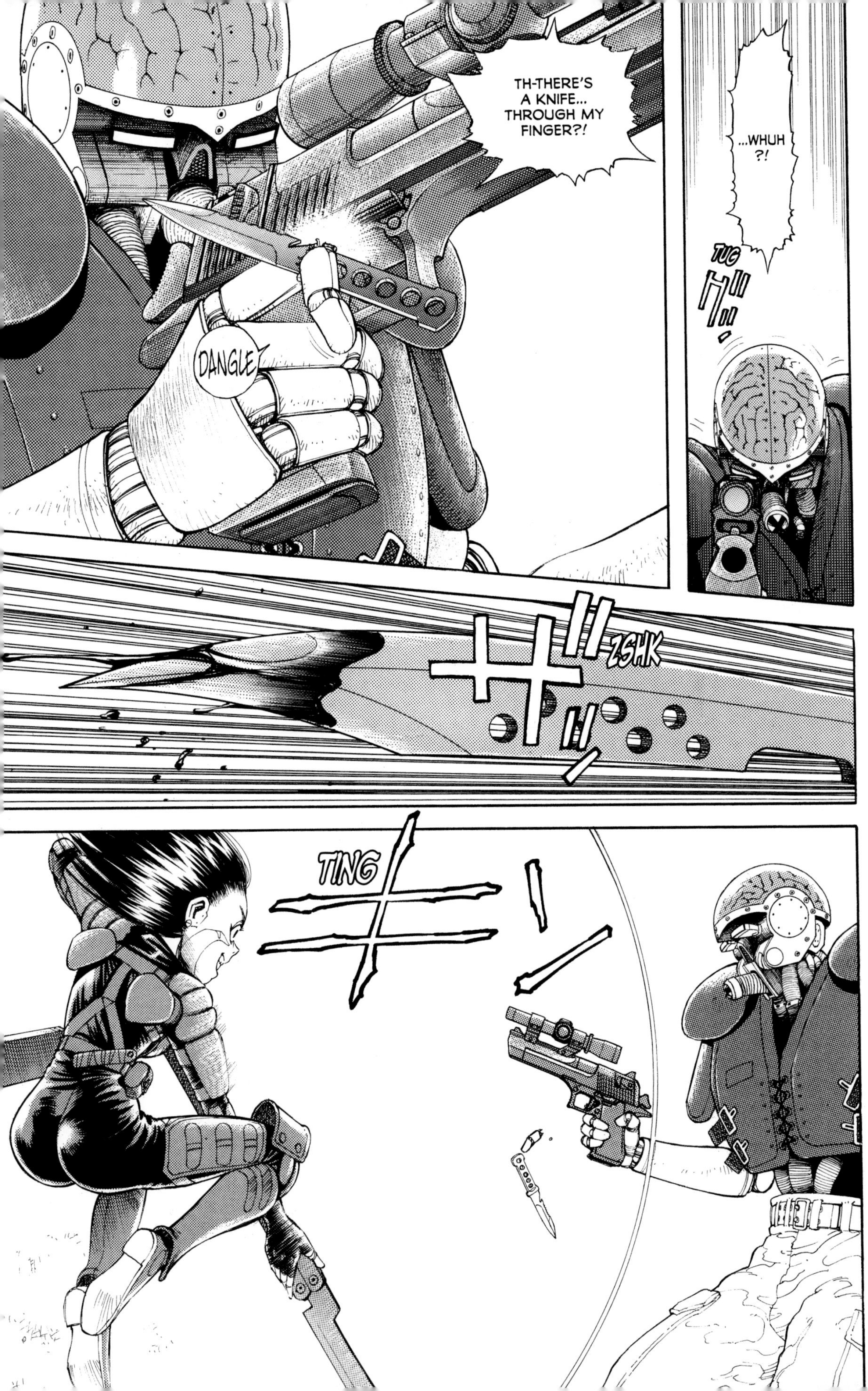
...WHUH ?!
TUG
TH-THERE'S A KNIFE... THROUGH MY FINGER?!
DANGLE
ZSHK
TING

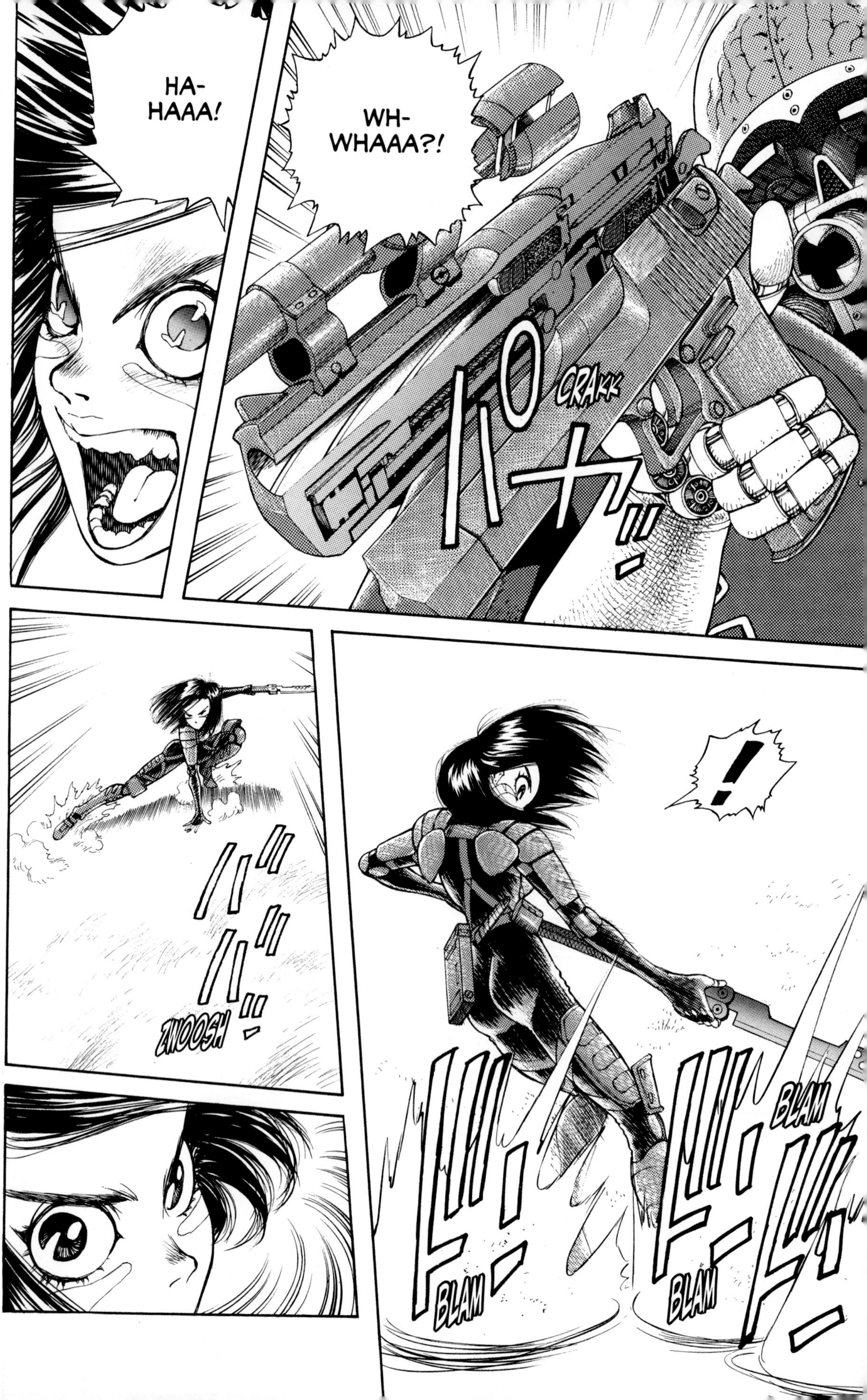
WH-
WHAAA?!
CRAKK
HA-
HAAA!
!
BLAM
BLAM
BLAM
ZWOOSH

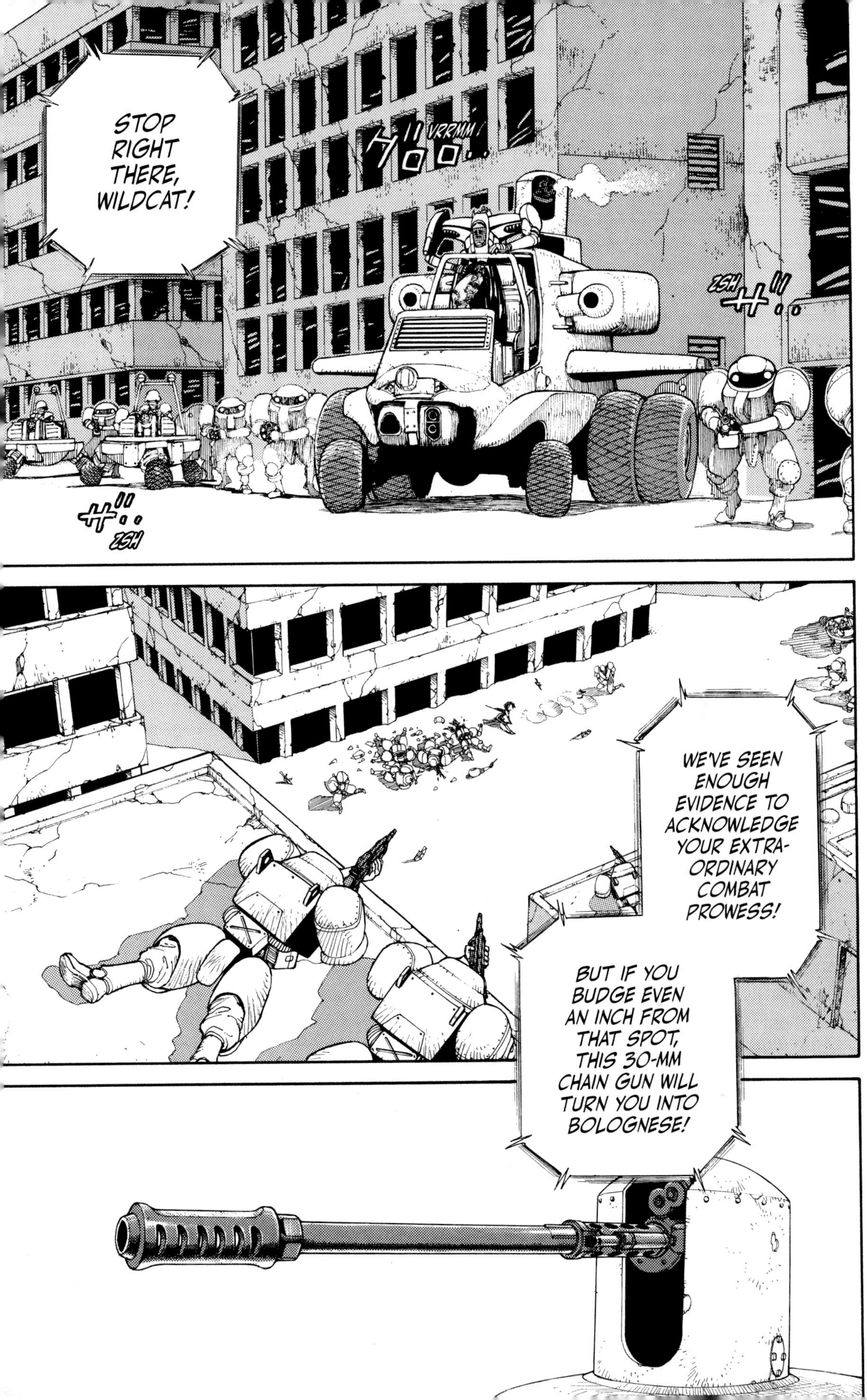
ZSH
VRRMM
STOP RIGHT THERE, WILDCAT!
ZSH
WE'VE SEEN ENOUGH EVIDENCE TO ACKNOWLEDGE YOUR EXTRA-ORDINARY COMBAT PROWESS!
BUT IF YOU BUDGE EVEN AN INCH FROM THAT SPOT, THIS 30-MM CHAIN GUN WILL TURN YOU INTO BOLOGNESE!

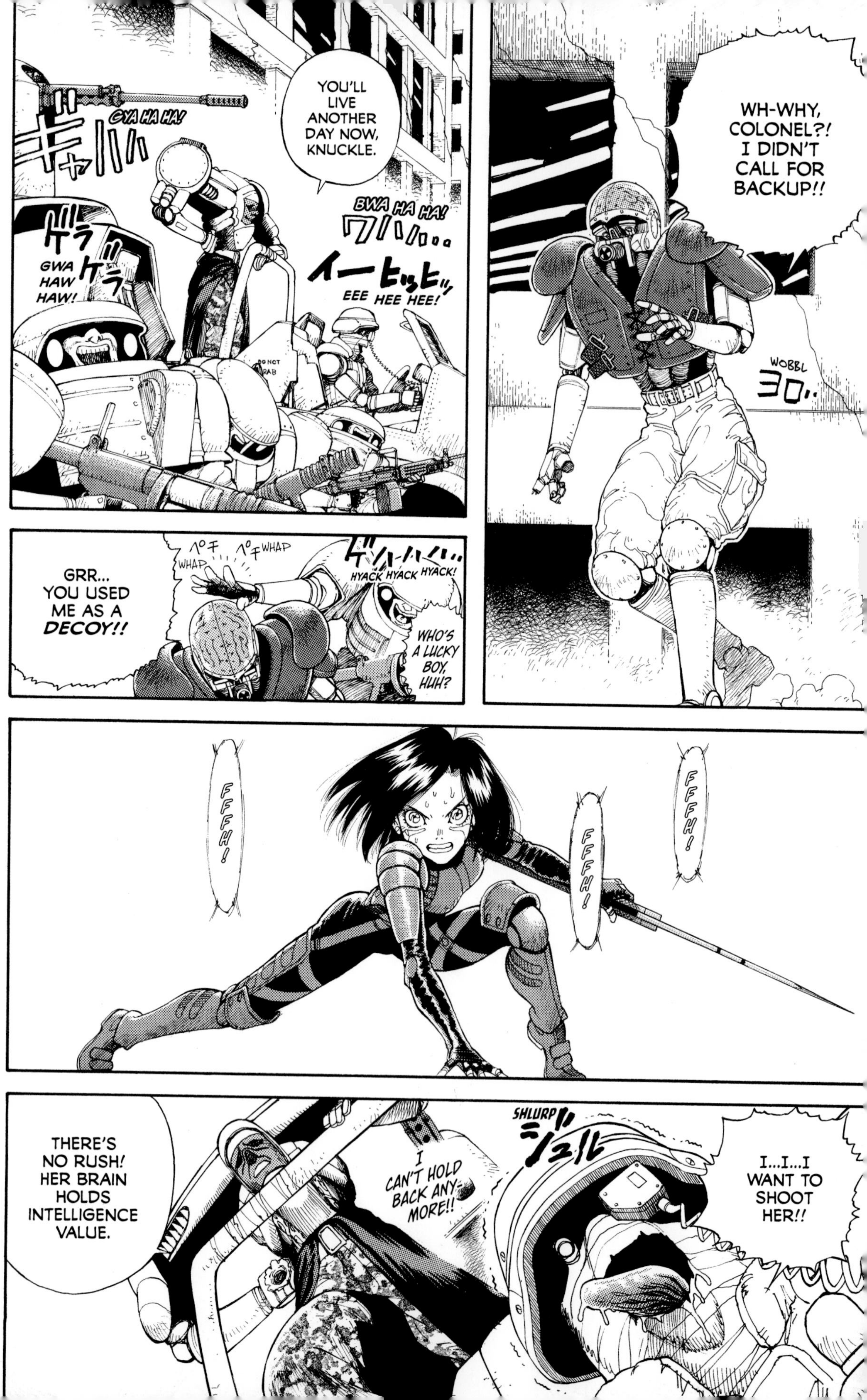

WH-WHY, COLONEL?! I DIDN'T CALL FOR BACKUP!!
WOBBL
YOU'LL LIVE ANOTHER DAY NOW, KNUCKLE.
BWA HA HA!
GYA HA HA!
EEE HEE HEE!
GWA HAW HAW!
DO NOT GRAB
WHAP WHAP
HYACK HYACK HYACK!
WHO'S A LUCKY BOY, HUH?
GRR... YOU USED ME AS A DECOY!!
FFFH!
FFFH!
FFFH!
I...I...I WANT TO SHOOT HER!!
SHLURP
I CAN'T HOLD BACK ANYMORE!!
THERE'S NO RUSH! HER BRAIN HOLDS INTELLIGENCE VALUE.

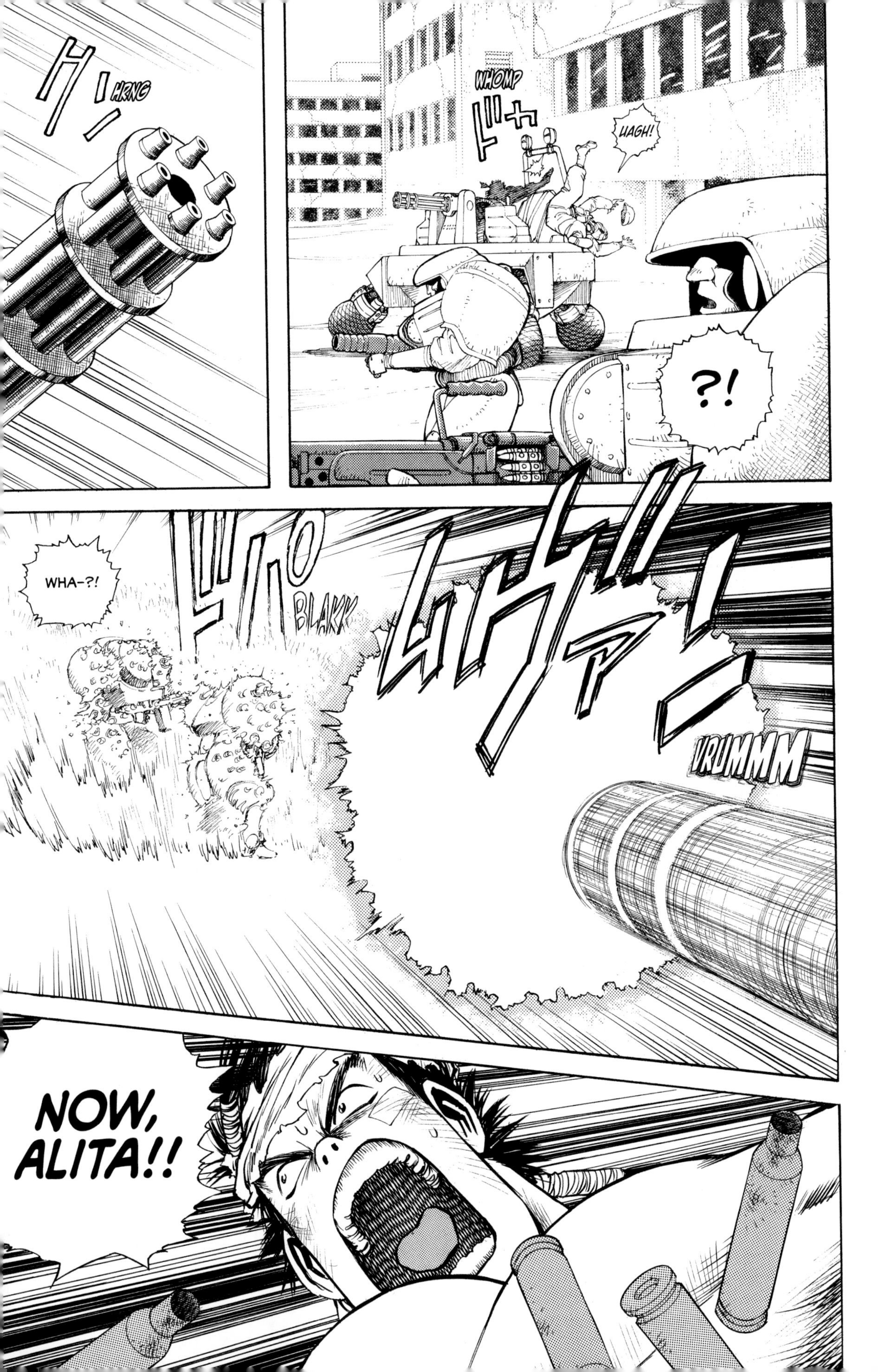
WHOMP
UAGH!
?!
HRNG
VRUMMM
BLAKK
WHA-?!
NOW, ALITA!!

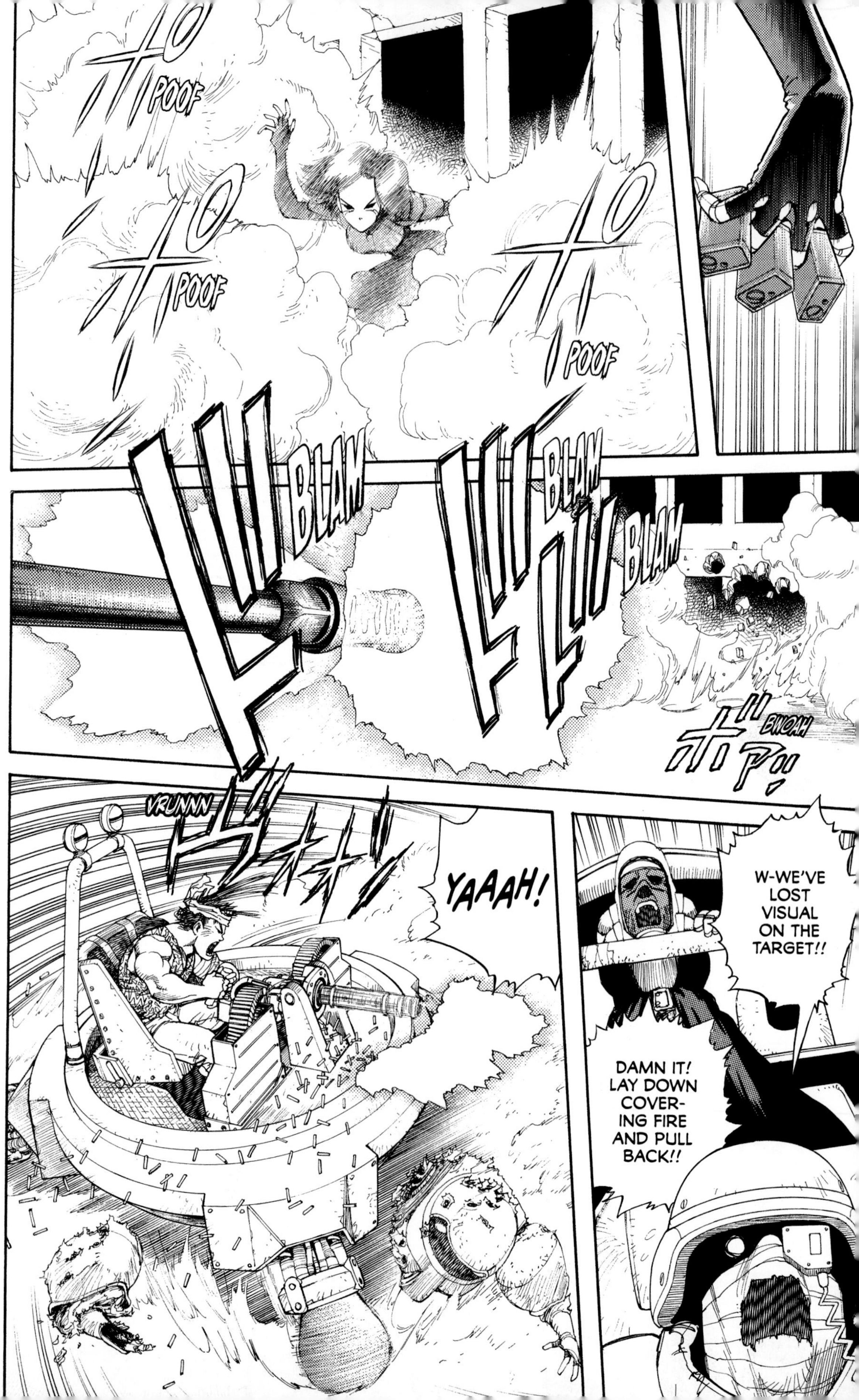
POOF
POOF
POOF
BLAM
BLAM
BLAM
BWOAH
W-WE'VE LOST VISUAL ON THE TARGET!!
DAMN IT! LAY DOWN COVER-ING FIRE AND PULL BACK!!
VRUNNN
YAAAH!

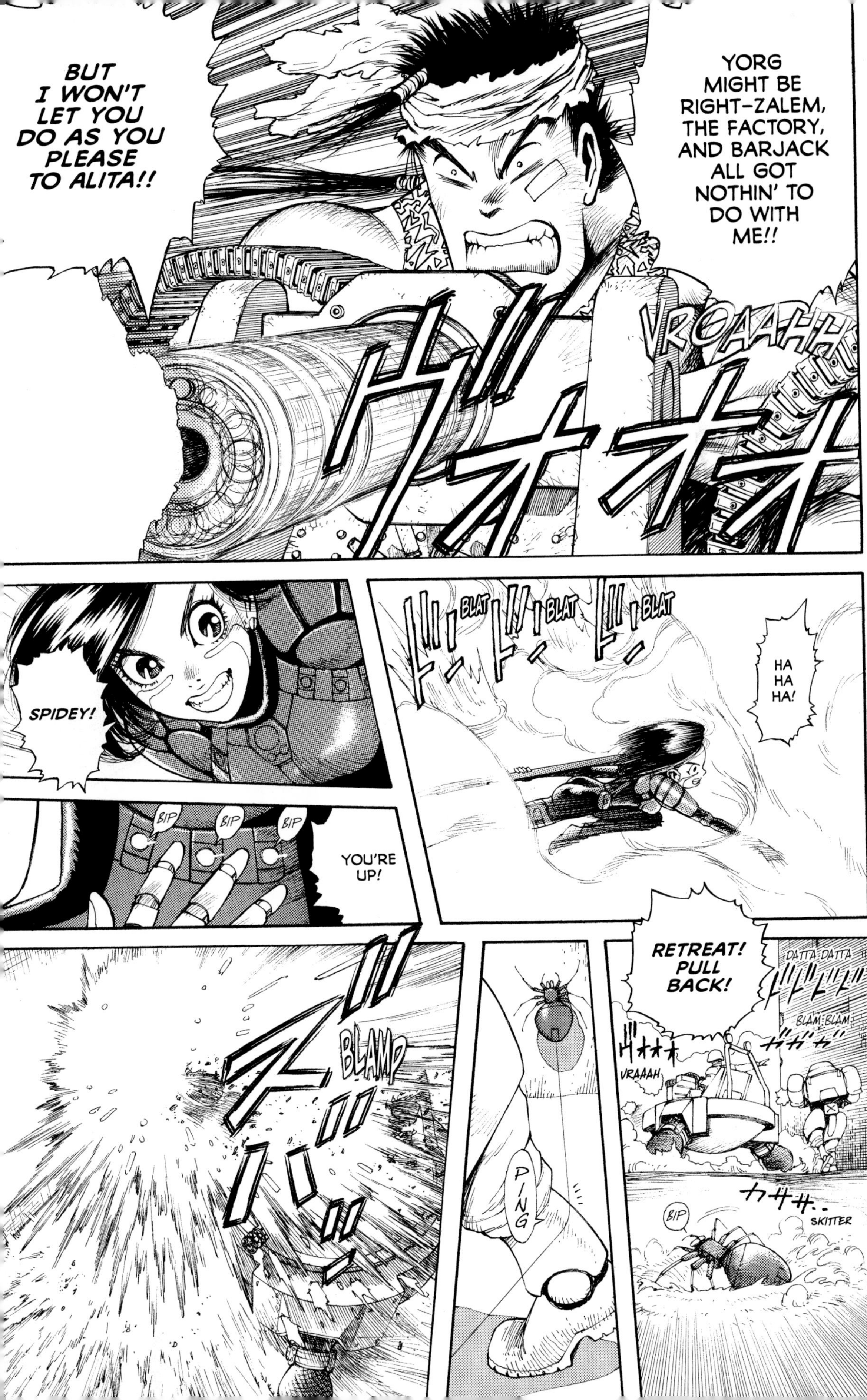
YORG MIGHT BE RIGHT–ZALEM, THE FACTORY, AND BARJACK ALL GOT NOTHIN' TO DO WITH ME!!
BUT I WON'T LET YOU DO AS YOU PLEASE TO ALITA!!
VROAAHH
BLAT
BLAT
BLAT
HA HA HA!
SPIDEY!
BIP
BIP
BIP
YOU'RE UP!
RETREAT! PULL BACK!
DATTA DATTA
BLAM BLAM
VRAAAH
BIP
SKITTER
PING
BLAMP

BOOOM
AAAH!
MORE ENEMIES TO THE REAR?!
RATATAT
BLAM BLAM
WHEN DID THEY SET UP A TRAP?!
*SPIDEY:
One of the special TUNED armaments. It's a Zalem-designed insectoid robot bomb that is programmed to set up traps according to the terrain. It can also be commanded externally, allowing for a wide array of tactical uses.
(When stored)
MISSILE BEES!
SHAK
FIRE!
BWEEE
FUMP
VWEEEE
BIP
TAKKA TAKKA
BIP

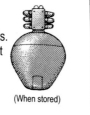

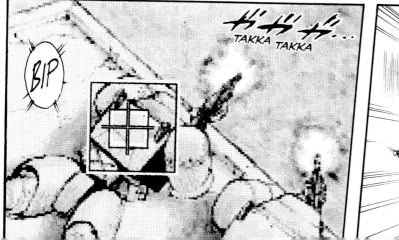

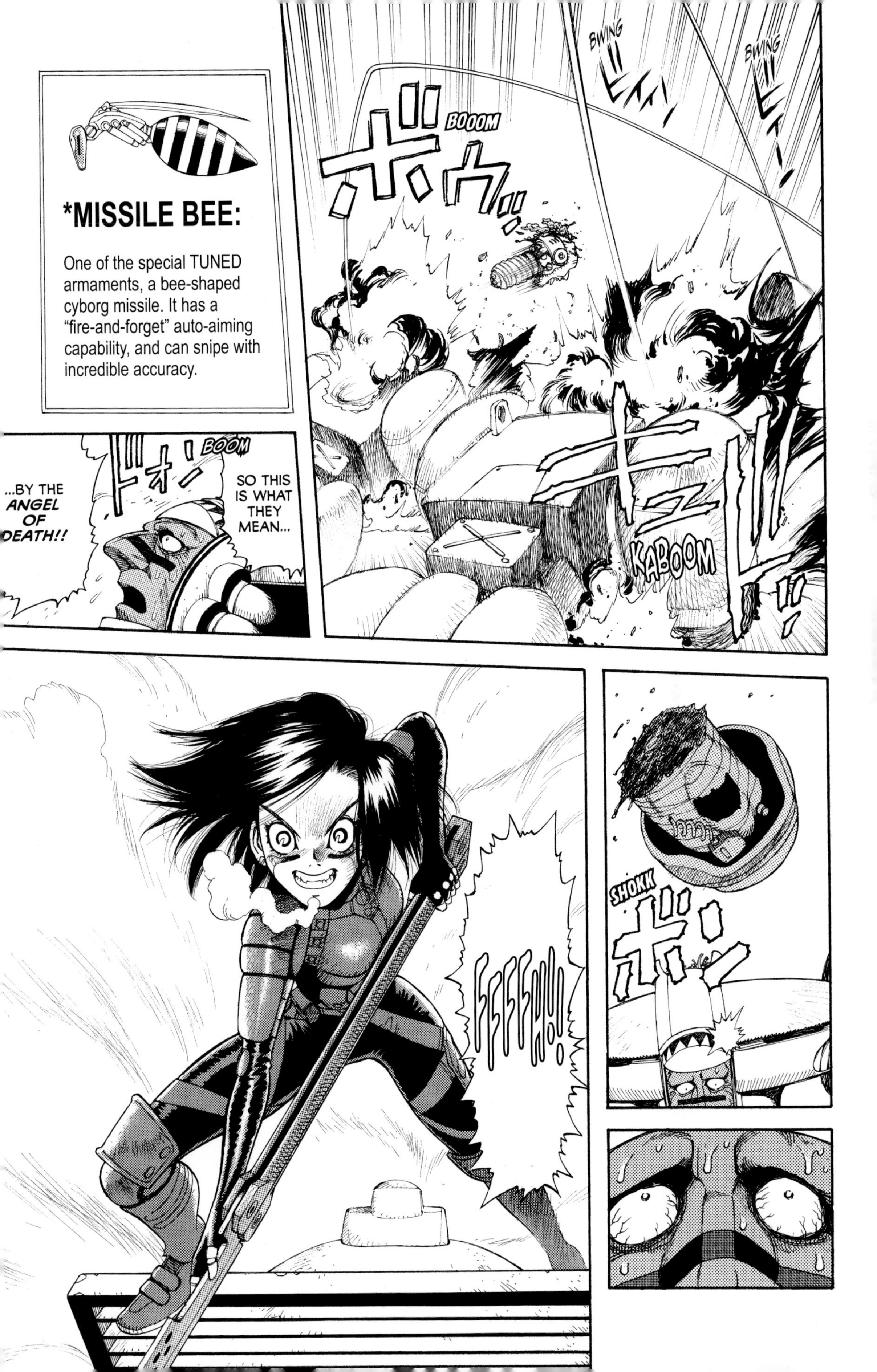
BWING
BWING
BOOOM
KABOOM
BOOM
SO THIS IS WHAT THEY MEAN...
...BY THE *ANGEL OF DEATH!!*
*MISSILE BEE:
One of the special TUNED armaments, a bee-shaped cyborg missile. It has a "fire-and-forget" auto-aiming capability, and can snipe with incredible accuracy.
SHOKK

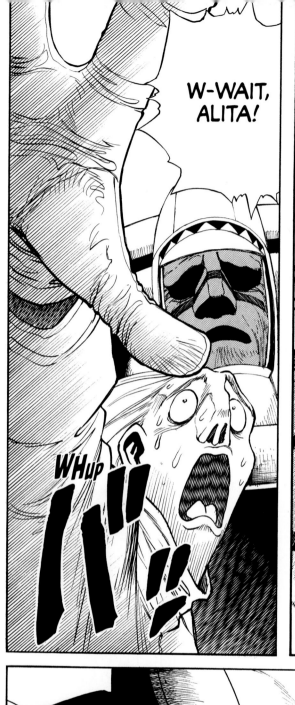

W-WAIT,
ALITA!

WHup

HAAAA.

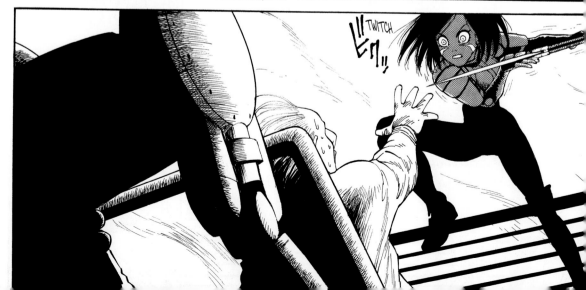

TWITCH

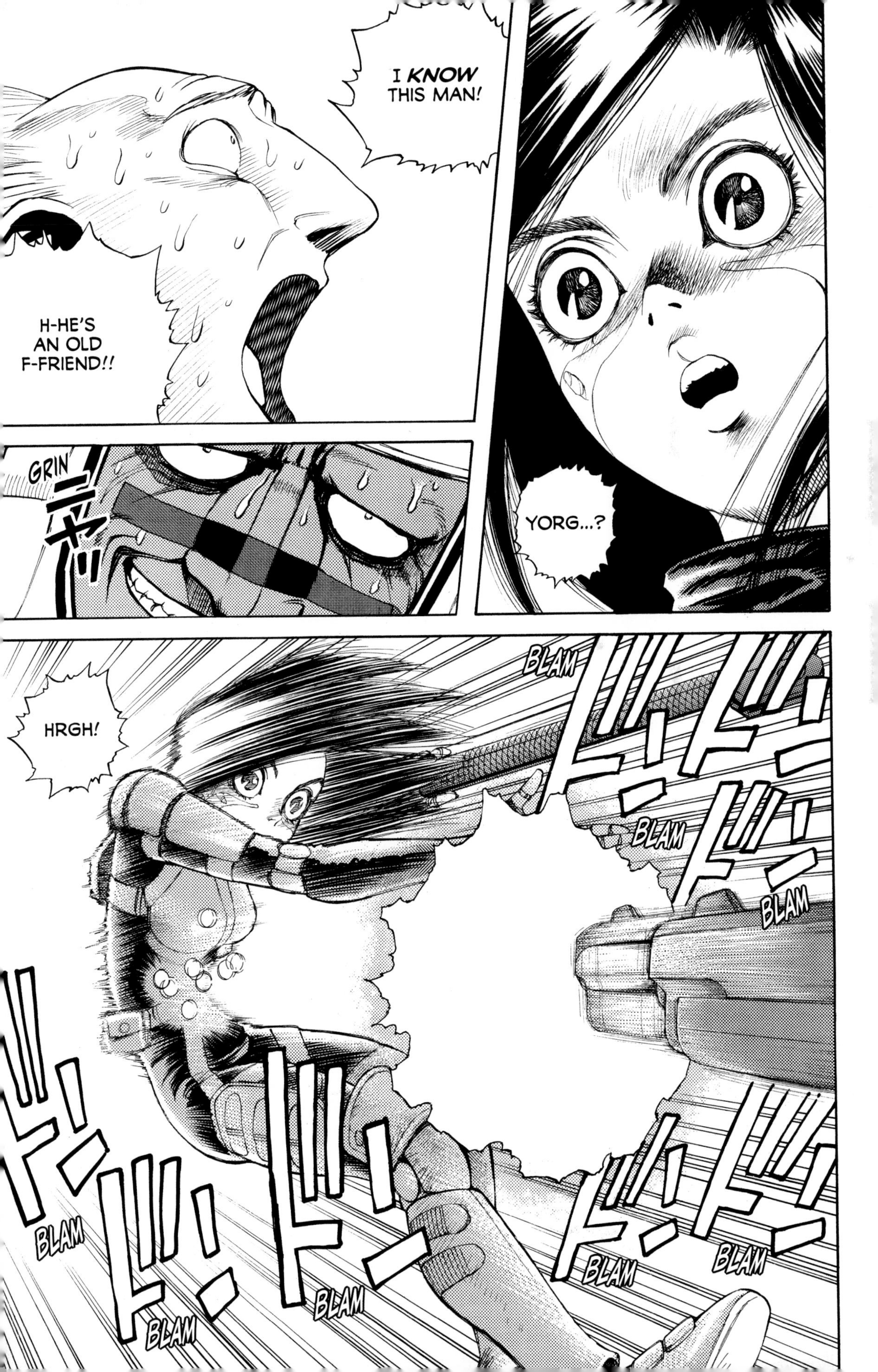
YORG...?
I KNOW THIS MAN!
H-HE'S AN OLD F-FRIEND!!
GRIN
ニヤッ
BLAM
HRGH!
BLAM
BLAM
BLAM
BLAM
BLAM
BLAM
BLAM

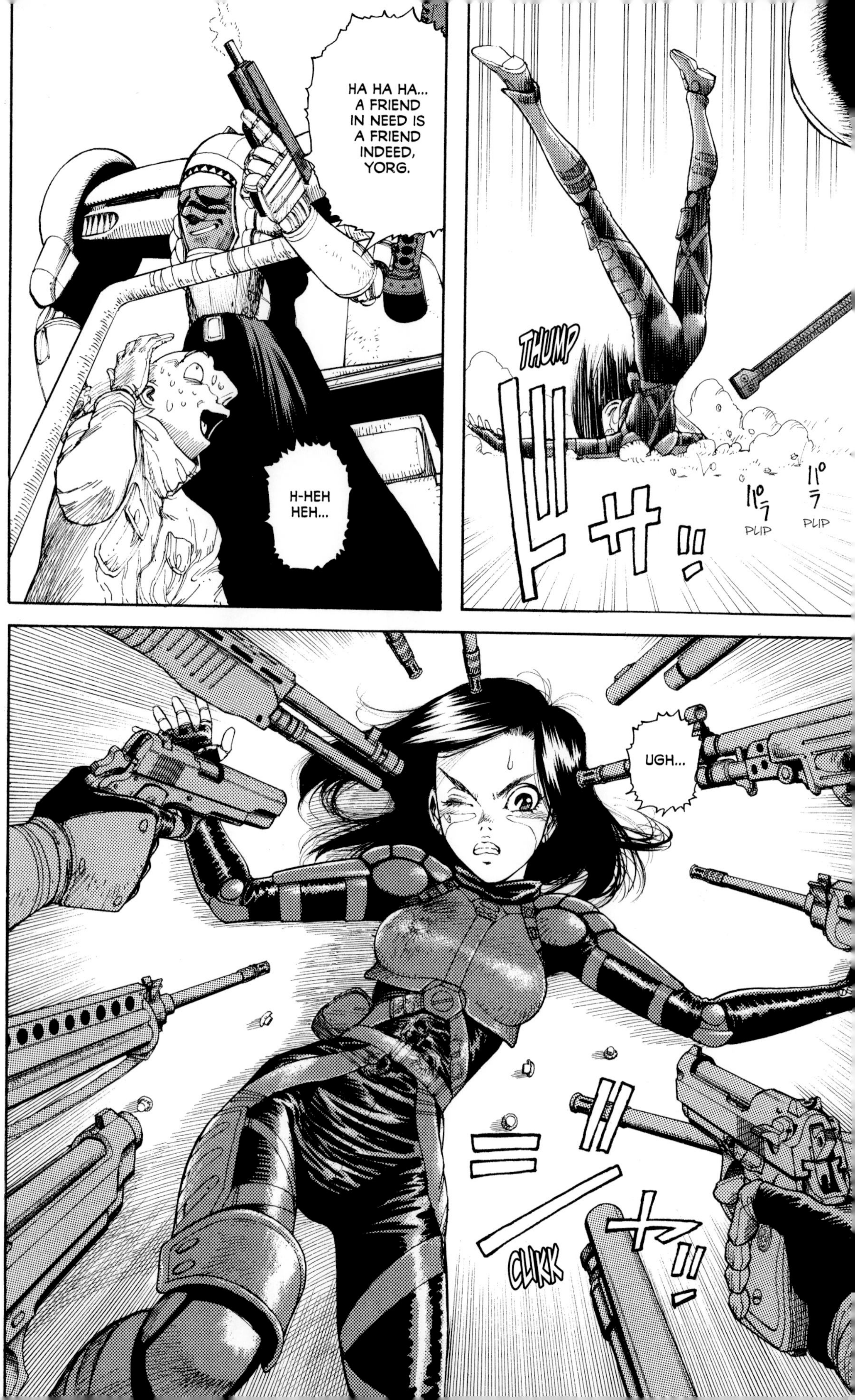
THUMP
ドサッ
パラ
PLIP
パラ
PLIP
HA HA HA... A FRIEND IN NEED IS A FRIEND INDEED, YORG.
H-HEH HEH...
UGH...
CLIKK

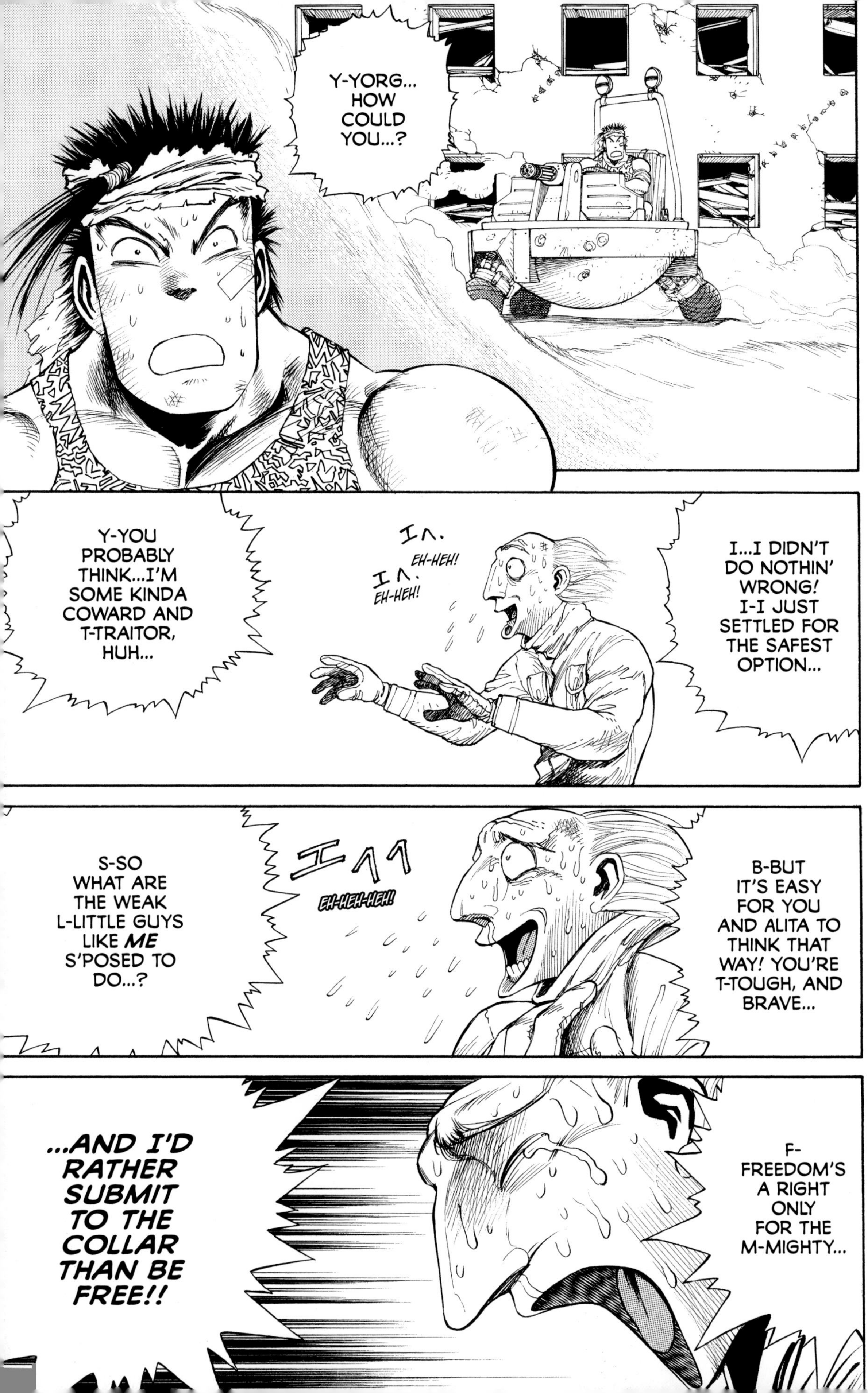
Y-YORG... HOW COULD YOU...?
I...I DIDN'T DO NOTHIN' WRONG! I-I JUST SETTLED FOR THE SAFEST OPTION...
EH-HEH!
EH-HEH!
Y-YOU PROBABLY THINK...I'M SOME KINDA COWARD AND T-TRAITOR, HUH...
B-BUT IT'S EASY FOR YOU AND ALITA TO THINK THAT WAY! YOU'RE T-TOUGH, AND BRAVE...
EH-HEH-HEH!
S-SO WHAT ARE THE WEAK L-LITTLE GUYS LIKE *ME* S'POSED TO DO...?
F-FREEDOM'S A RIGHT ONLY FOR THE M-MIGHTY...
...AND I'D RATHER SUBMIT TO THE COLLAR THAN BE FREE!!

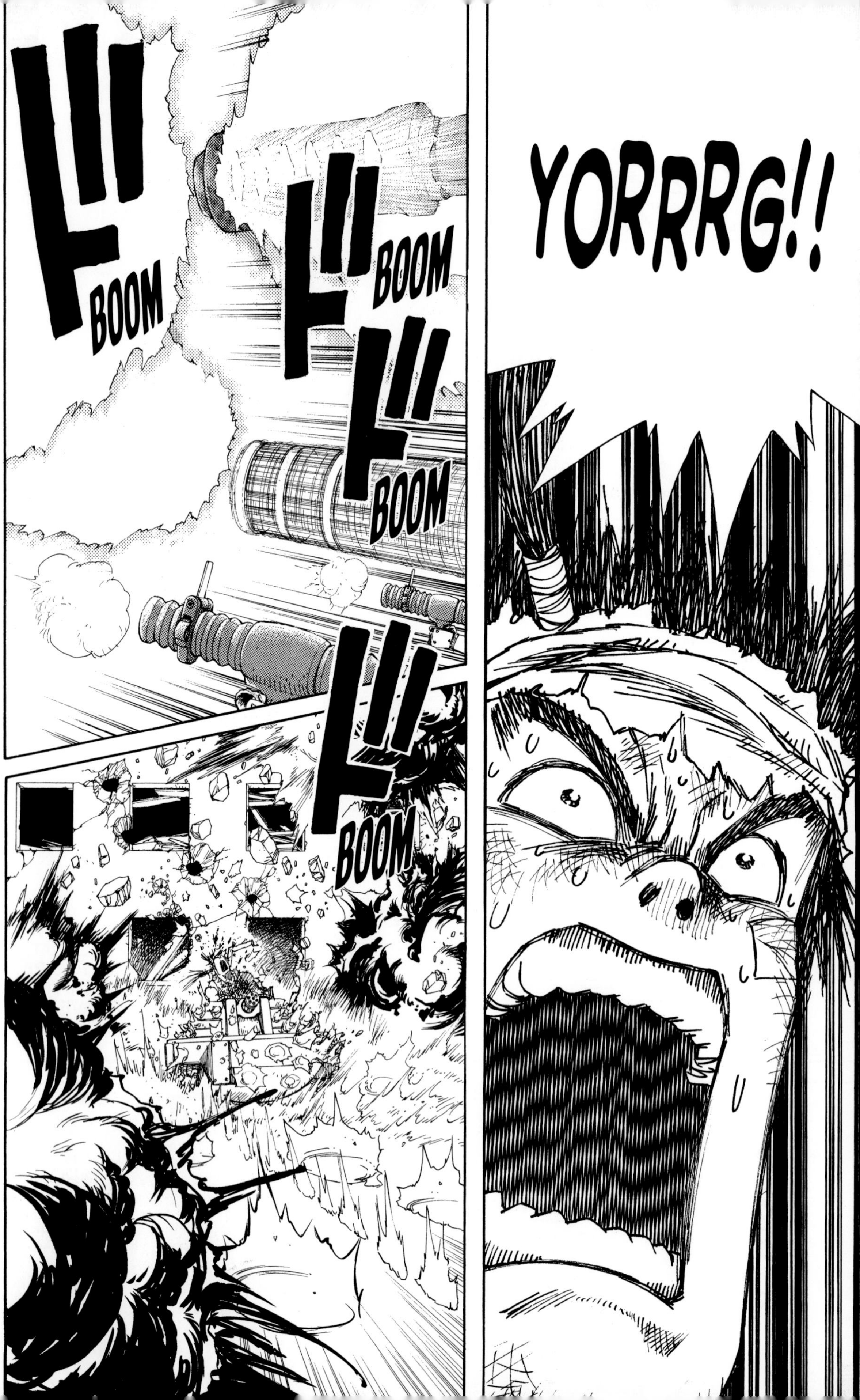
YORRRG!!
ド BOOM
ド BOOM
ド BOOM
ド BOOM

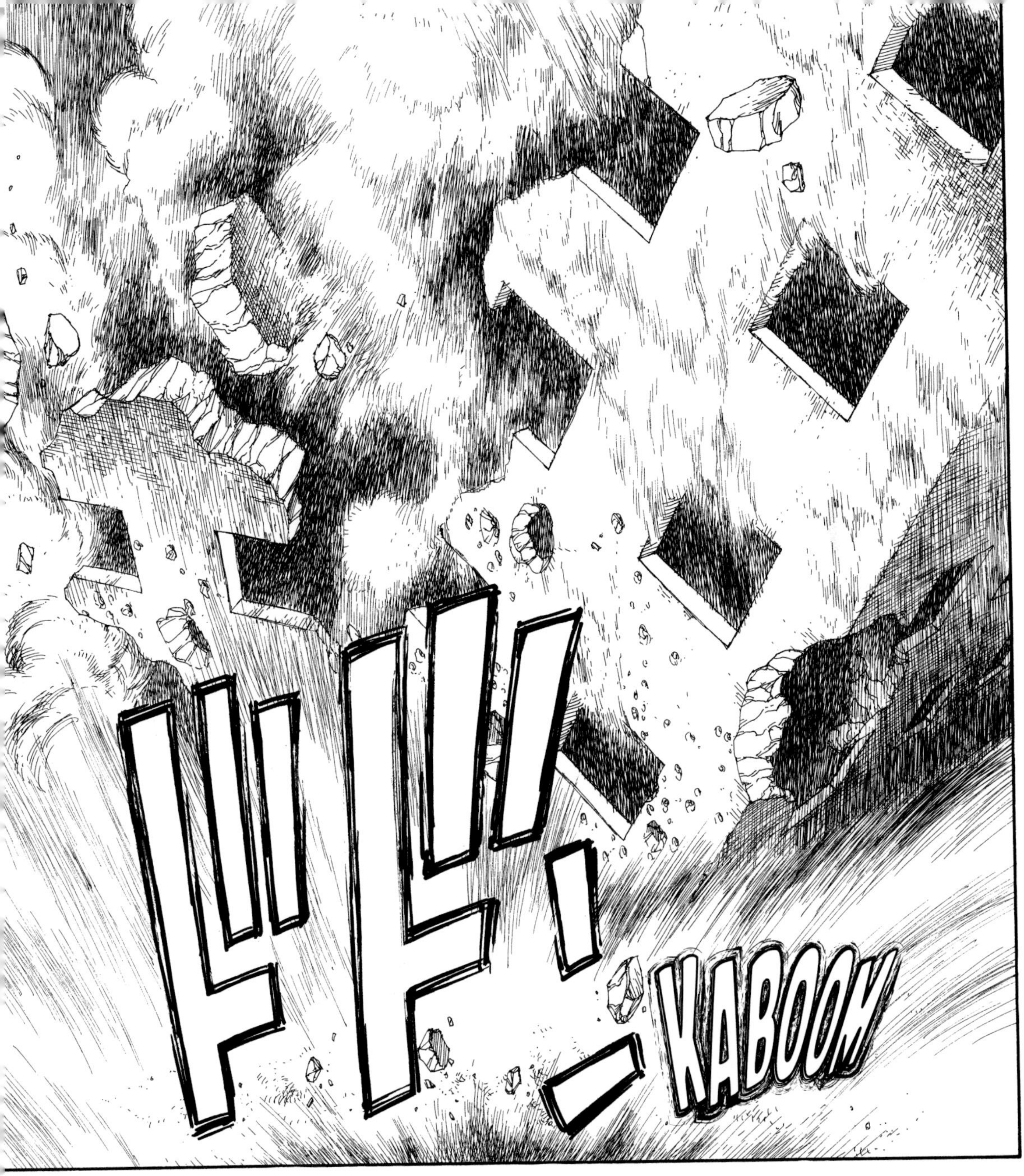
KABOOM
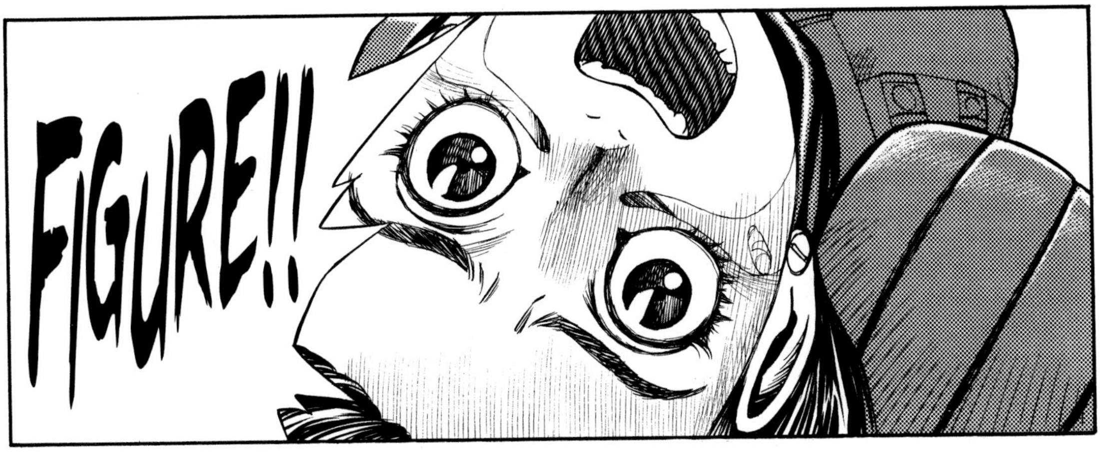
FIGURE!!

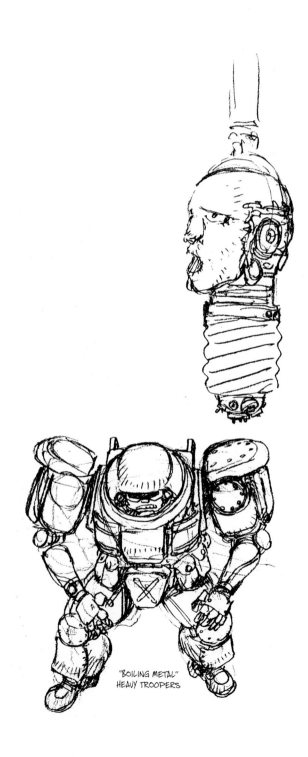

"BOILING METAL"
HEAVY TROOPERS

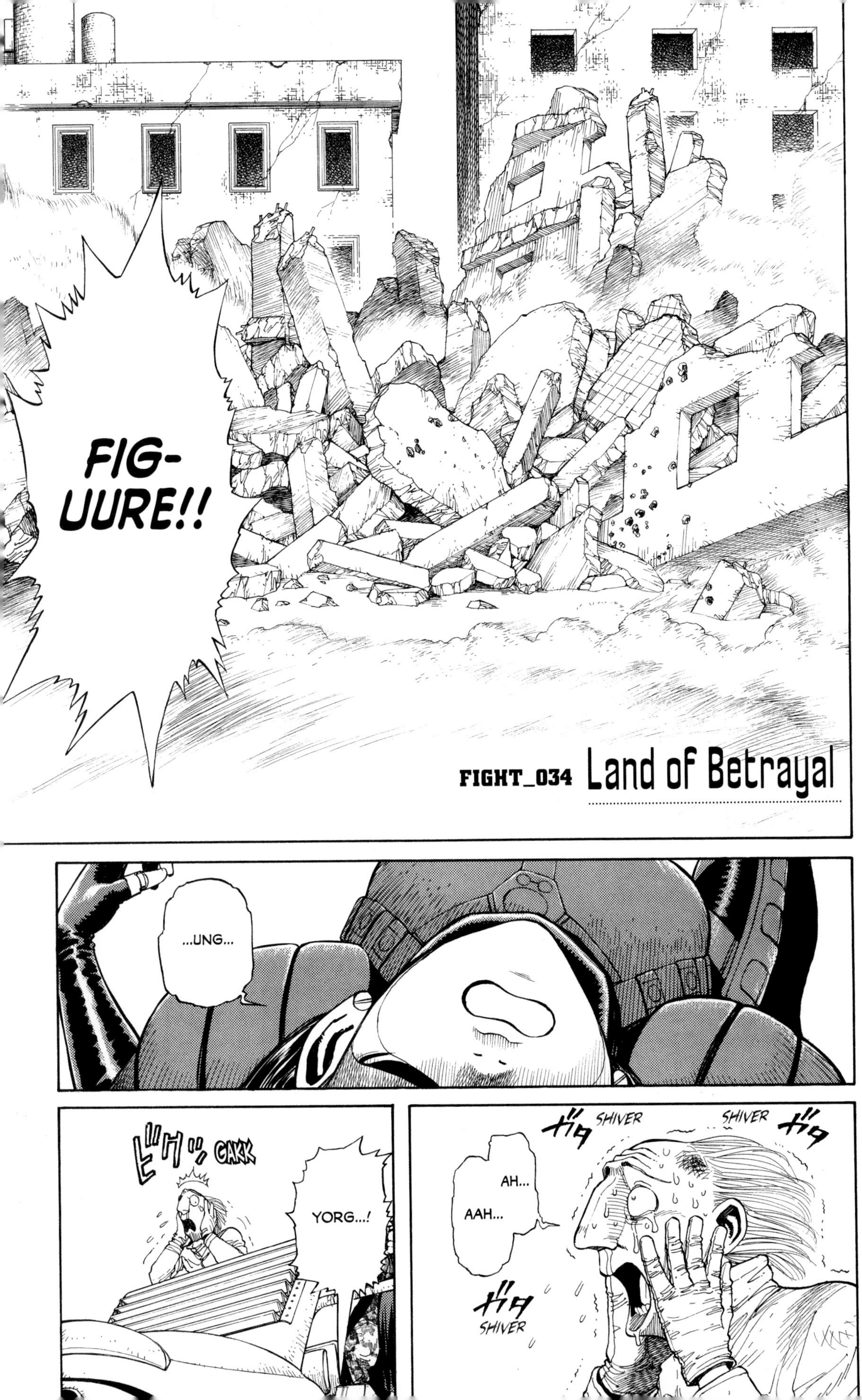
FIG-
UURE!!
FIGHT_034 Land of Betrayal
...UNG...
ガタ SHIVER
SHIVER ガタ
AH...
AAH...
ガタ SHIVER
ビクッ GAKK
YORG...!

FIGHT_034 Land of Betrayal

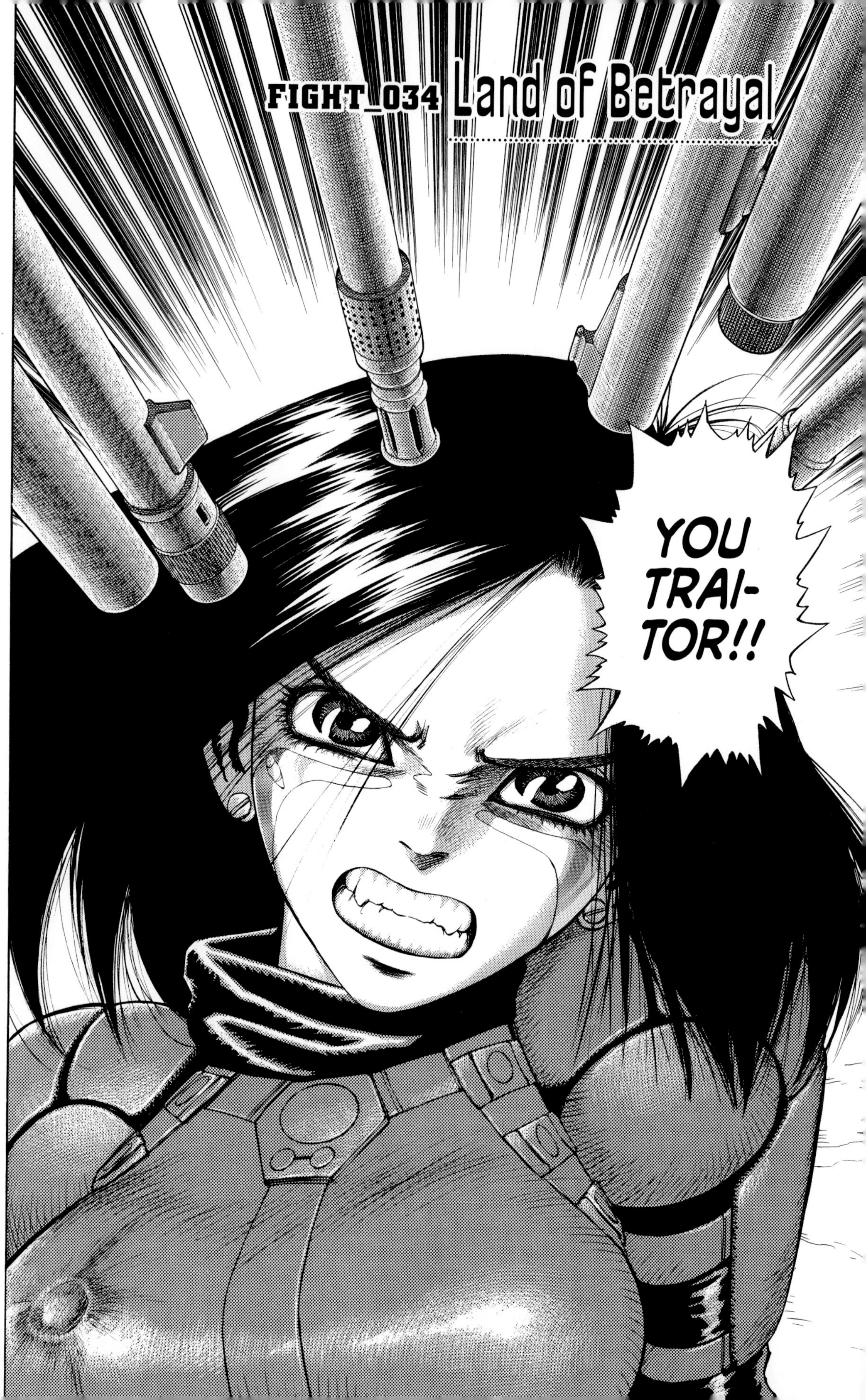
YOU TRAI- TOR!!

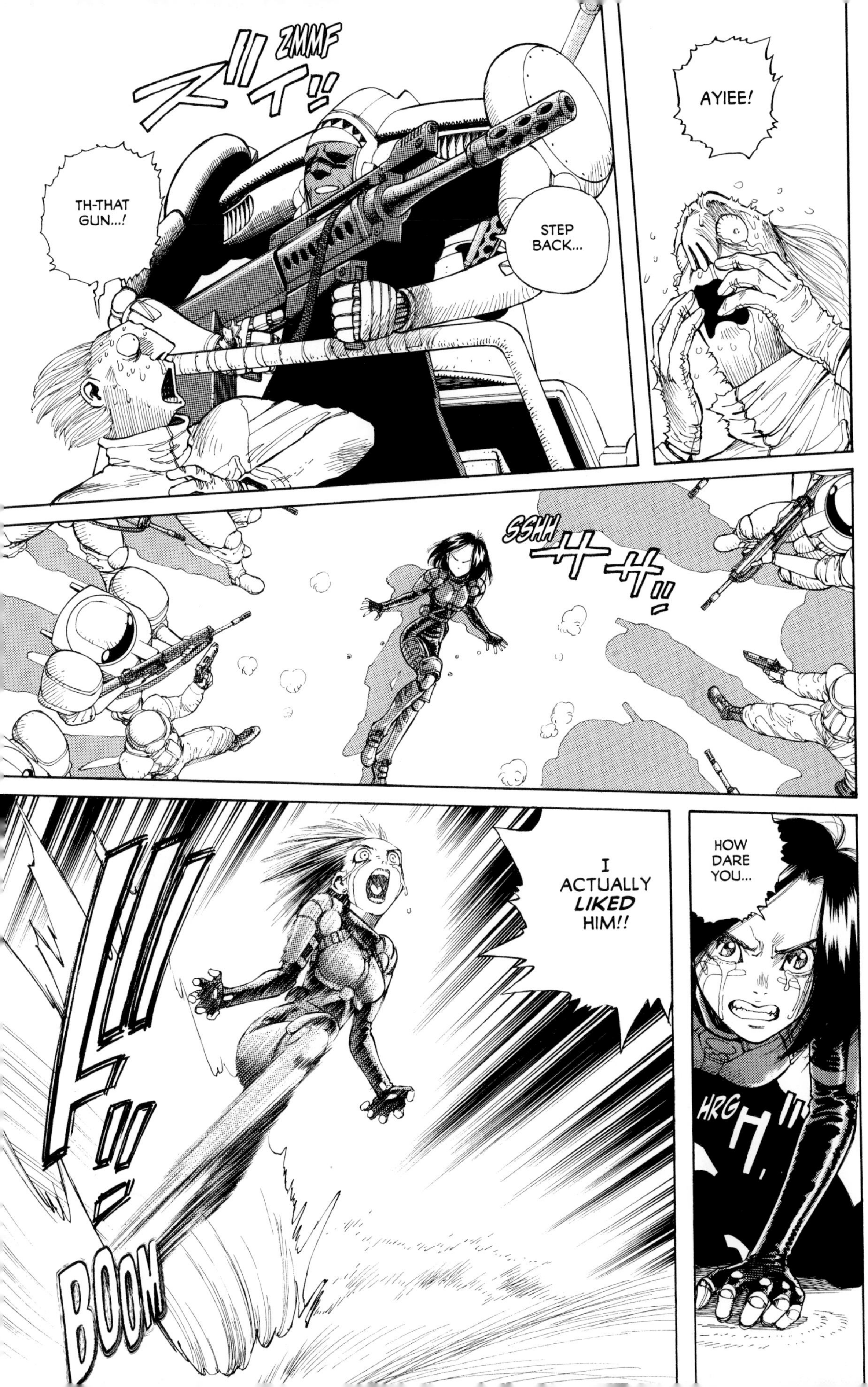
AYIEE!
ZMMF
STEP BACK...
TH-THAT GUN...!
SSHH
HOW DARE YOU...
HRG
I ACTUALLY *LIKED* HIM!!
BOOM

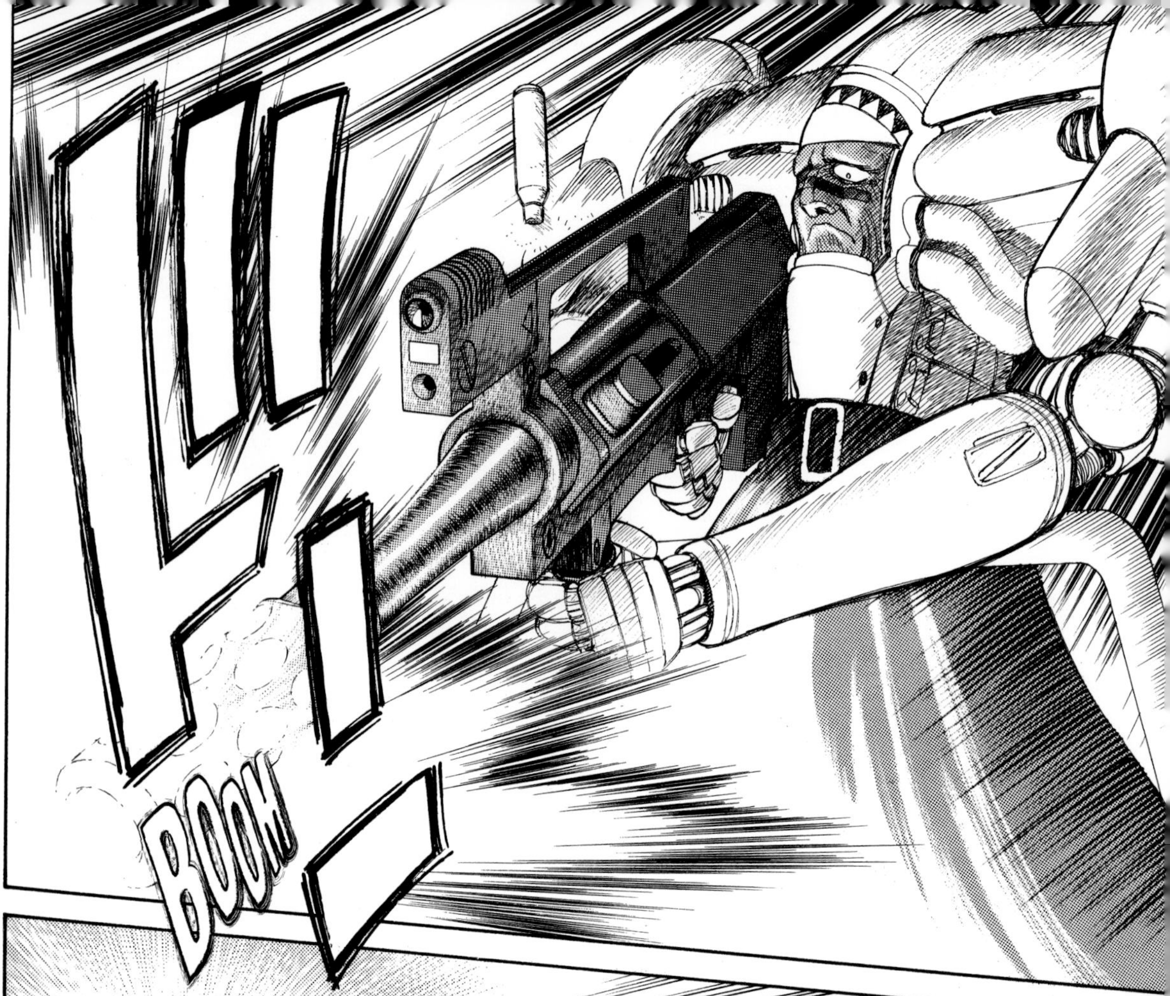
BOOM
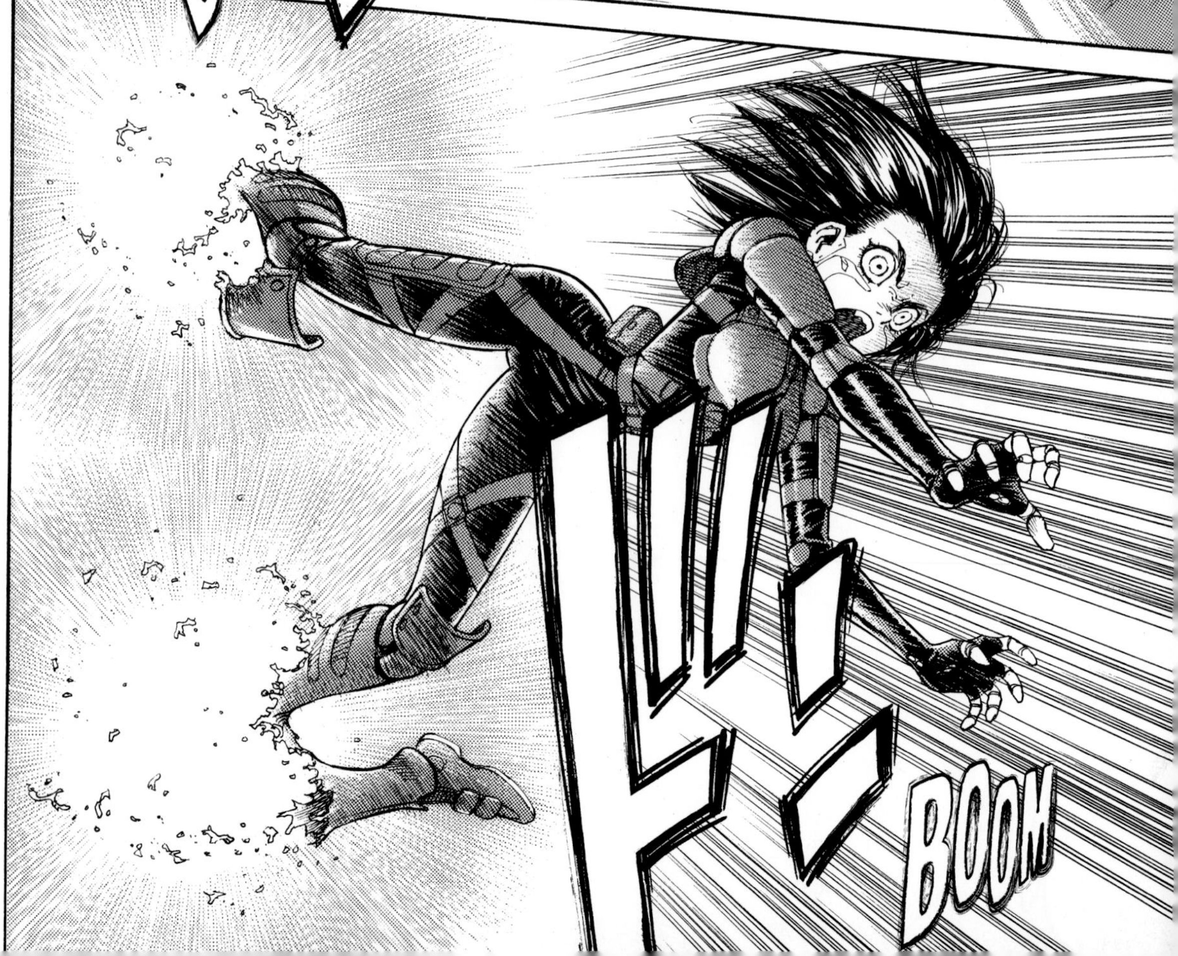
BOOM

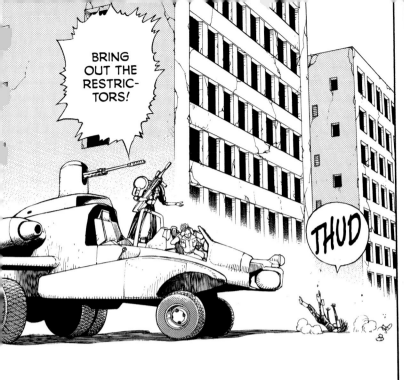

GANK
BRING OUT THE RESTRICTORS!
THUD
AUUGH!
BZZAT
HUFF!
HUFF!
...
SOUND OFF AND GET OUR NUMBERS!
BRING UP THE REAR GUARD AND LET'S RESUPPLY AS PLANNED!!

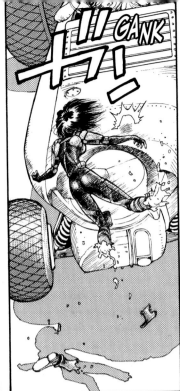

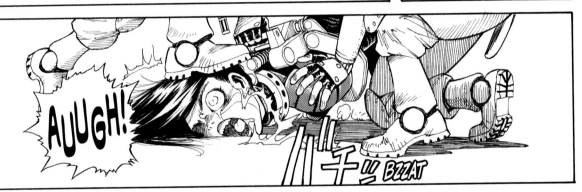

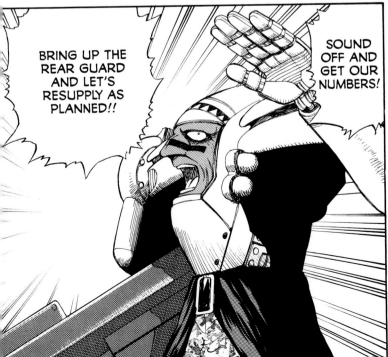

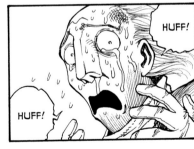

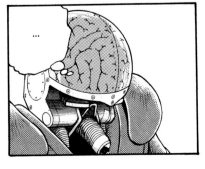

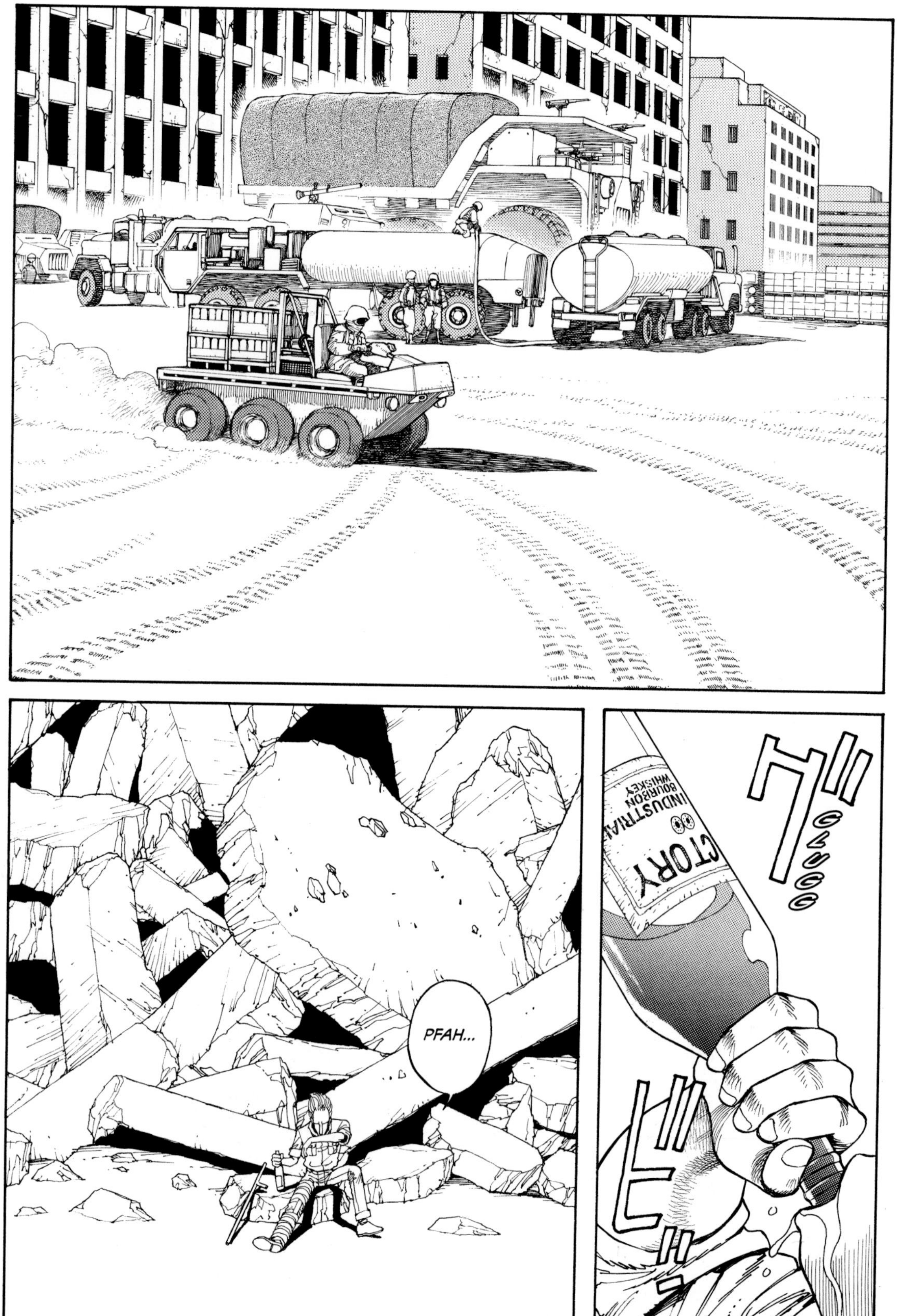
CTORY
INDUSTRIA
BOURBON
WHISKEY
GLUGG
PFAH...

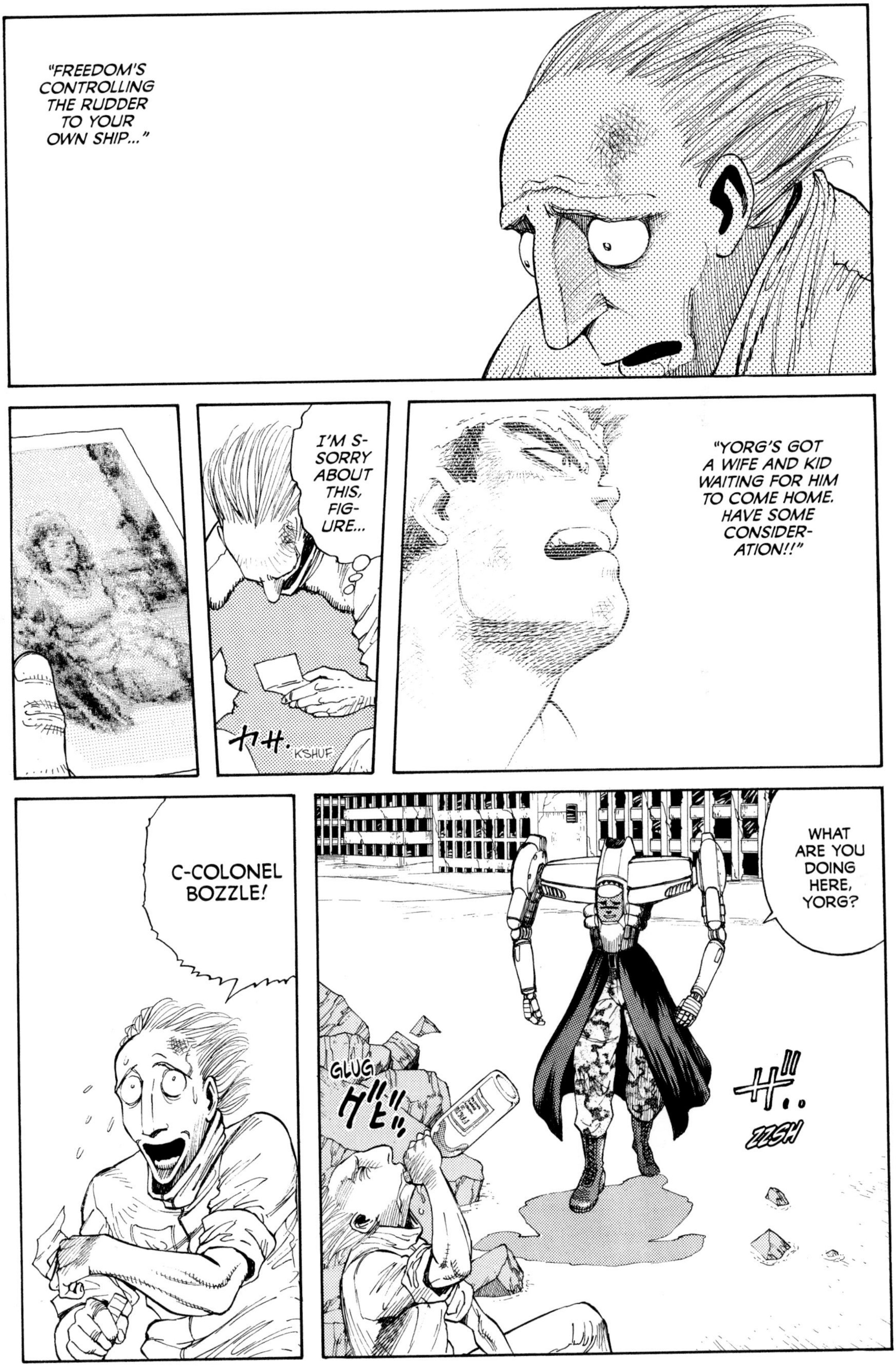
"FREEDOM'S CONTROLLING THE RUDDER TO YOUR OWN SHIP..."
"YORG'S GOT A WIFE AND KID WAITING FOR HIM TO COME HOME. HAVE SOME CONSIDER-ATION!!"
I'M S-SORRY ABOUT THIS, FIG-URE...
KSHUF
WHAT ARE YOU DOING HERE, YORG?
ZZSH
GLUG
C-COLONEL BOZZLE!

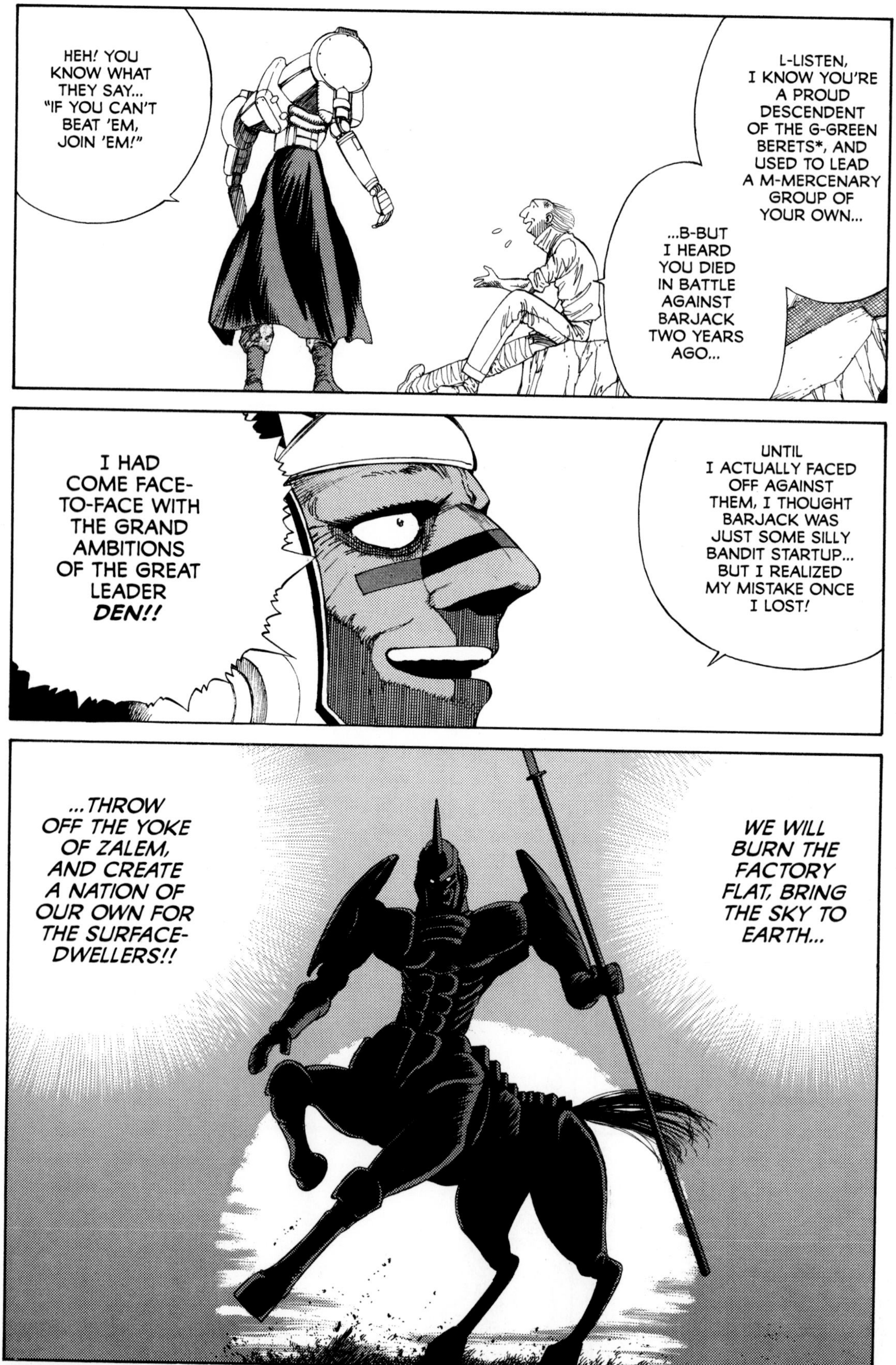
L-LISTEN, I KNOW YOU'RE A PROUD DESCENDENT OF THE G-GREEN BERETS*, AND USED TO LEAD A M-MERCENARY GROUP OF YOUR OWN...
...B-BUT I HEARD YOU DIED IN BATTLE AGAINST BARJACK TWO YEARS AGO...
HEH! YOU KNOW WHAT THEY SAY... "IF YOU CAN'T BEAT 'EM, JOIN 'EM!"
UNTIL I ACTUALLY FACED OFF AGAINST THEM, I THOUGHT BARJACK WAS JUST SOME SILLY BANDIT STARTUP... BUT I REALIZED MY MISTAKE ONCE I LOST!
I HAD COME FACE-TO-FACE WITH THE GRAND AMBITIONS OF THE GREAT LEADER DEN!!
WE WILL BURN THE FACTORY FLAT, BRING THE SKY TO EARTH...
...THROW OFF THE YOKE OF ZALEM, AND CREATE A NATION OF OUR OWN FOR THE SURFACE-DWELLERS!!

***Green Berets:** Referring to the special elite force of the American military. In this era, it seems to be considered the name of some powerful tribe of ancient warriors.

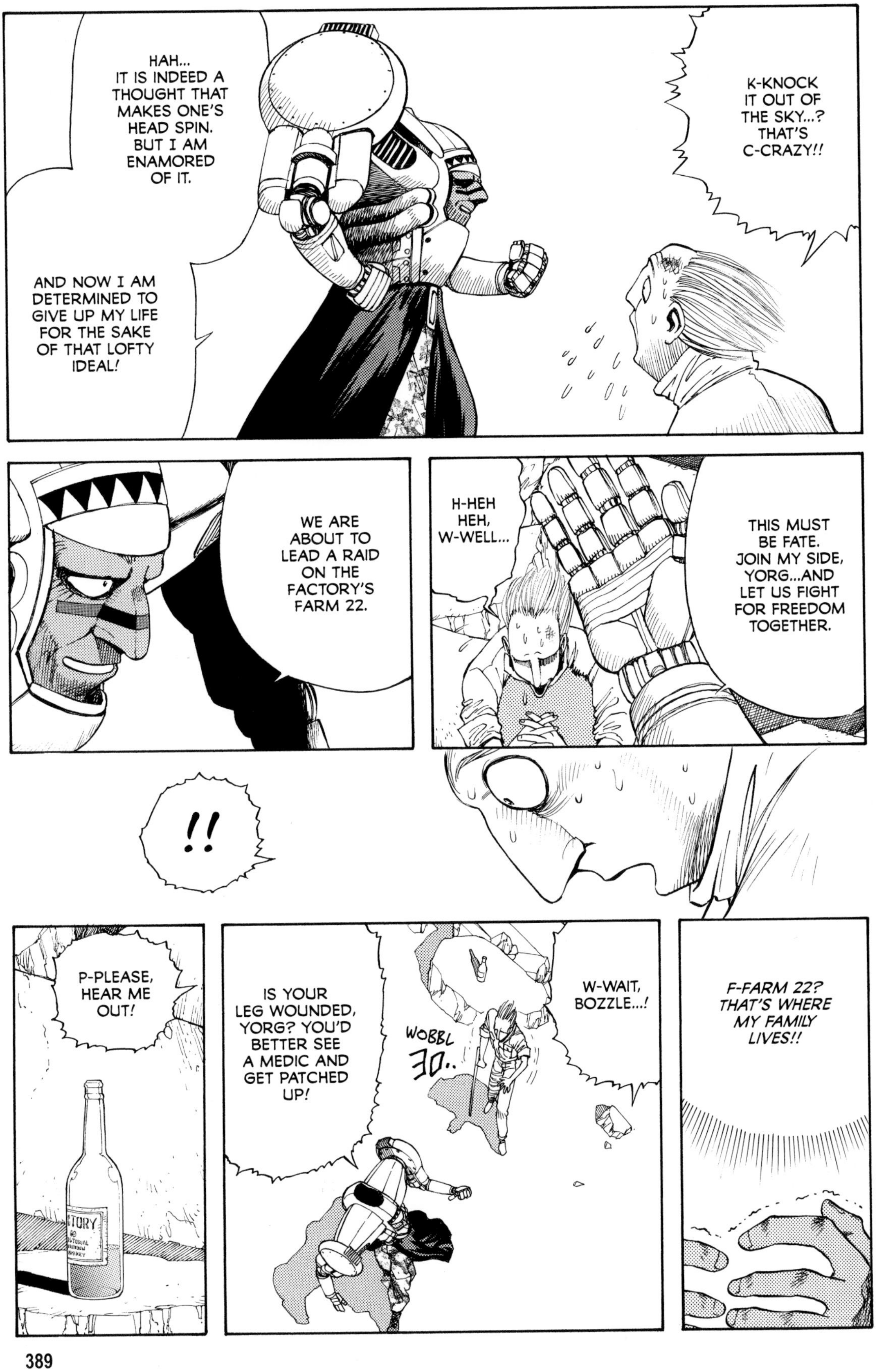
K-KNOCK IT OUT OF THE SKY...? THAT'S C-CRAZY!!
HAH... IT IS INDEED A THOUGHT THAT MAKES ONE'S HEAD SPIN. BUT I AM ENAMORED OF IT.
AND NOW I AM DETERMINED TO GIVE UP MY LIFE FOR THE SAKE OF THAT LOFTY IDEAL!
THIS MUST BE FATE. JOIN MY SIDE, YORG...AND LET US FIGHT FOR FREEDOM TOGETHER.
H-HEH HEH, W-WELL...
WE ARE ABOUT TO LEAD A RAID ON THE FACTORY'S FARM 22.
!!
F-FARM 22? THAT'S WHERE MY FAMILY LIVES!!
W-WAIT, BOZZLE...!
WOBBL
IS YOUR LEG WOUNDED, YORG? YOU'D BETTER SEE A MEDIC AND GET PATCHED UP!
P-PLEASE, HEAR ME OUT!

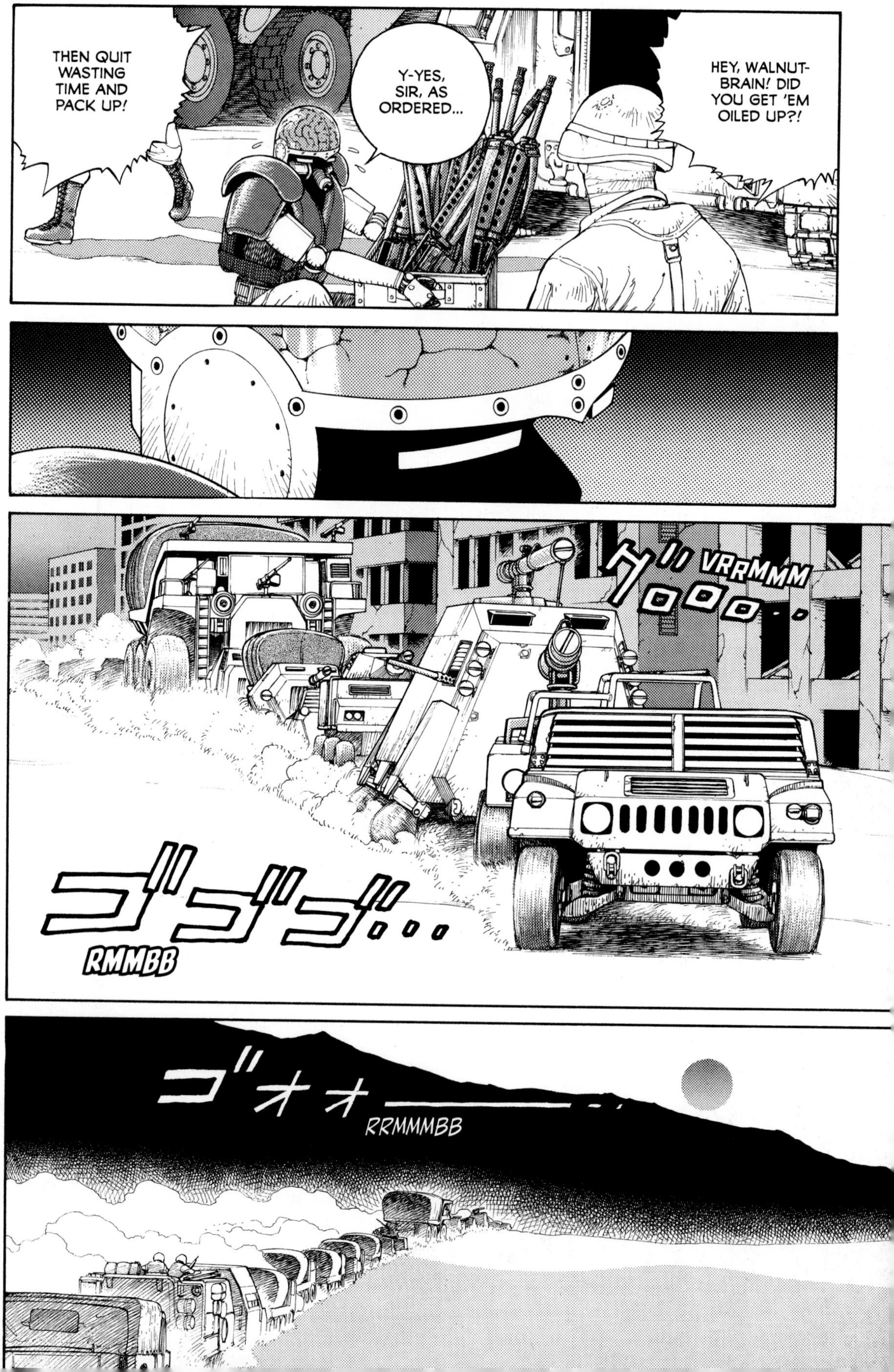
HEY, WALNUT-BRAIN! DID YOU GET 'EM OILED UP?!
Y-YES, SIR, AS ORDERED...
THEN QUIT WASTING TIME AND PACK UP!
VRRMMM
ゴゴゴ...
RMMBB
ゴオオ――..
RRMMMBB

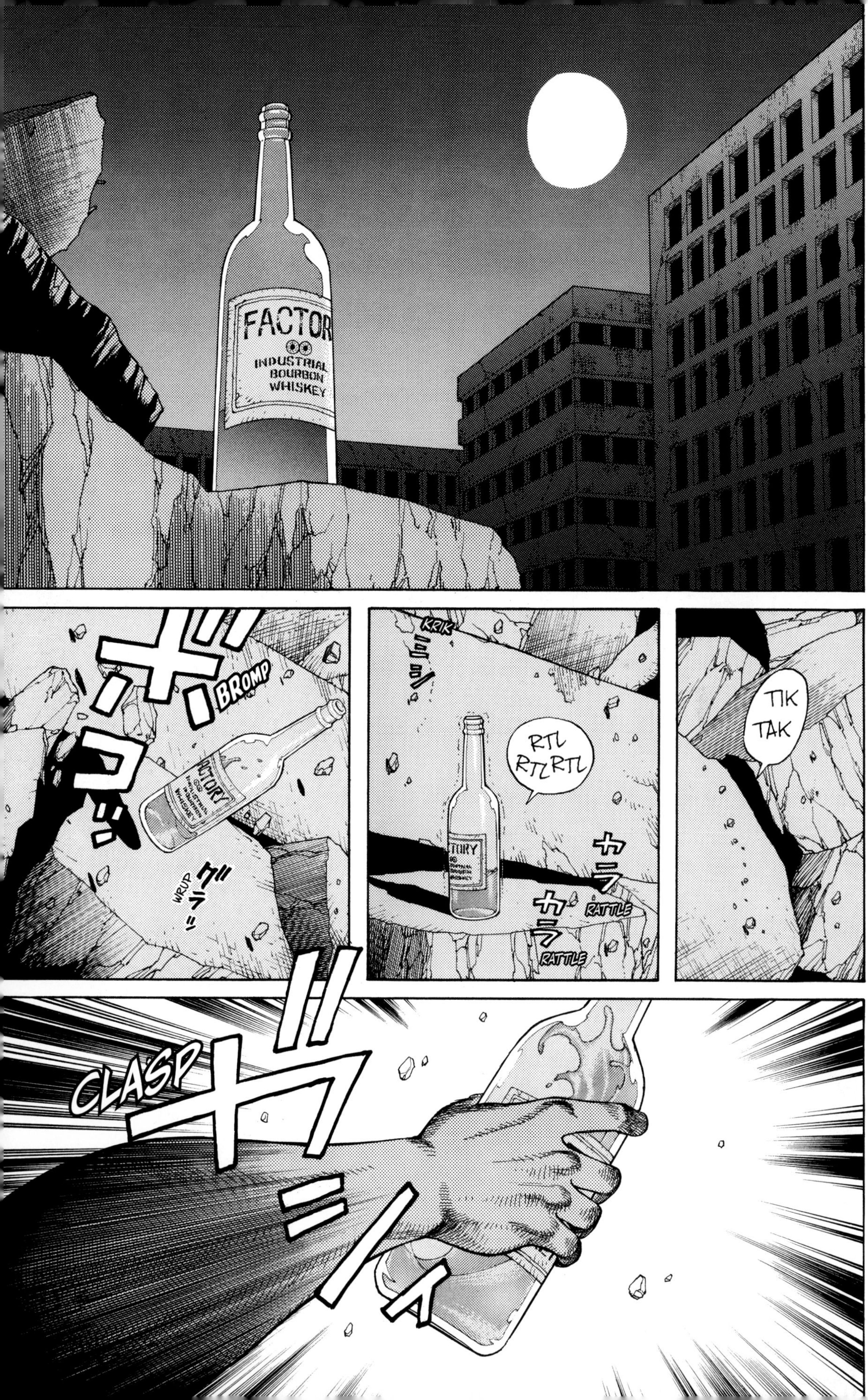
FACTOR
INDUSTRIAL BOURBON WHISKEY
TIK TAK
KRIK
RTL RTL RTL
RATTLE
RATTLE
BROMP
WRUP
CLASP

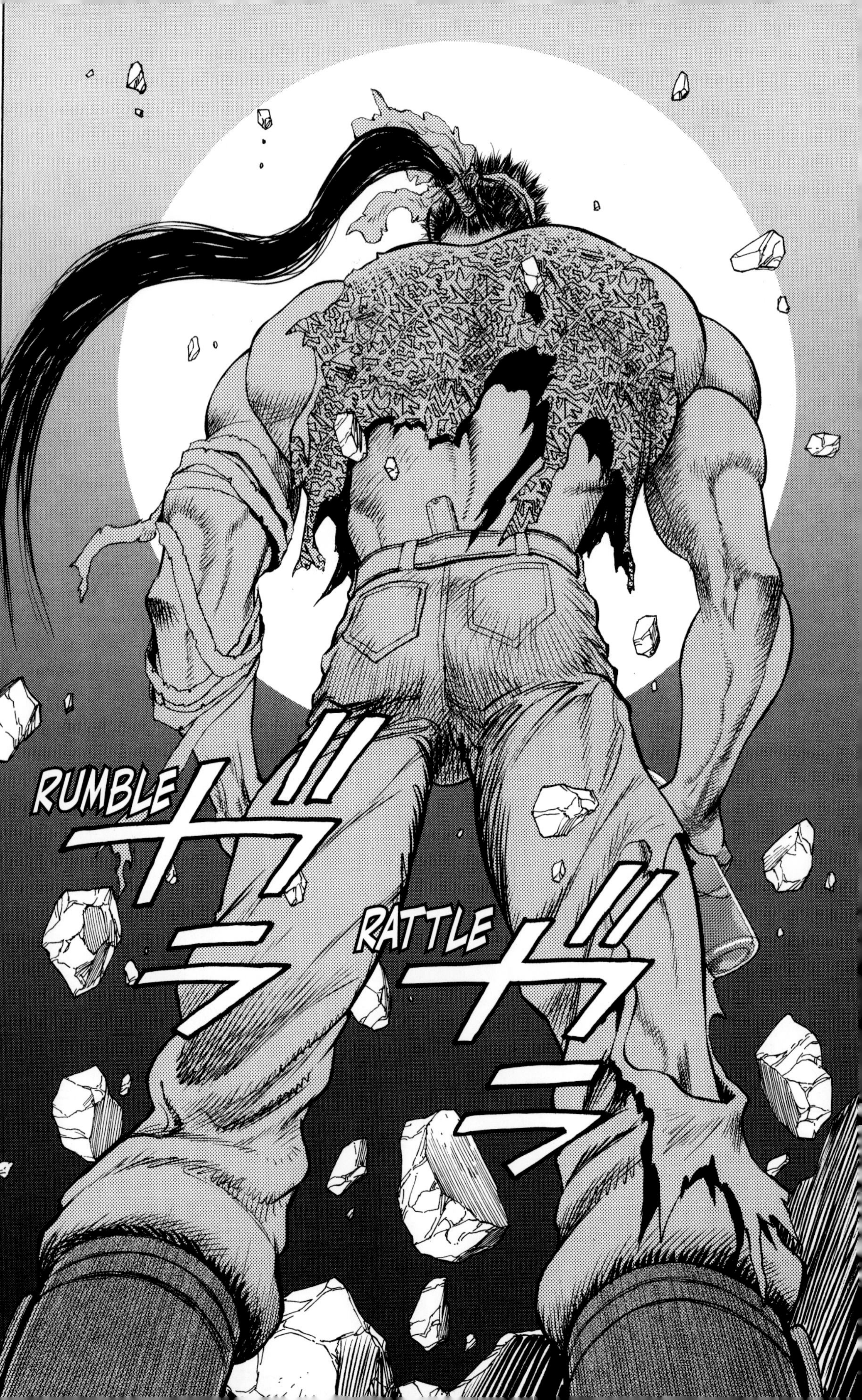
RUMBLE
RATTLE

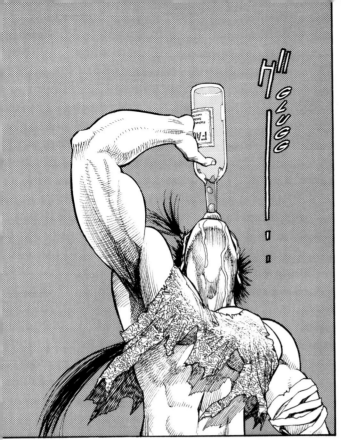

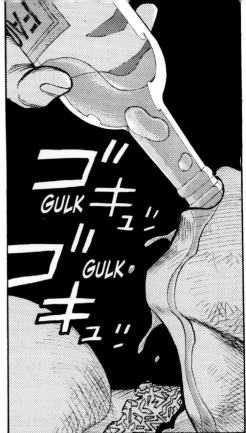

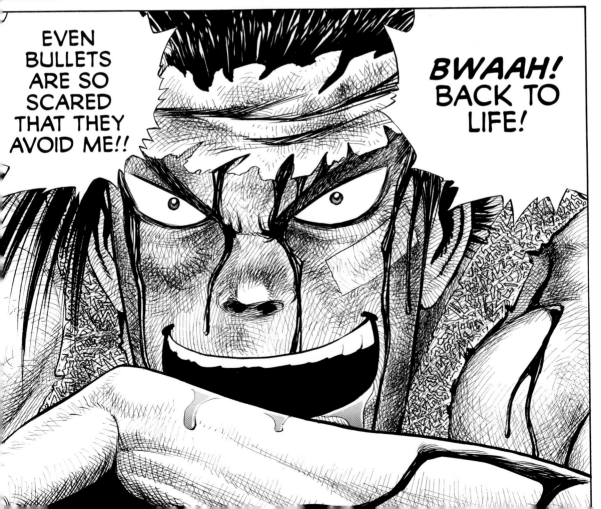

GULK
ゴキュッ
GULK
ゴキュッ
GLUGG
BWAAH! BACK TO LIFE!
EVEN BULLETS ARE SO SCARED THAT THEY AVOID ME!!

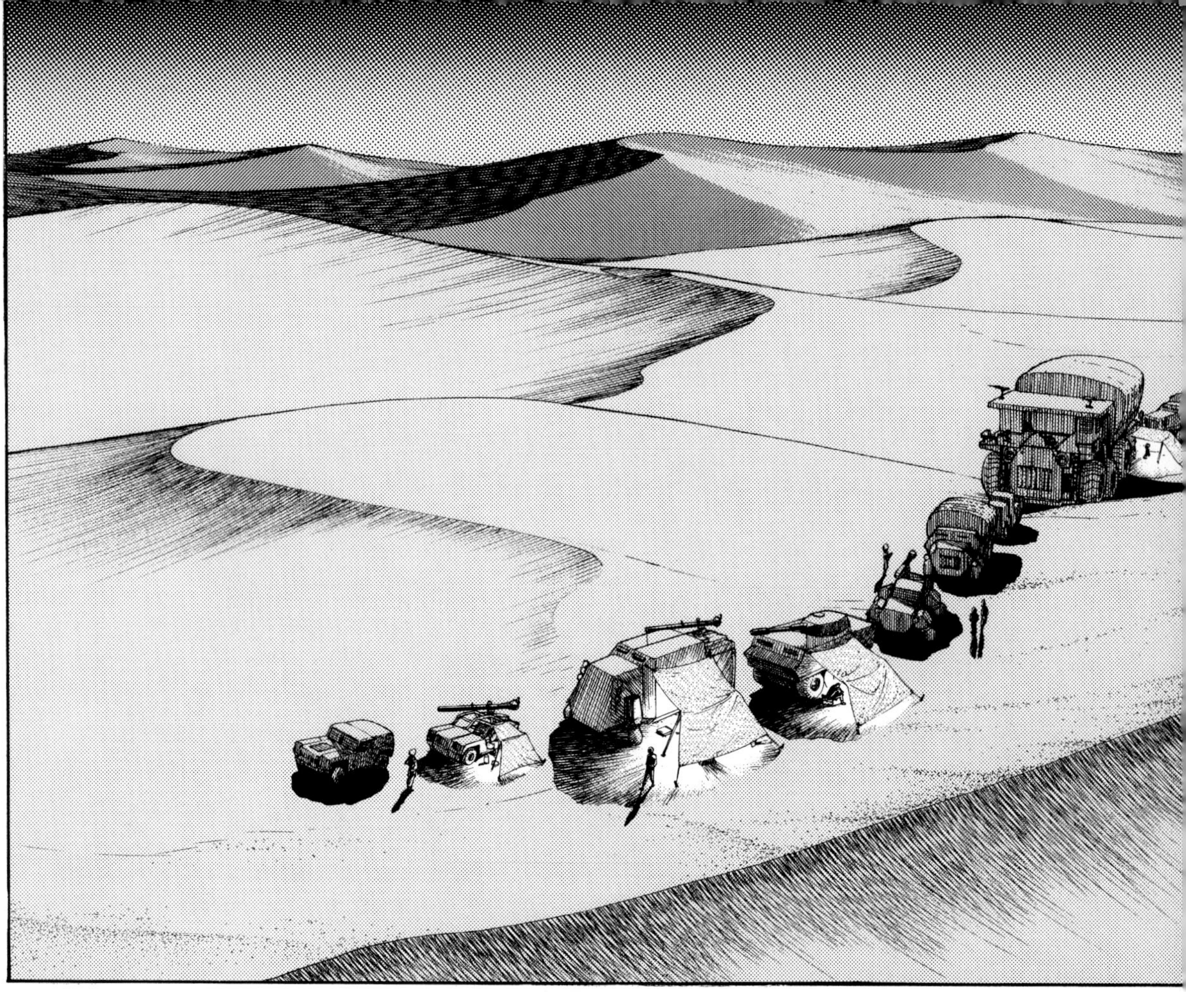

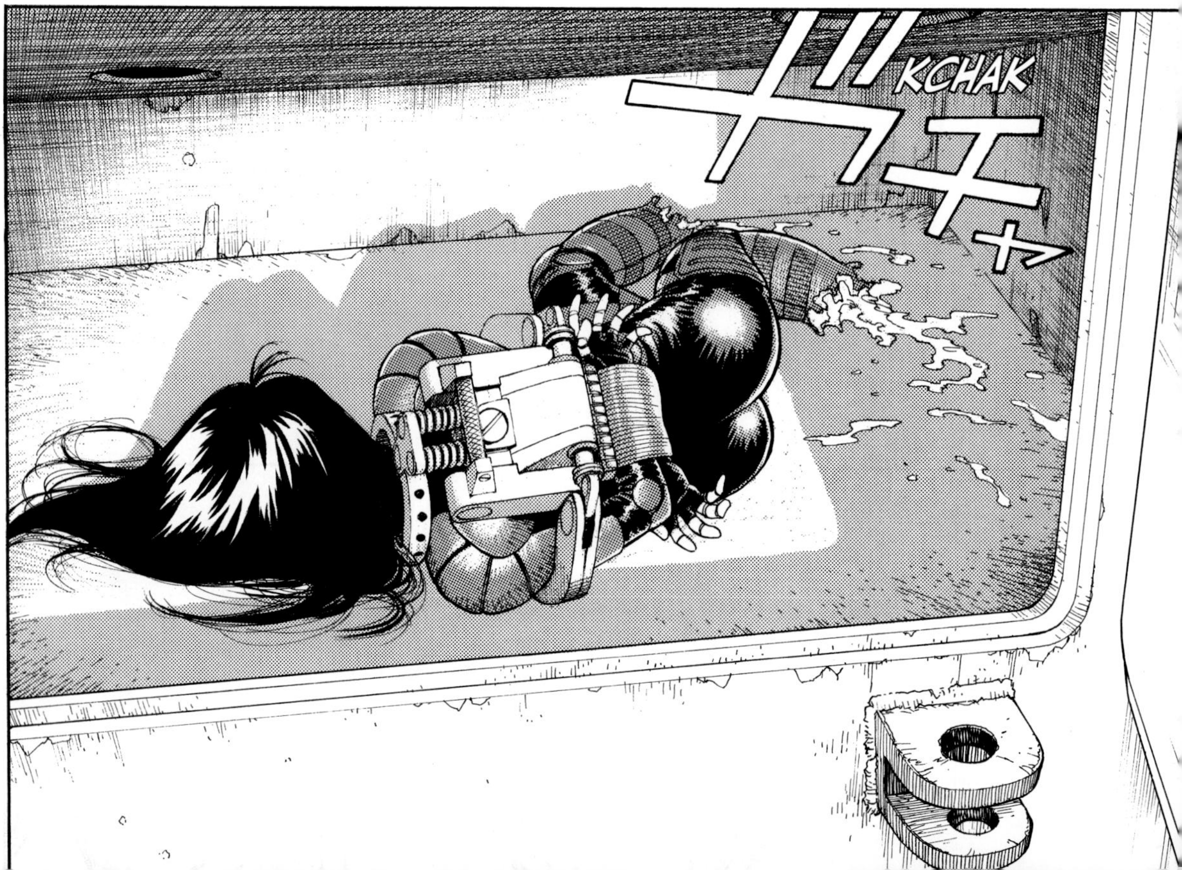
ガチャ
KCHAK

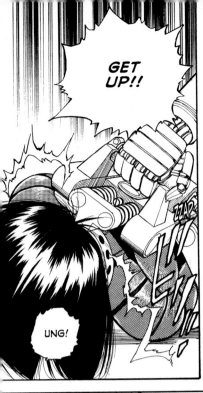

LOOKS LIKE SHE'S OUT COLD.
HEH! JUST LIKE YORG SAID, THIS DRYAD BUTTERFLY DID THE TRICK.
GET UP!!
UNG!
RISE AND SHINE, LITTLE ANGEL OF DEATH...
YOU'LL GET YOUR FULL INTERROGATION ONCE WE REJOIN THE MAIN FORCE...
...BUT I HAVE TWO OR THREE QUESTIONS TO ASK BEFORE THEN.
48... HOURS...
WHAT?!
IT'S BEEN OVER 48 HOURS SINCE I LOST CONTACT WITH ZALEM...
I SUSPECT... THAT MEANS... THEY'VE CUT ME LOOSE FROM THE *TUNED* PROGRAM...

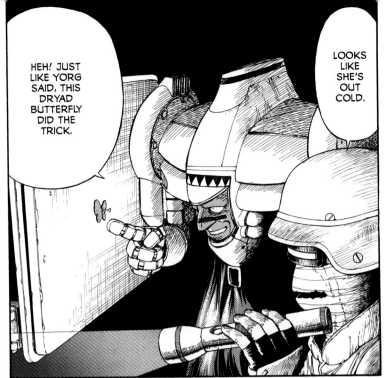

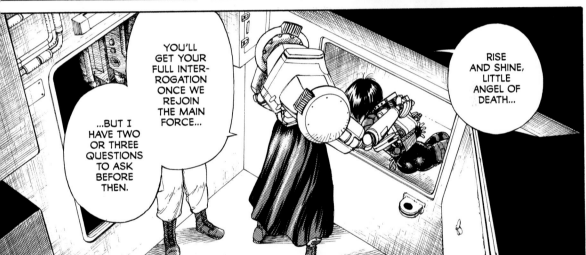

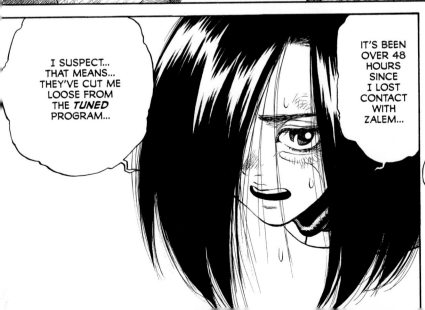

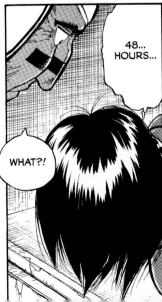

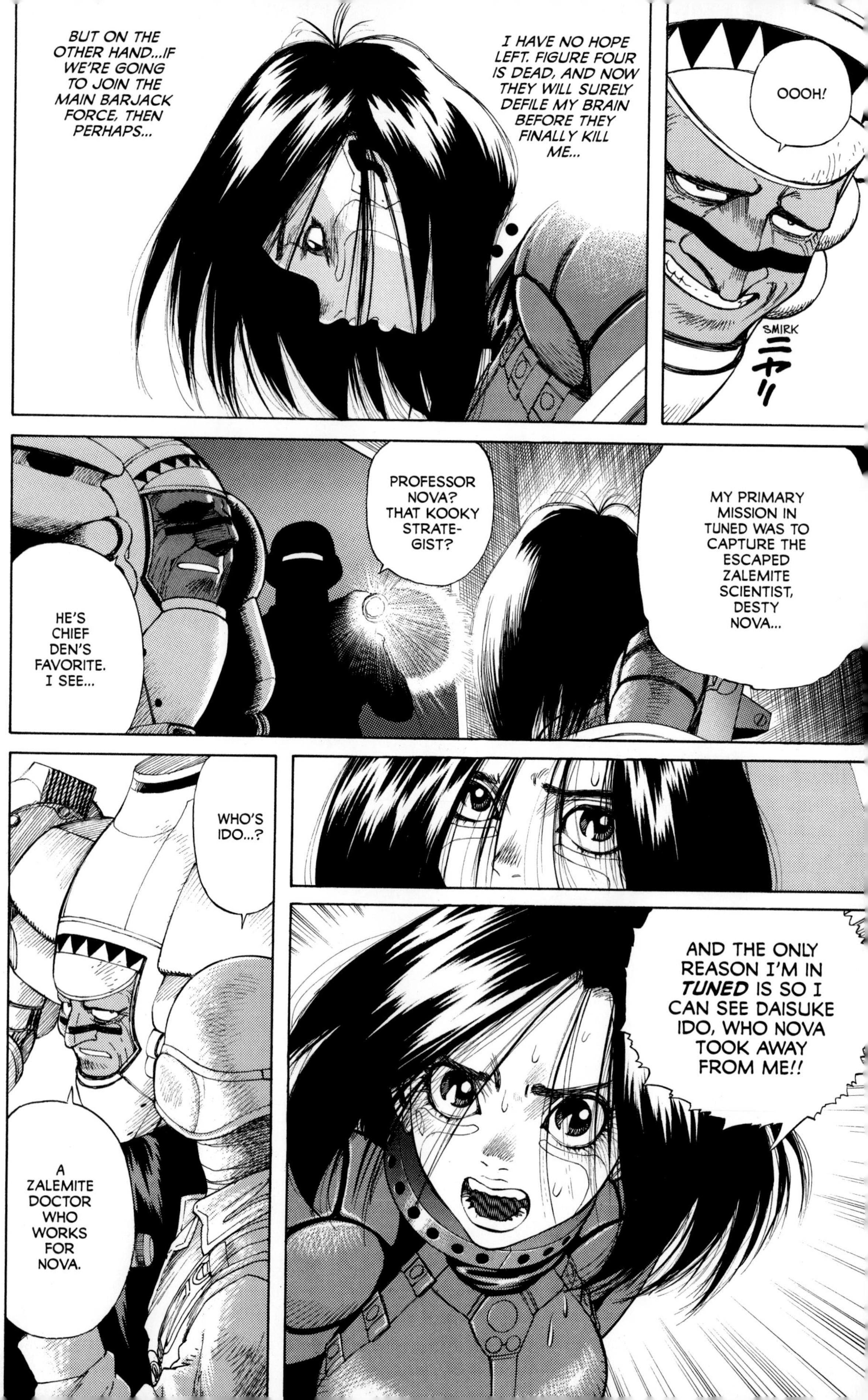

OOOH!
SMIRK
ニヤリ
I HAVE NO HOPE LEFT. FIGURE FOUR IS DEAD, AND NOW THEY WILL SURELY DEFILE MY BRAIN BEFORE THEY FINALLY KILL ME...
BUT ON THE OTHER HAND...IF WE'RE GOING TO JOIN THE MAIN BARJACK FORCE, THEN PERHAPS...
MY PRIMARY MISSION IN TUNED WAS TO CAPTURE THE ESCAPED ZALEMITE SCIENTIST, DESTY NOVA...
PROFESSOR NOVA? THAT KOOKY STRATE-GIST?
HE'S CHIEF DEN'S FAVORITE. I SEE...
AND THE ONLY REASON I'M IN *TUNED* IS SO I CAN SEE DAISUKE IDO, WHO NOVA TOOK AWAY FROM ME!!
WHO'S IDO...?
A ZALEMITE DOCTOR WHO WORKS FOR NOVA.

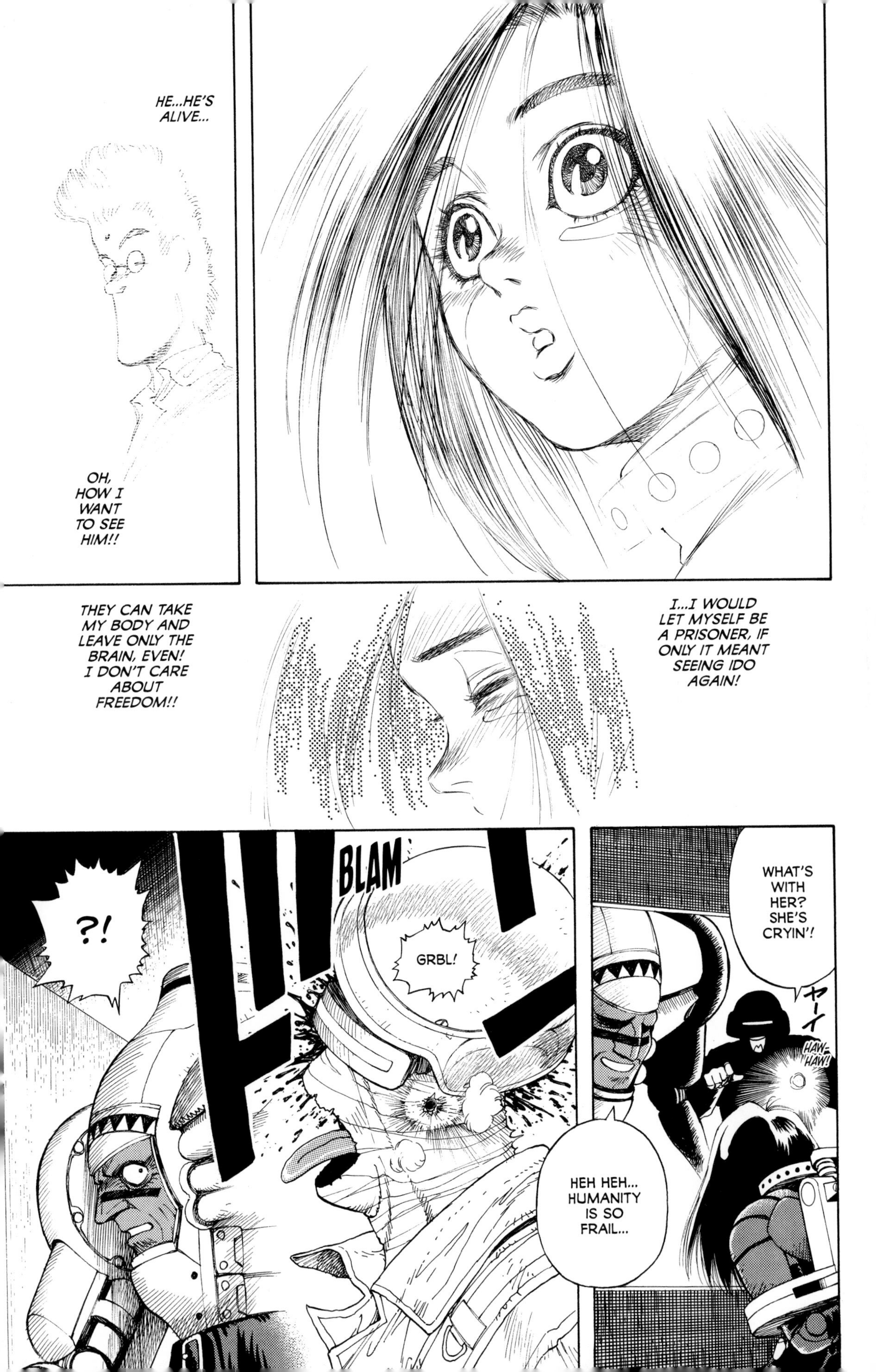
HE...HE'S ALIVE...
OH, HOW I WANT TO SEE HIM!!
I...I WOULD LET MYSELF BE A PRISONER, IF ONLY IT MEANT SEEING IDO AGAIN!
THEY CAN TAKE MY BODY AND LEAVE ONLY THE BRAIN, EVEN! I DON'T CARE ABOUT FREEDOM!!
WHAT'S WITH HER? SHE'S CRYIN'!
ヤーイ
HAW-HAW!
HEH HEH... HUMANITY IS SO FRAIL...
BLAM
GRBL!
?!

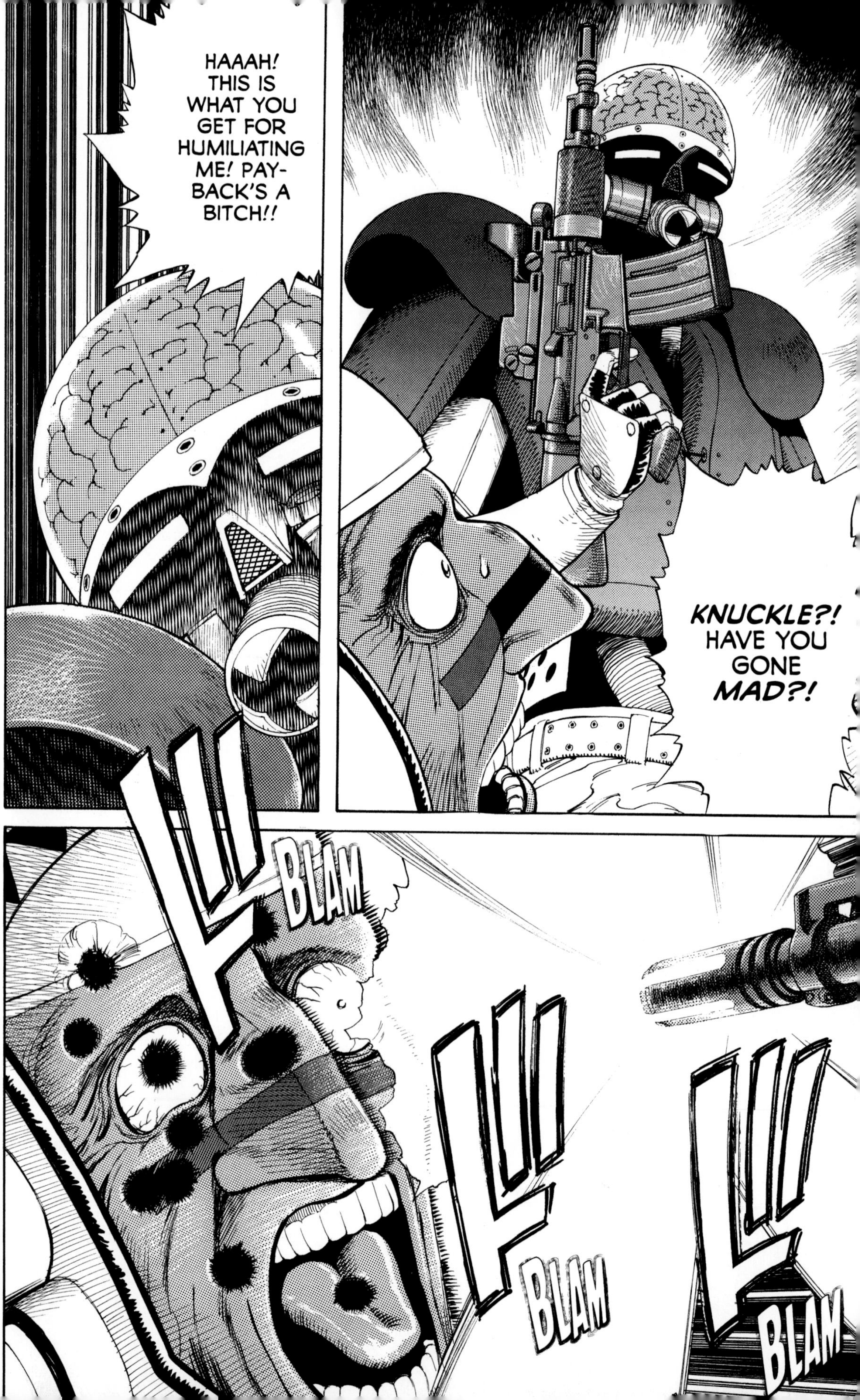
KNUCKLE?! HAVE YOU GONE MAD?!
HAAAH! THIS IS WHAT YOU GET FOR HUMILIATING ME! PAY-BACK'S A BITCH!!
BLAM
BLAM
BLAM

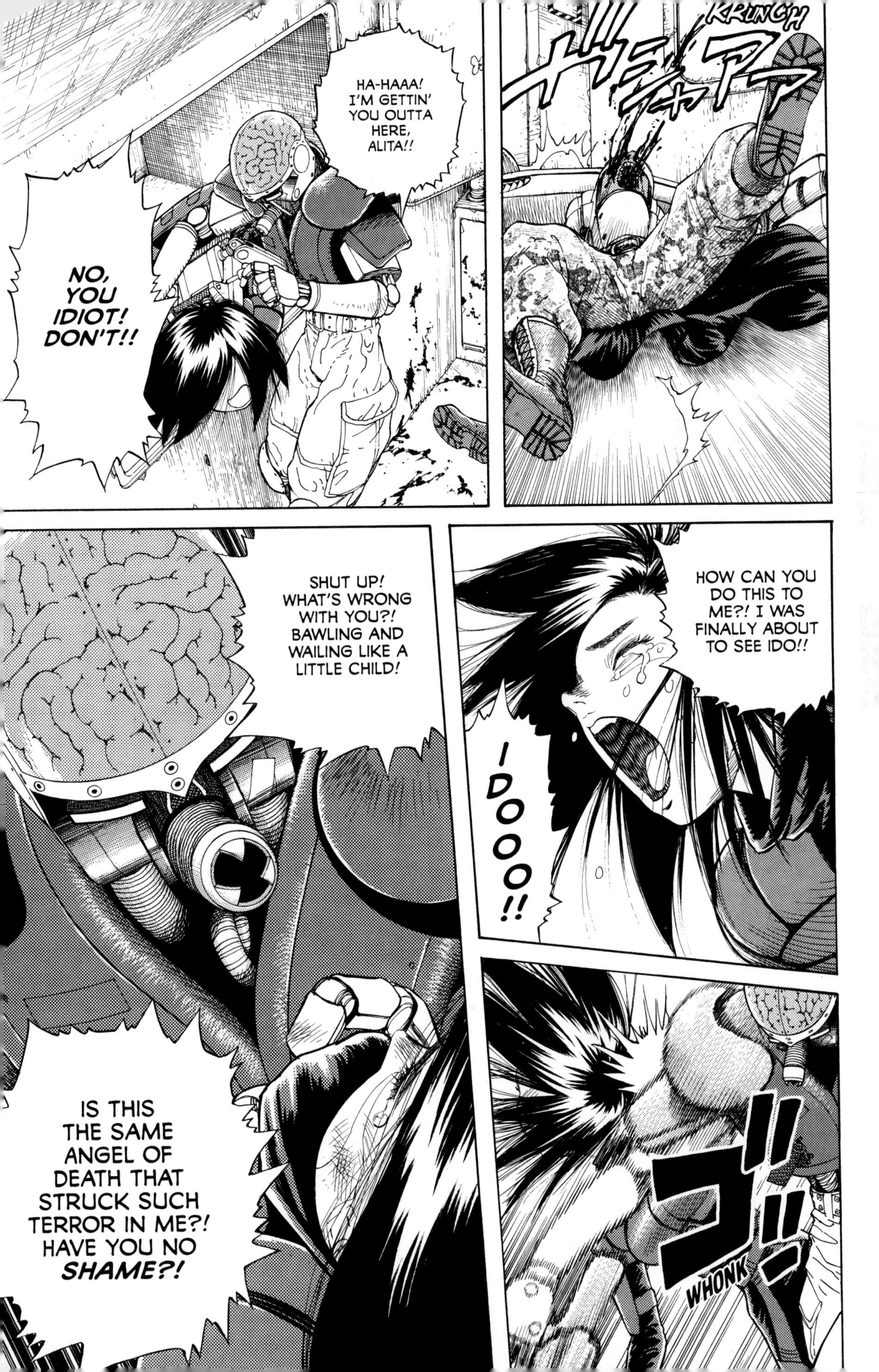
KRUNCH
HA-HAAA! I'M GETTIN' YOU OUTTA HERE, ALITA!!
NO, YOU IDIOT! DON'T!!
HOW CAN YOU DO THIS TO ME?! I WAS FINALLY ABOUT TO SEE IDO!!
IDOOOO!!
WHONK
SHUT UP! WHAT'S WRONG WITH YOU?! BAWLING AND WAILING LIKE A LITTLE CHILD!
IS THIS THE SAME ANGEL OF DEATH THAT STRUCK SUCH TERROR IN ME?! HAVE YOU NO *SHAME?!*

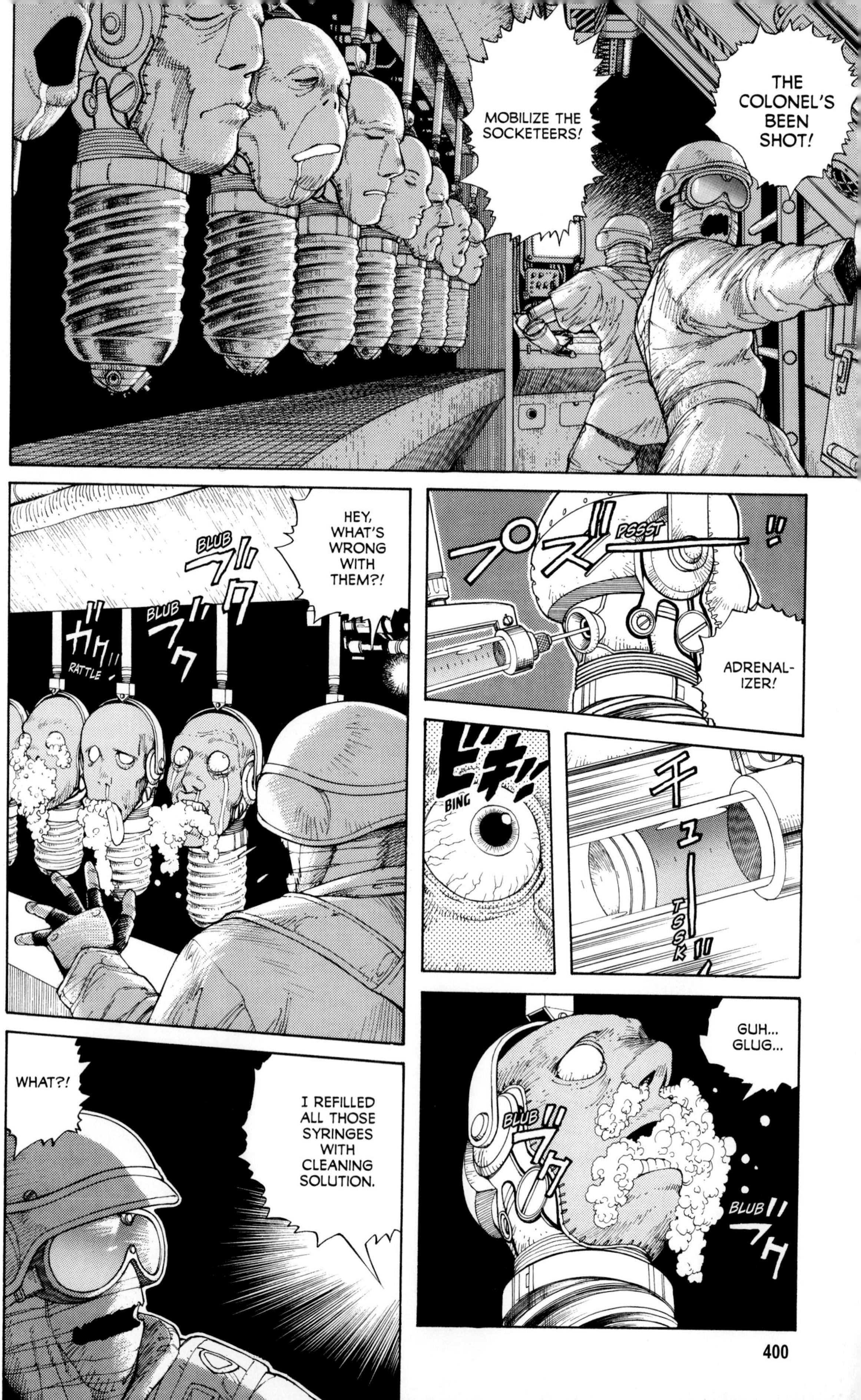

THE COLONEL'S BEEN SHOT!
MOBILIZE THE SOCKETEERS!
プス!! PSSST
!!
ADRENALIZER!
チュー TSSK!!
ビキ!! BING
HEY, WHAT'S WRONG WITH THEM?!
ブク BLUB
ブク BLUB
ガク!! RATTLE
GUH... GLUG...
BLUB!! ブク
BLUB!! ブク
WHAT?!
I REFILLED ALL THOSE SYRINGES WITH CLEANING SOLUTION.

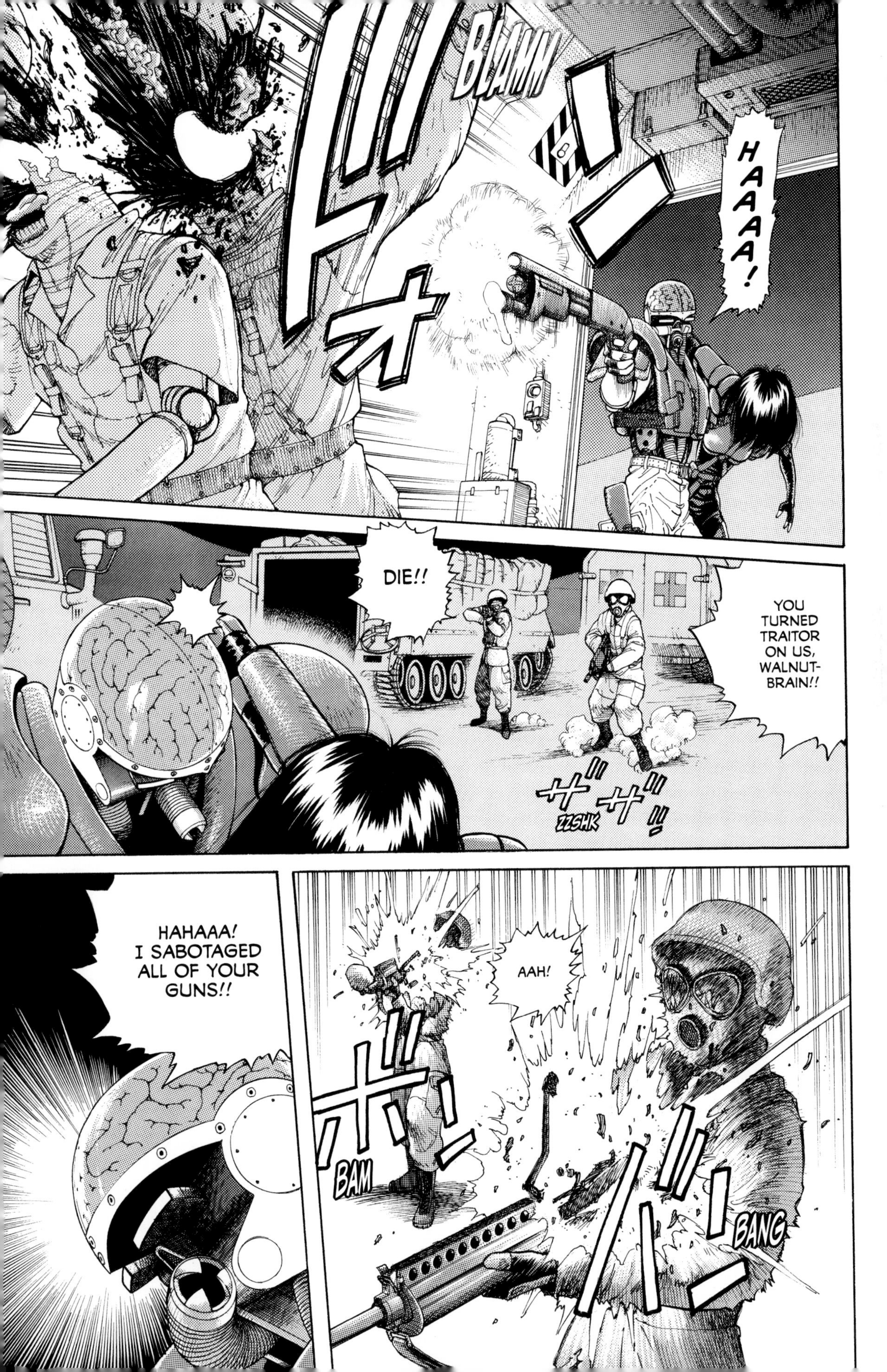
HAAAA!
BLAMM
YOU TURNED TRAITOR ON US, WALNUT-BRAIN!!
DIE!!
ZZSHK
BANG
AAH!
BAM
HAHAAA! I SABOTAGED ALL OF YOUR GUNS!!

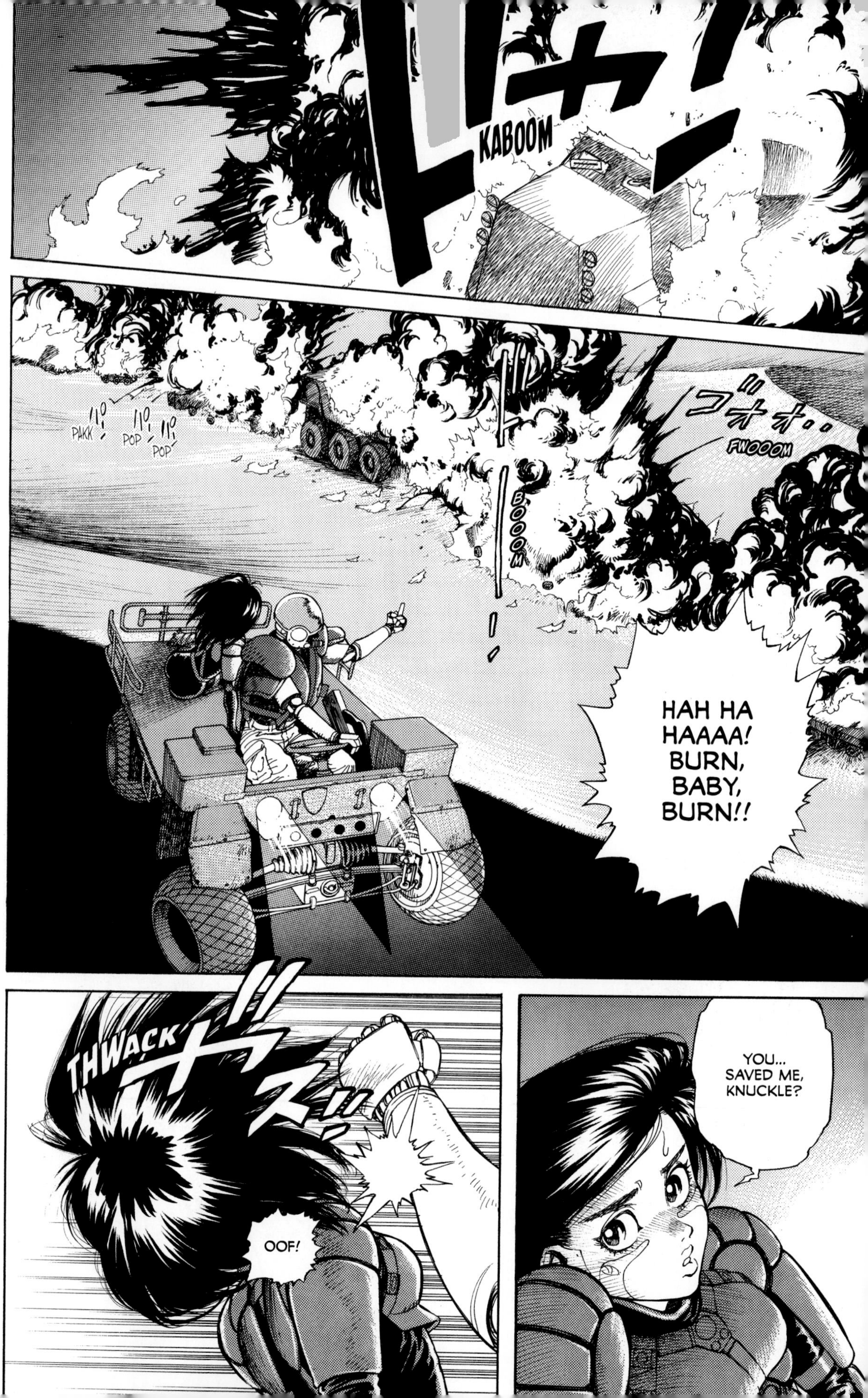
KABOOM
FWOOOM
BOOOM
PAKK
POP
POP
HAH HA HAAAA! BURN, BABY, BURN!!
YOU... SAVED ME, KNUCKLE?
THWACK
OOF!

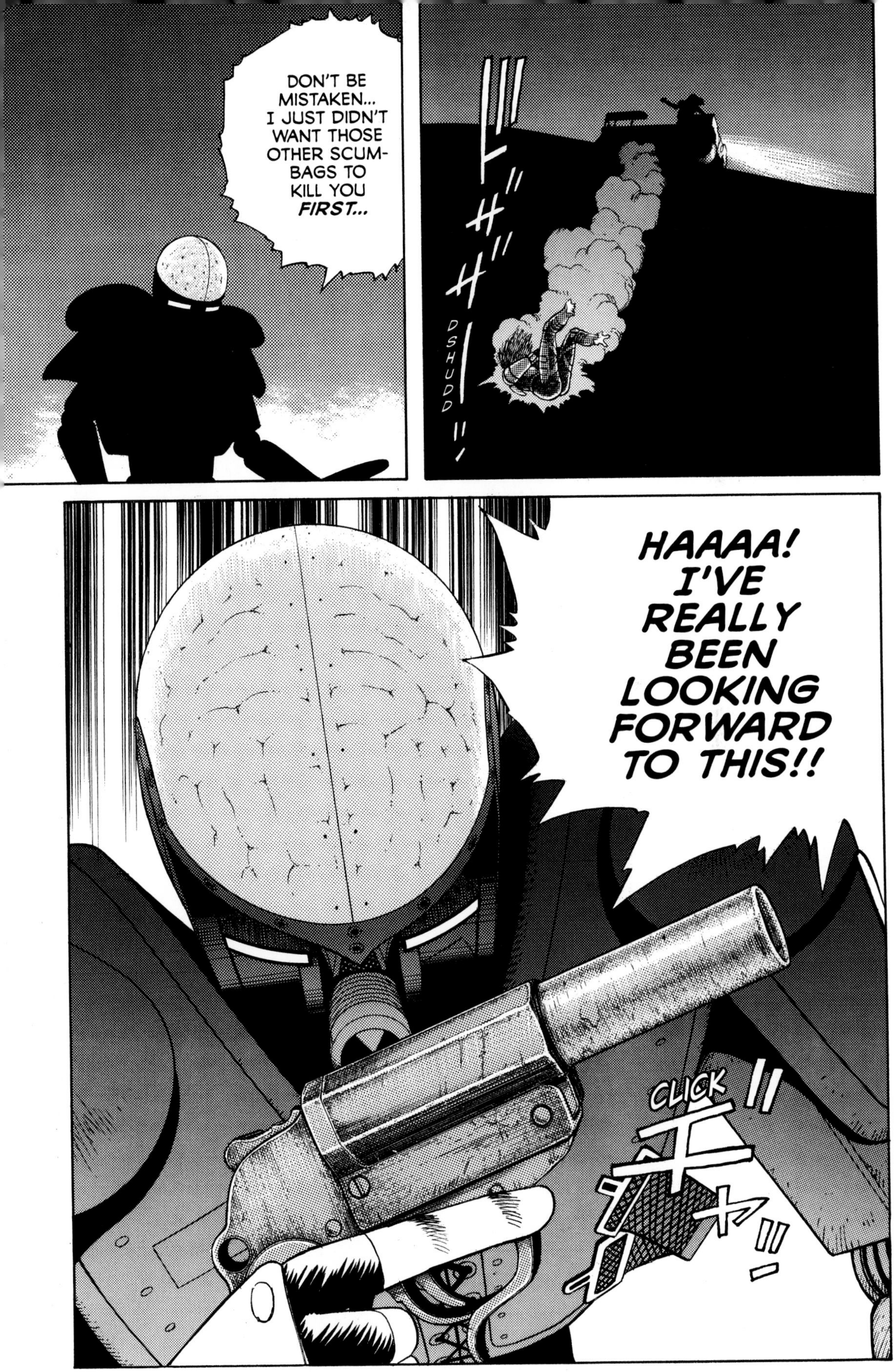
DSHUDD!!
DON'T BE MISTAKEN... I JUST DIDN'T WANT THOSE OTHER SCUM-BAGS TO KILL YOU *FIRST*...
HAAAA! I'VE REALLY BEEN LOOKING FORWARD TO THIS!!
CLICK!!

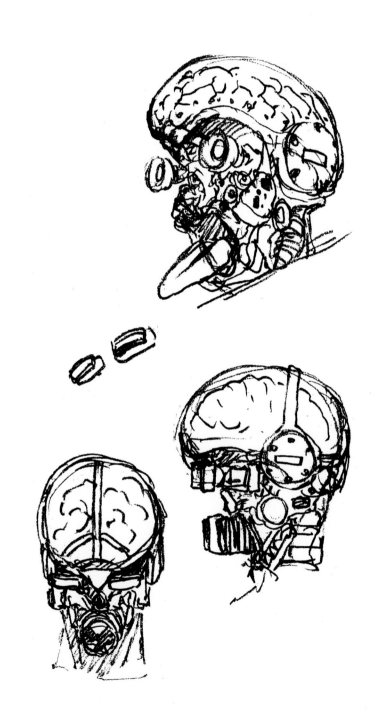

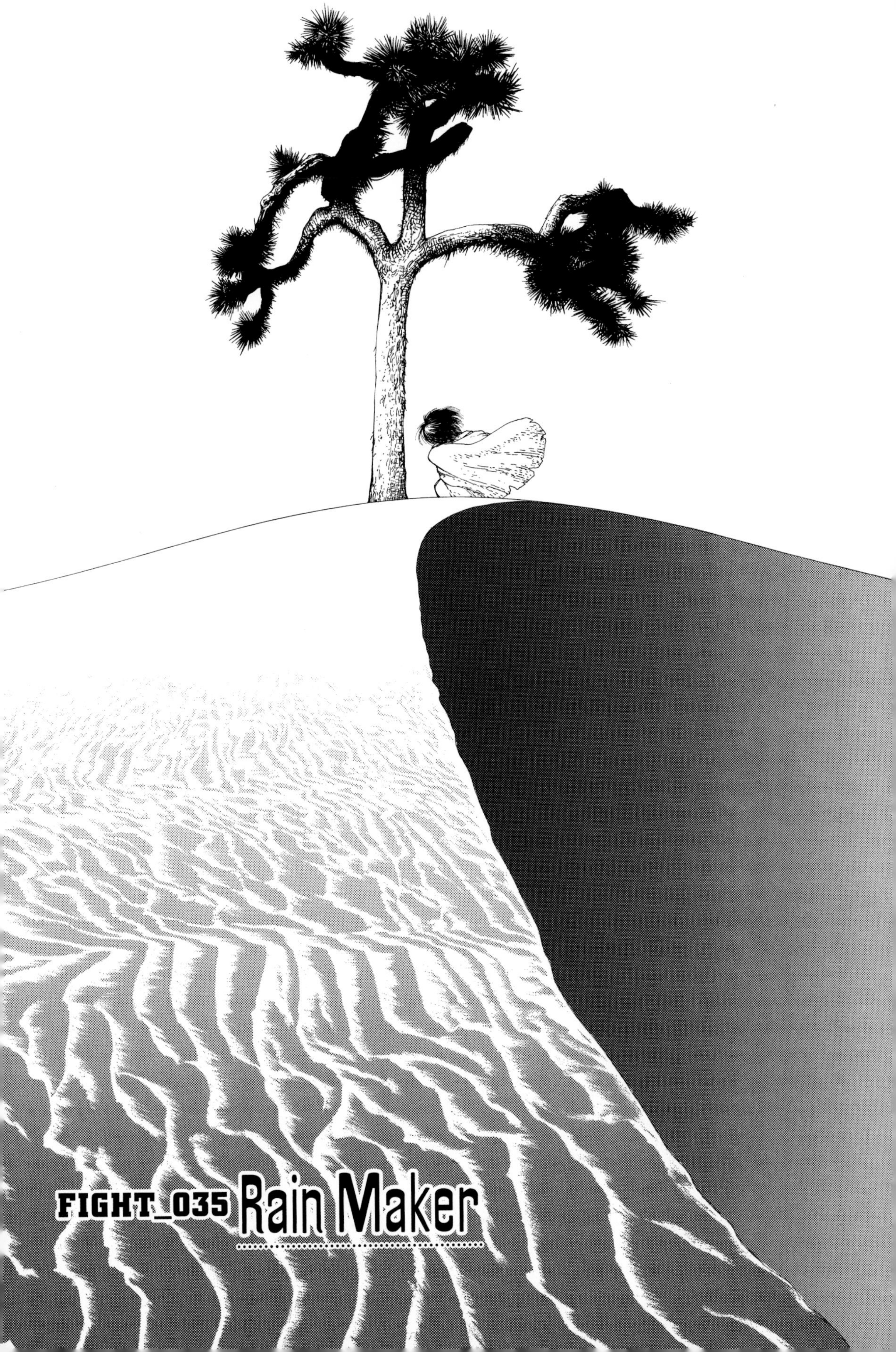
FIGHT_035 Rain Maker

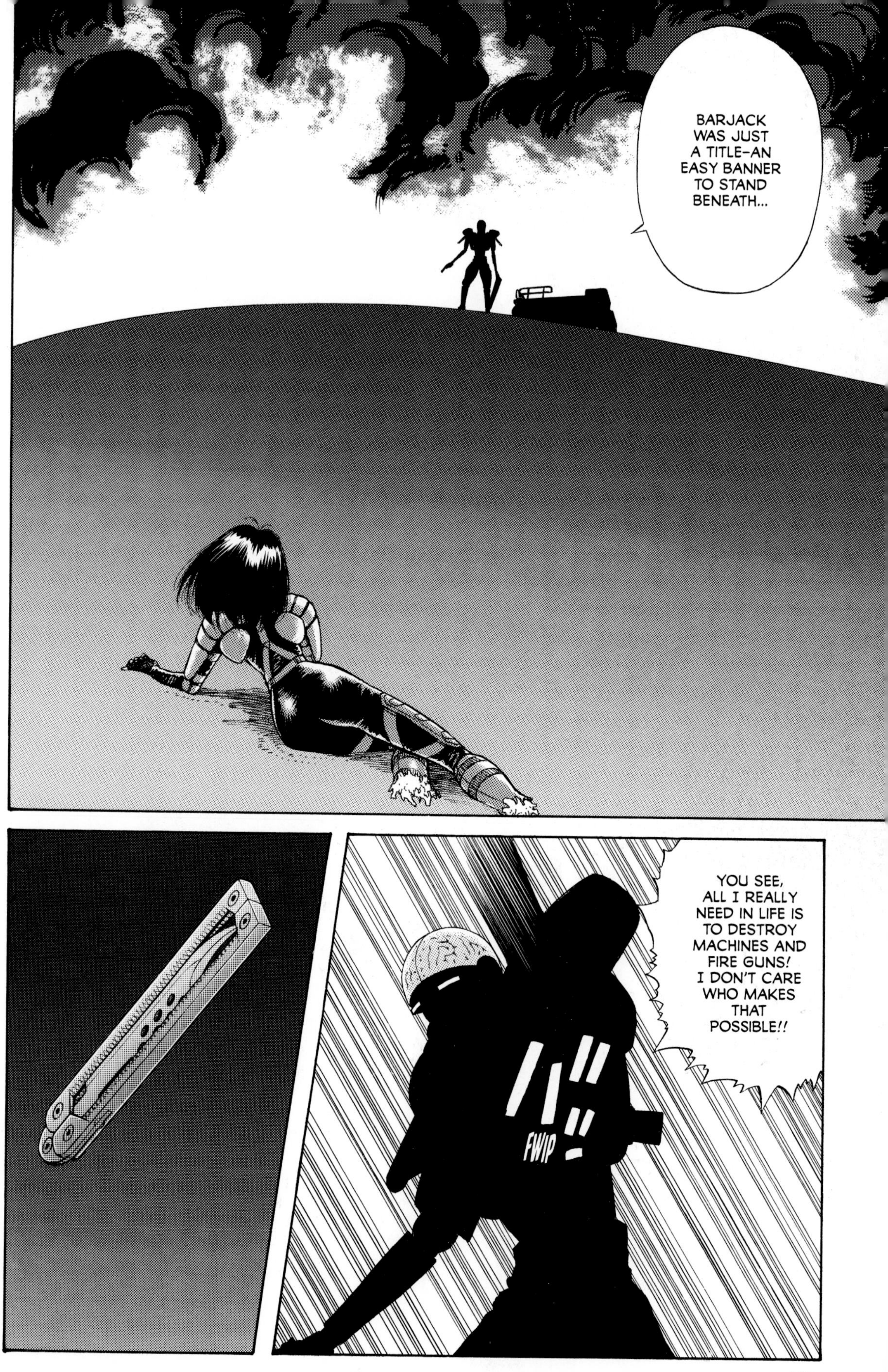
BARJACK WAS JUST A TITLE—AN EASY BANNER TO STAND BENEATH...
YOU SEE, ALL I REALLY NEED IN LIFE IS TO DESTROY MACHINES AND FIRE GUNS! I DON'T CARE WHO MAKES THAT POSSIBLE!!
FWIP

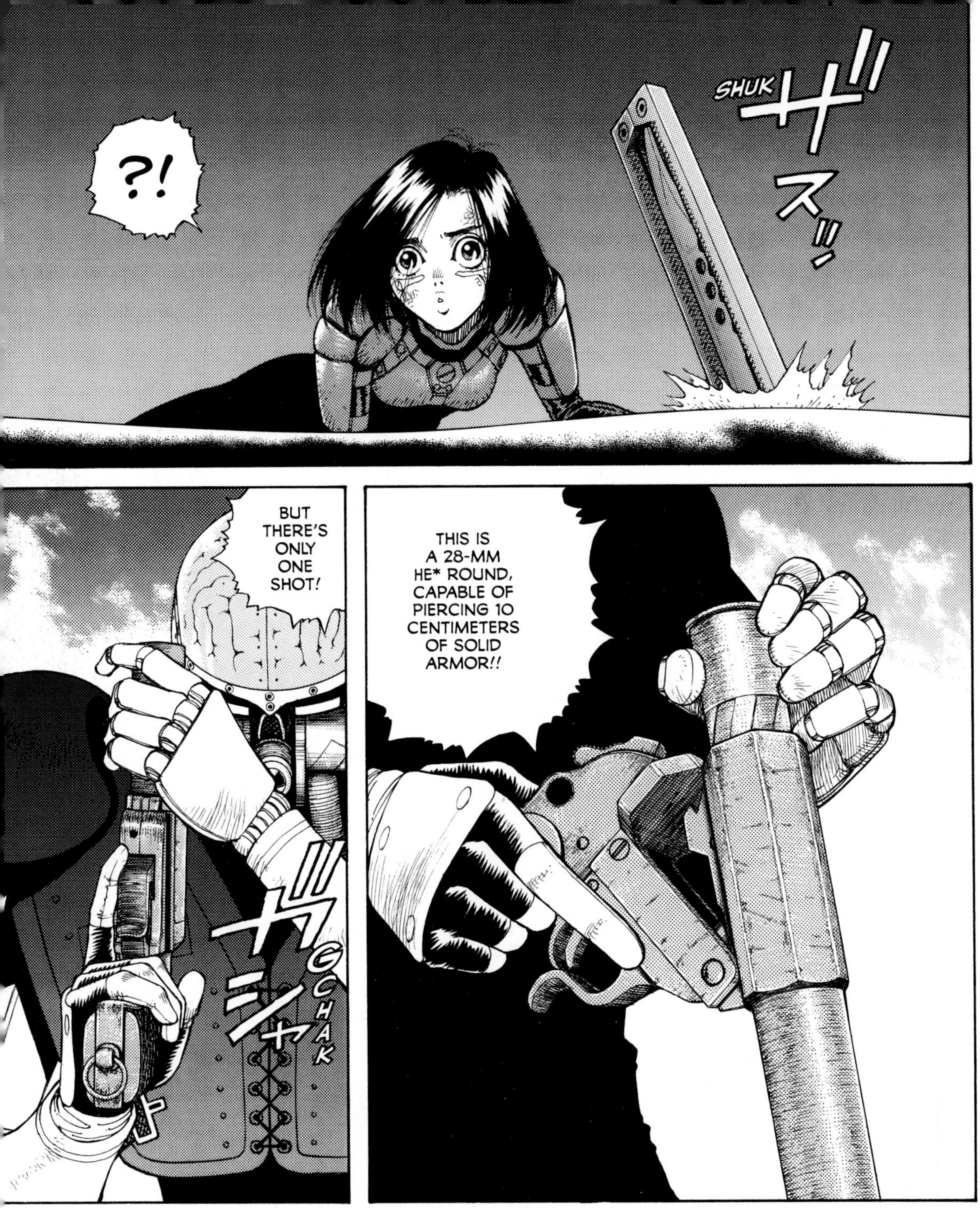
?!
SHUK
THIS IS A 28-MM HE* ROUND, CAPABLE OF PIERCING 10 CENTIMETERS OF SOLID ARMOR!!
BUT THERE'S ONLY ONE SHOT!
GCHAK

***HE ROUND (HIGH EXPLOSIVE)**

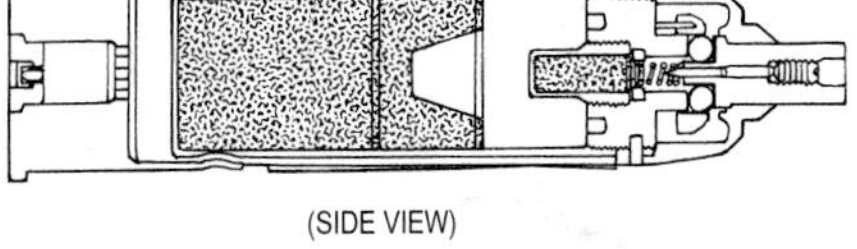

(SIDE VIEW)

The front of a shaped-charge explosive is hollowed conically, so that when it hits the target, all of the energy is focused and directed toward the point of the cone, utilizing a property called the Munroe effect. The penetrating effect of the HE round is roughly proportional to the diameter of the shell.

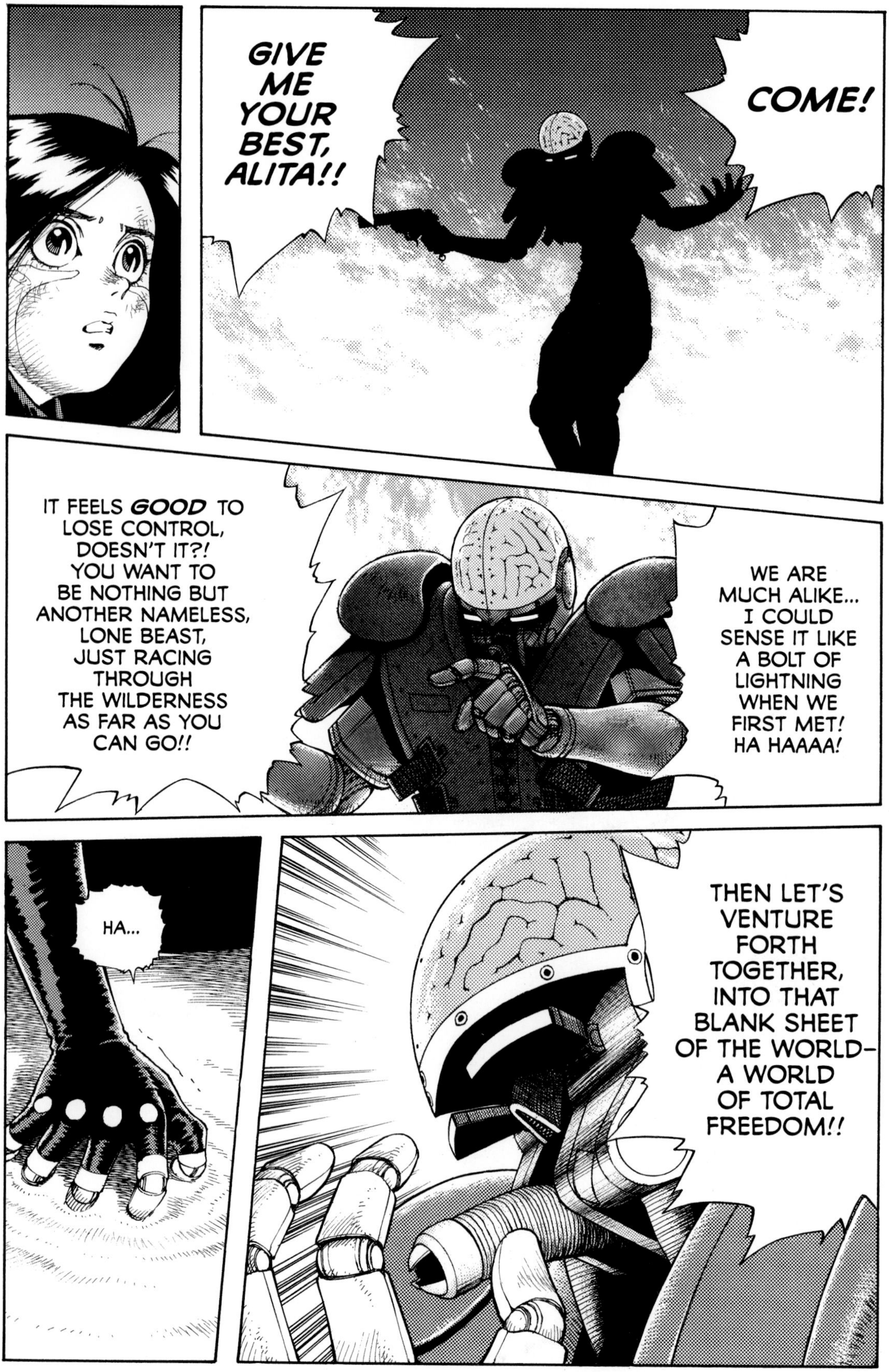
COME!
GIVE ME YOUR BEST, ALITA!!
WE ARE MUCH ALIKE... I COULD SENSE IT LIKE A BOLT OF LIGHTNING WHEN WE FIRST MET! HA HAAAA!
IT FEELS *GOOD* TO LOSE CONTROL, DOESN'T IT?! YOU WANT TO BE NOTHING BUT ANOTHER NAMELESS, LONE BEAST, JUST RACING THROUGH THE WILDERNESS AS FAR AS YOU CAN GO!!
THEN LET'S VENTURE FORTH TOGETHER, INTO THAT BLANK SHEET OF THE WORLD- A WORLD OF TOTAL FREEDOM!!
HA...

ZSHH
HA HAH!
HAH-HOO!
THAT'S RIGHT! COME TO ME!!
ZSH
HA HA!
HA...?!
HMM?!
WHUP

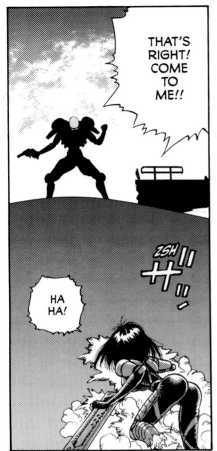

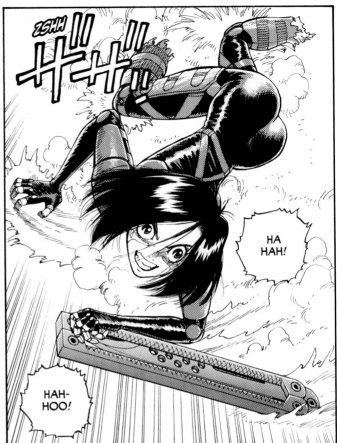

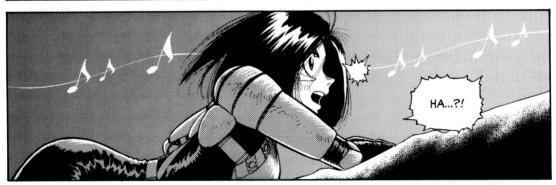

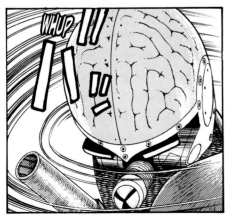

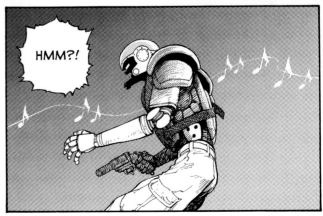

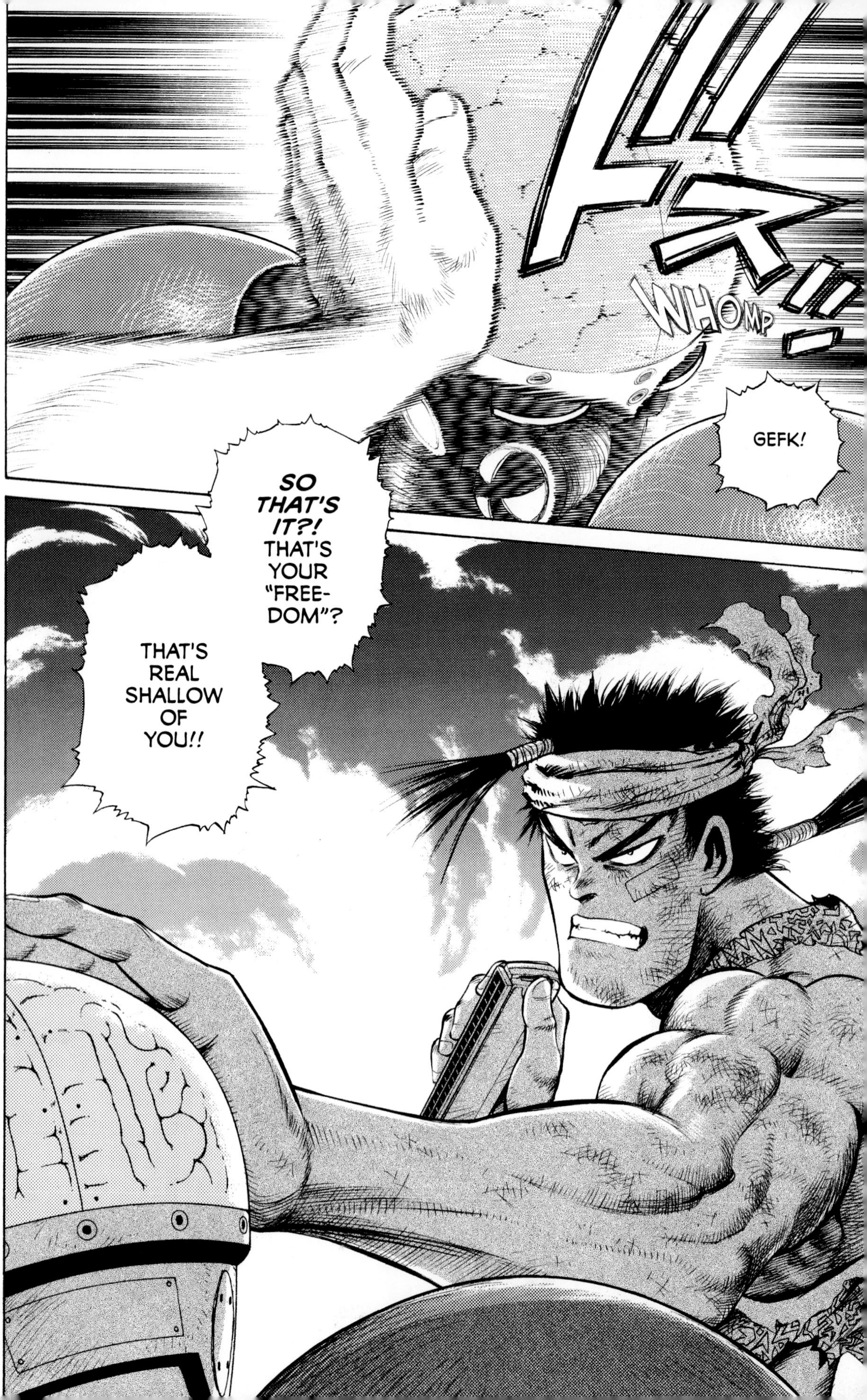
WHOMP
GEFK!
SO THAT'S IT?! THAT'S YOUR "FREEDOM"?
THAT'S REAL SHALLOW OF YOU!!

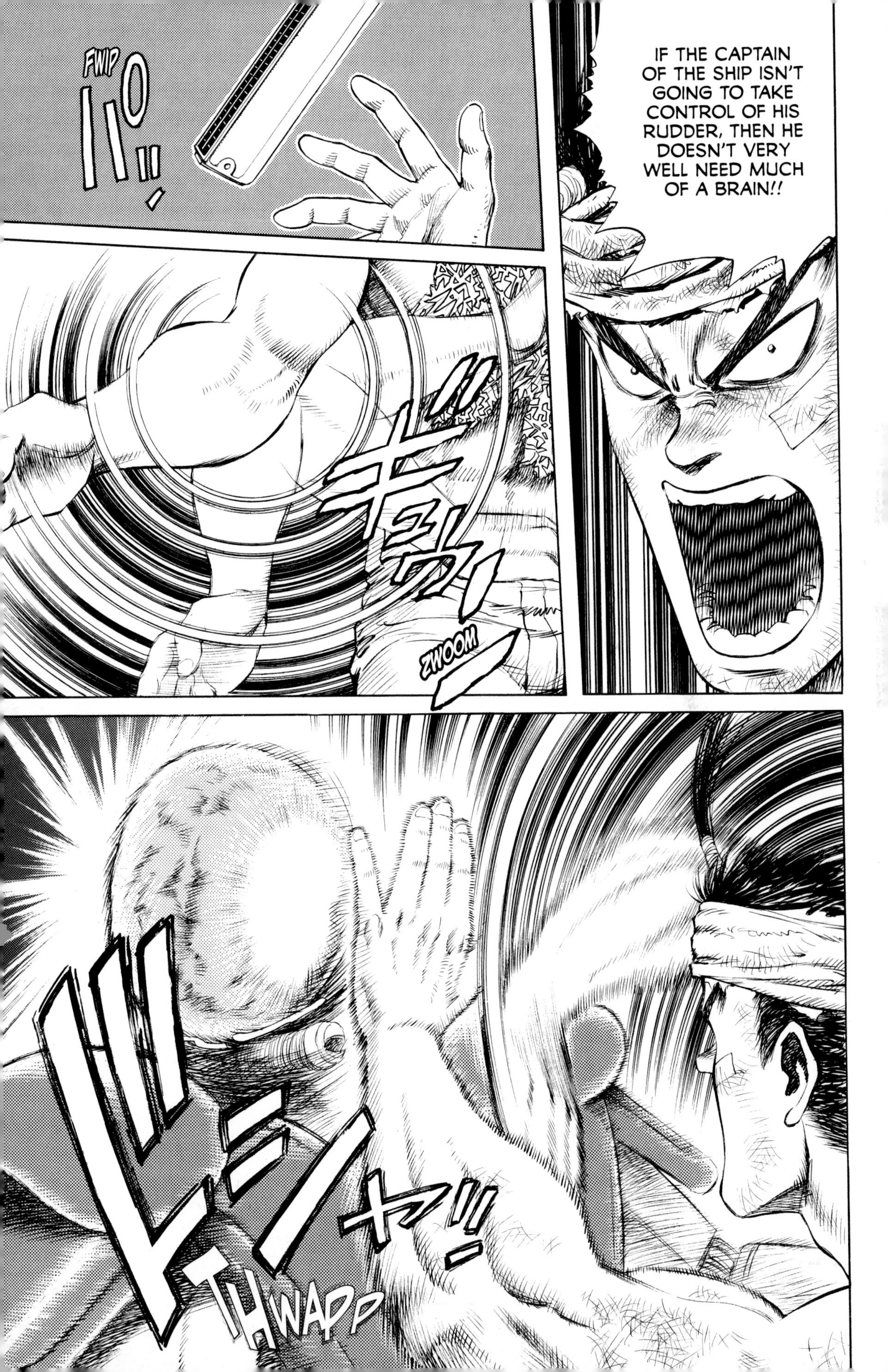
IF THE CAPTAIN OF THE SHIP ISN'T GOING TO TAKE CONTROL OF HIS RUDDER, THEN HE DOESN'T VERY WELL NEED MUCH OF A BRAIN!!
FWIP
ZWOOM
THWAPP

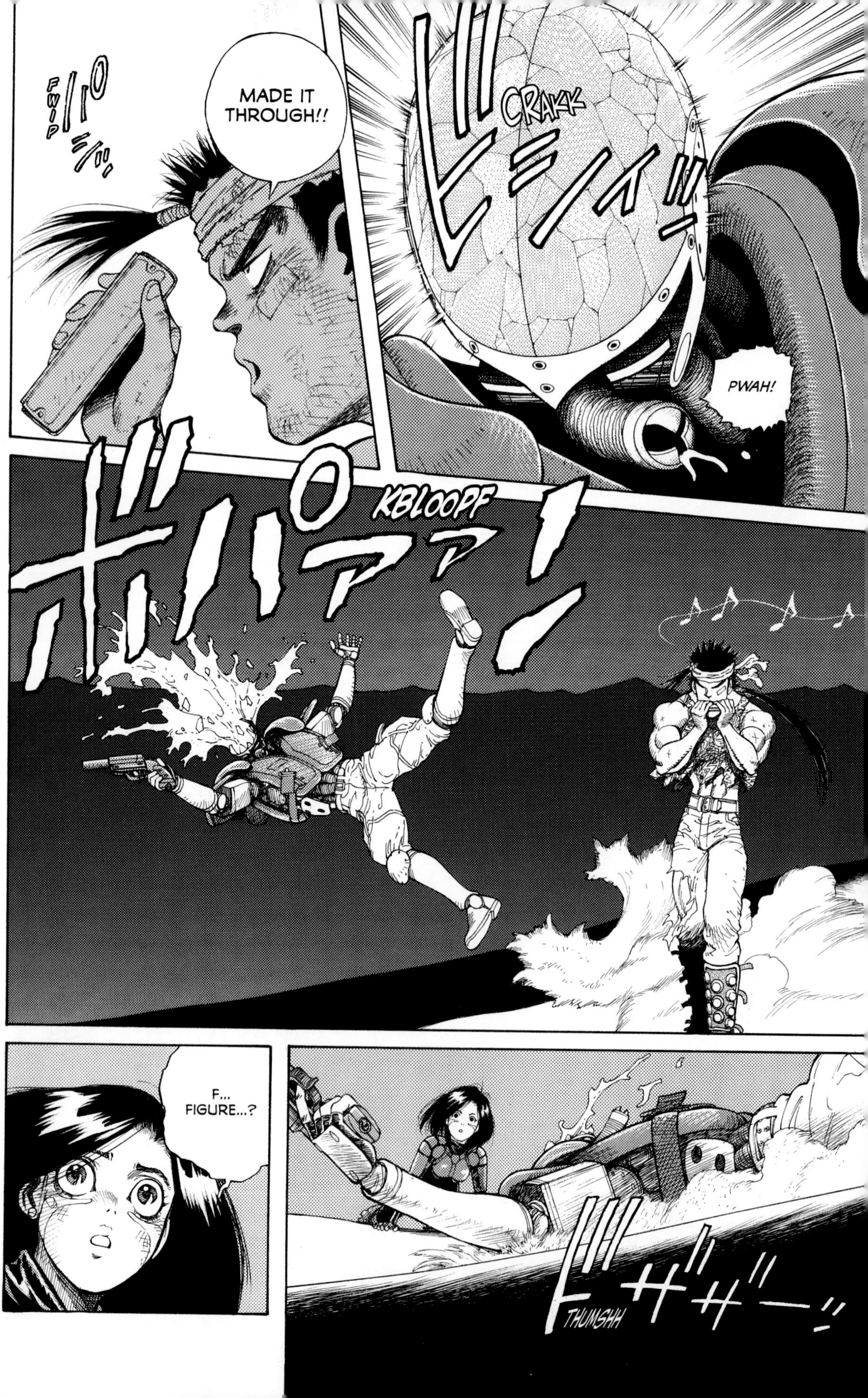
CRAKK
PWAH!
FWIP
MADE IT THROUGH!!
KBLOOPF
THUMSHH
F... FIGURE...?

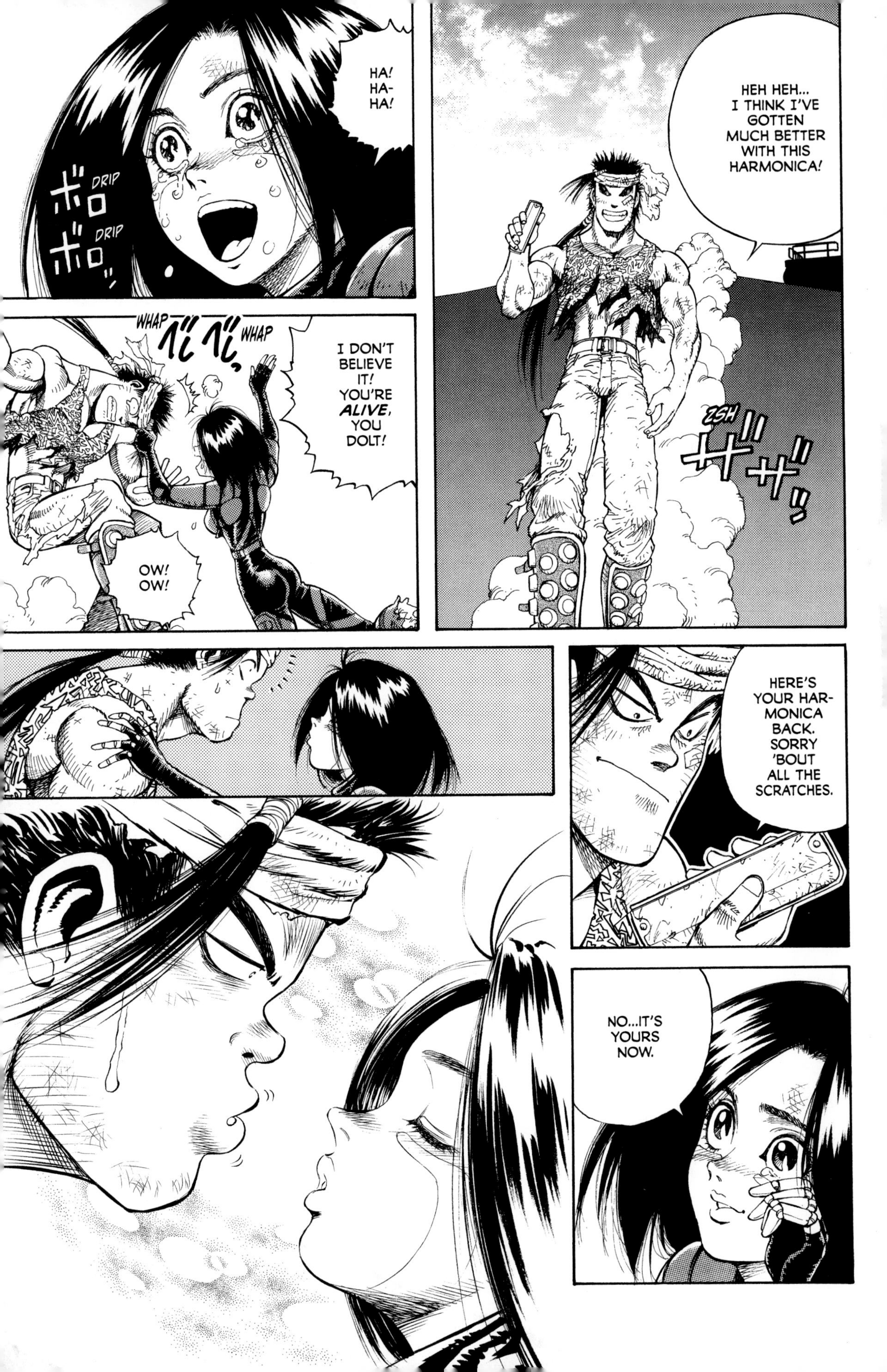
HEH HEH... I THINK I'VE GOTTEN MUCH BETTER WITH THIS HARMONICA!
ZSH
HA! HA-HA!
DRIP
DRIP
WHAP
WHAP
I DON'T BELIEVE IT! YOU'RE *ALIVE*, YOU DOLT!
OW! OW!
HERE'S YOUR HARMONICA BACK. SORRY 'BOUT ALL THE SCRATCHES.
NO...IT'S YOURS NOW.

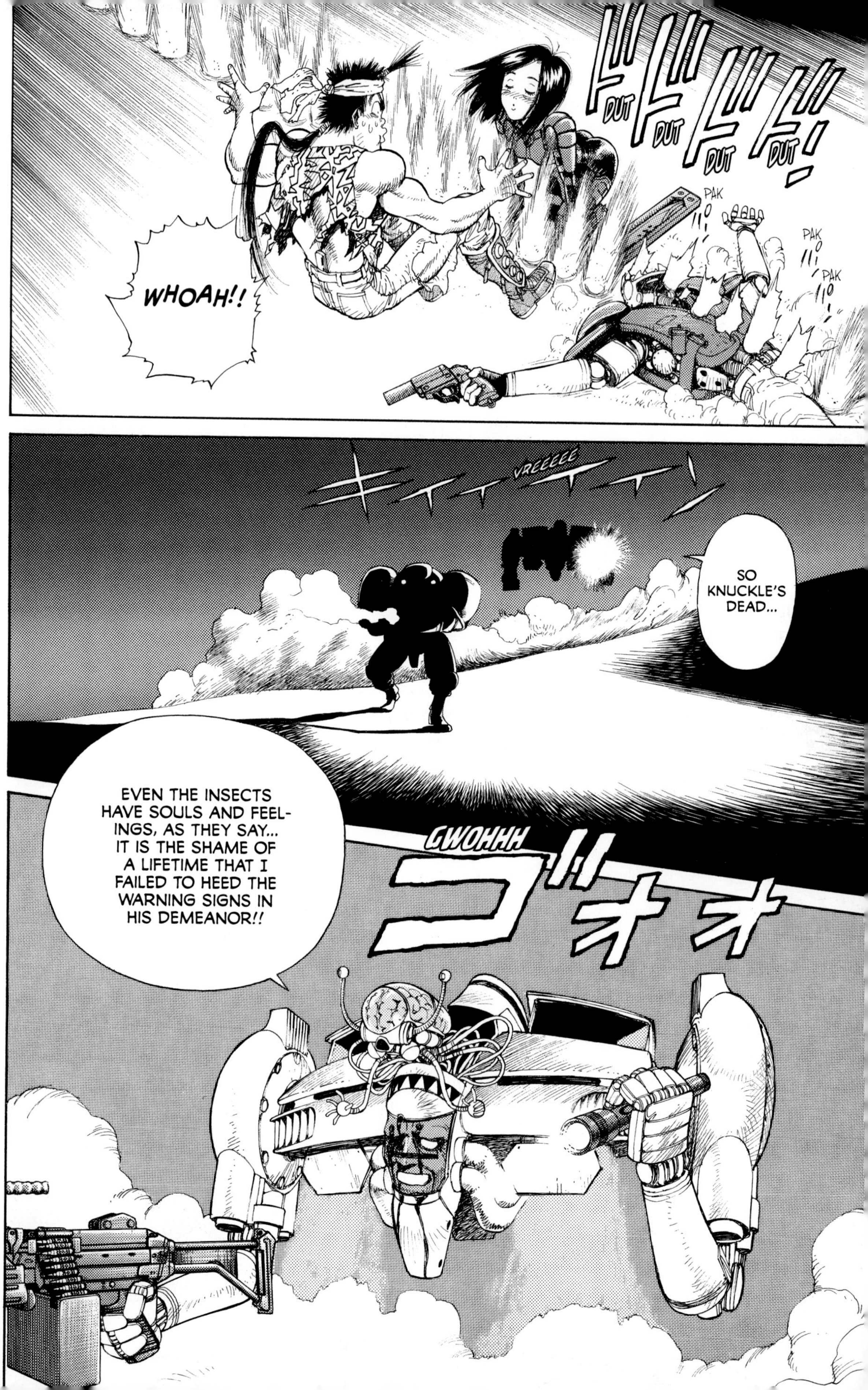
DUT DUT DUT DUT
PAK
PAK
PAK
WHOAH!!
VREEEEE
SO KNUCKLE'S DEAD...
GWOHHH
EVEN THE INSECTS HAVE SOULS AND FEEL-INGS, AS THEY SAY... IT IS THE SHAME OF A LIFETIME THAT I FAILED TO HEED THE WARNING SIGNS IN HIS DEMEANOR!!

NOTHING CAN BE ALLOWED TO STAND IN THE WAY OF THE REALIZATION OF OUR LOFTY IDEALS— NOT EVEN A BUG!

KILL THEM!

YORG!

Y...

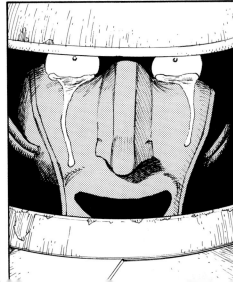

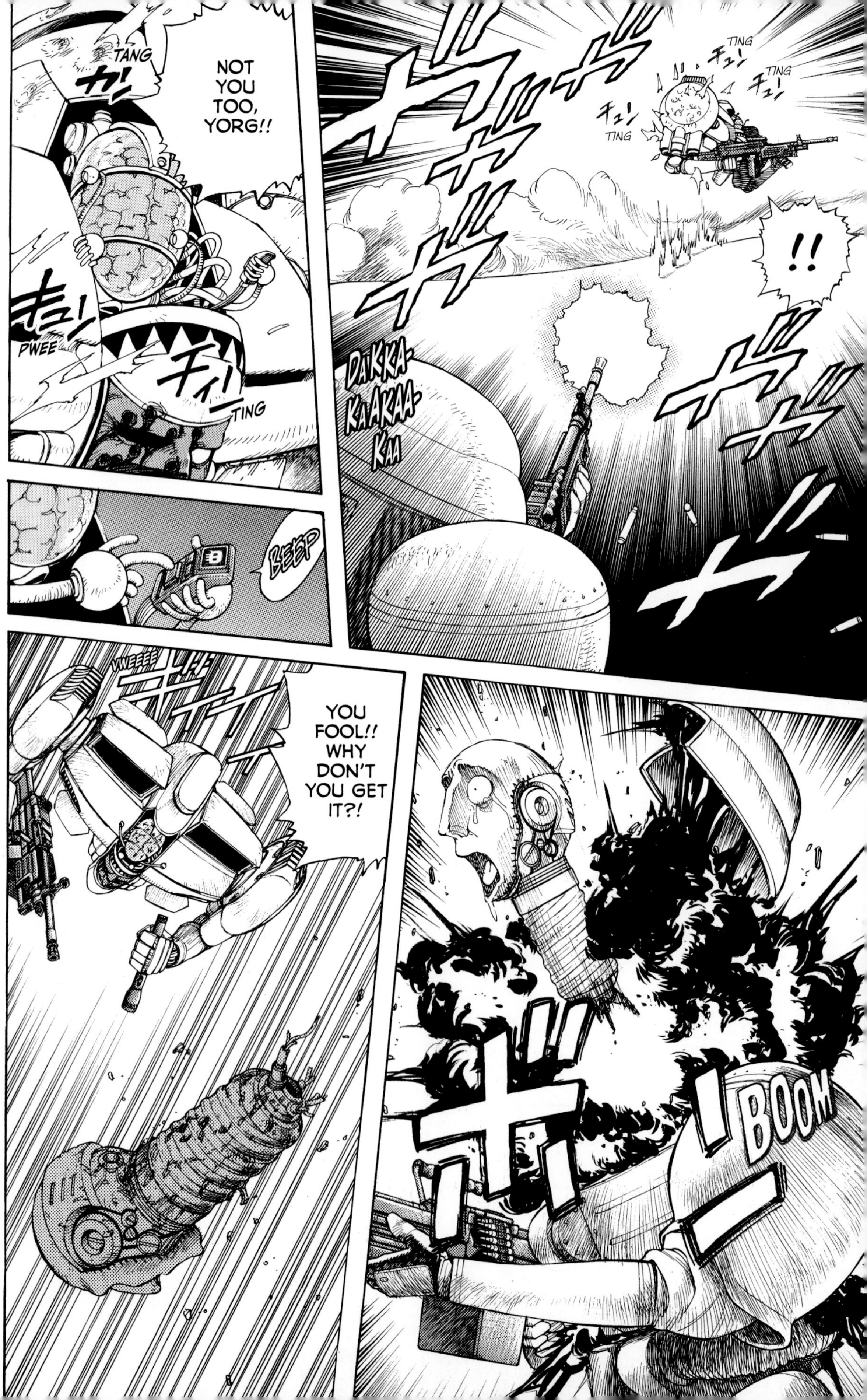
TING
TING
TING
!!
DAKKA KAAKAA KAA
TANG
NOT YOU TOO, YORG!!
PWEE
TING
BEEP
BOOM
VWEEEE
YOU FOOL!! WHY DON'T YOU GET IT?!

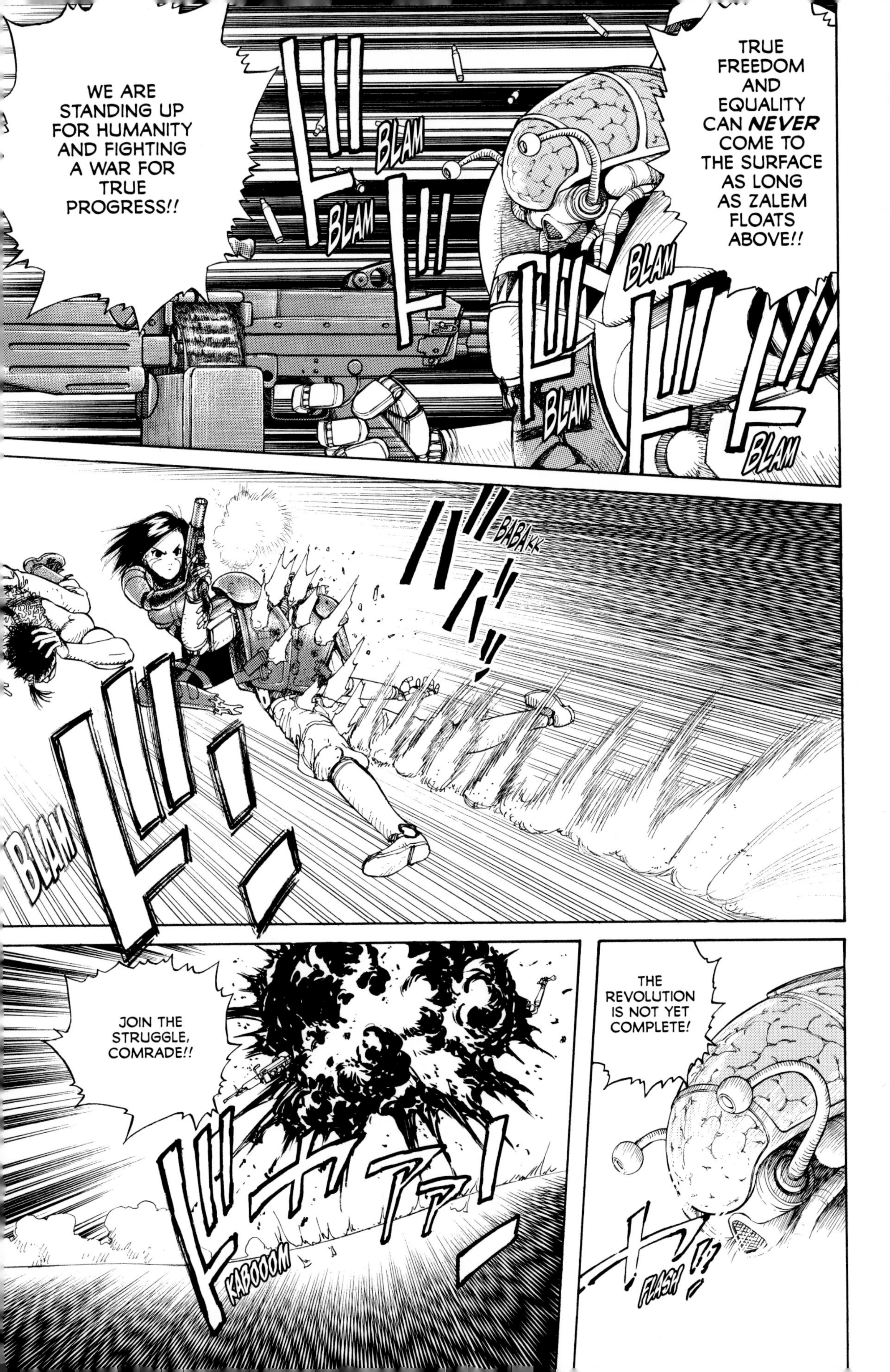
TRUE FREEDOM AND EQUALITY CAN ***NEVER*** COME TO THE SURFACE AS LONG AS ZALEM FLOATS ABOVE!!
WE ARE STANDING UP FOR HUMANITY AND FIGHTING A WAR FOR TRUE PROGRESS!!
BLAM
BLAM
BLAM
BLAM
BLAM
BLAM
BABAKK
BLAM
THE REVOLUTION IS NOT YET COMPLETE!
FLASH!?
JOIN THE STRUGGLE, COMRADE!!
KABOOOM

TWITCH

TWITCH

F-FORGIVE ME...FIGURE... ALITA... FORGIVE ME...

I'M...I'M NO GOOD, TOO WEAK...A-AND NOW I DON'T EVEN H-HAVE THE RIGHT TO SEE MY W-WIFE AGAIN. J-JUST...JUST...

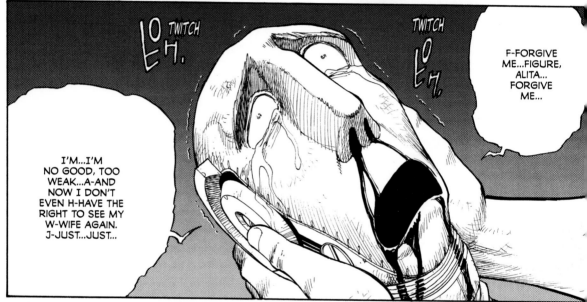

YORG...!

HRNG

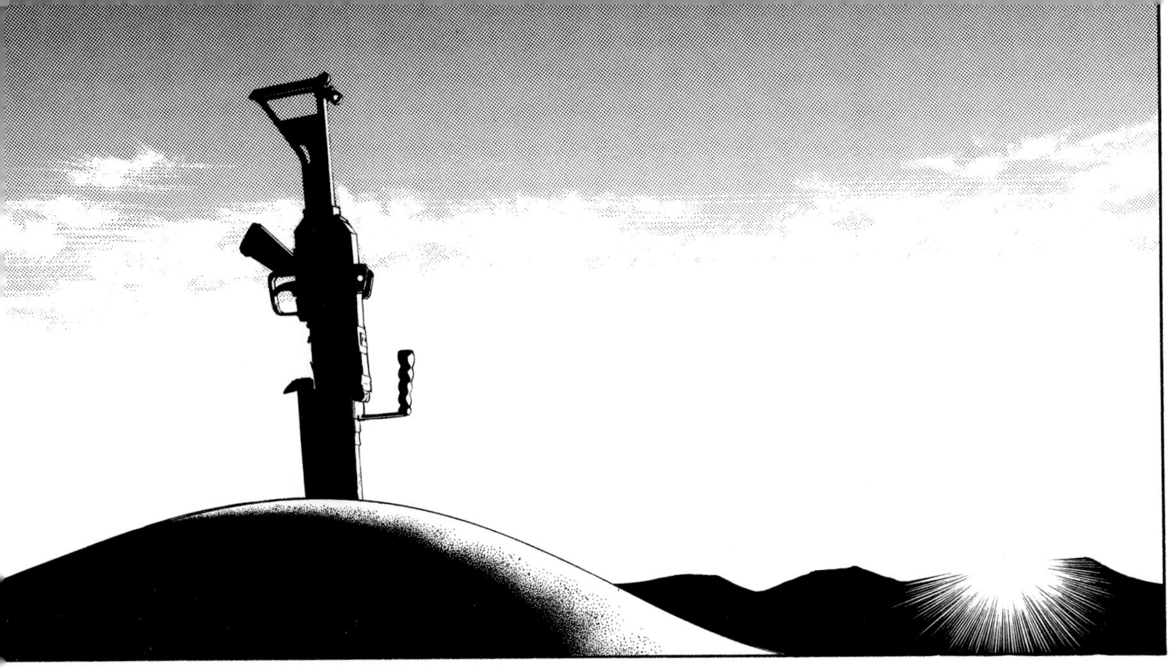

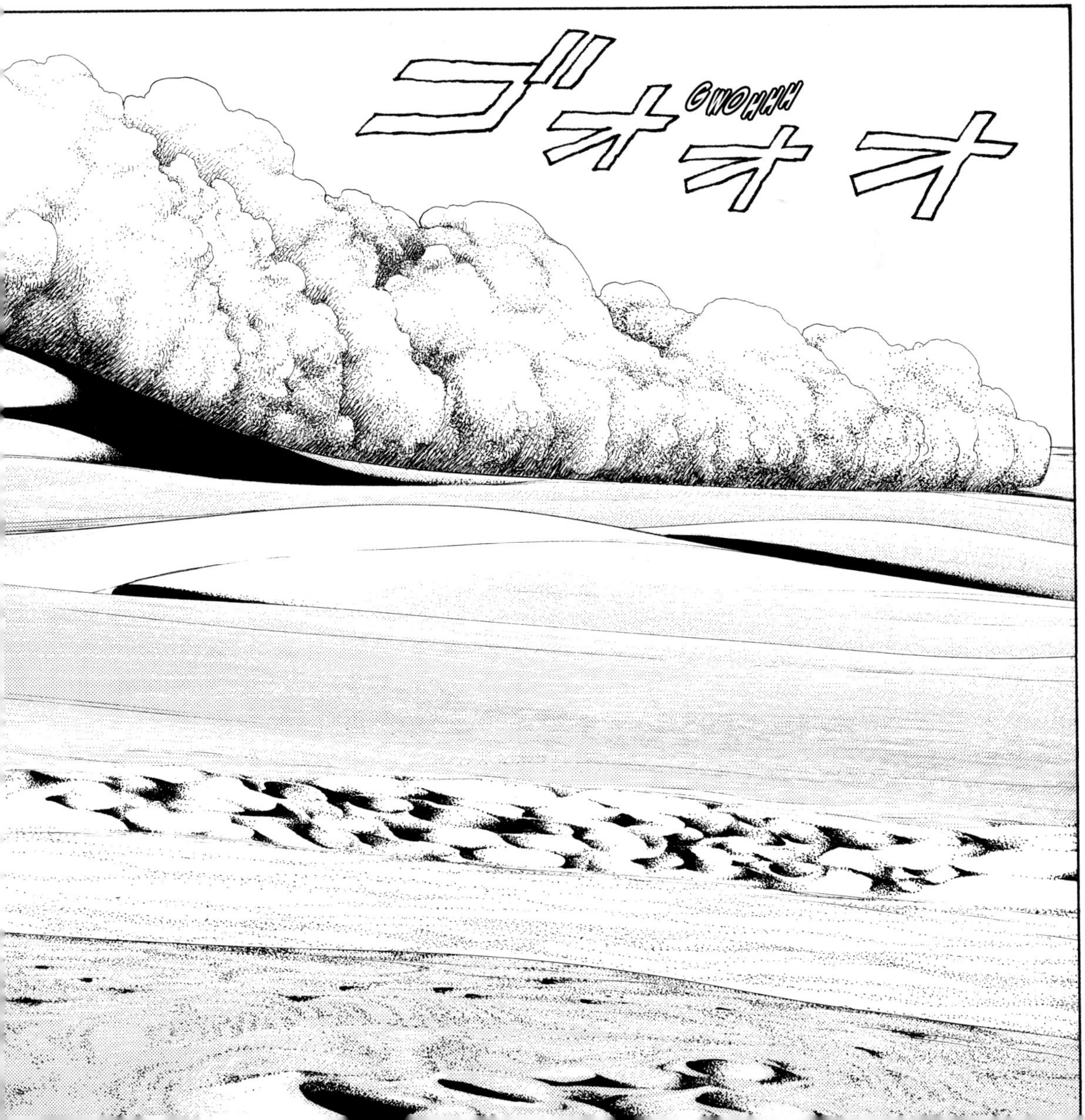
ゴオオオ
GWOHHH

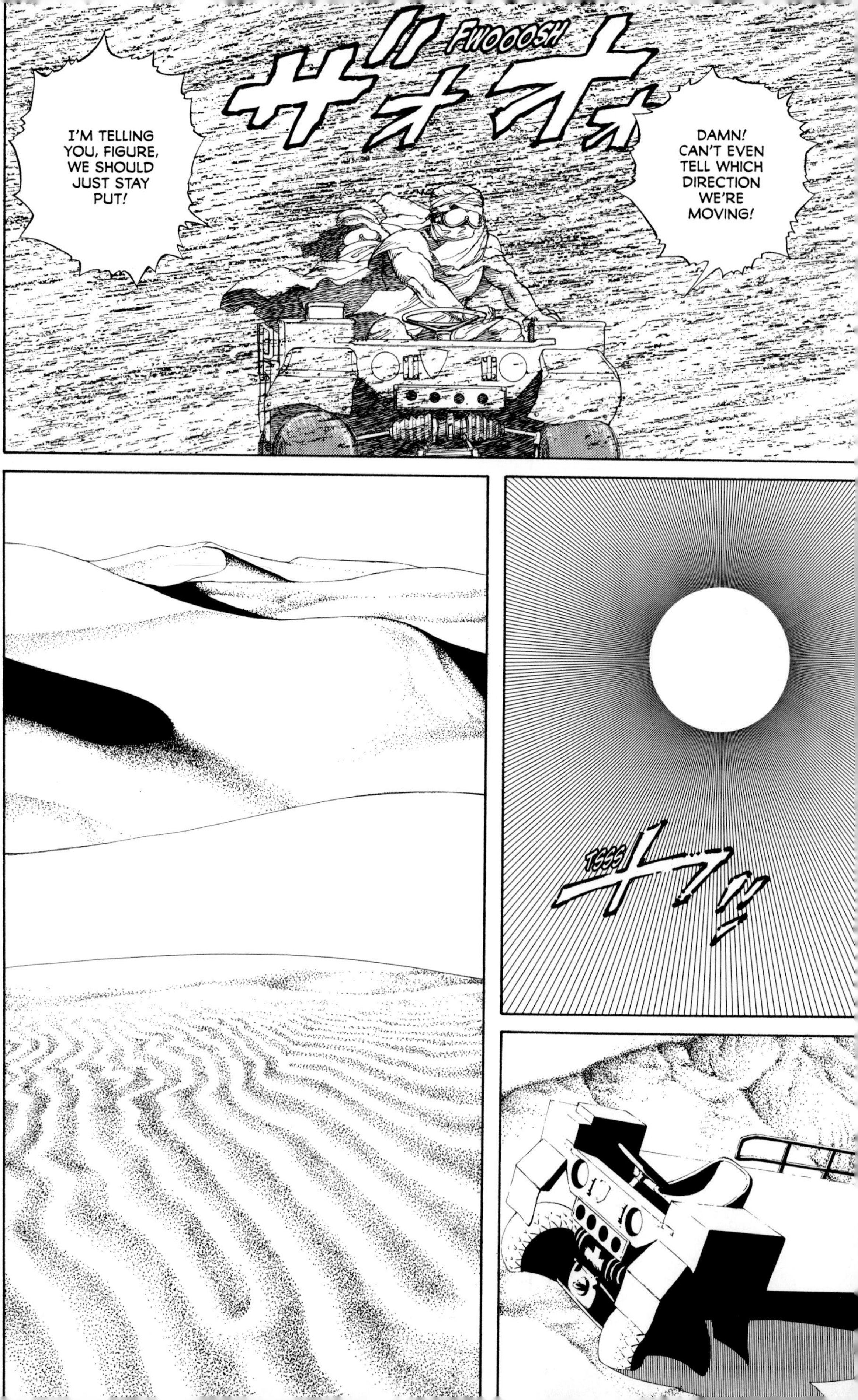
FWOOOSH
DAMN! CAN'T EVEN TELL WHICH DIRECTION WE'RE MOVING!
I'M TELLING YOU, FIGURE, WE SHOULD JUST STAY PUT!
TSSS

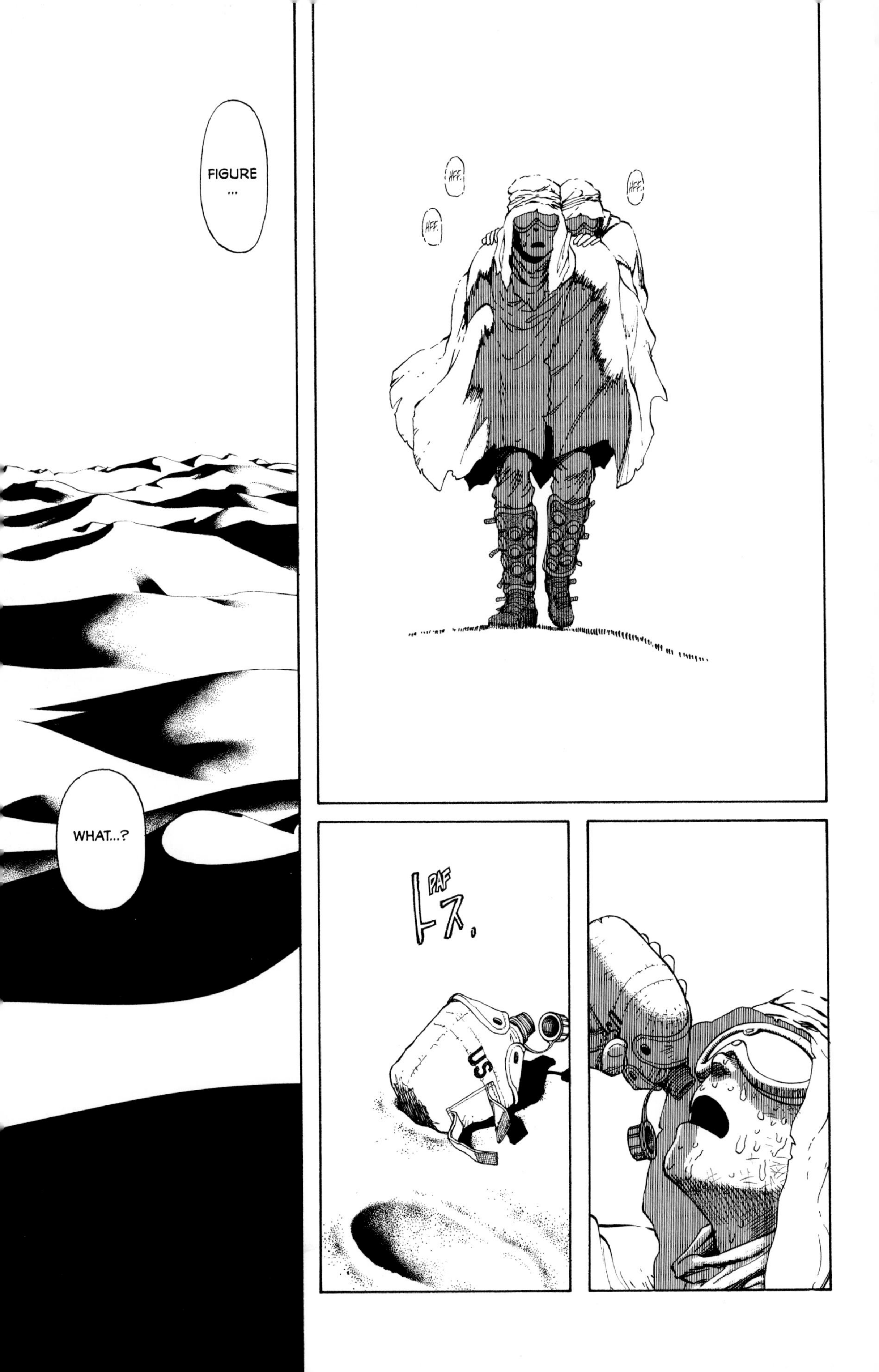
HFF.
HFF.
HFF.
トス
PAF
FIGURE ...
WHAT...?

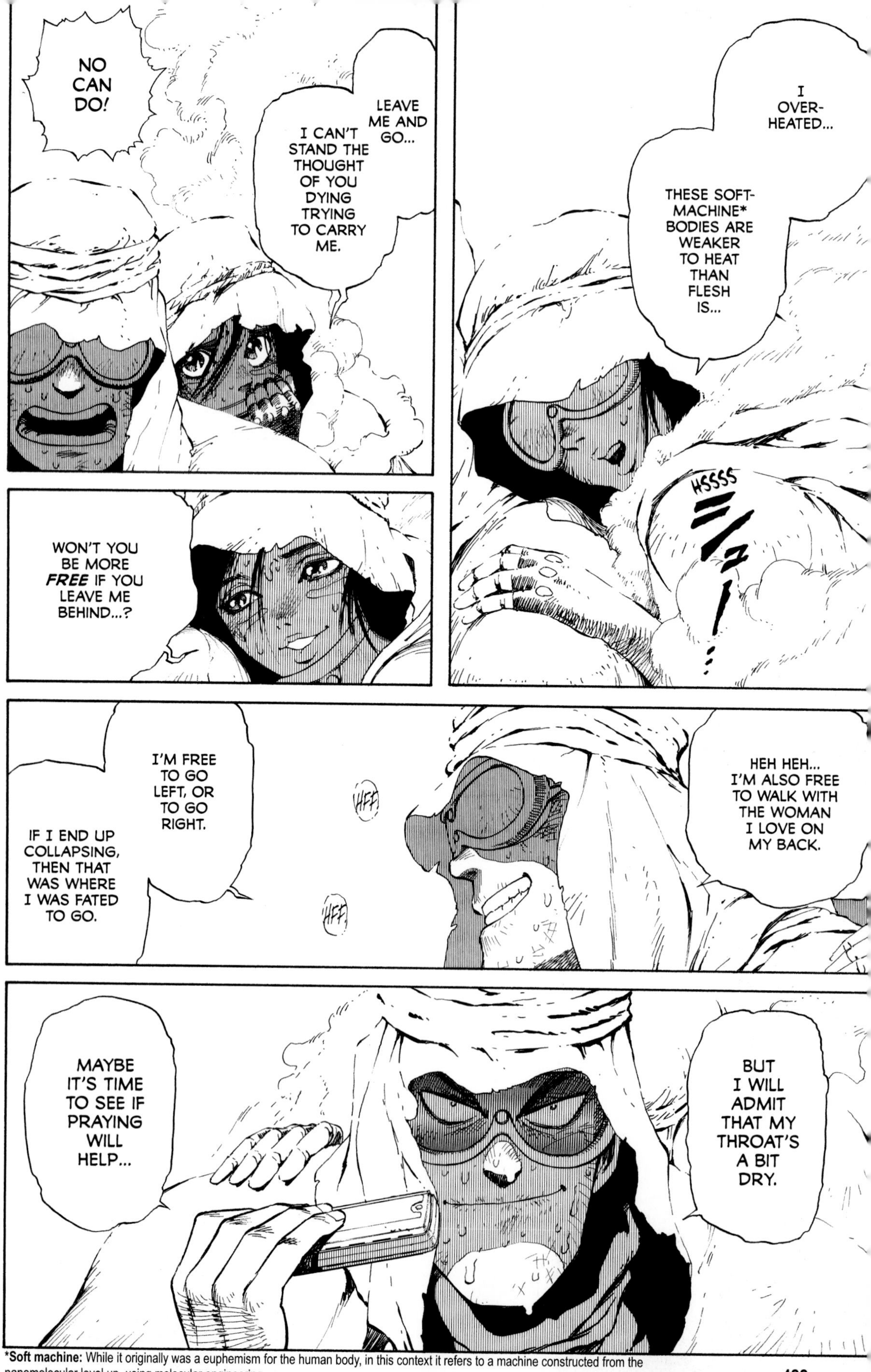
I OVER-HEATED...
THESE SOFT-MACHINE* BODIES ARE WEAKER TO HEAT THAN FLESH IS...
HSSSS
LEAVE ME AND GO...
I CAN'T STAND THE THOUGHT OF YOU DYING TRYING TO CARRY ME.
NO CAN DO!
WON'T YOU BE MORE *FREE* IF YOU LEAVE ME BEHIND...?
HEH HEH... I'M ALSO FREE TO WALK WITH THE WOMAN I LOVE ON MY BACK.
HFF
HFF
I'M FREE TO GO LEFT, OR TO GO RIGHT.
IF I END UP COLLAPSING, THEN THAT WAS WHERE I WAS FATED TO GO.
BUT I WILL ADMIT THAT MY THROAT'S A BIT DRY.
MAYBE IT'S TIME TO SEE IF PRAYING WILL HELP...

***Soft machine:** While it originally was a euphemism for the human body, in this context it refers to a machine constructed from the nanomolecular level up, using molecular engineering.

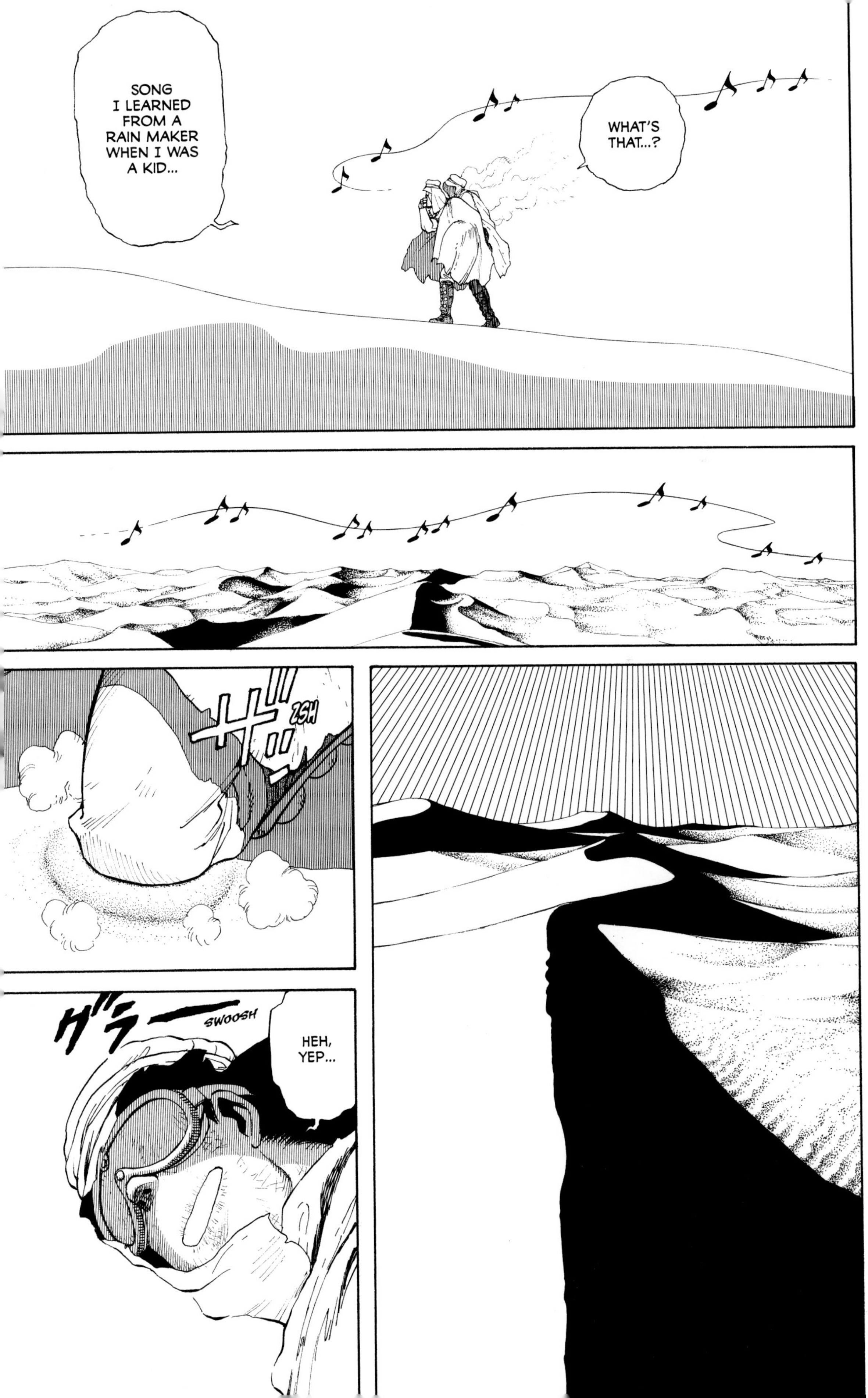
WHAT'S THAT...?
SONG I LEARNED FROM A RAIN MAKER WHEN I WAS A KID...
ZSH
SWOOSH
HEH, YEP...

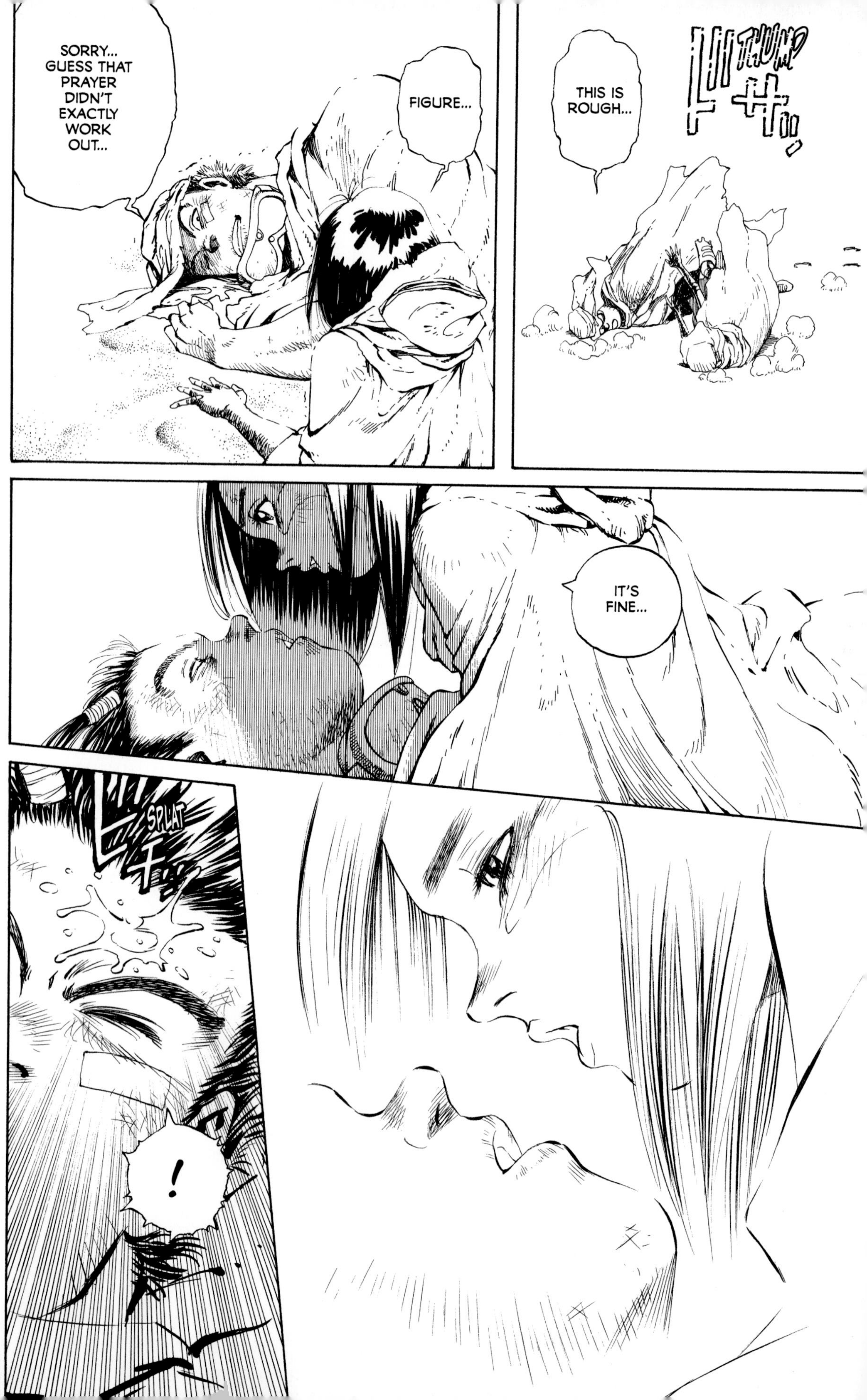
THUMP
THIS IS ROUGH...
FIGURE...
SORRY... GUESS THAT PRAYER DIDN'T EXACTLY WORK OUT...
IT'S FINE...
SPLAT
!

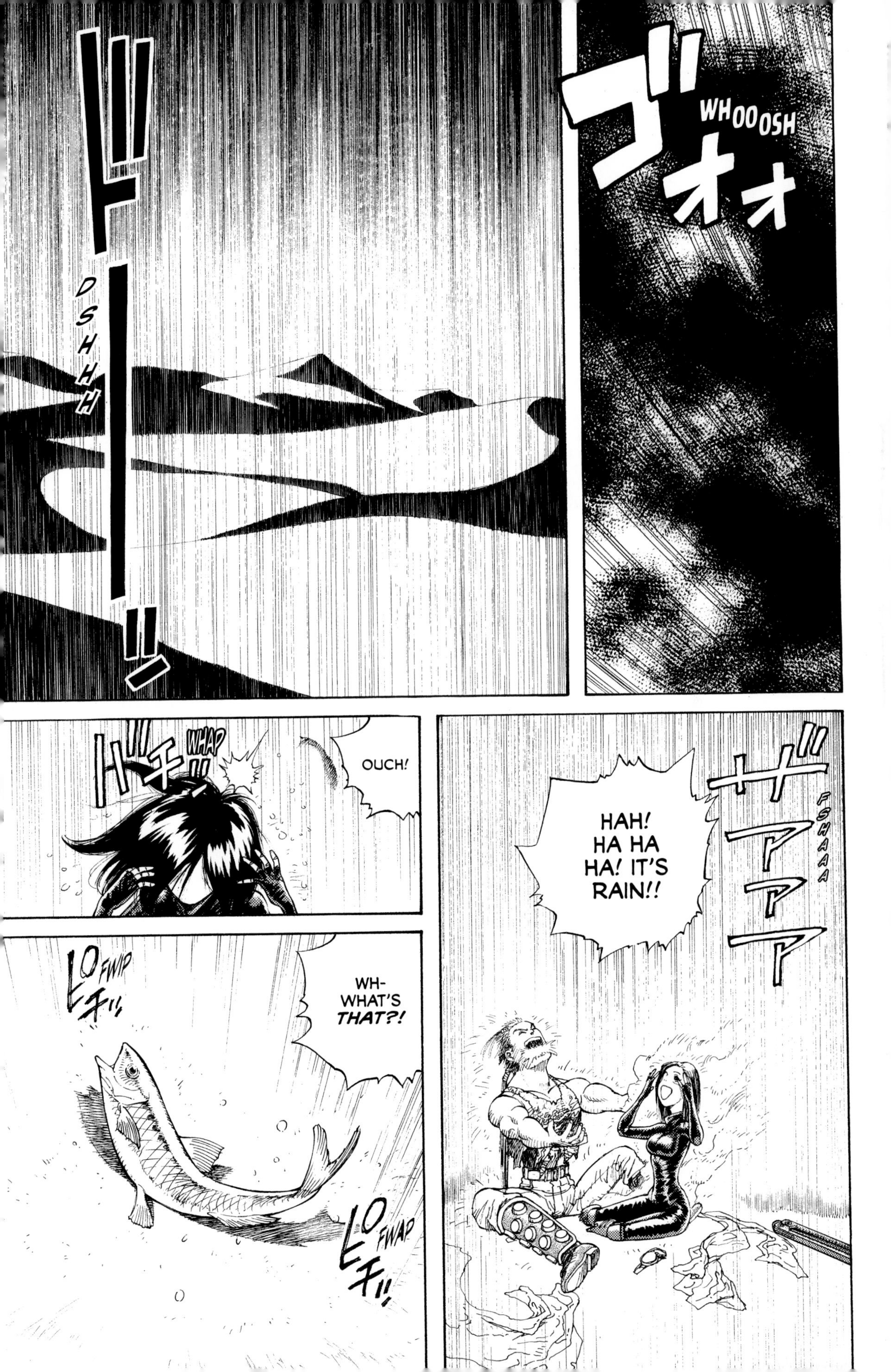
ゴオオ
WHOOOSH
ドドーーッ
DSHHHH
ザァァァ
FSHAAA
HAH! HA HA HA! IT'S RAIN!!
バチッ
WHAP
OUCH!
ビチッ
FWIP
WH- WHAT'S *THAT?!*
ビチッ
FWAP

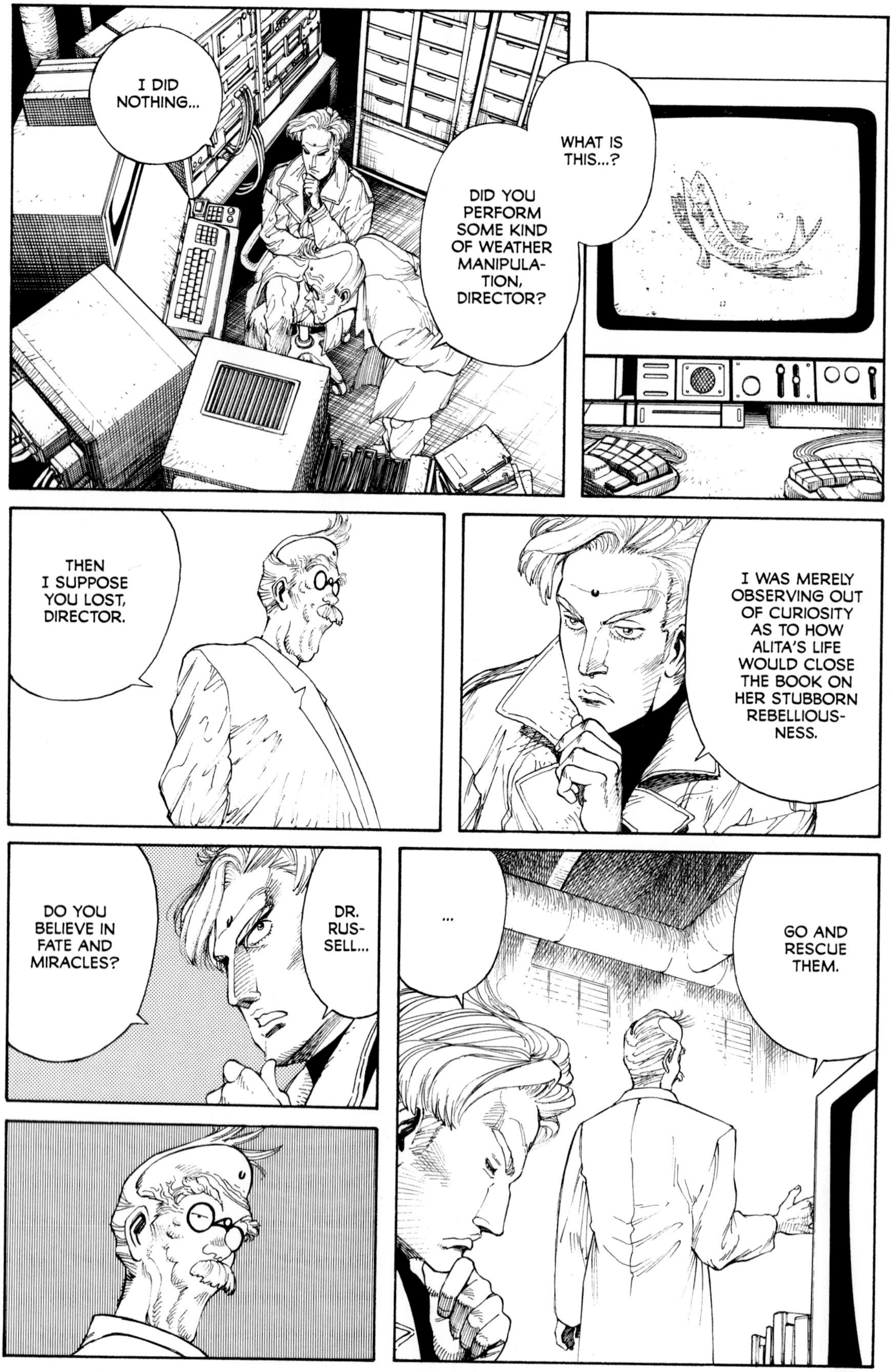
WHAT IS THIS...?
DID YOU PERFORM SOME KIND OF WEATHER MANIPULA-TION, DIRECTOR?
I DID NOTHING...
I WAS MERELY OBSERVING OUT OF CURIOSITY AS TO HOW ALITA'S LIFE WOULD CLOSE THE BOOK ON HER STUBBORN REBELLIOUS-NESS.
THEN I SUPPOSE YOU LOST, DIRECTOR.
GO AND RESCUE THEM.
...
DR. RUS-SELL...
DO YOU BELIEVE IN FATE AND MIRACLES?

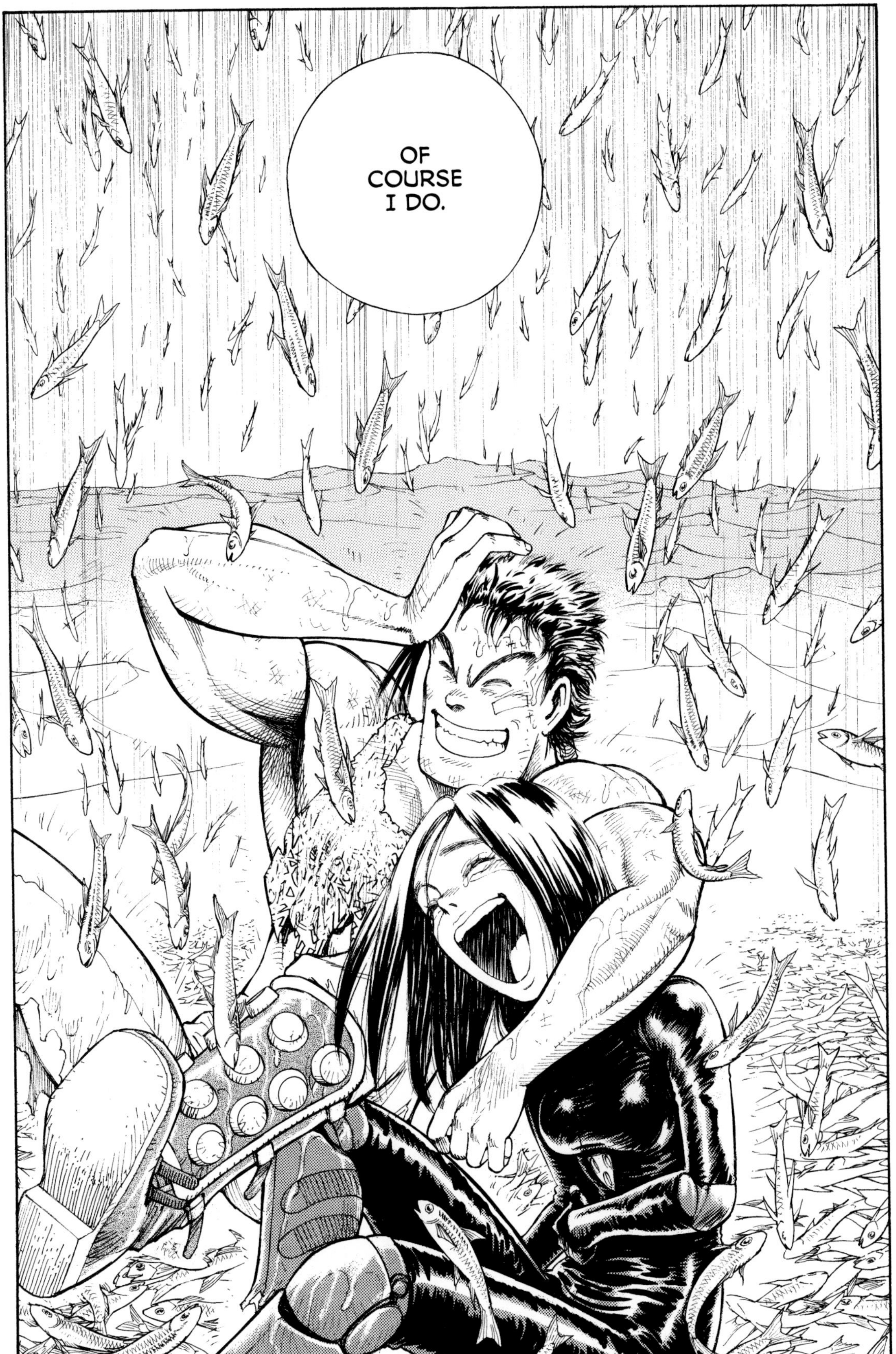
OF COURSE I DO.

Battle Angel Alita Part 6: Rain Maker / END

The Factory Trading System

EXPLAINED!

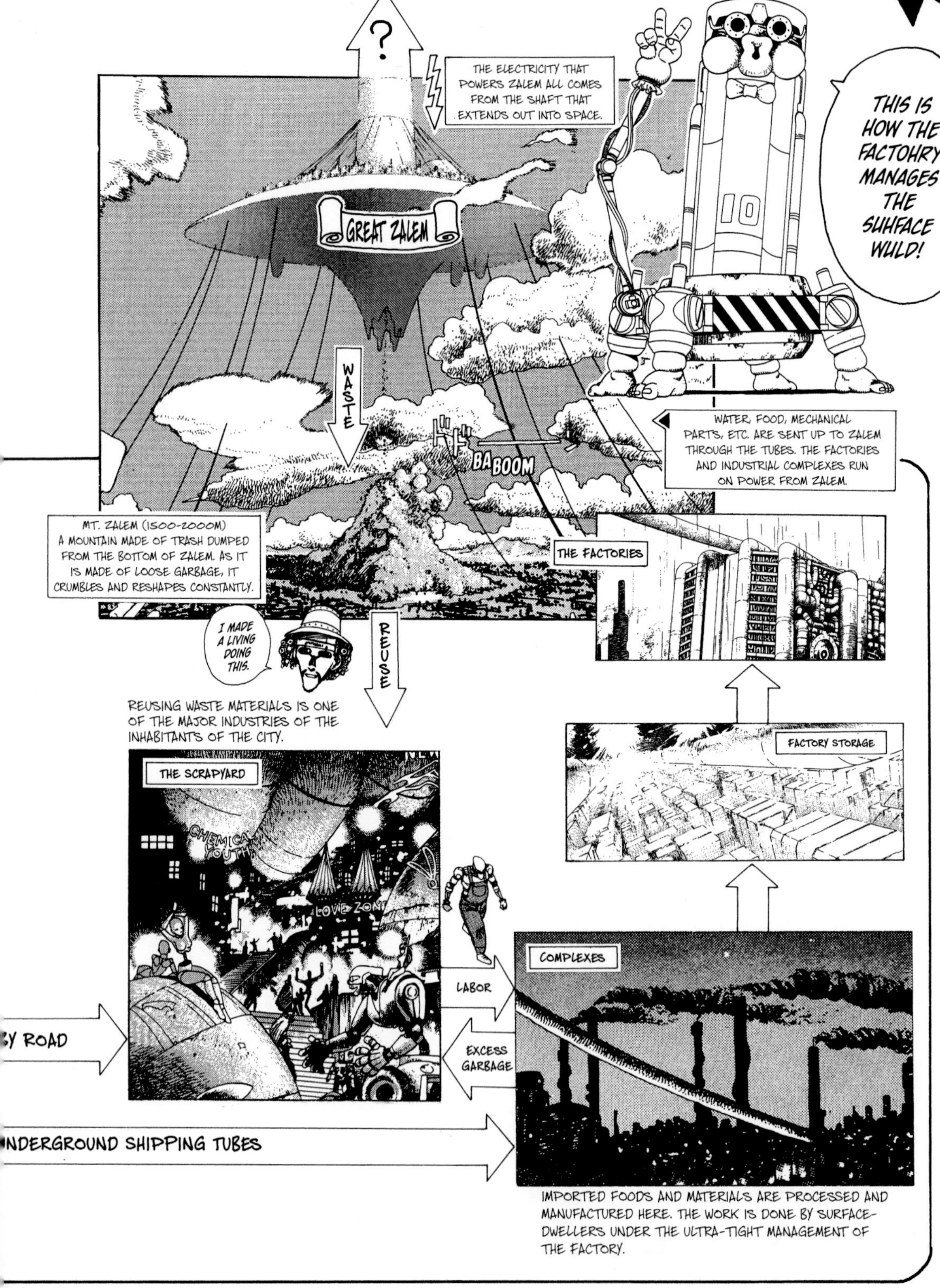

THIS IS HOW THE FACTOHRY MANAGES THE SUHFACE WULD!
?
THE ELECTRICITY THAT POWERS ZALEM ALL COMES FROM THE SHAFT THAT EXTENDS OUT INTO SPACE.
GREAT ZALEM
WASTE
BA BOOM
WATER, FOOD, MECHANICAL PARTS, ETC. ARE SENT UP TO ZALEM THROUGH THE TUBES. THE FACTORIES AND INDUSTRIAL COMPLEXES RUN ON POWER FROM ZALEM.
MT. ZALEM (1500-2000M) A MOUNTAIN MADE OF TRASH DUMPED FROM THE BOTTOM OF ZALEM. AS IT IS MADE OF LOOSE GARBAGE, IT CRUMBLES AND RESHAPES CONSTANTLY.
THE FACTORIES
REUSE
I MADE A LIVING DOING THIS.
REUSING WASTE MATERIALS IS ONE OF THE MAJOR INDUSTRIES OF THE INHABITANTS OF THE CITY.
FACTORY STORAGE
THE SCRAPYARD
CHEMICAL YOUTH
LOVE ZONE
COMPLEXES
LABOR
EXCESS GARBAGE
BY ROAD
UNDERGROUND SHIPPING TUBES
IMPORTED FOODS AND MATERIALS ARE PROCESSED AND MANUFACTURED HERE. THE WORK IS DONE BY SURFACE-DWELLERS UNDER THE ULTRA-TIGHT MANAGEMENT OF THE FACTORY.

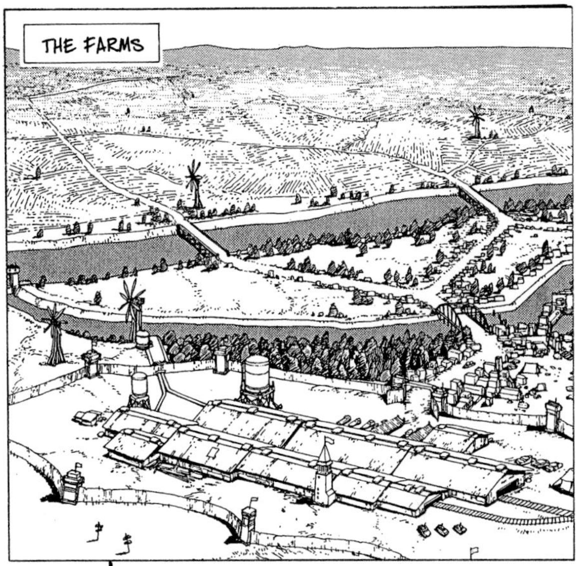
THE FARMS

FARMS WORKING DIRECTLY UNDER THE FACTORY. EACH STATION IS OVERSEEN BY A DECKMAN. IN ADDITION TO THE FACTORY ARMY, THE FARMS ARE PROTECTED FROM EXTERNAL ENEMIES BY CIVILIAN VIGILANTE GUARDS. WHILE FOOD IS PLENTIFUL ON THE FARMS, DOCTORS, AND CYBORG AND MEDICAL SUPPLIES ARE IN SHORT SUPPLY, MEANING THEY ARE RELIANT ON THE SCRAPYARD FOR HELP.

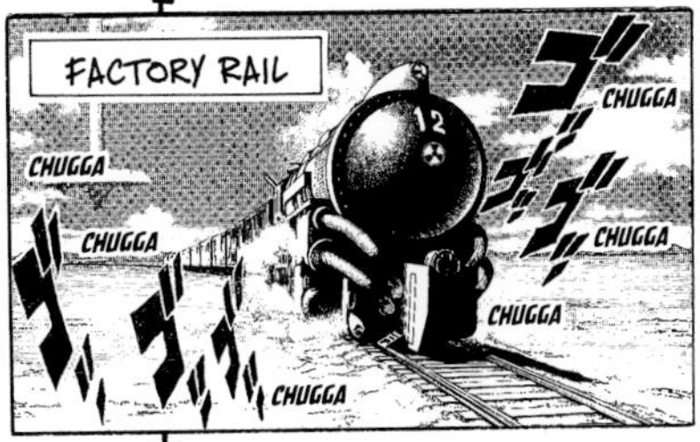
FACTORY RAIL
ゴゴゴ
CHUGGA
CHUGGA
CHUGGA
CHUGGA
CHUGGA
ゴゴゴ
CHUGGA
CHUGGA

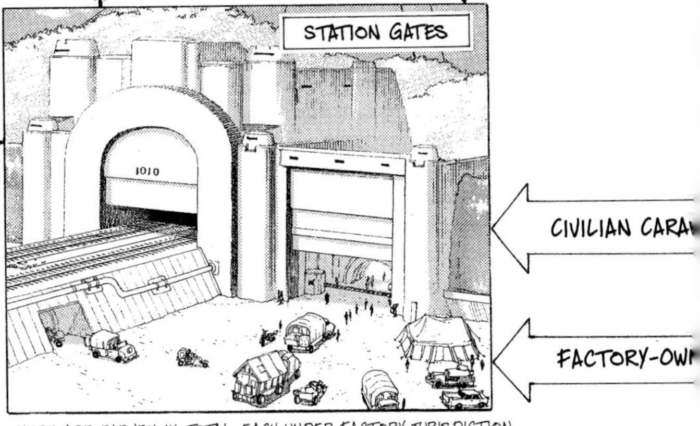
STATION GATES
1010
CIVILIAN CARA
FACTORY-OW

THERE ARE ELEVEN IN TOTAL, EACH UNDER FACTORY JURISDICTION. DUE TO ANTI-TERRORISM MEASURES, THE CUSTOMS CHECKS ARE QUITE SEVERE. THIS IS THE RELAY ROUTE VECTOR USED TO LURE YUGO INTO WORKING FOR HIM.

THE TRUTH OF THE WALL!

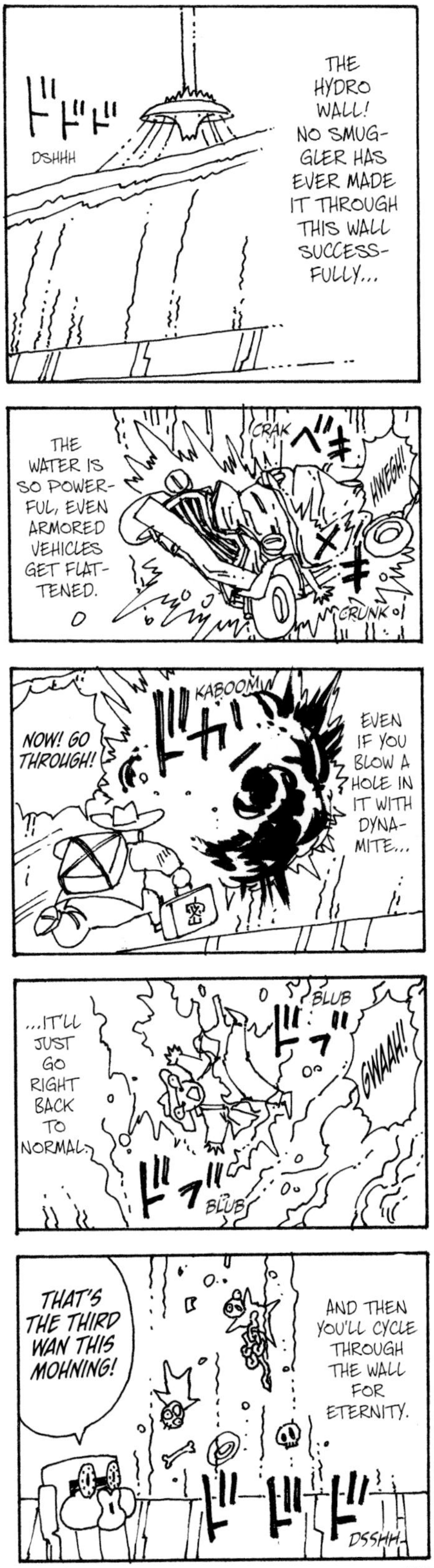
THE HYDRO WALL! NO SMUGGLER HAS EVER MADE IT THROUGH THIS WALL SUCCESSFULLY...
ドドド
DSHHH
CRAK
ベキ
HWEGH!
メキ
GRUNK
THE WATER IS SO POWERFUL, EVEN ARMORED VEHICLES GET FLATTENED.
EVEN IF YOU BLOW A HOLE IN IT WITH DYNAMITE...
KABOOM
ドカ
NOW! GO THROUGH!
BLUB
ドブ
GWAAH!
...IT'LL JUST GO RIGHT BACK TO NORMAL.
ドブ
BLUB
AND THEN YOU'LL CYCLE THROUGH THE WALL FOR ETERNITY.
THAT'S THE THIRD WAN THIS MOHNING!
ドドド
DSSHH

THE END.

YUKITO.
1993. 11. 21.

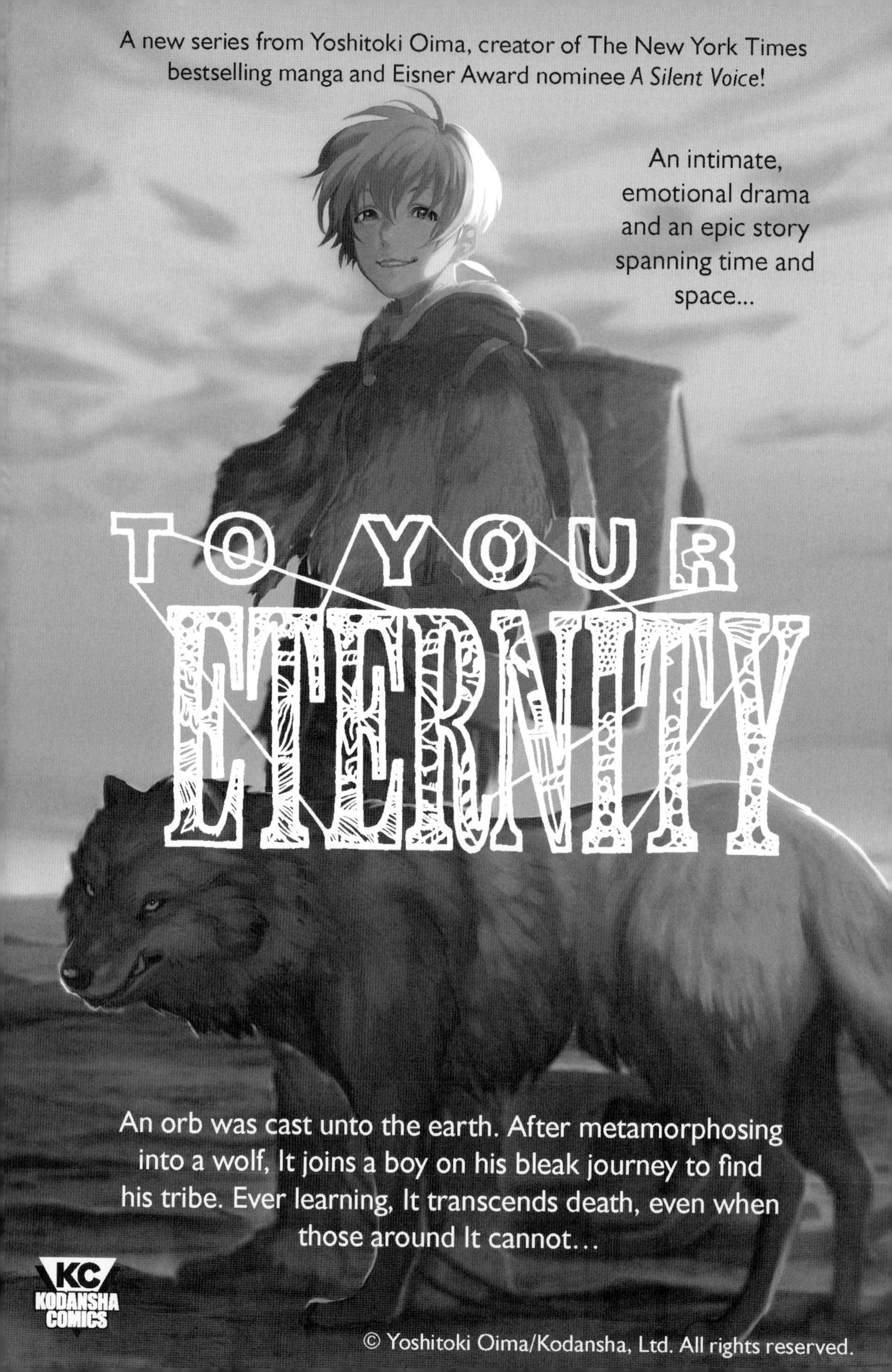
A new series from Yoshitoki Oima, creator of The New York Times bestselling manga and Eisner Award nominee *A Silent Voice*!
An intimate, emotional drama and an epic story spanning time and space...
TO YOUR ETERNITY
An orb was cast unto the earth. After metamorphosing into a wolf, It joins a boy on his bleak journey to find his tribe. Ever learning, It transcends death, even when those around It cannot...
KC KODANSHA COMICS
© Yoshitoki Oima/Kodansha, Ltd. All rights reserved.

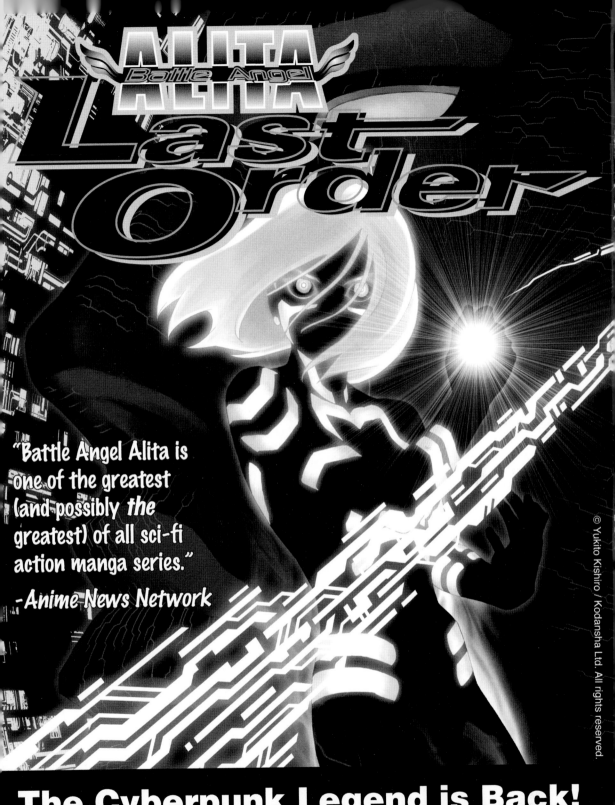

"Battle Angel Alita is one of the greatest (and possibly *the* greatest) of all sci-fi action manga series."

-Anime News Network

The Cyberpunk Legend is Back!

In deluxe omnibus editions of 600+ pages, including ALL-NEW original stories by Alita creator Yukito Kishiro!

KC
KODANSHA

The Black Museum: The Ghost and the Lady

By Kazuhiro Fujita

Deep in Scotland Yard in London sits an evidence room dedicated to the greatest mysteries of British history. In this "Black Museum" sits a misshapen hunk of lead—two bullets fused together—the key to a wartime encounter between Florence Nightingale, the mother of modern nursing, and a supernatural Man in Grey. This story is unknown to most scholars of history, but a special guest of the museum will tell the tale of The Ghost and the Lady...

Praise for Kazuhiro Fujita's *Ushio and Tora*

"A charming revival that combines a classic look with modern depth and pacing... **Essential viewing both for curmudgeons and new fans alike.**" — Anime News Network

"**GREAT!** The first episode of Ushio and Tora captures the essence of '90s anime." — IGN

OTOMO

大 友 克 洋

A GLOBAL TRIBUTE TO THE MIND BEHIND AKIRA

A celebration of manga legend Katsuhiro Otomo from more than 80
world-renowned fine artists and comics legends
With contributions from:
- Stan Sakai
- Tomer and Asaf Hanuka
- Sara Pichelli
- Range Murata
- Aleksi Briclot
And more!
168 pages of stunning, full-color art

**KC
KODANSHA
COMICS**

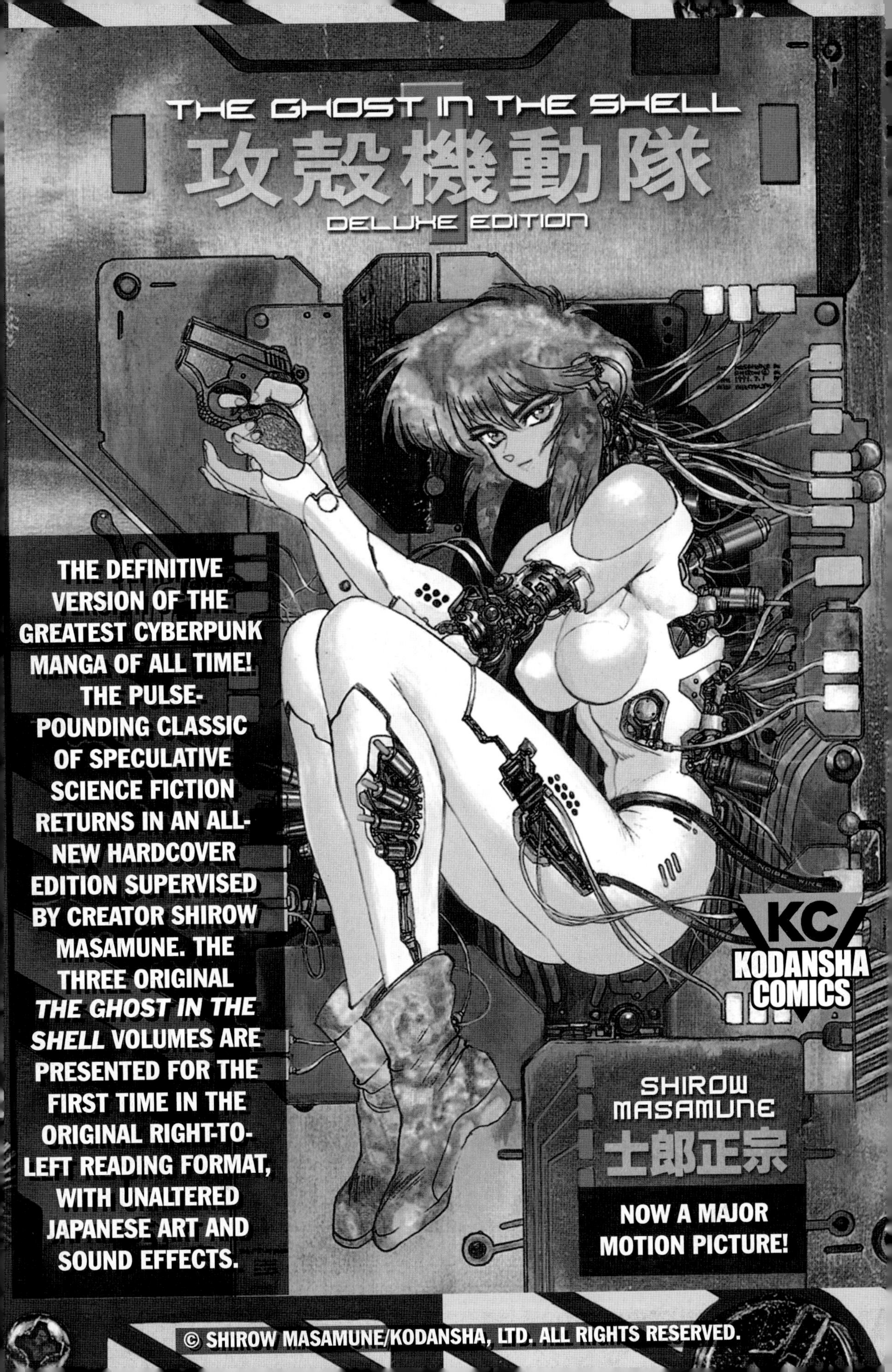

THE GHOST IN THE SHELL

攻殻機動隊

DELUXE EDITION

THE DEFINITIVE VERSION OF THE GREATEST CYBERPUNK MANGA OF ALL TIME! THE PULSE-POUNDING CLASSIC OF SPECULATIVE SCIENCE FICTION RETURNS IN AN ALL-NEW HARDCOVER EDITION SUPERVISED BY CREATOR SHIROW MASAMUNE. THE THREE ORIGINAL *THE GHOST IN THE SHELL* VOLUMES ARE PRESENTED FOR THE FIRST TIME IN THE ORIGINAL RIGHT-TO-LEFT READING FORMAT, WITH UNALTERED JAPANESE ART AND SOUND EFFECTS.

KC KODANSHA COMICS

SHIROW MASAMUNE

士郎正宗

NOW A MAJOR MOTION PICTURE!

Battle Angel Alita Deluxe Edition Volume 3 copyright © 2013 Yukito Kishiro
English translation copyright © 2018 Yukito Kishito

Published in the United States by Kodansha Comics,
an imprint of Kodansha USA Publishing, LLC, New York.

Publication rights for this English edition arranged through Kodansha Ltd., Tokyo.

First published in Japan in 2013 by Kodansha Ltd., Tokyo, as
Gunnm, volumes 5 and 6.

ISBN 978-1-63236-600-9

Printed in China.

www.kodanshacomics.com

9 8 7 6 5 4 3 2 1

Translation: Stephen Paul
Lettering: Scott O. Brown
Editing: Ajani Oloye
Kodansha Comics edition cover design: Phil Balsman